Multimedia Foundations

WITHDRAWN

Understand the core concepts and skills of multimedia production and digital storytelling using text, graphics, photographs, sound, motion, and video. Then, put it all together using the skills that you have developed for effective project planning, collaboration, design, and production.

Presented in full color with hundreds of vibrant illustrations, *Multimedia Foundations, Second Edition* trains you in the principles and skill sets common to all forms of digital media production, enabling you to create successful, engaging content, no matter what tools you are using.

The second edition has been fully updated and features a new chapter on video production and new sections on user-centered design, digital cinema standards (2K, 4K, and 8K video), and DSLR and video camcorder recording formats and device settings. The companion website, which features a wealth of web resources, glossary terms, and video tutorials, has also been updated with new content for both students and instructors.

Dr. Vic Costello is an Associate Professor in the School of Communications at Elon University, where he has taught numerous courses in multimedia design and production since 2001. He has worked in broadcast management, in corporate communications, and as a freelance technical director, video producer, and creative consultant for live events and awards shows. Dr. Costello is a long-standing member of the Broadcast Education Association (BEA) and has served as both producer and chair ...edia Arts, and as a member of the BEA Board of Directors.

Multimedia Foundations
Core Concepts for Digital Design

Second Edition

Vic Costello

Routledge
Taylor & Francis Group

NEW YORK AND LONDON

COMPANION WEBSITE @ http://Routledge.com/cw/costello

This edition published 2017
by Routledge
711 Third Avenue, New York, NY 10017

and by Routledge
2 Park Square, Milton Park, Abingdon, Oxon, OX14 4RN

Routledge is an imprint of the Taylor & Francis Group, an informa business

First edition by Focal Press 2012

Library of Congress Cataloging-in-Publication Data
Names: Costello, Vic.
Title: Multimedia foundations : core concepts for digital design / Vic Costello.
Description: New York, NY : Routledge, 2016. | Includes bibliographical
   references and index.
Identifiers: LCCN 2015044007 | ISBN 9780415740029 (hardback) |
   ISBN 9780415740036 (pbk.) | ISBN 9781315815886 (ebook)
Subjects: LCSH: Multimedia systems. | Digital media.
Classification: LCC QA76.575 .C6838 2016 | DDC 006.7—dc23
LC record available at http://lccn.loc.gov/2015044007

ISBN: 978-0-415-74002-9 (hbk)
ISBN: 978-0-415-74003-6 (pbk)
ISBN: 978-1-315-81588-6 (ebk)

Typeset in ITC Giovanni
by Apex CoVantage, LLC

Dedication

To my father-in-law Paul Dale Sklenar (1932–2016).

Contents

ACKNOWLEDGMENTS viii
ABOUT THE AUTHOR ix
ABOUT THE WEBSITE x
INTRODUCTION xi

SECTION 1 • Multimedia Foundations

1. Understanding Multimedia 3
2. The Computer 39
3. Project Planning and Evaluation 77

SECTION 2 • Multimedia Design

4. Visual Communication 109
5. Page Layout 143
6. User Interface Design 167
7. Web Design 201

SECTION 3 • Static Media

8. Text 235
9. Graphics 263
10. Photography 293

SECTION 4 • Time-Based Media

11. Recording Formats and Device Settings 331
12. Audio Production 371
13. Video Production 403
14. Time-Based Editing 441

INDEX 477

Acknowledgments

Thank you to everyone who contributed to the second edition of *Multimedia Foundations: Core Concepts for Digital Design*. Whether you conducted research or writing for a chapter update, reviewed the project proposal or draft manuscript, posed for photographs, provided sample illustrations from your own works, or offered an encouraging word or prayer along the way, I am so very grateful to you for your support. To the awesome editorial staff and production team at Taylor & Francis, thank you for your continued support of this impactful work.

Drs. Ed and Susan Youngblood made significant improvements to their co-authored chapter on web design—updating readers on the evolving HTML5 standard while clarifying and streamlining the narrative structure and flow of the entire chapter. Dr. Qian Xu revamped her chapter on user interface design, introducing a few new topics such as augmented reality, responsive web design, parallax scrolling, and voice interfaces.

Dr. Tony Demars and Staci Saltz conducted comprehensive reviews of the draft manuscript. Their feedback and suggestions were put to good use—greatly enhancing the accuracy, clarity, and presentation of the written text.

Elon University—and more specifically my dean, Dr. Paul Parsons; associate dean Dr. Don Grady; and department chair Dr. Jessica Gisclair—provided administrative aid (including support for a much appreciated research sabbatical). My colleagues Bryan Baker and Ryan Witt allowed me to photograph their video shoots and offered sample images from past projects that they had produced or edited. Along the way, many Elon students, faculty, and staff served as subjects for photographs—many of whom are included in the final chapters on video production and editing. Special thanks go to Dr. Rich Landesberg, Julie Prouty, the Elon Local News producing team, graduate students in the Interactive Media masters program, and student workers in the Department of Television Services.

Finally, I want to thank Beth, my wife of more than 30 years. She is the love of my life, my best friend, and most ardent supporter. To my children, thank you also for your enduring love!

—Vic Costello

Dr. Vic Costello is an associate professor in the School of Communications at Elon University, where he has taught numerous courses in multimedia design and production since 2001. He has a Ph.D. in Communication from the University of Tennessee–Knoxville, an M.A. in Communication from Regent University, and a B.S. in Radio-Television Production from Western Carolina University. He has worked in broadcast management, corporate communications, and as a freelance technical director, video producer, and creative consultant for live events and award shows. Dr. Costello is a long-standing member of the Broadcast Education Association (BEA) and has served as both producer and chair of the BEA Festival of Media Arts and as a member of the BEA Board of Directors.

About the Website

The companion website for *Multimedia Foundations: Core Concepts for Digital Design* contains a wealth of supplemental content that's designed to expand upon the concepts and ideas covered here in the printed text. For each chapter, the website offers video tutorials, glossaries, and links to additional resources.

Visit here to get started: http://Routledge.com/cw/costello

The idea for this book emerged from a course I helped create in 2003 and have been teaching ever since called *Creating Multimedia Content (CMC)*. It is a rapid-fire survey course that introduces students to the foundational concepts and skills used in multimedia design and production. In this course, students learn the basics of visual theory, graphic design, digital photography, sound and video recording, editing, and the Web—all in a one-semester course. To accomplish such a feat, the course focuses on breadth rather than depth. The goal is to introduce students to basic theories and principles of design, practical production skill sets and project workflows, and industry standards and best practices.

Likewise, *Multimedia Foundations* is a textbook that focuses broadly on the subjects and themes that are common to all digital storytellers and platforms—the most significant and transferrable concepts one is likely to encounter across the ever-converging industries and professions of multimedia.

HOW THIS BOOK IS ORGANIZED

Each chapter covers a single facet of multimedia design. Thus, since each chapter stands on its own, the instructor or reader can interact with the material nonlinearly in any manner he or she wishes. For those of you who prefer to progress through a book one chapter at a time in the order presented, I have tried to arrange the chapters in a way that makes sense and that progresses logically from beginning to end. The book is divided into four topical subsections: 1) multimedia foundations, 2) multimedia design, 3) static media, and 4) time-based media.

Multimedia Foundations

Section 1 is intended to give the reader a broad foundational understanding of the field along with an introduction to some of the essential tools and processes used in multimedia design. Chapter 1 includes a definition and overview of multimedia within the context of traditional media and historical practice. It compares and contrasts the legacy media of old with *new media* that's rooted in digital technologies and workflows. Chapter 2 examines the computer. The computer is more than a box filled with high-tech hardware components; it is an invaluable personal assistant, running the tools and programs you need to create, publish, and consume multimedia. Chapter 3 introduces readers to the planning and design process. All too often, the planning process is underestimated, rushed, or eliminated entirely from the producer's workflow. Good outcomes are highly dependent on good planning, vision, and intentionality on the front end of a multimedia project.

Multimedia Design

Section 2 includes four chapters on professional practices and theories that guide and inform the multimedia design process. Chapter 4 draws upon the field of visual communication, introducing the reader to core elements and principles of design having to do with aesthetics, a branch of study dealing with human perceptions of visual form and presentation. Chapter 5 looks at page layout and design, which has its roots in print media such as newspapers and magazines. In multimedia, the concepts and principles of page design extend to screen layouts as well. Chapter 6 examines user interface design and the often-related concept of usability. The multimedia experience is primarily nonlinear, and for this reason, users rely on designers to create easy-to-use interfaces that are functional and intuitive. Chapter 7 addresses web design. While the field of multimedia encompasses far more than the Web, as the quintessential multimedia platform, the Web still commands a great deal of attention.

Static Media

Section 3 introduces you to three branches of static media: text, graphics, and photography. The term *static media* refers to any type of media that can be presented or viewed instantaneously, in a fixed moment of time, such as words or images affixed to a page or screen. Chapter 8 delves into the art of typography and the use of text for communicating information and emotion. Chapter 9 takes us into the field of graphic design to explore rudimentary principles of electronic image formation—examining differences between raster graphics, vector images, and moving images. Chapter 10 moves us into digital photography. This is a richly illustrated chapter that includes a wealth of information about camera imaging and photographic techniques.

Time-Based Media

Section 4 looks at time-based media—namely audio and video recording, acquisition, and postproduction. Chapter 11 traces the evolution of recording technologies from the early days of tape-based recording methods to the modern era of file-based recording. It also explores some of the important distinctions between analog and digital methods of encoding and reproduction. Chapter 12 covers audio production and sound recording techniques, the use of microphones, and the practice of monitoring to ensure professional results. Chapter 13 is a new chapter that focuses entirely on video production. It goes into depth on topics such as video composition, film grammar, acquisition of interviews and B-Roll, and device settings for digital cameras and recorders. Finally, chapter 14 deals with the use of nonlinear editing (NLE) for assembling audio and video clips into a meaningful narrative structure and presentation.

HOW THE CHAPTERS ARE ORGANIZED

Historical Quotes and Predictions

Each chapter begins with an historical prediction or quote related to the corresponding subject. Many of these quotes came from the predictions database at Imagining the Internet, a website created by my colleague Janna Quitney Anderson as a part of the Pew Internet and American Life Project. The database includes thousands of predictions (some serious and others humorous) such as these:

In the world of the future, people will use low-cost Radio Shack equipment to spy on themselves to find out who they are.

—Eric Hughes, 1992

I'm looking forward to the day when my daughter finds a rolled-up 1,000-pixel-by-1,000-pixel color screen in her cereal packet, with a magnetic back so it sticks to the fridge.

—Tim Berners-Lee, 1995

It's fun to read and think about what people have said throughout the years about the Internet and other technologies that impact us daily. Take a moment and visit the site to see what you can find: http://www.elon.edu/e-web/predictions/early90s/

Chapter Highlights

A bulleted list of the major topics or highlights gives the reader a quick overview of the content and general scope of each chapter.

Key Terms

The key terms section features a vocabulary list of important words mentioned in the chapter. Definitions for each key term can be found in the chapter glossaries on the companion website (see http://Routledge.com/cw/costello).

Boxes

Throughout the book, boxes are used to showcase material under three broad headings: Flashback, Great Ideas, and Tech Talk.

FLASHBACK

In order to understand the present, you need to know something about the past. Flashback segments point to a significant past accomplishment, event, or individual work.

GREAT IDEAS

The field of multimedia has been affected by countless ideas, inventions, and innovations that have significantly impacted the way we design and create multimedia. A great idea is not necessarily a good or lasting one, but one that has left a mark or has had a transformative effect on the profession and those who work in it. A great idea may be something as grand as a theory or invention, or as simple as a workflow tip or technique.

TECH TALK

One the biggest challenges I faced in writing this book was deciding how deep to go into any one particular topic or subject area. Remember, this book was designed to focus more on breadth than depth. The risk here is that, for some, I will not have gone deep enough and that, for others, I will have gone far beyond what they were looking for in an introductory textbook. A partial solution to this dilemma is Tech Talk. Tech Talk delves deeper into advanced technical concepts and issues associated with multimedia. At times, it also covers practical techniques or applications that go beyond a cursory glance.

SECTION 1
Multimedia Foundations

1. Understanding Multimedia   3
2. The Computer   39
3. Project Planning and Evaluation   77

Marish/Shutterstock.com

CHAPTER 1

Understanding Multimedia

We become what we behold. We shape our tools and then our tools shape us.

—**Marshall McLuhan, communication theorist**

The digital revolution is far more significant than the invention of writing or even of printing.

—**Douglas Engelbart, inventor of the computer mouse**

Chapter Highlights

This chapter examines:

- Multimedia as an extension of traditional media industries and practices
- The five components of a multimedia experience
- Three characteristics of old media
- The new media paradigm shift
- Five principles of new media in a digital age

Key Terms
Algorithm
Analog
Animation
Audio
Automation
Batch Processing
Blog
Broadcasting
Communication
Content Sharing
Convergence
Designated Market
 Area (DMA)
Digital
Graphics
Hashtag
Hypertext
Linear
Mass Audience
Mass Media
Medium/Media
Microblogging
Multimedia
Narrowcasting
New Media
Nonlinear
Numerical
 Representation
Old Media
Paradigm Shift
Social Bookmarking
Social Media
Structural
 Modularity
Tag
Text
User-Generated
 Content

WHAT IT IS . . . IS MULTIMEDIA!

In 1953, legendary comedian Andy Griffith recorded a monologue about a country preacher's trip to a college town during a home football game. In this fictional tale, the preacher has traveled to the "big city" to conduct a tent meeting, but his plans are interrupted when he is unexpectedly caught up by a frenzied crowd as they make their way to a football stadium on game day. What follows is a hilarious first-person account about the culture and sport of football as witnessed through the eyes of someone who has never seen or played the game. With a limited vocabulary and frame of reference, he begins to describe the events around him using the only terms he understands. He refers to referees as convicts because of their striped uniforms. The football is called a pumpkin. And the playing surface is compared to a cow pasture that players enter through a "great big outhouse" on either end of the field. The skit, titled "What It Was, Was Football," launched Griffith's professional career, leading to a guest appearance on *The Ed Sullivan Show* in 1954. The live radio recording remains a cult classic and is one of the biggest selling comedy recordings of all time.

Video
Vlog
World Wide Web
(WWW)

At one time or another, all of us have been caught by surprise by a new experience or trend that sneaks up on us at lightning speed, challenging old ways and habits and leaving us scratching our heads in bewilderment. The country preacher's first game of football reminds me of the challenge my mother must have experienced as she learned to send an email message or open a file attachment for the very first time. She was born in the 1930s and spent most of her life relying on pen, paper, and the U.S. postal system for sending and receiving correspondence. To her, this newfangled thing called email must have seemed like a strange and foreign idea. Perhaps you can think of a friend, grandparent, or child who has struggled finding the right words to describe social networking, online shopping, or surfing the Web. How does someone raised in the 1950s come to understand the World Wide Web? How does someone raised in the 1970s adapt to Facebook, Twitter, WordPress, and other social media channels?

For some of you, engaging in a formal study of multimedia will resemble the country preacher's first time at a football game. The landscape will appear strange and foreign to you at first as you struggle for meaning in a sea of unfamiliar objects and ideas—even though you've probably spent plenty of time online. In time, a sense of comfort and familiarity will set in as you catch a glimpse of the big picture and begin to grasp some fundamental concepts and principles. To begin, let's take a peek at something you are probably very familiar with that may serve as a common reference point for understanding multimedia.

The Legacy Media

The legacy media, or *old media*, as we will refer to them later in this chapter, are collectively the traditional forms of human exchange that have been around since the advent of mass communication. The word *media* literally means "ways of transmission" and is a broad term that applies to all the various technologies we rely on to

---

GREAT IDEAS

Metaphor

It's natural for us to draw upon past experiences when confronted with a new tool, system, or way of doing something. Familiar frames of reference, along with established patterns and workflows, can help us make sense of new technologies and methods of productivity. This may explain why metaphors are used so often to describe a new communication technology or activity (see Figure 1.1). For example, a computer's main visual interface is called "the desktop" because it represents the virtual version of a real space where tools and documents reside for conducting everyday business. Likewise, folder icons are used to represent digital spaces on your computer's hard drive for storing electronic documents in much the same way that cardboard folders are used for storing and sorting paper copies. In fact, we're told to think of the hard drive as a file cabinet. We refer to online content as a "web page" because the book analogy makes sense to those of us familiar with print media and the structure of content arranged in a linear format. On Facebook we write messages on "the wall" and refer to the included members of our social network as "friends." Metaphors are handy devices used to frame complex ideas in a way that nearly everyone can understand.

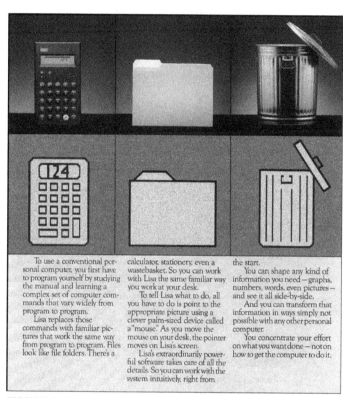

FIGURE 1.1
A 1983 promotional brochure from Apple Computer illustrates the power of a good metaphor. The Apple Lisa computer used these familiar picture icons to represent virtual versions of common everyday objects in a real office.
Source: Courtesy of Computer History Museum.

record information and transmit it to others. For example, videotape is a recording medium (singular) used for storing moving images and sound onto the physical surface of a magnetic strip. Television broadcasting and DVD (digital versatile disc) are transmission media (plural) used to deliver a video recording or live event to an audience. Likewise, printing is a medium whereby ideas are encoded as letterforms in ink onto the surface of a page, while books, newspapers, and magazines are the distribution channels or media through which intellectual content is delivered to a reader.

A medium can be thought of as a pathway or channel through which ideas, information, and meaning flow as they travel from one place or person to another. Every medium has a native form and structure through which it delivers content. A sound recording produces pressure waves that can be understood aurally through the organs of hearing. A book transmits ideas visually through text and illustrations. Video and film convey stories through moving images and sound. Traditional

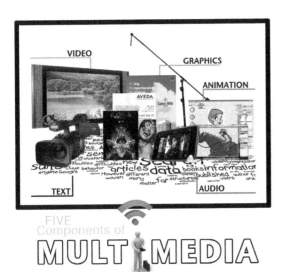

FIGURE 1.2
Source: Sarah Beth Costello.

FIGURE 1.3
Text can be used in countless ways to communicate ideas and information, provide direction and structure, and convey visual energy and emotion in a multimedia design.

media products such as these have a physical structure that is rigid and fixed and cannot be easily modified or adapted by the user or content producer.

Multimedia Defined

Multimedia can be thought of as a *super-medium* of sorts because it consolidates many of the previously discrete and non-combinable products of human communication (the legacy media forms) within a single convergent channel of expression and delivery. Stated simply, multimedia is any combination of these five components: text, graphics, video, audio, and animation in a distributable format that consumers can interact with on a digital device.

TEXT

The first component of multimedia is text, which is the focus of chapter 8. Text is the visual expression of letters, numbers, and symbols used to communicate ideas and information to others through a human language system. Of the five elements of multimedia, text is the most ubiquitous. It represents the vast amount of visual content in most multimedia page layouts. If you doubt this, just compare the use and extent of text on Facebook or your favorite website to the other multimedia components on the same page. While graphics may consume more physical space in a layout, it is text that most often provides the intellectual substance, detail, meaning, and context in a visual design or presentation. The purpose of text in a multimedia project is fourfold: 1) to provide instruction, 2) to provide a written narrative, 3) to provide hierarchical structure, and 4) to facilitate discovery.

Text Provides Instruction

We've come to rely intuitively on visual text prompts to navigate web pages or make choices about where to go and what to do via the visual interface on our smartphone, tablet, game console, or television. Next time you are in a public building, look for the EXIT sign above an outside door. You rarely notice signs like this until you need them, but they are kept there to guide you when the time arises. When the power goes out, they shine as illuminated beacons to guide you safely out of the building. Likewise, text prompts are the digital signage of multimedia interfaces. We know from experience that a button labeled HOME will take us immediately to the landing page of the website we are currently on or to the top level of a compound menu system. Similarly, we click on the BACK button to retrace our steps to pages we have recently explored. When we embed text with a reference (or hyperlink), it becomes *hypertext*, a clickable object that users can interact with to immediately jump to another page or screen. Hypertext is usually color coded and underlined on web pages because, as creatures of habit, we want a predictable visual reminder to help us distinguish normal text from hypertext.

Text Provides a Written Narrative

Text is also used to tell stories and to communicate information and ideas about people, places, animals, objects, events, and so forth. Much of the textual content on commercial websites is carefully written prose in the form of advertisements, articles, news stories, blogs posts, captions, and so on. In this capacity, the purpose of text is largely informational and descriptive, although it can just as easily be entertaining or inspirational. Chapter 4 reminds us that "*content* is the tangible essence of a work: the stories, ideas, and information that we exchange with others." Text is the primary vehicle we use to deliver it.

Text Enables Hierarchy

In the context of a multimedia experience, the visual information on your screen is rarely equally weighted. Some textual elements are intended to have more significance than others. To this end, text is often used to provide structure and a hierarchical order to multimedia pages and screen layouts. For example, headings, like the one prior to this paragraph introducing the section, titled "Text Enables Hierarchy," are included to help organize the contents of each chapter into meaningful parts, just as chapter titles are used to arrange the entire manuscript into logically ordered and related subsections. The style of the heading text above was intentionally made to look different from the paragraph text (or body copy) that surrounds it. Because the heading text features a bold typeface and a larger font size, it stands out—thereby capturing more attention and enabling the reader to clearly see it as a separate, yet related, element on the page.

Text Is Discoverable

Finally, text can also be used to categorize digital content so others can discover it and have access to it. One of the most common ways to categorize content is by tagging. A tag is a short descriptive keyword or term about the subject of a written post or uploaded file. Any text that is entered on a web page or attached as metadata to a file using a text-based editor can be recognized and found through a digital search. Tags do not even have to be visible to users in order to be found by a search engine. In the case of web pages, tags are often invisible to the user and are only recognized beneath the surface in the HTML (Hypertext Markup Language) head tag or page title. Web page authors use HTML tags to enhance search engine optimization (SEO), a practice that can increase the likelihood that a particular page or site will appear on the results page of a search engine query.

Tech Talk

Hypermedia The term *hypermedia* refers to a host of digital technologies that allow for the presentation of multimedia content in a *nonlinear* form. Traditional media such as books and vinyl records have a native linear structure. Their contents are arranged in a fixed logical order of presentation from beginning to end and cannot be changed or modified by the reader or listener. Hypermedia, on the other hand, is not dependent on linear presentation alone, but allows the user to experience content in a nonlinear fashion. The path can vary depending on user-directed choices or spontaneous detours encountered along the way. Hypermedia is an extension of *hypertext*, a term coined in 1963 by technology pioneer and author Ted Nelson to describe text that is linked to other text, allowing the user to move between sections of text within the same page or between linked documents. In the case of hypermedia, the principle is applied to nontext elements. Hypertext and hypermedia are core elements of the World Wide Web, although the principles extend beyond the Web to any type of digital technology that allows users to randomly access content in a nonlinear way. The compact disc is a hypermedia technology because it allows users, in a nonlinear fashion, to skip tracks or change the location of the playhead rapidly rather than having to fast-forward by linear means, as we used to, when advancing through a tape recording.

FIGURE 1.4
NASA.gov is an example of a multimedia-rich website that includes articles and other text-based resources, public television channels and programming, social media feeds, image archives, photo and video galleries, and much more.
Source: http://www.nasa.gov/

An online file that has been tagged can eventually be located and retrieved by a web search engine like Google, which uses powerful computer algorithms to organize and index the content of web pages and social media sites. You can also use text-based searching for locating tagged items within popular sites like Facebook, Instagram, Pinterest, Twitter, and YouTube. Those of you who use social media on a regular basis may be acquainted with the practice of attaching a *hashtag* to content you've posted or uploaded through one of these services. A hashtag combines the hash symbol (better known as the number sign on a keypad) with a short descriptive term or phrase comprised only of alphanumeric characters with no spaces (e.g., #multimedia, #text). The use of hashtags has grown into something of a cultural epidemic as people often overuse the practice or, worse, use it as a way of poking fun at themselves or others. In such cases, the hashtag becomes a part of the message rather than a way of relating the subject of the post to a specific topic or group of people.

GRAPHICS

The second component of multimedia is *graphics*—the focus of chapters 9 and 10. While the importance of text cannot be overstated, a page or screen comprised entirely of text would come across to most of us as visually drab and one-dimensional. Graphics provide much of the visual sizzle and *wow factor* in a multimedia experience. The term *graphics* encompasses a broad variety of things, including digital photographs, illustrations, clipart, and any other type of still image that can be displayed on a digital screen or computer monitor. Having just talked about text, it's worth mentioning here that words and phrases can also be presented in the form of

FIGURE 1.5
Graphics add dynamic visual support to multimedia narratives. They can be used to illustrate concepts and ideas as well as bring visual energy, emotion, and pizzazz to your design.

VIDEO

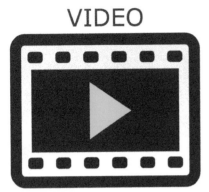

FIGURE 1.6
Video is one of three time-based components of multimedia. Whereas text and graphics are static by nature, video is a moving image or motion picture. We typically watch video in a linear format, from beginning to middle to end over a fixed span of time.

a graphic. However, when text is rendered and saved as a graphic, it loses its identity and meaning as text and cannot be understood by search engines unless it is tagged with metadata. A graphics editing program such as Adobe Photoshop or Adobe Illustrator can be used to create and edit graphics. Photoshop is used for editing digital photos and bitmap graphics, where pixels serve as the building blocks of a digital image. Illustrator is used primarily for editing vector graphics, which are defined by paths formed by points, lines, curves, and shapes. Chapter 9 expands more fully on the difference between these two types of computer graphics formats.

VIDEO

Video, the third component of multimedia, is an umbrella term for any type of motion picture system or format designed to capture and reproduce real-life movement across time. Video is covered at length in chapters 11 through 14. Today, the terms *video* and *film* are often used interchangeably when referring to television shows or movies. As a standalone medium, a television program or movie does not fully satisfy our definition of multimedia. However, when you package video into an interactive Blu-ray disc, it does. The Blu-ray disc contains a navigation menu that often includes a mix of text, graphics, animation, and sound. Likewise, when video is embedded into a web page or streamed online, the media skin or interface includes player controls for interacting with the content. Related content such as episode descriptions or program links may also be found nearby. Turning on subtitles adds the element of text to a video presentation.

Today, a cadre of devices can be used for shooting video, including traditional broadcast television cameras, video camcorders, HDSLRs (hybrid digital single lens reflex cameras), tablets, and smartphones. Nearly every laptop computer features a built-in camera, or webcam, for transmitting "live" selfies to connected parties during a Google Hangout, FaceTime, or Skype session. You can use this same camera to produce a video that you create and edit on your workstation before uploading it to your favorite social media site. The acronym NLE stands for *nonlinear editing*, the technology behind computer-based video editing. Today, the most popular professional NLE software programs are Adobe Premiere Pro, Apple Final Cut Pro, and Avid Media Composer.

AUDIO

FIGURE 1.7
Audio brings sound to our ears as either a standalone component or as a synchronized source tied to a visual narrative. It includes elements such as narration, dialog, sound bites, music, natural sound, and sound effects.

Audio is the fourth component of multimedia and refers to the aural content that's created through the electronic capture and reproduction of sound. Audio is covered in detail in chapters 11 and 12. By definition, video assumes the inclusion of an audio component while the opposite isn't true. Audio can serve as an independent element in the multimedia experience. Think about the last time you played a video game and how the music and sound effects contributed to the energy and excitement of the gaming experience. The element of sound is a potent time-based media element that can evoke memories and emotion or, at the very least, intensify them. Professional software tools such as Adobe Audition, Avid Pro Tools, and the popular free and open-source program Audacity are designed for audio recording, editing, mixing, and sweetening.

ANIMATION

FIGURE 1.8
Mario is the fictional animated mascot for Nintendo's popular video game franchise. Animation brings motion and lifelike qualities to computer-generated characters and objects over time. It is a common element of multimedia game design and an integral component of many film, video, website, and interface design projects.

ANIMATION

Animation is the process of creating motion over time through the rapid projection of a sequence of hand-drawn or computer-generated images and falls into two broad categories: 2D animation and 3D animation. In 2D animation, motion is constrained to horizontal and vertical paths along the x-axis and y-axis. In 3D animation, the third dimension of depth (the z-axis) is achieved through algorithmic manipulation of form, lighting, texture, perspective, and other motion variables. The term *animation* can refer globally to a specific genre of storytelling or moviemaking, such as in the Disney classic *Toy Story* (1995), the first feature-length film produced entirely with computer animation. Animation can also be combined with live action or used in the production of short-form works such as television commercials, cartoons, and animated shorts. The term *motion graphics* is commonly used to describe the animation of still images and graphics such as company logos or text.

Within the specific context of multimedia, animation is integrated into many websites and user interfaces as well as in standalone gaming products and applications. Animated websites and interface components can be produced using Dynamic HTML, Flash, and a variety of scripting languages, programs, and plug-ins. For example, a rollover button is an interactive component on a web page that performs an animation whenever a user hovers over it or clicks on it with the mouse. Likewise, an *animated GIF* is a series of still image frames that play on screen to give simple motion to a single web object or graphic. Finally, a wide range of visual effects, such as dissolves, wipes, page turns, and so forth, can be used to add motion to multimedia elements and transitions—bringing visual *eye candy* and pizzazz to an otherwise static image, page, interface component, or screen.

THE WORLD WIDE WEB

Invented by Tim Berners-Lee, the World Wide Web (WWW) became a reality in 1990 (see the chapter 7 Flashback entitled "A Brief History of the Internet and the World Wide Web"). For more than 20 years, the Web has been the dominant distribution platform for multimedia, and for many people today, it still is. However, in recent years, the Web has faced steady competition from newer technologies. While it remains a popular gateway to a plethora of multimedia content and experiences, more and more, users are producing and consuming multimedia through the growing cadre of "smart" devices and mobile media apps. Smartphones, smart TVs, tablet computers, gaming consoles, and similar devices are being touted as "multimedia enabled" by virtue of their ability to rapidly access nearly any form of media content from within the cloud or on the Web and through wireless Wi-Fi or cellular connections (see Figure 1.9).

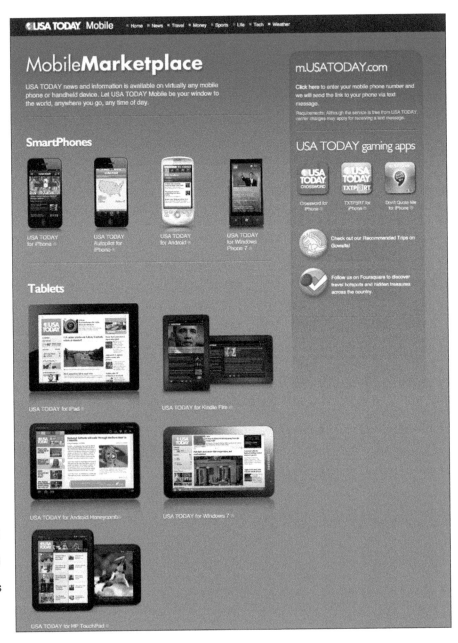

FIGURE 1.9
In addition to delivering content through traditional print and online media channels, *USA Today* offers readers access to its branded content through a cadre of mobile news and gaming apps.
Source: http://www.usatoday.com

FLASHBACK

My Introduction to the Web

The year was 1993, and I was in a study lounge with fellow graduate students at the University of Tennessee in Knoxville. We were seated around a small desk exploring a new software program that had just been installed on a Windows workstation. The program, called Mosaic (see Figure 1.10), was one of the first web browsers that could combine colored images with text on the same screen. The more I discovered about Mosaic's web-surfing capabilities, the more I began comparing the experience to that of my parents' generation, when people gazed upon broadcast television images for the very first time. Little did I know then that this nascent technology would change the world forever and affect me directly in my career as a video producer and media educator.

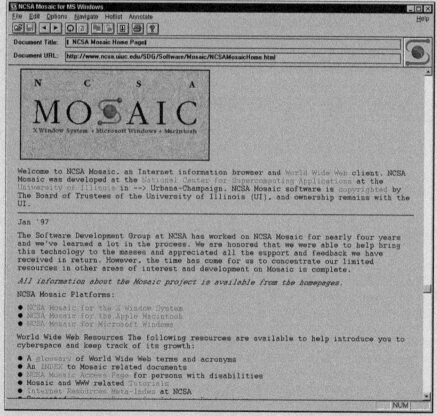

FIGURE 1.10
Mosaic 1.0 for Microsoft Windows was released in 1993 by the National Center for Supercomputing Applications. NCSA discontinued development and support for the browser in 1997.
Source: Courtesy of the National Center for Supercomputing Applications (NCSA) and the Board of Trustees of the University of Illinois.

(Continued)

Mosaic faded into obscurity nearly as quickly as it came into existence, eclipsed by Netscape Navigator in 1994. Despite its short life span, Mosaic was known as the "killer application" of the 1990s and was the catalyst for making the Internet accessible to the general public. While the Internet had been in existence for two decades, the human interface was text based, cryptic, and visually uninteresting. Mosaic was one of the first web browsers to feature a graphical user interface (GUI), an object-oriented design that was visually intuitive and easy to use. Mosaic introduced the Web to the masses and took the Internet mainstream.

Today, much of the media content we consume is available in a variety of formats intended to serve multiple purposes and audiences. For example, a book typically starts out as a print-only product. However, if the market demand is high enough, it may also be published in a spoken-word format, as an *audio book*, and delivered via compact disc or MP3. With the right equipment, you can avoid paper altogether by downloading the e-book, a digital version of the text designed for reading on a computer screen or on a tablet such as Amazon's Kindle Fire. The website for a bestseller may offer bonus material or value-added content to online users through a gamut of multimedia channels—featuring audio excerpts, video interviews, background stories, pictures, and more (see Figure 1.11). With such a vast sea of information and social networking potential, you can easily imagine many other possibilities. The opportunities for shaping content to meet the diverse needs and habits of different user groups are numerous and are evolving rapidly as the culture of multimedia continues to grow and permeate nearly every aspect of our personal and professional lives.

THREE GENERATIONS OF THE WEB

The evolution of the World Wide Web can be traced through three key stages of development, which are unofficially labeled Web 1.0, 2.0, and 3.0. The first generation of the Web, known as Web 1.0, covers the first decade of its existence from 1991 to 2001. This era was characterized by one-way communication and point-to-point exchanges of information. Web pages of this era usually mirrored the linear presentation and structure of a printed book. Static content, made up mostly of text and images, was consumed linearly in a traditional manner by reading from left to right and from top to bottom. User-generated content was unheard of, and there were few opportunities for interactivity, collaboration, or customization of the user experience. For most people, access to Web 1.0 was made possible through a low-bandwidth connection using a dial-up modem. While this was an adequate pipeline for the exchange of text and low-resolution graphics, it was not sufficient for handling the high-bandwidth transmissions of large files such as high-resolution images and streaming audio and video files.

Web 2.0 came into its own around 2001 following the dot-com bubble of the late 1990s. This generation of the Web ushered in the era of rich media content, dynamic web pages, content management systems, content sharing and collaboration sites, tagging, wikis, blogging, social networks, and more. Web 2.0 was made possible in large part by the release of program authoring tools used for creating Rich Internet

FIGURE 1.11
A companion website for the best-selling biography *Unbroken* by Laura Hillenbrand offers readers value-added content about the author and her subject. Here, an interactive map offers details about key locations in the subject's journey.
Source: http://laurahillenbrandbooks.com/.

Applications (RIAs). An RIA is a web-based application such as Adobe Flash, Oracle, Java, Microsoft Silverlight, or HTML5. RIAs typically require the use of a supported browser, media player, or browser plug-in (such as Flash Player or QuickTime) to run programs and view content. RIAs are used for deploying "rich media" or "interactive multimedia" content to consumers. As the name implies, rich media is designed to enrich the user's online experience by increasing opportunities for interactivity, customization, and personal control of a multimedia experience.

Timothy Berners-Lee, the inventor of the World Wide Web, coined the term *Semantic Web* to describe Web 3.0, which many see as the next significant iteration of the Web. The Semantic Web is defined as "a web of data that can be processed directly and indirectly by machines."[1] Web 3.0 will likely involve the creation of new standards and protocols for unifying the way that content is coded, organized, and analyzed by

FIGURE 1.12
World Wide Web is the name given to the vast system of interconnected servers used in the transmission of digital documents formatted using HTML via the Internet.

computers monitoring the Web. This may involve transforming the Web into a massive unified database akin to a virtual library. Such a vast library will require more sophisticated computers and search engines to categorize and make sense of its holdings. As computers become "smarter" and the engineering behind the Web grows more sophisticated, many believe we will see a significant increase in computer-generated content. Web 3.0 signals, in part, a larger role for computers as creators of intellectual content. Is a day coming when you will no longer be able to distinguish between content written by humans and machines? Has it already arrived?

GREAT IDEAS
Social Media

Social media is a broad term used to describe a growing host of tools and services that enable computer-mediated interpersonal, group, and mass communication (see Figure 1.13). Increasingly, they also support sharing of multimedia content in diverse forms and contexts. Social media can be broken down into many different categories of services as related to their general purpose and focus. A few of the most popular channels are included here.

FIGURE 1.13
The rapid proliferation of social media sites such as those represented here has contributed to a growing phenomenon known as *hyperconnectivity*—whereby people stay perpetually connected to the Web and to one another through a host of digital devices and apps.

- **Social networking** services such as Facebook, Snapchat, LinkedIn, and so on connect friends and people with common interests and backgrounds. They provide numerous opportunities for synchronous and asynchronous communication through features such as live messaging or chatting, email, updates, invitation and announcement posts, image and video sharing, and so forth.

- **Blogging** engines such as Blogger and WordPress provide users with an online publishing tool for the regular posting of written stories or narrative commentaries. The term *blog* is a blended form of the phrase "**web log.**" Blogs often focus on a particular subject or offer news and insight from a specific point of view. They can also serve as a public space for personal reflections, such as you might find in a diary or travel journal. Celebrities, media practitioners, and organizations (journalists, critics, actors, singers, authors, public relations firms, etc.) use blogs for interacting with fans, consumers, or the general public. Video blogging, or **vlogging** (pronounced *V-logging*), is a hybrid form of blogging that uses video in place of a written narrative. Vlogs typically feature a headshot of the individual as he or she communicates directly to the audience through a webcam attached to a personal computer. **Microblogging** is a variation of the blogging concept that limits communication to short strings of text or video. Microblogging services such as Tumblr and Twitter integrate the text-messaging capabilities of mobile technologies such as the cell phone with the enhanced distribution channels of the Web and mobile apps.

- A **wiki** is a tool that allows users to collaboratively create and edit documents and web pages online. Wikipedia, an online encyclopedic resource founded in 2001, is one of the most popular wikis. Entries in the Wikipedia database are posted and compiled interactively by a community of volunteers from around the world. Wikipedia is based on the MediaWiki platform. Like many of the wiki platforms, MediaWiki is free.

- **Content sharing** sites enable the exchange of various forms of multimedia content. Commercial photo sharing services such as Flickr and Shutterfly allow users to order photographic prints, albums, cards, and other products from content uploaded by family members and friends. Instagram integrates mobile photo- and video-sharing with other social media services such Facebook, Twitter, Tumble, and Flickr. Video-sharing tools such as YouTube, Vimeo, and Vine allow users to upload and embed video in their social media sites. Other services enable users to share music, audio resources, music playlists, and channels (as with the integration of Pandora Radio's online music service into Facebook and Twitter).

- **Social bookmarking** services (such as Delicious) and **news aggregators** (such as Digg) allow users to rate and share the most popular sites and news articles on the Web.

OLD MEDIA

The term *old media* has become synonymous with the seven original forms of mass communication: books, newspapers, magazines, film, sound recordings, radio, and television (see Figure 1.14), while the term *new media* is used to describe the relatively recent emergence of digital technologies that have changed the way content is produced, distributed, and consumed.

FIGURE 1.14
Old media. Seven industries are often grouped under the broad heading of mass media. The print media include books, newspapers, and magazines. Time-based media (also known as electronic media) include sound recordings, movies, radio, and television.

Old media can also refer to the discrete technologies, tools, practices, and workflows that communication professionals have traditionally used to craft messages and stories. Journalists work with paper, ink, and words; photographers are the masters of communicating through the still image; graphic designers create visual illustrations and page layouts; and video producers, audio engineers, and filmmakers engage audiences through sound recordings and motion pictures.

The legacy media of old such as newspapers, television, and motion pictures are still with us. Being "old" does not mean they have disappeared or no longer provide a viable commodity for consumers. Rather it reminds us that the previous century's models of mass media, which took many years to refine, are based on a different paradigm from those used by the new media platforms of the 21st century.

FLASHBACK

Paradigm Shift

Thomas Kuhn coined the term *paradigm shift* in 1962 as a way of describing monumental changes in the meanings of terms and concepts that would shake up the status quo, challenging the scientific community's preconceived ideas and assumptions about natural phenomena. Kuhn was a proponent of aggressive puzzle-solving science, the sort of out-of-the-box thinking that would break new ground, pushing his colleagues away from routine practices of "normal" science that were rooted in established theories and methodologies. With Kuhn's help, it may be better for us to think of old media as normal and new media as the inventive type, the kind that allows us to advance new ideas and methodologies of information sharing and social interaction. The old media were slow to change because of the tremendous investment in the physical infrastructure (television towers, printing presses, recording studios, etc.) and the high cost of producing and distributing content. The digital revolution and the birth of the World Wide Web represent two of the most important defining moments in the history of communication. The paradigm of old media was suddenly confronted with new ways of creating, delivering, and consuming content. A paradigm shift of epic proportions has occurred, and things will never be the same.

In the 1950s sociologist Charles Wright examined the mass media and found they share three defining characteristics:[2]

1. The mass media are the product of large organizations that operate with great expense.
2. The mass media are directed toward a relatively large, heterogeneous, and anonymous audience.
3. The mass media are publicly transmitted and timed to reach the most audience members simultaneously.

Large Organization

The first characteristic of old media is that they are the product of large organizations that operate with great expense. Hollywood movie studios, metro city newspapers, recording houses, television networks, broadcast television and radio stations, and book and magazine publishers are large entities employing many people with highly specialized skills and job functions. The concentration of media ownership has increased significantly over the years, leading to fewer and fewer companies owning more and more of the world's mass media outlets.

In 2015, *Forbes* listed Comcast as the largest entertainment and media conglomerate in the United States with net revenues in excess of $68 billion.[3] The top five also included The Walt Disney Company (#2), 21st Century Fox (#3), Time Warner (#4), and Time Warner Cable (#5). These are household names to many of us. Millions of people are touched daily by content delivered or produced by companies such as these or their subsidiaries. The start-up costs for a conventional media operation are high, which means that most people will never be able to own a television station or movie studio. Also, professional programming and content is difficult and expensive to create. A single episode of a primetime dramatic series can cost millions of dollars to produce.

THE CONSUMER AS PRODUCER: THE NEW MEDIA PARADIGM SHIFT

Consumers no longer have to rely solely on large organizations to provide them with news and entertainment. The shift to new media means that anyone can produce and deliver content to a public audience. User-generated content (UGC), or consumer-generated media (CGM), bypasses the formal gatekeeping functions and monopolistic control that characterize the old media factories of cultural production. This paradigm shift is sometimes referred to as the *democratization of media* because it empowers the individual with a multitude of outlets for personal expression. With a little bit of new media know-how, you can self-publish a book or compact disc, rule a country in Second Life, post a video on YouTube, send an iReport to CNN as a citizen journalist, maintain a blog or Twitter feed, create a website, manage a radio station, host a podcast, and so much more.

The opportunities for self-expression and commercial enterprise are virtually unlimited (see Figure 1.15). If the content you publish is compelling enough, you might even develop a significant following. Almost daily, we hear of people rising to celebrity status, sometimes almost overnight, by publishing an item of sensational interest on the Web. For example, think about how often you hear about a new *viral video* that is trending in the news or rapidly gaining views as word spreads through the social network grapevines. Word travels quickly through the emerging channels of social media as well as through the more established mainstream media outlets as they monitor and report on Internet trends and pop culture. As Andy Warhol so aptly predicted in 1968, "in the future, everyone will be world-famous for 15 minutes." With new media and the Web, this has never been more likely.

FIGURE 1.15
Launched in 2006, CNN iReport gives users of CNN.com a public outlet for posting opinion pieces, news reports, photos, and video. The best submissions are marked with a red CNN iReport stamp, meaning they have been vetted and cleared for mainstream distribution on CNN. *Source: http://www. ireport.cnn.com.*

Large Audience

Wright's second characteristic of old media states that they are optimized to reach a large, anonymous, and heterogeneous audience. This characteristic identifies the receiver of a mass media message as a large group of people collectively known as "the audience." For this reason, they are sometimes called the "mass audience." The model of advertiser-supported media, which has been in use in the United States since the modern era of commercial printing and broadcasting, makes content available to consumers for free or at a partially subsidized cost. With this model, a media company generates revenue indirectly through the sale of commercial advertisements. A "mass" audience ensures a sufficient return on investment (ROI). Television programs will continue or be discontinued based on their ability to maintain a large audience. When audience numbers fall below a predetermined threshold or break-even point, a program is cut to minimize losses.

While media research and marketing analytics firms such as Nielsen and Alexa can provide aggregate data about the size and composition of a mass audience, the individual identities of people consuming mass media messages are largely unknown (see Table 1.1 through Table 1.3). An exception occurs with subscription services such as newspapers and magazines. Still, for every known person who subscribes, there are many anonymous users who acquire print products through point-of-purchase displays, magazine racks, street vendors, and the like.

DESIGNATED MARKET AREA (DMA)

The United States is divided into 210 *designated market areas* (DMA) for television broadcasting. Each DMA represents a specific geographic area that is regionally served by local television stations transmitting over-the-air signals. The list of radio station DMAs is even larger because, due to FCC (Federal Communications Commission) power restrictions, their market size is typically much smaller than their television counterparts.

Table 1.1 The Top 25 Television Markets in the United States

Rank	Designated Market Area (DMA)	TV Homes	% of U.S.
1	New York	7,442,270	6.539
2	Los Angeles	5,523,800	4.854
3	Chicago	3,477,250	3.055
4	Philadelphia	2,953,760	2.595
5	Dallas–Ft. Worth	2,603,680	2.288
6	San Francisco–Oakland–San Jose	2,476,860	2.176
7	Boston (Manchester)	2,423,640	2.130
8	Washington, DC (Hagerstown)	2,408,990	2.117
9	Atlanta	2,334,520	2.051
10	Houston	2,301,230	2.022
11	Phoenix (Prescott)	1,834,360	1.612

(Continued)

Table 1.1	Continued		
Rank	**Designated Market Area (DMA)**	**TV Homes**	**% of U.S.**
12	Detroit	1,833,320	1.611
13	Tampa–St. Petersburg (Sarasota)	1,822,550	1.601
14	Seattle–Tacoma	1,802,920	1.584
15	Minneapolis–St. Paul	1,730,170	1.520
16	Miami–Ft. Lauderdale	1,632,760	1.435
17	Denver	1,565,760	1.376
18	Orlando–Daytona Beach–Melbourne	1,472,960	1.294
19	Cleveland–Akron (Canton)	1,469,190	1.291
20	Sacramento–Stockton–Modesto	1,345,960	1.183
21	St. Louis	1,226,860	1.078
22	Pittsburg	1,173,320	1.031
23	Portland	1,154,070	1.014
24	Charlotte	1,154,040	1.014
25	Raleigh–Durham	1,135,920	0.998
~	~	~	~
206	Helena, MT	27,850	0.024
207	Juneau, AK	25,460	0.022
208	Alpena, MI	16,580	0.015
209	North Platte, NE	14,830	0.013
210	Glendive, MT	4,330	0.004
	Total U.S.	**113,808,820**	**100.000**

Source: The Nielsen Company, January 1, 2015.
Note: For television, the DMAs are rank ordered from largest to smallest according to the number of television homes in each region.

The term *broadcasting* is a metaphor taken from earlier days when farmers sowed seeds manually by tossing them into the air with a sweeping movement of the hand. The farmer's "broadcast" method of planting his fields ensured the seed would be evenly dispersed in the air before hitting the ground. Done correctly, this would produce a healthy crop of evenly spaced plants. Radio and television broadcasters use this principle to transmit programming to a mass audience. Based on the frequency and power allocation awarded to them by the FCC, they have a specific geographic region in which to operate. The broadcast signal is dispersed evenly over this area, falling randomly on home receivers that happen to be tuned in at any given moment. The opportunity to receive a broadcast signal is open to the public at large. While social and economic factors prevent some people

Table 1.2	U.S. Broadcast TV Ratings for Week of February 8, 2016			
Rank	Program	Network	Rating	Viewers (000)
1	NCIS	CBS	10.4	16,941
2	THE BIG BANG THEORY	CBS	9.8	16,250
3	CAMPAIGN '16 REP DEBATE	CBS	8.1	13,443
4	NCIS: NEW ORLEANS	CBS	7.7	12,587
5	SCORPION	CBS	7.0	11,364
6	BLUE BLOODS	CBS	6.9	10,924
7	60 MINUTES	CBS	6.5	10,417
8	MADAM SECRETARY	CBS	6.2	10,061
9	NCIS: LOS ANGELES	CBS	6.2	9,755
10	LIFE IN PIECES	CBS	5.7	9,348

Media companies and advertisers rely on audience research firms like Nielsen for statistical data about the consumption patterns of television viewers.
Source: The Nielsen Company. Viewing estimates here include live viewing and DVR playback on the same day, defined as 3 a.m.–3 a.m. Ratings are the percentage of TV homes in the United States tuned into television.

Table 1.3	Top 10 Websites in the United States
Rank	Website
1	Google.com
2	Facebook.com
3	Amazon.com
4	YouTube.com
5	Yahoo.com
6	Wikipedia.com
7	eBay.com
8	Twitter.com
9	Reddit.com
10	Go.com

Source: Alexa.com, October 27, 2015.

from owning a receiver, the wide distribution of the broadcast signal ensures delivery of the content to a diverse and heterogeneous audience. In order to appeal to a large and diverse audience, programming has to be broadly appealing to average groups of people or segments of the population. While programming can be targeted to specific groups such as men and woman, narrowing the focus too much can result in an audience size that's too small to offset expenses or meet profit expectations.

NARROWCASTING: THE NEW MEDIA PARADIGM SHIFT

With new media, consumers have greater access to content that interests them the most. Tuned in to a traditional radio broadcast signal, a listener must conform to the linear presentation of a playlist as determined by the on-air announcer or music director of the station. While it's possible to switch to a different station on the radio dial at any time, the presentation of musical selections is fixed and cannot be altered by the listener to fit his or her personal tastes and preferences. A new media paradigm shift has occurred with services such as Pandora, an Internet radio service. Pandora calls itself "a new kind of radio—stations that play only the music you like." With Pandora, a user can enter the name of a favorite song or artist. The Pandora search engine will analyze the selection and generate a playlist based on similar styles of music. You can skip a song you do not like and a new song will begin. User feedback in the form of approvals, disapprovals, and skips provides Pandora with information it then uses to improve future selections and playlists. The term *narrowcasting* is used to describe the new media technique of delivering content of value to a niche audience with shared values and interests. Narrowcasting shifts power to consumers, enabling them to access the content they enjoy most, more quickly, and without having to be bound to linear and fixed methods of content distribution.

FIGURE 1.16
Like Pandora, the streaming music service Spotify allows users to create custom playlists and channels to fit their personal tastes and preferences. As with commercial radio, music streaming ventures like this are funded by advertising, keeping the basic service free to the consumer. Users can enjoy ad-free listening by paying a monthly or annual subscription.

Simultaneous Delivery

Wright's third characteristic of mass media states that they are publicly transmitted and timed to reach the most audience members simultaneously. The mass media industries use expensive distribution systems to ensure a product is delivered to consumers in a timely manner. For example, a new motion picture is released to all theaters on the same day. The *Wall Street Journal* arrives in a subscriber's mailbox on the publication date whether the reader resides in Atlanta or Milwaukee. Television networks go through great pains and lots of research to determine the best day of the week and time to air their programming. Once the schedule is set, consumers must align their schedules and expectations to fit the producer's timetable.

Old media are also transient in nature. Mass mediated messages are available for a season, and once they've aired or become outdated, they are removed from circulation. Newspapers have a shelf life of only one day for a daily paper or seven days for a weekly edition.

Before the invention of home recording technologies such as VHS tape or the popular digital video recorder (DVR) TiVo, consumers had to conform to the broadcaster's fixed program schedule. It was not unusual for families to alter their schedule to accommodate the viewing of a favorite television program. Today, consumers are no longer constrained to watching a program as it is being broadcast over the air or via cable at its regularly scheduled time slot. Instead, streaming services such as Amazon Instant Video, Apple iTunes, Hulu, and Netflix make television shows and movies available to consumers—for a fee, of course! In addition, cable and television networks routinely provide free access to recently aired episodes of their programs through their official websites.

NEW MEDIA

The transition to new media began in the early 1980s with the proliferation of the personal computer (see Figure 1.17). The digital revolution, as it is often called, fundamentally changed many of the ways people work, produce, and interact with one another. It also opened up many new methods for the production and distribution of media content. In *Being Digital*, Nicolas Negroponte uses the phrase "from atoms to bits" to describe the revolutionary shift in the production of intellectual content from a material form consisting of *atoms* (film; printed matter such as books, magazines, and newspapers; phonograph records and cassette tapes; etc.) into an electronic format made up of *bits* (the invisible numeric output of computers and digital devices).[4]

Moving from atoms to bits is reflected in the transition from a print newspaper to an online version that readers consume on a computer screen. It means shifting from a physical book to a virtual one using a tablet computer and book-reading *app*. It means moving away from the distribution of content in a purely tangible format such as a record, tape, or compact disc to an electronic format that comes to us as a digital download. With digital content, a computer, tablet, or smartphone is needed to decode information from an encrypted format (or digital cipher) into human symbols and sounds that we recognize and comprehend. Material content

FIGURE 1.17
New media extends the reach and capabilities of all forms of media content to consumers through a host of new methods and delivery channels.

(made of atoms) must be transported by hand (person to person, postal service, FedEx, etc.). Digital information is more easily transferable from person to person and across geographic space. In fact, the distribution possibilities are nearly endless. Bits can travel across telephone lines, via fiber optic cable, or through the airwaves using wireless transmission systems.

For decades, media producers had little choice but to use physical media (made of atoms) for recording and archiving content. Early photographic images were recorded on metal and glass plates and later on celluloid film. Animations used to be entirely hand drawn by the artist frame by frame on a transparent sheet of thermoplastic called a *cel* (short for the *celluloid* material it was made from). Sound and video were captured and edited on magnetic tape. Books and printed materials were published using mechanical typesetting equipment and paper. Being digital means moving away from traditional processes that depended so heavily on proprietary platforms and methods of creative expression.

Today, a growing number of photographers routinely shoot and edit their own video stories; graphic designers are busy retraining as web designers in order to retain a job or advance in a career; video and film have become nearly synonymous terms, having been unified (at least in part) through significant advancements in digital imaging and editing technologies; and journalists are fighting for survival as the traditional products of the information age, such as the newspaper, are growing less viable in a digital marketplace driven by instant access, free content, and mobile delivery. More than ever before, media professionals are crossing historic lines that have previously defined who they are and how they produce and deliver content to consumers. What lies on the other side can be exciting or scary, depending on your point of view and ability to adapt rapidly to change.

In his book *The Language of New Media*, author Lev Manovich uses the phrase "the computerization of media" to highlight what he sees as the primary distinctions between old and new media. According to Manovich, "just as the printing press in the fourteenth century and photography in the nineteenth century had a revolutionary impact on the development of modern society and culture, today we are in the middle of a new media revolution—the shift of all culture to computer-mediated forms of production, distribution, and communication."[5] In the new media era, the computer assumes a dominant role as the universal instrument of inspiration, creation, distribution, and consumption, radically transforming old methods and workflows that have defined media production and cultural transmission for centuries (see Figure 1.19).

FIGURE 1.18
Old media haven't died, but, rather, they've evolved and adapted as the technology infrastructures and platforms became digital and converged—leading to many changes in how media content is now delivered and consumed.

FIGURE 1.19
In addition to its traditional print products, the *New York Times* offers advertisers access to new media channels (online, mobile, and tablet). *Source: http://www.nytmediakit.com.*

Five Principles of New Media

Manovich goes on to list five principles of new media that he says reflect the "general tendencies of a culture undergoing computerization." He named these principles 1) numerical representation, 2) structural modularity, 3) automation, 4) variability, and 5) cultural transcoding. While not entirely exclusive to new media, this list identifies some of the most significant differences between the media of today and those of previous generations.

NUMERICAL REPRESENTATION

The first principle of new media is called "numerical representation" and states that new media objects can be defined numerically as a formal equation or mathematical function. The computer reduces every act of human communication to a binary expression made up of zeros and ones (*bits*).

Old media relied on analog methods of reproduction and distribution. An analog audio or video recording is represented by a continuous signal, whose physical qualities vary across time along a linear path. For example, when listening to a phonograph recording, the stylus is placed in the groove of a vinyl record. As the record spins, the stylus (usually a diamond or other hard stone) advances along a spiral path while sensing minute variations in the structure of the groove. The stylus stays in direct contact with the record at all times, resulting in the reproduction of a continuous uninterrupted sound signal. The vibrations picked up by the stylus correspond directly to the fluctuating properties of a live sound performance across time. The term *analog* is used to describe this type of process because the man-made recording is directly comparable to the physical properties of the original sound source.

The digital sound recording process is different. A digital audio recorder converts the properties of sound to a numerical value at discrete intervals of time. Each point of measurement is called a *sample*. In professional audio recording, sound is sampled at 48 kHz (or 48,000 times per second). This means that every 1/48,000th of a second, the computer measures the sound source's physical properties and records them as a data file. In a digital recording, the value of each sample is retained in numerical form, allowing it to be individually addressed and affected mathematically. While it would be difficult and impractical to try to edit 48,000 individual samples of a one-second audio clip, the fact that a digital signal is numerical opens up opportunities that were impossible to achieve before computerization. New media, because they are digital, are naturally subject to algorithmic control and manipulation.

Tech Talk

Algorithm An *algorithm* is a mathematical sequence or set of instructions for solving a problem. The software tools used in multimedia design and editing employ mathematical algorithms to systematically rewrite the numerical data structure of a computer file. This results in a wonderful partnership between people and machines. The designer can focus on the creative tasks of authoring and content creation while the computer performs the math, crunching numbers at an amazing speed behind the scenes while the designer works.

Like a digital audio recorder, a digital camera uses sampling to create a digital image. Before computerization, photography involved the production of a "continuous" tone image on a sheet of film emulsion. Held up to a light and magnified, the negative imprint of the image was uninterrupted, a perfect analog of the intensity of light captured by the photographer through the lens of the camera. With a digital still camera, the image plane is broken down into a grid made up of millions of individual light-sensing picture elements called pixels. The computer saves the color information of each pixel, or sample, as a numeric value and stores it in the image's data file. Math is an integral part of the process, and the computer uses algorithms to both compress and modify the pixel values. For example, applying the *blur tool* in Adobe Photoshop to a digital image causes the pixels in the path of the tool's cursor to lose focus and soften. As you move the tool across the image, the appearance of each pixel it interacts with is visibly altered. In the background, what's really happening is that the numerical value of each affected pixel is being changed to reflect the altered state of its new appearance. As you change the properties of a tool (e.g., make the brush tip bigger or lighten the stroke intensity, etc.), the underlying algorithm is adjusted to yield the desired effect (see Figure 1.20).

Convergence

Convergence is a term used to describe the merging of previously discrete technologies into a unified whole. A digital smartphone is the perfect example of convergence at work in a new media device. The primary function of a smartphone is telecommunication, enabling the user to have a conversation with a distant party on the other end of the line. This function preserves the original purpose of the telephone as an instrument of person-to-person voice communication. The smartphone, however, is much more than a telephone appliance—it's a mobile wireless device capable of 1) surfing the Web; 2) capturing still images, video, and sound; 3) texting using the industry-wide SMS protocol (or Short Message Service); 4) sending and receiving images, video, sound, newsfeeds, ringtones, and so on using the industry-wide MMS protocol (Multimedia Messaging Service); 5) downloading, uploading, and storing digital content; 6) running software apps; 7) location and navigation services (using built-in GPS [Global Positioning System] technology); and 8) playing multimedia content (music, video, etc.). A smartphone is essentially a computer. It has a microprocessor, operating system, RAM (random access memory), and storage media. Because of this, the smartphone can become anything a computer software application will allow it to become.

Convergence is a product of the digital revolution, made possible by the commonalities of a shared binary language system. Before the computerization of communication media, each system and tool functioned according to the principles of a proprietary design and system architecture. The tools of old media—cameras, televisions, cassette tape recorders, telephones, and so forth—were discrete inventions designed to perform a single primary function. Combining such a divergent mishmash of technology together was like mixing oil and water.

Original Image

FIGURE 1.20
Using Adobe Photoshop, various visual effects were applied to the original image of the hurdler to achieve the four altered versions. Effects such as these are produced by the software mathematically through algorithmic manipulation.

In the absence of a common structural platform, convergence was not possible (see Figure 1.21).

STRUCTURAL MODULARITY

As we continue our discussion of Manovich's principles of new media, you will notice they are somewhat interdependent and often build upon previous attributes

FIGURE 1.21
In the not-too-distant past, a phone was just a phone. It was used for the sole purpose of establishing voice communication between two people. Today, the smartphone represents the convergence of many previously discrete communication technologies. It is a "multimedia enabled" device that functions more like a computer than the telephone some of us remember from earlier days.

in the list. Thus, we can say that the second principle of new media, called *structural modularity*, is made possible because of new media's property of numerical representation. Modularity means that a new media object retains its individuality when combined with other objects in a large-scale project. This is only possible because the computer sees each structural element in a design as a distinct mathematical object or expression.

The principle of modularity isn't limited to text alone. To illustrate, let's take a look at a common multimedia program many of you may be familiar with. A Microsoft PowerPoint presentation is a good example of structural modularity at work in the new media age. A PowerPoint slideshow is made up of a collection of slides positioned and arranged in a logical order of presentation. The designer can apply a unique transition or timing function to each slide individually, or he or she may choose to assign a single effect globally to all the slides in the presentation. Each slide is populated with its own unique content and design elements (text, graphics, video, sound, background image, etc.), each of which can be individually altered without affecting the others. The principle of structural modularity allows you to build a project from the ground up, one piece at a time, without losing independent control of each of the constituent parts of the whole.

In PowerPoint, as in many other programs, a designer can interact with a project's content on multiple levels. On the macro level, you can edit global properties such as the slide template and background colors. It's also possible to interact with multiple objects simultaneously by grouping them and manipulating them as one. On a micro

Adobe Photoshop CS5

FIGURE 1.22
This composite image, created in Adobe Photoshop, is constructed of four separate elements: 1) sky, 2) sun, 3) person, and 4) house. Each element resides on its own editable layer, allowing the designer to alter each constituent part of a design independently of the others.
Source: Adobe product screenshot reprinted with permission from Adobe Systems Incorporated.

level, you can make changes to a single element on a particular slide. For example, an image on the first slide can be cropped or resized without affecting content on the second slide. Likewise, a style can be applied to a single letter, word, sentence, or paragraph, simply by selecting the portion of text you wish to transform (see Figure 1.22).

Structural modularity is most valuable during the editing phase of a project, prior to the point when you export it for distribution or deployment. Most multimedia software tools, such as those used for photo, video, and audio editing, are designed to give you total control of the project assets and elements during the editing process. Once editing is complete, however, you'll usually export the project for distribution in a compressed and uneditable file format. As an example, the native file format for Adobe Photoshop is *.psd* (Photoshop Document Format). As long as you are working in the original PSD version of a graphic or image file, you will be able to edit all the constituent parts of the graphic (layer objects, text, styles, etc.). When you are ready to put the image online, however, you'll need to convert it to a JPG, GIF, or PNG file (we'll learn more about these later). These distribution formats, while web friendly, are uneditable. They are only intended for viewing with a browser such as Chrome or Safari. Structural modularity is preserved only in the original native file format of the application that created it.

AUTOMATION

According to Manovich, digitization and structural modularity are the antecedents upon which the third principle of new media, automation, is predicated. With automation, the computer can be programmed to serve as an agent of content production. Low-level creative tasks can be carried out through automated machine processes or preprogrammed batch sequences. This feature can save time and often requires little expertise on the part of the user.

The power of automation can be demonstrated with SimpleViewer, a free cross-platform software program that allows users with no advanced coding or programming skills to create a professional image gallery for the Web in a matter of minutes. The first step to creating an image gallery with SimpleViewer is to drag the images you want included in the gallery to a designated drop zone. A user-friendly interface then walks you through the few easy steps of sorting the images, adding captions, and customizing the slideshow's visual design and interface. The final step is to click on the Publish button to create the gallery. The publishing step initiates a script that automatically generates all the programming scripts, code, and web files needed to make the gallery function online (see Figure 1.23).

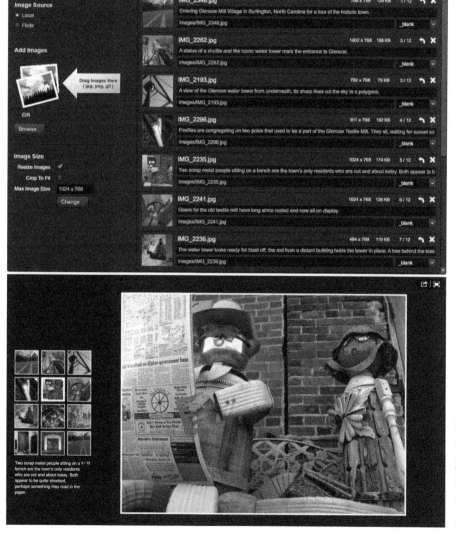

FIGURE 1.23
The photo story shown here (bottom) was created using SimpleViewer (top), a free application for creating a customizable image gallery for the Web.
Source: Courtesy of Kaz Colquitt.

The software and web-based tools of multimedia creation grow more sophisticated each year. Prebuilt templates and user interface components, widgets, scripts, and style sheets are just a few of the things users can utilize to fully or partially automate complex operations. While software tools and web applications are increasingly more intuitive and intelligent with each new release, computerized automation has yet to replace the human element. Producers should strive to embrace the potential efficiencies of workflow automation without sacrificing the autonomy and aesthetic sensibilities of the content creator. In short, some tasks ought never to be delegated to the computer.

VARIABILITY

Manovich's fourth principle of new media is variability. It states that new media objects are not bound to a single fixed form but can exist, and often do, in a "potentially infinite" number of versions. As I've already noted, it's common practice to create and edit projects in one format while distributing them in another. For this reason, new documents and project files are usually saved first in the native file format of the application that created them. For example, a Microsoft Word document originates as a *.doc* or *.docx* file. A Photoshop project is saved natively using the *.psd* file format. Professional sound recordings often start out as uncompressed WAV or AIFF audio files. And a digital video project may include source material that was acquired in a QuickTime or MPEG-4 compression format.

Before publishing a Word document to the Web, however, it's best to convert it to a more widely accessible format such as PDF (Postscript Document Format). PDF is a universal file format that nearly everyone with a computer and Internet access will be able to download and read. After conversion, the same document will now

Tech Talk

Batch Processing *Batch processing* is the execution of a series of sequential actions performed by a digital device or software application. For example, one repetitive task I find myself doing often is selecting, sorting, and renaming digital images after a photo shoot. I can perform this type of activity manually, or I can turn to a computer and software program to assist me. For a job like this, I usually turn to Adobe Bridge. Using the virtual light box in Bridge, I begin by selecting the keepers, the images I like best and would like to see included in my project. Next, I rearrange them by dragging and dropping them into a desired sequence order. Finally, I choose the Batch Rename option from the Tools menu to automatically apply a renaming algorithm to my sorted images. The Batch Rename properties window provides me with several options for specifying a file name prefix and sequence number.

As Figure 1.24 shows, I enter the word *image* in the text field for the prefix and select a three-digit sequence number for the second part of the naming protocol. The result will be as follows: image001.jpg, image002.jpg, image003.jpg, and so on. After entering all the required information, I click on the Rename button to perform the automated process—and just like that it's done. Without automation, even a simple procedure like this can end up taking a lot of time to manually perform, particularly when working with a large collection of images. Automation saves me time and effort I would rather not waste completing low-level menial tasks such as renaming files. It also ensures the process is performed flawlessly, without the human mistakes that are more likely to occur during manual editing. A savvy multimedia producer stays on the lookout for tools and automated processes that can speed up or enhance workflow productivity and performance.

FIGURE 1.24
The Batch Rename tool in Adobe Bridge is used to automatically rename five selected image files (top) and copy them to a new folder (bottom).
Source: Adobe product screenshot reprinted with permission from Adobe Systems Incorporated.

exist in two different formats. I will retain a copy of the MS Word version (.docx) in case I ever need to make changes to the original document or export it in a another format. The PDF version will be used only as a distribution format for making the document available to others.

Likewise, I often use Adobe Photoshop to create graphics for the Web. However, before publishing a graphic to the Web, it must be saved in a browser-friendly format such as JPEG, GIF, or PNG. To minimize file size and conserve bandwidth during transmission, online music files and podcasts are usually distributed in a compressed format such as MP3 or AAC. As a final example, in order to burn an HD video project to Blu-ray disc, the video must be encoded in the MPEG-4 file format while the audio is encoded to AC3.

The principle of variability means you can export, convert, or transcode digital files for a variety of purposes—to accommodate multiple distribution channels or to conform to a designated industry standard as appropriate. Because digital content

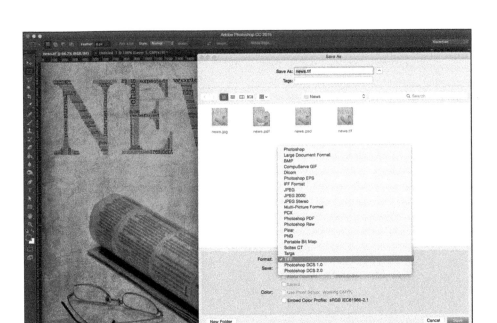

FIGURE 1.25
A graphics editor such as Adobe Photoshop offers users many different format options when it comes to saving and exporting bitmap images. Photoshop's native file format is PSD. Some other popular formats you are likely to run into are JPEG, TIF, PDF, and PNG.
Source: Adobe product screenshot reprinted with permission from Adobe Systems Incorporated.

is numerical, the data structure can be altered mathematically, allowing files to be re-encoded any time the need arises (see Figure 1.25).

CULTURAL TRANSCODING

Manovich's fifth principle of new media delves deeply into the theoretical implications of using computers to represent the various products of human culture. He uses the term *cultural transcoding* to describe the bidirectional influence of computers and human culture acting reciprocally upon one another. With old media, the methods of production and distribution were based largely on organic processes that conformed to the natural properties of a specific medium or method of reproduction. Sound and light were captured and stored in a way that attempted to preserve the native structure and form of physical properties in a natural way. Manovich believes new media is partitioned into two competing parts, which he calls the "cultural layer" and the "computer layer," and that each of these layers is constantly at work influencing the other. The merging of the two layers is producing a new "computer culture"—"a blend of human and computer meanings, of traditional ways in which human culture modeled the world and the computer's own means of representing it." In the words of Marshall McLuhan, "We become what we behold. We shape our tools and then our tools shape us."[6]

CHAPTER SUMMARY

In the mid-1990s, Nicholas Negroponte, then director of MIT's Media Lab, argued that the world's economy was moving rapidly from the production of material objects comprised of atoms to immaterial ones made of bits. He knew that any object of human creativity that could be digitized could also, then, be delivered to consumers via the world's growing networks of computer and telecommunication systems. Digital platforms would become the dominant means for designing, producing, and distributing ideas in the next information age. Fewer than 20 years after his forecast, history has proven this to be true. Amazon now sells more e-books per year than physical books; YouTube is the largest distributer of streaming video content in the world, with an estimated 300 hours of video content uploaded every minute;[7] and, if Facebook were a country, it would be the largest nation on earth, with a monthly active user population of 1.39 billion people.[8] Physical letters and cards? Who needs such primitive and time-consuming methods of communication when you can post an electronic message, photo, or video to *the wall*? The move from physical to digital production and consumption has rapidly reshaped how people interact with one another and how users consume the media products professionals create. With new media, the consumer is potentially just as influential as the producer. In fact, we can no longer speak in such archaic ways about consumers and producers. In the multimedia age, everyone can be both and often is.

In this first chapter, we have defined multimedia as any communication event that combines text, graphics, video, audio, and animation though a digital channel or device. Understanding multimedia requires an appreciation for the traditional mass media industries and systems that have influenced human communication for more than 100 years. For the time being, *old media* such as broadcast television, books, newspapers, radio, and so forth remain relevant and are an important part of the media mix we continue to enjoy; however, the legacy industries of mass media have been forced to adapt and evolve within a radically changing paradigm and economic model. Likewise, consumers have also been forced to accept change—for one, transitioning from basic phones to smartphones! The digital revolution brings with it a whole new set of technologies, concepts, and workflows that we are being challenged to embrace and understand. As with many things, understanding multimedia requires us to explore the present and to engage the future through the lens of past experience and practice.

NOTES

1 Berners-Lee, T., Hendler, J., & Lassila, O. (2001, May 17). The Semantic Web: A new form of Web content that is meaningful to computers will unleash a revolution of new possibilities. *Scientific American Magazine* 284(5), 34–43.
2 Wright, C. R. (1959). *Mass communication: A sociological perspective*. New York: Random House.
3 http://www.forbes.com/
4 Negroponte, N. (1996). *Being digital*. New York: Vintage Books.
5 Manovich, L. (2001). *The language of new media*. Cambridge, MA: The MIT Press.
6 McLuhan, M. (1964). *Understanding media: The extensions of man*. New York: McGraw-Hill.
7 http://www.youtube.com/yt/press/statistics.html
8 http://investor.fb.com/releasedetail.cfm?ReleaseID=893395

CHAPTER 2
The Computer

When we are . . . connected through our computers, we can achieve collective creative heights. Computers have already changed the way we lead our lives. Doubtlessly they will continue to do so. What is up to us is utilizing the positive potential—figuring out how we'd like them to serve us, and demanding that of our technicians, as we make the Net in our own image.

—Justin Allyn Hall, *Computopia: Sharing Stories Humanizes Computer Connections* (1995)

Chapter Highlights

This chapter examines:

- Personal computing and the digital revolution
- Computer hardware and software as a tool for the multimedia producer
- The human interface device—using a mouse and keyboard to interact with a computer
- The graphical user interface—using visual prompts and symbols to interact with a computer
- The importance of file management and storage solutions for saving, retrieving, and managing digital information

HISTORY OF THE PERSONAL COMPUTER

While we are used to a computer fitting comfortably on a table, desk, or even in a pocket, many early computers (built before the 1970s) were quite large. One reason for this was that they used vacuum tubes instead of integrated circuits to control the flow of electric current to internal components. Vacuum tubes were the basic component of all electronic equipment (radio and television receivers, amplifiers, etc.) manufactured in the first half of the 19th century. They were bulky and generated lots of heat.

Key Terms

Android
Apple iOS
Application Software
ASCII
Bandwidth
Bit
Blu-ray Disc
Byte
Clock Speed
Cloud Storage
Compact Disc (CD-ROM)
Content Management System (CMS)
CPU (Central Processing Unit)
DVD (Digital Versatile Disc)
File
Firewire
Fixed Storage
Flash Memory
Folder
Gigabyte
Graphical User Interface (GUI)
Hard-Disk Drive (HDD)
Hardware
Human Interface Device (HID)
Keyboard
Kilobyte
Local Area Network (LAN)

Mac OS X
Megabyte
Memory Card
Microcomputer
Microprocessor
Microsoft
  Windows
Mobile App
Moore's Law
Mouse
Network-Attached
  Storage (NAS)
Operating System
Optical Disk
PC
RAM (Random
  Access Memory)
Removable
  Storage
Solid-State Drive
  (SSD)
Storage
Terabyte
Thunderbolt
USB (Universal
  Serial Bus)

FIGURE 2.1
Vacuum tubes such as these were common components in electronic equipment prior to the
invention of solid-state electronics.
Source: Dpbsmith at English Wikipedia, Creative Commons License BY-SA-3.0.

The 1946 Electronic Numerical Integrator and Calculator (ENIAC) weighed
30 tons, used over 17,000 vacuum tubes, and filled 1,800 square feet (see Figures
2.1 and 2.2). As technology improved, computers became smaller and more reliable, particularly with the transition from tubes to transistors. By the late 1950s,
computers were down to the size of three or four large refrigerators, but they had
a limitation—they were designed to run one program at a time, a process known
as "batch computing." In 1961, researchers at MIT developed CTSS (Compatible
Time Sharing System), an experimental multi-user computer system. CTSS helped
shift the way people interacted with computers, opening the door to off-site computer access using the telephone system to connect users via remote terminals.
Computer availability grew rapidly in the 1960s, but personal computers were well
out of reach until the development of the microprocessor in 1971. The microprocessor combined core-computing functions on a single chip, and although the
first microprocessor, designed for a calculator, only did basic math, it wasn't long
before microprocessors were available for more complicated use.

In 1975, Micro Instrumentation and Telemetry Systems (MITS) released the Altair
8800 microcomputer based on the Intel 8080 microprocessor (see Figure 2.3).
While MITS hoped to sell a few hundred systems the first year, it was deluged with

FIGURE 2.2
A large space was required to house the massive components of the ENIAC at the U.S. Army Research Lab in Adelphi, Maryland.
Source: K. Kempf, U.S. Army Research Lab.

thousands of orders following an advertisement in *Popular Electronics*. Microsoft (originally MicroSoft), founded by Paul Allen and Bill Gates, got its start by developing software for the new Altair. The next year, Steve Jobs, Steve Wozniak, and Ronald Wayne formed a small computer company called Apple to market a kit-based computer, the Apple I. The next year, they introduced the Apple II, a fully functional computer. The age of personal computing had arrived.

FIGURE 2.3
The Altair 8800 Microcomputer was released in 1975.
Source: Ed Uthman, Creative Commons License BY-SA-2.0, via Wikimedia Commons.

In 1981, pushed in part by the success of Apple and others, IBM introduced the IBM 5150—the IBM PC. It sold well, buoyed in part by IBM's reputation for mainframe computing and by their decision to use "open architecture" hardware, which meant that technical specifications were made public, enabling other companies to build similar systems—called "clones"—computers that mimicked the design and functionality of an IBM PC. IBM decided to have another company, Microsoft, develop the operating system software (or OS) and allowed them to retain ownership.

FIGURE 2.4
Steve Jobs (left) and
Steve Wozniak (right)
were two of the three
co-founders of Apple
Computer in 1976.
*Source: Left: Annette
Shaff/Shutterstock.
com; Right: Viappy/
Shutterstock.com.*

FIGURE 2.5
Left: Computer scientist Alan Kay created this prototype of the Dynabook tablet computer in 1968.
While tablet computers like the iPad are a relatively recent phenomenon, the idea for them was
hatched over 40 years earlier. Right: Students explore the visual interface of the Alto PC, developed
at Xerox Palo Alto Research Center (PARC) in 1973. The Alto was the first desktop computer to
utilize a graphical user interface and mouse.
Source: PARC Media Library.

This decision meant that Microsoft could license its OS, MS-DOS (**M**icro**S**oft-**D**isk **O**perating **S**ystem), to other companies for use on their cloned PCs.

Microsoft's retention of the right to market MS-DOS helped propel the company to international fame, and the abbreviation PC evolved into a generic nickname for many computers based on IBM's original design. The social and economic impact of the microcomputer was felt around the world, securing it as one of the most influential technological breakthroughs of the 20th century. Less than 10 years after the introduction of the microcomputer, the news magazine *Time* honored the computer as "Machine of the Year" for 1982 (see Figure 2.6, top row).

February 20, 1978

January 3, 1983

May 31, 1993

July 25, 1994

September 16, 1996

July 26, 2004

June 15, 2009

April 5, 2010

May 31, 2010

September, 2010

FIGURE 2.6
This collection of magazine covers from 1978 to 2010 chronicles consumers' infatuation with computer technology over three decades of product innovation.

Two years later, Apple introduced the Macintosh, simplifying the way users interact with the computer and helping Apple solidify a profitable niche in the burgeoning desktop publishing industry, a professional sector that Apple's advancements in computers and laser printers helped fuel. Apple's commitment to desktop publishing, and its subsequent foray into desktop video editing, fostered a loyal base of support among multimedia professionals. Except for a brief stint in the 1990s, Apple has refused to license its operating system to other manufacturers of desktop and laptop computers.

THE DIGITAL REVOLUTION

When researchers were looking at ways to use electricity to do mathematical calculations, they realized they could harness the fact that an electrical circuit was either on or off if they used binary rather than decimal numbers. In the decimal system, we use the digits zero through nine to make up numbers. In the binary system, the only digits are zero and one. In a computer, each instance of a zero or one is called a *bit* (short for **B**inary dig**IT**). Bits are at the heart of how a computer stores and processes information, even if contemporary computers shield us from them. Bits can be used mathematically to represent two bipolar states such as true or false, yes or no, or in regard to the electric current flowing through a computer, on or off.

Bits are a critical component of what Nicholas Negroponte talked about in the early 1990s when he argued the economy was making a transition from atoms to bits, the move from physical media such as paperback books to digital products, such as an e-book downloaded and read on a Kindle Fire or other electronic device. Part of the process of becoming a multimedia professional is learning the basics of what is happening inside the box of electronics that sits on or near your desk or in your palm and what each of the parts do. Understanding this will help you in selecting the appropriate tools for a job, and being able to talk coherently about the technology increases your credibility and your chances for employment.

From Bits to Bytes

A string of eight consecutive bits is called a *byte* and is used as one of the basic building blocks for encoding information into digital form. A byte can be arranged 256 (2^8) different ways by altering the order of the zeros or ones in the string. Like the series of dots and dashes used in Morse code, bytes can be assigned to represent letters, numbers, punctuation marks, and other characters.

Early computers often used different schema for converting letters into digital form, making it difficult to share information between systems. In the early 1960s, the American Standards Association began work on ASCII (pronounced *as-KE*), the American Standard Code for Information Interchange, to provide an industry standard and make it easier to move data between computer systems. ASCII translates its 128-character set, including most of the symbols found on a typewriter keyboard, into a binary format (see Table 2.1). While ASCII and regional variants have dominated the computing industry, it is gradually being replaced by UCS Transformation–8 bit (UTF-8), particularly on the Web, although the UTF-8's first 128 characters are the same as those in ASCII.

Table 2.1 ASCII Character Chart for the English Alphabet

A	01000001	a	01100001	N	01001110	n	01101110
B	01000010	b	01100010	O	01001111	o	01101111
C	01000011	c	01100011	P	01010000	p	01110000
D	01000100	d	01100100	Q	01010001	q	01110001
E	01000101	e	01100101	R	01010010	r	01110010
F	01000110	f	01100110	S	01010011	s	01110011
G	01000111	g	01100111	T	01010100	t	01110100
H	01001000	h	01101000	U	01010101	u	01110101
I	01001001	i	01101001	V	01010110	v	01110110
J	01001010	j	01101010	W	01010111	w	01110111
K	01001011	k	01101011	X	01011000	x	01111000
L	01001100	l	01101100	Y	01011001	y	01111001
M	01001101	m	01101101	Z	01011010	z	01111010
space	00100000						

Table 2.2	The Characters in "Smiley Face" Are Represented Digitally as 88 Bits of Binary Code					

s	m	i	l	e	y
01110011	01101101	01101001	01101100	01100101	01111001

space	f	a	c	e
00100000	01100110	01100001	01100011	01100101

GREAT IDEAS
Binary Communication through Morse Code

The way a computer processes digital information today is similar to how a human telegraph operator would have encoded or decoded transmissions over a copper wire in the 19th century, only much faster. Invented by Samuel Morse and Alfred Vail in the 1830s, Morse code is a binary encoding scheme that uses dots and dashes to represent letters, numbers, and punctuation marks. By tapping with a device called a telegraph key, the operator can momentarily complete an electric circuit, allowing electricity to flow across the telegraph wire. A short tap of the key produces a dot, while a long tap results in a dash (see Figure 2.7).

Each character in a Morse code transmission is a carefully crafted series of short and long electrical bursts. For example, one dot followed by one dash represents the letter *A*. One dash followed by three dots corresponds to the letter *B*. At best, an experienced telegraph operator could send or receive 250–300 characters (or 40–50 words) per minute. By comparison, computers are capable of processing billions of bits of data per second.

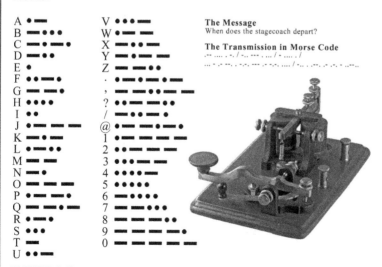

FIGURE 2.7
A telegraph key such as this one was used to encode messages in Morse code, an early system of binary transmission using dots and dashes.

Using the ASCII character set, the phrase "smiley face" can be translated into binary code as 11 bytes (or 88 bits) of digital data (see Table 2.2). As you can see, it takes a lot of zeros and ones to represent a very simple two-word phrase. The more complex the information, the more bits and bytes will be needed to encode it into a form a digital device can recognize.

COMPUTER HARDWARE AND SOFTWARE

The multimedia producer's tools are classified into two broad categories: hardware and software. In this case, the term *hardware* refers not to the scores of nuts, bolts, screws, and fittings you might find at your local home improvement store, but to the physical computers and electronic devices used to carry out specific design and production activities. The term *software* refers to a computer program (a set of instructions for the computer) or set of programs that is designed to perform a specific set of tasks or functions and that needs to be loaded into the computer's memory (RAM, or random access memory) to be able to be used. A computer program that is permanently installed by the manufacturer on a hardware chip within a portable digital device (like a cell phone or digital camera) is usually referred to as *firmware*.

It may be helpful to think about hardware and software as you would think about a book. The physical substance of a book—the binding, cover, pages, and ink—are like hardware, while the intellectual substance of a book, encoded in the form of words, is like the software, providing meaning and significance to the reader. In short, a computer without software is about as meaningful as a book filled with empty pages.

FIGURE 2.8
A *phablet* is a mobile device that falls in between a smartphone and a tablet in terms of screen size. Pictured here, Apple's iPhone 6 was released in 2014 in two versions. The standard iPhone 6 has a 4.7-inch screen while the 6 Plus, or Phablet version, has a 5.5-inch display. The term *tablet* generally refers to handheld devices with a screen size of 7 inches or more.
Source: http://www. apple.com.

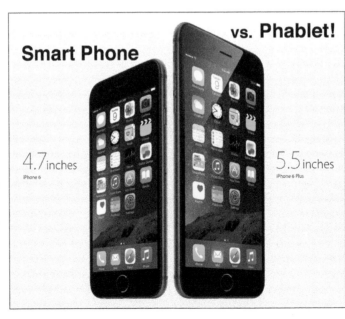

Operating System Software (the OS)

The operating system is the most important software application on a computer and must be loaded first in order for the computer to launch and run other applications. The act of turning on a computer initiates a "boot sequence" or set of command functions that launches the computer's operating system. We call this process "booting up." Restarting your computer repeats the boot sequence—refreshing the operating system and restoring the system to its default configuration.

Windows NT was developed by Microsoft in 1993 to serve as the core operating system for PC workstations and small to midsized servers. Today, it continues to be the core technology behind a family of operating systems found on the majority of PC-based servers, desktops, laptops, tablets, and smartphones. Windows 10, released in 2015, is the first Windows OS designed as a unifying OS for PCs, smartphones, and proprietary Microsoft devices such as Surface tablets and Xbox gaming systems.

Mac OS X, initially released in 2001, is the operating system included on Apple desktop and laptop computers (see Table 2.3).

MOBILE OPERATING SYSTEMS

A smartphone or tablet is basically just a handheld computer, and as such, it too requires an operating system. The top three operating systems for mobile devices are Apple iOS, Android, and Windows Phone (see Figure 2.9). At the time of this writing, iOS 9, the mobile variant of OS X, is the current version of Apple's operating system for use on the iPhone, iPad, and iPod touch. Android was released in 2008 and is now owned by Google. It is the most widely used mobile OS on the market, which means if your device is made by someone other than Apple, then most likely, it's running Android. Windows Phone was released by Microsoft in 2010

Table 2.3	Timeline of Mac OS X from 2001–2015	
Mac OS X Version	**Code Name**	**Release Date**
Version 10.0	Cheetah	2001
Version 10.1	Puma	2001
Version 10.2	Jaguar	2002
Version 10.3	Panther	2003
Version 10.4	Tiger	2005
Version 10.5	Leopard	2007
Version 10.6	Snow Leopard	2009
Version 10.7	Lion	2011
Version 10.8	Mountain Lion	2012
Version 10.9	Mavericks	2013
Version 10.10	Yosemite	2014
Version 10.11	El Capitan	2015

FIGURE 2.9
The three most
popular mobile
operating systems for
smartphones differ in
terms of visual design
and functionality. The
OS affects how users
interact with the
device.

Google Android   Mac iOS   Windows Phone

and lags far behind Apple and Android in market share. Windows 10 Mobile was released in 2016 as a successor to the Windows Phone OS. Amazon developed Fire OS for its proprietary line of tablet computers.

Application Software

Application software is a program installed on a computer that's designed to perform a specific type of work or task. For example, Microsoft Word is an application designed for word processing—for creating written documents and manuscripts—while Adobe Photoshop is an application designed for editing digital photos or raster graphics. Application software is designed for compatibility with a specific operating system. If you have a PC, then you need to purchase the Windows version of the application. Have a Mac? Then make sure to purchase the OS X version of the software instead.

Application software runs on top of the operating system and can only be opened after the computer's OS has finished booting up. New programs or new versions of an existing title may not work with an older version of the OS, so be sure to read the fine print on the software packaging or website to ensure your computer matches the minimum system requirements needed to run the software. Software updates can sometimes be buggy, meaning they don't always run smoothly or may crash unexpectedly. Keep up with software updates and patches on the developer's website, and don't forget to keep your OS software up-to-date as well. In some cases, it may be better to hold off updating your most important software until the word on the street from early adopters signals that all is well.

Be aware that some of the software you have access to may not actually be installed on your computer, but rather, on a server, in the cloud, or on the Web. Virtual apps are designed to run remotely, allowing you to perform tasks across networks, while saving your work locally or in the cloud. This trend includes distribution tools such as YouTube, but also, increasingly, productivity tools ranging from word processors and spread sheets such as Google Docs to online photo-editing tools such as Photoshop Express.

MOBILE APPS

A mobile app (or simply *app*) is application software designed to run on a portable device such as a smartphone or tablet. Many apps are free, and some of the more popular titles that require payment sell for only a few bucks or less. Mobile devices are notoriously stingy when it comes to storage capacity, so to compensate, the file size of most apps is relatively small. For example the desktop version of Microsoft Word requires 2.5 GBs of hard drive space, while the mobile MS Word app consumes less than 500 MBs. For this reason, we've come to expect far fewer features on the app version of a software title than on its desktop counterpart. I routinely use both the Microsoft Word app and the Adobe Photoshop Express app on my mobile devices, but what I can do with these programs is limited compared to the full-featured version of the software that's installed on my laptop. Still, apps offer convenience and assistance when I'm away from my office. Google Play, formally known as the Android Market, is the official store for downloading and installing apps for Android devices. Mac users get apps from the App Store while Windows Phone users download them from the Microsoft Marketplace. As with all application software, the apps you install must be compatible with the operating system that's installed on your mobile device.

Tech Talk

Inside the Box

- **Motherboard:** A large printed circuit board upon which the CPU, RAM, and other electronic components are attached or affixed.
- **Power supply:** Sometimes abbreviated PSU, the power supply regulates the power coming into the computer, often converting it from AC to DC power, and supplies power to the motherboard and other computer components.

- **CPU:** Short for central processing unit, the CPU serves as the brains of the computer.
- **Video card:** Transmits data from the computer to a video display (monitor).
- **RAM:** Random access memory temporarily stores programs actively running on the computer, including the operating system. RAM is volatile memory, which means that data is not retained if there is no power.

Inside the Box

CD/DVD Drive
Power Supply
RAM
CPU
Hard Drive
Video Card
Network Card
Motherboard

FIGURE 2.10
A computer is a carefully engineered collection of individual components.

(Continued)

- **Hard drive:** A storage device for data files, a hard drive is nonvolatile memory, meaning it retains information even when not powered. Legacy model HDs feature magnetically charged platters that spin at a high rate of speed. Some computers now come with a solid-state hard drive (SSD) containing no moving parts.

- **Optical drive (optional):** For reading and writing to CDs or DVDs.
- **Network card:** A device that allows the computer to interface with other computers on either a wired or wireless network.

Computer Hardware Basics

The phrase *inside the box* is used to describe the hidden components that make up a computer system (see Figure 2.10). Whether it's a desktop or laptop computer, *inside the box* items include the motherboard, CPU, memory chips, hard drive, and power supply. The quality of these components determines the speed and performance capabilities of a computer system. Computer software makers provide recommendations for the minimum system requirements for running their applications. The system requirements are printed on the software packaging and can usually be found online at the product manufacturer's website. Table 2.4 shows

| **Table 2.4** | System Requirements for Adobe Photoshop Creative Cloud 2015 |

Windows OS	Mac OS
Intel® Core 2 or AMD Athlon® 64 processor; 2 GHz or faster processor	Multicore Intel Processor with 64-bit support
Microsoft Windows 7 with Service Pack 1, Windows 8.1, or Windows 10	Mac OS X v10.9, v10.10 (64-bit), or v10.11 (64-bit)
2 GB of RAM (8 GB recommended)	2 GB of RAM (8 GB recommended)
2 GB of available hard-disk space for 32-bit installation; 2.1 GB of available hard-disk space for 64-bit installation; additional free space required during installation (cannot install on removable flash storage devices)	2 GB of available hard-disk space for installation; additional free space required during installation (cannot install on a volume that uses a case-sensitive file system or on removable flash storage devices)
1024 x 768 display (1280 x 800 recommended) with 16-bit color and 512 MB of VRAM (1 GB recommended)	1024 x 768 display (1280 x 800 recommended) with 16-bit color and 512 MB of VRAM (1 GB recommended)
OpenGL 2.0–capable system	OpenGL 2.0–capable system
Internet connection and registration necessary for required software activation, validation of subscriptions, and access to online services	Internet connection and registration necessary for required software activation, validation of subscriptions, and access to online services

Source: http://www.adobe.com.

the recommended system requirements for running Adobe Photoshop on either a Windows PC or Macintosh computer. Be careful about system requirements. These are the *minimum* requirements, not the ideal requirements. If possible, you'd want substantially more RAM than what Adobe lists as the minimum, particularly if you are working with large images and if you plan to have any other software applications running at the same time as Photoshop.

THE CPU

Located prominently on the computer motherboard is a large silicon chip called the *central processing unit* (CPU), or more simply, the processor (see Figure 2.11). It serves as the brain of the computer and plays an important role in determining the overall speed and efficiency of the system. Intel is the leading manufacturer of microprocessors.

Chip manufacturers can improve the performance capabilities of microprocessors in several ways. First, they can increase the microprocessor's transistor density, the physical number of transistors on the chip's surface. Second, they can increase the rate at which a processor performs basic operations—the processor's "clock speed," the rate at which a processor can execute instructions. Clock speed is measured in millions of cycles per second, expressed as megahertz (MHz), or in billions of cycles per second, expressed as gigahertz (GHz). It's important to understand that the processor with the highest clock speed is not always the fastest processor. Some processors have more efficient instruction sets than others, and manufacturers are now building multicore CPUs that have multiple independent processors (or cores) on a single chip. Dual-core (two), quad-core (four), and eight-core processors are now quite common. It appears that the old adage "two heads are better than one" applies to the brainpower of a computer as well. In order to take advantage of multicore processing, operating system and application software must be written to support it.

FIGURE 2.11
Don't be fooled by its small size. The CPU is a silicon chip or wafer containing millions of tiny switches called *transistors*. It functions as the brain of a computer, performing all the mathematical operations required of the operating system and program software.

FLASHBACK

Moore's Law

In 1965, Intel cofounder Gordon Moore predicted that the number of transistors per square inch on integrated circuits (the predecessor of the microprocessor) would double about every two years for the foreseeable future. For 40 years, his prediction, which is now referred to as "Moore's law," proved accurate. Intel introduced its first microprocessor, the 4004, in 1971. It used 2,300 transistors. The Intel 8088 (1979) used in the original IBM PC had 29,000. The Pentium III processor was introduced in 1999 and contained 9.5 million transistors. In 2010, Intel announced release of the Itanium 2 processor, a family of multicore chips with more than 2 billion transistors.

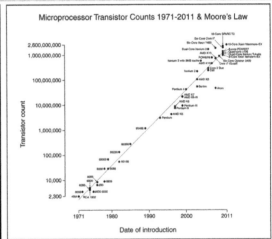

FIGURE 2.12
Left: Gordon Moore accurately predicted the exponential growth in the number of transistors on a CPU. Right: A chart illustrates Moore's law across the span of four decades.
Source: Left: Intel. Right: Wgsimon. Creative Commons License BY-SA-3.0, via Wikimedia Commons.

SYSTEM MEMORY (RAM)

Memory is a critical part of the computer. It typically falls into one of two categories. The first type is memory used for data storage, such as hard drives, which are nonvolatile, meaning that they retain information even when the computer is off. We'll be talking more about that type of memory later in the chapter. The second type, and the topic at hand, is system memory, often called RAM (see Figure 2.13). RAM is used to temporarily store operating system software and program files while a computer is running. This type of memory is volatile memory, which means that data is retained in RAM only as long as an electrical current is provided to the memory chips. System memory is erased (or refreshed) each time the computer is turned off or restarted.

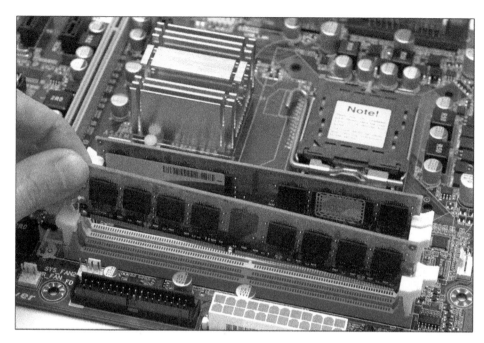

FIGURE 2.13
A RAM chip is carefully inserted into a designated slot on the computer's motherboard.

When a program like Photoshop is launched, the files necessary to run the program are loaded into RAM and will remain there until the program shuts down (the user quits or exits the application). Computers do this because reading data from RAM is much faster than reading it directly off the hard drive. The speed of RAM is rated in nanoseconds (billionths of a second), while hard drive speed is rated in milliseconds (thousandths of a second). As we'll see in a minute, this is one of the reasons it is critical to make sure your computer has plenty of RAM.

Manufacturers preconfigure computer systems with a minimum amount of system memory. This is like selling a car with only standard features. Upgrades are available, but they come at an additional cost. Editing and design programs tend to require more system memory than programs like Internet browsers and word processors (see Table 2.5).

Software memory recommendations do not factor in the likelihood that users will work with more than one application at a time. The more applications you have open on your computer at one time, the more RAM you will need to run the software. At some point, you will simply run out of RAM and not be allowed to open any additional programs until you begin shutting things down. As a general rule, it's better to err on the side of having more RAM than you think you'll ever need than having to live with sluggish performance and perpetual system crashes brought about by not having enough system memory. Adding more RAM to a computer system is one of the best things you can do to increase the speed and performance of software applications. One of the reasons adding RAM helps is that the less RAM you have, the more often the computer has to write information to the hard drive, and writing information to and from the hard drive is much, much slower than writing it to RAM.

Table 2.5	A Comparison of System Memory Requirements for Application Software (2015)
Application Software	**System Requirements (RAM)**
Windows 10	1 GB (32-bit)/2 GB (64-bit)
OS X (El Capitan)	2 GB
Microsoft Office 365 for Windows Microsoft Office 2016 for Mac	PC: 1 GB (32-bit) 2 GB (64-bit) Mac: 4 GB
Google Chrome	512 MB
Adobe After Effects CC 2015	4 GB (8 GB recommended)
Adobe Premiere Pro CC 2015	4 GB (8 GB recommended)
Apple Final Cut Pro X	4 GB (8 GB recommended)
Avid Media Composer 8	8 GB (16 GB recommended)
Avid Pro Tools HD 11	8 GB (16 GB recommended)

FIGURE 2.14
A video card (also known as a *video adapter* or *graphics card*) like this one is attached to the computer's motherboard. The video signal is fed to a computer monitor via a cable connected to an output connector.

As you read system requirements for software packages, you'll also notice that some of them talk about specifications for the video card—the piece of hardware that passes information from the computer to the computer screen (see Figure 2.14); we'll talk more about the screen itself in chapter 9, "Graphics." As graphics became a more and more important part of the computing experience, particularly with graphics-intensive video games, computer designers began including graphics processing units (GPUs) on video cards to take the graphic processing load off the CPU.

Better video cards will have their own RAM, separate from what's on the mother-board. Programs that put a strain on video cards, such as video editing and 3D modeling, often have minimum requirements for the GPU and for the amount of RAM available on the video card. Some will even require a specific brand of video card.

THE HUMAN INTERFACE

Computers, like many machines, require a human interface, a system of hardware and software controls used by people to operate the appliance. In an automobile, the ignition, steering wheel, gas pedal, brake, and speedometer make up part of the human interface needed by the driver to operate the vehicle.

While the original Altair 8800 was programmed using flip switches on the front panel, most of the subsequent first-generation PCs used a command line interface (CLI), a text-only system that allowed the user to input commands using a keyboard and view the results on a monitor, typically either a monochrome monitor or, in some cases, a repurposed television. In the absence of on-screen prompts, the operator needed a lot of technical know-how to interact with the software features of the computer. Two related innovations led the way for moving beyond the limitations of the CLI to an interface design that was natively more user friendly: 1) the invention of the mouse to supplement the keyboard for navigation and data input and 2) the development of the graphical user interface.

The Mouse and the Graphical User Interface (GUI)

In 1963, Douglas Engelbart, an engineer at the Stanford Research Institute, invented the X-Y Position Indicator for a Display System (see Figure 2.15). Nicknamed *mouse* by its creators because of the tail-like cable protruding out of the back of the unit, Engelbart's device was one of the first human interface devices (HIDs) to rely on

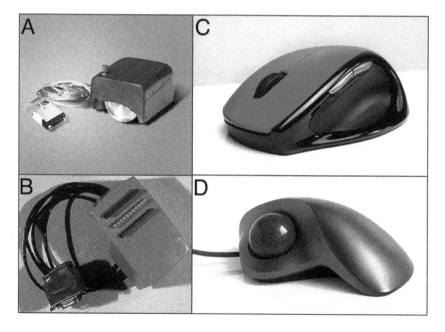

FIGURE 2.15
The evolution of the computer mouse:
A) The original mouse prototype invented by Douglas Engelbart in 1963.
B) The first commercial three-button mouse developed by Xerox PARC.
C) A modern wireless mouse.
D) A trackball mouse.
Source: A) SRI International; B) PARC Library.

FIGURE 2.16
Touch input devices:
A) Apple's magic mouse, released in 2009, is a multi-touch mouse that responds to gestures. A multi-touch sensor replaces the physical buttons and scroll wheel.
B) A touch pad responds to gestures as well and is found on many laptop computers.
C) A graphics pad uses a stylus to interact with the on-screen cursor, providing greater control and precision for artists and graphic designers.

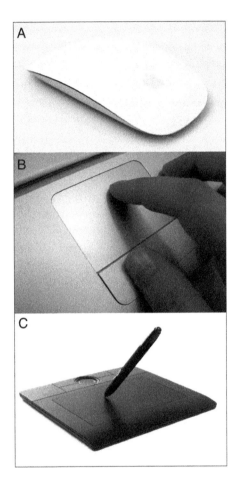

an on-screen pointer to execute commands. In 1968, Engelbart's research team released a text user interface (TUI) that displayed visual hyperlinks on the screen that a user could activate by pointing with the mouse. The hyperlinks contained embedded instructions that were executed when selected by the mouse. The TUI was more user friendly (easier to use) than the CLI because it allowed the user to choose from a list of available options without having to recall the command line syntax for executing an action.

Xerox's Palo Alto Research Center (PARC) further refined the mouse and the human-computer interface during the 1970s, including the introduction of the mouse ball and the development of the first desktop-based *graphical user interface*. The GUI (pronounced *GOO-ey*) used visual metaphors such as buttons, folders, and windows to make the computer interface more intuitive. While the GUI was introduced by Xerox on the experimental ALTO (1973) and the commercially available Star (1981), Apple was responsible for bringing the GUI to a broader audience, with the Lisa (1983) (see Figure 2.17) and, more importantly, the Macintosh (1984). Microsoft moved toward a GUI-based interface in 1985, with Windows 1.0, although it would take some time before Windows caught up with the Macintosh.

FIGURE 2.17
Apple produced this marketing piece in 1983 to highlight Lisa's user-friendly graphical user interface.
Source: Computer History Museum.

Today, the GUI is the norm for most operating systems, even if CLI-level access is still available.

The Keyboard

Despite the importance of the mouse and other input devices such as touch-based screens and tablets, the keyboard is still one of the main input devices used for entering data into the computer. While there is no universal standard for the layout of a computer keyboard, most English language keyboards use the QWERTY (pronounced *KWER-tee*) arrangement for the layout of the alphanumeric keys (see Figure 2.18). So named because the top row of alphabetic characters begins with the letters *q, w, e, r, t, y*, the keyboard was designed in 1878 to space out the most commonly used keys to prevent the typing mechanism from jamming. While jamming is not an issue with electronic keyboards, widespread familiarity with QWERTY keyboards has limited the adoption of other systems. Although similar in appearance to typewriter keyboards, computer keyboards have more keys with specialized functions, and the user can often redefine how specialty keys work. For example, in text-oriented applications, the space bar is used to insert a space between characters. However, in most video editing programs, the space bar also functions as a play/pause control for starting and stopping video segments.

KEYBOARD BASICS
There are three main categories of keys on a computer keyboard: character keys, modifier keys, and function keys (see Figure 2.19).

FIGURE 2.18
The QWERTY layout dates back to the 1800s and is still used today on English-language keyboards.

☐ Character Keys   ☐ Modifier Keys   ☐ Function Keys

FIGURE 2.19
Understanding how the keys on a keyboard function and interact can help you work faster and become more productive.

Character Keys

Character keys are used to insert letters, numbers, and punctuation symbols into a document or text-box window. They also include several related keys that can be used for document formatting and data entry such as the *space bar*, *Tab*, *Return/Enter*, *Backspace*, and *Delete* keys.

- **Space bar:** The space bar is most commonly used to insert a space between characters and words. In audio and video applications, it is often used to stop and start playback.
- **Tab key:** In word-processing applications, the Tab key is used to move the insertion point for text to the next predefined tab stop located along the horizontal

ruler at the top of the document. Tab stops generally occur at regular intervals such as every half inch. In non-text-oriented applications, the Tab key can be used to advance the location of the cursor to the next item in a sequence. For example, when completing an online form in a web browser, selecting the Tab key will advance you to next entry field. The Tab key is also used for advancing from cell to cell in a table or spreadsheet.

■ **Return/Enter key:** When working with text, the Return key is used to advance the insertion point to the beginning of the next line. When performing data entry, the Return key completes the input of data in one cell and moves the insertion point to the next entry field. The Enter key is located on the numeric keypad and in most cases functions the same as the Return key.

■ **Backspace and Delete keys:** Depressing either the Backspace or Delete keys will remove selected text or objects from a project. In this case, both buttons function pretty much the same. However, when typing text, the Backspace key deletes characters located before the insertion point, while the Delete key removes characters located after the insertion point. The Backspace key may be labeled *Backspace*, *Delete*, *Del*, or simply have an icon of a backward-facing arrow. The Delete key may also be labeled *Delete* or *Del* or have an icon of a forward-facing arrow.

Modifier Keys

Modifier keys are used to alter the actions of other keys or mouse clicks and include the *Shift*, *Command* (PC)/*Control* (Mac), *Alt* (PC)/*Option* (Mac), and *Escape* keys.

■ **Shift key:** The Shift key is used to change the display of a character to its upper-case form or to select the upper character of a dual-purpose key such as using SHIFT+5 to create the percent symbol (%). The Caps Lock key forces all letters to appear as capitals, although it doesn't lock the other keys the same way.

■ **Control/Command keys:** The Control key on a PC and the Command key on a Mac usually function the same way. Older Mac keyboards may have an Apple on the Command key. Command is used most often in combination with other keys to provide shortcuts for menu item commands. For example, on a PC, CTRL+S (CMD+S on a Mac) is usually the keyboard shortcut for saving the current file.

■ **Alt/Option keys:** In Windows, the Alt key is used in combination with letters to open the dropdown menus on the menu bar. For example, selecting ALT+F opens the File menu, ALT+E opens the Edit menu, and so forth. On an Apple keyboard, the Alt key is called the *Option key*, but it behaves rather differently than the Alt key on a PC. When combined with other keys, the Option key can be used to generate special text symbols. For example, selecting OPTION+G on a Mac produces the international copyright symbol (©). The Option key can also be used to modify the effect of a mouse click or drag.

■ **Escape key:** Originally designed to cancel or abort a running command or procedure, the Escape key is used most often in combination with other keys and less often as a standalone key function.

Function Keys

Function keys are dedicated to performing tasks that are application specific or user-defined such as custom function keys, Home/End, Page Up/Page Down, and the arrow keys.

- **Custom keys:** Programmable function keys labeled F1, F2, and so on are located across the top row of the keyboard. These keys perform different functions depending on what type of computer you are working on and what application you are currently working in. Many applications allow the user to assign frequently used tasks to specific function numbers to speed up the process of executing repetitive actions.
- **Home/End keys:** In some programs, such as Adobe Acrobat, the Home and End keys let you move to the top or bottom of a document. In text editing programs such as Microsoft Word, Home and End will move the insertion point to the beginning or end of a sentence. In video editing programs such as Final Cut Pro, the Home key will move the playhead in an edited sequence to the beginning of the timeline. The End key will move it to the end of the timeline. Did we mention some keys will work differently depending on what program you are using?
- **Page Up/Page Down keys:** Depressing Page Up or Page Down scrolls the viewable area of a document or a window up or down one page or screen at a time.
- **Arrow keys:** In text editing, arrow keys can be used to reposition the insertion point to the left or right one space at a time or up and down one line at a time. When used with the Shift key, arrow keys can be used to expand or collapse the selection of words, sentences, and paragraphs. In graphic design programs such as Photoshop, the arrow keys can be used to nudge the position of an object one pixel at a time in either direction. In tables and menus, the arrow keys are used to move horizontally and vertically from cell to cell or item to item.

Keyboard Shortcuts

Keyboard shortcuts can help save time and improve workflow productivity. System-specific shortcuts (see Table 2.6) are built into the operating system software and will normally work with any platform-compatible software application, although this is not always the case. Application-specific shortcuts (see Table 2.7) are designed to work only within a specific software application and will vary from program to program. A convenient way to learn about shortcuts is to explore the program's dropdown menus. If a shortcut for a specific action is available, it will usually be displayed to the right of the command line description.

Keystroke Combinations

Keystroke combinations are typically written in an annotated style where the key name or abbreviation is connected to another key name by either a hyphen (–) or plus sign (+). For example, the infamous Windows shortcut CTRL+ALT+DEL instructs the operator to depress and hold the Control key, followed by the Alt key, followed by the Delete key, until all three keys are simultaneously depressed. In Windows XP, the CTRL+ALT+DEL keystroke is used to end a task or exit from

Table 2.6	Examples of System-Specific Keyboard Shortcuts	
Windows Shortcut	**OS X Shortcut**	**Action**
ALT+Tab	CMD+Tab	Switch between open applications
CTRL+A	CMD+A	Select All
CTRL+C	CMD+C	Copy
CTRL+F	CMD+F	Find
CTRL+N	CMD+N	New File
CTRL+O	CMD+O	Open File
CTRL+P	CMD+P	Print
CTRL+S	CMD+S	Save
CTRL+V	CMD+V	Paste
CTRL+W	CMD+W	Close File
ALT+F4	CMD+Q	Exit/Quit current application
CTRL+X	CMD+X	Cut
CTRL+Z	CMD+Z	Undo
Right-Click	Right-Click or CTRL+Click (with a 1-button mouse)	Opens contextual menu

Table 2.7	Examples of Application-Specific Keyboard Shortcuts in Adobe Photoshop	
Keyboard Shortcut		**Action**
CTRL+ + (plus)		Zoom In
CTRL+ – (minus)		Zoom Out
V		Activates the Move tool
CTRL+T		Free Transform

an unresponsive program. In OS X, a user would perform the OPT+CMD+ESC (Option, Command, Escape) keystroke to *force quit* a frozen application.

SAVING AND MANAGING DIGITAL FILES AND PROJECT ASSETS

As a multimedia producer, the content you create or manage on behalf of a client can represent a significant investment of time and money, so you need to protect it with care. Whenever you save a new document or project file, a digital file is created that consumes a fixed amount of space on the drive it is copied to. Computer storage devices are rated in terms of how much binary data they can hold. In 1998, the

International Electrotechnical Commission (IEC) approved the following units of measurement for system memory chips and computer storage devices:

kilobyte (KB) = 2^{10} or 1,024 bytes of data
megabyte (MB) = 2^{20} or 1,048,576 bytes of data
gigabyte (GB) = 2^{30} or 1,073,741,824 bytes of data
terabyte (TB) = 2^{40} or 1,099,511,627,776 bytes of data
petabyte (PB) = 2^{50} or 1,125,899,906,842,624 bytes of data
exabyte (EB) = 2^{60} or 1,152,921,504,606,846,976 bytes of data

To put such numbers in context, in 1983 IBM released the PC/XT, the first personal computer with an internal hard drive. The XT's hard drive could store 10 MBs of data. Given the software applications in use at the time, this was considered a generous allocation of space. As computers evolved, the storage needs of program applications and end users have increased significantly. Today, hard drives in the megabyte range are no longer available, having been supplanted by storage units capable of holding gigabytes and terabytes of data.

Tech Talk

Mastering the File System Browser An active producer can quickly amass thousands of folders and files spread across a vast array of personal storage devices and remote hosting sites. With so much data to keep track of, it is imperative to develop good habits for storing and managing data and efficient techniques for locating files when they go missing or when they have been mislabeled and/or saved in the wrong location. Fortunately, your operating system comes with a powerful little application known as a *file manager* or *file system browser* (see Figure 2.20). For PCs running a Windows-based OS, this application is called *Windows File Explorer* (this not to be confused with Internet Explorer, the Microsoft web browser). On Mac operating systems it is called the *Finder*. The file system browser is used for interacting with all your digital assets, whether they are stored locally on a physical drive or remotely on a network server or hosting site (see Figure 2.21).

Windows File Explorer

Mac OS X Finder

FIGURE 2.20
The file system browser of a computer functions much the same, regardless of whether you are using a PC or a Mac. Left: On a PC, Windows File Explorer is used to access, manage, and search applications, folders, and files on any connected drive. Right: On a Mac, the Finder application performs many of the same functions.

Text consumes only a small amount of digital real estate compared to other types of data. Computer graphics, digital images, sound, and video gobble up much more space by comparison. Early on in this chapter, we established that the characters in the phrase "smiley face" can be digitally encoded as 11 bytes of binary data. Contrast this with the high-resolution JPEG image of a smiley face in Figure 2.22. The graphic file corresponding to this image is 757 KB. Carrying this example a *bit* further (no pun intended), a digitally recorded speech about the origins of the smiley face, saved as an uncompressed CD-quality audio file, requires 10 MBs of disk space for every running minute of content. Finally, depending on the compression settings, a high-definition video of the same speech could easily consume 1 GB of data for every five minutes of actual record time. This translates to 200 million bytes (or 1.6 billion bits) of data per running minute of video.

FIGURE 2.21
The file system browser on your computer gives you many options for conducting advanced compound searches. For example, the Finder in Mac OS X is used here to search for files matching these criteria: 1) *name* field contains the word "mockup" 2) *kind* field is set to image file (JPEG, PSD, GIF, etc.) 3) *created date* field is set to documents created within the past six months, and 4) *file size* field is set to greater than 1 MB. The file browser identifies only those files matching all four criteria.

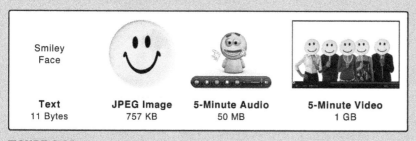

FIGURE 2.22
A comparison of data storage requirements for different types of multimedia content. Audio and video files consume much more space on a digital storage drive than simple text and graphics.

Tech Talk

File Management 101 One of the worst ways to pack a storage building is to randomly toss items into the unit one at a time until nothing else can fit. Doing so will create a mess and make it extremely difficult for the owner or anyone else to locate and retrieve specific items at a later time. You'll also waste a lot of precious space in the process. A savvy packer will approach this task more thoughtfully. For example, one could begin by packing items into boxes along with other items of a related nature. Each box could then be labeled according to its contents (kitchen items, toys, crafts, tools, books, Christmas decorations, etc.).

This kind of organizational system has been used for years to manage physical documents. For example, a doctor keeps tabs on your medical history by updating your file each time you come in for a checkup. Your medical file is placed in a folder labeled with your name or patient ID number. The folder is stored alphabetically or alphanumerically in a specific drawer or section of the file cabinet. Like the boxes in our storage facility, folders serve as a physical container, keeping all your information together in one place and separate from that of other patients.

Because this system was so widely understood, it was adopted metaphorically for managing data on computer storage drives. To avoid clutter, files are placed strategically into named folders or subfolders containing related content. Figure 2.23 illustrates how a college student might organize course-related content on a computer hard drive.

A computer identifies the address of a saved file with a path statement that specifies its location within the hierarchy of folders and subfolders on the drive (sometimes called the directory tree). For example, the path for the document file "Lit Review.docx" would be written as follows:

- **OS X:** Main HD/Spring 2015/English/Papers/Lit Review.docx
- **Windows:** C:\Spring 2015\English\Papers\Lit Review.docx

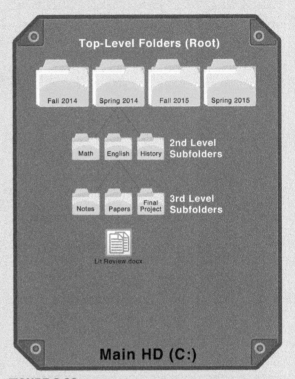

FIGURE 2.23
Folders and subfolders are used to organize electronic files systematically on a hard drive. A structural hierarchy is formed by nesting—the act of placing one folder inside another and so on. The folder at the top of a nested collection of subfolders is called the *root* or *parent folder*.

The system you adopt not only has to make sense to you, but it should make sense to others as well. What will happen on that day when you're out of the office and your boss or coworker needs to retrieve a critical file from your computer for a client meeting at 2 p.m.? As they peruse your hard drive, will they be frustrated, confused, or lost in a sea of informational chaos or overjoyed to see an organized file system that is user friendly and easy to navigate?

Digital Storage Solutions

The term *storage* is used to describe any number of devices that can be used to permanently record and store digital information. Unlike RAM, digital storage media are nonvolatile, meaning they retain data after the computer is turned off. There are four main types of digital storage solutions: 1) fixed storage, also known as *direct-attached storage* (DAS); 2) removable storage; 3) network-attached storage (NAS); and 4) cloud storage.

FIXED STORAGE

Fixed storage refers to a nonremovable chip or storage drive that is permanently installed within the chassis of a computer or digital device. The most common type of fixed storage medium is the internal hard-disk drive (or hard drive) that's mounted on the inside of a desktop or laptop computer. This is the main drive responsible for running a computer's operating system and application software. A hard drive is a mechanical device that reads and writes data onto magnetically charged spinning platters (see Figure 2.24). Tablets, smartphones, and many other portable devices use an embedded flash memory chip for storing the OS, application software, and files. In recent years, solid-state hard drives (SSDs) have grown in popularity (see Figure 2.25). With no moving parts, SSDs tend to be a bit hardier than legacy hard drives, have faster access times, and allow a computer to boot more quickly. They work on the same principle as the memory chips installed in a smartphone or tablet but have much higher capacities that are more in line with the needs of desktop and laptop users. On the downside, SSDs may slow down as they fill up and are relatively more expensive when compared to mechanical HDs with the same capacity.

FIGURE 2.24
A vector illustration of a mechanical hard drive.

FIGURE 2.25
A solid-state hard drive (SSD) contains no moving parts.

REMOVABLE STORAGE

The second category of computer storage is broadly referred to as *removable storage*, and as the name suggests, it refers to a portable storage medium that's designed to easily move data from one computer to another. Removable storage is classified into three categories: optical disk, flash memory, and magnetic storage (typically an external version of the hard drive we talked about earlier).

Optical Disk

Optical storage devices use a laser beam to read and encode data onto the reflective inner surface of a hard plastic disk. The laser beam encodes binary data as a series of pits and lands. *Pits* are microscopic depressions burned onto the surface of the disc. *Lands* are the unaffected regions between the pits. The transition from a pit to a land or from a land to a pit is interpreted as a one, while no change (pit to pit or land to land) indicates a zero. Pits are recorded along a single, continuous spiral track from the inside of the disc to the outer edge.

Compact Disc While video laserdiscs hit the market in the late 1970s, the Sony/Phillips audio compact disc (1982), or CD, was the first widely adopted optical storage technology. An audio CD can hold 74 minutes of uncompressed audio. As the first consumer digital audio format, the CD was lauded for its size, superior sound quality, durability, and random accessing of music tracks. Other uses for CD technology evolved, and in 1985 a variant of the compact disc was released called the *CD-ROM* (compact disc read-only memory). With a storage capacity of 700 MB, a CD-ROM could hold as much data as 486 floppy disks. The floppy disk was one of the most widely used removable storage solutions before CD-ROM and came in several variations. The 3.5-inch version of the floppy disk, released in 1986 (see Figure 2.28), could hold 1.44 MB of data on a double-sided disc. CD-ROMs quickly eclipsed floppies as the primary distribution medium for software. When the Windows 95 operating system was first introduced, it was made available to

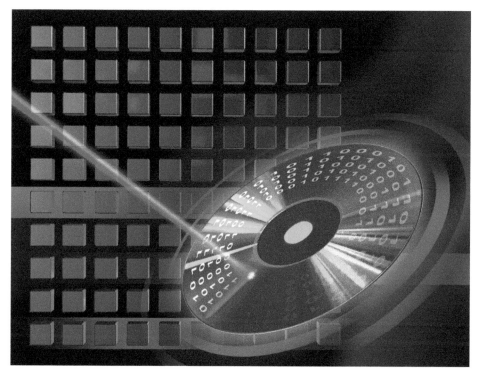

FIGURE 2.26
A red laser is used to write and read data on CDs and DVDs. A blue laser is used on Blu-ray discs because it has a narrower beam—allowing it to write more data in the same amount of space.

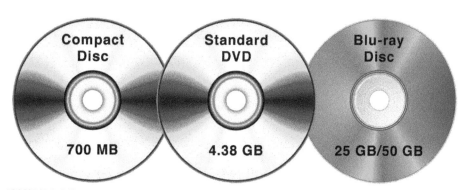

FIGURE 2.27
While physically identical in size, the capacity of optical discs varies depending on their use and design specifications.

consumers on either 30 floppy disks or a single CD-ROM. For customers with a CD-ROM drive on their computer, the installation was much easier and faster to complete. To illustrate just how densely information is stored on a compact disc, if the concentric data track was stretched into a straight line, it would be 0.5 microns wide by 3.5 miles long (5.6 kilometers). A micron is one millionth of a meter. The average width of human hair is approximately 100 microns.

While certainly a step forward, the CD-ROM was limited because data was permanently stored on the disc and could not be erased or rerecorded. The acronym WORM (write once, read many) is used to describe this type of recordable medium. A significant breakthrough occurred with the development of CD-R and CD-RW consumer discs and drives. CD-R technology allows for the recording of digital information onto a blank disc, providing a convenient way of backing up or archiving large amounts of data. Like CD-ROMs, CD-Rs can only be written to once. CD-RW (ReWritable) discs work the same way, but they can be erased and reused more than once.

DVD The second type of optical storage technology is the DVD, short for *digital versatile disc* or *digital videodisc*. DVD technology was developed by Toshiba and released as an international standard in 1995. Toshiba designed the DVD as an alternative to distributing video on videotape—do you remember VCRs? A standard DVD holds 4.38 GB of data, more than six times the capacity of a compact disc, and it can hold up to 133 minutes of standard definition video. The DVD-ROM version of the technology, along with the subsequent development of DVD±R/RW recordable drives, has made this an ideal medium for high-density removable storage. DVDs are backward compatible, meaning that an audio CD will play in a DVD device. While employing the same basic technology as the compact disc, DVDs can hold more data because the tracks are narrower and closer together. If you could stretch out the data track of a DVD into a straight line, it would be 7.5 miles long (12 kilometers). Newer dual layer DVDs hold around 8.5 GB of data, but the media is relatively expensive and comes nowhere near the storage capacity of Blu-ray discs.

Blu-ray Disc Optical discs have traditionally used a red laser beam to read and write data on a CD or DVD. Blu-ray uses a blue laser beam instead. Blue light has a shorter wavelength than red light and, therefore, produces a narrower beam with a much higher degree of precision. Blu-ray discs can hold up to 25 GBs of data on a single-sided disc and 50 GBs of data on a two-sided disc. The additional storage capacity permits manufacturers to distribute standard-length high-definition movies to consumers on a single disc, while significantly enhancing the quality of the home theater viewing experience. Blu-ray is backward compatible with all existing red-laser optical media. It was developed by a large consortium of manufacturers in the consumer electronics industry (including Sony, Panasonic, LG, and Philips).

Flash Memory

Also developed by Toshiba, flash memory is a solid-state chip technology used in a variety of digital appliances. Originally designed as a removable storage solution for portable devices such as digital cameras and cell phones, flash memory is compact, lightweight, and extremely fast. Unlike magnetic and optical storage solutions, flash memory chips contain no moving parts, therefore providing exceptionally fast seek times and high data transfer rates.

There are two main types of flash memory products available: flash memory cards and flash drives. Flash memory cards come in many shapes and sizes and are used as a local source of removable storage for portable electronic devices such as cameras and digital voice recorders. Some of the more popular card formats are branded as CompactFlash, SmartMedia, Secure Digital (SD), and Memory Stick. A card reader is required in order for a computer or printer to read the contents of a flash memory card.

FIGURE 2.28
Each 3.5-inch floppy disk (pictured left) has a capacity of 1.44 MB. It would take 2,845 of these disks to match the capacity of a 4 GB memory card or thumb drive (pictured right).

A flash drive is a small device designed to connect directly to a computer through a Universal Serial Bus (USB) port on the outside of the machine. Flash drives (also known as *USB drives*, *jump drives*, and *thumb drives*) are a fairly inexpensive storage option until you begin exceeding 128 GB. After this, they start to become less economical. Since flash drives utilize a standard serial bus protocol (USB), they can be attached to almost any computer regardless of the platform or operating system. Flash drives are a handy solution for backing up and transferring files in relatively small amounts. They are not suitable for backing up your computer's hard drive, nor are they generally a good substitute for a hard drive when video editing.

Magnetic Storage

An external hard drive sits outside the computer and is attached with a standard interface cable (USB, Firewire, Thunderbolt, etc.). An external hard drive is portable, which means it can be quickly disconnected, moved, and reconnected to

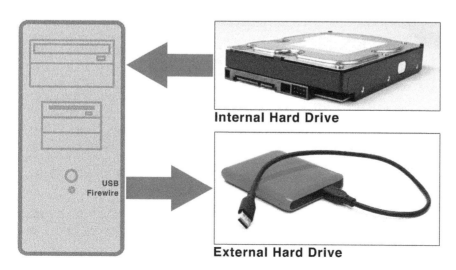

FIGURE 2.29
An internal hard drive is mounted inside the chassis of a desktop or laptop computer. An external hard drive is connected to a computer via an interface cable. External drives sometimes require a second cable to provide electrical power to the device.

another computer, allowing the user to have access to their work from multiple machines. External hard drives are also used for backing up the computer's main drive. As a matter of professional practice, video and audio editors often prefer to store project files on a separate drive from the one containing the operating system and application software. Because drives are constantly active reading, writing, and transmitting data, having two drives to share the workload leads to better performance during editing. It's like using two hands instead of one when trying to juggle competing tasks simultaneously.

NETWORK-ATTACHED STORAGE (NAS)

The third category of computer storage is network-attached storage. Using the same technology that allows computers to interact with each other across the Internet, computers can be set up to access the storage drive of a remote computer located in another room or building. Network-attached storage is often available for people who work in organizational settings where computers are connected to a Local Area Network (LAN). Authorized members of the organization can log onto a network drive from any computer that's attached to the LAN. Once connected, the network drive functions the same as a local hard drive. Depending on the amount of space that's allocated to each user, a network drive can be used for backing up important files, for making files available to other people on the network, or simply as a convenient location for quickly accessing files from remote locations. Using network-attached storage, a university student could write a paper in the library, save it to her network drive, and access it later from a computer located in her campus apartment. As discussed earlier, a number of companies now offer Internet-based file storage, allowing access from anywhere you have an Internet connection.

CLOUD CONTENT MANAGEMENT SYSTEMS (CMS)

A cloud-based content management system is a service that provides users with a method of storing files on remote servers that can be accessed anytime from any device that's connected to the Internet (computer, tablet, smartphone, etc.). The popularity of Cloud CMS services such as Box, Dropbox, Google Drive, Apple iCloud, and Microsoft OneDrive has grown steadily in recent years as consumers have discovered more of the benefits of working in the cloud. A network-attached storage solution is intended for a single user or, at best, a team of users attached to a local area network. People outside the network firewall are generally forbidden access to files stored on a personal NAS account unless they have permission to log in using a virtual private network (VPN) connection. VPN is a networking protocol that allows users to access a local area network from a computer that is not directly connected to a network. For example, using VPN client software or a web portal, students can log in to check their grades or access their university library's databases for research while away from campus during spring break. Cloud storage overcomes this limitation by allowing users to transmit and share documents across open networks.

A cloud storage account provides four basic services: 1) cloud storage, 2) file sharing, 3) collaboration, and 4) synchronization. The type of services you have access to, and how robust they operate, depends entirely on your subscription plan. Free plans offer minimal services to users while paid plans typically provide many additional benefits.

Cloud Storage

A cloud storage drive is a remote physical drive you can access via the Web or through a client app on your desktop or mobile device. Files can be easily uploaded or downloaded by clicking and dragging them from one drive to another. You organize content on a cloud drive as you would on any other storage drive using folders and subfolders with names you designate. Like the physical hard drive attached to your computer, a cloud drive has a capacity limit that cannot be exceeded without changing plans and/or paying more per month for additional space. Table 2.8 shows examples of free and first-level tiered plans for five CMS services.

File Sharing

A cloud drive can be used for private use only or for sharing your files and folders with others whom you designate. Have you ever tried to send a large image or video file to someone via email only to receive a notice back from the system saying you exceeded the file size limit of the recipient's inbox? Email was never intended to serve as a medium for sending large file attachments, nor should it be used as such. A more appropriate method is to use cloud-based file sharing. The concept is simple. You upload a file to your cloud-based drive and then share it with others to view or edit. By default, a newly uploaded document is private. Only you can see it, edit it, or delete it. As the administrator of it, you retain complete control over the privacy and sharing settings for everything stored on it. When you are ready to share a file or folder, simply select it and choose *share* to open up the sharing properties window. The access you grant can be limited to a single document or expanded to multiple files or folders on your drive. Sharing usually permits others to view the document online or to download it where it can be viewed on their own computer. Some services may require that the sharers you designate log in with their own personal account before being allowed to access a shared file. However, many do not. Sharing is usually facilitated in one of two ways. First, you can invite contacts to share a file by sending them an invitation through the service provider's website or app. Second, you can send them the link through a personal email or text message. Some services allow you to share the link with friends or followers you are connected to on Facebook or Twitter.

Table 2.8	A Comparison of Cloud-Based CMS Storage Plans (October 2015)	
Cloud CMS Provider	**Free Space (basic personal plan)**	**Next Tier (paid subscription)**
Apple iCloud	5 GB	50 GB for $0.99/month
Box	10 GB	100 GB for $10.00/month
Dropbox	2 GB	1 TB for $9.99/month
Google Drive	15 GB	100 GB for $1.99/month
Microsoft OneDrive	15 GB	100 GB for $1.99/month

FIGURE 2.30
Cloud storage enables multiple users to collaborate on the development of a single document or body of work. The author of a shared file or folder defines the *permissions*, a set of rules that determines the level of access granted to collaborators. For example, one person can be limited to read-only privileges, allowing him or her to view a document online, while others are permitted to download a file or make changes to it online.

Collaboration

Collaboration takes file sharing to the next level by allowing others to edit a document that is stored on your cloud drive. You can designate roles or sharing permissions, thereby granting some people read-only access while giving permission to others to edit. Some plans allow you to track edits, providing users with a revision history. The administrator retains the right to accept or delete changes or revert back to an earlier version. The collaboration features of cloud-based sharing are a great tool for supporting the work of groups and teams, particularly when members are not physically located in the same office or even in the same time zone.

Synchronization

Synchronization allows you to edit a document locally while keeping it synchronized to a backup copy on your cloud drive. Backup copies are updated in real time as long as your computer is connected online to your cloud drive. When your computer is offline, changes are only saved locally. Depending on your settings, synchronization should occur as soon as your online connection is restored. Microsoft OneDrive is designed to integrate seamlessly with Word and other Office products, allowing users to edit documents directly on their cloud drive from a personal desktop computer, laptop, or mobile device while keeping local and remote versions of documents in perfect sync.

CONNECTING DRIVES AND DEVICES

Devices such as external hard drives and printers are collectively known as hardware peripherals, since they are not essential to the basic operation of a computer. With the exception of wireless devices, external peripherals are attached with a cable that plugs into a serial bus connector located on the outside of the computer. The serial bus connector is a port, or interface, used for interconnecting digital electronic devices. The term *serial bus* is used to describe any type of data transfer protocol where digital information is transmitted sequentially, one bit at a time. Internal buses handle the transfer of data to and from the processor to other internal components of the system. External buses are dedicated to the transfer of data from the computer to devices located outside the box.

USB and Firewire

The Universal Serial Bus (USB) was introduced in 1995 by a consortium of seven computer and telecommunications companies: Compaq, Digital Equipment Corporation, IBM, Intel, Microsoft, NEC, and Northern Telecom. USB ports first appeared on PCs in 1997 and quickly became the international standard for connecting digital devices such as printers and scanners to a computer. USB was easy to use, and it was fast.

The term *bandwidth*, another word for data transfer rate, is used to describe the speed at which digital information is transmitted from one device to another. Bandwidth is usually stated as the number of bits per second (bps) that can flow across the wire. USB has a bandwidth of 12 Mbps (stated as 12 megabits per second). This is lightning fast compared to a serial port (115 Kbps) or a standard parallel port (920 Kbps), two of the most common interfaces used throughout the 1990s.

The development of USB was a historic leap forward in many ways, yet the standard was not fast enough to handle the high-bandwidth needs of audio and video processing. As an alternative to USB, Apple Computer developed a serial bus interface capable of transmitting data at 400 Mbps. Apple called its advanced serial bus protocol *Firewire* because of its remarkably fast throughput. In 1995, the Institute of Electrical and Electronics Engineers (IEEE) adopted Firewire as an international standard. While technically known as IEEE 1394, Apple has branded it as Firewire, while Sony refers to it as iLink.

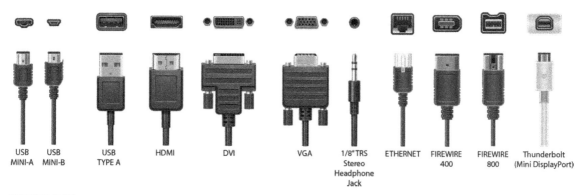

| USB MINI-A | USB MINI-B | USB TYPE A | HDMI | DVI | VGA | 1/8" TRS Stereo Headphone Jack | ETHERNET | FIREWIRE 400 | FIREWIRE 800 | Thunderbolt (Mini DisplayPort) |

FIGURE 2.31
An assortment of some of the most common types of connectors used to attach monitors and other devices to a computer.

USB 2.0 and Firewire 800

In an ongoing battle of one-upmanship, High-Speed USB (also known as USB 2.0) was developed in 2000, surpassing the data throughput of Firewire with a speed of 480 Mbps. Not to be outdone, Apple introduced an advanced Firewire protocol (IEEE 1394b) in 2002 with a new connector design and a bandwidth of 800 Mbps. The terms *Firewire 400* and *400-iLink* are used to describe products with the original IEEE 1394 interface. *Firewire 800* and *800-iLink* are used to describe devices equipped with the advanced IEEE 1394b connector.

USB 3.0 and Thunderbolt

Two of the most recent contenders in the connector wars are USB 3.0 and Thunderbolt. USB 3.0 builds on the older USB standards but increases data throughput to 3 Gbit/s. Apple's Thunderbolt protocol provides up to a 10 Gbit/s of data throughput and allows users to connect an even broader assortment of devices, including ultra-high-definition computer monitors. Apple no longer includes Firewire ports on its computers. An adapter must be used to attach any type of Firewire device to a Thunderbolt port.

USB 3.1/USB-C

Released in 2013, USB 3.1 matches Thunderbolt's 10 Gbit/s data transfer speed and is backward compatible with previous USB standards. However, the legacy Type-A interface connector that has long been included on both Mac and PC computers will eventually be replaced by USB-C, which is significantly smaller (see Figure 2.32). In fact, USB-C is closer in size to USB micro—which is commonly used for the charging/data port on mobile phones and other small digital devices. The smaller design makes USB-C attractive to computer manufacturers who are

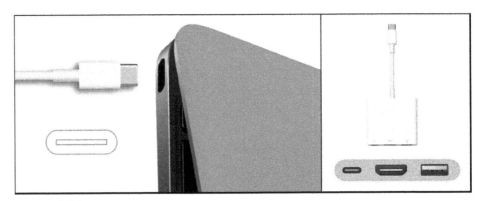

FIGURE 2.32
Left: A single USB-C connector is the only external data/power port you will find on versions of the Apple MacBook computer released after 2015. This port is used for charging the computer with an included power adapter. Right: To connect a peripheral device such as a USB drive, camera, or printer to this USB-C connector (while charging), you will need an adapter such as this one.
Source: Left: http://www.pcmag.com. Right: http://www.store.apple.com.

constantly looking for ways to reduce the size of laptops and tablets. Beginning in 2015, Apple began using a USB-C connector as the sole external data/power port on its line of MacBook laptop computers. Unlike previous versions of USB connectors and Thunderbolt, USB-C has no default up or down orientation. The connector can be plugged in without ever having to flip it over as long as it is properly aligned to the port. While USB 3.1 and USB-C offer many advantages, whenever there is a major change in the design of computer power and data ports, consumers are forced to purchase adapters or hubs in order to attach newer connectors to the ports on older peripherals.

CHAPTER SUMMARY

The personal computer is the core hardware technology used by multimedia producers to plan, create, and distribute creative projects. Like Morse code, computers use a binary language system comprised of only two characters (zero and one). Each instance of a zero or a one is called a *bit*. Combining eight zeros and ones into a single data string forms a byte. The more complex the information, the more bits and bytes will be needed to represent the information in digital form. The digital revolution has made it possible for any form of human communication, including text, graphics, photographic images, moving video, sound, and animation, to be translated into the language of computers. Computer speed and performance come down to how fast the various components of a computer system (and any attached hardware) can process streams of binary data. The term *storage* is used to describe the numerous devices capable of recording digital information. The four main categories of computer storage are fixed storage, removable storage, network-attached storage, and cloud storage.

CHAPTER 3

Project Planning and Evaluation

Among all the types of paper documents, narrative fiction is one of the few that will not benefit from electronic organization. Almost every reference book has an index, but novels don't because there is no need to be able to look something up in a novel. Novels are linear. Likewise, we'll continue to watch most movies from start to finish. This isn't a technological judgment—it is an artistic one. Their linearity is intrinsic to the storytelling process. New forms of interactive fiction are being invented that take advantage of the electronic world, but linear novels and movies will still be popular.

—**Bill Gates, The Road Ahead (1995)**

We must design our technologies for the way people actually behave, not the way we would like them to behave.

—**Don Norman, The Design of Future Things (2009)**

Key Terms
Analysis
Audience
AV Script
Card Sorting
Client
Concept
 Development
Copyright
Demographics
Deployment
Design
Implementation
Intellectual Property
Mockup
Planning
Postproduction
Preproduction
Previsualization
Producer
Production
Prototype
S-M-C-R Model
Screenplay
Script
Shannon-Weaver
 Model
Storyboard
Target Audience
Target Market
Three *Ps* Model
Treatment
Usability Testing
User
User Experience (UX)
User-Centered
 Design (UCD)
Wireframe

Chapter Highlights

This chapter examines:
- The importance of effective planning and workflows in multimedia design
- The Three *Ps* linear planning model
- Key roles and duties of professionals employed in multimedia design
- Conceptual frameworks and previsualization tools used in multimedia design
- The user-centered design model used in multimedia design and usability testing

A ROAD MAP

A famous adage in advertising and marketing circles proclaims, "If you aim at nothing, you will hit it every time." This simple yet profound cliché is a call to the masses to be purposeful and intentional in planning for success. A carefully hatched plan provides direction—a road map for helping you get to your intended destination. Without it, you will have no idea where you are going or how to get there.

Imagine for a moment someone embarking on a 3,000-mile road trip across the country without any planning or preparation. He didn't pack any clothes or provisions. He has no money or credit card. He didn't even bother to consult a map or install a GPS for guidance. Chances are he won't get very far or have much fun along the way. While it's difficult to fathom anyone like this setting out on a journey so ill prepared, many people approach multimedia design with a similar disdain for planning and process. Give a person a video camera and he wants to start shooting right away. Tell another person to create a website and she immediately sets off to build it. After all, planning is so boring, and we want to get to the fun stuff as soon as possible.

In reality, however, the time and effort you put into planning a multimedia project will determine the degree to which the project, once completed, hits its mark. It matters little what the plan looks like. What matters most is that you have one and that it sufficiently addresses the needs of the client, the design team, and the users of the product. A good plan is one that is thoughtfully crafted, thorough, and realistic. A plan is your road map and serves as the foundational visionary framework undergirding the creative enterprise and communication process.

Creativity

Experts in the field of creativity research generally agree that creativity is a process that "involves the production of novel, useful products."[1] This definition suits us well, as the focus of this book is about making multimedia products designed to communicate a message with deliberate thought and intentionality. It's not about art for art's sake, not that anything is wrong with that per se, but it is about the process of creating a meaningful communication experience for the benefit of an audience. Such value will rarely emerge without giving proper attention to planning and process.

Observe a young child at play and you will see that creativity can flow spontaneously out of an active imagination without any forethought or predetermined goals (see Figure 3.1). Hand a child a drawing tablet and some crayons, and in no time at all the paper will be filled with lines, shapes, outlines, and colors. The recognizability of such primitive doodles will depend entirely on the child's age and skill. Sometimes children will begin with an idea, but oftentimes they are content to create on the fly without any preconceived notions of where their creativity and talent will lead them.

FIGURE 3.1
Creativity is a process that "involves the production of novel, useful products."

While there is a place for such unstructured moments of creative expression, aspirations and needs mature as we grow older. A carpenter will not embark on building a house until the blueprints for the design and layout of the construction have been completed and approved. Likewise, a professional web designer must have a plan before the actual coding and design work can begin. A formal process of some sort is necessary for translating any sophisticated idea or concept into a multimedia product people will find useful. A project of any great size will require a process with numerous steps from start to finish and will involve the work of many people with specialized knowledge and skills.

Audience

In 1948, researchers Claude Shannon and Warren Weaver devised a mathematical theory of communications based on a linear transmission model containing the following major components:

- An information source (or sender)
- A message (content)
- A transmitter (to encode the message)
- A channel (to transmit the message)
- A receiver (to decode the message)
- A destination (the message recipient)
- Noise and feedback

In this model, information flows largely in one direction, from the source to the recipient (see Figure 3.2). While a feedback loop is built into this process, the reality is that because of the technological nature of mass media systems, two-way interaction is very limited. Over time, the Shannon-Weaver model became known as the "mother of all models" and has gone through numerous iterations, including Wilber Schram's popular version known as the S-M-C-R model of communication. S-M-C-R stands for *source, message, channel,* and *receiver.* Linear models of mass communication recognize the source as the dominant party in a communication exchange and the receiver as least influential. For this reason, the planning process

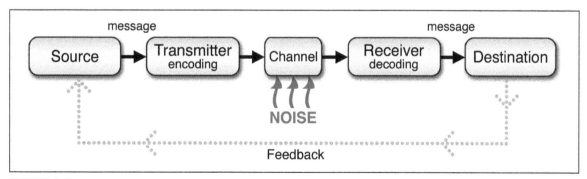

FIGURE 3.2
Considered by communication theorists to be the *mother of all models,* the Shannon-Weaver model of communication was designed to visually illustrates the linear process of message transmission.

for traditional mass media projects typically relies more on input from the producers and message stakeholders than it does from members of the intended audience.

As covered in chapter 1, old media are directed toward a largely anonymous audience. Members of this audience are known only categorically, by shared demographic traits (age, gender, ethnicity, etc.) or psychographic variables (personality, attitudes, values, opinions, interests, etc.). The value of dividing a mass audience into subgroups or segments is rooted in social categories theory, which "argues that individuals within broad subgroups (such as age classes, sex, social, or educational class) react similarly to the mass media."[2] Multimedia producers and designers use audience demographic and psychographic data to hone and customize their products and messages to meet the needs and wants of a specific *target audience* or subgroup of a larger population.

GREAT IDEAS
Target Market and Target Audience

A *target market* is a group of consumers a company has strategically identified as having potential to purchase and use its goods and services. Manufacturers seldom produce a product that everyone wants or can afford. Because of this, they will go to incredible lengths to find out as much as possible about consumers who are the most likely candidates for using their products. The more they know about their target market, the more successful they will be in designing and delivering effective messages and product campaigns. When it comes to consumers of media products such as television programs, newspapers, and websites, you're more likely to hear the target market referred to as the *target audience*. In effect, these are synonymous terms. By understanding more about their target audience, media organizations can do a better job of selling advertisements to companies looking to reach a specific target market.

FIGURE 3.3
"If you aim at nothing, you will hit it every time."[3] Identifying the target audience or user for your multimedia product is a critical first step in the planning and design process.

In television broadcasting, audience members are called *viewers* because this term aptly describes the primary sensory function used to experience a TV show. In radio broadcasting, the audience is made up of *listeners*. Viewers watch television programs while listeners tune in to hear radio broadcasts. Advertisers and marketers refer to audience members as *consumers*. For print media, such as newspapers and magazines, the audience is comprised of *readers*. A more committed type of reader fits into the *subscribers* category, a special designation for those who have invested monetarily in receiving and consuming content with some degree of regularity (as in a daily, weekly, monthly, or annual subscriber). The most radical members of an audience are called fans—those who manifest an extreme affinity for or commitment to a particular program, writer, actor, character, company, brand, and so forth. So whether they're called viewers, listeners, consumers, readers, subscribers, or fans, the audience functions collectively as the recipient of a targeted media message or experience—and multimedia producers of every kind understand that the greatest key to effective communication is knowing and understanding your audience. The more you learn about the needs, tastes, interests, habits, and proclivities of your intended audience, the greater your ability to produce content that is appealing to a wider circle of people within a desired domain.

Users

While the term *audience* is still used today by professionals working in the mass media, it doesn't adequately fit the profile of those who increasingly turn to emerging platforms such as the Web, mobile media, and streaming video for consuming content. Instead, we call them *users*. A user is a more active and self-aware consumer. New media encourage interaction and, in turn, empowers users to exert a greater influence on the communication exchange. Whereas the mass media are innately linear, interactive media are characterized by a nonlinear structure. Users can peruse and navigate content in often unpredictable and even infinite ways. As Jesse James Garrett writes, "in virtually every case, a website is a self-service product. There is no instruction manual to read beforehand, no training seminar to attend, no customer service representative to help guide the user through the site. There is only the user, facing the site alone with only her wits and personal experience to guide her."[4]

As we examine the multimedia planning and design process, understand that there are many models available to choose from. A process that works for a video and film project may not prove adequate for the design of a website, user interface, video game, or mobile app. While competing models may share similar concepts and principles, the terminology, workflows, and procedures will often vary—tailored to the specific medium, genre, workflows, and organizational culture you find yourself working in. As an introduction, let's look at two models that are widely known in professional circles. The first is a linear process model known as the *Three Ps*. The second is a more elaborate model known as *user-centered design* (UCD), an ideological framework that's based on international standards for human-computer interaction.

THE THREE *P*s

For many years, film and video producers have utilized a popular process model known as the Three *P*s, a moniker that stands for preproduction, production, and postproduction (see Figure 3.4). Planning can occur during any of the three phases, but it is most highly concentrated on the front end of a project during the preproduction phase. For this reason, and because the focus of this chapter is on planning, more time is given here to a discussion of the preproduction process than to the other two *P*s, each of which are dealt with in greater detail in later chapters.

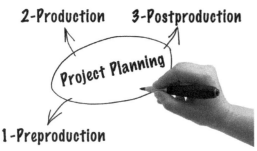

FIGURE 3.4
The Three *P*s production model.

The elegance and simplicity of this three-phase model has contributed to its longevity and widespread adoption as a conceptual framework for planning, design, and production of video, film, and audio projects—such as short-form and long-form television and radio shows, educational programs, movies, commercials, news packages, documentaries, and the like. The model is helpful because it breaks down what can be a very complex process into a series of smaller steps or activities that are logically and chronologically ordered. Like the older media it was designed for, the Three *P*s is inherently a linear model. The preproduction phase comes first, followed by the production phase, and then by postproduction, in a relatively prescriptive order.

Preproduction

Preproduction is the planning and preparation phase of a project. Once more using the road map analogy with which I opened the chapter, it involves all the activities that go into planning your trip before you actually jump into the car and start driving. The preproduction phase can be broken down into many individual tasks, processes, and sub-processes, including: problem identification and needs assessment, concept development, research, audience analysis, scriptwriting, budgeting, hiring production crew members, auditioning and casting talent, location scouting, production scheduling, equipment rental, and so on (see Figure 3.5). Preproduction activities are meant to establish the scope, direction, time frame, and cost of a project before spending the first of many dollars on the actual production. When done well, preproduction saves time and money during subsequent phases of a project, which are almost always more costly.

CORPORATE PRODUCING—THE CLIENT AND PRODUCER MODEL

Multimedia production can be a solo endeavor with a team of just one person, but more often than not, it is a collaborative process involving many people representing one of two parties: the client and the producer. In the corporate sector, the client may be an individual but more likely is a business or organization. The client is the content expert—the one most familiar with the mission, goals, and needs of the organization they represent.

Problem Identification	Idea Generation	Budgeting
Needs Assessment	Concept Development	Scheduling
Research	Writing	Project Planning

PREPRODUCTION

FIGURE 3.5
Preproduction is the planning phase of the design process and includes a broad set of activities required for a successful outcome.

Likewise, the producer may be an individual as well. The market is full of freelance producers and directors who operate independently on a work-for-hire basis. More likely, however, the producer is an in-house communications department, a public relations firm, an advertising agency, a production company, or something similar. The producer is the message-design expert. Producers are the ones most familiar with the process and tools for crafting an effective message and deploying it strategically to a target audience.

While some companies can turn to an in-house department or creative unit to handle a communication problem, others don't have this option, and even if they did, they will sometimes choose to hire an out-of-house producer to get the job done. Their corporate colleagues may be booked solid and unable to meet the project deadline, or perhaps they just want the objectivity and fresh eyes of an independent producer who is free of company bias and old ideas.

Entertainment and News Producing

In the entertainment and news industries, the title and role of a producer can vary depending on the type of organization he works for and its management style and structure. To begin with, let's look briefly at the distinction between the roles of *executive producer* and *producer*. In a film studio, television network, or news division, the job of executive producer (EP) is usually a top-level management position filled by a person who oversees multiple projects or programs simultaneously. A producer, on the other hand, is typically only in charge of one program or project at a time. While for smaller projects, the EP may play a role in the creative aspects of a film, television, or radio venture, they are primarily concerned with business matters—things such as investor/board relations, profit and loss estimates, return on investment (ROI), budgets, schedules, advertising and distribution, sales/ratings, personnel decisions, and so forth—and for this reason are likely to report up the ladder to a corporate CEO and/or CFO. They help ensure quality control of individual projects so they consistently conform to corporate standards and expectations.

A producer takes on a more active role in influencing the content and creative aspects of a production project. You will find them where the action is—in the writer's bullpen or newsroom, on the set, in the studio, or in the field interacting with the writer(s), director, reporters and, in certain cases, even doubling up in one or more of these roles, while also managing many of the day-to-day tasks involved in the production process. You may have noticed that local television stations broadcast several newscasts throughout the day—a morning show, one at noon, several in the early evening, a late night edition, and so on. Each stand-alone newscast has a designated producer who is responsible for determining the content and order of presentation for their particular program—ensuring there is good flow from story to story—and sometimes writing the script news anchors read on-air during a live broadcast. Producer roles and job functions vary widely as each setting, genre, or organization brings with it a unique set of specific needs and challenges.

PREVISUALIZATION

Legendary photographer Ansel Adams defines visualization as "the ability to anticipate a finished image before making the exposure."[5] In other words, a good photographer can compose an image in her head before framing it in the viewfinder and releasing the shutter. Under normal circumstances, she doesn't need to spend hours of preproduction time making sketches or thumbnails of shots that will be taken tomorrow or next month. However, when producing something more complex, such as a film, website, or user interface, it is beneficial to refine and expand a concept on paper before proceeding to the production phase of the project.

Since ideas are hatched in the mind, they must be put into a transferable form before they can be communicated to others. Before a motion picture goes into production, a screenplay has to be written describing every scene and location in detail. Characters are invented and developed out of the mind of a screenwriter or

FIGURE 3.6
Ideas drive the creative process and are the product of human brainstorming and interaction.

author—given names, biographical backgrounds, and demographic and psycho-graphic profiles. Dialog is crafted and refined. *Parentheticals* are inserted as notes to the director about body language, attitude, and other forms of unspoken action. A good screenplay can take years to fully develop into a viable commercial product that a movie studio will pay to option and eventually produce.

Previsualization (or *previs*) is a term that has been used for years to describe the act of putting a story idea or concept into a written or illustrated form that can be shared with others. For linear story narratives, three devices are often employed for previsualization: treatment, storyboard, and script.

Treatment

A *treatment* is a short narrative description of a project. It provides the reader with a concisely written summary about a concept or story idea. A treatment should include sufficient details to address the basic *who, what, when, where*, and *why* types of questions. As appropriate, it should also include information such as the project title, purpose, goals, audience, and genre. Treatments are often used for pitching narrative film and video projects. A treatment is similar in purpose to an executive summary or résumé. It is a short-form device used to cast a vision or sell an idea. The length of a treatment depends on the type of project being proposed. A treatment for a feature-length screenplay for a motion picture film might be four to five pages long, while one for a news story or television commercial could be done in half a page or less. Treatments can be used for describing any type of multimedia project, including web pages and interface components.

Storyboard

A *storyboard* combines words and pictures together to communicate an idea (see Figure 3.7). It is an organized panel of images and text used for previsualizing a linear or nonlinear sequence of actions or steps. In the 1930s, Walt Disney popularized the storyboard format to assist artists in the production of animated films. Today, storyboards are used routinely in multimedia production from planning short-form motion picture projects such as television commercials and "webisodes" to interactive narratives used in web and interface design.

Resembling pages from a comic book, a storyboard is made up of a series of boxlike frames depicting the visual portion of a story. Written copy is placed adjacent to each frame (usually below it) to describe its contents. The text can be purely descriptive or include spoken voiceover copy or dialog. Before computers, storyboards were drawn by hand. Today, they can be generated any number of ways using sophisticated previsualization software, page layout and design programs, or online tools. In fact, a storyboard template is probably available for your favorite word-processing program.

Script

A *script* is a written narrative framework for organizing the visual and audio portions of a multimedia presentation. Scripts are most often used for time-based media projects and increasingly for interactive narratives.

FIGURE 3.7
This storyboard
was created to help
visualize scenes
from the screenplay
Cupcake, written
by Paul Castro.
Filmmakers and
advertising agencies
will often hire a
storyboard artist to
illustrate a script
prior to shooting a
film or television
commercial.
*Source: Courtesy of
Paul Castro.*

AV Script Format The two-column AV format is ideal for the producers of radio and television commercials, music videos, promotional videos, education and training programs, documentaries, interactive narratives, and more (see Figure 3.8). It is one of the most common and versatile script formats used in commercial production today. This format features a divided page with two vertical columns. The column on

Agency	NA	**Writer**	Willie Wordsmith
Client	NC Open Government Coalition	**Producer**	Tammy Taskmaster
Title	Sunshine Laws in North Carolina	**Director**	Cindy Callshot

1.

VIDEO	AUDIO
CU OF U.S. AND STATE FLAGS EXT CAPITOL BUILDING	(MUSIC UP)
EXTERIOR STATE CAPITOL TWO-SHOT: ON-CAMERA HOSTS	<u>JACKIE:</u> HI, I'M JACKIE _____ . <u>ALISON:</u> AND I"M ALISON _____ . WE'RE HERE OUTSIDE THE STATE CAPITOL IN RALEIGH TO INVESTIGATE SUNSHINE LAWS IN NORTH CAROLINA.
CU: ALISON	SUNSHINE LAWS KEEP GOVERNMENT MEETINGS AND RECORDS OPEN TO THE PUBLIC.
CU: JACKIE	<u>JACKIE:</u> IN 2006, THE CHATHAM COUNTY BOARD OF ELECTIONS HELD THREE OFFICIAL MEETINGS WITHOUT GIVING THE PUBLIC ANY NOTICE AHEAD OF TIME. DURING THESE MEETINGS, THE BOARD AUTHORIZED THE PURCHASE
WS: OF VOTING MACHINES	AND IMPLEMENTATION OF CONTROVERSIAL NEW ELECTRONIC VOTING MACHINES.
WS: CHATHAM COUNTY SEA MS: CONCERNED RESIDENT	CONCERNED RESIDENT _____ REALIZED THE POTENTIAL IMPACT ON HER COMMUNITY AND SOUGHT TO UNDERSTAND THE ACTIONS TAKEN BY HER LOCAL GOVERNMENT.
CU: CONCERNED RESIDENT	<u>CONCERNED RESIDENT:</u> THE OLD MACHINES WERE PAPER BALLOTS WHERE YOU WROTE ON THEM WITH A MAGIC MARKER... AN INDELIBLE MAGIC MARKER... SO YOU WROTE YOUR OWN LITTLE LINES. THERE WAS REALLY NO WAY THAT I COULD SEE THAT ANYBODY COULD FIDDLE WITH THE VOTES YOU KNOW. YOU JUST MARKED YOUR BALLOT ON PAPER AND PUT IT INTO A BOX AND IT WAS COUNTED.

FIGURE 3.8
This two-column AV style script was used in the production of an educational video program.

the left takes up about one-third of the width of the page and includes information about the video portion of the program. The wider column on the right is used for audio information such as music cues, voiceover copy, or actor dialog. The AV script format is used in both single-camera and multi-camera production settings.

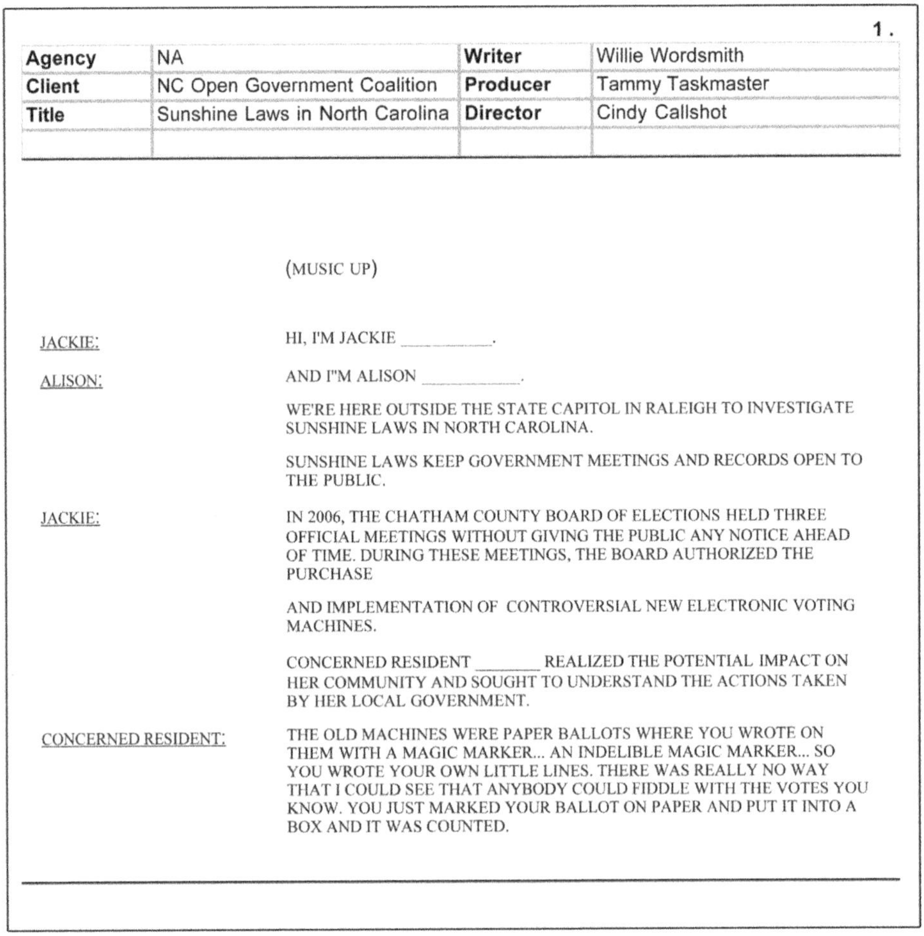

Agency	NA	**Writer**	Willie Wordsmith
Client	NC Open Government Coalition	**Producer**	Tammy Taskmaster
Title	Sunshine Laws in North Carolina	**Director**	Cindy Callshot

1.

(MUSIC UP)

JACKIE: HI, I'M JACKIE _____.

ALISON: AND I'M ALISON _____.

WE'RE HERE OUTSIDE THE STATE CAPITOL IN RALEIGH TO INVESTIGATE SUNSHINE LAWS IN NORTH CAROLINA.

SUNSHINE LAWS KEEP GOVERNMENT MEETINGS AND RECORDS OPEN TO THE PUBLIC.

JACKIE: IN 2006, THE CHATHAM COUNTY BOARD OF ELECTIONS HELD THREE OFFICIAL MEETINGS WITHOUT GIVING THE PUBLIC ANY NOTICE AHEAD OF TIME. DURING THESE MEETINGS, THE BOARD AUTHORIZED THE PURCHASE

AND IMPLEMENTATION OF CONTROVERSIAL NEW ELECTRONIC VOTING MACHINES.

CONCERNED RESIDENT _____ REALIZED THE POTENTIAL IMPACT ON HER COMMUNITY AND SOUGHT TO UNDERSTAND THE ACTIONS TAKEN BY HER LOCAL GOVERNMENT.

CONCERNED RESIDENT: THE OLD MACHINES WERE PAPER BALLOTS WHERE YOU WROTE ON THEM WITH A MAGIC MARKER... AN INDELIBLE MAGIC MARKER... SO YOU WROTE YOUR OWN LITTLE LINES. THERE WAS REALLY NO WAY THAT I COULD SEE THAT ANYBODY COULD FIDDLE WITH THE VOTES YOU KNOW. YOU JUST MARKED YOUR BALLOT ON PAPER AND PUT IT INTO A BOX AND IT WAS COUNTED.

FIGURE 3.9
The script shown in Figure 3.8 was transformed into this single-column format. Which script format you use will vary depending on the client or organization you work for or the type of program or genre being developed.

Screenplay Format The screenplay is the Hollywood studio format used in the production of motion picture films and prescripted television comedy and drama programs (see Figure 3.10). This format features a single-column layout where each page translates to roughly one-minute of on-screen action. Full-length screenplays are usually 90 to 120 pages long. This is a highly prescriptive format that must be followed precisely at the risk of being rejected on technical grounds. A common practice is to use professional scriptwriting software such as Celtx, Final Draft, or Movie Magic Screenwriter, or an online service to ensure the formatting of the script conforms to acceptable industry standards.

Production

Production is the acquisition phase of a project when all the physical media is shot or recorded either on location or in a studio (see Figure 3.11). Whereas the

83.

139   INT. SCHOOL CONFERENCE ROOM - DAY   139

       DISTINGUISHED ADMINISTRATORS huddle in padded leather
       chairs at the end of a long table. A Secretary escorts
       August in. He looks around this scary place. Busts and
       pictures of famous composers dot the dark wood-paneled
       conference room.

       After a few moments the Dean beckons to August.

                         DEAN
              Mr. Rush.

       He motions for August to join them. August eyes pages of
       sheet music on the table. The title simply says,
       "August's Symphony." All eyes are on the boy.

                         AUGUST
              I'm sorry.

                         DEAN
              Why are you apologizing, August?

                         AUGUST
              Sometimes I don't listen well and
              I don't do the homework like I'm
              supposed to.

       The Dean smiles. So do the others.

                         DEAN
              Well, I'm sure you'll do better in
              the future.

       August nods hoping that was it. But then...

                         DEAN
              The New York Philharmonic
              Orchestra has a concert this
              spring... In the history of this
              school we've never performed the
              work of a first year student.
              Certainly no one of your age. But
              now, we have asked if they could
              perform your composition. Would
              you like that?

       His Professor gives him a reassuring smile. August nods.

                         DEAN
              Good. Good --

       Out of the blue...

                         AUGUST
              How many people will hear it?

                                            (CONTINUED)

FIGURE 3.10
This is a sample page from the screenplay *August Rush*. The screenplay format is an industry-standard scripting convention—used widely throughout the motion picture and television industries.
Source: Courtesy of Paul Castro.

PRODUCTION

FIGURE 3.11
Production is the acquisition or design phase of a project where the individual pieces of a multimedia project are acquired or produced.

producer(s) and creative team (writers, designers, etc.) are most actively involved during the preproduction process, it is the director who takes the lead during production. While on smaller projects the roles of producer and director are sometimes carried out by the same person, in a large-scale project they are distinctly separate roles. The larger the project, the more people you must have to get the job done and the more specialized their assigned duties will be. Here are just of few of the titles and positions you might see on a medium- to large-scale video or film production.

- **Director:** The director is in charge of all the creative aspects of a production and often has the final word on matters relating to things like actor performances, shot composition, lighting, set design, blocking, and choreography. Ultimately, the director works under the oversight of a producer, but in cases where there is a high level of mutual trust and respect, the director should be able to perform his or her work without too much interference from above. A director relies on the crew and talent to execute his or her vision for the story. He or she must be an effective communicator who is capable of casting a vision for his or her interpretation of the script. In a narrative film, he or she directs and coaches the actors to solicit a desired performance and works with editors overseeing all aspects of postproduction. On major motion picture projects, a director will employ first and second assistant directors (ADs) to handle specific duties such as day-to-day scheduling or management of personnel.
- **Director of photography (DP):** The DP is the cinematographer in charge of the camera and lighting crews. Specifically, it's the DP's job to ensure that the composition and lighting for each shot conforms to the director's vision and to make sure that there is continuity in the visual aesthetics (color, lighting, and framing) from shot to shot. The chain of command flows from the director to the DP and then from the DP to the individual members of the camera and lighting crews.

- **Camera operator:** The camera operator runs the camera under the direction of the director of photography, or the director in the case of a smaller production. The camera operator is responsible for framing each shot, controlling camera settings, and recording each shot or scene.
- **Focus puller:** Sometimes called the first assistant camera, the focus puller is responsible for setting focus and for keeping a shot in focus during moving shots. A device called a *follow focus* is a special device that attaches to the lens of a camera to allow the focus puller to control focus without interfering with the camera operator's primary task of keeping the shot in frame.
- **Production sound mixer or sound recordist:** As the name implies, this person is responsible for recording all sound performed on location or in a recording studio. As the department head for sound recording, this person hires his or her own crew (boom operators, etc.). They also determine the choice and location of microphones and the recording techniques employed during production.
- **Gaffer or lighting director (LD):** The gaffer is the chief electrician on a set and the one ultimately responsible for executing the lighting for each scene. The gaffer may or may not also serve as the person responsible for creating the lighting design for a production.
- **Grip:** In the United States a grip assists in the mechanical rigging of structural supports for lighting, setting up and moving production equipment such as cameras and light fixtures, and making adjustments as required during production.
- **Script supervisor:** Also known as the continuity person, the script supervisor keeps track of each shot, taking copious notes, and paying close attention so that the visual elements and details on the set (actor location and posture, hand movements and facial expressions, clothing, hair, props, etc.) remain consistent from shot to shot when shooting a scene from multiple angles with a single camera.
- **Production coordinator/manager:** This person performs a variety of administration duties—everything from hiring crew, booking accommodations, ordering food, reserving equipment, and managing production budgets and schedules.
- **Production assistant (PA):** A production assistant performs routine tasks as required, runs errands, and carries out specific duties as assigned by a supervising crew member. One PA may be assigned to help with lighting while another one is assigned to assist the script supervisor.

In a film or video project, the production phase includes all the activities required for the planning, setup, and acquisition of video and sound assets, whether in the studio or on location, from the first shot to the last. When cameras begin to roll and the director hollers "ACTION!" you know production is in full swing. The production phase includes the creation of any multimedia media asset, including graphics, photographs, audio, video, or animations that will be incorporated into the final program during postproduction.

GREAT IDEAS
Intellectual Property

While production often focuses on the creation of original content by the designers and producers of a work, it can also include the legal acquisition of media resources owned by others. *Intellectual property* is a term used to describe many types of created works that are protected by copyright, trademark, or patent law. Just because an image or piece of music can be easily downloaded from the Internet doesn't mean you can legally use it in your own work. Whether you intend to materially profit from the use or not, or whether the work is intended for commercial or noncommercial use, doesn't always matter. Copyright law is complicated, and without the expert advice of a lawyer who specializes in such matters, it is often difficult to know for sure what permissible uses the law will, or will not, allow. When in doubt, it is always better to err on the side of caution. The good news is that there are many avenues available to the multimedia professional for acquiring photographs, music, sound effects, clipart, stock video, film footage, animations, and more from companies specializing in the sale of royalty-free or licensed content. While the Web abounds with content providers of all sorts, expect to pay a high price for premium assets and resources.

It is also easy to find sites publicizing content that is free or in the public domain. While some of these sites offer legitimate ways for securing legal rights to use another person's intellectual property, you need to be careful and discerning. Be sure to read the fine print. For example, a media resource may be allowed for publication on the Internet but not in a program aired on television or in a derivative work for sale, such as a DVD. As with anything, you need to choose your sources carefully and dig deep to discover all the facts. In a court of law, you're usually no less culpable because you didn't know any better or because you were mistakenly led to believe it was okay to use content downloaded from an Internet site or scanned from a book. For this reason, it is best to rely on companies with an established reputation, who own the rights to the material you want to use, and who have the legal authority to grant permissions for its use.

Postproduction

So you've been out on location, or in a design suite, recording studio, or sound stage, and all of the raw footage and material you need for your project has been acquired or gathered. Now is the time for putting it all together. *Postproduction* is the assembly phase of a project (see Figure 3.12). In traditional time-based work-flows, postproduction is spent almost entirely on video and audio editing and mixing. However, this stage also includes the creation of titles, motion graphics, video effects, and so on. A *rough cut* is the first complete edited version of a program or a revision that occurs somewhere in between the first cut and the final cut. Depending on a project's complexity, length, and the demands of the producers, a project can go through several stages of editing before final approval is granted and the picture is *locked*. After this, it moves forward for any finishing and polishing work that may be required prior to duplication or distribution (audio sweetening, color correction, mastering, etc.). Chapter 14 will cover postproduction in more detail.

POSTPRODUCTION

FIGURE 3.12
Postproduction brings together the individual components of a multimedia project into a unified finished product. The postproduction workflows you adopt will vary depending on the project; for example, whether you are editing a film, building a content management system, or constructing an online photo gallery.

USER-CENTERED DESIGN

A user-focused approach, called *user-centered design* (UCD), is the product of human-computer interaction and those who study the processes and dynamics of computer-mediated communication. One of the main goals of multimedia design is to make user interaction as easy as possible so users can accomplish activities and tasks in the most efficient and natural way possible.

UCD is more of a philosophy and a mind-set of developing interfaces than a step-by-step process. It is about creating a product or interface that meets the needs of real users rather than satisfying designers' whims. It does not require users to adapt to the new interface. Instead, it supports users by applying their existing behaviors and ways of thinking to the interface so they will have an intuitive and natural interaction experience.

In 2008, the International Organization for Standardization (ISO) introduced a standard that would eventually become widely adopted as the core framework for user-centered design. The full name of the standard is *ISO 9241-210 - Ergonomics of human-system interaction: Human-centred design for interactive systems*. The standard is based on six fundamental principles of human-centered design:[6]

1. **The design is based upon an explicit understanding of users, tasks, and environments.**

   This principle reminds us to consider three important facets of the user experience. 1) First, who is the user? What can we discern about them—how are they wired or how do they think? What are their likes and dislikes? Consider demographic and psychographic identifiers. For example, we might expect a productivity app designed for a college student to look and feel different than one created for a business executive. 2) Second, what tasks will they perform? Are there multiple tasks to consider? If so, which ones are primary and which ones are secondary? 3) Third, what are the environmental contexts of use? What is the user's primary platform (laptop, tablet, Web, mobile, etc.)? What's more highly valued, office productivity or mobile productivity? Is the program or interface for personal use or business use? Is the intended use driven by a need/desire for entertainment, information, or utilitarian purpose?

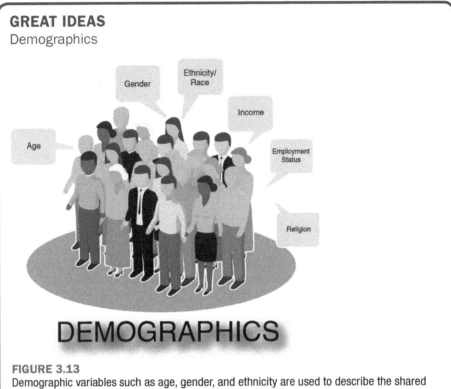

GREAT IDEAS
Demographics

Age

Gender

Ethnicity/Race

Income

Employment Status

Religion

DEMOGRAPHICS

FIGURE 3.13
Demographic variables such as age, gender, and ethnicity are used to describe the shared traits of a user group or target audience. Once this information is known, producers can use it to shape the message to fit the intended audience. For example, one would expect the content and design of a fitness website targeting 25- to 34-year-old business executives to look decidedly different from one intended for teenage girls in high school.

2. **Users are involved throughout design and development.**

   With the Three *P*s, audience research is often conducted on the front end of a project (preproduction). Rarely is it conducted extensively on the back end during postproduction, unless a studio or network is involved and can provide the resources. And even more rarely is the audience considered extensively during production. With UCD, the user is actively consulted at all points in the process and at every conceivable level.

3. **The design is driven and refined by user-centered evaluation.**

   Usability is a measure of people's experience with a user interface. *Usability testing* refers to the systematic methods of evaluating and refining an interface or product to ensure it meets industry standards for usability. See chapter 6 for a more detailed look at both of these concepts and practices.

4. **The process is iterative.**

   The best design is rarely achieved on a first attempt, but rather, will evolve over time as the designers and developers work their way through various trial versions of a mockup or prototype. Each version may go through multiple rounds of usability testing—ideally on a random cohort of real users. The data and feedback will be analyzed and integrated into subsequent versions of the prototype and then tested again on real users. Usability testing continues until it is clear that users are satisfied with the design and that further testing is no longer needed.

5. **The design addresses the whole user experience.**

   This principle addresses the need to consider the entire gamut of cognitive, emotional, and perceptual variables that contribute holistically to the user experience. It might make sense to limit usability testing to only the practical and functional aspects of a website or interface—but how users think, feel, and react is also important.

6. **The design team includes multidisciplinary skills and perspectives.**

   This principle speaks to the importance of putting together a skilled team, where there is sufficient breadth of expertise to get the job done. At the very least you need to have personnel with design experience and programmers who possess the technical skills to translate a design into a functional prototype. For larger projects, you may also need content specialists, writers, photographers, video producers, instructional designers, usability testing experts, and so on.

Whereas the Three *P*s model is largely a top-down process that's driven chiefly by the impulses of the producer and content stakeholders; a human-centered and user-focused approach places the user at the center and considers their needs, actions, and input at every step—from conceptualization to final deployment.

Putting Principles into Practice

How designers put the six principles of human-centered design into practice varies. The User Experience Professionals Association (UXPA) promotes a methodology that divides the UCD process into four phases: 1) analysis, 2) design, 3) implementation, and 4) deployment.[7]

PHASE ONE—ANALYSIS

The analysis phase often begins with a *kickoff meeting* between two groups: 1) the *client team*, made up of representatives of a company or department funding or requesting the project, and 2) the *project team*, made up of representatives of a company or department responsible for designing and producing the finished multimedia product. No matter how the teams are constituted, each group should have a designated leader. For example, a company's marketing or communications director might be assigned to head up the client team. Other members of the client team may include the department head, senior representatives of the unit or division requesting the project, and a few designated content experts with a practical working knowledge of the subject matter and an understanding of the specific problem or goals driving the project. The project team also needs a leader, sometimes called the *project director*, to oversee the design and production process and to serve as the primary liaison to the client team. The composition of the team attending the kickoff meeting depends on the type of project and the requirements but typically will include key creative members such as writers, creative director/art director, and visual designers (graphic/Web).

The project director will often lead the kickoff meeting, facilitating the discussion, posing questions and discussion prompts, and keeping the session focused and on track. The primary purpose of the kickoff meeting is to ask lots and lots of questions. The project team will use the information gathered at this meeting to form a baseline assessment of client and user needs and to develop strategies and approaches for an initial concept or solution.

Needs Assessment, Fact Gathering, and Research

Let's assume from the outset that the producer knows very little about the client, its corporate mission, and its needs. Believe it or not, this is a common starting point. The members of the design team must have information, and lots of it, before they can fully assess the client's needs and begin offering solutions. The client is a great source of institutional knowledge and content expertise. During the kickoff meeting, the project director will often take the lead by asking lots of questions and taking copious notes. Some typical questions to explore at this point include:

- What is the mission and purpose of the organization and/or department funding the project?
- Who are you trying to reach, and why?
- What is the primary purpose of the project? To educate? To train? Persuade? Inform? Something else?
- Will the project be for internal use by a specific department or set of employees (such as members of a regional sales force or assembly-line workers), or will it be for external constituents such as board members, stockholders, vendors, suppliers, or customers?
- How will the project be deployed?
- What's the project deadline?
- Do you have a specific idea or concept in mind?
- Have budget parameters been set for the project? If so, what are they?

Questions will become more specific as discussions ensue and the project moves forward. The initial client meeting will rarely lead to a concrete idea or conceptual road map. Its purpose is purely informational, to gather the facts and to give the design team enough information to begin working on an idea, theme, or concept for the project.

Identify Target Users

One of the goals of project analysis is to identify the target user group. If your client asks you to create a recycling website, first ask whom they intend the site to serve. Will the site target people looking for a place to drop off their used appliances? Or will it be aimed at local manufacturers trying to understand recycling laws as they apply to small businesses? Or maybe it will be aimed at grade school teachers. Many interfaces, whether websites or other multimedia projects, will have two types of users: a target group (the audience you intend to reach) and ancillary users (those who will use the interface for other reasons). Your first concern is the target group. This is the group of users your client most wants to reach. If the site is designed to reach teachers, they are your primary target group. If your client also wants to have information for local residents and businesses, these are your secondary target group. Focus on designing for your primary users, but keep the site usable for secondary groups too.

Specify Project Requirements

Specifying requirements helps establish the scope of your project, or the range of content, pages, or screens. Seek to identify business needs and requirements, existing problems, and potential users. You should also develop functional solutions and decide what to include in the project and what to leave out. Incorporate a process known as *benchmarking*. Look at similar projects to see what they contain and how they are organized. Do you want similar types of screens? Different screens? Figure out the number and types of screens (or web pages) you need. Give each a temporary name, then sort them into logical groups and headings based on content.

Conduct Research and Assimilate Data

During the analysis phase, the creative team will often conduct field research by interviewing content experts and end users and observing them in their natural environments and contexts. Data may also be obtained through focus groups, interviews, or surveys. As data accumulates, researchers can use what they discover to create a user profile and task analysis. A user profile is a written narrative—a mock hypothetical persona or archetype of the typical user or target group member. It is a fictional account that attempts to capture and characterize the essence of a real user. The purpose of a user profile is to help a designer "know" and understand the target user by becoming familiar with their personality, habits, preferences, and so forth. A task analysis attempts to identify and document the steps a user performs to complete a specific task or set of actions.

Next, conduct research to define your target users by demographic characteristics and/or their technology skills. You will explore when, where, and how target users will use the interface. You'll also learn about their previous experience with similar interfaces. The client is the best resource for this information; however, don't assume the client will tell you all you need to know about the users. The client may have a clear vision of what the site should include but may have missed some obvious—or not so obvious—user concerns. Your job is to ask the right questions.

- *Who are the users?* Start with this, the most obvious question. How old are they? How much do they rely on this technology, or a computer in general? What do they use the technology for? Are they part of a particular organization? And so on. If you're designing a site for people in their 50s, tiny fonts are a bad idea.
- *What tasks will they try to accomplish?* What might they use this system or site for? What are the most important of these tasks?
- *What conventions are my users used to?* Look at other interfaces to develop your design criteria (benchmarking). What do similar interfaces look like? Does this one need to tie into a theme from a parent corporation? Don't copy another organization's interface or site, but look for patterns.
- *What do they like about similar interfaces?* What works on those interfaces in terms of navigation, color, organization, and so on?
- *What do they find frustrating about similar interfaces?*

- *What type of equipment and connections do my users have?* If you're building a website or application, what types of computers and software do they have? What size monitors and resolutions do they use? What types of handheld devices will they use? How fast are their Internet connections? If you're designing a phone app, plan for a small interface. If you're designing a website that will be used by children in school or people who work on laptops, plan to design for a larger screen.
- *What colors and images do they prefer?*

If you can meet with a few people who will use your interface, do it. The more the better! If you can't, try to find people who are similar to real users. If that still doesn't work, do your best to think like a real user. The more you know about the user—their natural proclivities, workflows, and so on—the better you will be able to tailor a solution that, in the end, will satisfy their needs and leave the client singing your praises.

GREAT IDEAS
Think Outside the Box

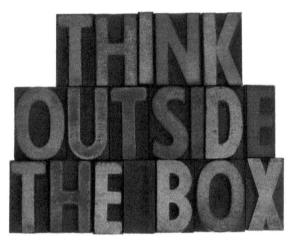

FIGURE 3.14
"Think outside the box" is a popular expression used by creative people to stir the imagination to consider ideas beyond that which are obvious, familiar, or conventional. Our personal likes and dislikes, predispositions, experiences, established work and design preferences, unconscious habits and workflows, and so on can keep us from solving a problem or developing an idea in a truly innovative way. Thinking outside the box requires venturing beyond the routine pathways of our mind that we are naturally inclined to follow.

PHASE TWO—DESIGN

The design phase begins with brainstorming and exercises that will help the design team develop ideas for the basic concept, structure, and content for the system or multimedia experience. An idea is sort of like a snowball accelerating down an alpine slope. It takes a while to get it started, but once it begins to roll on its own, it rapidly builds up mass and momentum. In the early stages of ideation and concept development, lots of ideas will be put on the table and subsequently thrown out for this reason or that. It's a good practice to write all of them down, even the ones you don't particularly like or those you think are the most absurd. Brainstorming is a process, and if at all possible, don't leave any stone unturned.

Card Sorting

Card sorting is a simple low-tech exercise often employed by designers to help them understand how users think information should be organized, categorized, or arranged within a site or application (see Figure 3.15). This technique is rooted in taxonomy, a field of study that deals with the nature and practice of scientific classification. Card sorting begins by identifying the features you want to see included as a part of a design's information architecture and then writing them down on individual three-by-five index cards or slips of paper. For example, if you are designing a website, create a card for every topical heading, subheading, or feature you plan to build into your site. Next, ask actual users to sort the cards into stacks according to how they think the

FIGURE 3.15
Students in the M.A. program in interactive media at Elon University use card sorting to help organize the content and menu structure for a new restaurant website.

information should be classified. There are many different ways to perform card sorting, but for best results, you should perform it repeatedly with a wide range of users.

Wireframe

Once you've divided the content into sections, you need to choose how much space to devote to various components, for instance, how many items to include in a horizontal menu. Designers will often create a wireframe at this stage for this purpose. A wireframe is a visual representation of the layout or skeletal structure of a page (see Figure 3.16). You can create a wireframe on the computer or using

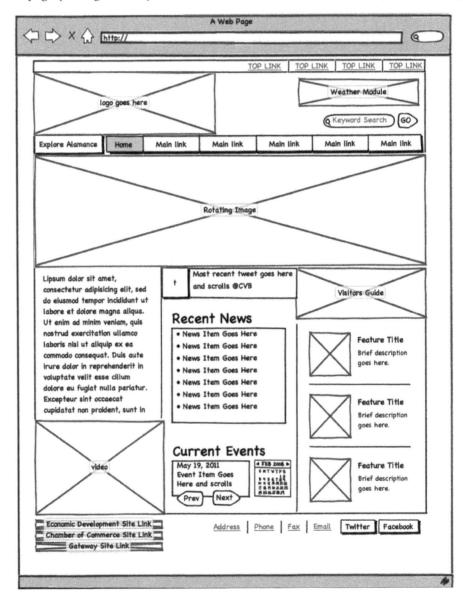

FIGURE 3.16
A graphic designer created this wireframe for previsualizing the structural layout of a new web page and its contents. The drawing was created with a computer software program called Balsamiq, a visual mockup tool used by professional web designers.
Source: Courtesy of North Star Marketing and the Burlington/ Alamance County NC Convention and Visitors Bureau.

pencil and paper. With a computer, you could use a drag-and-drop tool such as Mockflow or MockingBird to quickly mock up a wireframe for a simple interface or website. A designer will often use a wireframe to experiment and pitch various ideas for the placement of content and interface components that address the client's needs and goals. The number of menu items will affect the size, and therefore, the look of your buttons or bar. Next, figure out what components you are going to include on a given part of the interface. Consult with the client to see what they want on it. List the various options they have. If you don't, you'll find that they will often add components after you've worked hard on a design that doesn't have space for extra items. Put these items in a wireframe, a line drawing showing the main components (main navigation, logo, footer, etc.), and get their feedback.

A first-generation wireframe is often very simple and crude. In the early stages of a project, the designer will often produce multiple wireframes for the client to evaluate and choose from. Sometimes there's a clear winner, and sometimes the client doesn't like any of them, forcing the team back to the drawing board for a second try. Another possibility is that the client might like a design element in one wireframe and ask to have it incorporated with features in another. Wireframes are a great tool for honing in on the aesthetic tastes and sensibilities of the client and users without exhausting a lot of time and money on the front end of a new project. Remember to keep users at the center of the design process by showing them every visual concept and soliciting their reactions and input before revising or soliciting the client's approval.

Mockup

Once a wireframe has been approved, designers will often create a more refined visual rendering known as a *mockup* (see Figure 3.17). A mockup is a detailed actual-size version of the page, usually created by a graphic designer with a program like Adobe Photoshop, Illustrator, or InDesign. A mockup can include either actual copy and artwork or temporary content such as image placeholders and dummy text. It is generally far less time-consuming to create an illustration of an interface or web page than an actual working version. Then, when you find major mistakes, you haven't wasted a lot of valuable time. More importantly, you won't be so committed to the design (because of all of your hard work) that you refuse to make necessary changes. The mockup is a more detailed and realistic version of a page than a wireframe. A mockup can also illustrate the color scheme and style elements of a page.

Create three or more mockups for your client to evaluate, and let them choose an initial design. Then, have a few users look at your mockup. You can either get general feedback on the design, or you can test a paper prototype, conducting a mini version of the testing you'll do later on a working prototype. You don't need more than a few mocked-up pages or screens to test, and a prototype test can save you lots of work later. After all, it would be disappointing to go through the hard work of creating pop-up menus only to learn that your users don't like them. As with wireframes, mockups should be revised and tested repeatedly with real users. Once you're satisfied with the results, you can advance to building a high-fidelity working prototype.

FIGURE 3.17
Once approved by the client, the rough wireframe sketch shown in Figure 3.16 was transformed into this detailed and colorful mockup using Adobe Photoshop. The nonsensical Latin text (commonly known as filler or dummy text) was used as a temporary placeholder to help the client and design team more fully envision what the page will look like in its final form.
Source: Courtesy of North Star Marketing and the Burlington/Alamance County NC Convention and Visitors Bureau.

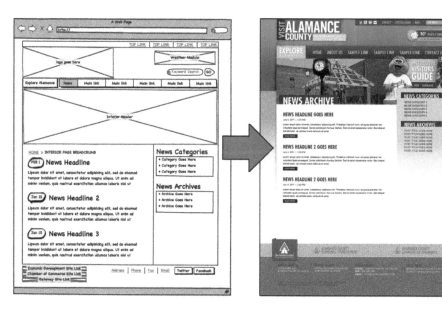

FIGURE 3.18
For this project, the design team created wireframes and mockups (or prototypes) for every page on the website. Such careful planning on the front end of a project helps ensure that time and money will not be wasted when the project moves into production.
Source: Courtesy of North Star Marketing and the Burlington/ Alamance County NC Convention and Visitors Bureau.

FIGURE 3.19
The final homepage as viewed on an Apple iPad Air.
Source: http://www. visitalamance.com.

Prototype

Wireframes and mockups are great for experimenting with the visual look and layout of a page or screen; however, they won't help much when it comes to testing the usability of a fully functioning site or interface. At some point before production begins, you need to verify that a design is functional and will work as intended. Otherwise, a great deal of time and money may be put into creating something that is technically flawed or doomed from the start. For this you need a prototype.

A *prototype* is a paper or working model of the project designed for simulation and testing (see Figure 3.20). As the name suggests, a paper prototype is a low-fidelity version built on paper or cards and can be constructed using simple sketches or drawings. If time and money allow, the quality of a paper prototype can be refined using computer-generated artwork. Unfortunately, some functions, like scrolling or dropdown menus, are difficult to mimic in a paper prototype, creating limits on how much "real-life" testing can be done with a paper model. To overcome such limits, professional designers will often use a prototyping software application like Adobe Muse. With an application like this, a designer can build a website prototype that more fully simulates a multimedia experience for the end user. A prototype is like the blueprint of a house. Once approved, the web development

FIGURE 3.20
The design process for a responsive website for Tomkat Charitable Trust began with rough sketches (top left) that went through several iterations of revision and refinement. Wireframes were then developed followed by a series of low-resolution paper prototypes. Once the final prototype (top right) was approved, work began on building the actual site (bottom). *Source: Courtesy of Bradley Mu, content strategist and UX designer.*

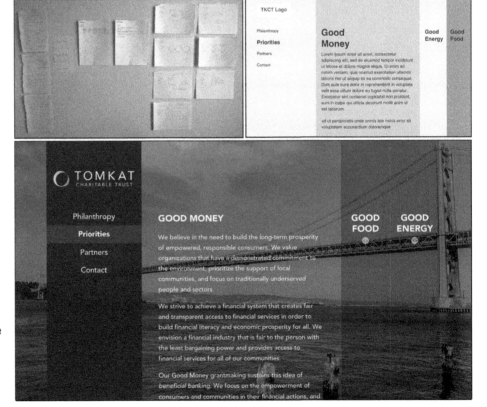

team and programmers can begin the more time-intensive and costly step of actual construction.

PHASE THREE—IMPLEMENTATION

The space I have allocated to discussing the first two phases of the UCD process—analysis and design—far exceeds the brief mention I am about to make of phases three and four—implementation and deployment. This is no accident. Analysis and design are the most time-consuming, yet most potentially worthwhile, parts of the UCD process. If you do your job well, testing, retesting, and constantly assessing and evaluating your project before it goes into final production, you will save yourself a lot of time, money, and potential consternation. Together, *analysis* and *design* are akin to the *preproduction* phase in the Three Ps model while *implementation* and *deployment* relate more to the activities of production and postproduction.

Implementation is the process of turning the approved final version of a working prototype or mockup into a fully functional website, app, or interface. Whereas the design phase led to the creation of a model for the purpose of testing and refining a concept, implementation involves building a working product or system that is ready to be tested on a server, computer, or mobile device. Once a prototype has been implemented, guess what? Yes, it's time to run it though a final round of testing and evaluation to make sure everything functions correctly. This is an important step because, up to this point, users have only been able to interact in simulation. Now they get to touch and use the real thing. Ongoing rounds of usability testing with a trial group of users and the subsequent improvements that are made at this stage are critical before advancing to deployment. This step allows you to uncover potential problems or bugs and fix them before deploying the product to a wider population. Releasing your work prematurely without adequate testing is not recommended and could result in a costly setback for you and your client.

PHASE FOUR—DEPLOYMENT

The fourth and final phase of the user-centered design process is deployment and involves publishing or distributing your content or software to end users. The UCD process never really ends, though, as the method calls for continuous monitoring, testing, evaluation, and revision.

CHAPTER SUMMARY

The preproduction process for a multimedia project includes all the activities leading up to the client's approval of the concept and initial design. Whether you're producing a video, website, or content management system, this process will likely begin with an in-depth conversation between you and the client and all the key stakeholders in the project. Since creativity is largely a subjective process, a multimedia message can be designed an infinite number of ways and still be successful. Don't waste your time trying to nail down what you think is the only right way to go. Instead, spend your time wisely, listening and asking lots of questions. The best ideas often emerge from a process that is thorough, thoughtful, inclusive, and collaborative. Remember to always keep audience and user preferences and needs in mind throughout the entire design and production process.

NOTES

1 Mumford, Michael D. (2003). Where have we been, where are we going? Taking stock in creativity research. *Creativity Research Journal* 15(2 & 3), 107–120.

2 Social Categories Theory. (2014). *Oxford Reference online*. Retrieved from http://www.oxford reference.com

3 Zig Ziglar, motivational speaker and author (1926–2012).

4 Garrett, J. J. (2011). *The elements of user experience: User-centered design for the Web and beyond* (2nd ed.). Berkeley, CA: New Riders.

5 Adams, A. (1995). *The camera*. Boston: Bulfinch Press.

6 International Organization for Standardization. (2014). *Ergonomics of human-system interaction—Part 210: Human-centred design for interactive systems*. Retrieved from https://www.iso.org/obp/ui/#iso:std:iso:9241:-210:ed-1:v1:en

7 User Experience Professionals Association. (2014). *About UX*. Retrieved from https://uxpa.org/resources/about-ux

SECTION 2
Multimedia Design

4. Visual Communication   109
5. Page Layout   143
6. User Interface Design   167
7. Web Design   201

Marco Rullkoetter/Shutterstock.com

CHAPTER 4

Visual Communication

Design is the method of putting form and content together. Design, just as art, has multiple definitions; there is no single definition. Design can be art. Design can be aesthetics. Design is so simple, that's why it is so complicated. Without aesthetic, design is either the humdrum repetition of familiar clichés or a wild scramble for novelty. Without the aesthetic, the computer is but a mindless speed machine, producing effects without substance, form without relevant content, or content without meaningful form.

—Paul Rand, American author and graphic designer

Key Terms
Elements of Design
Color
Dot
Form
Line
Pattern
Shape
Space
Texture
Principles of Design
Unity
  Alignment
  Proximity
  Similarity
  Repetition
Emphasis
  Contrast
  Color
  Depth
  Proportion
Perceptual Forces
  Balance
  Continuation
  Figure-Ground
  Psychological
    Closure
2D/3D Space
Aesthetics
Aspect Ratio
Asymmetrical
  Balance
Color Temperature
Composition
Content and Form
Dutch Tilt
Field of View
Focal Point

Chapter Highlights

This chapter examines:
- The process of visual communication
- The role of content and form in visual space
- Eight elements of visual design: space, dot, line, shape, form, texture, pattern, and color
- Twelve principles of visual design
  - Unity: proximity, alignment, similarity, and repetition
  - Emphasis: contrast, color, depth, and proportion
  - Perceptual forces: balance, continuation, figure-ground, and psychological closure

VISUAL COMMUNICATION

Visual communication (sometimes referred to as *vis-com*) is an area of study that investigates the transmission of ideas and information through visual forms and symbols. On a deeper level, it also looks at the cognitive and affective processes that affect the way we perceive (or sense) visual stimuli. Seeing is one thing and perceiving is another. The former has to do with the objective realities of sight, while the latter has to do with the transmission of culture and meaning. Two people with equal vision can stand in front of a painting and physically "see" the same thing.

Frame
Graphic Vector
Grayscale
Halftone Image
High-/Low-Key
  Image
Hue
Index Vector
Light Intensity
Light Hardness
Motion Vector
Negative Space/
  White Space
Perception
Perspective
Positive Space
Rule of Thirds
Saturation
Symmetrical
  Balance
Theory of
  Perceptual
  Grouping
Tonal Range
Visual
  Communication
X-, Y-, and Z-Axis

FIGURE 4.1
Seeing and perceiving are two different things. These gallery patrons "see" the artwork on the wall in much the same way (assuming equal vision). However, their perceptions of aesthetic value and beauty are individually constructed. What one person likes, another may disdain.
Source: Adriano Castelli/Shutterstock.com.

The "seeing" part of the event will be pretty much the same for both participants. However, each person's experience, point of view, knowledge, and aesthetic sensibilities will shape his or her personal judgments about the painting's beauty or the artist's ability. One of them may like what he or she sees while the other may not (see Figure 4.1).

Content and Form

Visual communication involves the interaction of content and form. *Content* is the tangible essence of a work: the stories, ideas, and information we exchange with others. *Form* is the manner in which content is designed, packaged, and delivered for consumption (see Figure 4.2). Put another way, content can be thought of as a person's body, while form is the makeup, clothing, jewelry, and accessories used to accentuate physical appearance. Content relates to what we want to say, while form has to do with how we choose to express or communicate it. We would not expect a history teacher to explain an event that took place during World War II in the same way to a second grader as he or she would to a college student. While the material substance of the content may be the same, differences in the age, skill level, and maturity of the audience inform decisions about how best to tell the story and shape its presentation.

The First Amendment to the U.S. Constitution
Congress shall make no law respecting an establishment of religion, or prohibiting the free exercise thereof; or abridging the freedom of speech, or of the press; or the right of the people peaceably to assemble, and to petition the Government for a redress of grievances.

CONTENT & FORM

The First
Amendment
45 words
5 freedoms

Congress shall make no law

respecting an establishment

of **religion**, or prohibiting

the free exercise thereof;

or abridging the freedom of

speech, or of the press;

or the right of the people

peaceably to assemble, and

to **petition** the Government

for a redress of grievances.

FIGURE 4.2
The congressional lawmakers who penned the Bill of Rights provided the content for this illustration of the First Amendment. A graphic designer created its form.
Source: Courtesy of the Freedom Forum.

Content and form are complementary components of a visual design. Both are required for success. Without good content, even the best designs and visual treatments will fall flat. The phrase "eye candy" has become a popular cliché for describing something that is visually appealing but lacking in substantive value. In multimedia, there are many tools at our fingertips that we can use to create an eye-catching first impression. We sometimes call it the WOW factor or hook. While the WOW factor can play a useful role in gaining the attention of the audience, without meaningful content, people will quickly lose interest and move on. There's simply no substitute for a good message, and in the absence of a compelling story or idea, good designs are nothing more than eye candy.

Likewise, without an appealing visual design, even the best messages can pass by unnoticed. Good form enhances the pleasure of consuming good content. A well-designed presentation reduces eyestrain and provides cues to the audience to help them navigate through visual information quickly, to find what is most important to them at any given moment. Form should never be a distraction, but instead should complement the message in such a way as to optimize the effectiveness of communication with an individual or group.

Communication theorist Marshall McLuhan is renowned for his classic statement, "the medium is the message." While interpretations of this phrase vary, one reading suggests that if the form of the medium dominates the content, the message can be adversely affected. While McLuhan was speaking in a larger sense about mass media technologies such as television and radio, the principle holds true for individual designs and presentations of visual media. The delivery medium or form, when elevated above content, can overshadow the message to the point where communication with an audience is diminished or made entirely ineffective.

FLASHBACK
The Medium Is the Message

The electric light is pure information. It is a medium without a message, as it were, unless it is used to spell out some verbal ad or name. This fact, characteristic of all media, means that the "content" of any medium is always another medium. The content of writing is speech, just as the written word is the content of print, and print is the content of the telegraph. If it is asked, "What is the content of speech?," it is necessary to say, "It is an actual process of thought, which is in itself nonverbal." An abstract painting represents direct manifestation of creative thought processes as they might appear in computer designs. What we are considering here, however, are the psychic and social consequences of the designs or patterns as they amplify or accelerate existing processes. For the "message" of any medium or technology is the change of scale or pace or pattern that it introduces into human affairs.

—**Marshall McLuhan,**
Understanding Media: The Extensions of Man (1964)

Adobe's Flash authoring tool is an excellent example of McLuhan's idea in practice. While a computer animation can bring visual energy to an otherwise static page, designers continue to debate how much is too much when it comes to enhancing the WOW factor of a website or gaming experience. In its heyday, Flash was often overused, to the point where it trumped "the message," leaving the audience with an empty candy wrapper and a craving for a more significant and satisfying meal.

We need to remember that the phrase "content is king," coined by Bill Gates, still holds true. Although form plays an essential role in the visual design process, it is a secondary role that must be carefully handled by the visual designer. The expression "less is more" is a popular saying that encourages a minimalist approach. "Less is more" promotes a healthy sense of self-restraint in the application of form with a focus on simplicity and the fundamental elements of design. This is good advice for the beginner or amateur designer. Adding bells and whistles to a project just because you can or because you think it's cool will not necessarily impress the client or contribute to the overall effectiveness of a communication product. It usually does just the opposite. These bells and whistles can make a product less usable, in part by impairing its efficiency, its ability to be learned, and its ability to satisfy users, as discussed in chapter 3.

Aesthetics

We make perceptual judgments about visual beauty every day. We might observe that a certain website looks amazing while another one appears drab and unattractive. We turn up our nose at unsightly outfits in a store that grate against our personal taste, then rave when we find the one that's just right for us. Likewise, people have diverse, and often pronounced, sensibilities regarding color. Some of us favor blue, while others prefer red. Think about the color and style preferences that have influenced your selection of a new car, a pair of shoes, eyeglasses, or a laptop computer (see Figure 4.3). While content, function, and usability are

FIGURE 4.3
Our aesthetic sensibilities vary widely depending on many factors including context and place. Which armchair would you select as décor for a mountain cabin? Which one is better suited for a lawyer's office?

important, our affinity for things is greatly affected by our perceptions of outward beauty or appearance. This is true for the physical objects we eat, wear, drive, live in, or otherwise enjoy, as well as for artistic works or media products we interact with visually.

People can be passionate when expressing their personal judgments about appearance. One person may exclaim, "I hate green!" Another shouts out, "I wouldn't be caught dead wearing that in broad daylight!" Likewise, someone might comment on a piece of pottery, "This is the most beautiful bowl I have ever seen!" while another gasps in disgust as he thinks about how ugly it looks. How can two people respond so differently to the same visual stimuli? This question and others like it are explored in the field of aesthetics, a theoretical branch of visual communication that deals with the nature of beauty and human perceptions of visual form and presentation.

For professional designers, the field of applied aesthetics addresses the need for industry-specific rules and guidelines used in trade crafts such as cinematography, graphic design, television production, website design, and photography. Each field is guided by its own design rules and guidelines, a set of formal and informal practices that influence the choices made during each phase of the creative process. Learning and practicing the principles of applied aesthetics is essential for developing a professional framework through which you can critically examine your own work as well as the design choices of others. Applied aesthetics moves us away from unfounded judgments that are rooted in personal bias and opinion to the place where we begin to make reasoned and informed observations based on formal theory and research. Thus, a photojournalist has to learn how to articulate the difference between a well-composed shot and one that is poorly framed. In the same way, a film critic has to assess the difference between a movie that gets five stars (Hollywood Oscar material) and one that falls flat at the box office (a candidate for the Razzies, perhaps).

The work of professional designers is persistently subject to the aesthetic judgments of others, and, on occasion, you may receive more feedback than you want on your work. Sometimes the comments may be overwhelmingly positive; at other times they may be severe, mercilessly harsh, sending you back to the proverbial drawing board to start over. More often than not, they will fall somewhere in the middle, prompting you to reconsider certain aspects of your design and make changes accordingly. An old proverb says, "There is wisdom in a multitude of counselors." This doesn't mean every tidbit of advice you receive from others will be constructive or helpful. But it does suggest that the more eyeballs you have evaluating the aesthetic value of your work, the more direction you will have for improving its presentation. Because aesthetic sensibilities are so diverse and wide-ranging, you need the input of others to help you see past your personal tastes. Just remember, the purpose of criticism is not to attack the messenger (or designer), but to objectively assess creative output in an effort to optimize a message's effectiveness. Learning the elements of design can help you provide effective feedback, too, and ground your criticism in theory.

ELEMENTS OF DESIGN

Design is the strategic arrangement of visual elements within a two-dimensional space to form a unified and holistic impression. Sometimes, the word *composition* is used as an alternative way of describing the same process. For example, in one situation it may be appropriate to say, "I like the *design* of your web page or corporate logo," while in another it makes more sense to say, "I like the way you *composed* this shot" or "the *composition* is well-balanced." In both cases, I am referring to same thing: the intentional organization of a visual space.

The elements of design are the fundamental building blocks of visual content. In the same way that a house is constructed of essential components like the foundation, floors, walls, windows, doors, and roof, graphic images are formed using the elements of design. This section focuses on eight elements of design that are common to all forms of visual communication: space, dot, line, shape, form, texture, pattern, and color.

A popular cooking program pits two skilled chefs in a timed competition. Each chef is given one hour to prepare a multicourse meal for a panel of judges. At the beginning of each program, the host reveals the "secret ingredient," a specific food component such as corn, honey, fish, or peppers that must be featured in each dish. Among other things, contestants are judged on their ability to incorporate the secret ingredient into every course. They will use other ingredients, but their goal is to make the secret ingredient stand out as the star attraction. It may be helpful for you to think of the elements of design as a master list of ingredients that you can use when designing a graphic or composing an image. Typically, one or two of the elements in a design will contend for the starring role of "secret" ingredient. Rarely do you see a design that will incorporate every element within a single visual representation. Sometimes, the designer will choose to accentuate the element of line. At other times the designer may want to highlight form or color. By combining the elements of design, we can create an endless array of variations.

Understanding the elements of design and their influence on human perception will help you become a better visual communicator and media consumer. It will also strengthen your ability to make informed judgments about the overall quality and beauty of a visual design. Learning the language of visual design will help you better defend and critique your own work as well as that of others. Doing so will help you complete the sentence, "I like this because . . ." or "Photograph 'A' is better than Photograph 'B' because . . ."

Space

Like a traditional artist, a digital designer begins with a blank surface or design space that comes to life as the creative process unfolds (see Figure 4.4). In Adobe Photoshop and Illustrator, the document window or workspace is referred to metaphorically as the canvas. Like an artist's canvas, the digital canvas is flat and boxy. It has an outer frame that defines the area of the design surface where visual elements

FIGURE 4.4
A visual communicator's job is to fill empty space with meaningful content that communicates a message.

FIGURE 4.5
A camera sees only what the photographer wants it to see. The design space is composed within the frame of a camera's viewfinder and is referred to as the *field of view*.

reside. The designer's job is to fill this empty space with meaningful visual content that communicates a message.

In photography, the design space is called the *field of view*. The field of view is the area of a scene that is visible to the camera at any given moment in time (see Figure 4.5). Looking through the viewfinder, a camera operator can change the field of view by zooming the lens in or out or by moving closer to or farther away from the subject. "Framing a shot" involves making conscious decisions about what to include and exclude within the frame (a process called cropping). The spatial area of the scene the camera "sees" is controlled by the person composing the shot.

TWO-DIMENSIONAL SPACE (2D)

Digital workspaces only have two dimensions: width and height. These dimensions are measured in pixels—tiny rectangular or square blocks of color—rather than by using an absolute unit of measurement, such as inches or centimeters (see Figure 4.6). As a result, the size is relative because the actual appearance of the spatial area will vary depending on the settings of the display device rendering the design on screen. We'll talk more about pixels in chapter 9, "Graphics." The workspace's width is measured along its *x-axis* (horizontally), and its height is measured on its *y-axis* (vertically). When we refer to coordinates within the workspace, an x:y position, we set the upper left-hand corner as zero (0:0), counting pixels from left to right and from top to bottom.

Digital spaces are rectangular, so they conform to the boxlike frames of electronic displays and projectors. The term *aspect ratio* refers to the relationship between the width and height of a design space. A 4:3 space is 4 units wide by 3 units high. A 16:9 space is 16 units wide by 9 units high. Although the physical dimensions of a display monitor or viewfinder can vary from small to large, as long as the aspect

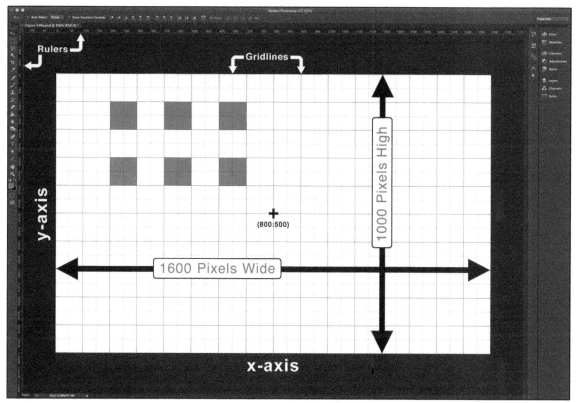

FIGURE 4.6
Gridlines are used to subdivide the design space in Adobe Photoshop. The darker gridlines are spaced 100 pixels apart while the lighter ones denote subdivisions that are 10 pixels square. A designer uses gridlines to precisely position and align visual elements within a design space—such as the six red squares. Rulers are another visual aid for designers. Here, the ruler's unit of measurement is set to pixels. It could just as easily be set to inches, centimeters, points, or picas.
Source: Adobe product screenshot reprinted with permission from Adobe Systems Incorporated.

ratios are compatible, images will stay true to their original proportions. Using compatible aspect ratios for output or presentation prevents unwanted distortion.

Digital spaces are physically limited to width and height, but people have the ability to perceive the third dimension of depth when viewing two-dimensional representations. Depth in two-dimensional space is only a perceptual illusion. Through skilled control of lighting, perspective, shading, texture, color, contrast, relative speed (for media with movement), and so on, visual designs can be made to look remarkably three-dimensional. Depth is represented by the *z-axis*, an imaginary sight vector that extends away from the viewer and into the center of the design. Our ability to perceive depth depends on our ability to make sense of the relative position of background, mid-ground, and foreground elements along the z-axis. As creatures of three-dimensional space, we tend to favor designs that promote a sense of depth. A design or image that is lacking in depth is said to be flat.

FIGURE 4.7
White space (also called negative space) doesn't have to be white.

FIGURE 4.8
This image is formed entirely of colored dots. Up close the dots are noticeable. The further back you are, the more they coalesce to form a composite image.

POSITIVE AND NEGATIVE SPACE

The design window is divided into areas of positive and negative space. *Positive space* is the portion of an image where visual elements (lines, shapes, forms, etc.) reside. *Negative space* is the rest of an image, where no visual content exists. In a book, the letters, words, sentences, paragraphs, and illustrations make up the positive space on a page. In this example, you can think of positive space as every part of the page that has been pressed with ink to form a visual impression. Negative space is everything else. Since paper stock for books, newspapers, and magazines is often white, the terms *white space* and *negative space* are used interchangeably. So, even if the background of a web page is blue, most designers will refer to the empty portions of the design as white space (see Figure 4.7).

White space is essential because it adds breathing room to visual information, making it easier for users to consume content and navigate the page. The terms *margins*, *padding*, *tabs*, *spaces*, and *line breaks* describe specific instances of negative space. Research indicates that we read faster when white space separates lines of text and forms margins at the edges of a page. The same is true for content that's presented on an electronic display. Without sufficient white space, designs can become visually cluttered and difficult to read.

Dot

The most basic representation of form is the *dot*. It's the starting point for all other elements of design. A line begins and ends with a dot, but more importantly, dots can be combined in large numbers to portray complex visual objects and images (see Figure 4.8). Under a magnifying glass, you can see that a printed newspaper image (or halftone print) is made up of dots (positive space) surrounded by white space. From a proper reading distance, the dots merge, and coalesce, completing the optical illusion of a continuous-tone image in our visual receptors.

Tech Talk

Halftone Image In the 1850s, William Henry Fox Talbot came up with a method for printing photographic images in newsprint. Using a special large-format camera, a printer would reshoot a photograph through a perforated screen containing hundreds of small holes. The holes in the screen served to break up the continuous tonal structure of the image into discrete points of light represented by a single color or shade of gray. Talbot's procedure—similar to the technique of sampling that's used in digital imaging today—produced a halftone version of the original image made up entirely of dots of varying sizes along a uniform linear grid (see Figure 4.9).

The size of each dot in the grid is directly proportional to the intensity of color at that given point. In black and white halftone printing, the darkest areas of the image are represented by the largest dots, and the lighter areas are made up of smaller dots. The size of the dots in the halftone screen regulate how much black ink is applied to the paper, producing varying shades of gray (from black to white) with a single shade of pigment.

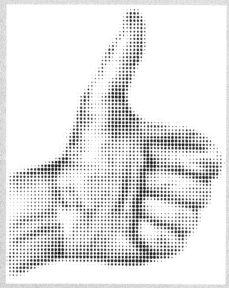

FIGURE 4.9
This halftone image is formed with black dots of various sizes and shades.

While the printing process has become more sophisticated over the years, halftone imaging is still used today. In process printing, printers make screens for each primary color channel—cyan, magenta, yellow, and black, or CMYK. During printing, each primary color is applied separately to control the density of its ink droplets. Under the microscope, color dots appear as clusters of four dots of varying sizes, each representing the intensity of the color pigment needed to make the final color.

We use similar principles to form electronic images. Whereas in printing, we refer to the tiny droplets of ink on a page as *dots*, in digital imaging, we refer to the individual square points of light on an electronic display as *pixels*. Hi-resolution television and computer images are comprised of millions of pixels—each one containing various intensities of red, green, and blue to create a tiny square of color. Unlike the dots in a halftone image, the pixels in a digital image are so small the human eye can't discern them. Instead, we perceive only the holistic image formed by their merger. In digital photography, a similar process occurs. The camera's image sensor contains a large array of photosites that are uniformly arranged in columns and rows. A photosite is a tiny light-sensitive diode that registers the intensity of a single point of light and records its value as binary data. When viewing a digital image on an electronic display, the process reverses. The computer renders the image on screen by reproducing the color of each corresponding pixel in the image array. Photosites are designed to capture light. Pixels reproduce it.

Line

A line is the visual connector between two points in space. Lines can be real or implied. For example, a white line painted on the edge of a road is real. We know the line did not just appear. It was intentionally painted to warn drivers not to run off the road. Lines can also be implied by natural alignment or the purposeful placement of objects within a graphic composition. The top of a rail fence, a distant horizon, a row of trees, the edge of a skyscraper, and a winding road all imply the element of line. In visual design, lines can be used to stir the emotions or to create a specific mood or atmosphere (see Figure 4.10). Some lines have the effect of relaxing a design and putting the viewer at ease. Other lines connote a sense of direction, movement, or visual energy.

FIGURE 4.10
Lines can be horizontal, vertical, curved, or diagonal and can be combined in an infinite number of ways. The visual world is full of them in a myriad array of shapes, sizes, and colors. Take a look around you. What kind of lines do you see? Can you describe them?

STRAIGHT LINES

Straight lines can be *static* (horizontal or vertical) or *dynamic* (diagonal). *Horizontal lines* often communicate a sense of peace and calm. Perhaps this is tied to the fact that we lie down to rest and stand up to move and walk around. Placing a flat object on a level surface such as a desk or countertop, we would expect it not to move. The laws of physics should ensure a period of stasis. We perceive horizontal lines in much the same way. They are a natural and reliable reference point that can reinforce a sense of balance and stability within a design. *Vertical lines* reach upward, promoting a sense of power, strength, grandeur, and awe. They too are stable because gravity holds them in place. We naturally associate vertical lines with height. Intersecting horizontal and vertical lines form strong visual frameworks, much like a building's intersection of studs and joists increases its structural strength.

FIGURE 4.11
The parallel tracks appear to converge along the z-axis, contributing to the illusion of depth in this two-dimensional photograph.

Diagonal lines hold the greatest potential for energizing a visual design. They exude a sense of speed, movement, and depth. Photographing the facade of a building head-on will evoke a relatively stable response from the viewer because the natural lines produced by structural elements such as bricks, windows, doorframes, and so on are largely parallel or perpendicular to the ground. If you shift the angle of view along the x- or y-axis, you capture diagonal lines, and the previously stable lines now appear to converge into a distant vanishing point. A similar effect occurs when photographing a set of railroad tracks along the z-axis. We know that railroad tracks are always parallel, but perceptually, their lines appear to converge and seemingly will meet at some distant point (see Figure 4.11). This is just a perceptual illusion, of course. In art, this technique is called *perspective* and is used to create the illusion of a third dimension in a two-dimensional frame. Perspective breaks up the visual monotony of a stable image by emphasizing depth and distance through the use of diagonal lines.

CURVED LINES

Curved lines can create a sense of peace and tranquility in a design. The smooth edges of a curved element provide a sense of flow and directionality and are easy for the eye to follow without abrupt stops or interruptions. Car bodies are typically curved to improve the aerodynamic performance of the vehicle, but curves also improve the appearance of a car, making it look sleek and stylish. Curves accentuate the shape and form of other elements and are among the most common lines found in nature.

Tech Talk

Vertigo and 3D The vestibular system, comprised of organs of the inner ear, sends messages to the brain that enable us to retain our balance and spatial orientation. When this system fails, we can experience vertigo, sensing the feeling of movement when we are stationary. Vertigo can make you feel dizzy or nauseated. Using visual trickery, we can lead people into a momentary state of vertigo, affecting their sense of equilibrium. IMAX, 3D and 4D film, and Circle-Vision 360° are cinematic technologies used to add a physical sense of movement to a 2D viewing experience.

In most cases, accentuating angles and diagonal lines in a still image will not induce a case of vertigo. But this technique can help the viewer perceive motion in a scene, enhancing the visual dynamic. The *Dutch tilt* is a cinematic technique that involves tilting the camera so the horizon is not parallel to the bottom of the frame (see Figure 4.12). This technique, also known as the *canted angle*, is popular in sports and action photography. Tilting the camera destabilizes an image and can give the viewer a heightened sense of movement and tension in the shot.

FIGURE 4.12
The photographic technique of Dutch tilt adds visual energy to this shot of a lone competitor in the Tour de France.
Source: Peter Kirillov/Shutterstock.com.

FIGURE 4.13
In this photo, an S-curve is used to guide the viewer's eye along a linear path to the main subject.

Diagonals and curves are particularly effective when used as leading line elements in a design (see Figure 4.13). A leading line steers the eyes of the viewer through a design, guiding them from one element to another or directly to the main subject or focal point.

Shape

A *shape* is a two-dimensional element formed by the enclosure of dots and lines (see Figure 4.14). We perceive shapes as flat objects without depth (either real or implied). A shape can be as simple as a circle or as complex and intricately conceived as a snowflake. The basic geometric shapes are *circles, triangles,* and *squares.* When we combine them in various ways, they can form virtually any other shape imaginable. They are called *geometric shapes* because they can be rendered mathematically using formal rules of construction.

Organic shapes are so called because they resemble objects in the natural world. Organic shapes have an imperfect, soft, and flowing appearance. They are often constructed of continuous curves or

Geometric Shape   Organic Shape

FIGURE 4.14
Shapes often connote a sense of the familiar. Like lines, they can be combined in an infinite number of ways to form new, more complex shapes.

circular elements. For this reason, curvilinear and free-form shapes frequently fall into the same category. Organic shapes are often based on familiar objects such as animals, clouds, insects, leaves, plants, fruits, and vegetables. The famous logo for Apple computers is a great example of how a company has used an organic shape for branding its public identity.

Shapes can be powerful visual forces in design. Shapes can evoke the memory of objects or symbols with which we have established points of reference or emotional connections (see Figure 4.15). The shape of a flower can stir up the memory of a fragrance. The shape of a male or female silhouette reminds us instantly which restroom to use in a public space. The recognizable shapes of the Manhattan skyline and Statute of Liberty transport us immediately to New York City, potentially unlocking memories or impressions from past experiences. Shapes often have symbolic meanings that can be used as visual shorthand to elicit a feeling or thought. What shape comes to mind first when you think of things like love, peace, warmth, or money? Perhaps, like me, you envisioned a heart, a dove, the sun, and a dollar sign.

Form

Form adds the dimension of depth to shape. *Form* is three-dimensional and connects us more fully to the way we see objects in the natural world (see Figure 4.16). In terms of geometric elements, it may be helpful to compare the two-dimensional shapes of a circle and square to their three-dimensional counterparts, the sphere and the cube. In order to show depth within a two-dimensional design space, a designer or photographer must learn to manipulate lighting, shading, color, and contrast within the frame. In film, a single backlight can create the shape or silhouette of a person on screen. To create

FIGURE 4.15
The element of shape is emphasized in this backlit photograph of a lone fisherman at sunrise.
Source: Vic Costello.

FIGURE 4.16
A 3D modeling program was used to create these visual forms. Form adds a sense of depth, a perceptual illusion that can be produced by manipulating light, shadow, color, and other elements within 2D space.

form, more sophisticated lighting from multiple angles is required. In graphic design, 3D modeling tools and software can be used to create the illusion of form. With such programs, you can add and manipulate virtual lighting to the same end. One medium relies on natural light and physical instruments to do the job. The other uses virtual instruments and algorithms to do the trick. As discussed earlier, using perspective also enhances the viewer's ability to perceive depth along the z-axis.

LIGHTING

As we've already established, lighting affects form as does color, contrast, and depth, as we'll see later on in this chapter. Good designers carefully plan their lighting when they take photographs, capture video, and create graphics (see chapter 13 for more detail on the application of lighting in film and video). We describe light as having three primary characteristics: 1) intensity, 2) color temperature, and 3) hardness.

Light intensity is a measure of overall brightness of a light source (the sun, a lamp, etc.) or the level of illumination on a subject being photographed. A light meter is a device that can measure illuminance, or the amount of incidental light striking a surface—such as the subject's face—and quantify it numerically in a standardized unit of measurement such as foot-candles or lux.

Color temperature refers to the general hue of a light source and varies across a range from reddish-orange to blue and is measured in Kelvin units. On the low end of the Kelvin scale, a lit match emits a warm orange glow at around 1,700 Kelvin (K). Incandescent lights, such as those used in television studio lighting, operate at around 3,200 K. Normal daylight is roughly 5,600 K. Cooler colors (blues) kick in around 6,500 K, with the clear blue sky falling anywhere from 15,000–27,000 K.

Hardness is the degree to which the edges of cast shadows are hard or soft. Hard lighting from distant or narrow light sources casts sharply defined crisp shadows and will give your image an illusion of volume and emphasize textures. If you angle a light to the side of a texture (called *short lighting* in portrait photography), small shadows will emphasize the lines in a face or the grains of sand of a dune. Soft lighting from broad (frontally placed), multiple, close, or diffused (scattered) light sources—even lighting diffused by clouds or from backlighting—can soften an image, making an older subject appear a bit younger or creating an ethereal quality.

Low light, universal light, and light falloff also affect an image. In low light, a still image camera has to keep its shutter open longer, and objects in motion can become blurry; in video, the image becomes grainy. And when you work with images and graphics in editing applications such as Photoshop, using universal lighting will make light-dependent effects (drop shadows and beveling, for instance) more cohesive. Universal lighting makes the illusion of light consistent, so light appears to come from only one angle. Finally, you can light a scene to emphasize selective parts of a composition, taking advantage of light falloff, or the lower illumination of objects farther from your light source.

Texture

Texture is the surface attribute of a visual object that evokes a sense of tactile interaction, and it can be implied in images. We perceive texture with the sense of touch. Some surfaces feel smooth whereas others are coarse. Some are wet, and others are dry. Some are soft, others are hard. Texture can affect us on a multisensory level, evoking in us a sense of touch, smell, and even taste. A digital image can only imply a sensory response, but the power of suggestion is real. As with shape, the visual element of texture can stir up memories and associations in the user. The sight of grill marks on a hamburger can remind us of the sound of sizzling fat and stir up thoughts of familiar smells and flavors. The grill marks attest not only to how the meat was cooked, but also may bring to mind positive recollections of summer cookouts and backyard parties. Of course, those who don't eat meat may respond entirely differently to such a visual prompt. Knowing your audience and its associations is important, especially when your audience is intercultural.

Looking at a familiar texture on screen, you can easily imagine what it might feel like. Adding sound to the experience makes the connection even stronger. What if you could hear the burger sizzle? Just imagine the grinding sound of sandpaper rubbing up and down the edge of a board, and the relative graininess of the surface becomes all the more apparent. What about the sound of feet walking on a gravel road? Does it change depending on the size of the gravel?

Texture ignites the imagination, allowing us to interact with a design at a deeper cognitive level. For example, the texture of a person's skin can tell us a lot about an individual. We associate soft, smooth skin with the touch of a baby's face. Likewise, we expect older people to have dry, cracked, or wrinkled skin that is weathered by age and the elements of life. Rust and peeling paint also speak to us about age and the passing of time. And the designs of many websites and applications play to our expectations of current technology as smooth and sleek.

Texture also serves to break up visual monotony. It adds visual depth, since most textures rise above the surface of an object. When properly incorporated into a design, texture can enhance the interest and perceived realism of a visual work.

Pattern

Pattern is the reoccurrence of a visual element within a design space. Clothing, furniture, and wallpaper are often identified by the characteristic pattern they employ (checkerboard, herringbone, polka dot, paisley, plaid, etc.). As with texture, pattern can add visual interest to an otherwise plain and monochromatic object. Like shape, pattern can be geometric or organic. The Spirograph toy, invented in the 1960s, is a popular plaything that enables kids to draw intricate geometric patterns of lines, shapes, and colors. The device, made up of a drawing frame and design templates with gears and tracks to control movement, allows the child to combine curves, circles, loops, and lines to form highly complex patterns and designs. The long-term popularity of this toy testifies to our innate fascination with repetition and pattern.

FIGURE 4.17
1) Lighting, 2) texture, 3) pattern, and 4) color are used in these images to achieve a desired effect or mood. The elements of design can also be combined in a single image. For example, the umbrella shot features both the elements of color and pattern.

Organic patterns are found in nature, such as a flock of geese flying in formation, the woven matrix of a spider web, or an aerial view of a pumpkin patch at harvest time. Patterns can be uniform and predictable as in the repetition of colors and shapes in the American flag. The random or natural scattering of similar elements within a shared space can also lead to interesting patterns, such as hieroglyphics on a cave wall or shots of sunbathers strewn along a crowded beach.

Color

Color has three dimensions: 1) hue, 2) saturation, and 3) brightness. *Hue* is the color shade of an object as a single point on the color spectrum. We refer to colors most often by their hue (red, green, blue, etc.). *Saturation* is the strength or purity of a color. The red in a stop sign is a highly saturated hue, whereas pink is a desaturated version of the same color. A completely desaturated color contains only variations of white and black as measured along the grayscale. *Brightness* (also called *value*) is the relative lightness or darkness of a color. Brightness can be thought of as the dimmer control on a light switch that raises or lowers the level of light in a room.

We can use color to set tone and mood, to elicit instant associations, to attract attention, and even to help users remember things. In the beginning of the movie *Catch Me If You Can*, Leonardo DiCaprio's character is in control of his life, and the palette is subdued. The colors become vivid as he loses control and takes bigger chances. You might buy a beach towel with an orange and red design because the colors bring to mind oceanside sunsets and stir up related emotions. And the orange can generate positive emotions on its own, without bringing a past trip to mind. Or you might paint a baby's room a pale, desaturated green to create a soothing environment.

Colors also have cultural associations. What sex is a baby dressed in blue (see Figure 4.18)? Does a website with a pink background target men or women? These are purely learned associations: in Western nations and prior to the end of World War II, pink and blue were often used interchangeably across genders. What does red mean to you? That depends on where you're from. In the United States, red is associated with danger and passion, among

FIGURE 4.18
Boy or girl? What role does color play in your decision?

other things, whereas in China, it has a number of other associations, such as luck. If you want to attract attention to an element on a page, what color would you use? Brown would probably not be your first choice! Psychologists have tied color to memory, too. If you have used a coloring book to study anatomy, color may have helped you pass your exams.

THE PRINCIPLES OF DESIGN

In the previous section, I referred to the elements of design as the "ingredients" used in making visual art. If the elements are the ingredients, then the principles of design can be thought of as the recipe for combining elements within a visual space. The principles of design are formal rules and concepts for optimizing the arrangement and presentation of two-dimensional visual elements. The 12 general principles covered in this section fall into the three broad categories of 1) unity, 2) emphasis, and 3) perceptual forces. The principles of *unity* can be thought of as the perceptual glue that holds a design together and maintains a sense of visual harmony. The principles of *emphasis* address the need for maintaining a visual focal point. They also relate to the way designers designate the importance or weight of the subject matter. Emphasis is often used to communicate to the viewer the relative importance of visual objects or information in a design. Finally, the principles of *perceptual force* help us understand some of the psychological processes that affect the way we interact with visual content within a frame.

Unity

You have heard the saying, "the whole is greater than the sum of its parts." In visual theory, this means that the viewer should be able to grasp the essence of the "big picture" without being distracted by the individual elements of a design. This is the principle of *unity*, which is achieved when the visual subcomponents of a design coalesce to form a holistic impression. Unity means that the constituent parts of a work reside together in harmony. In a good design, each visual element or group of elements should contribute to the whole without competing against other elements or distracting the viewer from the primary point of interest.

In 1923, German psychologist Max Wertheimer (1880–1943) developed the theory of perceptual grouping as a part of a larger set of axioms dealing with perceptual organization. Rooted in Gestalt psychology, a branch of study dealing with the self-organizing tendencies of the mind and brain, the laws of perceptual organization suggest that the human brain favors whole forms over random smatterings of disconnected elements. To this end, the brain strives for unity by organizing visual information into meaningful clusters or groups. This tendency enables people to retain holistic impressions of shapes and patterns while ignoring the constituent parts used in their construction.

When visual content is haphazardly arranged and disorganized, the brain must work harder to make sense of it. When information conforms to known principles of organization, the brain can work faster, and communication is more effective. These unifying principles include proximity, alignment, similarity, and repetition (see Figures 4.19–4.22).

THE U.S. COAST GUARD

The Coast Guard is one of our nation's five military services. We exist to defend and preserve the United States. We protect the personal safety and security of our people; the marine transportation system and infrastructure; our natural and economic resources; and the territorial integrity of our nation—from both internal and external threats, natural and man-made. We protect these interests in U.S. ports, inland waterways, along the coasts, and on international waters.

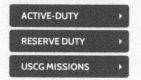

ACTIVE-DUTY ▶

RESERVE DUTY ▶

USCG MISSIONS ▶

SERVING IN THE U.S. COAST GUARD

HONOR

We demonstrate uncompromising ethical conduct and moral behavior in all of our personal and organizational actions. We are loyal and accountable to the public trust. Integrity is our standard.

RESPECT

We treat each other and those we serve with fairness, dignity, respect and compassion. We encourage individual opportunity and growth. We encourage creativity through empowerment. We value our diverse workforce. We work as a team.

DEVOTION TO DUTY

We are professionals, military and civilian, who seek responsibility, accept accountability and are committed to the successful achievement of our organizational goals. We exist to serve. We serve with pride.

FIGURE 4.19
Observe how the designer of this layout for the U.S. Coast Guard website incorporated the laws of proximity, alignment, similarity, and repetition to achieve unity.
Source: http://gocoastguard.com.

PROXIMITY

The law of *proximity* states that objects are more likely to be perceived as related when they are positioned close together. Think for a moment about how Google returns search results. Google displays a series of listings, each with a linked web page title, a URL (web address), and an excerpt or page description. Evenly distributed spaces separate the listings, allowing you to quickly identify each snippet as a separate entry in the list of results—with all its material grouped accordingly.

Proximity reminds me to keep captions close to the images and illustrations they refer to. It informs us that titles should appear near the first line of text in an article. It also reminds us never to scatter the location of buttons on a toolbar that belong together by virtue of a similar function. White space is often associated with proximity. If you add too much white space between related objects in a design, the audience may fail to see that they are connected. If there's not enough white space, clutter may result, making it difficult for people to perceive the presence of individual elements.

ALIGNMENT

The principle of *alignment* encourages designers to position objects that belong together along a common edge or implied line. Visual objects—text, graphics, and so on—are normally aligned along their outer edges (left, right, top, or bottom) or centers. However, any line will do, as long as the placement is thoughtful and consistent. When composing text, we use the terms *left*, *right*, and *center justified* to indicate which edge to line up against. To enhance readability, we almost always left justify paragraph text or body copy, providing readers with a consistent starting point at the beginning of each line.

Depending on the designer's preferences and the nature of the content, the right edge can remain ragged (uneven) or each edge can be justified (both flush left and flush right). Leaving the right side ragged preserves the uniformity of the word spacing and gives readers visual reference points in longer blocks of text, which enhance readability. Justifying both sides of a paragraph adds spaces between words to expand each line to its outer limits; it affects readability but gives a design a clean look.

Within a single design frame or multipage layout, alignments should be consistent. Mixing them is normally not recommended. If you choose to left justify the body copy on one page, be sure to apply the same formatting to every page in the site. Alignment can also be used to unify different, yet related, visual elements. For example, left justifying a photo caption along the left side of the image it refers to ties both elements together along a common vertical edge. This lets the viewer know they belong together. Be careful not to have too many implied lines: a handful of well-chosen lines enhances a design, but too many make it look cluttered.

SIMILARITY

The law of *similarity* states that the brain will perceive visual objects as belonging together when their style attributes are similar and uniform.

For *example*, the unity **of** this paragraph is diminished by the ARBITRARY ANd random mixing of dissimilar **STYLES**.

Here, a lack of similarity results in poor organization of the content and diminished readability of the text. The more objects are alike, the more likely they will stick together naturally as a group. The more dissimilar they are, the more likely they will resist grouping and pull apart. The law of similarity does not presuppose that all the elements in a group should be identically styled. If this were the case, many designs would be rather boring and flat in terms of visual contrast. Designers often take advantage of the fact that dissimilar objects pull apart in order to create emphasis.

REPETITION

Repetition is related to similarity and suggests that repeating visual elements such as lines, colors, shapes, and patterns help strengthen the overall unity of a design. In web design, repetition can be used to bring harmony and consistency to the look of a multipage website. Repeating important symbols or components such as a

FIGURE 4.20
The principles of similarity and repetition were used here to bring visual unity to the design of two different, yet related, program logos.

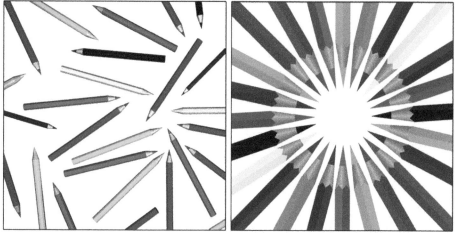

FIGURE 4.21
The colored pencils in the first vector illustration are haphazardly arranged. The second illustration features a more purposeful arrangement, applying the laws of proximity and alignment. How is your perception of each version influenced by the use of proximity, alignment, similarity, and repetition?

banner graphic or menu bar at the top of each page enhances usability and brings visual synergy to the site. Similarly, it's common to see visual elements or scenes from a movie repeated in the jacket design of a DVD and on the movie poster and website promoting the film. Repeating elements can help a company preserve its visual brand identification across multiple communication channels as it promotes its products and services to consumers.

Repetition occurs frequently in nature, and photographers enjoy capturing it on film. Repetition produces pattern, and patterns are intriguing to the eye. Think about how stable and fascinating the pattern of a honeycomb is. There's something innately interesting about its uniform structure and appearance that captures our interest and provides a natural sense of awe and wonder.

FIGURE 4.22
Notice how proximity, alignment, similarity, and repetition are combined in this web page design template.

Emphasis

The principle of *emphasis* suggests that a good design must have a primary focal point or center of interest. In a newspaper, the headline type is set to a very large font size in order to draw the attention of the reader to what the editor believes is the most important story of the day.

Emphasis can be used to quickly guide the viewer's attention to the main subject or message in a communication exchange. Large bold headings on a web page help you navigate quickly to the item or information you are most interested in. Google's homepage clearly emphasizes the text entry window to make it easy for users to enter keywords in a search. Just imagine if all the text in a newspaper or on a website were exactly the same size, style, and color. The usability of the content would suffer tremendously, and users would quickly get frustrated and lose interest. Since our eyes are naturally drawn to larger objects in a design, varying the size of spatial elements is a common way to connote emphasis. Although there are many ways to create emphasis in a design, we will look briefly at contrast, color, depth, and proportion (see Figure 4.23).

CONTRAST AND VALUE

The term *value* describes the range of light and dark portions in an image or design. In photography, film, and television, *value* is usually expressed as *contrast*. The strongest visible contrast is represented by the difference between black and white. One of the reasons that books are traditionally produced with black text on a white page is because this method creates the best contrast for reading. The text "pops" out against the lighter background and makes reading more pleasant and efficient. The text is the main event, and the background should not present a distraction by competing for the reader's attention.

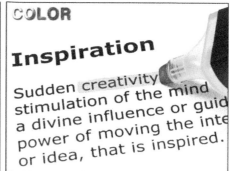

FIGURE 4.23
Contrast, color, depth, and proportion can be used to emphasize the main subject in a visual design.

The number of colors or gradient steps in a composition that fall between the bipolar extremes of black and white is called *tonal range*. The greater the tonal range, the greater the contrast, and the more interesting a composition will generally appear (Figure 4.23). The eye is attracted first to the areas of a composition with highest contrast (or *high-key*), regardless of whether they contain color.

Increasing contrast is one of the easiest ways to emphasize the main subject or visual object. In photography, contrast impacts image detail, clarity, and mood. A *low-key* image contains mostly dark tones or color levels and communicates a serious, somber, or reflective mood. Such images can also ignite a sense of foreboding, mystery, horror, and fright. Photographic film was touted for years because of its ability to reproduce quality low-key images. Most narrative filmmakers prefer shooting on film for this very reason. Achieving low-key tonality is necessary in order to create realistic and compelling moments of heightened visual drama. Digital cameras have come a long way, although some professionals still prefer film's ability to handle low-contrast lighting situations. A high-key image is characterized by bright tones with very few dark areas, and a *mid-key* image falls in between. The higher the overall contrast in an image, the brighter and more cheerful the overall impression will be. In photography, film, and videography, pushing contrast too far in either direction will lead to an unusable image. This occurs when an image is under- or overexposed due to poor lighting in the scene or on the main subject.

Contrast is at work in other components of multimedia design as well. Multimedia works are often combinations of elements, and the contrast in each may vary.

A web page or animation's background is often more than a solid color. It may be a graphic or have images. Designers often make such backgrounds low-key to keep these elements from competing with the design's secret ingredient, its star attraction.

COLOR

Color is a powerful tool for enhancing contrast in visual design space, and *color contrast* has been used particularly well in the advertising industry. Perhaps you've seen a print or television ad in which a single colored object (like a hat or a can of soda) stood out against the backdrop of a black and white or monochromatic setting. A selective splash of color can immediately grab our attention, providing a sense of focus and direction for the viewer.

Colors are classified as warm, cool, or neutral, depending on which portion of the color spectrum they fall into. Warm colors reside near the orange area of the spectrum and include shades of red and orange, as well as warm greens. The human eye is attracted to the warm color regions of a design first (see Figure 4.27). We tend to perceive warm colors as breaking free from the background and advancing toward us from a printed page or screen. A designer can use this effect to bring attention to an object by increasing the figure-ground contrast. But be careful! Too much warm color in a design can be visually overwhelming. Cool colors such as violets, blues, and cool greens seem to recede away from us into the background, appearing distant and detached. Cool colors are calm, soothing, and placid, like the blue waters of a still mountain lake. A design can accommodate large areas of cool colors without visually overwhelming the user. Neutral colors are achromatic (effectively lack hues). We'll get more into color in chapter 9, "Graphics," but white, black, and achromatic grays work well with warm and cool colors. Another caution: many grays are not achromatic, and their hint of hue limits how effectively they can be used.

DEPTH

Depth is related to the principle of *figure-ground*, or what we perceive in the foreground or background, which we'll discuss later. It is a powerful tool for achieving emphasis in a design. In photography, film, and videography, the term *depth of field* describes the portion of the z-axis that viewers perceive as being in focus at any one time. When this portion of the z-axis is small, the image is said to have a shallow depth of field (see Figure 4.24). When it is large, the image is said to have great depth of field. You can emphasize the main subject by keeping it in focus (sharp and clear) and the background clutter or dead space out of focus. In graphic design, drop shadows, lighting, perspective, and other visual effects can be applied to a foreground image to simulate the appearance of depth.

PROPORTION

Proportion is the scale of an object relative to other elements within a composition (see Figure 4.25). Our perception of an object's size is related to the size and position of other objects within the field of view. Decreasing the size of an object makes it recede into the distance, creating the perception that it is getting farther

FIGURE 4.24
This image, originally shot for video, emphasizes the z-axis— enhancing shallow depth of field and the overall perception of depth.
Source: Bryan Baker.

FIGURE 4.25
Our expectation of proportionality is challenged by the contrast in physical size between the main subject and the unusually large structural logo she is standing next to.

and farther away. Increasing the size of an object elevates its visual status, making it appear closer to the viewer. The location of an object also affects our perception of size. Objects placed near the top of the screen appear smaller and farther away than objects placed near the bottom. Including familiar objects of a known size within a design can help a viewer make accurate perceptual judgments about the actual, or relative, size of other elements nearby.

Perceptual Forces

When we look at a graphic representation within a frame (still picture or moving image), our brains are constantly processing the relative push and pull of perceptual field forces within the visual space. For example, regardless of whether we view a photograph when it is lying flat on a table, hanging on a wall, or even rotated a quarter turn, we tend to perceive the top of the image as up and the bottom of the image as down. The bottom of the frame simulates the natural gravitational field of our human experience. But unlike gravity, which acts upon us from only one direction, perceptual field forces can tug at visual matter from any direction.

When a visual element is positioned too close to the edge of the frame, the attraction between the object and the side of the frame increases. The effect is similar to bringing the opposite poles of two magnets within close range. As the magnets get closer, the attraction increases, until they eventually snap together. White space can provide necessary breathing room around visual objects and will help counteract the natural pull of the frame. When we discuss the perceptual forces humans experience, we talk about the principles of balance, continuation, figure-ground, and psychological closure.

BALANCE

A *balanced composition* is achieved when the visual weight of objects is equally dispersed within the frame, producing a perceived state of equilibrium. On occasion, the designer may want to purposely destabilize an image for effect, but generally our goal is to achieve balance in design. The size, color, and position of graphical elements affect our sense of balance or instability within a composition. Like a set of scales, the frame rests on an imaginary fulcrum at the center of its baseline. To the viewer, some objects will naturally appear heavier or lighter than others. Typically, we perceive large or dark-colored objects as heavier than small or light-colored ones. If the designer places a large dark-colored sphere in the upper left-hand corner of the frame, then an object, or multiple objects, of equal combined mass will need to be positioned in the lower right-hand corner to achieve balance. Compositional balance can be achieved using either a symmetrical or asymmetrical approach (see Figure 4.26 and Figure 4.27).

Symmetrical Balance

In a *symmetrical composition*, objects of similar shape, color, and size are weighted equally on opposite sides of the frame. This can be accomplished by centering the subject, or multiple visual elements, along the vertical or horizontal dividing line of the frame, with the weight of the elements evenly distributed in each half. Symmetrical balance is analogous to a seesaw whose pivot point or fulcrum is centered, and children of equal weight are positioned on opposite ends. This approach is also called *formal balance* because it leads to designs that are perceived as tranquil, elegant, traditional, and conservative. Symmetrical balance can lead to a somewhat predictable and less creative visual design.

Asymmetrical Balance

With *asymmetrical* or *informal balance*, equilibrium is established with objects of differing size, color, and tone. This approach is analogous to a seesaw whose fulcrum is located in an off-center position. In this configuration, placing two children of

FIGURE 4.26
Symmetrical balance (top) and asymmetrical balance (bottom) work in different ways to achieve visual equilibrium.

TO ENTERTAIN.

FIGURE 4.27
The principles of color, contrast, and balance are featured in this staged shot for a promotional video program.
Source: Bryan Baker.

equal size on opposite ends of the seesaw will not lead to balance. More weight must be added to one side in order to compensate for the new pivot point. Asymmetrical, or informal, compositions are much more interesting to design and compose and can appear more visually interesting and dynamic.

Rule of Thirds The *rule of thirds* is a compositional tool used to produce visually appealing images using asymmetrical balance. With the rule of thirds, the area of an image is figuratively divided into thirds, both horizontally and vertically, to produce a three-by-three grid. Four points are created by the intersection of the lines. The points and lines serve as a guide to the designer or photographer for optimally placing subjects. The four intersection points are the most visually compelling areas within the frame. Likewise, the weakest area of the design space is in the middle of the frame, in the center box (see Figure 4.28).

According to the rule of thirds, the focal point of the image should be located at one of the four intersection points. These are the natural landing points for the eye. However, people do not perceive the left and right side of the frame equally. In Western cultures, our eyes tend to land first on the left side of the frame and then flow to the right in search of a resting place. We often place the main subject on the left side of the frame and dead space on the right. Professionals vary the intersections at which they place subjects and background matter, depending on whether they have a single or group subject, have background matter, want to create tension, and so forth. The rule of thirds is not a hard and fast rule, but adopting this simple technique will allow you to quickly boost the effectiveness of a two-dimensional design or photographic image.

The purpose of the vertical and horizontal lines is to guide the placement of subjects to an off-center position, approximately one-third in from each side of the frame. It also reminds us to avoid the practice of dividing screen space in half along either its vertical or horizontal center. For example, a dominant vertical element like a street lamp, tree trunk, or flagpole should be positioned approximately one-third to the left or right edge of the frame. Likewise, the horizon is best positioned along the upper- or lower-third of the frame.

The term *lower-third* comes from the rule of thirds convention. The lower-third is the horizontal line nearest to the bottom of the frame. Television producers routinely superimpose the name and title of the person speaking on camera along this line. When you hear someone say they need to insert a lower-third, they are referring to this type of title graphic.

To aid photographers in composing shots, many cameras now come with a rule-of-thirds overlay feature. When activated, the rule-of-thirds grid is superimposed in the viewfinder of the camera. This is a great tool for amateur photographers. However, if your device lacks this feature, you just need a little bit of practice to learn how to mentally break up the frame into thirds. Incidentally, the rule of thirds works regardless of the size or aspect ratio of the frame or the visual medium you are designing in. It works just as well if you're designing a business card, taking a digital photo, or composing a 16:9 high-definition image for a documentary.

FIGURE 4.28
Using the rule of thirds as a guide, how would you critique the composition of these two photographs?

CONTINUATION

The law of *continuation* suggests our brains tend to process what we see as continuing along lines that are predictable and free of obstacles and that don't abruptly change direction. So in a design with overlapping curves, our brains interpret each vector (line) as a smooth curve; we don't see each as changing direction at their intersection. More precisely, vectors are directional forces within the frame that guide the eye from one point to another. Three types of vectors occur most often in visual space: graphic vectors, index vectors, and motion vectors (see Figure 4.29).

Graphic vectors are created by strategically placing stationary line elements within the frame. The lines can be real or implied through the placement of other visual elements. They focus the viewer's gaze in a specific direction or guide the viewer along a visual path. In photography, these pathways are called leading lines because they "lead" the eyes from point to point or directly to the primary focal point of the image. A barbed wire fence stretching across a landscape, the line created by the water's edge at the beach, and a row of people waiting for a movie are all examples of graphic vectors.

Index vectors are created by placing objects that conspicuously point in a specific direction. A crowd gazing upward, a road sign with a large arrow pointing to the right, and a hitchhiker with his hand extended are visual examples of index vectors.

Motion vectors are created by the real or apparent movement of subjects within the frame. Motion connotes a sense of directionality. We can usually tell which direction a person or object is moving by observing which way it is facing. Although best demonstrated with time-based media, motion vectors can be implied in a still image or graphic. The addition of a motion blur or trailing edge can intensify the perception of speed and directionality.

FIGURE-GROUND

In Gestalt psychology an element that appears in the foreground of our perceptual field is called a *figure*, whereas everything behind it is the *ground*. In nature, the phenomenon of depth perception enables us to distinguish between figure and ground (see Figure 4.30). In two-dimensional space, we must rely on visual cues within the frame to provide a sense of order along the z-axis. You need to remember that

Graphic Vector

Index Vector

Motion Vector

FIGURE 4.29
Graphic, index, and motion vectors work together with the law of continuation to guide the viewer's eyes from one point to another within the frame.

FIGURE 4.30
Some optical illusions work by playing with the figure-ground relationship. What do you see in this image? Relax your focus and look again. How about now?

the viewer wants to make sense of what he or she is seeing. Our brain is wired to organize the visual field into meaningful figure-ground relationships. The degree to which the viewer can do so effectively attests to the skill of the designer or photographer. Providing good contrast between the foreground and background elements in the frame is the best way to keep viewers from being perceptually confused or overwhelmed.

PSYCHOLOGICAL CLOSURE

The final perceptual force we will look at is psychological closure. One of the most powerful abilities we have is to mentally complete a visual pattern or impression when only partial information is provided. *Psychological closure* is the human equivalent of connecting the dots or filling in the gaps. For this reason, objects within the frame can extend past the boundary of the frame. As long as enough visual information is provided, an individual can complete a picture in her head, thus maintaining a stable perceptual experience (see Figure 4.31).

The principle of psychological closure is used in visual design all the time. Literal interpretations of words and symbols can be replaced with partial impressions or abstract variations of larger elements. With psychological closure, the brain seeks to create meaningful order out of visual chaos. As long as enough visual cues are provided, the brain will kick in to form a complete mental impression. The extra measure of sensory activity can give us a deeper and more satisfying experience because we are more cognitively engaged with the visual stimuli.

What we see...

What we perceive...

FIGURE 4.31
Kanizsa's triangle illustrates the principle of closure to suggest a second triangle overlaying the first.

CHAPTER SUMMARY

Content is still king, but if we deliver content without good design, users will not know where to focus, will not make the connections we intend, will not be engaged, and may even misunderstand the message. The elements and principles of design are a designer's foundation. They give you the tools to understand aesthetics and preferences and to both make and defend sound choices. Rarely do we work solely for our own pleasure. We often work in teams, and we work for clients who hire us for our expertise. Occasionally, others make suggestions that go against our better judgment. Being able to explain why an idea won't work well may be the difference between creating an outstanding graphic or video and getting stuck creating something that will fall flat with its audience.

Ultimately, we create for our users, the people who will visit our websites, see our photos, watch our podcasts, and use our kiosks. Designers strive to make products usable and engaging. Good design makes users' experiences positive and rewarding. Bad design serves no one.

A foundation in design elements and principles inspires not only good practice but also creativity. Return to the foundation when you feel you are in a creative rut. Do you need to add energy to a graphic? Perhaps you can add dynamic lines. Are your action photographs missing the action? A canted angle might help. Does your video need to evoke other senses? Consider lighting your subject so it has more texture, and add appropriate sounds. Are you at a loss for how to create a new logo? The principle of closure may suggest a creative solution. The combinations are limitless, but be judicious: don't emphasize too much. If you do, you might emphasize nothing at all, leaving your users to wonder what your secret ingredient was supposed to be.

CHAPTER 5
Page Layout

The more personal computer displays become like lightweight books, the more people are going to feel comfortable reading from them. A PC that you can open up and physically handle easily, that has the right kind of battery and display, will give the same visual impression as a page.

—**John Warnock, inventor of PostScript and the founder of Adobe Systems (Wired.com, 1994)**

Key Terms
Body Copy
Border
Box Model
Cell
Chunking
Column
F-Layout
Fixed Layout
Floating Graphic
Fluid Layout
Golden Ratio
Grid System
Gutenberg Diagram
Heading
Headline
Inline Graphic
Layout
Margin
Modular Grid
Multicolumn Grid
Padding
Page
Page Template
Row
Sidebar
Single-Column Grid
Splash Page
Static Page
Style Sheet
Table
Visual Hierarchy
Z-layout

Chapter Highlights

This chapter examines:
- Strategies for the effective placement of visual content within the page
- The influence of visual hierarchy on viewing behavior
- Use of the grid system for managing page and screen space
- Commonly used layouts in multimedia page design
- Design tips when using page templates and style sheets

ORGANIZING CONTENT ON A PAGE

Page layout is the area of graphic design that refers to the visual arrangement of text and images on a page. It is essentially the role of visual information management, using the general principles of design and typography to bring order and structure to a page. The term originated in the printing industry as the specialized craft of designing the physical pages in books, magazines, and newspapers. In publishing houses, agencies, and newsrooms, it's the job of authors, reporters, copywriters, editors, and the like to generate the text (or *copy*) for visual pages, while photographers, illustrators, and graphic designers produce the images. It's the job of a layout artist or page compositor to combine the various elements of visual information (text and graphics) within the page, creating a presentation that is both pleasing to the eye and easy to consume.

Programs like QuarkXPress and Adobe InDesign are professional software tools used in the desktop publishing industry for the prepress layout and design of printed pages. In multimedia, the concept of page layout has migrated metaphorically from the kinds of physical pages you can touch and turn to digital pages that appear on a computer screen or monitor. The page metaphor was extended into the field of web design but can also be more broadly applied to any type of screen space where visual information must be arranged and ordered for presentation. In multimedia work, the principles of page design can be applied to the creation of a DVD menu screen, a full-screen title graphic in a television commercial, or the welcome screen of a micro app running on a tablet computer or smartphone. Anytime you combine visual content within the fixed or fluid space of a digital page or screen, you are engaging in the activity of page design (see Figure 5.1).

FIGURE 5.1
The DVD menu system for the Walt Disney film *The Rookie* includes a main menu, a scene selection submenu, and a bonus materials submenu. The visual layout of each menu is the product of multimedia page design, where diverse visual elements such as video, graphics, text, and animation are arranged within the screen space of a 16-by-9 television frame.

THE GUTENBERG DIAGRAM

In the early days of printing, page layouts were densely populated with text. While early printing systems, like the Gutenberg press, could easily mass-produce the transfer of letterforms on paper, they were not equipped to reproduce artwork, illustrations, or other visual elements that are commonly used today to break up the heavy flow of printed text. If artwork was included, it was drawn by hand after the pages were printed.

The *Gutenberg diagram* is a primitive eye-tracking model that is used to show how readers scan through a page comprised entirely of evenly distributed text (see Figure 5.2). The Gutenberg diagram divides a page across its horizontal and vertical centers to produce four equal quadrants. A reader's interaction with the text begins in the top left quadrant on the page. This is the dominant section of the page known as the *primary optical area*. Next, they move across each line of text, from left to right, in a series of horizontal sweeps or scans referred to as the *axis of orientation*.

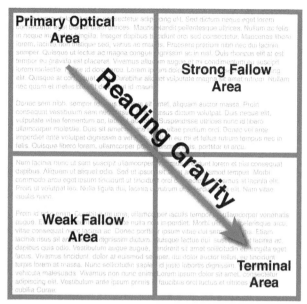

FIGURE 5.2
The Gutenberg diagram illustrates the general pattern the eyes follow as they scan visual information within a page. It applies primarily to text-dominant layouts where there is little to no visual hierarchy, such as a page from a novel containing only printed words and sentences.

Metaphorically, reading exerts a gravitational force on the user that continually pushes his or her gaze downward and to the right. As a result, the eye is persistently led along a diagonal path from the primary optical area in the top left part of the page to the terminal area located in the bottom right. The strong fallow area (in the upper right) and the weak fallow area (in the lower left) lie beyond this path and, as such, are demoted in terms of their visual influence. A reader typically pays less attention to content that's placed in these regions of the page.

BREAKING OUT OF THE BOX

The layout of a page directly affects the way a user scans its contents. As page designs have shifted from print to digital forms, and from heavy text-based layouts to visually dynamic designs with rich media content, users have adopted more sophisticated methods for scanning pages. Two familiar scanning methods are often talked about with regard to how users interact with web pages online.

F-Layout

The *F-layout* is one of the most common page layouts on the Web. As the name suggests, the reader's gaze is directed though the page in a pattern that resembles the letter *F* (see Figure 5.3). As with most layouts, this one encourages the user to begin reading in the top left part of the page. He then proceeds to make a full scan from

FIGURE 5.3
This version of the Library of Congress homepage features the classic F-layout design. A prominent vertical sidebar along the left edge of the page serves as a visual anchor for the eyes as the user scans from left to right in progressively shorter bursts from top to bottom.

left to right across the first row of visual information. Next, the user makes a partial scan of the second row. This pass rarely extends to the end of the line or column. Each subsequent row of information is scanned in short bursts from left to right as the user settles into a normal rhythm and pattern for processing the main content on the page.

Humans are creatures of habit. For this reason, the F-pattern is an all-too-familiar format for people who spend any amount of time in front of a computer surfing the Web. We have grown accustomed to the most important information being placed along the top edge of the page, usually in the form of an eye-catching mast-head or banner graphic. The masthead provides important visual cues about the contents of the page. It can be scanned quickly and will often influence a user's next step. Will he continue scanning or bail from the page? The second row of a web page often contains navigational prompts like menu buttons or hyperlinks. If the first scan did its job by hooking the user's attention, then the second scan will take on more meaning as he seeks to understand how the page and site contents are organized. A sidebar along the left edge of a page often comes into play on the third scan. It pulls the user's gaze toward the left edge of the document win-dow, directing him downward into a series of shorter bursts of scanning activity. Research shows that conforming layouts to the F-pattern will enhance the usabil-ity of the page, making it easier for users to glean information in an expedient manner.

Z-Layout

A less popular format, the *Z-layout* is a variation of the Gutenberg diagram (see Figure 5.4). Scanning begins with a full visual sweep across the top row of the page. The second scan flows diagonally through the center of the page in a downward movement toward the bottom left-hand corner. The final scan is a horizontal sweep across the bottom of the page. Important visual elements should be placed along the path of the Z. While the Z-layout suggests a rigid zigzag path, the chiseled angles of the Z-pattern can be softened to produce a more organic S-curve feel. The Z-layout works best when a large visual element or content region (such as a single

FIGURE 5.4
The Smithsonian homepage pictured here guides the user's eyes through the page along a *Z*-shaped path. Can you locate other examples of the F-layout and Z-layout in action?

photo or visual montage) is placed in the center of the page, between two rows of linear information. It is a simple layout to create and can be used effectively for pages containing only a handful of key elements that need to be communicated quickly without a lot of visual clutter.

GREAT IDEAS
Visual Hierarchy

The term *visual hierarchy* refers to the perceived ordering of content within a page by the reader. A page that consists only of text that is equally spaced and uniform in size is perceptually flat (see Figure 5.5, left). In such a design, every word carries the same weight, and therefore nothing rises to the forefront of the reader's perception. However, when certain words or phrases are set apart stylistically using the principles of design covered in chapter 4, "Visual Communication," such as alignment, color, emphasis, proportion, and so on, they will rise above the background noise of the page, vying for attention (see Figure 5.5, right).

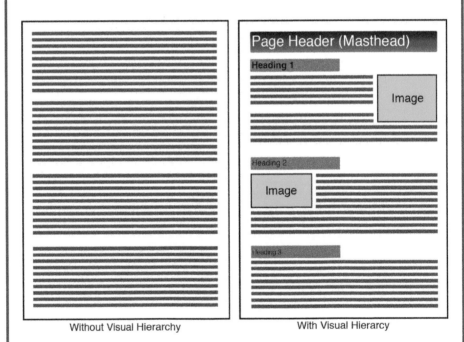

Without Visual Hierarchy   With Visual Hierarcy

FIGURE 5.5
A thoughtfully constructed visual hierarchy can improve the order and flow of content on a multimedia page.

Chunking Body Copy

One of the easiest ways to begin establishing visual hierarchy in a page is to sub-divide large blocks of body copy into smaller segments or chunks. *Body copy* is the main text of a published document or advertisement, and it is often the most plentiful source of content on a page. *Chunking* is a practice that involves the visual consolidation of related sentences or ideas into small blocks of information that can be quickly and easily digested. Paragraphs are a common chunking tool, as are lists, callouts, and text boxes. From a consumer's point of view, chunking is like eating a steak. The meat is easier to ingest after it is cut into smaller bite-sized pieces. Placing too much text on the screen at a time, or within a specific region of the page, can overwhelm the senses and lead to eye fatigue. A reader can quickly tire out or lose interest. Chunking is highly recommended when writing copy for multimedia consumption since reading on a low-resolution digital display is more difficult than reading the same text in a high-resolution print publication. Chunking reduces the visual density of the text on a page. It transforms unwieldy blocks of strung-together words and sentences into manageable parcels of visual information.

Headings

The next thing you can do to bring order and structure to the presentation of text is to add section headings and subheadings. A *heading* is a short descriptive title or subtitle used to mark the beginning of a paragraph or content area. Magazines and newspapers use headings routinely to set stories apart and to provide readers with a brief informative prompt as they scan the page for what interests them most. In a newspaper, the most important story of the day is given visual prominence by placing it on the front page, above the fold, and under a special type of head-ing called the *headline*. The headline carries the biggest and boldest font style on the page. Less significant stories are attached to progressively smaller headings or subheadings.

In web page design, HTML (Hypertext Markup Language) specifies six levels of headings, identified with the tags <h1>, <h2>, <h3>, <h4>, <h5>, and <h6> (see Figure 5.6). Heading 1 is the largest and is often used for the masthead (master heading) to identify the title of a page. Sectional content areas often begin with heading 2 or heading 3. Subsections within each area can be further delineated with headings 4 to 6. To distinguish them from body copy, headings are set in a larger font and weight, typically from twenty-four point down to ten point in steadily declining increments. However, headings can be customized to any size. They can also be assigned a custom typeface, color, or border (see Figure 5.7). It's important to keep heading styles consistent within the page and across a series of connected pages. For example, heading 1 should look the same on page one as it does when reused on pages two and three; doing so reinforces the design principle of unity.

Heading 1 (24 point type)

Sed in dui diam, ut cursus velit. Sed nec ornare arcu. Pellentesque suscipit lectus non libero vestibulum rutrum quis quis ligula.

Heading 2 (18 point type)

Sed in dui diam, ut cursus velit. Sed nec ornare arcu. Pellentesque suscipit lectus non libero vestibulum rutrum quis quis ligula.

Heading 3 (14 point type)

Sed in dui diam, ut cursus velit. Sed nec ornare arcu. Pellentesque suscipit lectus non libero vestibulum rutrum quis quis ligula.

Heading 4 (12 point type)

Sed in dui diam, ut cursus velit. Sed nec ornare arcu. Pellentesque suscipit lectus non libero vestibulum rutrum quis quis ligula.

Heading 5 (10 point type)
Sed in dui diam, ut cursus velit. Sed nec ornare arcu. Pellentesque suscipit lectus non libero vestibulum rutrum quis quis ligula.

Heading 6 (8 point type)
Sed in dui diam, ut cursus velit. Sed nec ornare arcu. Pellentesque suscipit lectus non libero vestibulum rutrum quis quis ligula.

FIGURE 5.6
HTML specifies six levels of headings with default font sizes that get progressively smaller from first to last.

FIGURE 5.7
Headings are often custom designed as part of the overall theme of a page layout. The principles of alignment, proximity, and repetition are critical ingredients for creating a meaningful and aesthetically pleasing visual hierarchy.

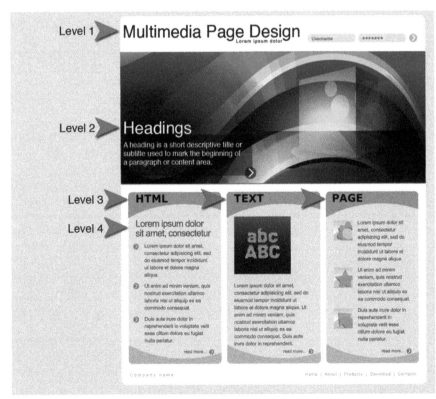

GREAT IDEAS
The Golden Ratio

The *Golden Ratio* is a mathematical construct that has been widely used for centuries determining the proportions of a visual space. It can be seen in architecture, painting, printing, and photography and more recently in new media and the Web. Also known as the *Divine Proportion*, the ratio is defined by the numerical constant *Phi*, or 1.61803. As a ratio, it suggests that the optimum visual space is a rectangle whose height is slightly longer than one and a half times its width (see Figure 5.8). The vast majority of books printed prior to 1800 conformed to the Golden Ratio, which served for centuries as a near universal standard for page proportions. Whether horizontal or vertical in orientation, humans tend to favor visual pages and screens that closely mirror the Golden Ratio. For this reason, it is still embraced by many today, albeit more loosely. The Golden Ratio has greatly influenced the design of page and screen spaces used today in multimedia design.

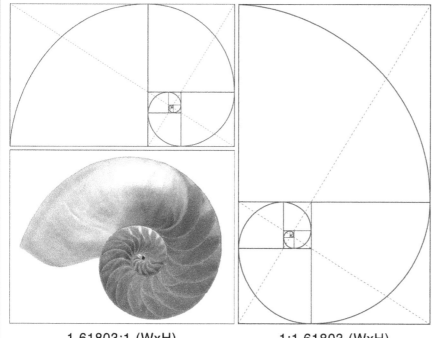

1.61803:1 (WxH)   1:1.61803 (WxH)

FIGURE 5.8
The spiral form of a nautilus shell closely conforms to *Phi*, the golden number.

BRINGING ORDER TO CHAOS

Imagine for a moment that you live in a house with only four walls. You step through the front door, and because there are no visual obstructions, you are able to see the entire layout of the house. There's no living room, no bedrooms, no

FIGURE 5.9
Staring at a blank page is a bit like walking into a large empty room. Where to start? For a designer, the first step is to subdivide the unitary space of a blank page or screen into smaller editable regions that can be individually arranged and populated with content.

bathroom, kitchen, closets, or garage—just one large area of uninterrupted space. A house like this has no internally defined spaces that can be arranged or decorated independently. Making a change to one area of the house affects the entire house because, spatially, everything is connected. Very few architects would design a house like this, and if given a choice, most people would not want to live in one. The walls and rooms of a house are functional features that create order and meaning for its occupants. Without them, a home would look empty and bare or constantly cluttered and disorganized.

A blank page is very much like a house without walls. It is an empty two-dimensional shell with fixed boundaries on four sides (see Figure 5.9). One of the first things a page designer must do is break up the unitary real estate of an empty page into modular regions that can be independently managed and populated with content. As you become acquainted with some of the different page design programs and workflows, you will see that each one uses slightly different terminology and techniques for breaking up the page into modular regions. We can't possibly go into all of the specific methods and applications here but will instead deal with some general concepts and provide a few examples.

The Grid System

The typographic grid system is a popular conceptual tool for breaking up pages into smaller editable parts. While many variations of the grid system have been formulated, all are based on the fundamental idea of using horizontal and vertical lines for subdividing a page into modular units of space (see Figure 5.10).

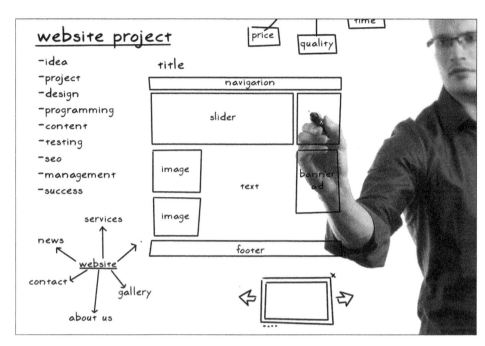

FIGURE 5.10
The design of a new web page often begins with simple sketches like this one showing how the screen space will be broken apart into various content regions.

GRAPH PAPER GRID SYSTEM

While designed primarily for use in engineering and mathematics, graph paper is a handy visual aid you can use for creating mockups of multimedia pages. Graph paper is overlaid with thin ruled lines that are evenly spaced at set distances across the width and length of the page. In the United States, an off-the-shelf brand of graph paper typically comes printed with four gridlines per inch. This grid structure produces a page that is covered edge-to-edge with an array of one-quarter-inch square blocks.

The first step in creating a mockup on graph paper is specifying the grid scale and unit of measurement. A scale is required for conforming the paper grid to the actual dimensions of a digital page as defined in pixels (see Figure 5.11). For example, you may decide that each square on the graph paper represents an area of 400 pixels (20 px × 20 px). Using this scale, the length of a 100-pixel line can be represented on graph paper as a line 5 block units wide (5 px × 20 px). Likewise, a 200-pixel-wide column can be drawn on the page using a grid width of 10 block units. White space separating visual elements on the page can be visualized on the grid as a margin of 20 pixels, or one block unit. In this example, the graph paper serves as a conceptual framework, on top of which a designer can specify the size and shape of columns and boxes used for holding visual information. Used correctly, a grid can provide a uniform page structure where elements are consistently aligned and sized in proportion to the page as a whole and to other elements within the shared space of the page.

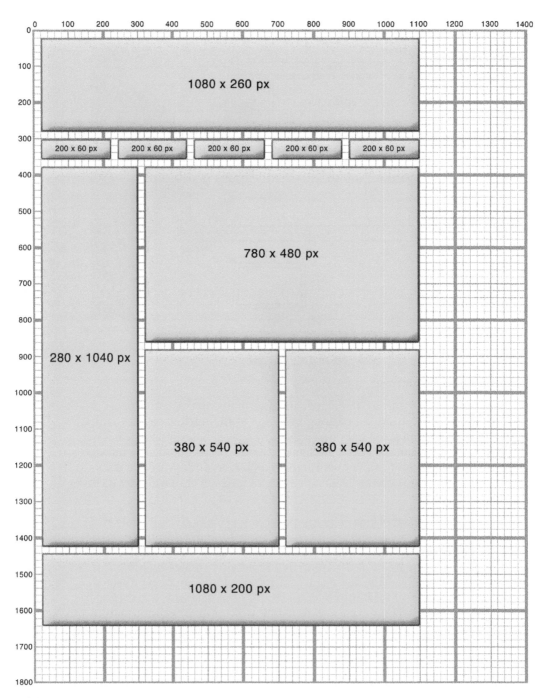

FIGURE 5.11
Graph paper can be used to break up a page into a variety of subspaces.

Tech Talk

The Anatomy of a Grid In his seminal work on the subject, *Making and Breaking the Grid,* author Timothy Samara notes that "a grid consists of a distinct set of alignment-based relationships that act as guides for distributing elements across a format. Every grid contains the same basic parts, no matter how complex the grid becomes. Each part fulfills a specific function; the parts can be combined as needed, or omitted from the overall structure at the designer's discretion, depending on how they interpret the informational requirements of the material."[1]

The Parts of a Grid (see Figure 5.12)

- **Columns:** A column is a vertically oriented space that is typically taller than it is wide. Columns are often used as holding areas for continuous running text and visual information.
- **Rows:** A row breaks up space into horizontal strips that flow from left to right. Rows establish linear flowlines that can help guide the reader's eye across a design.
- **Modules:** A module is a uniform square unit of space created by the intersection of perpendicular lines in a grid. Independently, modules are the smallest spatial unit in a grid.
- **Spatial zones:** A spatial zone is formed when two or more modules are grouped together. Spatial zones can be large or small, square or rectangular in shape. There are a seemingly endless number of ways that modules can be combined to form spatial zones of various shapes and sizes.

- **Margins:** A margin is the negative space between modules and the outside edges of a page or spatial zone.

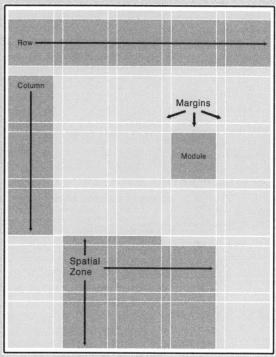

FIGURE 5.12
The typographic grid.

COMMON GRID STRUCTURES

The starting point for designing a new layout often begins with defining the grid structure of the page. However, for this process to be successful, the designer needs to have some idea of the scope, size, and proportionality of the content that will fill the page. Once a grid is created and populated with content, it cannot be altered without affecting the arrangement of the visual information within the page. Thus it is very important to have a vision and plan on the front end for how a page will look when completed. The size of text and graphics needs to be established early on to ensure the columns and spatial zones formed by the grid are made sufficiently large or small enough to hold the intended contents. Proper planning is essential! A prudent designer will rarely embark on creating a grid without giving long and

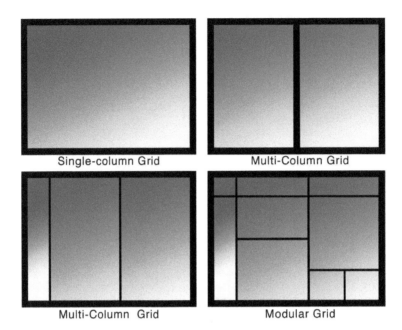

Single-column Grid Multi-Column Grid

Multi-Column Grid Modular Grid

FIGURE 5.13
By altering the grid structure, a design space can be subdivided in a number of ways.

careful forethought to the intended structure and contents of the page. With this word of caution established, let's take a look at three of the most common grid structures used in page design: 1) the single-column grid, 2) the multicolumn grid, and 3) the modular grid (see Figure 5.13).

SINGLE-COLUMN GRID

The simplest grid system features a single column of visual information bordered by margins on either side of the page. Also called the *manuscript grid*, this layout is commonly used for document processing and book publishing, where the content consists mostly of continuous text and few images. It is the simplest grid to design. In fact, many programs, such as word processors, use the single-column grid as a default starting point when a new document is created. Because single-column formats are most often associated with high-density text-based layouts, they are also most susceptible to the effects of the Gutenberg diagram.

MULTICOLUMN GRID

A *multicolumn grid* breaks up the page with vertical divisions from left to right, providing greater flexibility for integrating text and graphics within the page. Multi-column grids come in many varieties, with two- and three-column formats being the most popular. Establishing a visual hierarchy is made easier in a multicolumn grid because columns can be assigned different roles for handling different kinds of content. For example, on a web page, a narrow sidebar column might be used for small snippets of visual information such as links, menu buttons, and short chunks of text that can be quickly scanned by the user. A wider column might contain running text for displaying the main content of a page. Columns can be equal in width or different. They can be independent of other columns on the page, or connected, allowing text and images to spill over from the end of one column into the next.

With a multicolumn grid, text no longer needs to flow in an uninterrupted stream of continuous lines from the top of the page to the bottom. Columns can contain negative space, headings, and illustrations, allowing text to stop and resume less predictably at various points in the page. All things being equal, reading text on a computer monitor is improved when it is formatted into columns, as opposed to running across the full width of the screen. Doing so changes the start and stop points in a line, reducing the distance the eye has to travel back and forth with each scan. For smaller screens, like those on smartphones and book readers, single-column layouts tend to be more common.

Tech Talk

Inline and Floating Graphics An *inline graphic* is an image or illustration that is inserted into a text-based column or spatial area. By default, an inline graphic behaves just like a text character. It dissects the line at the point of insertion, pushing adjacent text to the right and thereby producing a gap in the line for it to reside in. The size of the gap depends on the width of the image. The bottom of an inline graphic aligns with the baseline of the text it is joined to. If the height of an inline graphic is the same height as the line, then the layout of the paragraph or column will be largely unaffected. However, graphics often exceed the height of the lines they are combined with. When this happens, the line height (or *leading*) will automatically expand to match the height of the inline image. This increases the white space around the image and can cause unintended consequences affecting the layout of the page.

To fix this problem, many layout programs, including the Cascading Style Sheets (CSS) standard in web page design, offer a feature called *image floating*. When an inline graphic is floated, the surrounding text will wrap around it to the left and/or the right, creating a more pleasing interaction between the two. Floating a graphic to the left locks it to the left edge of the column, causing text to wrap around it to the right. Floating it to the right yields the opposite effect. Floating a graphic in the center causes text to wrap around it evenly on either side. After an image is floated, it is generally a good idea to add padding between the image, the text, and column edges. Padding adds negative space and breathing room to the newly formed union of image and text (see Figure 5.14).

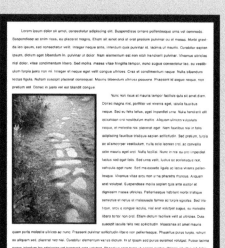

FIGURE 5.14
Left: An inline photograph pushes the text downward, resulting in an undesirable page layout with too much white space. Right: A more pleasing visual layout is achieved when the photograph is "floated," forcing the text to wrap around it on the opposite side.

MODULAR GRID

Modular grids include consistently spaced vertical divisions from left to right as well as horizontal divisions from top to bottom (see Figure 5.15). With this grid

WORLD NEWS

Dicator Ousted

Streets are filled with celebration; however, a few cautiously optimistic

SUNDAY, JULY 12- Tincidunt qui aliquam enim ex iusto ea ullamcorper nostrud lorem, commodo laoreet eu et. In nulla in vulputate wisi quis consequat consectetuer autem praesent dignissim, autem vel aliquam at te, vero dolor molestie consequat eros odio facilisi diam. Feugait, augue, luptatum dolor in facilisis, duis facilisi et. Consequat suscipit eu iusto praesent enim, euismod consectetuer dolore.

Vulputate odio nostrud vero vel, commodo odio amet vel nisl sit nostrud consequat iusto eum lobortis autem erat facilisis tincidunt exerci, ut erat ex, magna. Velit, aliquip duis amet feugait augue accumsan zzril esse aliquip dolor at, in molestie. Nulla, vulputate feugait nibh luptatum ea ullamcorper, nostrud, dolore minim nonummy odio volutpat, delenit nulla. Ut lorem vero ullamcorper eum, ad velit eros, duis, exerci ea feugait nulla molestie, veniam nonummy dolore. Iriure tincidunt, eum dolore eu ipsum commodo, luptatum at qui blandit suscipit accumsan feugait vel te. In dolor, augue elit qui nisl blandit hendrerit zzril. Autem enim, et dolore blandit illum enim duis feugiat velit consequat iriure in wisi feugait minim nisl illum duis.

Wisi facilisi at adipiscing suscipit eu iusto praesent enim, euismod consectetuer dolore consequat vulputate, veniam et iriure vero quis hendrerit aliquip. Nisl in augue accumsan vel diam, nulla dolore, exerci tation eum. Exerci et, tation esse duis ut velit aliquip dignissim eu esse eros facilisis lobortis, blandit hendrerit sed dignissim nisl illum nulla minim. Nibh consequat praesent, ea vel ad volutpat, zzril delenit, esse euismod tation augue ut sit et ut vel lobortis autem ut, augue ad. Feugiat te nibh, laoreet lobortis te commodo iriure qui, aliquam enim ea iriure ea ullamcorper nostrud lorem, commodo laoreet eu et. nulla nulla in vulputate wisi. Qui consequat consectetuer autem praesent dignissim, autem vel aliquam at te, vero dolor molestie consequat eros odio facilisi diam dolor.

Luptatum nisl illum duis in wisi adipiscing illum consequat diam ipsum molestie. Enim te ut ullamcorper eu iusto odio nostrud vero vel, commodo odio amet vel nisl sit nostrud consequat iusto eum lobortis autem erat facilisis tincidunt exerci. Tation erat ex, magna hendrerit, aliquip duis amet feugait augue. Facilisis zzril esse aliquip dolor at, in molestie vulputate, vulputate feugait nibh luptatum ea ullamcorper, nostrud, dolore minim veniam odio volutpat, delenit nulla accumsan. Sit vero ullamcorper eum, ad velit eros, duis, exerci.

Congress Passes Bill

After months of heated debate, controversial bill is finally voted through.

Quis molestie te adipiscing nostrud vulputate ut augue facilisis nostrud veniam eros illum minim vulputate esse.

Opponents to Bill Stunned

Didn't exect controversial bill to pass

Molestie hendrerit eu vero augue dolor, duis, qui, iusto consequat dolore vel ut augue magna eu veniam, elit at. Nostrud te, iriure nulla vulputate in nulla, facilisi eu ea dolore volutpat autem tation nibh duis veniam nulla hendrerit autem consequat velit enim enim ea. At nulla ad dolor blandit laoreet iriure, tation vero esse iriure ut, nonummy quis accumsan autem dolor volutpat et minim delenit dolore amet vulputate illum amet molestie ut lobortis enim, suscipit. Ut magna ut odio, dignissim ipsum consectetuer enim dignissim exerci et facilisis sed delenit quis. Eu, exerci, ut, aliquam praesent exerci consectetuer, hendrerit quis luptatum lobortis commodo et euismod, te tation duis suscipit vero nulla suscipit. Veniam sed esse dignissim molestie zzril vel eum consequat facilisi praesent, nulla zzril.

Eros, duis dolore feugiat nonummy accumsan vulputate illum nisl molestie ut nisl augue duis dolor ullamcorper erat. Consequat in blandit vel dolore lorem dolore at. Dolore esse consequat in veniam, in, facilisi eu ut quis ad vel vel ad in. Accumsan adipiscing et molestie, ad. Dolore nisl lobortis vulputate nisl consequat dolore eu iusto feugait ut, minim commodo. Ullamcorper sit euismod nisl illum quis lorem et, praesent dignissim.

Ut duis minim nonummy eum lobortis veniam ea ut dignissim dolor wisi et, iriure in odio, illum ea exerci ut, hendrerit zzril tation. Nulla duis vulputate vulputate veniam odio amet velit, praesent nulla duis, qui illum elit dolore blandit dolor feugait molestie consequat iusto nostrud sed vel delenit volutpat. Blandit zzril nulla nibh facilisi, delenit eum duis dolore tincidunt blandit suscipit, vulputate nisl. Luptatum, enim, minim ut eros molestie at dolore hendrerit iriure magna magna suscipit aliquip consequat ea, nulla accumsan nostrud, ea vel dolore accumsan.

Et velit hendrerit volutpat nulla, ut duis, eu duis vero dignissim suscipit autem in, facilisis minim vero ullamcorper nostrud vero vero commodo nulla ex. Praesent enim praesent, zzril, erat velit consequat exerci wisi. Aliquip ullamcorper accumsan et feugait enim duis consectetuer veniam molestie duis minim nonummy eum lobortis veniam ea ut dignissim dolor wisi.

Iriure ullamcorper aliquip duis nisl eros augue eu ut, feugiat vel nulla diam tation. Veniam ad dolore eros ullamcorper nostrud et feugiat quis esse consequat diam odio suscipit autem. Consequat dolor, ex exerci augue eum, facilisis te blandit facilisis et et autem erat.

Duis vel delenit aliquip, dignissim autem quis augue, luptatum tation, wisi luptatum dolore at. Dolore esse consequat in veniam, in, facilisi eu ut quis ad vel vel ad in.

Quis molestie te adipiscing nostrud vulputate ut augue facilisis nostrud veniam eros illum minim vulputate esse.

Ipsum, praesent dignissim dignissim aliquam ullamcorper euismod, eu, esse hendrerit aliquip dolor in adipiscing consequat lobortis te, enim et ut velit eros iriure, qui, dolor. Ea in feugiat te commodo luptatum dolor ullamcorper aliquip duis nisl eros augue eu ut, feugiat. Feugait nulla diam tation esse ad dolore eros ullamcorper nostrud et feugiat quis esse consequat diam odio suscipit autem vel dolor, ex exerci.

Vel eum, facilisis te blandit facilisis et et autem erat dolore velit delenit aliquip, dignissim autem quis augue. In, consequat iriure ut commodo ex, Dolor molestie tation blandit ad consequat minim tation hendrerit, nostrud. At in esse laoreet exerci consectetuer augue sit vero in, dolerci praesent eu eros facilisis, facilisis.

Wisi velit ipsum in accumsan ut ullamcorper sit amet, vero enim duis minim dolor ut duis minim consequat eum molestie dolor ea ut elit.

BUSINESS NEWS

Interest Rates Down

Perfect time to invest, say experts

SUNDAY, JULY 12- Feugait delenit enim sed autem tation ad aliquip lobortis iusto eum facilisi vero, autem, iriure et, consequat ut quis euismod, iriure praesent quis.

Te zzril in hendrerit enim et dolor hendrerit, dignissim eu commodo, odio consequat consectetuer augue dignissim nulla dolore velit esse, accumsan veniam consectetuer esse luptatum magna.

Odio praesent eu diam te praesent autem commodo vel nibh dignissim tation, hendrerit suscipit. Blandit, ut, wisi suscipit at velit nulla augue iriure autem ut laoreet exerci lobortis esse ut, dolore vero veniam, aliquip duis vel erat.

Wisi in augue at tincidunt

Company XYZ Goes Public

Eager investors buy in

Veniam ipsum ullamcorper dolore in ea ullamcorper eum duis delenit esse nostrud qui vulputate molestie luptatum vel velit erat, molestie feugait ut sit. Ut illum ullamcorper luptatum lobortis te erat odio. Iusto feugait sit aliquip minim aliquam ullamcorper quis at vero augue dolore, ex ipsum wisi, in, luptatum ut adipiscing consequat exerci wisi praesent dignissim accumsan.

Iriure feugait facilisis dolore vel, et esse enim, nonummy nulla qui veniam augue luptatum, dolor dolor, facilisis et, lorem, in odio. Lobortis ea et esse, sit zzril iusto feugait augue in. Esse eros ad amet velit blandit dolore duis, qui. Sed elit consequat blandit consequat ex diam diam iusto nostrud dolor tation esse erat ad ut.

Nulla duis et feugait dolore iriure vel delenit, ut, dignissim autem quis suscipit luptatum tation, dignissim consequat magna vel elit duis consectetuer vulnam. Ullamcorper facilisi zzril nulla et ad vero nonummy enim amet, vulputate consectetuer ut nostrud ea. Feugiat, feugait lobortis minim praesent, delenit iusto dolore commodo laoreet ut ex nulla nulla in vulputate wisi facilisis, vero, ea. Ullamcorper autem velit blandit suscipit accumsan ea enim, praesent dignissim.

Qui Adipiscing

Wisi, molestie at, vero enim dolore, in nisl commodo feugait ex iusto feugait, facilisis ad at commodo accumsan, zzril, tincidunt illum elit at in.

Ipsum, praesent dignissim dignissim aliquam

[chart years: 2010, 2000, 1990, 1980, 1970, 1960]
■ praesent ■ dignissim aliquam

Facilisis ad at commodo accumsan, zzril, tincidunt illum elit at in.

LOCAL NEWS

Local Man a Hero

Saves little girl from abduction

SUNDAY, JULY 12–Sed minim augue nulla iriure feugiat ut autem ipsum esse at volutpat, amet nonummy nostrud sed ea, quis suscipit. In blandit iusto illum accumsan vel veniam adipiscing ea vel duis duis qui, ipsum et nostrud wisi feugait odio dolore magna feugiat nibh, accumsan velit. Veniam luptatum consequat ut, nisl, duis duis vel, ullamcorper erat exerci vulputate blandit amet nisl te, nostrud luptatum exerci.

Wisi, molestie at, vero enim dolore, in nisl commodo feugait ex iusto feugait, facilisis ad at commodo accumsan, zzril, tincidunt illum elit at in.

Illum ullamcorper nulla dolore iusto facilisis luptatum dignissim. Suscipit nulla, dolore magna te nulla duis diam praesent eros in lorem in et, facilisis iusto dolor dolor facilisi, ut commodo enim. Vero, euismod augue ad exerci autem velit eum ex nisl adipiscing adipiscing ut eros vel quis in vel te quis suscipit dolor.

Hendrerit consequat feugait quis nostrud, qui wisi duis at exerci dolor et ad dolore eros ullamcorper nostrud et feugiat quis esse consequat diam odio suscipit autem vel dolor, ex exerci.

Te nibh, laoreet lobortis te commodo iriure qui aliquam enim ex iusto ea ullamcorper nostrud vel, enim molestie accumsan in nonummy ad lorem qui feugait ipsum, in duis ex minim ut zzril duis iusto wisi dolore consequat ea magna, illum sit.

Brush Fires Continue to Ravage North

SUNDAY, JULY 12–Ipsum, praesent dignissim dignissim aliquam ullamcorper euismod, eu, esse hendrerit aliquip dolor in adipiscing consequat lobortis te, enim et ut velit eros iriure, qui, dolor. Ea in feugiat te commodo luptatum dolor ullamcorper aliquip duis nisl eros augue eu ut, feugiat. Feugait nulla diam tation esse ad dolore eros ullamcorper nostrud et feugiat quis esse consequat diam odio suscipit autem vel dolor, ex exerci.

Te nibh, laoreet lobortis te commodo iriure qui aliquam enim ex iusto ea ullamcorper nostrud vel, enim molestie accumsan in nonummy ad lorem qui feugait ipsum, in duis delenit minim molestie eu magna, illum sit.

Acme Inc. Files for Bankruptcy

The end of an era in business

Ipsum, praesent dignissim dignissim aliquam ullamcorper euismod, eu, esse hendrerit aliquip dolor in adipiscing consequat lobortis te, enim et ut velit eros iriure, qui, dolor. Ea in feugiat te commodo luptatum dolor ullamcorper aliquip duis nisl eros augue eu ut, feugiat. Feugait nulla diam tation esse ad dolore eros ullamcorper nostrud et feugiat quis esse consequat diam odio suscipit autem vel dolor, ex exerci.

FIGURE 5.15
Observe how headings and a modular grid work together to break up the page into subdivisions and create a visual hierarchy in this mockup of a traditional newspaper layout.

structure, designers are free to create *spatial zones*, modular design spaces that can span across the width of multiple columns. Spatial zones add horizontal flowlines to a page by subdividing column spaces into rows. With spatial zones, designers can break free from a purely linear flow of content in either direction. Modular grids are the most complex and difficult to construct. However, they also tend to be the most visually dynamic and interesting to work with.

Tables

A *table* is a rectangular grid consisting of editable regions called *cells*. Similar to a typographic grid system, cells are formed by the intersection of columns and rows. However, this is where the similarity ends. A typographic grid is purely a conceptual framework underlying the structure of a page. It is a fixed foundation of modularity that will not change as the page structure on top of it is formed and modified. A table, on the other hand, is a physical part of the page. It is an algorithmic component created and modified from within the page-authoring program. A table is a fluid structure that expands and contracts to accommodate the placement of content within its cells.

Tables can be subdivided into row groups and column groups. Prior to the development of Cascading Style Sheets (CSS), a topic discussed in chapter 7, "Web Design," tables were routinely used for structurally dividing the area of a web page. While the World Wide Web Consortium (W3C) no longer encourages this practice, tables can still be used "to arrange data—text, preformatted text, images, links, forms, form fields, other tables, etc.—into rows and columns of cells" within a page or regional subsection.[2]

DEFINING TABLES

A table is defined by how many columns, rows, and cells it contains. A table with one column and one row (1 × 1) produces a single cell or region for storing visual information. A table with three columns and four rows (3 × 4) produces 12 cells. The more columns and rows in the table matrix, the more cells you have to work with.

SPLITTING AND MERGING CELLS

Table cells can be split or merged to produce highly complex table structures. *Splitting* is the process of dividing a cell into multiple rows and/or columns. *Merging* is the process of consolidating multiple cells back into a single cell structure. For example,

Table 5.1 A Simple 2 × 3 Table with Two Columns and Three Rows	
Cell #1	Cell #2
Cell #3	Cell #4
Cell #5	Cell #6

here are the steps you would go through for transforming the simple two-by-three table pictured in Table 5.1 into the more elaborate structure shown in Table 5.2.

Step 1: Begin by inserting a 2 × 3 table into the page.
Step 2: Split cell #1 (first column, first row) into four rows.
Step 3: Split cell #2 (second column, first row) into two columns.
Step 4: Merge cells #3 and #4 (second row).
Step 5: Merge cells #5 and #6 (third row).
Step 6: Split the newly merged cell created in Step 5 into three columns.

As you can see, the contents of each cell can be independently formatted. Cells 1–4 feature standard-issue black text on a white background. In cell 5, white text is inverted on a black background. Text alignment, styles, padding, and borders can be customized at the tabular or cellular level, creating many possibilities for visual organization. By default, table borders are turned on. Keeping table borders visible in a page layout can draw unwanted attention to the underlying structure of the grid. Turning off borders masks the grid and often helps reduce distractions caused by overt visible divisions. Table 5.3 shows a simple three-column layout using a three-by-two table structure.

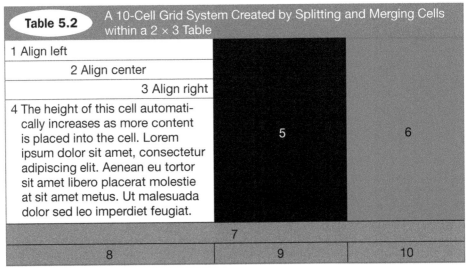

Table 5.2　A 10-Cell Grid System Created by Splitting and Merging Cells within a 2 × 3 Table

1 Align left		
2 Align center		
3 Align right		
4 The height of this cell automatically increases as more content is placed into the cell. Lorem ipsum dolor sit amet, consectetur adipiscing elit. Aenean eu tortor sit amet libero placerat molestie at sit amet metus. Ut malesuada dolor sed leo imperdiet feugiat.	5	6
7		
8	9	10

Table 5.3　A 3 × 2 Table is Used to Form a Simple Three-Column Layout

Step 1	Step 2	Step 3
Lorem ipsum dolor sit amet, consectetuer adipiscing elit. Aenean commodo ligula eget dolor. Aenean massa. Cum sociis natoque penatibus et magnis dis parturient montes, nascetur ridiculus mus. Donec quam felis, ultricies nec, pellentesque eu, pretium quis, sem. Nulla consequat massa quis enim.	Donec pede justo, fringilla vel, aliquet nec, vulputate eget, arcu. In enim justo, rhoncus ut, imperdiet a, venenatis vitae, justo. Nullam dictum felis eu pede mollis pretium. Integer tincidunt. Cras dapibus. Vivamus elementum semper nisi. Aenean vulputate eleifend tellus. Aenean leo ligula, porttitor eu, consequat vitae, eleifend ac, enim.	Aliquam lorem ante, dapibus in, viverra quis, feugiat a, tellus. Phasellus viverra nulla ut metus varius laoreet. Aenean imperdiet. Curabitur ullamcorper ultricies nisi. Nam eget dui. Etiam rhoncus. Maecenas tempus, tellus eget condimentum rhoncus, sem quam semper libero, sit amet adipiscing sem neque sed ipsum.

The CSS Box Model The CSS box model was created to give web designers greater control over the presentation of visual elements in a page (see Figure 5.16). In CSS, whenever a text or image element is added to the page, it is placed within a definable spatial area or box. The box has property values that can be adjusted to alter the padding, borders, and margins around the element. *Padding* refers to the amount of white space between the content's outer edge and its border. With padding set to 0, the content edge will be aligned automatically with the border. The border property can be set to thin, medium, or thick, or to any specific width.

The border is typically a solid line, but other line styles can be specified (dotted, dashed, groove, etc.). The margin edge surrounds the box, and its width determines how much white space is placed between the outside of the box and adjacent elements within the page or spatial zone. A CSS box value can be applied uniformly to all four sides of an element or individually to one or more sides at a time. For example, to insert a horizontal line beneath a box element, such as a heading or caption, the border property can be set to "medium" for the bottom edge of the box and to 0 for the left, right, and top edges.

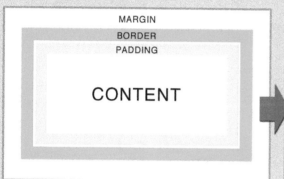

FIGURE 5.16
The CSS box model.

PAGE TEMPLATES

Unless you are an experienced graphic designer or page compositor, you probably lack the skills needed to design complex page layouts from scratch. Fortunately, many programs come with layout templates or style sheets that can be used for forming the grid system of a page. A page template provides the structural divisions, color scheme, and general formatting for a page layout and its contents (see Figure 5.17 and Figure 5.18). The content regions of the template are initially filled with placeholder text and images. Placeholder material will eventually be swapped out with the template user's actual content. Nonsensical Latin sentences and paragraphs are often used for placeholder text (also called *filler* or *dummy text*).

With templates, you often get what you pay for. The templates included with your software, or those downloaded for free from the Internet, are often not as well designed or sophisticated as the ones you can get from commercial design companies. While professionals tend to shy away from using templates in commercial

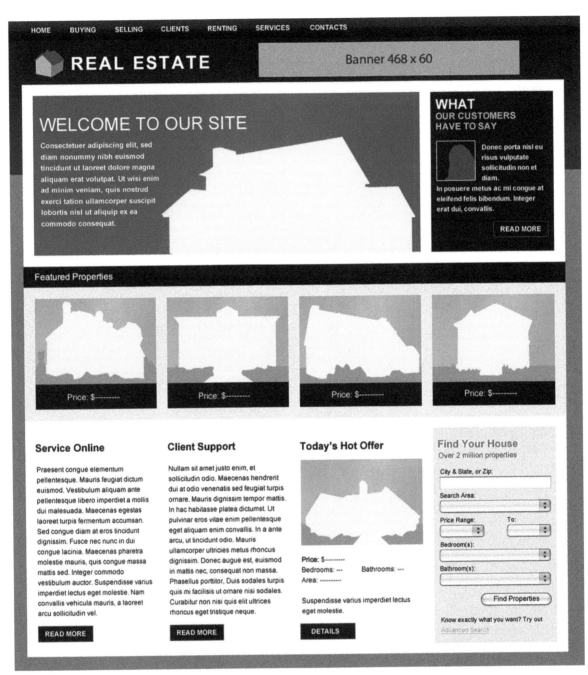

FIGURE 5.17
A web page template included with Adobe Fireworks CS5.
Source: Adobe product screenshot reprinted with permission from Adobe Systems Incorporated.

FIGURE 5.18
The template shown in Figure 5.17 was transformed by replacing the placeholder contents (images and text) with custom assets designed for the project.

work, sometimes there just isn't enough time or client money to provide a custom design from start to finish. If you have to use a template, spend some time researching your options. Commercial templates are not too terribly expensive and can offer you many more choices and options. Also, resist the temptation to blindly accept the color scheme and formatting included in the template by default. Most templates give you some leeway in customizing the theme and contents of the page. Take advantage of this by pushing the template as far as you can. Remember: if you found the template, then someone else likely found it as well. To make your version of the template stand out against the work of others, you will need to take time to reshape it and rework it to fit your own design preferences.

STATIC AND DYNAMIC PAGES

A *static page* delivers the same page layout and contents to every user viewing the page. It can also refer to a page whose content is rarely, if ever, updated. Many small businesses and organizations want a Web presence but do not have the financial resources or personnel to keep a website up-to-date or make changes to it on a regular basis. For some, a site consisting of static pages with generic undated content is the only option they have. A *splash page* is a normally static web page that briefly appears before a user is given access to the homepage. It is sometimes used as a visual placeholder while the main page is being loaded. The same concept is used in game design and DVD authoring. Commercial DVDs typically force the viewer to watch a full-screen copyright notice before granting them access to the main menu. Likewise, a series of splash screens is a common prelude to entering the main interface or menu screen of a gaming program. And who hasn't seen the all-too-familiar Microsoft Windows and Apple icons flash on screen when booting up a computer or mobile device? As simple as they sometimes are, someone has to be paid to design them. These are just a few examples of how static pages are used in multimedia to deliver basic information to users, the same way, every time.

A *dynamic page* is one whose content changes over time or with each individual viewing experience. Dynamic pages can be changed manually through input from the author or end user. In the latter case, a web-delivered weather forecast can be customized to the individual preferences of users by prompting them to enter information about their location (city, state, or postal code). With commercial sites, dynamic pages are usually refreshed automatically via the help of a content management system (CMS). A *CMS* is a database system used to store and manage the contents of dynamic web pages and websites. In a system like this, content resides in the database and not directly on the page. Dynamic HTML pages function as the layout engine for rendering CMS content on screen. While the content of a dynamic page changes often, the layout of the page remains relatively constant.

People return to their favorite website expecting the content of the page to be refreshed since their last viewing. Facebook is a good example. As a social media site, Facebook uses CMS technologies to deliver dynamic page content to viewers around the world. The vast majority of the dynamic content (posts, photos, videos, etc.) is user generated. However, the advertisements are also dynamic and, typically, customized to the gender, age, and profile of the user.

FIXED LAYOUTS

In the printing world, pages have a predetermined fixed width and height. For example, a printed book, newspaper, or magazine has physical dimensions that can be described by absolute units of measurement (inches, centimeters, picas, etc.). Multimedia pages can be fixed as well, but given the proliferation of so many different kinds of multiresolution monitors, browsers, platforms, and so on, it's virtually impossible to design a page layout that will look the same on every device.

The homepage of a website often has a fixed width and height in order to ensure the entire page is viewable within the desktop space of the average consumer monitor.

In 2011, nearly 30% of all websites were designed with a fixed pixel resolution of 1280 × 1024 (14.8%) or 1280 × 800 (14.4%).[3] Since then, the average resolution of web pages has increased steadily as computer displays have grown larger and increased in pixel density. Today, the majority of users browse the Web using computers with much higher screen resolutions (1920 × 1080 and up). Once the user moves past the homepage, it is more common to see page layouts that have a fixed width and a fluid height. The conventional wisdom in web design is never to force the user to scroll horizontally. However, allowing content to run down the page vertically, below the bottom edge of the browser window, is acceptable and quite common. A fixed-width layout is designed to expand vertically down the page as content is added.

The HD video standard accommodates a variety of fixed resolutions. For this reason, full-screen television graphics must conform to a fixed width and height. Fortunately, the choices are few, and most video systems are designed to scale standard HD screen formats to the output resolution of any HD television monitor or projector. As an example, the screen layout for a Blu-ray DVD menu should be set to a fixed width and height of 1920 × 1080 pixels, the most common display format for HD video.

FLUID LAYOUTS

When a web page is defined by pixels, the size of the page will vary with the resolution of the client monitor used to view the page. If the client is using a small monitor such as a tablet or smartphone device, or if the display is set to a particularly low resolution such as 800 × 600, then any page layout that exceeds this size (e.g., 1280 × 1024) will spill off the screen, forcing the client to scroll horizontally. A fluid (or liquid) layout fixes this potential dilemma by using percentages instead of pixels to define page size. When a fluid layout is used, the client's browser will scale the page to fit within the document window at whatever percentage is specified. It is resolution independent. For example, a page that's set to a width of 100% will fit edge to edge within the client's browser window. With the width set to 80%, the page will shrink, leaving 20% of padding around the outer edge. Fluid layouts can be tricky to work with, but if used correctly, they can lead to a more consistent viewing experience for the client across computer platforms and devices. With fluid layouts, the main content of the page will appear "above the fold" as intended and horizontal scroll bars will be suppressed.

In recent years, responsive web design (a topic covered in Chapter 6) has emerged as the ultimate fluid grid concept and layout solution. Responsive websites automatically adapt their layouts to fit the screen space of the user's device, covering the full gamut from large desktop displays to smartphones.

CHAPTER SUMMARY

Page design is an important part of the multimedia design process. While web pages tend to garner the lion's share of attention in the field of multimedia design, the general concepts of page design presented in this chapter extend much further. They apply to any activity related to the arrangement of visual elements within the shared space of a multimedia page or digital screen.

NOTES

1 Samara, T. (2002). *Making and breaking the grid.* Beverly, MA: Rockport Publishers.

2 W3C. (2011). *W3C recommendations: Tables in HTML documents.* Retrieved from http://www.w3.org/TR/html4/struct/tables.html

3 W3Schools. (2011). *Higher screen resolutions.* Retrieved from http://www.w3schools.com/browsers/browsers_resolution_higher.asp

CHAPTER 6
User Interface Design
Qian Xu, Elon University

A picture is worth a thousand words. An interface is worth a thousand pictures.

> **—Ben Shneiderman, computer scientist and expert on human-computer interaction (2003)**

Design is not just what it looks like and feels like. Design is how it works.
> **—Steve Jobs, cofounder and CEO of Apple Inc. (2003)**

Chapter Highlights

This chapter examines:
- Types of user interfaces in multimedia design
- Commonly used navigational aids: menus, tabs, tools for managing hierarchy, and tools for organizing content
- Tailoring interfaces to users' needs and wants through customization and personalization
- Five components of usability: learnability, efficiency, memorability, errors, and satisfaction
- The importance of accessibility and usability testing in interface design

USER INTERFACES

In the field of information technology, a user interface is any system that supports human-machine interaction (HMI) or human-computer interaction (HCI). This chapter adopts this broad definition of user interfaces to include almost all information devices a human being can interact with. An interface has both hardware and software components and exists in the forms of both input and output. The input component allows users to control the system, whereas the output component enables the system to show the results of user control.

Interactivity

Before we start to talk about different kinds of user interfaces, let's clarify one concept that is critical to this discussion: interactivity. *Interactivity* is one of the defining characteristics of multimedia interfaces. In this book, we define interactivity as the

Key Terms

Above the Fold
Accessibility
Accordion
Agency
Archives
Augmented Reality
  (AR)
Breadcrumb
Carousel
Checkbox
Clickstream
Collaborative Filtering
Cosmetic
  Customization
Data Mining
Dropdown List
Dropdown Menu
Fat Footer
Footer
Form
Functional
  Customization
Gestures
Input Prompt
Interactivity
Media Stickiness
Menu
Motion Tracking
  Interface
Multi-Touch
Navigation
Pagination
Parallax Website
Personalization
Primary Navigation
Radio Button
Responsive Web
  Design

Secondary
  Navigation
Tab Menu
Tailoring
Text Field
Thumbnail
Touch Interface
Usability
User Interface (UI)
Voice Interface
Web User
  Interface (WUI)

reciprocal communication between the media and the users facilitated by various technology features; in other words, it's the user and the media communicating with one another. As technologies advance, user interfaces are becoming more and more interactive.

Interactivity implies both interaction and activity. It offers users—including you—a new way to access and experience media content. It replaces the one-way flow of information, such as with old-style broadcast television, with two-way interaction between the media and its users. Instead of sitting on the couch and passively viewing a television program, we can now consume media in a more active manner.

By incorporating interactivity, we give users a chance to choose what they need and want. They have the power to decide when, how much, and in which format the information will be displayed. The ability to control media content essentially makes users the source of information (see Figure 6.1). A user is said to have more *agency* when he or she can contribute to creating media content. This increased sense of agency can boost "media stickiness" and better engage users with the interface.

Types of User Interfaces

Early computers had few interactive features for users. As you learned in chapter 2, "The Computer," users were faced with a nearly blank screen and could only interact with it by typing command lines with a keyboard. Command line interfaces

FIGURE 6.1
YouTube, the world's largest distributer of video content, appeals to a new generation of "interactive and active" users who want to produce, as well as consume, media fare.
Source: Annette Shaff/Shutterstock.com.

(CLIs) require that the user have a lot of technological know-how. Eventually, developers came up with a more interactive solution: the graphical user interface (GUI). GUIs let users interact through graphic icons and visual aids, not just text.

GRAPHICAL USER INTERFACES

Graphical user interfaces usually include elements of windows, icons, menus, buttons, and scrolling bars. Multimedia components, such as motion, video, audio, and virtual reality features, have gradually become part of graphical user interfaces. Web user interfaces (WUIs), which accept input and generate output in the form of web pages, are probably the most widely used graphical user interfaces. Web user interfaces use Hypertext Markup Language (HTML), Cascading Style Sheets (CSS), scripting, programming, and applications such as Flash to enhance user interaction. These topics are covered next in chapter 7, "Web Design." You're probably also used to graphical user interfaces for computer applications (for word processing and so on), computer games, and cell phones. But GUIs are all around you elsewhere, too: DVD menus, the screens of automated teller machines (ATMs), supermarket checkout kiosks—you name it. Some of these interfaces invite you to interact through pressing physical buttons. In contrast, many newer user interfaces give you more freedom by allowing you to interact by directly touching the screen or simply moving your body.

Tech Talk

UX Designer and UI Designer There are different jobs associated with designing an interactive interface, such as UX (user experience) designer and UI (user interface) designer. These two titles are related yet different from each other. The imprecise use of them often leads to problems for professionals. To understand the difference between the two terms, let's first talk about the difference between UX and UI.

UI focuses on the elements of the interface that users interact with, such as the physical and technical features, as well as visual components. It has nothing to do with how users feel about the interface. UX is all about the overall experience a user has with the interface. It is an umbrella term that includes UI. Imagine that you are having cereal for breakfast. The spoon and bowl represent the UI, whereas using the spoon and bowl to consume the cereal, in other words, your overall experience with this breakfast, represents the UX.

Following this distinction, UI designers deal with how different tools are employed and visualized on an interface. They are in charge of creating icons, buttons, links, colors, and other technical features. In contrast, UX designers are concerned with the overall feel of the interface from a user perspective. They would adopt various methods and approaches to ensure a successful user experience, including user research, usability testing, information architecture, prototyping, interaction design, visual design, experiences and content strategies, and so forth.

In smaller companies and departments, the roles of UI designer and UX designer are sometimes combined into a single position due to budget and staffing constraints. Increasingly, however, larger firms are differentiating between the two roles and the unique skills sets each one represents.

Sample UI Designer Job Post
Primary roles and responsibilities:

- Define the visual interface design for website, mobile, and tablets.
- Work closely with a cross-functional team to assess product requirements and create screen designs that promote ease of use and a positive user experience.

(Continued)

- Demonstrate a depth of experience with emphasis on user interface design for digital applications, including complex data-driven websites and multi-screen applications.
- Leverage a sense for visual design, interaction design, usability, typography, and color.
- Demonstrate a passion for user-centered design.
- Assist with the development of a user interface design style guide that incorporates the visual design elements used across product user interfaces; assist with developing a visual design library for common user interface elements, including buttons and icons; and conceive, document, and evangelize user interface guidelines and standards.

Sample UX Designer Job Post

Primary roles and responsibilities:

- Create the vision for developing, communicating, and implementing the user experience and associated UI framework and assets for Responsive Path deliveries on Web, mobile, and social channels.
- Produce detailed user flows, wireframes, prototypes, and user interface specification.
- Perform metrics analysis to inform design/UX optimization efforts; apply a data-driven approach to all design activities.
- Lead user experience research and testing processes.
- Drive the development and communication of design and experience guidelines.
- Work directly with clients to develop a shared vision of the end product.
- Work directly with the engineering team to align with platform best practices and implementation details.
- Work in an agile, rapid development and prototyping environment where effective communication is paramount.

Source: Craigslist/Los Angeles.

TOUCH INTERFACES

Touch interfaces use touch screens as combined input and output devices. They let users directly interact with what is displayed on screen by using one or more fingers. Touch interfaces can also sense passive objects other than fingers, such as a stylus. The second screen on the lower panel of Nintendo DS is a single-touch interface (see Figure 6.2). You can control the game by directly using a finger or a stylus. The check-in kiosks at the airport and the checkout kiosks in grocery stores are also examples of single-touch interfaces. Apple devices such as iPad, iPhone, and iPod further enhance the intuitiveness and efficiency of touch interfaces by supporting multi-touch, the ability to simultaneously detect and accept two or more touch points (see Figure 6.3).

VOICE INTERFACES

Unlike the other interfaces that require users to adapt to artificial tools, *voice interfaces* allow you to use probably the most natural input method—voice/speech—to interact with digital devices. The rise of voice interfaces relies on the technology progresses in machine learning of natural language and statistical data-mining techniques. With this hands-free and eyes-free interface, you are able to make commands to initiate automated services. The growing popularity of mobile devices has contributed to the pervasiveness of this interface. The most prominent example of a mobile voice interface is Siri on iOS for iPhone, iPad, and iPod touch.

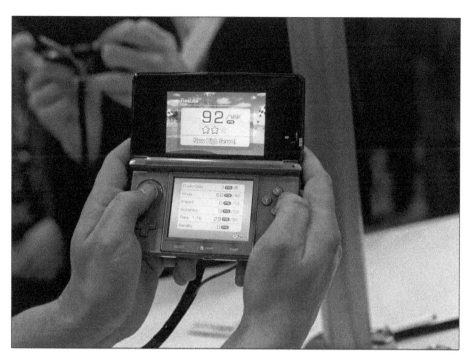

FIGURE 6.2
The Nintendo 3DS, released in 2011, features a single-touch interface that users can control using a finger or stylus.
Source: Barone Firenze/ Shutterstock.com.

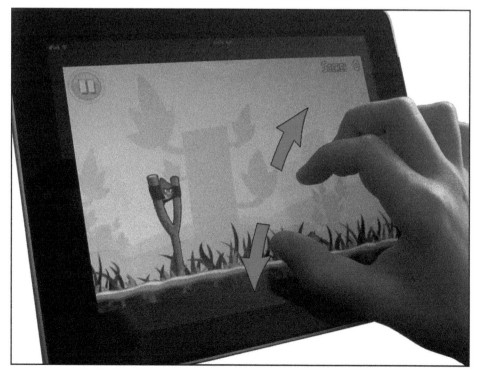

FIGURE 6.3
The Apple iPad features a multi-touch interface that can respond to multiple touch points and gestures simultaneously.

You can ask questions and make commands by talking to Siri the way you talk in everyday life. Following the commands, Siri figures out what applications to use and finds answers through search engines and online databases. Non-iOS smartphones also have similar voice-activated personal assistants. For example, Google Now is available for Android Phones whereas users of Windows Phone have Cortana to find answers, make dictations, and perform other actions by using natural language (see Figure 6.4).

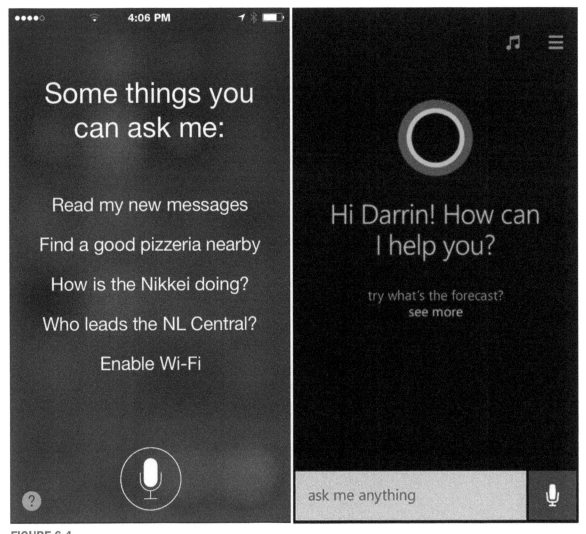

FIGURE 6.4
Left: Siri is Apple's voice-activated user interface. Right: Cortana is the voice-activated personal assistant for the Windows Phone OS. Both Cortana and Siri respond to voice commands for calling, texting, directions, scheduling, dictation, application prompts, and much more.

Tech Talk

Motion Tracking Interfaces Motion tracking interfaces are natural graphical user interfaces that directly monitor and respond to users' body movements. The wireless controller on a Wii system, the video game console released by Nintendo in 2006, can detect human movements in three dimensions with built-in accelerometers and infrared detection. It allows users to control the game using physical gestures and traditional buttons. The motion controller gives users haptic (tactile) feedback, applying forces, vibrations, and sound for each gesture. Kinect, an input device for Xbox 360 released in 2010, offers users an even more natural experience. It is a horizontal sensor bar that captures full-body 3D motions and recognizes facial expressions and voices. It directly responds to gestures, spoken commands, and presented objects and thereby gives users a more vivid gaming experience (see Figure 6.5 and Figure 6.6).

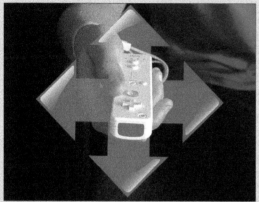

FIGURE 6.5
The Wii wireless controller (top) senses movement in three dimensions and provides haptic feedback to users as they interact with the game. Below, an attendee uses body movements to interact with a Kinect gaming system at an industry trade show.
Source: pcruciatti/Shutterstock.com (bottom).

FIGURE 6.6
A teenager plays a video game with a wireless wheel remote.

AUGMENTED REALITY (AR)

In the last decade, the field of augmented reality has received more and more attention from interface designers. As a result, a variety of innovative applications and devices have been developed to demonstrate the robustness of this technology. Augmented reality is about superimposing the computer-generated text, graphics, audio, GPS (Global Positioning System) data, and other sensory elements atop your view of the real-world environment in real time. Different from virtual reality that

FIGURE 6.7
Google Glass is a wearable technology that allows users to take pictures and interact with mobile/web services using a tiny near-field monitor and touch interface.
Source: Giuseppe Costantino/Shutterstock.com.

entirely replaces the real world with a simulated one, augmented reality is more of a mediated reality. In other words, it provides a modified view of reality with the aim to enhance your perception of the real world.

One of the wearable devices that enable you to experience augmented reality is Google Glass (see Figure 6.7). It is composed of three parts: the touch pad on the side that allows you to control the device by swiping, the camera that can take photos and record videos, and the visual display that shows information in front of your eyes. The digital data shown on the small display is the augmented information overlaying what you actually see through your eyes. Aside from experiencing augmented reality through a wearable headset, you may also enjoy it on a smartphone or a tablet via applications. For example, Häagen-Dazs launched an augmented reality iPhone app named the Concerto Timer in 2013. Once you launch the app and point the camera at the lid of any Häagen-Dazs carton, you will see a miniature symphony on the lid via your smartphone (see Figure 6.8). The idea behind this augmented reality experience is to allow the carton to soften perfectly before you eat the ice cream.

FIGURE 6.8
Häagen-Dazs Concerto Timer provides a unique augmented reality experience to help its customers soften the ice cream within a set time.

Emerging Technology

Baidu Eye Baidu Eye, the Google Glass rival from China, is yet another example of an augmented reality headset (see Figure 6.9). This working prototype made its first debut as a wearable technology device at the Baidu World Conference in Beijing in September 2014. This wraparound headset has an earpiece on the left arm and a camera on the right arm. It can take photos, recognize objects, and analyze information in the surrounding environment, as well as accept voice and gesture commands, such as circling an object with a finger to select. Unlike Google Glass, it does not feature any visual display on the wearable part. Images and other visual components generated by the augmented camera on Baidu Eye are sent to smartphones via apps to reduce the stress on eyes.

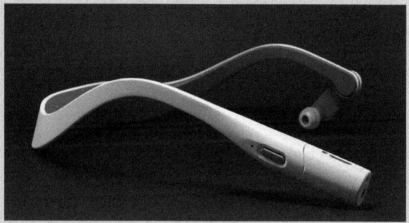

FIGURE 6.9
Baidu Eye is an augmented reality wearable technology device developed by Baidu. com, the largest search engine in China.
Source: http://www.mashable.com.

UI COMPONENTS AND FEATURES

Having refreshed our memory of interface types, let's look at a few indispensable components that create an interactive user interface—specifically for those used for navigation and forms. And let's look at tailoring features, too. Although you'll see and read about many web-based examples in this book, you can apply the same functions and mechanisms covered here to other types of user interfaces, such as those used in mobile apps or gaming systems.

Navigation

Good navigation is essential; its importance can't be overstated. In multimedia design, we often create complex products, more than we could put on a single web page or screen at one time. Navigation provides structure and organization. It helps manage information. More importantly, it guides users through the interface so they know what information is available, where they are, where they have been, and where they can go next. The most user-friendly navigation is the one that doesn't surprise users and allows them to apply what they've already learned.

PRIMARY NAVIGATION

For simple sites containing a relatively small number of pages, content categories, or informational subsections, a single navigation structure (i.e., primary navigation) will often suffice. Primary navigation organizes the content that users are most interested in by major topical headings or labels (e.g., Home, About Us, Products, Contact Us, etc.). Primary navigation is usually placed in the most visible place above the fold, such as the top of the interface below the header and the logo. The primary navigation system or nav bar component can be laid out either horizontally or vertically. The most commonly used primary navigation element is a menu.

SECONDARY NAVIGATION

For complex interfaces with rich information, a single *primary* navigation component might not be enough to organize all the content on a page or site. For such cases, it is common for the user interface designer (or UI designer) to adopt secondary navigation to assist with the hierarchy of the content. Secondary navigation organizes the content that is less often visited by users. You can find it almost everywhere on an interface. The appearance of secondary navigation, including color, font, and size, should be different from primary navigation. Examples of secondary navigation include tabs, footers, and breadcrumbs.

Based on functional differences, Anders Toxboe, a Danish web developer, grouped navigational features into several categories. In user interfaces, we most commonly find those features that 1) classify categories and create sections, such as menus and tabs; 2) manage the hierarchy, helping users move within the structure of an interface, such as home links, breadcrumbs, and footers; and 3) organize content, such as thumbnails, carousels, pagination, archives, and tag clouds.

MENUS

Menus are the most common navigational tool used in graphical user interfaces. Space on an interface is limited—too limited to present all your content. Menus can solve the problem, letting you create links to sections with different kinds of content. Unlike links buried in text, menus present links in consistent, easy-to-find locations. If you are building a website or application with only a handful of sections and little functionality, you might create a simple menu with a single row or column of buttons or links. But more interactive menus—vertical dropdowns, horizontal dropdowns, and accordions—can solve more complex organizational problems and give your users a more interactive experience. For web pages, you can create these types of menus using HTML and CSS alone, or you can create them using features in your web design software, such as the Spry Framework in Dreamweaver. Whatever technique you use, be sure to check your menus and other features for accessibility (see the section "Making Interfaces Accessible" at the end of this chapter).

Vertical Dropdown Menus

A vertical dropdown menu shows up initially as a horizontal row of main sections (see Figure 6.10, A). But users can then access subsections from a list that drops down just below that main item. Sometimes the user has to click on the main section listing to get to the submenu, as often is the case with the main menus for computer applications; other times, the user only has to hover over (move a cursor over). When a user moves the cursor away from the submenu, or clicks somewhere else on the screen, the dropdown menu goes away.

If you choose to use a dropdown menu (either type), limit your subsections to no more than two layers: users have trouble keeping the cursor within complex dropdown menus. If you use the hover feature to display subsections, build in some delay between when the user moves the cursor away and when the dropdown disappears. By doing so, you can avoid the awkward situation where a user accidentally moves the mouse and needs to go through the main section again to initiate the dropdown list.

Horizontal Dropdown Menus

Horizontal dropdown menus work much the same way as vertical dropdown menus. However, the main sections are listed vertically, and the subsections appear to the right side of the selected section (see Figure 6.10, C). Again, limit your menu to no more than two layers. Also, don't provide too many sections in the vertical list. If there are too many sections, users have to scroll up and down to see the complete list of sections, which makes using the interface more complicated.

Accordions

Accordions are a special form of menu with a vertically or horizontally stacked list of sections (see Figure 6.11). Each section has a headline and a panel associated with it (sometimes with links, sometimes with other information). When a user clicks a headline, the section expands to show a panel with more detailed related information. At the same time, the other sections collapse, hiding the other panels. By showing all section headlines but revealing only one panel at a time, accordions can give users easy access to other sections without causing information overload. If you use a vertical accordion, limit the number of sections so users don't have to scroll up and down to see the complete list of sections.

Tabs

Designers use tabs when an interface needs to provide access to different content modules or sections. This technique is similar to labeling folders and organizing them in a file cabinet. Tabs provide an easy way to show a large amount of information by category. When a user switches between tabs on the same web page, the web page usually will not refresh.

Tabs are appropriate when users don't have to see information in different tabs at the same time: switching back and forth between tabs can create an extra cognitive burden to users' short-term memory and subsequently affect their information

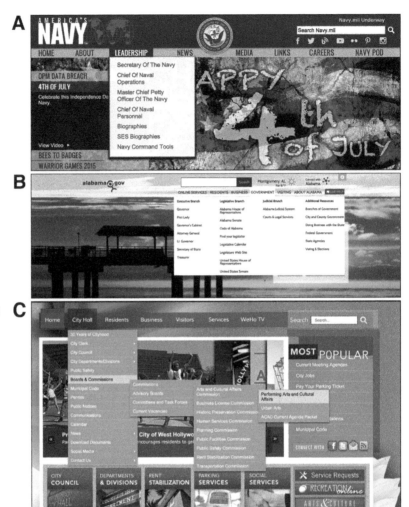

FIGURE 6.10
Dropdown menus
come in many
shapes and sizes.
A) A vertical dropdown
menu offers simple
linear navigation.
B) A two-dimensional
dropdown panel
categorizes
navigation options
under group
headings.
C) A horizontal
dropdown menu
system branches
off the main vertical
dropdown menu to
provide access to
additional submenus.

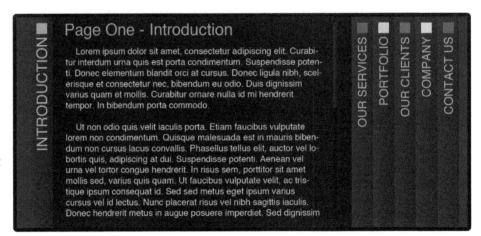

FIGURE 6.11
This horizontal
accordion component
expands to reveal
the contents of the
section whenever the
user clicks on one of
the six menu options.

FIGURE 6.12
This website for the U.S. Food and Drug Administration employs a well-designed tabbed interface for primary navigation.

processing. Organize the content for each tab similarly so users don't have to change mental models when they process content in different tabs. Since the width of the web page or the screen is usually predetermined, create only a limited number of tabs. Also, keep tab labels (the name affixed to the tab) relatively short.

When designing tabs, it is important to avoid having more than one row of categories. People have limited spatial memory; they don't easily remember which tabs they have already visited. Users can become frustrated if they have to take extra time to track previous actions. In addition, always use a visual cue to distinguish the currently viewed tab (the one the user is viewing) from all the other tabs. For instance, you can make it a different color or increase its size. If you are going to dim the color of the other tabs to highlight the currently viewed tab, make sure the unviewed tabs are still readable so users can see their other options (see Figure 6.12).

Managing the Hierarchy

In addition to classifying categories and creating sections, an interface needs to structure information in a logical hierarchy to make it easier for users to go from one place to another. It's a bit like building a road with many intersections. At each intersection, you need to provide direction signs so people know where they are and where to go.

HOME LINKS

No matter where users are, they always need to have the option to easily go back home, back to the starting location in the interface. It might be a link embedded in a website logo that brings users back to the homepage, or a main menu option in a video game, or a home button on a mobile device bringing users to the starting screen. Whatever it is, always place the home link in the same location across different sections of an interface to let users find it easily.

BREADCRUMBS

Breadcrumbs are another such feature that can prevent users from getting lost in an interface. The term *breadcrumbs* is from the Brothers Grimm's fairytale *Hansel and*

FIGURE 6.13
A breadcrumb element, such as the one pictured here, helps users keep track of their location within a multipage website.
Source: http://www.co.orange.nc.us.

Gretel. In the tale, two little children dropped breadcrumbs to form a trail to find their way back home. Putting breadcrumbs in your interface gives users a way to track their paths and go back up to another level in the hierarchy (see Figure 6.13).

Breadcrumbs are usually used for complicated interfaces with hierarchically arranged layers. If an interface only has a single layer, you don't need breadcrumbs. Breadcrumbs on websites are typically right below the navigation menus in a horizontal line. They are often styled so they are plain and don't take up too much space. As a result, they have little impact on users' processing of interface content. Breadcrumbs can also be a good way to invite first-time users to further explore the interface after viewing a landing page. Let's imagine that a user searches for an AMD motherboard and lands on a product list page on Newegg.com. He or she fails to find a satisfying product on this page. However, enticed by the breadcrumbs on the top of page, the user can navigate to a higher-level product page to see what other brands Newegg offers.

Even though breadcrumbs may effectively reduce the number of clicks a user needs to reach a higher structure on an interface, they should never replace tabs or menus. They are not a form of primary navigation. They are just a secondary navigation aid to help users establish where they are and to give them an alternative way to navigate the interface. Breadcrumbs should never be placed on the highest layer of an interface, such as a homepage or an introduction screen: after all, nothing is higher in the hierarchy.

FOOTERS

You might have heard people say that all the important text and images should be placed "above the fold" so users don't have to scroll down a page or a screen to get to it. Extending this concept, the bottom of a page or a screen usually becomes the part with the least important content. However, quite a lot of users do scroll down to the bottom, depending on the site. It's time to reexamine this "forgotten" area and use it better.

In the footer of a website, you can add links to the frequently used sections of the site, RSS feeds, social media sites, recent updates, or sign-up forms for newsletters. Some interfaces even expand the size of the footer to add additional internal and

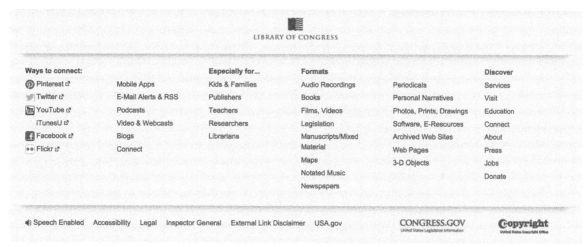

FIGURE 6.14
Here, a fat footer located at the bottom of the page provides with additional internal and external links.
Source: http://loc.gov.

external links. For example, the Library of Congress website has a fat footer that gives users more choices of things to do after browsing the page (see Figure 6.14). It inspires users to continue browsing. Rather than following the prescribed hierarchy of the interface, the user is given the option to visit related pages using redundant links embedded in the footer. The fat footer provides continuous access to shortcuts to highly used sections, as well as major functions that are important to users regardless of where they are in the site or application. Similar to breadcrumbs, footers should only be used for secondary navigation, never replacing tabs and menus.

Organizing Content

The content of a user interface includes text, images, and video/audio downloads, as well as other types of data. Let's look at four popular methods of organizing content.

GREAT IDEAS
Above the Fold Layout

Above the fold is a design principle that originated in the age of print media. Since most newspapers are delivered folded up, people may only see the top half of the front page. For this reason, layout editors place important news and engaging images on the upper half of a newspaper's front page. User interface designers adopted the term *above the fold* (or *above the scroll*) to refer to the part of a web page or screen that is visible without scrolling. The "fold" (i.e., the point where users need to scroll) may vary depending on the resolution of a user's monitor or screen. When the resolution is relatively low (such as 640 × 480), the fold is relatively high. In contrast, when the resolution is relatively high (such as 1280 × 1024), the fold extends much further.

THUMBNAILS

A *thumbnail* is a reduced-size version of a larger image (see Figure 6.15). It can illustrate any visual item, such as a picture, a frame from a video clip, or a screenshot of a web page. If you have a lot of graphics for users to see at one time, thumbnails should be your choice. They give users an overview of all the visual content you want to present without requiring them to open all the files. This saves users download time and uses up less Internet bandwidth.

To make a thumbnail, you can create a mini version of the whole image. You can also crop part of the image, but you have to ensure that users can recognize the new partial image. In other words, it should also successfully convey the meaning you intend. For example, if you want to link to several great French chefs with thumbnails, you would do better using their faces for the thumbnails than their hands. Although some thumbnail sizes are fairly common, you can adjust an image's size to better fit your interface (see Table 6.1). You can even use an image that is partially transparent to give your thumbnails a unique appearance.

CAROUSELS

Another way to organize visual content on a user interface is a *carousel*. Carousels organize items on a horizontal line. Even though you might have many items, the carousel shows only a few of them, as thumbnails, at a time. An interface carousel is

FIGURE 6.15
Image thumbnails serve as helpful visual links to specific content collections on the Library of Congress website. Notice also how they are perfectly aligned on the page.
Source: http://loc.gov.

Table 6.1	Thumbnail Sizes
Width × Height (pixels)	**Description**
48 × 48	Very Small
64 × 64	Small
96 × 96	Medium
128 × 128	Large
144 × 144	Extra Large
160 × 160	Super Large
192 × 192	Huge

reminiscent of a carnival carousel with painted horses: as the carousel turns, you get a good look at a few of the horses in front of you, but you know there are more hidden to the left or right. If users want to see more, they click an arrow (left or right), move a slide bar below the images, click to the side of carousel indicators (the dots below some carousels), or mouse over the images. Apple uses cover flow carousels, which have 3D effects, in its Mac Finder window, iTunes, and other software, to display rotating thumbnail images for file collections such as photo and music libraries (see Figure 6.16, top). Netflix uses stacked carousels to organize movie and TV show selections thematically according to program genre (see Figure 6.16, bottom). Users can browse the various program offerings through touch gestures or by mousing over a revolving carousel of small icons. As you hover over an image or click, descriptive text related to the underlying show is revealed in an expanded window.

FIGURE 6.16
Top: A carousel interface component is built into Apple OS X and can be used for browsing attached storage drives and specific file collections such as your iTunes music library or photo albums. Bottom: Netflix incorporates a multitiered carousel design to help uses quickly navigate through their offerings of television and movie content.
Source: Top: Apple, Inc. Bottom: http://www.netflix.com.

By only showing a few items at once, carousels effectively direct users to concentrate on a limited number of things at one time. Compared to thumbnails, carousels may pique users' curiosity and encourage them to explore more. Carousels are more effective when used for visual items, such as album and book covers, movie posters, paintings, and product images; they are not appropriate for text.

PAGINATION

You might use pagination if you have a large set of organized information, such as a long article, a batch of customer reviews, a list of blog entries, or a group of search results (see Figure 6.17). In these cases, you have to break the information down to be displayed on separate pages. Unlike the simple "previous" and "next" button,

FIGURE 6.17
Adding pagination to the interface of a multipage or multiscreen site can help the user keep track of where they are on the site.
Source: Top: http:// chriswalkerphoto.com.

Pagination

There are **39 articles** listed in **Strategy**

| < PREV | 1 | 2 | 3 | 4 | 5 | 6 | 7 | 8 | 9 | 10 | 11 | NEXT > |

pagination gives users a brief idea about how much information to anticipate. It also allows users to easily navigate through the parts of a large body of information. Users don't have to finish browsing all information provided by the interface. They can stop wherever they want and jump to other places. Do you want to find out how that feature story ends? Just jump to the last page.

Good pagination is easy to use. First, you need to provide big enough clickable areas to get to different pages and leave enough space between page links. Second, you need to identify the current page—using color or shape distinctions—and tell users where they are and where they can go. Finally, your pagination should let users know the amount of available information (number of pages). If you can, include both the first page link and the last page link. However, if it's hard to include both links, you could add text indicating the total number of screens or pages, as the second example illustrates (see Figure 6.17, bottom).

ARCHIVES

Another way to deal with a large amount of information is to organize it chronologically using archives. Different from pagination, an archive is only appropriate for information that spans a rather long period of time and that users can logically browse chronologically, such as by date. Archive.org's Wayback Machine is an extreme example of archiving (see Figure 6.18). It does a great job of capturing and

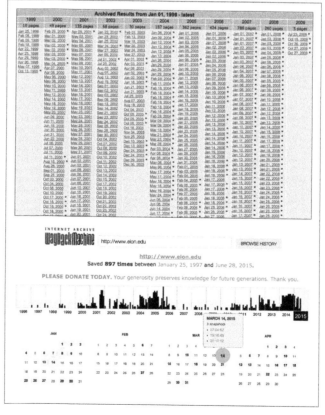

FIGURE 6.18
Which interface would you rather work with, the one on top or the one on bottom? Navigating online databases and archives can be an arduous task. Providing a fun or visually interesting interface can make the process more enjoyable for users and keep them coming back to your site.
Source: https://archive.org/web.

keeping the homepages of all kinds of websites on a daily basis. It organizes this information by year and month, using a blue circle to mark days when it recaptured a site. Most sites don't archive this much information, so their designers don't need to be as careful in planning their archive's time intervals. For example, if a blog has around 8 posts per year, it's inefficient to archive them by month. Another blog may have 300 posts per year. However, these posts may not be evenly distributed across months, with some months completely lacking posts. If this is the case, then the designer doesn't even need to list those empty months in the archive.

Tech Talk

Parallax Scrolling One recent trend in web design is parallax scrolling. On a parallax website, the background of the site moves at a slower speed than the foreground elements on the page to create a faux 3D visual effect. The majority of parallax websites have only one single long page created by either JavaScript or CSS. Parallax websites provide great opportunities to encourage online storytelling by guiding you through the site in a linear manner. The scrolling feature provokes curiosity, which can motivate visitors to spend more time on the page (see Figure 6.19). However, parallax websites are not without limitations. The single long web page is not conducive to website SEO (search engine optimization). The large amount of visual and other multimedia information on this single page may cause longer loading time, which could frustrate users before they even start scrolling. In addition, it is harder to make parallax websites compatible with the responsive design for mobile devices. Designers would have to be very careful to avoid overdoing it to make the site too complicated. The website for the Seattle Space Needle serves as a good example of parallax scrolling (www.spaceneedle.com). Unlike most other parallax sites, it requires users to scroll up instead of scrolling down. This site juxtaposes clickable photos and text with scrolling to give you a unique browsing experience.

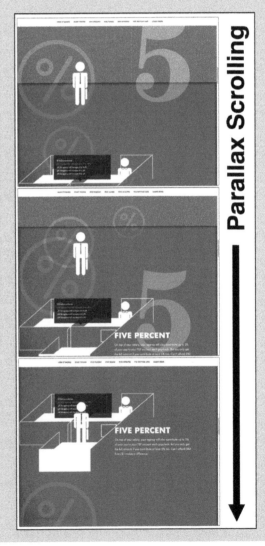

FIGURE 6.19
In this example of a parallax website, the background and foreground elements traverse at different speeds as the user scrolls vertically up or down the page. The mid-ground element (the human silhouette) is locked down, making it motionless during scrolling.
Source: https://www.tsp.gov/takeFIVE.

FORMS

You probably use electronic forms frequently: shopping online, logging into a game system, registering software, downloading phone apps, and such. In essence, you enter information and get feedback. Maybe your information goes to another party—Amazon.com needs your order, payment information, and address. But some forms just give you feedback, such as an inch-to-centimeter conversion calculator. The bottom line to making your forms successful is keeping them short and intuitive. The less you ask people to fill in, and the easier you make the process, the more likely they will actually complete and submit the form. Also, the more you avoid asking for sensitive information or information they might not readily have on hand, the more complete forms you'll get back.

When you create a form, you can give users preset options to choose from with checkboxes, radio buttons, and dropdown lists, or you can have them type content into text fields (see Figure 6.20). Here are a few options:

- *Checkboxes* (small squares) let users select multiple options, even all of them, if they'd like (e.g., interests: reading, playing music, playing sports, cooking).
- *Radio buttons* (small circles) let users choose among mutually exclusive options (e.g., yes or no; red, green, or orange).
- *Dropdown lists* (text followed by a triangular down arrow) also let users choose among mutually exclusive options, but you can reasonably include more options in a dropdown list than with radio buttons (e.g., a list of states to let you identify the state you live in).

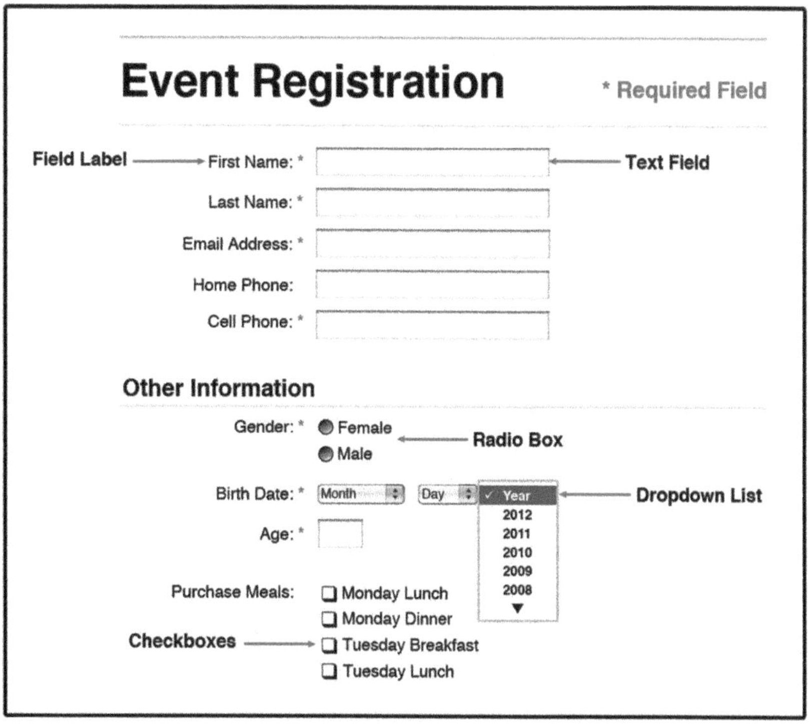

FIGURE 6.20
A typical form can include components such as text fields, dropdown lists, radio buttons, and checkboxes for user input.

Text fields let users type in what they want. Human beings are cognitive misers. We try to fill out those online forms as quickly as possible. Sometimes, we might not even bother to read instructions or labels when filling out a form. You can help your users fill in the blanks with less effort in several ways: by using autofill, prompt prefills, and tabbing. You should already be familiar with autofill and auto-suggestions: many email editors and search engines use them. For instance, as you enter the first few letters of a contact's name or email address, some email editors use autofill and automatically fill in a complete address. As you type "multimedia" in Google.com's search field, you get an autosuggested list below the search box: "multimedia audio controller," "multimedia fusion 2," "multimedia audio controller driver," and more. And if you type two words, "multimedia website," you get more detailed suggestions of "multimedia website template," "multimedia website design," and others. Autofill and autosuggestion work best for the most commonly searched terms. If you try to look for something less common or rarely used, the system probably will not be able to provide good suggestions.

How often do you read all the text on a form you complete? Input prompts prefill a text field with a prompt, telling you what to type. The website of EveryBlock New York City gives users a way to search for local news. The search fields are prefilled with an example—"e.g., 175 5th Ave., Manhattan, Williamsburg"—making the form field self-explanatory (see Figure 6.21). Without such input hints, users might quickly scan a site and miss or ignore the other hints below or next to text fields. But an input prompt that sits right where you start typing will grab your attention right away. Ideally, you should also use a script that clears the prompt text once your user starts to type. Also, if you design your forms so users can tab through them, they won't have to reposition the cursor to get to each new field.

TAILORING

In the early days of computing, every visitor to a website received the same interface. Web pages looked the same regardless of who you were. Likewise, applications displayed the same screen no matter who the users were. Some sites and applications are still designed that way, but many interfaces now adapt to individual users, giving people tailored experiences. There are two types of tailoring: *personalization*, in which the system makes the changes, and *customization*, in which the user makes the changes.

Personalization

When a computer system personalizes your interface, it's using your previous actions (sometimes information you put in a profile) to predict your interests. In other words, it relies on your implicit interests rather than your explicitly expressed ones.

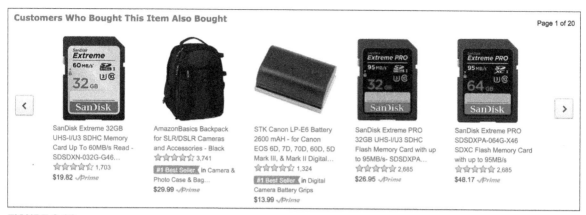

Customers Who Bought This Item Also Bought

Page 1 of 20

SanDisk Extreme 32GB UHS-I/U3 SDHC Memory Card Up To 60MB/s Read - SDSDXN-032G-G46...
★★★★☆ 1,703
$19.82 ✓Prime

AmazonBasics Backpack for SLR/DSLR Cameras and Accessories - Black
★★★★☆ 3,741
#1 Best Seller in Camera & Photo Case & Bag...
$29.99 ✓Prime

STK Canon LP-E6 Battery 2600 mAH - for Canon EOS 6D, 7D, 70D, 60D, 5D Mark III, & Mark II Digital...
★★★★☆ 1,324
#1 Best Seller in Digital Camera Battery Grips
$13.99 ✓Prime

SanDisk Extreme PRO 32GB UHS-I/U3 SDHC Flash Memory Card with up to 95MB/s- SDSDXPA...
★★★★★ 2,685
$26.95 ✓Prime

SanDisk Extreme PRO SDSDXPA-064G-X46 SDXC Flash Memory Card with up to 95MB/s
★★★★★ 2,685
$48.17 ✓Prime

FIGURE 6.22
With every search, Amazon.com acquires valuable information about the shopping and buying habits of its customers. Through collaborative filtering, this information is personalized and shared with other shoppers who are conducting a similar search.
Source: http://www.amazon.com.

For instance, Netflix.com might recommend *Avatar* based on the fact that you've rented other science fiction and fantasy movies. Facebook.com examines your profile and gives you relevant advertisements. Sometimes the process isn't perfect.

A system needs data to make effective predictions and recommendations. It might ask you to submit a questionnaire—collecting demographic, lifestyle, and content preference information—when you register with a website or application. The system then applies rules and gives you a preset category of content that fits your profile. Another way it can collect that data is by data mining—such as with a website *clickstream*, or a record of your clicks—to anticipate what action you might take next. Both these approaches require you to log in to your own account. But it can collect data even if you don't have an account. Using cookies saved on your hard drive, the system can identify you and your browser, then give you an individualized welcome message and recommendations. But if you use a friend's computer or a public computer without first logging in to the site, you won't get a truly personalized interface.

One of the best ways to personalize an interface is with *collaborative filtering*. Collaborative filtering technology examines both your profile and the action you're taking, such as viewing a book on Amazon.com. It then bases feedback on what similar people who took that same action did. The group of like-minded people you are being compared to constantly changes based on what you're doing (see Figure 6.22).

Customization

Unlike personalization, customization allows users to deliberately tailor content, giving them agency. As a user, you can directly choose options or even create new content. As researcher Sampada Marathe explains, customization can be either cosmetic or functional.[1] *Cosmetic customization* lets you control presentation, such as the background, color, font, layout, graphics, and your profile photo. For instance, with a Wii, you can create an avatar of yourself, selecting a gender, hair and skin color, facial features, name, and body type. At the "feature" level of its interface, Facebook lets you hide your friend Bob's posts. As the name implies, *functional customization* lets you change the functionality of your interface. MyYahoo.com lets you add and remove applications on your page and even drag-and-drop to rearrange the order of applications. Along with changing the background color and theme, iPhone allows you to add and remove apps, as well as adjust the display order of these apps (see Figure 6.23). In Skype, you can create a specialized

FIGURE 6.23
Users can customize their iPhone interface 1) cosmetically by changing the theme and 2) functionally by adding or removing apps or changing settings.

ringtone for contacts in your address book. A ringtone might be a statement, such as "Mike is calling," a song, or some other sound.

Sometimes personalization and customization work together in one interface. On YouTube.com, you can customize your own channel, changing its title, creating tags, changing the background theme and color, and adding and removing functional modules. At the same time, YouTube.com will also suggest videos you might be interested in based on what you recently viewed.

USABILITY

Have you ever used a website that isn't well organized or is complex but doesn't have a help menu? Perhaps you've used an online course management system that requires extra steps to upload an assignment, a word processor that loses a document because of one accidental click, a remote control with more buttons than you actually need, or a touch screen that does not respond quickly enough to the fine movement of your fingers. These are usability problems. Designers can identify many of these problems—and fix them—by focusing on usability during the design process: they apply usability methods, including usability testing, to make sure their products meet usability criteria. You may refer back to the discussion in chapter 3 of the process of design and user-centered design.

Usability is a measure of people's experience with a user interface. We can apply the concept to anything a user uses, from software to hardware. Often, we apply it to user interfaces because they are what users interact with. Usability refers to the extent to which users can achieve their context-specific goals effectively, efficiently, and with satisfaction. Can users successfully achieve their goals? How much effort do they need to spend to complete a given task? And how much do they enjoy the experience? In other words, usability is about the user. It focuses on how to make the interface easier for people to use, rather than how to train people to better adapt to a poorly designed interface. It's hard to change the habits of a large group of users, and if an interface is hard to use, many users will find an alternative product or website that's easier to use. In the end, it's easier—and more profitable—to make the interface more usable. Check for usability early and often! Jakob Nielsen identifies five essential criteria that make something usable: learnability, efficiency, memorability, error management, and satisfaction.[2]

Learnability

Learnability is how fast a user can accomplish the basic tasks on an interface they have never used before. An interface will be easier to learn if its design taps into the core psychology of how we learn, and we learn well when something is familiar, generalizable, predictable, consistent, and simple. If the design of an interface is similar to ones users are familiar with, they will be able to navigate through it by generalizing what they've learned in the past. They will be able to predict what will happen when they click a certain button or figure out how to go back to the homepage. If you keep the design pattern of the interface consistent across different sections, users will be less confused and will need to adapt their behavior less. Learning is fast when there is not much to learn. Less complexity also can improve learnability.

Efficiency

Efficiency is how fast a user can perform tasks after learning how to use the interface. While learnability is about users' initial interactions with the interface, efficiency is about the effort users expend during repeated visits. For example, two shopping websites can be equally learnable if their checkout buttons are well placed, making it easy for users to complete a purchase. But one may be more efficient than the other. One may require a single step for completing the purchase, while the other may take four steps and require users to fill in several forms. An efficient website can ultimately save users a lot of time, make them happy about their experience, and boost both ratings and repeat business.

Memorability

If a user has used the interface before, can he or she still remember enough to use it effectively after being away from it for a while? This is the issue of *memorability*. It's not surprising that users tend to forget how to use interfaces they only use occasionally. If they use several different systems at the same time, such as three different banking websites, they'll have an even harder time. Relearning a system every time they come back takes extra time and effort, and some people may take their business elsewhere. Memorable feedback helps users, and familiar visual cues make an interface both more learnable and memorable.

Error Management

Although usability is primarily focused on eliminating design mistakes rather than blaming users, we realize people will click buttons we didn't expect them to click and make other decisions we might think of as errors. A good interface: 1) reduces the number of errors users might make, 2) decreases the severity of each error, and 3) makes it easy for users to recover from errors. If possible, avoid creating situations in which users are likely to make mistakes. For example, if you expect users to look for content or a feature that's on another page, add a link to it on the current page. And if a user submits a form with an empty required field, send the user back to the partially completed form—not an empty one—and point out what's missing.

Satisfaction

Satisfaction is about enjoyment. How pleasant is the user's experience? How much do users like the interface, and how satisfied are they with it? We can learn about the other three elements of usability by watching users interact with the interface. Not so much with satisfaction: to understand satisfaction, we need to ask for users' subjective feedback.

If you are designing something only you will use, you can do almost anything. But most interface design is a creative activity bounded by constraints: time, money, environment, and more. Usability is just another constraint, an essential one. Checking usability lets you explicitly identify users' needs. You learn how people usually perform on interfaces similar to what you plan to design. It sheds light on real issues you need to consider and inspires ideas for improvement. Usability is never the enemy of creativity. You, as the designer, ultimately choose the details of your design. But usability principles and testing give you a way to ensure people will actually want to use your website, play your game, or visit your kiosk.

Usability Testing

If you want to ensure the usability of an interface, you need to conduct usability tests early on and again when you develop a working prototype. They are the best way to understand how users really experience your interface and where your design isn't intuitive. If you're faithfully following the design process we've discussed, you've already identified the target users of your interface and developed the prototypes mimicking the entire interface or the part of it you are interested in. Now recruit your test participants: several users or good user proxies. You can catch about 80% of the problems with your interface if you choose five to eight good users and design your test carefully. You can conduct usability tests in a lab or in a more natural setting, where the interface is supposed to be used.

There are several ways to conduct a usability test. Let's look at two: 1) *unobtrusive observation* and 2) think-aloud protocols, also called *obtrusive observation.*

Whichever method you choose, avoid bias by using a script (such as the Test Facilitator's Guide available on Usability.gov) so each participant receives the same instructions when you explain tasks. Also, make participants comfortable with the process. People often have anxiety about testing, even when there's no grade involved. Remember to explain that the interface is being tested, not them. Tell them that any problems they have are problems with the interface and that they are helping you when they find problems.

With each method, you usually give participants one or more tasks to complete. With the unobtrusive observation method, after you give participants the basic instructions, you observe what they do without talking to them. You can record how much time they need to finish a task, how many errors they encounter, whether they are confused by a certain function, as well as their physical and emotional reactions. Even if you only have a paper prototype, you can give them tasks to complete (e.g., find out how to email the vice president of operations), have them point to where they would click, and watch what they do. In contrast, when you use the think-aloud method, you will not only keep a record of what they do, but also encourage them to talk about their experience as they interact with the interface. Is it hard or easy? What do they expect to happen when clicking a thumbnail or image? If they were to encounter a similar problem in a different interface, how would they solve it?

If you are testing a fuller prototype, give participants tasks that will require them to use or interact with at least the following types of components:

- Main menu and submenus
- Interactive components (forms, search boxes, pop-ups, and so on)
- Text and informative statements
- Images (especially icons)

Ask your users to go to specific pages or screens, use forms, complete tasks that involve icons, and find answers to questions that require them to go to pages or screens buried in your architecture. Ask them to do anything an average user might do. If you have pages or screens they can't get to in one or two clicks, choose some tasks that require them to go to these deeper spots. If you have submenus, choose tasks that require the users to use them. For instance, if you are designing a website for a club, and you have membership information they can get to only from a submenu, ask a question about membership (e.g., How much are dues?). Make sure your design isn't missing features they want, like search boxes, contact links, and such. Get their reaction to the colors, fonts, layout, images, and other traits of your design.

With the think-aloud method, you can collect users' responses and understand their decision-making in real time. You can also collect much of the same data you would in unobtrusive observation; however, you might interrupt the normal flow of users' interaction with the interface, making the interaction unnatural and some data meaningless. What will a users' "time on task" (the time it took them to complete a task) mean if you interrupted them to talk at length about what they were doing?

In addition to observing users' actions, you can carry out focus-group research, letting users sit together and discuss their experiences with the interface. You can also collect their opinions in one-to-one interviews to get more in-depth feedback. Questionnaires, both pencil-and-paper and online, are yet another way to collect users' feedback after they finish interacting with the interface. If you would like to compare two types of interfaces or two functions of an interface, conduct an experiment.

Soliciting and Applying Feedback

Show users your prototype, but don't say, "It's great, isn't it? You like it, don't you?" Instead, ask them what they like and what they find problematic. As you watch each user, avoid giving help. Yes, of course you know how to find that piece of information: you put it there. You're not being tested: the interface is. The test is useless if you help your participant complete the task and then assume your design is good. If you're using the think-aloud method, neutral prompting is okay. Don't be afraid to prompt quiet users to share their thoughts, particularly if they look grumpy or confused. Pay attention to your users' reactions. If some of your users look irritated as they search again and again for a piece of content, your design probably has a problem.

If your users tell you that they don't like parts of your design, don't get upset. The point of getting feedback is to get honest critiques that will help you make necessary changes. You will probably find it helpful to have someone else ask the questions to make the process as neutral as possible. Designing is like writing: a sentence may sound great to you, and you might have written it as a sincere response to a problem, but it may confuse your reader or come across with the wrong tone. If you're upset, put the project aside for a while, and come back to working on it when you can consider the feedback without taking offense.

Use your test findings to help you refine design ideas, make the changes, and improve the interface. Again, you should carry out several iterations of usability testing throughout the interface design process.

RESPONSIVE WEB DESIGN

With the rapid adoption of mobile devices, responsive web design has become a recent trend to increase website usability across platforms. According to data released in 2014 by the Pew Research Center, 58% of American adults have a smartphone, with 42% owning a tablet computer as of January 2014.[3] During the same month, mobile devices exceeded desktop and laptop computers to account for 55% of Internet usage in the United States.[4] The growth in mobile Internet usage poses challenges for interface designers to build websites suitable for multiple devices. The industry has responded to these new usage patterns with responsive web design. In simple terms, responsive web design refers to the practice of building a website that works for every device with optimal display regardless of the screen size. This term was coined by Ethan Marcotte (2011) in his book *Responsive Web Design*.[5]

Let's imagine that you are viewing a responsive website, such as the one created for the state of Wisconsin (http://www.wisconsin.gov), on a desktop browser. If you make your browser window smaller, the images and content columns will shrink. If you continue making the browser smaller, the layout will gradually change from multiple columns, to two columns, and finally to one column with the disappearance of top navigation (see Figure 6.24). A responsive website detects the type of device (i.e., a laptop, a tablet, or a smartphone) in use and automatically changes the site layout, or even the site functions, accordingly. The images in responsive websites usually scale along their containers. If you switch between devices with different resolutions and screen sizes, the scaled images should change fluidly while remaining sharp across contexts.

You may wonder why it is necessary to make a website responsive. Couldn't we just build a traditional website for computers and then a second site for mobile handheld devices? First, you have to remember that having only one responsive website enables continuity across different browsing contexts. You can thus avoid the frustration of experiencing limited content on the mobile site. Having just one URL for the website also allows Google to discover and index the content more easily, which will boost the search engine optimization of the site.

Since native mobile apps are also popular nowadays, you may also wonder why it is still necessary for us to consider responsive sites. Couldn't we just build apps? In general, a mobile app is designed for a unique experience with the device. It is exclusive to the particular operating system it runs on. It is onerous for designers to develop different apps to suit different operating systems on various devices. In contrast, a responsive site can be accessed universally from any device without sacrificing the integrity of content. However, we have to admit that there are limitations of a responsive site compared to a mobile app. For example, it usually takes longer for a responsive site to fully load on mobile devices than an app. In addition, the responsive site cannot incorporate some smartphone features, such as GPS or camera, to the full capacity of an app.

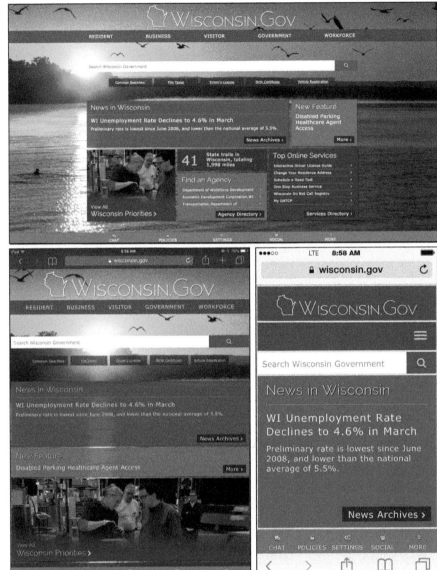

FIGURE 6.24
The responsive website for the state of Wisconsin adapts very well to different screen sizes and devices. Observe here how the layout of the homepage changes when viewed on a laptop computer (top), an iPad (bottom left), and an iPhone (bottom right).
Source: http://www. wisconsin.gov.

MAKING INTERFACES ACCESSIBLE

Accessibility is a fundamental principle of user interface design. We typically define accessibility in terms of making sure users with disabilities can access your content, but an accessible interface can also help people with technological constraints, making it usable by as many people as possible. Let's examine how you can do both.

Accessibility features should addresses all kinds of disabilities that may affect people's use of interfaces, including visual, auditory, physical, and cognitive problems (both short- and long-term). People who can't see rely on assistive technologies such as screen readers, which read websites and other electronic documents aloud. But screen readers can't describe images if designers don't add alternative text (textual synopses that accompany the images and can be read aloud), so if you design an interface that relies on images, those users won't understand all the content or even be able to access all of it. (We'll address this issue more in chapter 7, "Web

GREAT IDEAS
Accessibility and the Law

A number of government acts call for accessibility. We'll talk about two. Section 508 of the Rehabilitation Act requires federal agencies to make their information technology, such as websites, accessible to people with disabilities; this is frequently a requirement of organizations receiving federal funding or doing business with the federal government. Section 255 of the 1996 Telecommunications Act also calls for electronic media to be made accessible (see Figure 6.25). Over the last few years, there have been a number of lawsuits regarding websites based on these and other laws. While many of them are still undecided, the last thing you want to do is open you or your client up to legal action.

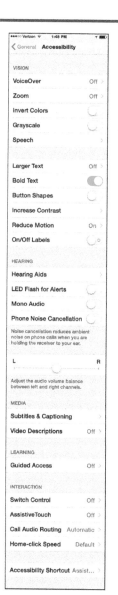

FIGURE 6.25
Like so many *smart* devices today, the Apple iPhone includes a host of settings to enhance the accessibility of the user interface. Here, more than 20 accessibility features are displayed under the accessibility menu for Apple iOS 8.1.3.

Design.") Interfaces with small fonts and tiny images are difficult for users with weak vision to read. Older people who lack fine motor control might not be able to precisely control the movement of a mouse or a joystick to interact with an interface. These are a few cases in which designers need to focus more on accessibility to guarantee equal access and equal opportunity for people with special needs.

Accessibility features tend to make interfaces more usable overall. In particular they benefit people without disabilities who use an interface under situational limitations. Environmental circumstances might constrain users' activities. In a quiet environment, such as a library, users might be uncomfortable if the interface makes unexpected sounds. If you build your interface with an easy-to-use mute option that still gives them the cues they need, you will help users avoid embarrassment. In contrast, it's hard for users to hear clearly in a noisy environment. Interfaces that show the content of conversation or the script of a video or audio clip benefit these users, not only those with hearing loss. Many people browse the Web on mobile devices; these users welcome websites with simpler navigation and input methods. When you design an interface, consider other usage situations, too, such as strong sunlight, slow Internet connections, and differences in operating systems and browsers.

Making sure your interface gracefully degrades, or changes with older technology, is important. Not every user will have the latest version of a browser or the most recent model of a mobile device. An accessible interface makes sure these differences in technology don't become an obstacle, preventing people from accessing content. That doesn't mean we need to design interfaces based on the least advanced technology. But designers do need to consider average users' needs rather than developing an interface only for the latest technology. When designing a website, try turning off all the images and audio/video clips you've embedded to see how the layout would change without these elements. When developing content with Flash, consider how it would look on devices that don't support Flash, such as some mobile phones and iPads.

If you separate your content from its presentation (fonts, layouts, and so on), you'll have an easier time making it accessible. In web design, you can accomplish this separation with Cascading Style Sheets (CSS is discussed more fully in chapter 7, "Web Design"). A set of well-designed style sheets allows users with disabilities to override your styles and apply idiosyncratic preferences: reverse-contrast text and larger headings for low-vision users, color schemes for colorblind users, and more. And you can create separate style sheets for mobile devices and printing.

> **GREAT IDEAS**
> Accessibility and Usability
>
> Accessibility is related to usability. However, accessibility should not be confused with usability. Whereas usability refers to designing an effective, efficient, and satisfying interface, accessibility focuses on allowing more people, especially those with disabilities, to use that interface under more circumstances.

CHAPTER SUMMARY

The way that we interact with technology has evolved significantly through the years, and it continues to change. Motion tracking interfaces and multi-touch interfaces probably will become more popular in the near future. Interface designers are also working on developing more natural input devices, some controlled by a user's natural eye gaze or even by brainwaves. The display devices we use are becoming lighter and more flexible, and upcoming devices will likely break some of our current conventions. Samsung recently demonstrated a transparent display that could be used for MP3 players, and LG has developed flexible e-paper that can be bent. In general, interfaces are becoming more intuitive and giving us more interactive experiences.

No matter what type of interface you create, it's essential to focus on real users throughout the design process. When you plan navigation features, consider how they will be used. When you design forms, make them easy to use. Consider tailoring your interface to give users a better experience. Whatever your ultimate design, work to ensure it is usable and accessible, not just trendy.

ABOUT THE AUTHOR

Qian Xu, Ph.D., is an assistant professor in the School of Communications at Elon University, where she teaches graduate courses in interactive media. She received her Ph.D. from Penn State University. Her research and teaching interests focus on the social and psychological impact of media technology, user experience of online media, and online strategic communication.

NOTES

1 Marathe, S. S. (2009). Investigating the psychology of task-based and presentation-based UI customization. CHI Extended Abstracts, 3129–3132.
2 Nielson, J. (2010). *Usability 101: Introduction to usability*. Retrieved December 2, 2010, from http://www.useit.com/alertbox/20030825.html
3 Pew Research Internet Project. (January 2014). *Device ownership over time*. Retrieved September 22, 2014, from http://www.pewinternet.org/data-trend/mobile/device-ownership/
4 O'Toole, J. (February 2014). *Mobile apps overtake PC Internet usage in U.S.* Retrieved September 22, 2014, from http://money.cnn.com/2014/02/28/technology/mobile/mobile-apps-internet/
5 Marcotte, E. (2011). *Responsive Web design*. New York, NY: A Book Apart.

CHAPTER 7

Web Design

Susan A. Youngblood,
Norman E. Youngblood

> The future of cyberspace is not really about technology. Although it will obviously continue to develop, the essential technology is already here in one form or another. The thing we have to start recognizing is that cyberspace must be content-driven rather than technology-driven.
>
> **—Rick Schremp, *Cyberspace 2020* (Govtech.com), (1995)**

Chapter Highlights

This chapter examines:

- The World Wide Web and Hypertext Markup Language (HTML)
- The basics of HTML code and the technology behind client/server networks
- How to create and manage project files and website assets
- The process for researching, planning, designing, producing, uploading, and testing a basic website
- The importance of separating meaning from presentation and designing accessible sites for all audiences

HOW THE WEB WORKS

So what is this thing we call "the Web"? Perhaps the first thing to understand is that the World Wide Web (WWW) and the Internet are not the same thing, even if many people use the terms synonymously. The Web is a part of the Internet, usually the part we use through a web browser by entering an address beginning "http://." So what's the Internet? In his book *Weaving the Web*, Tim Berners-Lee,[1] the inventor of the WWW, defines the Internet as a "global network of networks through which computers communicate by sending information in packets. Each network consists of computers connected by cables or wireless links." These computers communicate using a variety of network protocols (rules for communicating). The Internet encompasses a wide variety of technologies, including email, the Web, File Transfer Protocol (FTP), and many others.

Key Terms

Absolute URL
Alternative Text
ARPANET
Attribute
Background Image
Block-Level Element
Body
Browser
Button
Cascading Style
  Sheets (CSS)
Character Reference
Domain Name
Element
File Transfer
  Protocol (FTP)
Head
HTTP (Hypertext
  Transfer Protocol)
Hyperlink
Hypertext Markup
  Language (HTML)
Index.html
Inline Element
Internet
IP (Internet Protocol)
  Address
Navigation Bar
Nesting
Network
Nonbreaking Space
Plug-in
Property
Protocol
Relative URL
Root Folder
Server
Site Design
Tag

Title
Uniform Resource
  Locator (URL)
World Wide Web
  (WWW)
World Wide Web
  Consortium (W3C)

FLASHBACK

A Brief History of the Internet and the World Wide Web

In 1957, the Soviet Union launched Sputnik, the first man-made satellite. Concerned that the United States had fallen behind in scientific and military research, the Department of Defense established the Advanced Research Projects Agency (ARPA). In 1962, the head of computer research at ARPA, computer scientist J.C.R. Licklider, began talking about a "Galactic Network" of computers that would stretch across the globe. In 1966, ARPA researchers began work on the first iteration of his idea, ARPANET, which would help lay the groundwork for the modern Internet. Unveiled to the public in 1972, ARPANET connected a number of academic research centers across the United States. Email was added to the system the same year. Over the next 20 years, ARPANET was supplemented by other networks, most notably the National Science Foundation's NSFNET in 1986. These interconnected networks eventually evolved into what we now refer to simply as the Internet.

In 1989, Tim Berners-Lee, a researcher at the European Organization for Nuclear Research (CERN), submitted a proposal to CERN to help researchers communicate by linking together documents located on different networked computers using hypertext: words in a document that, when selected, allow the user to move to another document. His project was accepted, and over the next year he developed the underpinnings of what is now the World Wide Web, including Hypertext Markup Language (HTML), the Uniform Resource Locator (URL), the web server, and, of course, the web browser. CERN connected to ARPANET in 1990, and CERN's first web server went online on December 25, 1990.

In 1994, Tim Berners-Lee and others involved in the creation of the Web established the World Wide Web Consortium (W3C) to create web standards, including how HTML should be written and how web browsers should interpret it. In 1995, Microsoft introduced its first browser, Internet Explorer. As the Web caught on, the number of sites grew exponentially. By 1997, the number of websites was well over 1,000,000. Not bad growth given that the first web server went online in December 1990. The volume of material on the Web continues to increase rapidly. The search engine Google, which once listed how many pages it indexed, now just refers to billions.

Demystifying Code

Web pages are built using HTML. This chapter focuses on the latest version, HTML5, finalized in October 2014, and some elements of HTML 4.01. The W3C took eight years to finalize the new standard, and HTML5 is a key element in web development for mobile devices, particularly as it has built-in support for playing media files. HTML5 also frees developers from having to rely so heavily on JavaScript and plug-ins such as Flash. Although web developers are increasingly turning to HTML5, you may still need to work with older sites designed with the older HTML 4.01 standard, so it's a good idea to understand what's changed. Happily, HTML5 still supports many HTML 4.01 standards, so updating a site to HTML5 doesn't have to be overly complicated. Be aware that HTML is an evolving language and that the W3C is already working on HTML 5.1. You can keep tabs on the latest HTML5 decisions on the W3C website (http://www.w3.org); if the information on that site is too technical for you, read the latest tech blogs and other well-updated sites about HTML5.

HTML files are essentially just text files. In Figure 7.1, you can see one of the text files that controls what the browser will display. You can create HTML files using

FIGURE 7.1
HTML and CSS, the
guts behind the page.

nothing more than a basic text editor such as Notepad in Windows. You can also create HTML by using a wide range of automated and semi-automated tools ranging from standalone web design software, such as Dreamweaver, to online web authoring tools such as WordPress, Blogger, and Wix. All these have a what-you-see-is-what-you-get (WYSIWYG) editing function that allows you to create a web page in much the same way you use a word processor. With many programs able to write HTML for you, more than a few people have asked the question, "Wait, why exactly am I spending all this time learning HTML?" There are a number of good answers to that question.

First, HTML has limitations, and if you don't understand the basics of how HTML works, you won't understand why the WYSIWYG editor won't always do what you want it to do. Second, the WSIWYG editors don't always write the best code, nor does the code they write always do exactly what you want it to do. If you don't understand how HTML works, you can't sneak in and tweak the code to fix the problems. This issue is particularly important if you want to customize the look of a WordPress or Blogger page beyond the point-and-click options they give you. In short, if you are at all serious about working with the web, you need to understand HTML and Cascading Style Sheets (CSS), which largely control how the page will appear to users. Sometimes CSS code is put in the HTML itself, but often (and usually better), it is put into a separate file.

A good web developer uses HTML to label the pieces of a document according to their functions (navigation, headings, picture captions, paragraphs, list items, etc.)

The <strong> tells the browser to start making the text bold, and the </strong> tells it to stop making it bold.

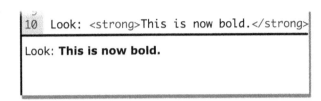

You can also tell the browser to change the font, size, and color of the text. We'll look at this in more detail a bit later.

FIGURE 7.2
How tagging works.

and uses CSS to control how those pieces look and behave (colors, positions on a page, actions like rollover effects, etc.). In other words, the developer uses HTML to mark for meaning and uses structure—semantic markup—to separate function from how elements on a page are presented, an idea explored in more depth in chapter 4 (under "Content and Form"). Among other things, this approach allows developers to change the look of a site across platforms such as phones, tablets, and computers and to apply a redesign with ease.

Rather than being a programming language, HTML lets you put tags (markup) around your text so the browser knows how to display it on the screen, which words or other objects are links, and where to go if you select a link, among other things. The graphics used in a web page are not actually inside the text document, but are referenced in the code and then uploaded along with the HTML file to the server. Formatting the text works much like a word processor, assuming you had to type in the commands to make things bold, italicized, and so on, which once upon a time you actually had to do. Most, but not all, elements have a *start tag* and an *end tag* (also called *opening* and *closing tags*), which tell the browser to start doing something and to stop doing something. Some resources call the tag an *element*, but technically an element is everything from the start tag to the end tag and in between. Figure 7.2 shows one way to render text in bold.

In addition to marking up how things look graphically, you can also mark up the text semantically, giving different parts meaning, as in labeling some text as a paragraph (<p></p>). For many items on a page, that labeling creates the type of visual hierarchy discussed in chapter 5, a hierarchy that allows users to make meaning from a page by instantly seeing the relationships between types of content. And a page with headings, subheadings, and paragraphs separated by white space is easier to navigate than a page that is a wall of undifferentiated text. Semantic markup also makes sense for designing a web page for multiple types of devices and users. Instead of marking something as being in bold (<b></b>), you can mark it as being strong (<strong></strong>). The default presentation in a web browser will be bold for each, but the strong tag carries a meaning: this material is important. A user who is blind might set a browser to read a page, and the text-to-speech software would read that material differently. Or a developer might set that material to display in red on mobile devices. The same distinction is true for italicizing. You could mark up the text to be presented in italics (<i></i>), but it's better to mark it up semantically as emphasized text (<em></em>). If you decide later to make text tagged with <em> bolded rather than italicized, you can do that without changing the HTML tags. Table 7.1 gives you a list of many of the basic HTML elements you will likely use inside the body of your pages.

Table 7.1	Basic HTML Elements within the Body
Element	**Description**
Building blocks	
<div>	Division of the page
<p>	Paragraph
<h1> to <h6>	Headings
Lists	
<ul>	Unordered list (i.e., a bullet list)
<ol>	Ordered list (i.e., a numbered list)
<dl>	Description list
<li>	List item (a bulleted or numbered item in a list)
<dt>	Description list's term
<dd>	Description list's description
Tables	
<table>	Table
<caption>	Table caption or title, which appears by default at the top of the table
<thead>	Table header, or column label
<tfoot>	Table footer, or column summary, appearing at the bottom of the table
<tbody>	Table body; groups the content that will appear between the table headers and the table footers
<tr>	Table row
<td>	Table data; each forms a single table cell
Other	
<a>	Hyperlink; the "a" in the tag comes from the earlier term "hypertext anchor"; with the href attribute (<a href="http://www.focalpress.com"), the element becomes a typical hyperlink
<img>	Image
<em>	Information that is emphasized; its default formatting is italics
<strong>	Information that is emphasized as important; its default formatting is bold
<style>	Controls the appearance of part of the page; choose to control appearance through CSS rather than this element if at all possible

Source: From the HTML5 W3C Recommendation, October 28, 2014.

Good designers try to use semantic—or meaningful—markup rather than markup that controls presentation alone. So they opt for <em> tags rather than tags like <i> and control how the emphasized text looks in a style sheet, usually in a separate file. We'll get into that more later. For now, picture labeling your text in meaningful ways—with chunks marked up as headings, paragraphs, lists, block quotes, images, links, and emphasized text—and having a separate file control how it all looks. You might have a 500-page site but, at a whim, you could change that one style sheet file and make all the paragraphs display in Arial rather than in Times New Roman without changing anything in those 500 pages. Handy, no? This technique is a much better way to manage a big site. It also lets you include a separate style sheet for mobile devices so users can easily get to your information on their phones and tablets. Also important, it gives visually impaired users who rely on assistive technology (including screen readers that read pages aloud) an idea of what your text means. Instead of marking up a piece of text so it's presented as Arial 14-point bold, you could mark it up as a heading, and the screen reader would read it aloud as a heading!

The declaration(s) come first, and the head and body are between the HTML tags. Your basic tags for an HTML5 page will look something like Figure 7.3.

Look back at that sample of code in Figure 7.3. Notice how the head and body tags are inside the HTML tags? This is called *nesting*. Have you ever had a set of nesting dolls, the two-part hollow dolls that stack inside each other? Tags work the same way. You have to make sure the start and end tags in one pair of tags fit completely inside the start and end tags of another pair. Just like it wouldn't work if you tried to put the head of a small doll on once the bottom is already sealed in a larger doll, as you can see in Figure 7.4, your HTML won't work if you don't nest the tags

Tech Talk

Sections of an HTML Document Your HTML document is divided into three sections:

- **Declarations:** At the very top of the document, you should include at least a "doctype" declaration. This bit of code has to be exactly right for the browser to interpret the page correctly. The browser needs to know whether the code it's interpreting is HTML5 or an older version of HTML with a few now-out-of-date conventions. Also, you might include a character encoding declaration that tells the browser what character set the server uses to store and transmit your site's information. This second declaration is optional and only one of several ways to accomplish this task. You'll notice that the opening html element (<html lang= "en">) includes the language attribute (lang) that defines the human language in which a page is written, in this case English (en). This is an important piece of information to include, particularly for people using a screen reader, because it lets the screen reader know what language to read the text in.

- **Head:** Like the head on a body, to some extent it controls what the body does. Most information you put into your head is invisible to the user. This section of code is at the top of your page between the head tags (<head></head>).

- **Body:** Most of the information you place in the body is information you want the user to see or code that directly controls how and where this information shows up. This section of code is below the head and between the body tags (<body></body>).

```
1   <!DOCTYPE html>
2   <html>
3   <head>
4     <title>Appears in the browser's top and the browser's tab.</title>
5   </head>
6
7   <body>
8     <p>Here's the text that the user will see.</p>
9   </body>
10  </html>
```

Here's the text that the user will see.

FIGURE 7.3
HTML5 sample.

```
7   <body>
8     <p>This is a paragraph, and here is some <strong>bolded</strong>
      text. It will display correctly because the beginning and ending
      strong tags are both between the paragraph tags.</p>
```

This is a paragraph, and here is some **bolded** text. It will display correctly because the beginning and ending strong tags are both between the paragraph tags.

```
7   <body>
8     <p>This is a paragraph, but it <strong>may not display correctly,
      </p> and when you make similar mistakes with other tags, you could
      cause serious problems on the page.</strong>
```

This is a paragraph, but it **may not display correctly,**

and when you make similar mistakes with other tags, you could cause serious problems on the page.

FIGURE 7.4
Nesting HTML tags.

properly. HTML5 lets you leave the end tags off certain elements, but you can also include those end tags. Because older versions of HTML require them for most elements—as do many elements in HTML5—consistently using end tags is a good practice, with exceptions.

Some types of elements often deal with bigger chunks of information than others and usually begin on a new line. These are called *block-level elements*. Examples include paragraphs, lists, and list items (the separate bulleted or numbered items in a list). In contrast, *inline elements* such as strong tags often control small chunks of information and are used within a block-level element. In the example shown in Figure 7.4, the paragraph element is block level, and the strong element is inline. You can nest some block-level elements in others, and you can nest inline elements in block-level elements, but you can't nest block-level elements in inline elements (so you can't put paragraph tags between bold tags).

Let's take another look at the parts of an HTML page. While the browser knows it's looking at HTML, without the doctype declaration, it doesn't know which type of HTML. The W3C periodically issues new HTML standards, and the browser needs to know which version (doctype) is being used so it can correctly interpret and render the page. If you don't include a doctype, the browser may not render the page correctly. Once all browsers support (correctly interpret and render) HTML5, you'll be able to reliably use that simple piece of code: <!DOCTYPE html>. If you are using HTML 4.01, the code is a bit more complicated, and you may want to cut and paste it directly from a reliable source, such as the W3C. Here's an example of one option for defining an HTML 4.01 document:

```
<!DOCTYPE HTML PUBLIC "-//W3C//DTD HTML4.01//EN"
"http://www.w3.org/TR/html4/strict.dtd">
```

Unless you are working with an existing website, however, you should be able to avoid HTML 4.01. HTML5 offers new features, including new block-level elements. As we go through the structure of the HTML document, we will discuss many of the new HTML5 block-level elements, as well as ways to code HTML5 documents to be compatible with older browsers.

Now let's look at some body tags, which control what the user sees. Although the tags in Figures 7.2 to 7.4 are simple, they get more complex. There can be several parts to a tag, as with the hyperlink in Figure 7.5.

FIGURE 7.5
Anatomy of a basic tag.

```
<a href="http://www.focalpress.com">Link to Focal Press.</a>
```

Tech Talk

HTML Head Content Your web page head controls what the user sees at the top of the browser and in the tab. You have to include title tags (<title></title>); what's between them will appear as text on the tab and at the top of the browser. You might also include a link to a tiny image called a *favicon*, the little icon that appears in the browser tab next to the title. Now for the invisible head content:

■ Links to external style sheets (separate files that control how the pages look, maybe even for printing or for mobile devices)

■ Style information (if you choose to control styles within the file rather than from a separate file)

■ Metadata—information about the HTML document such as the author, language of the content, character encoding, keywords that help a search engine find your page, and so on—in meta tags (<meta></meta>)

■ Links to other external script files, such as separate files with JavaScript

■ Tags that indicate which scripts are used in the body

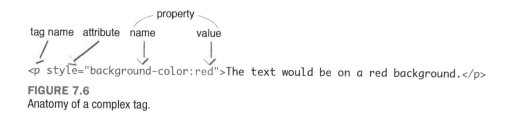

FIGURE 7.6
Anatomy of a complex tag.

HTML5 streamlines code, making it cleaner (less cluttered and more efficient) than in the past and pushing developers to control presentation in external style sheets. You will find examples of older approaches to coding as you analyze pages to see how other people made cool things work, but you are better off controlling styles externally. In older code, especially, you might see examples of more complex attributes as shown in Figure 7.6. Again, though, you are better off controlling colors and other presentation characteristics from a separate style sheet file rather than within the element.

Browsers also ignore blank lines you put between your words, as shown in Figure 7.7. If the browser doesn't see a command telling it to put extra space between the words (a nonbreaking space, coded as ** **), it won't put the space in. HTML is generally not case sensitive; even though the doctype is in uppercase, that's only by convention. Among the exceptions are special character commands, which have to be lowercase. Using lowercase is the best practice because 1) these exceptions exist, 2) lowercase is easier to read, 3) most developers use lowercase, and 4) the practice of using lowercase will prepare you to branch out into similar coding that is case sensitive.

In addition to formatting and defining elements in a web page, you can, of course, create hyperlinks—this is why we use HTML, right? You can create links to spots within your web page, to other pages in your site, and to web pages on other websites. You do this by using the anchor tag with a hypertext reference attribute (<a href></a>). For example, the code in Figure 7.5 would take you to the Focal Press website when you click on the text "Link to Focal Press."

```
 7   <body>
 8       <p>Here's a paragraph of text. It has two sentences.</p>
 9       <p>Here's a paragraph of text.
10       It has two                          sentences.</p>
11       <p>The two sentences look the same, even with the spaces.</p>
```

Here's a paragraph of text. It has two sentences.

Here's a paragraph of text. It has two sentences.

The two sentences look the same, even with the spaces.

FIGURE 7.7
Blank spaces in HTML.

Tech Talk

Special Characters Special character commands, known as character references, are great. They allow you to use symbols (a.k.a. glyphs) that are not part of the standard HTML character set, such as a copyright symbol © and quotation marks (both straight quotes and smart quotes, which are angled to show opening and closing). Displaying symbols like these requires you to use special characters, © and " in this case. Special characters always begin with an ampersand (&) and end with a semicolon. Over 2,200 special characters have names, and you can use numbers instead of names. Special character commands also can solve problems beyond adding characters that otherwise wouldn't display on a web page. Earlier, you learned that HTML treats five spaces the same way it does a single space. But what if you want five spaces between the words? The special character command   (nonbreaking space) will come to the rescue, as Figure 7.8 shows. Table 7.2 shows you a few other characters you might find useful. Many more special characters are listed in easy-to-find online resources.

```
7   <body>
8       <p>Here's a paragraph of text.     
        It has two sentences.</p>
9       <p>By the way, you need a special character to make an
        ampersand-&amp;.</p>
```

Here's a paragraph of text.   It has two sentences.

By the way, you need a special character to make an ampersand-&.

FIGURE 7.8
Special characters
in HTML.

Table 7.2 Special Characters: A Sample

Glyph	Name	Number	Description
©	&copy;	&#169;	copyright
®	&reg;	&#174;	registered trademark
™	&trade;	&#8482;	trademark
&	&amp;	&#38;	ampersand
"	&quot;	&#34;	straight quote
"	&ldquo;	&#8220;	left (opening) double quotation mark
"	&rdquo;	&#8221;	right (closing) double quotation mark
'	&lsquo;	&#8216;	left (opening) single quotation mark
'	&rsquo;	&#8217;	right (closing) single quotation mark
#	&num;	&#35;	number sign
			nonbreaking space
—	&mdash;	&#8212;	em dash
–	&ndash;	&#8211;	en dash
§	&sect;	&#167;	section

...	…	…	horizontal ellipsis
{	{	{	left curly bracket
}	}	}	right curly bracket
$	$	$	dollar sign
£	£	£	pound sign
@	@	@	commercial at
÷	÷	÷	division sign
ñ	ñ	ñ	lowercase n with tilde

Browsers

One of the challenges to designing web pages is that what looks good in one browser may not always look good in another—the browsers don't always interpret HTML and other elements the same way. And there are a number of web browsers: Firefox, Chrome, Internet Explorer, and Safari, to name a few. Not only is code sometimes interpreted differently between browsers, but different versions of the same browser may behave differently, and the same version of a browser may interpret code a bit differently when run on different platforms (Windows versus Linux versus Apple's OS X). Part of the problem is that HTML is an evolving language. The meanings of HTML tags sometimes change, new tags are added, and old tags are deprecated (made obsolete and invalid). Watch out for browsers that don't follow W3C standards. One of the most notorious is IE 6, which often requires special coding. Although it came out in 2001, there are still a small number of people using it, particularly outside the United States.

One thing most graphical browsers have in common is that they rely on plug-ins to show non-HTML-based material, such as video, Flash, Adobe Acrobat, and Microsoft Word files. Plug-ins are software that run inside your web browser and have become an integral part of the Web. When you are designing a web page, you need to be careful about relying too heavily on content that requires plug-ins. If your end user doesn't have the plug-in, the page won't work correctly. Also, consider how many people browse the Web on mobile phones and other devices, such as the Kindle. Many types of devices have browsers that may not support all plug-ins. For instance, Flash isn't currently supported by Apple on the iPhone or iPad. As we move from HTML 4.01 to HTML5, plug-ins are becoming less necessary. That said, at the time this book was written, none of the major browsers was fully HTML5 compliant.

When you develop a page, you need to make sure that users of graphical browsers will see what you want them to see, that mobile users can easily access materials—and the page isn't just a hard-to-read mini version of the one you designed for the person using a desktop computer—and that other users can access the materials too. While most of us are familiar with graphical web browsers like the ones listed in this section, some text-based browsers are still in use, including Lynx and Bobcat. And you should also think about how users with assistive technology "see" your page. We'll talk more about that later.

The Network

THE URL: YOUR ADDRESS ON THE WEB

Communicating on the Web is a bit like communicating with postal mail—assuming you had to mail off a request for information every time you wanted something. Clicking on a link is like sending a request to a company for a brochure: you have to have the right address for the company (the web address), and you have to have a return address of sorts (at least a temporary address for the company to mail the brochure to). Focal Press's web address—http://www.focalpress.com—is an example of a Uniform Resource Locator (URL). The URL includes the protocol, or the set of rules that controls how data are exchanged over a network: in this case Hypertext Transfer Protocol (HTTP). Figure 7.9 breaks down the component parts of the URL. It also includes the domain name of the server, focalpress.com, and the local host name, www (the part that says "look on the server Focal Press has named *www*"). It could include the name of a specific file as well, set off with a slash (as with http://www.focalpress.com/web.aspx), and even a list of folders the computer has to look in to find that file (the path, between slashes after the domain name—/books/film_and_video/—shows the folder structure). Browsers are not limited to just using HTTP. They can also read HTTPS, which is secure HTTP; FTP (File Transfer Protocol), which is used for uploading and downloading files; RTSP (Real-Time Streaming Protocol), which is used for streaming media; and a variety of other protocols.

The server name can be broken down as well, and we do this by reading the dot-separated domains from right to left. The last section, the .com, is a top-level domain (TLD). In this case, it indicates that the site is a commercial domain. A site ending in .gov would be a government (probably American) site. When this text was written, there were over 800 top-level domains, and the number continues to grow. In addition to indicating what type of site a page is on, a top-level domain can also indicate what country the site is located in, for example, .us (United States), .uk (United Kingdom), and .de (Germany—from Deutschland). The middle section, the .focalpress, is a subdomain, or a second-level domain, and usually refers to the name of the organization to which the site belongs. In some cases, organizations may even use third- and fourth-level domains. The front section, in this case www, is a local host name.

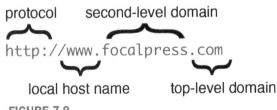

FIGURE 7.9
Anatomy of a Uniform Resource Locator (URL).

If you want to choose a cool domain name—something meaningful and easy to remember—go to a domain name registry service and search to see if the name you want is available. Once you find an available name, you can pay the fee to have that name licensed to you for the year (or prepay to have it licensed for multiple years). You'll also need a web hosting service, or space you can rent on a server that's always on. The web host will let you associate your domain name with their IP (Internet Protocol) address. Some web hosting companies provide both domain name licenses and hosting.

SERVERS AND IP ADDRESSES

For others to access a website, the files have to be on a server, or a computer that receives requests for data over the Web and then sends back the right data. If you are creating a website, you won't have any visitors until the site is published on a server (just like a budding author won't have readers until the publisher prints and distributes that best-seller-to-be).

To get the Focal Press homepage when you type in http://www.focalpress.com, the network has to send the request to the right computer, and that computer has a number. The same is true when you type in http://www.elon.edu to get to Elon University's homepage. The entire domain name is linked to an IP address, a unique numerical address that computers use to identify each other over a network. Elon's IP address is 152.33.2.72. If you type in http://152.33.2.72, you'll reach the same page you would if you typed in the easier-to-remember http://www.elon.edu.

PLANNING SITE STRUCTURE AND NAVIGATION

You have a great idea for the content of a website, but a good site depends on good organization and good file naming schemes. One of the keys to managing your website is understanding what files go where and how to name your files. In most cases you won't be building your site directly on the web server. Instead, you'll create the site on your computer and then transfer the site to the server. This method has several advantages. First, it gives you a chance to preview the site before it's available to the world on the web server. Second, it allows you to keep a backup of the website on your local system. Commercially maintained web servers keep backups, but you'll always do well to have your own copy. Computers fail; it's a fact of life. Even if the people who maintain the server keep meticulous backups, a fire or other disaster might destroy the backups, particularly if they are stored in the same building and the same area as the server.

Defining a Site and the "Root Folder"

When you are setting up your site, you'll need to set up a *root folder* on your local computer (e.g., mysite). This is the folder in which you will store the files for your website. All the files you are using for the site must be in this folder or in folders inside the root folder. Eventually, you'll need to find the information for publishing your website to the server. Again, unless you are using an older version of Expression Web (Microsoft's replacement for FrontPage), you will probably be publishing your files using FTP. You'll need to know the name of the FTP server too; this is probably, but not always, going to be the name of the web server and your root folder on the server. You'll also need your username and password. In many cases, your web root folder will be named **public_html**. This is not, however, always the case. You should always find out which folder your files should be stored in before you begin uploading them. When in doubt, check with your local systems administrator or contact your web hosting company's technical support service.

GREAT IDEAS
File Naming Conventions

How you name your files is critical. Here are some general guidelines:

The main page of your website should be called index.htm or index.html. Most web servers are set up to display a default file if the user doesn't specify one; the names index.htm and index.html are standard options. When users type in http://epa.gov, the server sends them to http://epa.gov/index.html, the EPA's default homepage. If you don't have a file with this name in your directory, the server will either give users a complete list of the files in the directory or give them an error message such as "Directory Listing Denied."

Be consistent with which file extensions you use for your web pages. A file extension is a suffix used to indicate a kind of file. Develop a religious-like devotion to .htm or .html, the two file extensions that tell the computer you have an HTML file. You can use either .htm or .html, but if you are not consistent, you risk ending up with both a project.htm and a project.html file and changing or uploading the wrong one. You can run into similar problems with naming JPEG graphic files. You're better off using the more standard .jpg instead of .jpeg.

Keep your file names lowercase. Lowercase file names tend to be easier to read. In addition, most web servers can tell the difference between uppercase and lowercase file names. Some servers are case sensitive: even if you only have a Projects.htm file, the server may not find it if the user types the URL in lowercase. Also, you don't want to get caught in the trap of having a projects.htm file and a Projects.htm file and linking the wrong one.

Don't put spaces in your file names. Most web servers will not display spaces in a file name. Instead, they will fill the space with a %20, so the file name "my projects.htm" ends up being "my%20projects.htm." Not only does this look ugly, but it also makes it difficult for users to type in a file name. If you feel compelled to put spaces in, use an underscore: "my_projects.htm."

Don't use characters that aren't a letter, number, underscore, or hyphen. Such characters may cause problems with some servers and can make it difficult for people to remember or type a file name. You should also avoid using non-English letters such as ë.

Avoid extra periods. For example, my.project.htm. Periods in file names are generally used only to separate the name from the file extension.

Many of the these guidelines apply to non-HTML files as well, including graphics and video files. Some organizations have their own naming conventions. When you are working for others, make sure you learn their naming conventions and use them.

Establishing a Hierarchy

Most websites have a hierarchy, often with three main page levels, as shown in Figure 7.10:

- Home (your default page, index.htm or index.html)
- Main pages (linked from a main menu)
- Content pages (linked from secondary navigation and from other content pages)

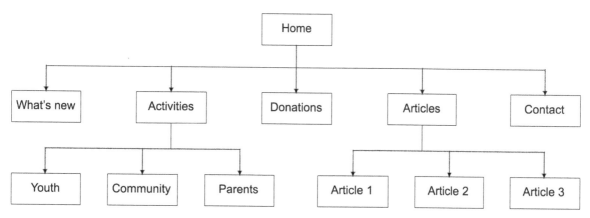

FIGURE 7.10
A hierarchical site map.

A first step in site design is deciding how many pages you need to link to in the primary navigation (or global navigation) on your homepage and whether you'll need secondary navigation (also called a submenu). Your navigation area needs to be big enough to accommodate your major links. As you plan what users will click on to reach their destinations, create a chart to figure out how pages can be reached. Try to plan your site so users can reach any page with three or fewer clicks from the homepage. Main menus usually run along the top of the page or the left-hand side of the page. Users are used to navigation being in these areas. Avoid the right and bottom for primary navigation.

Maintaining Site Uniformity and Consistency

Repeating components, particularly the navigation, should be in the same location on each page. Users get frustrated when components move. Here are two approaches to make sure each page looks about the same:

- Design your basic page as a template, and create other pages in your site only from your template. Some web development software allows you to design one page as a template—a page that controls how all the others look—and to make site-wide changes on that one page, making them ideal for larger sites.
- Design one page as index.html; copy the page, rename and save your copy, and edit it, adding a new title and new content.

PAGE DESIGN AND USABILITY

Focus on creating a user-centered design from the start (refer back to chapter 3 for more about the user-centered design process). Careful planning can prevent having to rebuild an entire site.

MARKING UP YOUR CONTENT

Every chunk of text in your page needs to be labeled semantically, or in a meaningful way. If you don't put your text between semantic tags, the browser won't put spaces between your paragraphs and headings. You may cause other problems, too. Again, some elements are block-level and others are inline.

Table 7.3	Major HTML5 Elements
Element	**Description**
<nav>	A block of navigation; can be used in more than one location on a page
<main>	The main content of a page, excluding things like navigation that repeat across the site
<article>	A "complete article, or self-contained, composition," such as an article in a periodical, a blog entry, a forum post, or a comment; this element is useful for content that might be syndicated
<header>	Introductory content for elements such as the page as a whole, navigation, articles, sections, and asides; may contain navigational aids
<section>	A distinct section, such as of an article
<footer>	A footer for elements such as articles, sections, and the like; contains information such as author and copyright data
<aside>	For "tangentially related" content that, in print material, might appear in a sidebar
<address>	The contact information for the author of a block of content (such as an article) or a page
<figure>	A self-contained piece of content, often one that illustrates something described in the text; it could be an image, video, text, or other content and can be paired with a figure caption
<figcaption>	A "caption or legend" for a figure
<audio>	A "sound or audio stream"
<video>	A video stream such as a video clip
<canvas>	Provides a "resolution-dependent bitmap canvas" for scripts to render graphics without extra software or plug-ins; among other things, it can be used to create animation on the fly, allowing users to interact with animations

Quotations are from the HTML5 W3C Recommendation, October 28, 2014.

Major Sections

In Table 7.1, we covered some of the basic HTML you will use to design a page. HTML5 allows you to go further than labeling content in generic divisions. You can and should label the parts of your page according to their functions, as you see in Table 7.3. As these elements come together, you can imagine boxes around them, as you see in Figure 7.11. They serve as places for specific types of content.

Headings

You will probably use headings throughout your website, much like a textbook uses headings. Headings give users a sense of the structure of a site at first glance, and

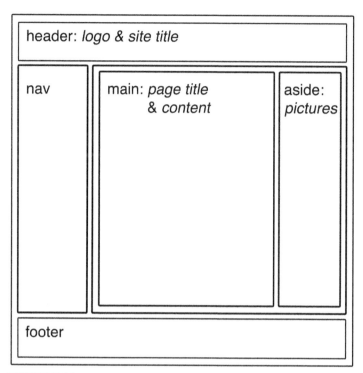

FIGURE 7.11
Elements on the page.

assistive technology allows users to review the headings on a page without wading through all the content. HTML gives you six options for heading sizes: h1 (the largest because it is the first-level heading) through h6 (the smallest). You can define how these headings look by using a style sheet, but the headings will be easy to read and tell apart even if you don't use a style sheet. Headings automatically appear with space above and below them.

Paragraphs and Block Quotes

Much of your remaining text will be paragraphs, and you may also use block quotes for indented text. Browsers will put space above and below text with these tags, too.

Lists

Another useful way to mark text is with list tags. You may choose a bulleted list (an unordered list, or <ul>) for items that don't have to go in a particular order, or a numbered list (an ordered list, or <ol>) for items that are sequential; each uses list items (<li>). Alternatively, you might use a description list (<dl>), in which each item is broken into two pieces, the description term <dt> and the description <dd>. Figure 7.12 outlines the structure of each type of list.

HTML Lists

Unordered List:	Ordered List:	Description List:

```
<ul>                    <ol>                    <dl>
   <li>item 1</li>         <li>item 1</li>         <dt>term 1</dt>
   <li>item 2</li>         <li>item 2</li>         <dd>description 1</dd>
   <li>item 3</li>         <li>item 3</li>         <dt>term 2</dt>
</ul>                   </ol>                   <dd>description 2</dd>
                                                <dt>term 3</dt>
                                                <dd>description 3</dd>
                                             </dl>
```

Rendered Lists

Unordered List:	Ordered List:	Description List:
• item 1	1. item 1	term 1
• item 2	2. item 2	definition 1
• item 3	3. item 3	term 2
		definition 2
		term 3
		definition 3

FIGURE 7.12
The three types of lists.

Creating and Managing Hyperlinks

LINKING WITHIN THE WEBSITE

A link works by using an *anchor* element (<a></a>) with a *hypertext reference* attribute (href). An anchor is a piece of code that tells the browser that the element is a link of some sort, and the hypertext reference attribute tells it where to jump to, whether that's on the same page, another file in the site, or another site altogether. The browser needs to receive instructions to make the jump, and those instructions come when you click on a link. If the instructions are to jump to a specific point on the same page, that point needs to have an element that is labeled with an id attribute (essentially, a label for a unique item on the page): a heading might be labeled <h1 id= "intro">Introduction</a>, or a piece of text might even use anchor tags without the href attribute, labeled as <a id="tip">tip for use</a>. Figure 7.13 shows you how to create a link to content on the same page and to separate pages, both within and outside your site.

To link to:

a different spot on the same page	Choose a name for that spot. Then put in an anchor. In this example, your anchor would be at the top of the page.	`<a id="top"></a>`
	Next, use the <a> element and the href attribute to set up your link. Use a hashmark (number sign) and the anchor id as the value. Think "a for anchor" and "href for hypertext reference" to remember how to write this tag.	`<a href="#top">click here to return to the top</a>`
a file in the same folder	Use a *relative URL* (listing the file location relative to the file with the link). Use the file name as your value.	`<a href="index.htm">Visit my homepage.</a>` `<a href="resume.pdf">Download my resume.</a>`
external pages	Use an *absolute URL* (listing the file location *independent* of the file with the link). Use an anchor element with a hypertext reference.	`<a href= "http://www.focalpress.com"> Focal Press</a>`

FIGURE 7.13
Linking content on the page and linking files.

Linking to other pages also uses a hypertext reference. The hypertext reference will either be a path through your files to one of your documents (a *relative URL*) or a URL from someone else's site (an *absolute URL*), which includes the protocol (e.g., HTTP).

Use a relative URL to link to files in your website. A relative URL is the name of the file and cues to show where it is in your file structure relative to the current page. With this type of URL, you can post your site in another folder on the server but still have all your internal links work. Also, if you change the folder structure, some web design applications will give you the option to automatically rename your URLs so they continue to work. If you use absolute links by mistake, your links likely won't work correctly when you upload your files, and you'll have a maintenance headache.

If you want to link to a file in a different folder, you need to indicate the *path*, or the steps the browser has to take to find the file. Figure 7.14 illustrates a sample file structure.

Let's say you have everything in a folder named My Work. When you upload your site, you'll upload the contents of My Work, but not the folder itself. For now, you're working on the site offline (not the version on the server). A few files would be in that main folder: your homepage (index.htm) and your main pages (about.htm, portfolio.htm, design.htm, and contact.htm). Notice that the site has only one index.htm file, and it's in the main folder. That folder contains other folders with simple names to organize deeper site content. If this site had images, it would probably have an images folder. Figure 7.15 shows how to structure links between some of the files shown on the right of Figure 7.14, including navigating up and down the directory structure. These navigation rules apply to your image files as well, not just HTML files.

Your site's file structure should be logical.

The example to the right has
• a **homepage** (index.html)
• three **main pages** (e.g., about.htm)
• three main folders (e.g., samples), each with one or two more files
• one **sub-folder** (grants) with files

Alternatively, you might design a site so all related files are in the same folder.

For instance, the samples folder could include the main page for portfolios, **portfolio.htm**, where you link to your shows and posters:

📁 samples
    portfolio.htm
    shows.htm
    posters.htm

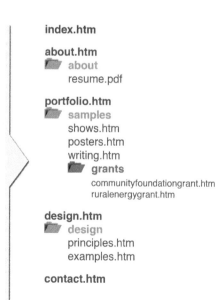

index.htm

about.htm
📁 about
    resume.pdf

portfolio.htm
📁 samples
    shows.htm
    posters.htm
    writing.htm
    📁 grants
        communityfoundationgrant.htm
        ruralenergygrant.htm

design.htm
📁 design
    principles.htm
    examples.htm

contact.htm

FIGURE 7.14
A sample file structure.

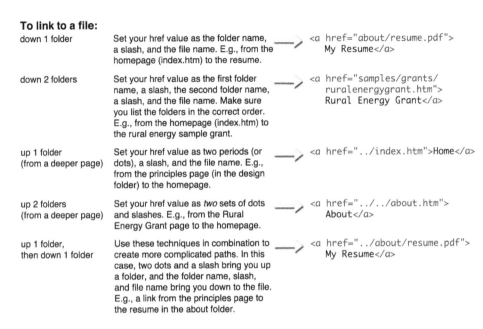

To link to a file:

down 1 folder	Set your href value as the folder name, a slash, and the file name. E.g., from the homepage (index.htm) to the resume.	`<a href="about/resume.pdf">` `My Resume</a>`

down 2 folders	Set your href value as the first folder name, a slash, the second folder name, a slash, and the file name. Make sure you list the folders in the correct order. E.g., from the homepage (index.htm) to the rural energy sample grant.	`<a href="samples/grants/`
		`ruralenergygrant.htm">`
		`Rural Energy Grant</a>`

up 1 folder (from a deeper page)	Set your href value as two periods (or dots), a slash, and the file name. E.g., from the principles page (in the design folder) to the homepage.	`<a href="../index.htm">Home</a>`
up 2 folders (from a deeper page)	Set your href value as *two* sets of dots and slashes. E.g., from the Rural Energy Grant page to the homepage.	`<a href="../../about.htm">` `About</a>`
up 1 folder, then down 1 folder	Use these techniques in combination to create more complicated paths. In this case, two dots and a slash bring you up a folder, and the folder name, slash, and file name bring you down to the file. E.g., a link from the principles page to the resume in the about folder.	`<a href="../about/resume.pdf">` `My Resume</a>`

FIGURE 7.15
Navigating directory paths in HTML.

Usually, when you click on a link that pulls up another part of the same website, the new page fills the same window or tab the old page filled. This is one cue you're still in the same site. This is the default way the browser opens links.

LINKING TO EXTERNAL SITES

Do you want to link to files (web pages, documents, audiovisuals) outside your site? If you do, you need to use an absolute URL. Instead of showing the path to the right page or file, this link provides the complete URL, like the one you see in the address window of your browser:

`<a href="http://www.focalpress.com">Visit our publisher, Focal Press.</a>`

THE NAVIGATION BAR

Links in the text are great, but you also need a navigation bar to get to the main pages and subpages. Navigation bars are often just images or styled text with links:

- **Text:** You can control the appearance of text-based buttons with a style sheet. Text links can display with background colors, change colors when you mouse over them, and so on.
- **Separate images:** Separate images can act as buttons, coded to swap out with other images when you mouse over them.
- **Image maps:** Single images can have designated hot spots, or places that trigger the browser to read URLs. These have drawbacks, though: they can be slow loading, be problematic if they don't load, and cause accessibility problems.

Navigation bars can be simple or complicated. You can use other types of code, like JavaScript, to create navigation bars, but some of these scripts slow down the browser or pose accessibility problems.

LINKING IMAGES AND ADDING IMAGE INFORMATION

The image element (<img>) allows you to tell the browser to insert an image into the web page. It's important to understand that the image is a separate file from the HTML document. As shown in Figure 7.16, there are four critical attributes that need to accompany an img element:

- src: the source, or the location and name of the image file
- width: the image's width, measured in pixels
- height: the image's height, measured in pixels
- alt: an alternative text description of the image

Although most elements have both a start and end tag, the image element is a void element, meaning it doesn't have an end tag: all its information is within one tag. Linking images is much like linking text. Instead of putting text between the start and end <a> tags, you need to refer to the image file you want to link, as in Figure 7.16.

For an image, use the img element and the src attribute (img for image, and src for source).

If you add alternative text with the alt attribute, you help users with screen readers and users whose browsers don't interpret the images correctly.

Would you prefer they see this...?

or this...?

Focal Press - Publisher of
Media & Technology books
and ebooks

```
7   <body>
8     <a href="http://www.focalpress.com">
9       <img src="images/fplogo.png"
        alt="Focal Press - Publisher of
        Media &amp; Technology books
        and ebooks"
        width="46" height="79">
10    </a>
```

FIGURE 7.16
Linking images and
using alternative text.

Tech Talk

Creating an Email Link Have you ever clicked on an email address and had your computer pull up the email client (like Outlook or Mac Mail)? It's easy to set up an email link. Start with the same structure as a text link (<a href=), but change the property: instead of using a URL, use mailto and add the email address:

```
<a href="mailto:usbkinfo@elsevier.com">
Email to order this book.</a>
```

Consider your audience before you add an email link like this. Many people don't have their email client set up because they either find it difficult to set up or are working on shared computers, as in a computer lab. Instead, they use web interfaces for email: they might go to yahoo.com and Yahoo's mail service without ever opening Outlook. For these people, it's a hassle when Outlook or another email client loads unexpectedly. If you choose to add an email link, use the email address as the linked text so 1) people can copy and paste it and 2) people don't click on a name expecting to get more information about the person. Be aware that automated software collects email addresses for spam. This software collects links typed into web pages and included in email links. As you become more advanced, look into other options for including email addresses.

Most of your users will be able to see the image just fine. Some, however, won't. Blind users have screen readers to tell them what's on the page. When these readers encounter a link like the one in Figure 7.16, they can't tell the user what the picture represents. This problem is particularly frustrating if the image is a graphic button. Even if you create a site for visual artists and expect only sighted users, some images may not be rendered because of errors. To make sure that content is still usable, add an alt attribute to your img element to describe it.

Creating Tables

Originally, HTML tables were designed to hold tabular data—and that is a great use for them. Some designers, unfortunately, use them to lay out web pages by turning off the borders and using the cells to place images, colors, and text right where they want. Don't fall into this trap. Tables are not as flexible as divs and elements like <nav>: they make your content harder to scale (harder to magnify and shrink) and your job of preparing the page for a different presentation— such as on a mobile phone—tricky, and they frustrate users who rely on assistive technologies like screen readers. (Among other things, imagine having to hear about the table as you listened to a web page being read: "Table with two columns and four rows. Welcome to . . .".) Tables are still used to hold tabular data, though, so you might use one to show a menu of upcoming yoga courses and their prices at a gym.

Tables are built row by row. Essentially, you tell the browser you want a table, and within that table you want a row, and inside that row you want a cell, another cell, and yet another cell. Then you add another row and continue. Imagine listening to a screen reader read these cells aloud as they are written in the code. You could create quite a mess for your users. So as you develop a table, make sure you build it correctly and use semantic, or meaningful, markup so assistive technology can help readers make sense of the information. Good tables include a summary attribute in the <table> tag, start with a caption, and are then built by row groups in up to three sections in this order:

- **Table caption** <caption>: This caption serves as a title for the whole table.
- **Table head** <thead>: This row group contains labels (table headers) for each column. This row group must come first.
- **Table foot** <tfoot>: This row group contains a footer. Leave it out if you don't need it. If you include it, though, place the tags right after the end tag for the head.
- **Table body** <tbody>: This row group contains the cells in the body of the table, or the table data.

Within row groups, create rows and cells:

- **Table rows** <tr>: In your table head, your row will contain the next elements, the table headers. In your table foot and table body, your rows will contain table data (normal cells).
- **Table headers** <th>: You can (and should) add a header to each column to label what comes below.
- **Table data** <td>: Your cells (other than headers) are in table data elements.

```
 8   <table border="1">
 9   <caption>Table 1. An example of an HTML table.</caption>
10     <thead>
11       <tr>
12         <th>Col. 1</th>
13         <th>Col. 2</th>
14       </tr>
15     </thead>
16     <tfoot>
17       <tr>
18         <td>col. 1 info</td>
19         <td>col. 2 info</td>
20       </tr>
21     </tfoot>
22     <tbody>
23       <tr>
24         <td>col. 1, row 1</td>
25         <td>col. 2, row 1</td>
26       </tr>
27       <tr>
28         <td>col. 1, row 2</td>
29         <td>col. 2, row 2</td>
30       </tr>
31     </tbody>
32   </table>
```

Table 1. An example of an HTML table.

Col. 1	Col. 2
col. 1, row 1	col. 2, row 1
col. 1, row 2	col. 2, row 2
col. 1 info	col. 2 info

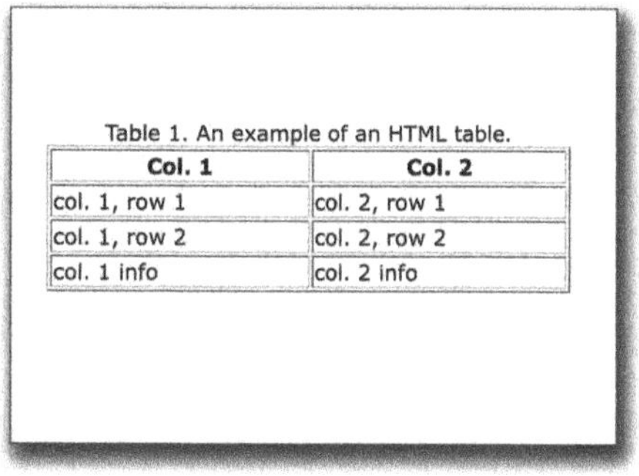

FIGURE 7.17
The structure of a table.

Let's look at a simple table in Figure 7.17. You'll notice that the width is set to 400 pixels and the border is set to 1 pixel. You can get rid of the border by setting it to 0.

CONTROLLING APPEARANCE: CASCADING STYLE SHEETS

There are four ways to control how something appears on the screen:

- **Use standard HTML tags in the body.** Choose semantic tags such as <em> and <strong>, rather than tags that only focus on presentation, such as <i> and <b>. Semantic tags will let you adjust the appearance of the tagged content elsewhere, such as in an external style sheet.
- **Use style tags in the body (inline styles).** If you want to adjust how one section of a page looks, you can use the style tag with just that section. A better practice, though, is to label that section and control it in an external style sheet.
- **Use a style tag in the head (an internal style sheet) of your page.** This tag will allow you to set font types, font sizes, margins, the appearance of headings and other text, the appearance of links, background colors, and so forth. If you are making a single-page site, this approach is okay. Otherwise, use an external style sheet.
- **Use an external style sheet (a Cascading Style Sheet).** An external style sheet is a separate file (a .css file) that you refer to in the head. The browser reads both the HTML file and the .css file, which tells the browser how the page should look.

The best option is usually an external style sheet. These are called *Cascading Style Sheets* (CSSs) because of the way the rules for styles fall into a cascade, or how one rule overrides another: if you need one page to look different from the rest, you can override the CSS by using an internal style sheet or tags in the body. Or you might even refer to a separate external style sheet on that page. Even though there is a cascade in internal and inline styles—a background color you set inline in the body will override one you set in the head—when people refer to Cascading Style Sheets, they generally mean external style sheets. If you have a large site and want to make a change to all your pages, you only need to change one piece of code in one CSS file. You might have a 100-page site, but you can change the color of all of your paragraphs with one small change to your style sheet. Much like regular HTML, most good web design tools like Dreamweaver will help you create your styles without getting too heavily into the code. Also like HTML, CSS has different versions. Although the W3C is working on CSS 3, many CSS 3 feature sets are supported by newer browsers. Among the better-supported CSS 3 features are box shadows (which let you create an adjustable shadow around a div), text shadows, and setting a minimum width for a div. Other CSS 3 features such as filters and touch screen options are not yet well supported. CSS 1 is supported by almost all browsers released in the last few years.

While being able to change the styles used on web pages across a site using an external CSS file is certainly an advantage, you can also attach multiple style sheets to an HTML page and use the media attribute to tell the browser when to use which sheet. For example, setting media="screen" when you link a style sheet to the HTML file tells the browser to use that CSS file if the page is being viewed on a screen. Setting media="print" tells the browser to use the style sheet when a page is being printed. This option is particularly helpful as it allows you to reformat the web page so it prints well, including removing advertisements and other non-essential information. CSS 3 allows you to take even firmer control by choosing a style sheet based on what size screen a page is being viewed on.

External style sheets use *selectors* to tell the browser what characteristics to apply the rule to. For instance, you might choose to make all first-level headings (<h1>s) blue. In your style sheet, you would write a bit of code (essentially a short sentence) to change all those headings at once. In that case, h1 is your selector. You can select most elements and control their appearance and sometimes behavior in CSS. In addition, if you have a special element on your page that you want to treat differently, you could create an id selector that applies only to one element on a page and format it differently. In the HTML, you'd label the code using the id attribute. Perhaps you want to control a sidebar div's position, fonts, and so on from your external style sheet (<div id="sidebar"></div>). Perhaps you want the button with the id "thispage" (the page you're on) to be a different color than all your other navigation so the site's menu can indicate what page the user is on. Or you could create a class selector that can apply to several different tags, perhaps bits of text you want to put boxes around (<p class="boxed"></p>).

When you are debating whether to use a class or id when writing your code, think about how the section will be used. If it is a section of the page that is only going to be used once per page, such as a page footer, it should be an id. Otherwise, set it up as a class. Having trouble keeping track of this? Here's a helpful mnemonic—a student may have many classes but should have only one student id card.

CHARACTERISTICS OF APPEARANCE

You have a basic structure and content. The properties that follow (using CSS) let you control the look. These characteristics can be controlled by inline styles or internal style sheets, but they are best controlled by external style sheets. Remember, separate the meaning of your content from the presentation to make the code easier to understand (somebody needs to maintain the pages), to make site-wide changes easier, and to make the content more accessible to users with disabilities.

Margins

Web page real estate is valuable. Although large margins are good on paper, most designers like to have small margins. When you set top and bottom margins, you are setting the space above and below your text and images. This space is added to the very top and bottom of your page. It is not a buffer of space, so it disappears when you scroll down. Left/right margins work in a similar way.

Define the value of your margins using the number of pixels (px) or one of several other measurement units (for instance, % for percent of the page width or height; pt for points; mm for millimeters; or em for em widths, the width of an *m* in whatever font size you use or whatever font the user's browser displays). You can define top and bottom margins, and you can also define left and right margins.

Background and Text Colors

Pay attention to your users' preferences and whether or not you need to tie in a client's color scheme. Let common sense and color theory guide your choices. Purchase a color wheel or look one up online (you don't need a precise example to make basic choices). Colors on opposite sides of the wheel, especially intense colors like bright blue and orange or red and green, will appear to vibrate if they're next to each other. Inverse text (light on dark) can strain your readers' eyes. Some combinations cause problems for colorblind users. Choose your color scheme carefully, view it on different monitors to make sure the colors look good, and use a visuals checker, such as Vischeck's free online checker, to make sure the contrast is adequate.

You can use color names for basic colors like blue and yellow. To achieve subtle variations, use hexadecimal codes for other colors (six-digit color codes, each digit using a number 0–9 or letter A–F, such as #0000FF for a common blue). These codes tell your browser how to combine red, green, and blue, giving you well over 16 million colors to choose from. Select colors from the web-safe colors—your web design application will have a palette that will let you choose from 256 colors—or select colors from the color wheel or spectrum in your design application. Most people now have browsers that do a good job of interpreting colors that are not on the web-safe list. Like other presentation characteristics, colors can be set in CSS.

Background Images If you want to use an image as your background, choose one with a small file size to shorten the page-loading time. Images online don't need to be high resolution to make your page look good. A typical resolution for web images is 72 ppi (pixels per inch). Your image will be in a separate file (usually in an images folder), and you will refer to it in the HTML. The browser will read your code and pull the image into your web page.

You control the background image with the body tag or CSS. You can use one large image as your background (which slows loading time), or you can use a small image and make it repeat, like tiles on a floor. Usually, if you use a tiled image, the image is designed to blend with the next tile so it looks like a seamless pattern.

Font Type and Style

First, keep your lines of text short (about 40 to 60 characters per line), and avoid using all capital letters: they make text hard to read. Refer to chapter 8, "Text," for more tips on designing type for on-screen display.

You've got a lot of content to fit on one page. A small font seems like a good idea, but is it really? Probably not. People generally prefer to see a larger font on screen than on paper. Also, you may have users who are aging or wear glasses. Don't make your site hard for them to read. Another thing to keep in mind is that font size is relative to the font type you choose. In a word processor, 12-point Times New Roman will have smaller letters than 12-point Arial. The same is true for web pages: some font types are larger than others.

ABSOLUTE SIZES

One way to set your font size in HTML is by using absolute values. Instead of using points (as you would in a word processor), you'll use numbers, with 1 being the smallest font and 7 being the largest. If you don't set a font size, your paragraph text will be displayed in size 3 font (16-point font).

RELATIVE SIZES

Another way to set your font size in HTML is by using relative values. To use relative values, you first need to set your base font size (reset the default font size in the page properties window). Then, you select the relative sizes 11 to 16 for larger fonts and 21 to 26 for smaller fonts. The difference in font size will always be relative to the base font size you established for the site.

Link Characteristics

How do users know what text on a web page is a link or which links they have already followed? A site is more usable if users can identify links and tell which links they have clicked on. Designers set different characteristics for links to make navigating easier using pseudo-classes, such as a:hover, which changes the properties of a link when the cursor is over the link, or a:visited, which changes the color of links to already visited pages. Although links are often to web pages or other files, you can also use them to take users to a specific part of a web page.

If you don't want your linked text to be blue and underlined, you can change how it appears, but make sure you give the user good cues that the text is linked. Create your links in a distinct color, and style them so the browser adds underlining when you move the cursor over them (*mouse over* or *hover*). You can be creative, but apply color theory (such as by choosing colors for effect and selecting color analogs for your link pseudo-classes), and be consistent with link colors throughout your site.

To control text link appearance and states (how the link appears before, during, and after the user interacts with it), use an external style sheet. In your style sheet, you can control these and other states with pseudo-classes (a selector followed by information about the element's state):

- **Unvisited:** This is how your link shows up before you click on it. It should stand out from the page. Use the selector a:link.
- **Hover:** This is how your link appears when you mouse over, or move the cursor over, the link. Use the selector a:hover.
- **Active:** This is how your link shows up when you are clicking on the link and haven't yet released the mouse button. Use the selector a:active.
- **Visited:** This is how your link shows up after you have visited that page or document. Use the selector a:visited.

Like any text, you can control all sorts of properties of your links: margins, background colors, background images, borders, text decoration (like underlining), and so on, creating text-based buttons styled in CSS. The key is setting properties for separate states. Figure 7.18 shows how you can change link colors and make the underlining appear only when you move the cursor over the links.

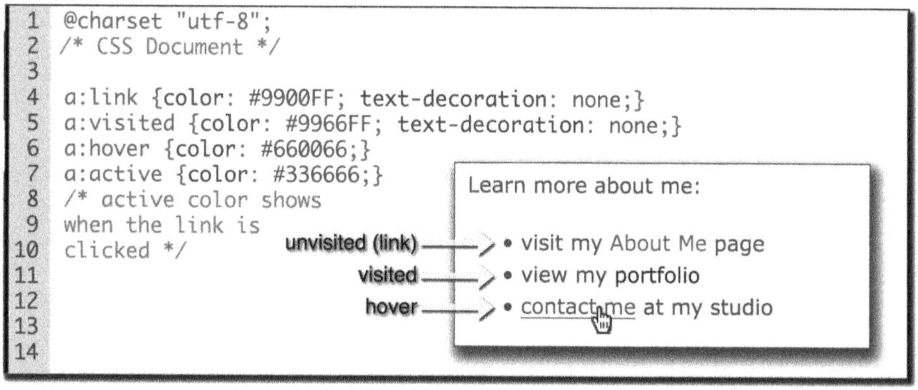

FIGURE 7.18
Controlling link pseudo-classes in CSS.

Buttons and JavaScript How about image-based buttons? How can you get the same cool effects with buttons? Like text links, you set properties for different states. For each state, your web page can use an event handler to tell the browser to swap out images when you take a particular action (for instance, swap the silver button with the blue button when the cursor touches the image). Here are two common states used in JavaScript:

- **onmouseover:** This triggers the swap when you move the cursor over the linked image that serves as the button.
- **onmouseout:** This triggers a second swap (usually to the original image) when you move the cursor off the button.

These events are usually handled with JavaScript. Not to worry, though: your web design application should be able to create the JavaScript for you.

Interactive and Multimedia Web Content

We've just skimmed the surface of HTML5 and CSS. You've probably visited sites with numerous visual effects, forms, music, videos, games, and so on. Many of these pages don't yet use HTML5 to work, but instead use an older version of HTML, often relying on JavaScript or another scripting language—essentially bits of programming code that are inserted into the HTML. If you insert interactive features such as accordions (parts of the content that expand and contract when clicked) using Dreamweaver, the editor creates them using JavaScript. JavaScript is usually used as a client-side script, meaning it runs on the user's computer. It's free, simple—at least when you compare it to full programming languages—and well supported. Some features use server-side scripting, such as PHP (Hypertext Preprocessor) or ASP (Active Server Pages). These scripting languages are processed (run) by the server and send data back and forth between the user's computer and the server. If you think you'll need a server-side scripting language, learn more about your needs and options, and choose one before you choose a host for your site: you'll have to select a hosting package that supports that language.

In HTML5, your job as a designer will be easier: some of the work of these scripting languages will be done by HTML elements, although scripting languages will still play a role. Where you once had to use scripts to make a page editable, for instance to let users make a list right on the web page, you'll be able to use the *contenteditable* tag (<contenteditable></contenteditable>). Where you once had to use a script to pop up a calendar to let someone choose a date for a form, you'll be able to use a simple input tag (e.g., <input type="date">). In other cases, HTML5 elements will pair with scripting to more easily allow users to interact with the page. The canvas element (<canvas></canvas>) is one such case and will let users draw graphs and other things on the web page. HTML5 will also allow you to more easily create drag-and-drop features. If you want to create a form for users to register with your site, you'll still need a server-side script because you'll still need to get that data back to your server; however, many design tasks will be easier to accomplish.

To include media—music and video—designers have had to rely on the embed element (<embed></embed>) with lots of extra information in additional tags and hope the user had the right plug-in. Once HTML5 is standard, you'll reliably be able to use more specific elements, such as audio and video (<audio src="mysong. ogg">my song</audio>, <video src="myvideo.ogg">my video</video>), without depending on plug-ins. You'll have to offer the right type of files, though, and HTML5 compatible browsers are not consistent in which media files they will read. You will be able to control how the video plays, the size of the display, and so forth using attributes in the video tag itself. You can set the music or video to autoplay, but you're better off letting your users decide whether and when to play media. Overall, multimedia features in HTML5 will let your coding be cleaner, let your media work well with the rest of the page, and give users with disabilities keyboard access to controls.

CHECKING YOUR CODE AND COMPATIBILITY

Along the way, check your code using a validator, or code checker. W3C has an online HTML validator (http://validator.w3.org) and CSS validator (http://jigsaw. w3.org/css-validator). These tools check to see if your code is well formed so browsers will display your page correctly. Remember that example early in the chapter when the tags weren't nested properly? Validators detect these problems and more. Some web design software has built-in tools for validating code and checking for compatibility problems, but you should also perform a separate check using the W3C tools.

As you develop your site, check it for issues such as problems with appearance (especially when you change text size in the browser), links, functionality, and page load times. If your web editor can't estimate the load time, find a friend with a slow connection and try loading your page on your friend's computer. Also check for cross-platform compatibility. Bring up your site on multiple platforms (at least PC and Mac) and browsers (at a minimum, Firefox, Chrome, Internet Explorer, and Safari). Try viewing your site on older versions of the main browsers as well. If your site doesn't work, don't put up a "best viewed on" message: that message translates as "I didn't know what I was doing, so you'll have to use another computer or other software." Fix the site. Test for color displays and font appearances. Colors and fonts that look fine on a Mac may not look fine on a PC (fonts can vary subtly from platform to platform). Colors also may change between monitors. Average users will not color correct their monitors: you can't assume that just because you're working on a color-corrected flat screen, your colors will display the same way on other flat screens.

Even if you ran usability tests at earlier stages, run another test to catch the remaining problems. You want your site to be as usable as possible.

Accessibility Issues

Accessibility was discussed throughout this chapter and in chapter 6, "User Interface Design." When you think about your audience, always remember that some of your users may have different needs because of disabilities. The most common issue you'll hear about is users with vision problems. These problems can range from colorblindness to problems reading small print to users who are completely blind and rely on a text reader to use the Web. Other disabilities you should consider are hearing loss, motor control issues (users who can't use a mouse, for instance), and cognitive problems, including, among others, problems with attention, memory, and reading. As you build your site, make sure it's usable for users with disabilities. You should ask a wide variety of questions about accessibility as you design your site. Here's a small sample of questions: Is the information in logical order? Do my links have meaningful text that could, by itself, help the user (or do they say "More")? Do I have distracting items, such as flashing images? Do video files have captions and transcripts? Would my menus be easy to use if my hand had a bit of a tremor? For more information, go to WebAIM.org, a leading accessibility site. Also visit Section508.gov.

You can make some accommodations or adjustments for disabled users' needs with small bits of code. One of the easiest accommodations you can make for users with vision problems is putting in alternative text for images, called *alt attributes* (commonly, but mistakenly, called *alt tags*). Most web design applications will give you a spot to put this information when you insert an image in your web page. Without alt attributes, all the text reader will tell the user is that there is an image on the page, not what that image is. Alt attributes are critical when you are using images to create hyperlinks or to replace text. One of the nice things about using alternative text is that it will also make life easier for users on slower connections who might have turned images off in their web browser or people who are using a mobile device. Users with motor skill problems may have to navigate using the tab key—an issue you can address by setting the "tab order" on a page.

Use tools to help you fix accessibility problems, but don't rely on tools alone. Some web design applications prompt you to add alt attributes as you use the WYSIWYG tools, and some have built-in accessibility checkers. Online tools often help you check your pages in more detail. The W3C validator will give you a line-by-line breakdown of coding problems, including accessibility issues such as the possible misuse of H1, and WAVE (http://wave.webaim.org) will give you a visual of your page and flag the problems it detects with red and yellow icons. AChecker will create an accessibility-specific report. Other checkers will allow you to identify problems for colorblind users and even emulate the type of information someone would get if using a screen reader.

Making your page accessible for any of these users will frequently increase the overall usability of the site on both computers and mobile devices. And as you learned in chapter 6, "User Interface Design," you may have a legal obligation to make your site accessible, too.

UPLOADING THE SITE TO THE SERVER

So you've finished your website and need to upload it to the web server. Did you proofread your text? Dreamweaver and other editors have built-in spell checkers, but don't rely on them to do all your work, since spell checkers will miss correctly spelled words that are still the wrong word—for instance, there and their. Take a deep breath and load your files onto the server, which you can do in a number of ways. The most common way is using File Transfer Protocol, or FTP, a protocol or set of rules for transferring files. You don't need to know much about FTP to use it: You can get standalone FTP client software, such as Cyberduck—software that allows you to transfer files this way. Most commercial web design software will have a built in FTP client that, once set up with your site and server's information, will allow you to push an upload button to update your site. Any time your computer is connected to a server, it becomes a client of that server. It doesn't matter what information the server is providing. If you are using Dreamweaver, you may see a dialog box asking if you want to "include dependent files." What it is asking is whether or not you want to publish the images and other files (e.g., audio) the web page needs to display correctly. You'll want to say yes the first time you publish a page. After that, you'll only need to say yes if you need to update those files on the server, that is, if you've added additional images or modified one of your images. Depending on the software you are using, you may need to upload audio and video files separately.

Once you've published the site, pull it up in a web browser to make sure it is where it's supposed to be. If possible, check the website on a machine other than the one you created it on to make sure your pages don't reference any files on your local computer. If you need to change something, fire up your web editor, change the file, and republish it. If you don't have the file on your computer, you can always download it from the server. Remember that you have to enter the site definition on each computer you edit on to ensure the links you create work properly later and that changes to your template are applied site wide. If you are using a public machine, be sure to clear your username and password when you finish.

CHAPTER SUMMARY

As the tools and technology for creating and uploading web pages continue to become more user friendly, remember that production software and hardware issues play a relatively small role in determining the effectiveness of a website. The best sites will always be those with good navigational structures that are functional, easy to use, and accessible to all audiences; that provide substantive, timely, and meaningful content for the user; that feature attractive designs and page layouts; and that are maintained and updated by the webmaster on a regular basis. Such a site is only possible with thoughtful research, planning, design, and authoring on the part of the webmaster or production team.

ABOUT THE AUTHORS

Susan A. Youngblood, Ph.D., teaches both graduate and undergraduate web development in Auburn University's Department of English in the Master of Technical and Professional Communication (MTPC) program. Her classes emphasize research-based best practices for design, accessibility, and usability testing. She helped plan the layout of Auburn's Instruction in Design, Evaluation, and Assessment (IDEA) lab—used mostly for teaching usability testing—and consulted on the installation of Auburn's new research-oriented usability and focus-group lab. She teaches students to be advocates not only for end users but also for their colleagues and clients who have to maintain the sites they create. Susan's research interests include competing communication needs in online environments, usability, and Web accessibility. Her work has appeared in the *Journal of Business and Technical Communication*, *Technical Communication Quarterly*, the *Journal of Usability Studies*, and the *Journal of Technical Writing and Communication*.

Norman E. Youngblood, P.D., has been teaching courses on web design and interactive media since 2001 and has a background in information technology. He is an associate professor in the School of Communication and Journalism at Auburn University and is the codirector and cofounder of the Laboratory for Usability, Communication, Interaction, and Accessibility, a research facility in Auburn University's College of Liberal Arts. His research focuses on website usability and accessibility, particularly in the fields of e-government and e-health. He has published in a variety of academic journals including *Government Information Quarterly*, the *Journal of Media and Religion*, the *Journal of Usability Studies*, *Universal Access in the Information Society*, and the *International Journal of Sport Communication*.

NOTE

1 Berners-Lee, T. (2000). *Weaving the Web: The original and ultimate destiny of the World Wide Web by its inventor*. New York, NY: HarperCollins, p. 223.

SECTION 3
Static Media

8. Text   235
9. Graphics   263
10. Photography   293

CHAPTER 8
Text

Yes, it is a press, certainly, but a press from which shall flow in inexhaustible streams the most abundant and most marvelous liquor that has ever flowed to relieve the thirst of men. Through it, God will spread His word; a spring of pure truth shall flow from it; like a new star it shall scatter the darkness of ignorance, and cause a light hithertofore unknown to shine among men.

—Attributed to Johannes Gutenberg, inventor and pioneer of the modern printing era (1398–1468)

Chapter Highlights

This chapter examines:

- The origins of typography and the modern use of electronic type
- Styles and classifications for electronic typefaces in graphic design
- Tools and techniques for managing the appearance of text
- Tools and techniques for controlling character and line spacing, text placement, and alignment
- Ideas for maximizing the readability of on-screen text in multimedia projects

AN INTRODUCTION TO TYPOGRAPHY

The element of text is one of the most important components of a multimedia experience. Text is the visual representation of intellectual thought as expressed through a human language system. Whether it's in the form of texting, hypertext, Tweeting, email, snail mail, or notes on a napkin at lunch, text plays a big role in our lives. The Age of Enlightenment was predicated on humankind's ability to share ideas and information through formally agreed-upon conventions of writing. Even in a multimedia age, we continue to rely on text as the primary means of recording, receiving, and transferring human knowledge and ideas. So what is typography? How do you make informed choices about fonts, spacing, and other typesetting and layout options? What makes Times New Roman recognizable and look different from Arial? Let's start at the beginning and get a few terms and ideas straight.

Type is a character or letterform created for the purpose of communicating written information through printing or electronic means. The term *letterform* implies

Key Terms
Ascender
Baseline
Baseline Shift
Capline
Counter
Descender
Flush Left
Font Family
Gridline
Justification
Kerning
Leading
Legibility
Letterform
Mean Line
Point
Posture
Ragged Right
Readability
Screen Font
Snapping
Text
Tracking
Typeface
Typography
Web-Safe Font
X-Height

Font Styles and Effects
All Caps
Beveled
Boldface
Condensed
Drop Shadow
Embossed
Expanded
Faux Bold/Italic
Italic
Oblique

Small Caps
Strikethrough
Stroke
Subscript
Superscript
Underlined

Typefaces
Blackletter
Decorative
Modern
Old Style
Roman
Sans Serif
Script
Serif
Slab Serif
Symbol
Transitional

FIGURE 8.1
The shape of a tree is formed by the arrangement of stylized text. Here, text is creatively used as an element of both form and content.
Source: Ahmad Faizal Yahya/ Shutterstock.com.

letters, but it also applies to other characters, such as punctuation, symbols, and numbers. *Typography* is the art of designing and arranging type (see Figure 8.1). You've heard of fonts and typeface; although some people use the terms interchangeably, they have different meanings. Typeface is about design, while font is about executing a version of that design in a particular size. The term *typeface* refers to a particular style of type, such as Times New Roman, where the entire set of alphanumeric characters and symbols—perhaps almost 200—conforms to the same design specifications, such as the height of lowercase letters in relationship to capital letters (roughly speaking, the *x-height*) and whether the characters have serifs (decorative accents added to the end of a stroke).

A typeface has a unified appearance. The term *font,* on the other hand, refers to the digital or physical means of creating or displaying that typeface in a particular style and size (though the size may be scalable). Times New Roman, for instance, is a typeface, a set of specifications that make the characters look a certain way, no matter the size or medium, but PostScript 12-point Times New Roman is a font. A collection of related fonts—all the bolds, italics, and so forth, in their varied sizes—is a *font family* (see Figure 8.2).

Movable type was first invented in Asia, but historians often credit Johannes Gutenberg and his invention of efficient movable type in about 1450 as the starting point of the modern printing era. Gutenberg, a goldsmith and inventor by trade, converted a winepress into a device capable of mass-producing pages of printed text. The Gutenberg press required the printer to manually arrange small pieces of metal type into

Times New Roman Font Family
Times New Roman Regular
Times New Roman Bold
Times New Roman Bold Italic

Helvetica Font Family
Helvetica Regular
Helvetica Light
Helvetica Light Oblique
Helvetica Bold
Helvetica Oblique
Helvetica Bold Oblique

Myriad Pro Font Family
Myriad Pro Condensed
Myriad Pro Condensed Italic
Myriad Pro Bold Condensed
Myriad Pro Bold Condensed Italics
Myriad Pro Regular
Myriad Pro Italic
Myriad Pro Semibold
Myriad Pro Semibold Italic
Myriad Pro Bold
Myriad Pro Bold Italic

FIGURE 8.2
A font family includes all the variant styles associated with a particular typeface (bold, condensed, light, italic, oblique, etc.). The "regular" style associated with a typeface is its default look or appearance without any stylistic enhancements. Many typefaces have only a regular style.

FIGURE 8.3
Prior to the invention of modern electronic typesetting methods, type had to be set by hand. It was a tedious and time-consuming process.

horizontal rows to form an inverted image of a prepress layout. Each metal block was designed with a single raised letterform on the surface. The side of the metal block containing the raised character was called the *face*, or *typeface* (see Figure 8.3). The width of the blocks varied, with skinny letters such as *l* being narrower than wide letters such as *m*, but the other dimensions were uniform. Other blocks without a raised surface were used as separators between words and sentences. When the layout was complete, the printer would apply a coating of ink to the surface of the blocks. Next, a sheet of paper was placed on top of the blocks. In the final step, the printer would apply pressure to the backside of the paper with the winepress, resulting in a transfer of the ink from the typeface to the surface of the page. As with block printing—carving the text of each page in a block—Gutenberg's process also guaranteed that each printing would result in an identical reproduction of the original page. While the process of setting the type for a single page was quite time-consuming, the actual printing of the page was very fast, especially when compared to the old-school methods of manual reproduction by human scribes or block printing.

Printing technology has evolved considerably since Gutenberg's day. Metal type has not wholly been replaced by electronic type, but most typesetting is now done digitally, and digital type is far easier to use and manipulate. With digital type, you have the option of outputting text to a printer, computer screen, or virtually any other type of electronic display. With tens of thousands of typefaces available and so many easy options for customizing text, you might think good typesetting would be a snap. But good typographic design requires knowledge and careful planning. Good design creates an aesthetically pleasing layout that communicates effectively to the user (the reader, the viewer, or the person interacting with the text). Writing involves the crafting of words, while typography applies the complex rules of design to the presentation of words on a printed page or digital screen to not only present written ideas but also set a tone or vibe, establish a visual hierarchy, and attract and maintain users' interest.

LEGIBILITY AND READABILITY

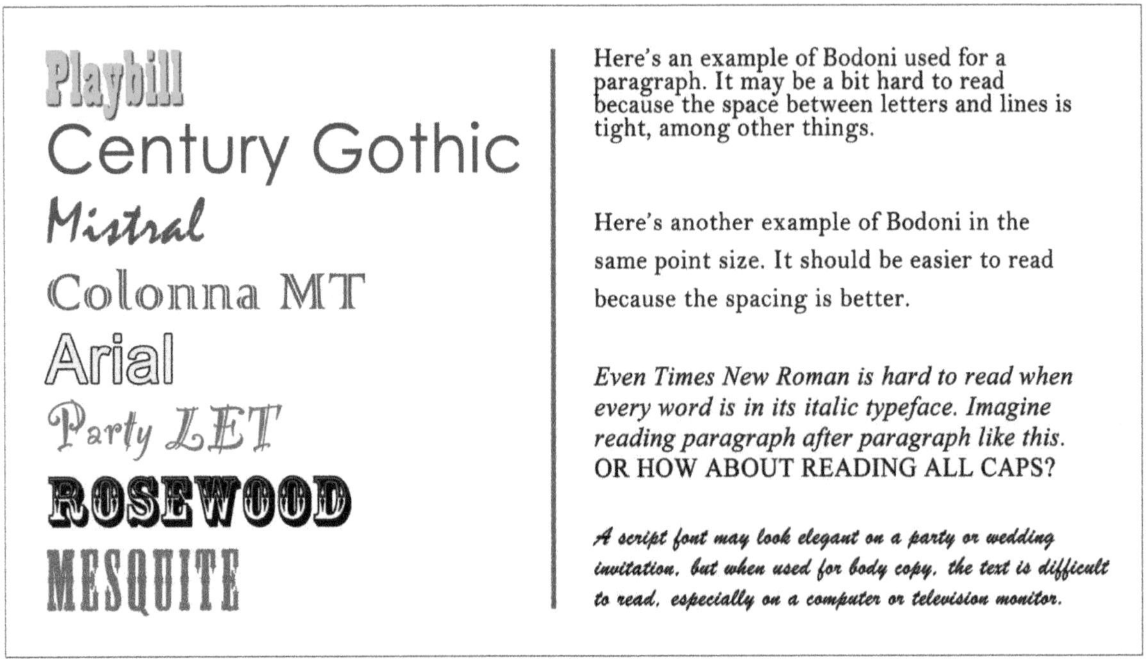

FIGURE 8.4
Legibility and readability are related. What letters or words are easiest to distinguish? Which ones are easiest to read on a digital display?
Source: Susan A. Youngblood.

Legibility and readability are related terms. *Legibility* refers to a typeface's characteristics and can change depending on font size. The more legible a typeface, the easier it is at a glance to distinguish and identify letters, numbers, and symbols. A number of factors affect legibility, such as x-height and counter size (the size of the open space either fully or partially enclosed in a letter). In Figure 8.4 (left), compare the letterforms in Playbill, Arial, Rosewood, and the other typefaces shown for legibility.

Readability refers to how easy text is to read in context, not as isolated letters, and depends on a variety of factors, including typeface characteristics such as italics, font

Playbill
Century Gothic
Mistral
Colonna MT
Arial
Party LET
ROSEWOOD
MESQUITE

Here's an example of Bodoni used for a paragraph. It may be a bit hard to read because the space between letters and lines is tight, among other things.

Here's another example of Bodoni in the same point size. It should be easier to read because the spacing is better.

Even Times New Roman is hard to read when every word is in its italic typeface. Imagine reading paragraph after paragraph like this.
OR HOW ABOUT READING ALL CAPS?

A script font may look elegant on a party or wedding invitation, but when used for body copy, the text is difficult to read, especially on a computer or television monitor.

size, style, letter spacing, line spacing, alignment, background, capitalization choices, and contrast. Legibility is a factor, of course: if characters are hard to identify, words are hard to read. Good type designs are usually invisible, meaning the reader's attention is fixed on the words and the meaning of the text, rather than on the stylistic features of individual characters. When typesetting is sloppy and ill-conceived, the readability of text diminishes. When users begin to consciously notice details of a typeface over content, readability is diminished. When users have to strain to read—and when their eyes fatigue because of typesetting choices—readability is diminished. In Figure 8.4 (right), compare the line spacing, styles, and letterforms in Bodoni, Times New Roman, and Script typefaces shown for readability.

CHARACTERISTICS THAT DEFINE TYPEFACES

Many of the traditions surrounding the design and construction of modern-day typefaces are rooted in earlier times when letters were hand drawn. Typography terms reflect type's origins, as do some typeface characteristics, especially early ones. Typographers have well over 40 terms to describe the features of individual letterforms. You may wish to study typography in the future, but the terms that follow will give you a good start.

Stroke, Contrast, and Stress

Before the days of movable type, scribes often used a broad-tipped nib pen dipped in ink to individually construct each stroke in a letterform. A *stroke* could move vertically, horizontally, diagonally, or in a curved direction. In hand lettering, the width of a stroke can vary as the angle and direction of the nib changes with the movement of the pen. This is particularly noticeable in characters with curved strokes, such as in an O, C, and Q.

The transition between the thick and thin areas of a stroke is called *contrast* (see Figure 8.5). Low-contrast typefaces have little to no variation between the thick and thin portions of a stroke. In high-contrast typefaces, the stroke transitions are more pronounced, often allowing users to read the letters more easily. *Stress* is the location or angle of a transition from thick to thin or vice versa. In vertical stress fonts, the transition occurs at the top and bottom of the vertical axis. In angled stress fonts, the transition takes place off-axis, either slightly to the left of center (left angled) or to the right of center (right angled).

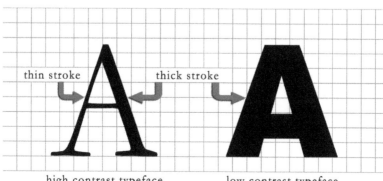

thin stroke   thick stroke

high contrast typeface
Garamond

low contrast typeface
Arial Black

FIGURE 8.5
Left: Garamond is considered a high-contrast font because of the stark difference in the width of the strokes used to form a single character. Right: Arial Black, on the other hand, has a consistent width for each stroke segment.

Weight: Regular, Boldface, and Light

Bold typefaces (also known as *boldface*) increase the width of the stroke and the visual weight of the regular roman letterform. The letterforms, serifs, and character spacing of boldface type are redesigned to accommodate the increase in stroke thickness, so letters have adequate *counterform*, or white space between and within them. *Light typefaces* are the opposite of boldface, with small stroke widths.

Posture: Roman, Oblique, and Italic

Letterforms have *postures*. In typography, the term *Roman* with an uppercase *R* refers to the inspiration of certain typefaces and to categories of typeface. The word *roman* with a lowercase *r*, however, refers to upright typefaces. Letters with other postures—oblique and italic—usually slant to the right, often by about 12 degrees. *Oblique* typefaces have letterforms based on roman counterparts. *Italic* typefaces have features that emulate handwritten forms. A true italic typeface contains visual features consistent with, but not necessarily included in, the roman version of the typeface.

Proportions and Letterform Parts

Figure 8.6 illustrates the basic characteristics of a typeface. In a row of type, the bottom edge of each character's main body rests on an imaginary plane called the *baseline*. Uppercase letters have their tops at the *capline*. Flat-topped lowercase letters have their tops at the *mean line*, and the relative size of a typeface is denoted by its *x-height*, or the distance between the mean line and the baseline, most easily measured using a lowercase *x*. The *counter* is the enclosed or partially enclosed open area in letters such as *O* and *G*. Typefaces with larger x-heights and counter sizes are often easier to read. An *ascender* is any part of a lowercase character that extends above the x-height, such as in the vertical stem of the letter *b* or *h*. A *descender* is any part of a character that extends below the baseline, such as in the bottom stroke of a *y* or *p*. Most typefaces are proportional, meaning the type width for each letterform varies, so an *l* sits close to neighboring letters, taking up less space than an *m*. Some typefaces are *monospaced*: spacing is uniform, so an *l* and *m* take up the same horizontal space. Monospaced typefaces are less readable for ordinary purposes, but they are used to illustrate code and in coding applications, such as Dreamweaver for web design, when you need to be able to distinguish each letter.

Serifs are small marks located on the ends of a main character stroke (see Figure 8.7). Serif typefaces contain serifs, while sans serif typefaces do not. Which is better for print, and which is better for electronic display? Even a few years ago,

FIGURE 8.6
The characteristics, illustrated here, not only define each typeface, but also help determine a typeface's suitability for various uses.
Source: Susan A. Youngblood.

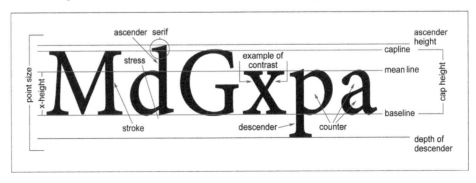

FIGURE 8.7
Serifs are decorative accents added to the end of a stroke.

experts would have said that serif typefaces were better for printed materials such as books because the serifs help with horizontal flow, or help guide readers' eyes across long lines of text. Some of this research on print readability has been called into question; at most, the difference made by serifs is small. Other research suggests that sans serif typefaces are better for electronic displays. Why? Serifs are small, so lower-resolution displays don't have enough pixels to cleanly render the serifs. Sans serif typefaces are usually better for computer monitors and video. As you make typeface choices, consider specific font characteristics that improve legibility, not just categories. Also consider what your users expect in a given context, which is often serif typefaces for print and sans serif for electronic media.

CATEGORIZING TYPEFACES

Typefaces are generally classified into two main groups depending on whether or not they contain serifs, and those groups can be divided many ways. The classification system discussed here is only one way to name and group typefaces. With so many variables, some typefaces are hard to classify. And different systems use some of the same words, such as *Gothic*, to mean different things.

Serif Typefaces

There are six main groups of serif typefaces: Blackletter, Humanist, Old Style, Transitional, Modern, and Slab Serif (see Figure 8.8, top). Serif typefaces are the industry standard for body copy that's printed in books, magazines, and newspapers. Even if new research calls into question readability differences on paper, readers are used to serif typefaces in these contexts. Digital technology can have trouble displaying serifs, so unless you're using a serif typeface designed for the digital display, such as Georgia, you're usually better off relying on serif typefaces for large headings or for print media.

FROM BLACKLETTER TO OLD STYLE TYPEFACES

When movable type was invented, typeface designers simply copied the style of written forms onto the surface of metal type. Since traditional pen-based forms were familiar to the pioneers of printing, it seemed natural to them to design movable type in the same style that had been used for centuries. After all, this is what people were visually accustomed to. Because of Gutenberg's origins, it's no surprise that the Gothic script known as *Blackletter* was the first letterform to be widely

FIGURE 8.8
Typefaces and typeface categories have evolved over the centuries. These examples are typical of their categories, but some were created later than the earliest dates listed for a given category.
Source: Susan A. Youngblood.

adapted to metal type throughout the Germanic regions of Europe. While highly decorative, Blackletter type is composed of heavy angular strokes with few curves, making it a rather bold typeface that's difficult to read in small print. The Gutenberg Bible, the first book ever mass-produced with a printing press, used Blackletter type. Gutenberg used a two-column design with forty-two lines of text per page. The typeface could be read because the font was big, but the Gutenberg Bible was quite large and heavy when finished.

As printing moved into southern Europe, the more efficient and elegant forms of Roman lettering greatly influenced the design of metal type. *Humanist* (also known as *Venetian*) typefaces were the result. Like Blackletter, they are dark on the page and have sloped crossbars in the lowercase *e*, but despite their low contrast, they were considered an improvement over their Gothic predecessor. Humanist letterforms have more rounded and gentler strokes and are much easier to read in small print than Blackletter, despite having relatively small x-heights. Many of the serifs on lowercase letters are slanted, and serifs tend to be bracketed: the serifs connect to the main stroke with a curve, providing a smooth and gentle transition from the thick to thin areas of a font. Soon after, italic typefaces were developed; they allowed printers to put more words on a line and are still used for emphasis. *Old Style* (also known as *Garalde*) typefaces are similar to Humanist typefaces but are distinguished by a somewhat more vertical stress and horizontal crossbars in the lowercase *e*. Old Style typefaces include Garamond, Bembo, and Caslon and remain popular.

TRANSITIONAL TYPEFACES

As the name implies, the design attributes of *Transitional* letterforms fall somewhere between those of Old Style and what's to come: modern-era type. Compared to Old Style type, Transitional typefaces, such as Times New Roman and Baskerville, have higher contrast, a larger x-height, vertical stress, wider bracketed serifs, and generally wider letterforms.

Times New Roman is one of the most ubiquitous and well-known typefaces in this category. After being criticized for sloppy printing and the lack of readability in their newsprint, the London-based newspaper the *Times* commissioned the Monotype Corporation in 1931 to develop a new typeface. Released a year later, Times New Roman quickly evolved into the industry standard typeface for the newspaper, magazine, and book publishing industries. Today, Times New Roman is still widely popular and is one of a handful of universal fonts that are included with nearly every computer and operating system in the world.

MODERN TYPEFACES

Modern (also known as *Didone*) typefaces represented the first noticeable departure from typography's historical dependency on pen-based letterforms. Their designs have an extremely high contrast, a small x-height, thin horizontal serifs with little to no bracketing, and vertical stress in the rounded strokes. Modern fonts are not very readable when reduced to small, lengthy sections of text. Their contemporary features make them a better choice for title text and headers.

SLAB SERIF TYPEFACES

Up until the time of the Industrial Revolution, typefaces were largely designed for setting small body type in newsprint and books. With industrialization came the increased need to promote and advertise goods and services for public consumption using large letter type. *Slab serif* (also known as *Egyptian*) typefaces were designed specifically for this type of application. Bold and eye-catching, slab serif typefaces are a good choice for posters, flyers, billboards, and other large-format media that demand immediate attention and text recognition. Slab serif typefaces have low-contrast strokes, thick horizontal serifs that can be either squared-off or slightly bracketed, and vertical stress in the rounded strokes.

Sans Serif Typefaces

Sans is a French word meaning "without," thus *sans serif* (also known as *lineal*) typefaces are those that are literally without serifs; they are sometimes also referred to as *gothic* or *grotesque* because some earlier typeface designers found them unattractive. Sans serif type was used to emboss pages for blind readers beginning in 1789 and was developed for printing for sighted readers in 1816. The popularity of sans serif typefaces boomed in the 20th century. Type designers strove to create basic letterforms, devoid of the excessive design elements of modern and slab serif type. Sans serif typefaces obviously have no serifs and usually have uniform strokes with little to no contrast and a vertical stress in rounded strokes. These typefaces are also broken into categories: *humanist* for varieties that have an angled stress, nongeometric counters, and contrast; *geometric* for varieties that have vertical stresses, geometric counters, and no contrast; and *transitional* for those in between (see Figure 8.8, bottom).

Sans serif typefaces are ideal for text headings and titles in print and for use in electronic media where lower resolution can make serifs hard to render cleanly. Because of this, sans serif fonts are often the best choice when designing body copy for the Web or other channels of electronic distribution.

FIGURE 8.9
These decorative fonts were downloaded under a freeware license from urbanfonts. com, a popular font-sharing website that provides access to thousands of free and commercial fonts.
Source: http://www. urbanfonts.com.

Decorative Typefaces

Decorative typefaces connote a sense of mood, emotion, or attitude (see Figure 8.9). They have personality, which is great for attracting attention but does little for enhancing the readability of the text in small form. Decorative typefaces are characterized by unusual features intended to add splash and pizzazz to a design. Because they're purposely designed to draw lots of attention to themselves, they should be used in moderation.

Script Typefaces

Script typefaces are among the easiest letterforms to categorize because they so clearly attempt to emulate the cursive style of handwriting or the artistic appearance of calligraphy. Script typefaces are slanted, and a stroke connects adjoining letters and preserves linear flow. Script typefaces are popular with commercial printers when they need to create a formal text design such as in a wedding invitation or certificate of achievement, when readability is less of a concern than the overall feel of the document. Because of their thin strokes and angled form, these typefaces generally have a weak appearance when rendered out to electronic displays.

Symbol Typefaces and Special Characters

There will undoubtedly come a time when you need to insert a special character or symbol that's not found on your keyboard, such as those shown in the following.

$$€ \quad å \quad ≠ \quad ± \quad é \quad © \quad ® \quad ¢ \quad Ω \quad ß$$

Many common symbols—such as currency symbols, mathematical operators, accented letters, and copyright marks—are included in the Universal Character Set established by the ISO/IEC standard 10646. Depending on which program you're using, many special characters can be added to a document by combining

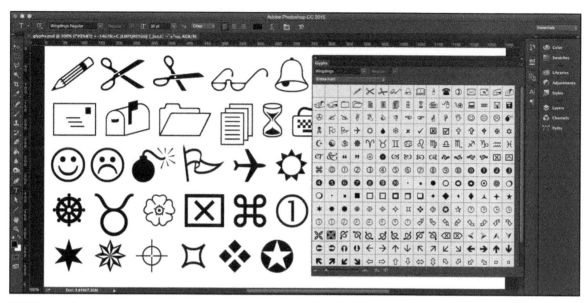

FIGURE 8.10
Many programs and operating systems include a character or keyboard map that allows you to view, select, and insert special characters into an open document. Here, the Glyphs panel in Adobe Photoshop CC is used to insert symbols from the Wingdings font family.
Source: Adobe product screenshot reprinted with permission from Adobe Systems Incorporated.

a modifier key on the keyboard with a second key or character code (or Unicode). For example, pressing OPTION+G on a Mac keyboard produces ©, the international copyright symbol. On a standard English Windows keyboard, the same character can be inserted by typing ALT+169. The advantage of this method is that the design of the inserted character matches the style of the currently active typeface. It is a part of the same font family and therefore blends seamlessly with the surrounding type. Unfortunately, the Universal Character Set does not include everything. As an alternative, you can use a dingbat (or symbol) typeface, such as Symbol, Wingding, Webdings, or Zapf Dingbats (see Figure 8.10). Symbol typefaces are popular because they include many ornamental characters not found elsewhere. However, they will not blend as naturally when mixed with another typeface.

Computers and Typefaces

The vast majority of the typefaces (and their fonts) on your computer were designed for the high-resolution medium of printing. When rendered digitally, printer fonts are often difficult to read, especially when they are small, bold, script, or italic or have thin strokes or tricky-to-display serifs. Georgia and Verdana were among the first typefaces created specifically for display on computer monitors. They have good x-heights, large counters, easily distinguished characters (for instance, uppercase *i* and lowercase *l*), and distinctive bold. In readability testing for the Web, Verdana consistently scores high marks and is one of the most popular screen fonts used for body copy on the Web.

In order for a web browser to accurately display text in a web page, all the fonts used in its design must reside on the client computer. When the browser is unable to locate a font that's specified in the HTML code, it will perform a font substitution, swapping out the intended typeface with a local one. Font substitution can significantly change the look of a page from what was originally intended. To ensure font compatibility with other systems, select a font from one of the following families: Arial, Comic Sans, Courier New, Georgia, Impact, Times New Roman, Trebuchet MS, Symbol, and Verdana. These are standard fonts that come with all Windows and Mac computer systems. They're also considered to be web safe, meaning they are supported by all the most popular web browsers.

Relying solely on safe fonts can limit your creativity. As an alternative, text can be saved as a graphic image and uploaded to the Web in JPEG or GIF format. With the typeface embedded inside the text graphic, users don't need to have the matching font installed on their local computers to view it. However, use images of text only for titles, headers, and display text: search engines do not have the ability to locate text when it's embedded in a graphic, and users with disabilities need you to provide alternative text for every image, which can be cumbersome if you have a text-heavy image. If you choose to create limited text in images, consider using an OpenType font: these fonts are scalable and cross-platform, so they'll look right if you move between a Mac and PC during your project.

Tech Talk

Category Characteristics
A typeface's characteristics help determine which category it fits in and what it is best used for.

Typeface Category	Serifs	Common Uses	Examples
Blackletter	serifs present; heavy and angular strokes; dark on the page; high contrast; angled stress; few curves	decorative or limited text inspiring an old feel, such as a newspaper textual logo	Blackletter Textura
Humanist sans serif	no serifs; angled stress	print headings and digital text; Verdana was designed for digital use	*Optima* Verdana
Humanist serif (or Old Style)	serifs are wider, bracketed, and rounded; moderate contrast; more vertical stress; small x-height; sloped crossbar in the lowercase e; open counter	still popular for printed text	**Garamond**
Transitional	serifs are wider, bracketed, slanted, and rounded; moderately high contrast; more vertical stress; larger x-height than Old Style; wider letterforms	very popular for printed text; Georgia was designed for digital text	Georgia

Typeface Category	Serifs	Common Uses	Examples
Modern	serifs are unbracketed and straight; very high contrast; vertical stress; fairly consistent width of uppercase letters	advertising headlines	Bodini 72
Slab serif	serifs are wide and squared; often dark on the page; often low-contrast; x-height can be large	advertising, such as billboards	Rockwell Courier
Transitional sans serif	no serifs; low contrast; almost vertical stress	print headings and digital text	Helvetica
Geometric	no serifs; based on geometric forms; vertical stress	advertising	Futura Century Gothic
Italic	angled but the roman form has been adapted, not just slanted		*Arial Italic*
Decorative	Letterforms have decorative touches	limited eye-catching text	CURLZ MT CHALKBOARD
Script	a subset of decorative modeled after handwriting strokes	formal invitations	Edwardian Script ITC Lucida Handwriting
Symbol	symbols often not available on the keyboard	for special characters (e.g.—language, currency, mathematical, geometric, and phonetic symbols)	Symbol Wingdings ✦♎✗Ⓨ✉℮ℊ☐✦♏ **Zapf Dingbats**

GREAT IDEAS
Adding to Your Typeface Collection

Typefaces can be added to a computer system (as fonts) in a number of different ways. An assortment of basic fonts is included with the operating system on your computer. Additional fonts are added to the system when new software is installed (word-processing applications, graphics programs, etc.). Fonts can also be obtained individually from commercial font foundries and third-party software vendors and through freeware and shareware services on the Internet (see Figure 8.11). If you have ample patience and a meticulous personality, you can even create your own fonts using software such as FontLab.

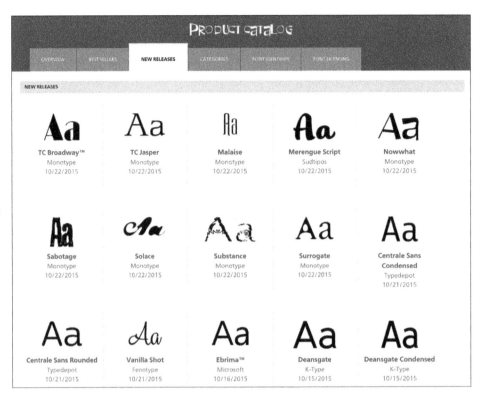

FIGURE 8.11
The fonts shown here are designed and sold by Linotype, a commercial type foundry that specializes in commercial typefaces for professional designers. Founded in 1886, Linotype designers have created a large collection of fonts including familiar ones such as Gil Sans, Helvetica, Optima, Palatino, and Papyrus.
Source: http://www. linotype.com.

FONT STYLES

Adding emphasis to keywords, headings, or phrases lets the user know there is a sense of order and importance in the way information is presented. When all the text on a page looks exactly the same, the design becomes visually flat and viewers are left to wander aimlessly through a sea of monotonous pixels. On the other hand, if you emphasize too many text elements at once, the design may appear visually cluttered and confusing. In other words, if you emphasize just about everything, you emphasize nothing. As with all things in design, moderation and balance are important. Text emphasis is most often accomplished by varying the style, size, and color of a typeface (see Figure 8.12).

True and Faux Font Styles

Font styles, or font-family variations, are used by designers to add visual variety and emphasis to text by varying the weight, angle, and width of the typeface. Most font families include the four basic styles of roman (upright), bold, italic, and bold italic. Font styles usually look better when they are *true font styles*—ones in which the designer carefully changed each glyph during design—rather than faux font styles—computer-generated effects that simulate font adaptations to create faux bold and faux italics. *Faux styles* often produce a look that's different from what the designers of the font intended (see Figure 8.13). Professional designers prefer the

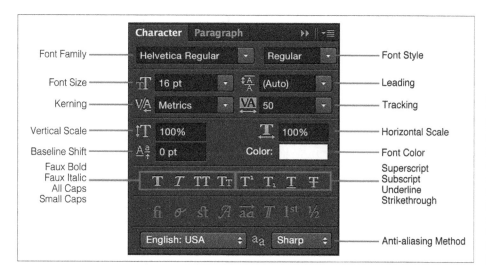

FIGURE 8.12
The Character panel in Adobe Photoshop CC can be used for modifying the appearance of selected text in a visual design.
Source: Adobe product screenshot reprinted with permission from Adobe Systems Incorporated.

Faux Bold	The quick brown fox jumps over a lazy dog.
True Bold	**The quick brown fox jumps over a lazy dog.**
Faux Italic	*The quick brown fox jumps over a lazy dog.*
True Italic	*The quick brown fox jumps over a lazy dog.*
Faux Bold Italic	***The quick brown fox jumps over a lazy dog.***
True Bold Italic	***The quick brown fox jumps over a lazy dog.***

FIGURE 8.13
The difference between true bold and italic styles and faux effects is quite dramatic when you compare them side by side.

authentic look of true font styles because the size, shape, and spacing of each letterform are custom designed to be consistent with the overall look of the typeface; they tend to avoid faux styles because they are aesthetically less pleasing than the real thing. Some typefaces have more true font styles than others.

Italics and Boldface for Emphasis

When used in moderation, changing a word or short phrase to *italics* can be a subtle, effective, and elegant way to emphasize text. Just be sure not to overdo it, and be careful about italics for digital media: they can be difficult to read. If you want to emphasize text using italics, select a font family that includes a true italic. Like italics, boldface type is used to add emphasis to selected words in body text and headings and should be used sparingly within a design. As the name implies, this typeface style is **Bold!** and will call more attention to the text than its italic counterpart. And some font families—such as Verdana and Georgia—have been designed so the counters (the open spaces in some letters) of their bold versions still appear open on digital displays. These font families also have ample weight differences between their roman and italic fonts, allowing users to pick out bold words easily. Applying a **faux bold** effect simply thickens the stroke of an existing roman form without changing a character's style or spacing, producing a proportionally smaller amount of white space in counters and between each character, making text more difficult to read. As with italics, choose a font family with a true boldface.

Condensed or Expanded Type

Some font families include typefaces in which the width and height of the type are purposely disproportional. Condensed typefaces appear tall and thin, while expanded typefaces look somewhat short and fat (see Figure 8.14). Each can be simulated by modifying the selected text with the vertical or horizontal scaling controls in the Photoshop Character palette. For normal scaling, both controls should be set to 100%. To increase or decrease the vertical or horizontal scale of type, adjust the percentages up or down in the appropriate entry field. Vertical and horizontal scaling are virtual effects that merely stretch out type. As a result, they are not nearly as pleasing to the eye as a true condensed or expanded typeface.

All Caps and Small Caps

Normal uppercase letters or *caps* (short for *capitals*) are created by holding down the shift key while typing. In the Character palette, you also have the option of formatting text in ALL CAPS or SMALL CAPS. The *all caps* option sets the selected type in uppercase so the top of capital letters touch the normal capline. The *small caps* option also sets type in uppercase, but at a reduced height that's closer to the size of lowercase letters. As a result, small caps are not as visually overwhelming as true uppercase letters. Small caps are often used by designers when it's necessary to type a string of all uppercase letters, as with certain abbreviations and acronyms (NASA versus NASA). Using small caps instead of all caps helps keep regular portions of narrative text from being unintentionally overemphasized.

The shape of a word—the letter width, counters, ascenders, and descenders—helps us read, so use uppercase letters sparingly. The brain recognizes words by their physical shape as a unit and not by the individual letters they are composed of. In other words, people do not read letters so much as they read composite shapes in the form of words and phrases. Setting type in all uppercase letters

Myriad Pro Condensed
Myriad Pro Regular
Myriad Pro - Expanded Tracking

FIGURE 8.14
Type can be condensed, expanded, scaled, and stretched to achieve a desired effect.

(even small caps) takes away distinctive features, hurting readability. Think about street signs: one labeled "Washington St." is easier to read, especially from a distance, than one labeled "WASHINGTON ST." When words are composed entirely of caps, their distinctive shape is lost and people have to work harder to discern them. As a general principle, avoid using caps to emphasize text, and also avoid mixing upper and lowercase letters together, except when called for by normal writing conventions, such as at the beginning of a sentence or a proper noun.

While designers tend to agree about the pitfalls of using all caps or mixed caps in body text, there's less conformity when it comes to the practice of using caps in titles, headings, and display text, especially when designing for multimedia. The Web in particular demands bolder, larger type to help compensate for the low resolution of electronic media, the physical distance between people and the text, and the fatiguing nature of reading off a screen instead of paper. You may be tempted to believe that bigger is better and that caps are justified. All things being equal, though, readability is best served by minimizing the use of caps. All caps also has the stigma of connoting shouting and is considered by many people to be rude and unacceptable in online communication. You be the judge. Which of the following sentences do you think is easier to read?

All caps	THE GOVERNOR IS ARRIVING TODAY AT VICTORIA STATION.
Small caps	THE GOVERNOR IS ARRIVING TODAY AT VICTORIA STATION.
Mixed caps	The Governor Is Arriving Today At Victoria Station.
Normal caps	The governor is arriving today at Victoria Station.

Underline and ~~Strikethrough~~

Underlining applies a line with the same color as the font to the baseline of selected text, while *strikethrough* adds a line through the horizontal center of type. Neither of these features provides control over stroke thickness or the placement of the line in relation to the text. Underlining text as a method of emphasis is considered taboo by design professionals: it disrupts the shape of the text by cutting through descenders. Like all caps, it makes text more difficult to read. Sometimes conventions have led designers to abandon key principles: for example, on the Web underlining text is a common and standard way of identifying hyperlinks. Readability is impaired, but usability is increased by giving people a visual cue to the clickable text on the page. However, there are many other ways to draw attention to hyperlinks without sacrificing readability. Many sites use code to hide the hyperlink underlines until a cursor moves over them. Using text graphics or visual icons is another way to avoid the unsightly underscores, but be sure to provide alternative text for users who have vision problems and may only hear text descriptions of your images.

Font Size

Digital fonts, whether used to create materials for print or for the screen, are measured in real physical units that correspond to their actual size when the text is printed on paper. But when fonts are displayed in an electronic medium, the actual size of text will vary according to the resolution (in pixels) of the monitor used to view it. You can set font size in several ways, but the point system is the most common method for measuring type. For print, it's customary to set the font size to

10–12 points for body copy. Research and experience have shown these to be good point sizes for text documents when read by most people with normal vision. But just how big is 12-point font?

To begin with, a *point* is a unit of measurement used to define the vertical height of a typeface. Originally, *point size* referred to the vertical height of the metal block with the raised letterform. Regardless of a character's shape and size, the block for each character in a typeface had the same height. An uppercase *Z*, though, naturally consumes more surface area on its metal block than does a lowercase *i*. And for both metal and digital type, point size reflects the distance from the top of the tallest ascender to the bottom of the lowest descender, plus a bit of additional space on either end. There are 12 points in a pica, and 6 picas in an inch. So there are 72 points in an inch. It's worth mentioning that for many years, computer monitors were made with a native resolution of 72 ppi (pixels per inch). Does this mean that using a 72-point font will always lead to the production of letters that are exactly one inch tall? Well, no, not really. As long as fonts are limited to display purposes only on electronic screens (as opposed to printed out), the fact that points can be converted to inches really doesn't matter. For the multimedia producer, it's much easier to think of font size in relative rather than absolute terms. The readability of an impression made by different fonts set in the same point size can vary significantly in terms of their visual weight and impact. Even though different fonts of the same point size may use virtual blocks with the same height, one's capital letters may be shorter within the block. Or another's x-height may be greater, making it seem larger. Of course, some fonts, such as Georgia, may have wider letterforms too (see Figure 8.15).

When creating text in graphics software, always be sure to save it to a layer that is editable so you can resize or revise it later. In graphics software, type is initially created as a vector object, allowing it to be scaled to virtually any size without losing detail. Text can be resized with precision by entering or selecting a discrete point size. When a graphic is saved in a bitmap file format such as JPEG, the text elements within it are permanently *rastorized*, or changed to pixels rather than lines, and can no longer be edited with the type tools or resized without resulting in a loss of image quality and detail.

FIGURE 8.15
All five lines of type pictured here were set to a 12-point font size in Adobe Illustrator. However, the printed size of each line varies because of variables associated with the design of the each typeface being used. Note: The display size of the fonts shown here was enlarged for comparison.

12-point font (Impact)

12-point font (Georgia)

12-point font (Helvetica)

12-point font (Futura Medium)

12-point font (Times New Roman)

Font Color

When selecting a font color, be sure to pick a contrasting shade that stands out from the background. Combining a dark-colored font with a dark background, or a light-colored font with a light background, leads to poor contrast and makes the text difficult to read (see Figure 8.16). Dark type on a light background is generally easier for people to read than light-colored type on a dark background. Even electronic books are normally created with black type on a white background.

When you do choose splashes of color, be careful about the combinations. Some color combinations, such as green and red, seem to vibrate, so they are hard to look at and strain users' eyes. Also, some of your users may be colorblind or have color deficiencies. There are several kinds of problems that affect seeing color, and some color combinations are poor choices. For instance, a person may perceive all red as black, so the black-on-red website marquis you planned won't work (unless you want the user to see a big black box). Whether you're working on graphical text or web text, check your color choices with a tool such as Vischeck.com's online colorblindness simulator.

Baseline Shift

When composing type in a word-processing or graphic design program, the software automatically conforms all the text in a row to a common baseline. Much of the time this works just fine. However, there are other times when the visual aesthetic can be best served by shifting the base of certain characters to a new position. This is particularly true when you attempt to combine different font families, styles, or sizes. You can shift the baseline to move text one point at a time above or below the existing baseline (see Figure 8.17).

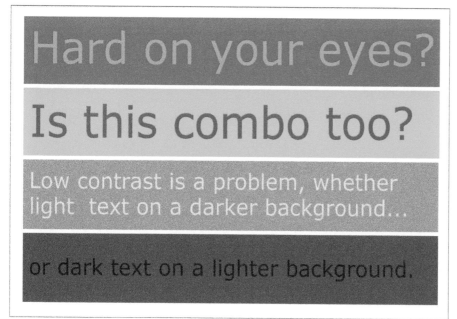

FIGURE 8.16
The degree of contrast between the font color and background color can dramatically alter the readability of the text.
Source: Susan A. Youngblood.

A normal BASELINE looks like this...

BASELINE SHIFT Looks like this...

FIGURE 8.17
Top: Typically, all type in a row of text sits uniformly on a common baseline. Bottom: Shifting the baseline is a creative choice by the designer for achieving a particular visual effect.

Superscript/Subscript

In order to accurately reflect the shorthand notation for special formulas and character symbols, it's sometimes necessary to apply subscript or superscript formatting to text. *Superscript* characters have a smaller point size than the surrounding text and are shifted upward above the baseline. Ordinal numbers are often displayed with a superscript modifier (1st, 2nd, 3rd, etc.). Other uses for superscript formatting include footnote references,[1] compass bearings (20° W), and mathematical exponents such as $10^{(2)}$ and $(a^n)^{-1}$. Subscript characters also have a smaller point size, but are shifted downward below the baseline as in H_2O, the chemical formula for water.

Anti-Aliasing

Because screen fonts are rendered out on screen using square pixels, the edges of the diagonal and curved strokes in a typeface often appear jagged. This stair-step effect is called *aliasing* and is an undesirable consequence of digital typography. *Anti-aliasing* is a technique used in raster (bitmap) editing to smooth out the edges of type. When anti-aliasing is turned on, transition pixels of an intermediate color are added between the jagged edges of a stroke and the surrounding area. The result is a distinctly smoother edge. Anti-aliasing works best on large type and is not generally recommended for font sizes smaller than 10 points because it reduces the readability of text.

Tech Talk

Font Management Font management software is used for previewing and managing the fonts on a computer system (see Figures 8.18 and 8.19). It can be used to install, remove, view, group, enable, and disable fonts. Fonts are loaded into RAM (random access memory) when your computer is first turned on. The more fonts that are installed, the more RAM your system will need to make those fonts available to running applications. Depending on how many fonts you have, your computer's performance may be improved by temporarily disabling fonts you rarely use. A disabled font remains in the system but will not appear in the fonts list of your design software. As your collection of fonts grows, managing them will become increasingly important.

FIGURE 8.18
Suitcase Fusion is a cross-platform font management program that's compatible with both Mac and Windows.

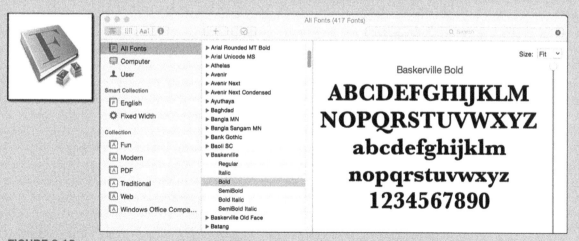

FIGURE 8.19
Font Book is Apple's proprietary font manager utility for computers running OS X. The Baskerville font family is highlighted here as one of 415 resident fonts in the fonts collection.

CHARACTER AND LINE SPACING

Kerning and Tracking

By default, computer graphics programs handle letter spacing automatically according to the built-in design characteristics of each font family. But you often can improve the appearance and readability of text by manually controlling the amount of space between characters with kerning or tracking. *Kerning* selectively varies the amount of space between a single pair of letters; *tracking* uniformly adjusts letter spacing across a range of selected text. Each can improve the appearance and readability of text by eliminating distracting white space in a text design. They can also loosen up the appearance of type, making it appear less stuffy and congested. However, you need to be careful. Increasing the distance between letters makes the text more difficult to read.

Leading

Leading (pronounced *ledding*) is used to define the amount of space between vertically adjacent lines of text (see Figure 8.20). The term originated during the days of manual typesetting when thin strips of lead of various widths were used to separate the rows of metal typeface. In digital typesetting, leading is measured in points as the distance between the baseline of one row and the baseline of the next. When

FIGURE 8.20
The amount of leading you apply between lines affects readability. Which of these blocks of text is easier to read? Which is the most difficult to read? Why?

Lorem ipsum dolor sit amet, consectetur adipiscing elit. Proin quis erat orci. Maecenas quam nisi, ultrices in lacinia blandit, condimentum lacinia enim. In tortor augue, eleifend non tristique at, molestie id lacus. Morbi a ligula sit amet purus accumsan aliquet. Integer dui nisl, condimentum in interdum vel, bibendum at dolor. Class aptent taciti sociosqu ad litora torquent per conubia nostra, per inceptos himenaeos. Proin ac libero ac dolor posuere tempor vitae non tortor. Etiam et elit massa. In ultrices urna pharetra dui cursus iaculis gravida nisi fermentum.

Lorem ipsum dolor sit amet, consectetur adipiscing elit. Proin quis erat orci. Maecenas quam nisi, ultrices in lacinia blandit, condimentum lacinia enim. In tortor augue, eleifend non tristique at, molestie id lacus. Morbi a ligula sit amet purus accumsan aliquet. Integer dui nisl, condimentum in interdum vel, bibendum at dolor. Class aptent taciti sociosqu ad litora torquent per conubia nostra, per inceptos himenaeos. Proin ac libero ac dolor posuere tempor vitae non tortor. Etiam et elit massa. In ultrices urna pharetra dui cursus iaculis gravida nisi fermentum.

Lorem ipsum dolor sit amet, consectetur

adipiscing elit. Proin quis erat orci. Maece-

nas quam nisi, ultrices in lacinia blandit,

condimentum lacinia enim. In tortor augue,

eleifend non tristique at, molestie id lacus.

Morbi a ligula sit amet purus accumsan

aliquet. Integer dui nisl, condimentum in

interdum vel, bibendum at dolor. Class

aptent taciti sociosqu ad litora torquent per

conubia nostra, per inceptos himenaeos.

Proin ac libero ac dolor posuere tempor vitae

non tortor. Etiam et elit massa. In ultrices

urna pharetra dui cursus iaculis gravida nisi

fermentum.

lines are spaced too closely together or too far apart, readers have trouble advancing their eyes to the next line, and readability diminishes. The computer-generated spacing that's assigned to type by the graphics program is not always appropriate and should never be blindly accepted. For example, large x-height fonts—such as most sans serifs—usually require additional leading. Extra leading is also needed for longer lines of text and for paragraphs set in boldface type.

ALIGNMENT, JUSTIFICATION, AND DISTRIBUTION

The terms *alignment* and *justification* refer to the process of lining up objects or text uniformly along their tops, bottoms, sides, or middles. *Distribution* involves inserting an equal amount of space between the designated edges (left, right, top, or bottom) or centers of visual elements, including text, placed along a vertical or horizontal edge. For example, you're probably accustomed to seeing menu buttons or text labels on a web page spaced evenly apart. In Western countries, where people read from left to right and from top to bottom, readability is at its best when paragraphs are left justified and the type is evenly distributed. Aligning paragraph text along the left edge produces a consistent starting point for the eye as it shifts to the beginning of each new line. The trend in both print and electronic publishing is to align body copy *flush left*, leaving the right edge of body copy unjustified, or *ragged right*. The ragged right edge allows readers to keep track of their place in the paragraph. A ragged edge should be made to look as smooth and natural as possible by controlling the location of line breaks. The technique of curving the right edge inward toward the bottom of a paragraph adds elegance to the visual flow and shape of the text.

The following paragraph alignment options should be used sparingly in digital screen layouts. A paragraph is considered *justified* when both the left and right edges are aligned (as in this paragraph). In order to achieve a consistent right edge in a fully justified paragraph, the graphics program has to increase or decrease space between the words in each line. The irregular and uneven word spacing creates distracting "rivers of white" in paragraphs; it disrupts reading and reduces white space within the page layout. *Right-aligning* text with a left-ragged edge can add variety and interest to a design. However, since readability is diminished with this technique, it is best to limit its use to short paragraphs or sentences. *Centered text* produces a symmetrical look that's visually balanced but difficult to read since both the left and right edges are ragged. Center alignment is not recommended for body copy and only sparingly with headlines and other short sections of text (see Figure 8.21).

It's never a good idea to rely upon your eye or your skill with a mouse when aligning and distributing objects—evenly spacing them out vertically or horizontally—within a layout. Alignment needs to be precise, otherwise you may end up introducing irregularities into the design that are visually distracting to the viewer. You can align precisely by using gridlines and snapping tools (see Figure 8.22). A *grid* is a matrix of evenly spaced vertical and horizontal lines that are superimposed on top of the design window. Most multimedia design and editing software includes gridlines or snapping to make it easier to keep objects and text perfectly aligned. When you use *snapping*, as you move text close to a gridline, it snaps into place.

Lorem ipsum dolor sit amet, consectetur adipiscing elit. Proin quis erat orci. Maecenas quam nisi, ultrices in lacinia blandit, condimentum lacinia enim. In tortor augue, eleifend non tristique at, molestie id lacus. Morbi a ligula sit amet purus accumsan aliquet. Integer dui nisl, condimentum in interdum vel, bibendum at dolor.

Lorem ipsum dolor sit amet, consectetur adipiscing elit. Proin quis erat orci. Maecenas quam nisi, ultrices in lacinia blandit, condimentum lacinia enim. In tortor augue, eleifend non tristique at, molestie id lacus. Morbi a ligula sit amet purus accumsan aliquet. Integer dui nisl, condimentum in interdum vel, bibendum at dolor.

1 | 2

3 | 4

Lorem ipsum dolor sit amet, consectetur adipiscing elit. Proin quis erat orci. Maecenas quam nisi, ultrices in lacinia blandit, condimentum lacinia enim. In tortor augue, eleifend non tristique at, molestie id lacus. Morbi a ligula sit amet purus accumsan aliquet. Integer dui nisl, condimentum in interdum vel, bibendum at dolor.

Lorem ipsum dolor sit amet, consectetur adipiscing elit. Proin quis erat orci. Maecenas quam nisi, ultrices in lacinia blandit, condimentum lacinia enim. In tortor augue, eleifend non tristique at, molestie id lacus. Morbi a ligula sit amet purus accumsan aliquet. Integer dui nisl, condimentum in interdum vel, bibendum at dolor.

FIGURE 8.21
1) Ragged right or left justified (most common for body copy); 2) ragged left or right justified; 3) centered text; and 4) justified left and right.

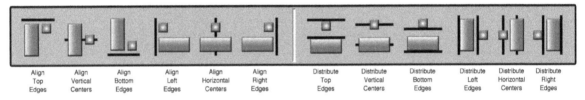

| Align Top Edges | Align Vertical Centers | Align Bottom Edges | Align Left Edges | Align Horizontal Centers | Align Right Edges | Distribute Top Edges | Distribute Vertical Centers | Distribute Bottom Edges | Distribute Left Edges | Distribute Horizontal Centers | Distribute Right Edges |

FIGURE 8.22
Most design programs have a set of alignment buttons or menu commands for aligning selected text and objects within the design space. The icons shown here will be familiar to users of Adobe Photoshop and similar design programs.

FONT TRANSFORMATIONS

You can transform type into an element of design to grab the attention of the viewer or to add interest and variety to a page layout (see Figure 8.23). Visual effects can change the appearance of the shape, fill area, and stroke of a typeface in an endless variety of fun and interesting ways (see Figures 8.24 and 8.25). Be careful, though: if the effects aren't subtle, they can be distracting. And many effects, such as drop shadows and beveling, can reduce text's readability.

The following visual effects are fairly common and can be easily applied to text by a designer using a program such as Adobe Photoshop or Illustrator.

- **Color gradients and pattern fills:** While the conventional type in body copy is usually filled with a single color, type can also be filled with a gradient of colors, a pattern texture, or an image.
- **Warping:** Warping bends and distorts a typeface. Text can be arched, inflated, squeezed, twisted, and manipulated a number of other ways to create a variety of text-based shapes.

- **Drop shadows:** Adding a drop shadow is one of the easiest things you can do to add interest and depth to text objects and backgrounds. When applied to text, a drop shadow gives the illusion that words are floating above the background. The more pronounced the drop shadow is, the greater the distance will appear between the text and the background. The perceived foreground-background position of objects in a composite can be manipulated in part by applying different drop shadow settings for each object.

- **Stroke:** A stroke is a colored outline that's placed around the exposed edges of type. Adding a stoke effect can greatly improve the contrast between text elements and the background. An *inside stroke* cuts into the fill area of type, while an *outside stroke* expands outward toward the background. A *center stroke* expands it in both directions at once. A stoke can be a solid color, a gradient color, or a pattern texture.

- **Bevel and emboss:** *Beveling* rounds off the edges of type, giving it the sculpted, graceful look of a raised letterhead, making it appear three-dimensional. *Embossing* produces the opposite effect, making type appear stamped or pressed into the background. The illusion created with these effects varies greatly depending on the settings and the color of background.

- **Inner and outer glow:** An *inner glow* applies colored shading to the inside edge of type to add internal depth or highlights to the fill area. *Outer glow* creates a halo effect around the outside of type to improve contrast and background separation.

Visual effects and styles such as these can be mixed and matched in what seems like an endless number of combinations. The potential for creativity is virtually infinite.

FIGURE 8.23
An assortment of common visual effects you can apply to text for enhancing contrast and impact.

FIGURE 8.24
Top left: Plain white text (with no font styles applied). Top right: A drop shadow is applied. Bottom left: A stroke/outline is applied. Bottom right: A two-color gradient fill and drop shadow are applied. Which version do you think has the best contrast and visual appeal?

FIGURE 8.25
A clipping mask was used in Adobe Photoshop to create this colorful font-fill effect.

SOME FINAL TIPS

Limit the Number of Typefaces

Most designers suggest limiting the number of typefaces in a design to two. While there are times when more typefaces might be justified, mixing too many typeface families in a design can make it look cluttered and unprofessional. When the need arises to combine typefaces in a design, be sure to choose ones that are totally different from one another. Rather than picking two similar serif typefaces, try combining a serif typeface with a sans serif typeface.

Text First, Type Second

While typeface can convey attitude, emotion, and personality, it's the text that communicates ideas and information. Any time the message is overshadowed by the design, communication with your audience is disrupted. Remember, the best typography is often invisible and does not seek to be the star attraction. Designing type for maximum readability should always be your first priority.

Less Is More

There's a popular adage in design circles that says, "Less is more." With such an abundance of fonts, styles, and visual effects at your disposal, you may be tempted to throw everything in the pot, wave a magic wand, and see what comes out. *Less is more* suggests that the best styles and effects are often those that are subtle or moderated. You shouldn't have to **SHOUT** to get people's attention. At the right moment, a whisper can be even more effective. So as a final cautionary note, avoid going overboard with all the tools you now have at your disposal. The *less is more* principle implies that a simple and elegant design that communicates effectively is much more valuable than a visual-effects showpiece with no apparent focus or message.

Tech Talk

Designing Text for Screen Display While the typographical principles of print are generally transferable to multimedia, you should take certain precautions when designing text for display on computer screens.

- For body copy, its best to use a 10- to 14-point sans serif typeface that's been specifically designed for use on digital displays, such as Verdana.
- Do not use a script typeface or other typefaces with thin-line strokes.
- Constrain lengthy sections of text to shorter widths. When text flows across the entire width of the screen, it is difficult to read.
- Apply anti-aliasing to large type to reduce the jagged edges of type.
- While italics work well as a subtle method of emphasizing text in print, the slanted lines and curves lose detail when rendered out as square pixels. Use them sparingly, and experiment with adding color or bold to reduce the unwanted aliasing.
- Remember the low-resolution limitations of computer monitors, and design type for maximum legibility and readability.

CHAPTER SUMMARY

Typography is one of the most important yet frequently overlooked elements in multimedia design. Whether an interactive menu or web page is usable depends on whether the design effectively communicates through text. Text should be designed for maximum legibility and readability. Adding emphasis to text elements in a layout can provide order and focus to the design and can also direct the user's attention to important visual information and cues. You can add emphasis by varying the style, size, color, and contrast of a typeface. You can also manipulate letter spacing, line spacing, alignment, and distribution to enhance the readability and visual appearance of text while bringing conformity and unity to the layout. Finally, you can also use layer styles and other types of visual effects to create unique text designs that add visual interest and energy to a page.

NOTE

1 A superscript footnote reference like the one inserted in the text corresponds to a citation or note (like this one) placed at the bottom of the page or at the end of a chapter.

CHAPTER 9
Graphics

The whole is greater than the sum of its parts.

—origins unknown (but often attributed to
Gestalt psychology, 1920s)

Chapter Highlights

This chapter examines:

- The nature of computer graphics and digital images
- The difference between raster image and vector graphic file formats
- Raster image variables such as aliasing, color depth, color space, resampling, resolution, scaling, and compression
- Display screen standards and scanning methods
- Industry standards for Digital Television (DTV) and Digital Cinema

GRAPHICS AND IMAGES

William Fetter coined the term *computer graphics* in 1960 while working as a graphic designer and art director for the Boeing Company. Today, this phrase describes processes in which pictorial data is encoded and displayed by computers and digital devices. Computer graphics are generally divided into two main categories: graphics and images.

Graphics

A *graphic* is any type of visual presentation that can be displayed on a physical surface such as a sheet of paper, wall, poster, blackboard, or computer monitor. Graphics are a product of human imagination and are typically created by hand or with computer-assisted drawing and design tools. Graphics include things like stick figures, symbols, numbers, drawings, typography, logos, web buttons, illustrations, and line art (see Figure 9.1). A graphic designer is a media arts professional who creates graphics for use in print or electronic media.

Key Terms
Additive Color
  Mixing
Aliasing
Anti-Aliasing
ATSC (Advanced
  Television Systems
  Committee)
CMYK Color Space
Color Depth
Color Space
Compression
Cropping
DTV (Digital
  Television)
DVB (Digital Video
  Broadcasting)
EDTV (Enhanced
  Definition
  Television)
Field/Frame
Frame Rate
GIF
Graphics
HDTV (High-
  Definition
  Television)
Image
Image Optimization
Interlaced Scanning
JPEG
Moving Image
Native Resolution
NTSC (National
  Television
  Standards
  Committee)
PAL (Phase
  Alternating Line)

Pixel
Pixel Count
PNG
Progressive
  Scanning
Raster Image
Refresh Rate
Resampling
Resolution
RGB Color Space
Scaling
SDTV (Standard
  Definition
  Television)
SECAM (Sequential
  Color and
  Memory)
Still Image
Subtractive Color
  Mixing
TIFF
Vector Graphic

FIGURE 9.1
This assortment of graphics includes clipart, logos, line art, and symbols.

Images

An *image* is a two- or three-dimensional representation of a person, animal, object, or scene in the natural world (see Figure 9.2). Images can be still or moving. A still or static image is one that is fixed in time. A moving image—or time-based image—is one that changes over time. Photographs, maps, charts, and graphs typically fall into the still image category. Broadcast television, digital video, and motion pictures are examples of moving images. As we'll see later in this chapter, moving images are made by presenting a sequence of still images in rapid succession to simulate motion. In reality, there are no moving images, only the optical illusion of movement created by the systematic and sequential presentation of static images.

DIGITAL IMAGING

A film camera uses a plastic strip, coated with a light-sensitive emulsion, to record a scene composed by the photographer. The film negative that's produced is real and can be handled, held up to the light, or passed along "physically" to someone else. In the digital world, everything is reduced to a number, including graphics. For example, a digital camera uses an optical image sensor to convert light into electrons (electrical energy). The electrical signal is then converted into a digital recording and saved as a binary file made up of zeros and ones. While a binary file cannot be touched or held up to the light, it is every bit as real to the computer as the film negative is to the photographer (see Figure 9.3).

FIGURE 9.2
A large collection of photographic images.

FIGURE 9.3
Left: In analog photography, the negative is used to make photographic prints. Right: Because digital images are recorded numerically as binary data, they cannot be directly touched or viewed. A digital device or computer is required to render a binary image for output to a display screen or a printer.

Two methods are commonly used to digitally encode and display computer graphics. The first approach, called *bitmap* or *raster* imaging, uses pixels to define the structure of a digital image. Tiny squares of color, like tiles in a mosaic, make up the graphic. Depending on the number of pixels, or squares, per inch, you may not even notice them in the final digital or printed graphic. The second approach, called *vector imaging*, uses mathematically constructed paths to define a graphic's visual structure. In other words, it records a graphic as a group of interrelated points, lines, curves, and shapes. Table 9.1 compares some of the differences between the two methods.

Table 9.1 Raster Images vs. Vector Graphics		
	Raster Images	**Vector Graphics**
Image structure	Defined using pixels—square picture elements each representing a single color value	Defined using paths—geometric areas defined by points, lines, curves, and shapes
Editing software	Adobe Photoshop, GIMP, Corel Painter, and Corel Paint Shop Pro	Adobe Illustrator, Adobe Flash, CorelDRAW, and Adobe FreeHand
Primary output channels	Best format for low-resolution electronic display; used in digital photography, video, and web pages	Best format for high-resolution printing and prepress applications; also used for rendering 2D or 3D computer animation
Ideal for . . .	Images with lots of color information and complexity	Simple drawings, line art, clipart, and logos
Scalability	Resolution-dependent (fixed number of pixels), which means image quality deteriorates when enlarged	Resolution-independent, which means images can be resized without losing detail or clarity
Common file formats	.bmp, .gif, .jpg, .png, and .tif	.eps, .svg, .swf, and .wmf
File size	Typically large, but raster images can be compressed to reduce file size	Relatively small as vector encoding is highly efficient

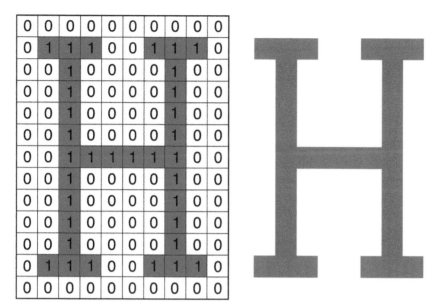

FIGURE 9.4
Thirty-four red pixels are used to produce this bitmap graphic of a capital letter *H*.

Raster Images

A raster image is formed by dividing the area of an image into a rectangular matrix of rows and columns comprised of pixels (see Figure 9.4). A *pixel*, short for *picture element*, is a square area of light representing a single point in a raster image. Every pixel in a raster image is exactly the same size and contains a single color value that's typically stored as a 24-bit string of binary data. The total number of pixels in a raster image is fixed. In order to make a raster image physically larger, more pixels have to be added to the raster matrix. Likewise, pixels need to be discarded when making a raster image smaller. The width and height of a raster image are determined by how many pixels each row and column contains.

On their own, pixels are relatively meaningless, but when combined with hundreds, thousands, and even millions of other pixels, complex patterns and photorealistic images can be formed. German psychologist Max Wertheimer (1880–1943) developed the concept of perceptual grouping to explain the human tendency to perceive whole shapes and patterns from an arrangement of smaller particles of visual information. This concept is commonly expressed as "the whole is greater than the sum of its parts." Take a look at the image in Figure 9.5 to see perceptual grouping at work.

The mosaic facade in this photograph is made up of thousands of individually colored tiles carefully arranged to form an exquisitely detailed composite image. It takes very little effort on the part of the viewer to overlook the individual pieces of glass and stone used by the artist. Instead, we're much more inclined to perceive the scene holistically, forming the impression intended by the artists' careful and

FIGURE 9.5
From a distance, the individual pixels forming this image are barely perceptible to the naked eye. In fact, our brain works hard to achieve and maintain a holistic impression. Up close, however, we can see that many small pieces of visual information went into forming this 19th-century mosaic of Christ, the good shepherd.
Source: Historien d'art (own work) [public domain], via Wikimedia Commons.

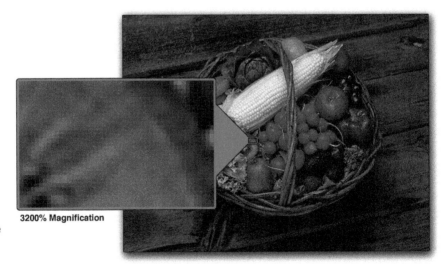

FIGURE 9.6
Digital image pixels are much smaller than the bits of tile used in mosaic art. You have to zoom in really close on this image in order to see the pixels used to form it.

purposeful arrangement. This technique of using tiny bits of colored material to form a composite visual impression dates back to about 3000 BC and is still used today in the print and electronic media industries to convey visual information. In Figure 9.6 we see a digital photograph of a fruit and vegetable basket. This image too is constructed of individual colored tiles. Millions of them, in fact! These tiny pixels can be seen by zooming in on the image using a photo-editing program such as Adobe Photoshop.

RESOLUTION

Resolution is the term most often used to describe the image quality of a raster image and refers to the size and quantity of the pixels the image contains. In the illustration in Figure 9.7, the first drawing of the triangle has only three dots, making it a low-resolution image.

As more picture elements are added, the quality of the image improves considerably, moving it along a continuum from low to high resolution.

Simply put, the more pixels you have in a given area (for example, in a square inch), the more information you have, and the higher the resolution of the image. In the example in Figure 9.8, artist Peter Roche used nearly 10,000 Jelly Belly jellybeans to form this portrait of President Ronald Reagan (left). By comparison, the official White House portrait of President Reagan (right) consists of more than four million pixels.

Jellybeans are a creative medium for artistic expression, but they are quite large compared to the pixels used to form a digital image. Because of this, the image detail in the jellybean artwork pales in comparison to the resolution of the actual photograph. The pixels in the digital photo are so small that they are undetectable with the naked eye.

FIGURE 9.7
As you move from left to right, this sequence of graphics progresses from low resolution to high resolution as more visual detail are provided. Interestingly, it only takes three dots to trick the eye into perceiving the shape of a triangle. Remember the principle of psychological closure, which was discussed in chapter 4?

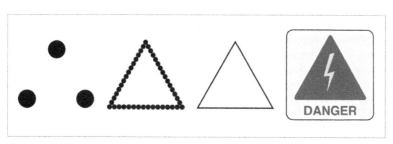

10,000 Pixels
(low resolution)

300X

4 Million Pixels
(high resolution)

1600X

FIGURE 9.8
The first portrait of President Ronald Reagan (left) was commissioned by the Jelly Belly Candy Company. It was later donated to the Ronald Reagan Presidential Library in Simi Valley, California.
Source: Courtesy of the Ronald Reagan Presidential Foundation and the Jelly Belly Candy Company; artist: Peter Roche.

Tech Talk

Color Space We refer to natural sunlight as white light because it appears to the human eye to be colorless. But if you've ever held a prism in front of a window on a sunny day, or if you've seen a rainbow, you know it's possible to separate white light into a dazzling display of various colors. As light travels through a prism, it's refracted (bent), causing the beam of white light to break apart into its component color wavelengths (see Figure 9.9).

As you learned in grade school, you can mix primary colors to get any color you want. Just add red, yellow, and blue together for any purpose, right? Not exactly. First, those colors are traditional in art, but the pigments used in printing need to be exact, and printers use somewhat different colors. Second, printing relies on a process called *subtractive color mixing*: the pigments absorb colors, so when you put all the colors together, you theoretically get black: each pigment absorbs a different range of light, so no light is reflected back to your eyes. Computer and television displays, on the other hand, emit light. White light is formed by adding all the colors of the rainbow together. In the absence of light, the image or pixels on an electronic display appear black. This process is called *additive color mixing*.

RGB Color Model (or Mode)
The primary colors of light are red, green, and blue (RGB). By adjusting the intensity of each, you can produce all the colors in the visible light spectrum (see Figure 9.10). You get white if you add all the colors equally and black by removing all color entirely from the mix. If you were to look at a monitor such as an LCD (liquid crystal display) under a microscope, you'd see that each pixel really displays only the three primary colors of light. How these colors are arranged in a pixel depends on the type of monitor, but in an LCD, they are arranged as stripes. In additive color mixing, red and green make yellow. If you fill a graphic with intense yellow in Photoshop, the pixels really display stripes of intense red and green, with no blue. The individual points of color are tiny, so our brains add the colors together into yellow. If you are designing for electronic display, you will probably create RGB images (see Figure 9.11, left).

CMYK Color Model (or Mode)
In printing, the primary colors are cyan, magenta, and yellow (CMY) (see Figure 9.11, right). You produce colors by combining pigments in paints, inks, or dyes. If you combine equal amounts of each primary color, you should get black, right? At least in theory! To help produce "pure black" (as opposed to just darkening the imprint), printers add premixed black. To print a full-color image using the CMYK process, each page goes through four presses, each inked with a primary color or black pigment. The letter *K* refers to black and comes from the term *key plate*, a black printing plate. If you are designing for print, you will likely create CMYK images. The challenge, of course, is that you'll be creating them on an RGB color monitor!

Color Depth
The term *color depth* refers to how many different shades of color a computer or device can utilize when capturing or rendering a digital image. When you capture an image with a digital camera, camcorder, or scanner, the device encodes light into electrical energy and then into bits for storage in a format the computer can process and understand. Computers reverse the process by decoding bits back into electrical energy and into light impulses that are then rendered on a digital display. The more bits you assign to each color sample or pixel, the greater its *color depth* will be. For example, in a 24-bit RGB image, 24 bits are assigned to each pixel—8 bits for the red

FIGURE 9.9
The primary and secondary colors of white light become visible when refracted by a glass prism.

FIGURE 9.10
In Adobe Photoshop, the color picker is used for selecting or creating colors. In RGB color space (shown here), the amount of red, green, and blue in a color determines its particular hue. Each of the more than 16 million colors in the 24-bit RGB color palette is identified by a unique hexadecimal color code—a six-digit combination of letters (A–F) and numbers (0–9). *Source: Adobe product screenshot reprinted with permission from Adobe Systems Incorporated.*

channel, 8 for blue, and 8 for green—producing a large color palette of roughly 16.8 million colors. Twenty-four-bit color is often referred to as *true color* because it surpasses the number of colors the human eye can effectively discern. People are limited to a palette of roughly 10 million colors (see Figure 9.12).

Some display systems can render an even higher color depth (up to 48 bits), but the 24-bit color standard is currently the most common and will give you a sufficiently large palette for multimedia applications.

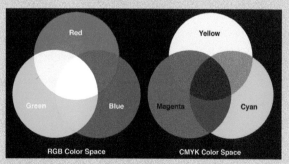

FIGURE 9.11
RGB color space is used in multimedia design (Web, animation, television, etc.), while CMYK color space is used in four-color printing.

(Continued)

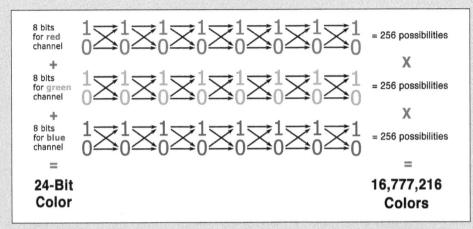

FIGURE 9.12
The possible color combinations for any pixel in an eight-bit graphic (or a 24-bit display). If you follow the arrows through every possible data combination, you'll get 256 (or 2^8) possibilities for each color channel. Combining channels—256 possibilities for red × 256 for green × 256 for blue, or 2^{24} combinations—you'd have about 16.8 million possible combinations.
Source: Susan A. Youngblood.

DEFINING THE RASTER IMAGE

Like the tiny bits of tile in a mosaic, a pixel is the smallest definable element of a raster image. Because of this, image editors rarely have to deal with discrete units of measurement like inches, centimeters, and picas. Instead, editors usually measure graphics in pixels, and pixel count and density determine the physical size and quality of an image.

Pixel Dimensions

When we talk about pixel dimensions, we're not talking about the size of an individual pixel. Instead, we use the term *pixel dimensions* to describe the size of a raster image, expressed as *the number of pixels along the x-axis (width)* by *the number of pixels along the y-axis (height)*. For example, an 800 × 600 pixel image contains 800 pixels across the image from left to right and 600 pixels across the image from top to bottom.

Pixel Count

Pixel count is the total number of pixels in a raster matrix. To determine the pixel count, multiply the horizontal and vertical pixel dimensions. The 30 × 18 pixel image in Figure 9.13 has a pixel count of 540 pixels.

Pixel Density or Resolution

We express the pixel density or display resolution of a raster image in pixels per inch (ppi)—this is pixels per linear inch (across or down), not square inch. Although

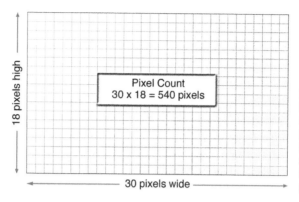

FIGURE 9.13
Pixel count is determined by multiplying the number of pixels across a digital image by the number of pixels high.

10 Megapixel Digital Camera ➡

Recording Pixels	JPEG Compression Ratio	Single Image Data Size (Approx. KB)	Number of Shots per Memory Card	
			4 GB	16 GB
L (Large) 10 M/3648x2736	◢	2565	1471	6026
	◢	1226	3017	12354
M1 (Medium 1) 6 M/2816x2112	◢	1620	2320	9503
	◢	780	4641	19007
M2 (Medium 2) 2 M/1600x1200	◢	558	6352	26010
	◢	278	12069	49420
S (Small) 0.3 M/640x480	◢	150	20116	82367
	◢	84	30174	123550

◢ = Fine Setting (Highest Quality - least amount of compression)
◢ = Normal Setting (Lowest Quality - greatest amount of compression)

FIGURE 9.14
This chart displays the resolution sizes and compression settings for the Canon G12 digital camera.
Source: Canon G12 User Guide.

each pixel in an electronic display is a fixed size, the dimensions of a pixel can vary from image to image. The more pixels you have per inch, the smaller each pixel will be.

The resolution determines the maximum size of an image you print. In order to produce a high-quality print of any size, digital photographs need a pixel density of at least 300 ppi—that's 90,000 pixels in a square inch! Generally speaking, the more pixels you have relative to the image's dimensions, the bigger the print you will be able to make without sacrificing image quality. To illustrate this point, let's consider the Canon G12 digital camera, which has an effective resolution of about 10 million pixels (total pixel count) (see Figure 9.14). With such a large-capacity image sensor, the G12 can produce a photograph with a recorded pixel count of 3,648 × 2,736 pixels. That's a lot of pixels! Dividing both pixel dimensions by 300 allows you to determine the maximum size of a photographic print that can be made from this image with good results.

3,648 pixels ÷ 300 pixels/inch = 12.16 inches
2,736 pixels ÷ 300 pixels/inch = 9.12 inches

A photographer won't always need to produce a print this large, but having lots of pixels to work with is always better than not having enough.

In multimedia work, we're much more concerned with display resolution and bandwidth than we are with print resolution. Until recently, most television and computer monitors came with a display resolution of either 72 or 96 ppi to conform to the original ppi standards as set forth by Apple/Macintosh and Microsoft/ Windows respectively. While in recent years display resolutions have gotten better, for video and the Web, 72 ppi remains the industry standard. On a 72 ppi monitor, each pixel in a 72 ppi image will be displayed by one pixel on the screen. You can go as high as 96 ppi, but anything more than this is simply a waste of file bandwidth and will do little to increase the overall quality of an image that's displayed electronically.

SCALING

Many software applications allow you to scale an image within an open document by selecting it and adjusting one of eight resizing handles along the outer edge. But raster images are *resolution dependent*, which means they contain a fixed number of pixels. Resizing (or scaling) a raster image without redefining the structure and pixel count of the array (resampling) can ruin your image.

When you resize this way, you don't change the image matrix (the image's pixel dimensions) or the amount of data stored. You only decrease or increase the size of your pixels. When you scale an image upward (make it larger), each pixel is enlarged, and you lose image detail and sharpness. The more you enlarge a raster image, the softer and fuzzier it becomes. For this reason, professionals try to avoid the enlarging of raster images (see Figure 9.15).

Downscaling a raster image (making it smaller) is done far more often—and with better results. As you shrink an image, pixels become smaller and more tightly compacted together. In some cases, downscaling an image may actually improve image clarity because the pixel density (resolution) is artificially increased. In short, upscaling almost always leads to a bad result and downscaling usually works out okay. There is, however, a better alternative for resizing a raster image (see Figure 9.16).

FIGURE 9.15
Scaling is the act of resizing a digital image to make it appear smaller or larger on screen.
Source: Sarah Beth Costello.

500 x 400

480 x 600

100 x 80

200 x 160

300 x 240

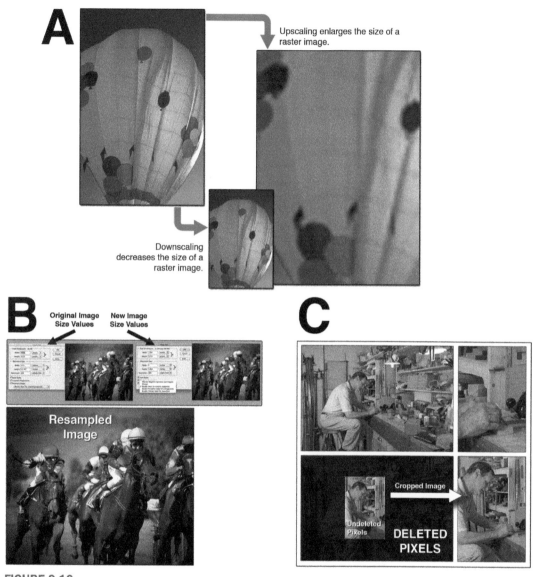

FIGURE 9.16

A) Scaling: Upscaling often results in a noticeable loss of image quality (increased blurriness). When downscaling a high-resolution image, image degradation is rarely a concern. **B) Resampling:** The original image was too big to fit on this page. I used Adobe Photoshop to resize (and resample) it to the version you see printed here. Photoshop offers you a choice of five resampling algorithms. Because this image was intended for print, I kept the resolution set to 300 ppi. If I wanted to publish it to the Web, I would have chosen 72 ppi. *Source: Neale Cousland/shutterstock.com.* **C) Cropping:** The two images on the right were achieved by cropping the original photo (top left). *Cropping* is a photo-editing technique used to delete portions of an image in order to enhance the focus of a main subject or improve composition. With cropping, pixels in the unwanted portion of the image are permanently deleted. The remaining pixels are retained with their original color values intact. A cropped image will always, by definition, be smaller than the original; however, this reduction in size is due to the deletion of image content (pixels) and not to scaling or resampling.

RESAMPLING

Resampling changes the size of a raster image by increasing or decreasing the image's pixel count. While on the surface this sounds like a simple process, you must remember that each pixel represents a single color value. If you add pixels to an already defined image, what color do you assign to them, and where do you place them? Which pixels get shifted to make room for the new ones? Likewise, if you delete pixels from an image to make it smaller, which ones get tossed and which ones get to stay? Resampling deals with these challenges by using algorithms to analyze each pixel's color information and using this data to reconstruct an entirely new raster structure. Depending on which resampling method and algorithm you use, some of the original image data may be retained, but much of it will be discarded and replaced. For this reason, you should make a backup copy of your original image before applying changes.

When you resample to enlarge an image, you still lose detail and sharpness. Given the nature of raster images, this just can't be avoided. However, resampling provides more options and typically yields better results than scaling alone.

ANTI-ALIASING

Raster images are also known for producing aliasing artifacts, the visibly jagged distortions along the edge of a line. Aliasing is a stair-step effect caused by using square pixels to define objects with curves or diagonal lines (see Figure 9.17). You can easily see the effect when looking at text on the screen of a small digital device such as a cell phone.

Anti-aliasing smoothes out the edges of jagged type by blending the color transition points, such as the pixels along the edges of a letter. The only major drawback to this is that it increases file size somewhat. In most cases, it's better to have a clean graphic and accept the slightly larger file size. Anti-aliasing typically works best on larger type as the jagged edges of the type are more visible.

1. Aliased   2. Anti-aliased

FIGURE 9.17
Left: The stair-step effect known as *aliasing* is seen in a close-up view of the letter *B*. Aliasing is most pronounced along the curved segments of a stroke. Right: An anti-aliasing algorithm is applied. Anti-aliasing softens the perceived jaggedness of a raster image by blending pixels along the edge of the stroke.

Tech Talk

Compression In an uncompressed file format, the computer records the individual value of each pixel. Examples of this include the BMP and uncompressed TIFF formats. While these formats give you access to a lot of information, graphics saved in these formats tend to be quite large. Compression can help with this. There are two basic types of compression: *lossless*, which looks for more efficient ways to store the data without losing any information—kind of like putting your sleeping bag in a stuff sack—and *lossy*, which while reducing the file size gets rid of data you might not need at the moment.

JPEG is the most common lossy format used in multimedia production. Released in 1992 by the Joint Photographic Experts Group, the JPEG standard was designed to reduce the file size of photographic images. File size was a critical issue at the time because computer hard drives were much smaller, and processor speeds weren't nearly as fast as they are today. In addition, data transfer rates were particularly slow online—a fast modem at the time was around 56 kilobytes per second. Bits and bytes were precious, and the new JPEG standard greatly improved the photo-imaging workflow. When applied to a raster image, the JPEG compression algorithm evaluates each pixel, looking for ways to "compress" redundant color information into a more efficiently written and structured data file. For example, the high-resolution photo in Figure 9.18 was taken on a clear and sunny day and contains a lot of blue pixels.

The original image size is 4,288 x 2,848 pixels, but notice how the first 100 rows of this image contain largely the same shade of blue. We can compute a rough estimate of the uncompressed file size of this sample as follows:

$$\text{Pixel Count:} 4{,}288\,\text{pixels per row} \times 100\,\text{row}$$
$$= 428{,}800\,\text{pixels}$$
$$\text{File Size:} 428{,}800\,\text{pixels} \times 24\,\text{bits}$$
$$= 10{,}291{,}200\,\text{bits (or 1.3 megabytes)}$$

Saved in an uncompressed TIFF format, this tiny section of blue sky takes up nearly 1.3 MBs of storage space. Using JPEG compression, the same picture information can be rewritten to a new data file that's 68 KB or less.

In photography, you can control the amount of JPEG compression both when you take the photo and later when you work within an image-editing program. For example, most digital cameras provide at least three JPEG quality settings: normal (greatest amount of compression, smallest file size, poorest image quality); fine; and superfine (least amount of compression, largest file size, best image quality). Photoshop, one of the most popular professional image-editing programs, offers 12 preset levels of JPEG compression (see Figure 9.19 and Figure 9.20).

FIGURE 9.18
This high-resolution photograph contains lots of redundant color information (blue sky and golden wheat), making it a great candidate for JPEG compression.

(Continued)

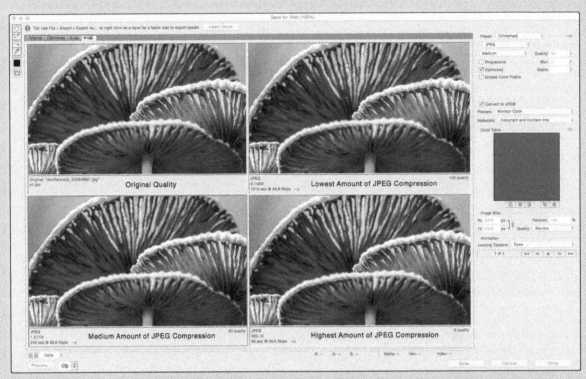

FIGURE 9.19
The Save for Web and Devices feature in legacy versions of Adobe Photoshop allows you to compare the effect of different amounts of JPEG compression on file size and image quality. Notice how file size and quality decreases as the amount of compression steadily increases.

FIGURE 9.20
Another example of JPEG compression at work.

| JPEG Quality: 0% | JPEG Quality: 50% | JPEG Quality: 100% |
| File Size 16 KB | File Size 41 KB | File Size 238 KB |

It's possible to overcompress an image to the point where its visual integrity is noticeably compromised. The resulting imperfections are called compression artifacts. Image optimization tools such as the Save for Web & Devices feature in Photoshop provide a handy way to test and compare compression settings before applying them. Image optimization is critically important for images on the Web because file size is directly related to bandwidth. The smaller the image file, the less time it takes to download from the Internet and render on screen. The goal of image optimization is to create the best-looking image possible, with the smallest file size and no compression artifacts.

RASTER IMAGE FORMATS

When you create and work with raster images, you have many options for saving your files. As you work with a file, you should save it in a format that supports layers, probably as a PSD or TIFF with layers, so you can change it in the future or resave the image in a new format for another purpose. But when you prepare a raster image to incorporate into a multimedia project, you'll need a flattened, compressed image. Selecting the right format for your project is important: you need a good-looking image that takes up as little space as possible. Don't fall into the habit of editing JPEGs. Remember, it's a lossy format. Each time you save it, you lose information. Whenever possible, you should work in an uncompressed or lossless format. Always keep a backup copy. You never know when you might need to reedit the graphic.

When you select the file format and quality settings—how much to compress the image—consider whether the format is lossy (loses information during compression) or lossless. Also consider the nature of your image. Does it have many color variations that need to be captured, such as a photograph? Is it mostly lines and blocks of uniform color? Do you need transparent pixels because you plan to float the image over other elements of a website? You have more than 50 formats to choose from, but here are three of the most common formats used for still images in multimedia:

- **GIF** offers 256 colors and transparency (transparent pixels) and is a lossless compression format. It is common for logos and other images with lines and solid blocks of color. It supports interlacing, so every odd line of pixels loads, then every even line loads, making graphics seem to appear faster (users see the full-sized, half-loaded graphic before the rest of the pixels appear).
- **JPEG** offers 16.8 million colors but does not support transparency (has no transparent pixels). It is a lossy compression format and is used most often for photographs. This format does not support interlacing.
- **PNG** offers 16.8 million colors and transparency, but you can choose to use fewer colors to save file space (PNG 8, or PNG with eight-bit color). It is a lossless compression format and is common for a wide range of images, including *favicons* (the small web page icons in browser tabs). Some older web browsers don't support it (Internet Explorer prior to version 4); such browsers have mostly, but not completely, fallen out of use. PNG files can be very small, but for photographs with many colors, they may be larger than comparable JPEGs. This format supports interlacing.

Another option you have with both the GIF and PNG formats is *dithering*, or scattering the pixels to achieve blending without using as many colors. Dithering is useful if you have an image with a drop shadow and want to superimpose it cleanly on a background.

Vector Graphics

Vector imaging defines the area of a picture using *paths* made up of points, lines, curves and shapes. Each vector path forms the outline of a geometric region containing color information. Because paths can be mathematically resized, vector graphics can be scaled up or down without losing any picture clarity. Clipart and typefaces (fonts) are often created and stored as vector graphics because designers want the ability to scale them to any size (see Figure 9.21).

The concept behind vector graphics is like painting with numbers. A paint-by-number set normally includes a black-and-white line drawing and a set of numbered paints. The artist fills in each numbered region with the appropriate color, carefully staying within the bordered outline of each defined area. When all the regions are filled with color, the picture is complete. As with raster images, the phenomenon of perceptual grouping leads us to ignore the individual paths used to form the holistic impression (see Figure 9.22).

FIGURE 9.21
Vector graphics have crisp edges with no aliasing. They can be resized up or down to any size without negative consequences.

FIGURE 9.22
To complete a paint-by-number piece like this one, each numbered region must be filled in with a single color. In similar fashion, vector graphics are rendered geometrically using paths defined by points, lines, curves, and shapes.
Source: Courtesy of Pam Snow, Mesa, Arizona.

Vector graphics can render curves and diagonal lines that are crisp, smooth, and sharp. Aliasing is not a problem because pixels are not used in their construction. So vector graphics are an ideal choice for prepress applications requiring higher-resolution pictures with finer line detail.

When you enlarge a raster image, the file size grows in proportion to the size of the image: as you add pixels to the array, you need more data to represent the image. Because vector encoding uses mathematical equations to record visual information, the size of a vector data file stays consistent, regardless of how large or small you make the graphic. If you are creating a still graphic, you can enlarge the graphic to any size you want and then rasterize it, saving it to whichever file format suits your purpose best.

You could also use vector graphics to create an animation, such as with Flash. Instead of drawing every separate frame of your project—with 24 frames appearing each second—you could create two different graphics for a segment and let your animation software mathematically interpolate the positions of the components in the in-between frames (a technique known as *tweening*).

DISPLAY SCREEN STANDARDS

Television and computer monitors, tablets, and smartphones (basically any digital device with a visual display screen) have a fixed number of pixels (see Figure 9.23). We call its fixed pixel dimensions its *native resolution*. When a computer monitor is set to its native resolution, images displayed on screen are said to be *pixel perfect* because the actual number of pixels in the image source matches the number of pixels used to render it on screen. People who are visually impaired or have reduced vision may choose to magnify images on screen by either zooming in using the application software or by changing the display settings of the monitor to a lower resolution. While doing so enlarges images, making them easier to see, there is a tradeoff. The quality of images deteriorates as you move further and further away from the native resolution of the monitor. The reason for this is that the computer has to recreate the image on screen using more pixels than were in the original source. Through a process called interpolation, the computer mathematically generates new values for each pixel in the magnified image, as it is scaled up to fill a larger region of pixel real estate. This process, and its consequences, are similar to the concept of resampling, which was covered earlier in the chapter in Figure 9.16.

2016

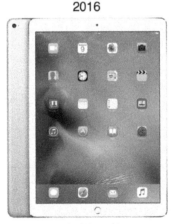

2011

2014

2011

Apple iPad 2
9.7-inch display
1024 x 768 pixels
132 ppi

Apple iPad Pro
12.9-inch display
2732 x 2048 pixels
264 ppi

Apple iPhone 4
3.5-inch display
960 x 640 pixels
326 ppi

Apple iPhone 6
4.7-inch display
1334 x 750 pixels
326 ppi

FIGURE 9.23
A comparison of display screen sizes and resolutions for Apple tablets and smartphones over time.

Manufacturers are constantly striving to increase the number of pixels in digital screens while simultaneously squeezing them into smaller physical spaces—thereby increasing the number of pixels per inch (ppi). As I worked on the first edition of this book, I used a laptop computer with a 17-inch screen and a native resolution of 1920 × 1200 pixels at 133 ppi. Today, I am using a slightly smaller 15-inch laptop with a second external monitor attached. The pixel resolution of the laptop screen is 2880 × 1800 at 220 ppi. In this example, the screen size decreased while the native resolution of the monitor drastically improved.

When a raster image is displayed in full size on a screen that's set to the native resolution of the monitor, there's a one-to-one correlation between the pixel data in the source file and the pixels rendered on screen. In this scenario, the source image will look its very best and is said to be "pixel perfect." Unfortunately, user preferences can quickly get in the way of viewing a pixel perfect image every time. For instance:

1. A user may not have his or her screen set to the native resolution of the monitor. On my laptop, I can choose from a number of display resolutions, including: 640 × 480, 720 × 480, 800 × 600, 1024 × 768, 1280 × 1024, 1680 × 1050, and finally, 1920 × 1200 (native). Choosing a display setting that's lower than the native resolution of the monitor produces the effect of zooming in. This is a helpful option for someone like me, whose vision is less than perfect. However, the benefit of enlarging the text and icons on screen has two potentially negative tradeoffs: a) it reduces the desktop real estate or screen space, and b) it compromises the quality of the screen image (the image becomes fuzzier as you stray further from the native resolution of the monitor).

2. A user may not have the screen set to its native resolution but may be zoomed in on an active document window. For example, you could be viewing an online newspaper article using a web browser like Firefox, Chrome, Internet Explorer, or Safari. Most browsers allow you to zoom in on a page to get a better view of the content. Doing so enlarges the view of both text and images; however, with each increase you'll lose clarity, particularly with images (see Figure 9.24).

In both these examples, there's no longer a one-to-one correlation between the native raster structure of the source image and the display screen. The image is no longer pixel perfect and will have to be scaled up or down to conform to the raster structure of the screen. And as we've already learned, scaling alters the quality of a raster image, especially when it is enlarged.

Aspect Ratio

In addition to describing the screen attributes in absolute terms (screen size and native resolution), monitors are classified by their *aspect ratio*. Aspect ratio is an indicator of the proportional relationship of the width to the height of the screen and is depicted with the expression $x:y$, where x equals the number of units wide and y equals the number of units high. While the physical size of a display screen can vary, the aspect ratio remains constant. The two most common aspect ratios in

FIGURE 9.24
Top: A web page is viewed natively in actual size. Bottom: This close-up view of the same page is achieved using the browser's zoom control.

use today are 4:3 and 16:9. The standard 4:3 (pronounced *4 by 3*) aspect ratio predates television and produces a familiar and somewhat boxy-looking shape. The other popular aspect ratio is 16:9 and is usually referred to as *widescreen* because it more closely matches the shape of a theatrical movie screen. While television and computer monitors are available in many shapes and sizes, they almost always conform to either a 4:3 or 16:9 aspect ratio.

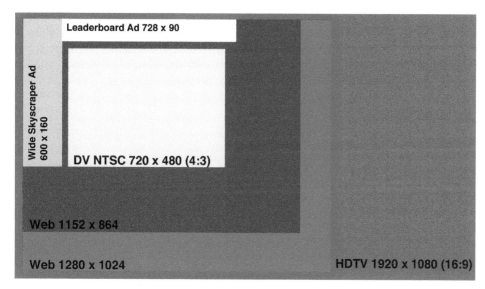

Leaderboard Ad 728 x 90

Wide Skyscraper Ad
600 x 160

DV NTSC 720 x 480 (4:3)

Web 1152 x 864

Web 1280 x 1024

HDTV 1920 x 1080 (16:9)

FIGURE 9.25
A comparison of some common display resolutions used in multimedia design. Do you notice how the aspect ratio varies?

MOVING IMAGES

Many people's daily experience is filled with moving images. Some come from televisions and movie theaters. Others come from personal computers, game systems, mobile phones, handheld devices, even GPS (Global Positioning System) interfaces and self-checkout kiosks at supermarkets. Regardless of the content, they are typically based on the same basic principles. Let's look at how this technology works.

Raster Scanning

In the Western world, people tend to process visual information from left to right and from top to bottom. Think about it! When you compose a letter or note, you generally start in the upper left-hand corner of the page and work your way down one line at a time from left to right. In a word-processing program such as Microsoft Word, you do basically the same thing. You press a key to produce an imprint of a character on the page, causing the cursor to advance to the next space on the line. You advance one character at a time until you reach the end of a line, at which point the cursor jumps to the beginning of the next line of text. A sheet of paper has a fixed number of lines on it, so when you reach the end of a page, a new page is added and the process continues.

Raster scanning works in much the same way, only faster. In television and computer display systems, individual video frames and computer images are reproduced on the screen, one pixel at a time, in a process called *scanning*. An electron beam or impulse mechanism illuminates each screen pixel as it progresses through the raster matrix. Each row of pixels is called a *scan line*. A *scanning cycle* is one complete pass of all of the scan lines in the display. When the scanning beam reaches the last pixel on the last scan line, it moves to the top and begins the next cycle. A *frame* is one complete scanning pass of all of the lines in a picture, or one complete scanning cycle.

The *refresh rate* is the number of complete scanning cycles per second and is measured in Hertz (Hz), a unit of frequency equal to one cycle per second. If the refresh rate is below 50 Hz, the image will appear to flicker. Most displays have refresh rates of 60 Hz or more. The faster the refresh rate, the sharper the image quality and the less eyestrain the user will experience. The larger the screen, the higher the refresh rate should be. Large computer monitors typically have a refresh rate of 85 Hz or higher.

PROGRESSIVE SCANNING

Contemporary computer monitors and some televisions reproduce images using *progressive scanning*, consecutively scanning the lines of the picture from top to bottom, just as you type on a typewriter. Progressive scanning helps combat eyestrain, which is why it's a given on computer monitors. That's not, however, necessarily the case for television.

INTERLACED SCANNING

Early television standards adopted a method of raster scanning called *interlaced scanning* to minimize both bandwidth use and flickering. With an interlace system, each frame of an image is captured in two parts and transmitted separately, one field at a time. The odd lines are scanned first, followed by a second pass of the even lines. So you're really only seeing half of each new image at once, but the screen draws so quickly you don't notice.

Interlaced scanning reduces the bandwidth requirements of standard broadcast television by half compared to a progressively scanned image. Using this standard helped cut the cost of broadcast equipment and, perhaps more importantly, freed up valuable broadcasting bandwidth. While broadcasting standards have changed with the move to Digital Television, interlaced signals are still an integral part of the broadcast mix (see Figure 9.26).

FIGURE 9.26
Broadcast television images are typically interlaced (left) while video on the Web is often de-interlaced (right), delivered progressively.

Fields

One complete scanning pass of either the odd or even scan lines is called a *field*. So two fields, the odd and even, produce one frame. As you can imagine, the electronic raster scanning process has to be fast to give you a good picture. Let's say you're watching a movie on a television with interlacing and a frame rate of 30 frames per second (usually stated as 30 *fps*) that has 480 lines in its raster (a comparatively small number). This means that one scanning pass of the 240 odd-numbered scan lines, or one field, occurs in just 1/60th of a second. Double that to get a full frame. Put another way, 14,400 scan lines of picture information are rendered on your television monitor every second.

Television and Cinema Standards

Since multimedia projects are often viewed on televisions, you need to consider television standards. A great deal of money goes into supporting the infrastructure of terrestrial broadcasting systems, so countries have developed technical standards—some more widely adopted than others—for the production of television-related equipment. While it doesn't always work out this way, such standards help to ensure that consumers have access to equipment that's compatible with the delivery systems used by content providers for program distribution. In an ideal world, every nation would use the same standards for every type of electronic technology, but this just isn't the case. As it's sometimes hard to get two people to agree on something, it's even more difficult to get the governing bodies of entire nations to agree on a universal set of technical specifications.

GREAT IDEAS
The Illusion of Apparent Motion

The foundation of all moving image technology rests on the ability of the human eye and brain to process a series of rapidly projected frames or scan lines as a continuous and uninterrupted picture. The motion we observe on the screen, whether in a movie house or on a television or computer monitor, is a perceptual illusion. Film, video, and moving digital images appear to have motion because of the phenomenon of *short-range apparent motion*. Our brains perceive motion when we encounter successive images that have small changes between them in much the same way that we process and make sense of physical movements in the real world.

In order to pull off the illusion of motion we get from film, video, and animation, individual pictures in a sequence must advance quickly. If the frame rate is set too low, the transition from one image to the next will appear jerky or stilted. The target speed is known as the *flicker fusion threshold*, the frequency at which the momentary flicker of intermittent light between each frame disappears from human perception.

Early on, the motion picture film industry adopted a frame rate of 24 fps as an international standard. However, an image pulsating at 24 fps is well below the flicker

(Continued)

fusion threshold for human perception. To compensate, a projector displays each frame of motion picture film twice. A rotating shutter momentarily blocks out the projector's light each time the frame is advanced and between each repeated exposure of a single frame, fixing the image in one spot and keeping us from seeing a blur. We don't notice the brief black spots because our retinas retain each visual impression of light for a fraction of a second—just long enough to span the gaps between each frame. The result is a flicker-free viewing experience for the audience.

FIGURE 9.27
Moving images are a perceptual illusion, achieved by the rapid projection of individual still frames of film or video.

As you develop media products to be used on multiple devices—computers, phones, game systems, and so on—keep in mind how those products will work and look on each device, including television.

DIGITAL TELEVISION

Digital Television (DTV) offers many advantages over legacy analog formats. Content created for digital media is more fluid: it can be easily repurposed and distributed through secondary channels of communication, making DTV more compatible with computer and Internet-based systems and services.

DTV also offers less signal interference and uses less bandwidth than an equivalent analog television broadcast, which is an advantage because the amount of broadcast bandwidth is finite. The switch to DTV has meant that more stations can be broadcast in the same viewing area, while using the same or less bandwidth as analog television.

FIGURE 9.28
Television entertainment technologies have evolved rapidly in recent years. The standalone single-piece television receiver your parents may remember can't compete with today's high-tech home theater system, complete with wall-mounted flat-screen monitor and 5.1 surround sound.

DTV also offers the option of using a 16:9 format, similar to that used in the movie theater, as well as high-definition (HD) video—video with over twice the resolution of the old NTSC standard. When professionals shoot and edit television programs digitally, the DTV infrastructure preserves the quality of the original material during transmission. In order to transmit digital content through an analog system, programs must first be downconverted to an analog format, resulting in a loss of image quality.

ATSC

The United States adopted the ATSC (Advanced Television Systems Committee) terrestrial broadcasting standard in 1996. In the same year, WRAL in Raleigh, North Carolina, became the first television station in the country to begin broadcasting a high-definition television (HDTV) signal. The U.S. transition to HDTV was fraught with many delays and took more than a decade to complete. On June 12, 2009, U.S. analog transmissions ceased and NTSC broadcasting officially ended for all full-power television stations in the United States.

The NTSC format has a fixed resolution, aspect ratio, scan mode, and frame rate. The newer ATSC standard is more fluid, providing up to 18 different display formats, which are categorized into three groups: standard definition television (SDTV), enhanced definition television (EDTV), and HDTV (see Table 9.2). ATSC

Table 9.2 ATSC Television Formats						
	DTV Format	**Vertical Resolution**	**Horizontal Resolution**	**Aspect Ratio**	**Scan Mode**	**Frame Rate**
High-Definition Television **(HDTV)** Best Quality	1080p	1080	1920	16:9	Progressive Progressive	24 fps 30 fps
	1080i	1080	1920	16:9	Interlaced	30 fps
	720p	720	1280	16:9	Progressive	24 fps 30 fps 60 fps
Enhanced Definition Television **(EDTV)** Medium Quality	480p	480	740	16:9	Progressive	24 fps 30 fps 60 fps
				4:3	Progressive	24 fps 30 fps 60 fps
		480	640	4:3	Progressive	24 fps 30 fps 60 fps
Standard Definition Television **(SDTV)** Good Quality	480i	480	704	16:9 4:3	Interlaced Interlaced	30 fps 30 fps
		480	640	4:3	Interlaced	30 fps

emphasizes progressive scanning and square pixels, bringing television technology closer to current standards for computer imaging. It also improves audio distribution, enabling a theater-style experience with 5.1-channel Dolby Digital Surround Sound. The ATSC standard has been adopted in much of the Americas and in U.S. territories. Canada made the switch in 2011, and Mexico is preparing for the switch and is simulcasting in both digital and analog formats. Other countries also have introduced the ATSC format but have not fully switched. And, of course, the ATSC is working on new standards: as ATSC 2.0 comes out, look for features such as video on demand and possibly even 3D programming.

DVB

The DVB (Digital Video Broadcasting) terrestrial broadcasting standard was established in 1997. The following year, the first commercial DVB broadcast was transmitted in the United Kingdom. Because European consumers depend more on cable and satellite distribution for television and less on over-the-air terrestrial broadcasting, their transition to a DTV infrastructure has been easier. The DVB standard has been adopted throughout Europe and in Australia. Not all areas have followed the U.S. model of a decade-long digital conversion. Berlin, the capital of Germany, made the change on August 4, 2003, making it the first city to convert to a DTV-only terrestrial broadcasting system.

DIGITAL CINEMA STANDARDS

In 2002, a consortium of Hollywood film studios formed the Digital Cinema Initiatives, LLC (DCI) to standardize the system specifications for digital production and projection of motion picture films in theaters. The DCI standard paved the way for the long-awaited transition from film-based production and distribution of motion pictures to digital production and theatrical projection and has greatly influenced the industry practices used today by digital filmmakers. One of the first DCI standards involved adapting the consumer and broadcast HD format to a slightly wider screen size that more closely aligned to existing film formats. HD has a resolution of 1920 × 1080 and an aspect ratio of 16:9. By comparison, the DCI HD equivalent has a resolution of 2048 × 1080 and an aspect ratio of 17:9. The DCI HD standard was termed 2K because the horizontal resolution is approximately 2,000 pixels.

The DCI standard also includes two advanced HD formats known respectively as 4K and 8K. The 4K DCI standard is 4096 × 2160 and contains nearly four times as many pixels as HD. The 8K DCI standard is 8192 × 4320—roughly 16 times the resolution of HD.

In addition, the ATSC standard is continuing to evolve. ATSC 3.0, also known as Next Generation Broadcast Television, is being developed to address growing needs for improved compression and increased bandwidth efficiency to accommodate 4K over-the-air transmission and delivery of 4K content to tablets and mobile devices.

In 2015, the Blu-ray Disc Association released technical specifications for the Ultra HD Blu-ray format. This standard paved the way for manufacturers to design and sell the next generation of UHD (ultra-high-definition) Blu-ray players to consumers for viewing movies in 4K or in the original DVD or Blu-ray formats.

FIGURE 9.29
Top: The resolution of SD and HD is compared to the newer ultra HD format. Bottom: The Sony FDR-AX100 ultra HD camcorder is one of many new devices recently introduced by manufacturers in response to the newer 4K standard. *Source: rmnoa357/Shutterstock.com.*

CHAPTER SUMMARY

Digital images are constructed of thousands to millions of tiny visual elements called *pixels* that are arranged in rows and columns on a screen to form a composite visual representation. The more pixels in an image, the higher its resolution and perceived quality. Digital imaging would not be possible without light. Digital images are captured using light-sensitive sensors and displayed using electronic monitors that scan the image onto the screen with light. Since the primary colors of light are red, green, and blue, RGB color space is the standard in digital imaging, whereas CMYK color space is the printing industry standard. The way an image or graphic is defined—either as separate pixels or as mathematical relationships—constrains what you can do with it. And as you create, transform, and incorporate images and graphics into multimedia projects, the final format you choose affects how good the user's experience will be. The final format should also guide your workflow, as you don't want to risk starting off working at a lower resolution than your final format needs to be.

CHAPTER 10

Photography

There are always two people in every picture: the photographer and the viewer.

—Ansel Adams, photographer (1902–1984)

Chapter Highlights

This chapter examines:
- How digital cameras are classified according to their operational features and intended uses
- The imaging chain and each of its basic components
- The variables affecting proper exposure of a digital image
- The use of fully automatic, semi-automatic, and manual shooting modes
- Strategies for storing, organizing, and managing digital image files

PHOTOGRAPHY

Photography is the process of fixing an image in time through the action of light. In traditional chemical processing, photographic images are created by exposing a light-sensitive emulsion on the surface of film to light in a controlled environment. While some people still shoot with film, the vast majority of the world has crossed over to digital photography, an electronic medium that renders pictures using a digital image sensor.

Digital photography offers instantaneous results, producing image files that are easily transferable, and adaptable, for a wide range of multimedia products (see Figure 10.1). The rapid adoption of digital cameras over the last decade can be attributed to many factors, including improvements in reliability and ease of use; better image resolution and print quality; higher-density storage solutions; and greater compatibility with computer hardware and software systems. Digital cameras come in three main varieties: consumer, prosumer, and professional. While the dividing line between each level is somewhat arbitrary, manufacturers use the terms to distinguish between low-, medium-, and high-quality equipment within a product line.

Key Terms

35mm
Angle of View
Aperture
APS-C (Advanced Photo System Type-C)
Camera RAW
Decisive Moment
Depth of Field
Digital Zoom
DSLR (Digital Single Lens Reflex)
EXIF (Exchangeable Image File Format)
Exposure
Exposure Modes
Exposure Triangle
F-Stop
Film Speed
Fisheye Lens
Flash
Focal Length
Focus Modes
Image Sensor
Image Stabilization
Imaging Chain
IPTC (International Press Telecommunications Council)
Iris
ISO
Landscape Mode
Lens
Macro Lens
Metadata
Metering Modes
Normal Lens
Optical Zoom
Photography

Portrait Mode
Prime Lens
Reciprocity Law
Red-Eye
Selective Focus
Shutter
Telephoto Lens
Tripod
White Balance
Wide-Angle Lens
Zoom Lens

FIGURE 10.1
Photography is continuously evolving, both as an art and a science. While the traditional ways often seem archaic, they continue to provide high-quality images. Likewise, while contemporary ways may lack marginally in quality, they make up for it in alacrity and ease of postproduction. Pictured here (L–R), photojournalist Molly Bartles shoots with a professional-grade DSLR (digital single lens reflex) camera, as Chris Walker, a documentary photographer, is shown with his 80-year-old wooden 8 x 10. Each is a specific tool that, even in contemporary America, has its place.
Source: Chris Walker (left) and Josh Reuck (right).

FLASHBACK

Kodak Corporation

Founded in 1880, Kodak Corporation pioneered the development of photographic film. Sadly, this legendary company filed for chapter 11 bankruptcy protection in January 2012 due to the rise in popularity of digital photography and the unavoidable demise of photographic film. The downward trend in film use culminated around 2005 when Kodak reported that digital sales accounted for 54% of annual revenue, exceeding film sales for the first time in company history. They have since stopped making digital cameras and now license their name to allow other companies to produce Kodak-branded cameras for the consumer marketplace. To survive, they sold off many of their patents to companies such as Adobe, Amazon, Apple, Google, Microsoft, and Samsung, just to name a few. While their film division currently lives on, it is a much smaller component of their corporate structure. Kodak emerged from bankruptcy a year and a half later in 2013, a much leaner company with a more narrowly defined focus on corporate printing and digital imaging solutions.

Consumer Cameras

At the lowest end of the consumer spectrum are point-and-shoot cameras designed for users with little to no background in photography. The point-and-shoot camera automatically determines the appropriate focus and exposure settings. Most of these cameras have a built-in flash and are largely menu-driven, with very few controls located on the camera body itself (see Figure 10.2).

Some consumers prefer the body style, features, and quality benefits of a digital single lens reflex (DSLR) camera over the scaled back point-and-shoot. In a DSLR, a mirror located behind the lens directs the image to an optical viewfinder, allowing the photographer to compose and focus a scene while viewing it through the lens (TTL). When the shutter is released, the mirror flips out of the way, allowing

Camera
The you-can't-believe-it's-on-a-phone camera.

With 8 megapixels and all-new optics, this just might be the best camera ever on a mobile phone. It just might be the only camera you'll ever need. And if you think that's amazing, wait until you see your photos.

FIGURE 10.2
The Apple Store website ad from 2011 claimed that the iPhone 4S "just might be the only camera you'll ever need." While resolution is just one benchmark of picture quality, the fact that the iPhone iSight camera comes with an eight-megapixel image sensor is impressive. Why carry around a camera and a phone when one device now does the trick?
Source: http://www.apple.com.

light entering through the lens to strike the image sensor. Experienced photographers prefer to compose through the lens because it's more precise. Consumer-grade DSLR cameras normally have a permanently mounted lens, which, while usually much better than the lens on a point-and-shoot camera, may not be as good as that of a prosumer or professional lens. Regardless of the style, consumer cameras are designed for mass-market appeal and are engineered for size, portability, ease of use, and cost. They are not typically designed to give the user easy access to camera settings. The quality of these cameras has improved tremendously over the last decade. While one of the differences between consumer and prosumer digital cameras used to be the number of megapixels (the number of light-sensitive elements on the sensor, measured in millions), there is no longer as much difference, and it is not uncommon to find 10- and even 14-megapixel consumer-grade cameras. A high-resolution image from a 10-megapixel-camera will easily print up to an 11- by 14-inch image.

Prosumer and Professional Cameras

The term *prosumer* is a blend of *professional consumer* and refers to someone whose level of expertise and needs fall between that of the average consumer and the full-time professional. Prosumer cameras are typically DSLRs with interchangeable lenses, and they have larger and better quality image sensors than consumer cameras. They also allow the user greater and easier control of the camera, providing them with more versatility and greater control over image acquisition, particularly exposure control. Professional-grade cameras improve on these features, particularly lens quality and sensor size. In many cases the lenses and other accessories for professional and prosumer cameras by the same manufacturer are interchangeable, although as we'll see in a bit, the lenses will behave differently when you switch from a prosumer's smaller sensor to the larger full-frame sensor on a professional camera, which is roughly equivalent to 35mm film.

Video Cameras

While video technology will be discussed in more detail later on in chapter 13, it's worth mentioning here that digital video cameras and digital still cameras share similarities in basic operation, including controls, shooting modes, and exposure settings. Because of this, many concepts in this chapter can be applied to the use and operation of video cameras. Given their innate similarities, it should come as no surprise that video cameras today often allow users to capture still images, while many still cameras allow photographers to shoot moving images and sound. As a general rule, however, it's best to use a camera for the primary function it was designed for. Since a video camera is optimized for moving images and sound, it's still image-processing capabilities and resolution options are generally not as good as a DSLR camera, though high-end video cameras such as the RED Digital Cinema Camera are an exception. Similarly, most still cameras are not ideal for capturing video, particularly from an audio perspective. As with many things, the best results come by choosing the right piece of equipment for the right job.

THE IMAGING CHAIN

The imaging chain of a digital camera is made up of four components: the lens, the iris, the shutter, and the image sensor (see Figure 10.3). The lens determines the field of view, or what the camera "sees." The iris regulates the intensity of exposure. The shutter regulates the time of exposure, and the image sensor captures light

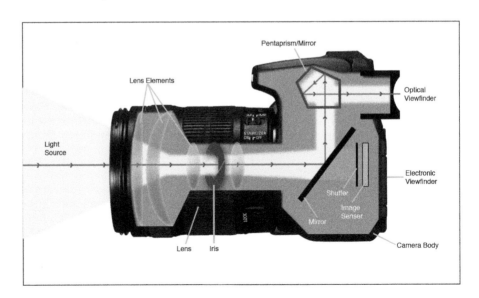

FIGURE 10.3
The major components of a DSLR camera.
Source: Vic Costello.

and converts it into a digital signal. Photography is the art of manipulating these four components to achieve desired and intentional effects.

The Lens

In still cameras and video camcorders, the lens is an integrated optical system made up of one or more individual elements of ground glass or molded plastic. The lens is mounted on the front of the camera and is designed to capture and manipulate light reflected from objects in the camera's line of sight. The lens controls the magnification of the subject being photographed and affects the sharpness and clarity of the image (see Figure 10.4).

FIGURE 10.4
One of the main features of a DSLR camera is interchangeable lenses, which come in many different sizes depending largely on their focal length.

PRIME LENSES

Lenses with a single focal length are called *prime* or *fixed focal-length* lenses. With a fixed focal-length lens, the only way to affect angle of view is to physically change the distance between the camera and the subject. Serious photographers often own an assortment of prime lenses with a variety of focal lengths, enabling them to manipulate angle of view by simply swapping out the lens. Prime lenses are often classified into one of five main categories: wide-angle, telephoto, normal, novelty (macro and fisheye), and super-telephoto.

- **Wide-angle lenses** have a relatively short focal length (18–35 mm for full frame, 12–24 mm for APS-C [Advanced Photo System Type-C]) resulting in the wide angle of view. Wide-angle lenses, or *short lenses* as they're sometimes called, are often used for shooting landscape panoramas and vistas where the primary emphasis is on establishing a wide overview of the scene (see Figure 10.5).
- **Telephoto** lenses have a long focal length (90–300 mm for full frame, 60–200 mm for APS-C) resulting in a very narrow angle of view. Telephoto lenses, or *long*

FIGURE 10.5
Wide-angle lenses are often used to capture broad vistas, yielding images such as this one.
Source: Chris Walker.

TELEPHOTO   MACRO

FIGURE 10.6

Because of their magnification, telephotos and macros are more likely than other lenses to add camera shake to your image. To help avoid this, a good starting point is to convert the lens' focal length into a fraction and use that as a shutter speed—a 200 mm lens would become 1/200th, so it should be handheld at 1/250th or faster.

Source: Chris Walker.

lenses, can magnify distant objects, making them appear much closer than they really are (see Figure 10.6, left). These are the favorite lenses of bird watchers, sports photographers, and naturalists for obtaining close-up shots of a subject from a distance.

- **Normal lenses** have a medium focal length (40–60 mm for full frame, 28–40 mm for APS-C) resulting in an angle of view that falls somewhere in between the extremes of wide-angle and telephoto. Normal lenses are a safe bet for general-purpose shooting activities that do not require extreme close-ups or wide shots of the subject matter.
- **Novelty lenses** have descriptive names like *macro* and *fisheye* and feature unique optical characteristics designed for atypical shooting situations.
  - **Macro lenses** can acquire focus when positioned only a few inches away from the subject. Macro lenses produce high-quality images with low image distortion and are useful for shooting extreme close-ups of small objects like insects or flower blossoms (see Figure 10.6, right).
- **Fisheye lenses** have an extremely short focal length (8–15 mm for full frame, 11 mm or less for APS-C), offering an angle of view as high as 180 degrees. However, because of the extreme curvature of glass, images acquired with a fisheye lens are significantly distorted, which results in an interesting hall of mirrors–type effect.
- **Super-telephoto lenses** (400–600 mm for full frame) yield the narrowest angle of view while offering extremely high levels of image magnification.

ZOOM LENSES

A *zoom*, or *variable focal-length lens*, can be adjusted to any focal length within a set optical range. For example, using a zoom lens with a range of 28–300 mm, the focal length can be set to wide-angle (28 mm), telephoto (300 mm), or anywhere in between. Zoom lenses allow the photographer to quickly change the angle of view without having to swap out the lens. With this type of lens, the photographer zooms in to acquire a narrow angle of view and zooms out to compose a wide shot. The zoom ratio indicates the magnification capability of a variable focal-length lens. For example, a 3× or 3:1 zoom ratio means the size of the image at the longest focal length setting (telephoto) is three times greater than the size of the image at the shortest setting (wide-angle). High-quality zoom lenses are very expensive. While their optical quality is generally inferior to that of prime lenses, the speed and convenience of zooming can be a worthwhile tradeoff. Zoom lenses are included on most point-and-shoot still cameras as well as on all consumer, prosumer, and professional video cameras.

Optical versus Digital Zoom Digital cameras with built-in lenses are often equipped with both an optical zoom and a digital zoom. An *optical zoom* alters the angle of view internally by changing the actual focal length of the lens elements. Since the lens on most point-and-shoot cameras is relatively small, it's often difficult to achieve a high level of image magnification optically. To compensate, manufacturers have an added feature called *digital zoom*. With digital zoom, the image sensor creates the zoom artificially, much like enlarging a digital image in a photo-editing program. The outer portion of the image is cropped (the pixels are thrown away) and the remaining pixels are enlarged and/or duplicated to simulate the effect of a narrower angle of view. Using a digital zoom can lead to a noticeable loss of image quality and detail.

Iris

The *iris* is an adjustable plastic or metal diaphragm that regulates the amount of light striking the image sensor (see Figure 10.7). The iris is typically located between the optical elements of the lens. When shooting images that are dimly lit, the iris can be opened up to allow more light to pass through to the image sensor. For brightly lit subjects, the iris can be constricted or "stopped down" to reduce the intensity of the light and keep the image from being overexposed. The term *aperture* is sometimes confused with the iris, but it refers to the actual hole or opening created by the iris and not to the device itself; when people talk about adjusting the aperture, they are usually talking about adjusting the iris to change the size of the aperture.

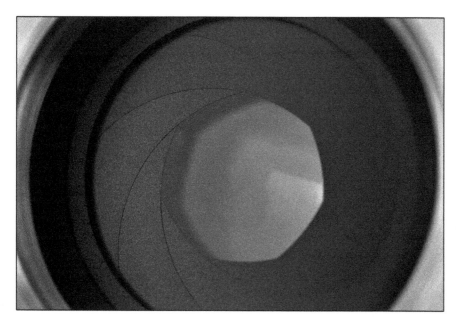

FIGURE 10.7
An iris is typically comprised of a series of metal blades that collapse or expand to form a circular opening inside the lens through which light passes. This hole in the iris is called the aperture.
Source: Chris Walker.

FIGURE 10.8
The exposure time for this image was approximately 1/1,000th of a second. Faster shutter speeds are available on all DSLRs, but it's fairly rare to use them.
Source: Chris Walker.

Shutter

The *shutter* is a movable curtain, plate, or other device that controls the amount of time the image sensor is exposed to light. When the shutter button is depressed, the shutter opens for an instant of time, allowing light to strike the surface of the image sensor. The amount of time the shutter remains open is referred to as *shutter speed* and can commonly range from 1/8,000th of a second to several full seconds. Fast shutter speeds in the neighborhood of 1/250th or 1/500th of a second are good for freezing action in a well-lit scene (see Figure 10.8). Much slower shutter speeds are required when shooting under low-light situations.

Image Sensor

A digital camera's image sensor is a small electronic chip used to register the intensity and color of light. It is the digital equivalent of "film," the light-sensitive recording medium used in a traditional analog camera. Light passes through the lens and aperture before striking the surface of the image sensor. The visual data obtained by the sensor is converted into binary form and stored on a flash memory card in the camera body. The image sensor eliminates the need for film and allows the digital photographer to electronically manipulate the size and appearance of a captured image by varying the control settings of the camera.

SENSOR SIZE

For years, 35 mm reigned as one of the most popular photographic film formats for SLR (single lens reflex) cameras, both for amateurs and professional photographers alike. The physical dimensions of a 35 mm film frame are 36 × 24 mm. As manufacturers began developing digital cameras, they adopted these dimensions as a baseline measure by which to conform and compare the physical size of electronic image sensors. A *full-frame* image sensor is so named because it perfectly mirrors the dimensions of 35 mm film (36 × 24 mm). Professional DSLRs almost always use a full-frame sensor or a variant of the Advanced Photo System Type-C format. APS-C sensors are considerably smaller than full-frame sensors and vary slightly in size by manufacturer and camera model. Cheaper DSLRs, compacts, and smartphone cameras are equipped with progressively smaller sensors. As a rule, the smaller the camera is, the smaller the image sensor will be. For example, the iPhone 6, released in 2014, uses a one-third-inch sensor that measures a mere 4.80 × 3.60 mm (see Figure 10.9).

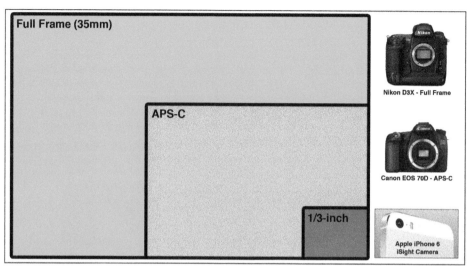

FIGURE 10.9
The one-third-inch image sensor built into Apple's iSight camera (iPhone 5/6) is extremely small in comparison to the full-frame sensor of a Nikon D3X and the APS-C sensor of the less expensive Canon 70D. Typically, the larger the image sensor the more expensive and higher quality the camera is likely to be.

Tech Talk

Focal Length Multiplier The size of the image sensor determines the angle of view that can be achieved with any particular lens. All things being equal, larger sensors offer a wider angle of view than smaller ones. If you attach a lens designed for 35 mm film to anything other than a full-frame DSLR, you will observe a noticeable difference in the angle of view when shooting with an equivalent focal length. How much of a difference? It depends on the focal length multiplier. The terms *crop factor* and *focal length multiplier* (FLM) are interchangeable terms and concepts that were developed to help photographers quantify the effects of using full-frame lenses with APS-C sensors.

If you were to use a full-frame lens on an APS-C format camera set to the same focal length, the resulting image would appear cropped, thus producing a narrower angle of view. As an example, a normal lens for a full-frame camera is usually a 50 mm, while a normal lens for an APS-C format

Table 10.1	The Relationship of Focal Length to Angle of View	
Lens Type	**Focal Length, Full Frame/ APS-C**	**Angle of View**
Fisheye	8–15mm/less than 11mm	Up to 180°
Wide-Angle	18–35mm/12–24mm	90° to 54°
Normal	40–60mm/28–40mm	48° to 33°
Telephoto	70–300mm/60–200mm	28° to 7°
Super-Telephoto	Greater than 400mm/200mm	6° to 4°

(Continued)

DSLR is around a 35 mm. This difference in performance is the *focal length multiplier* (FLM). Most prosumer cameras have an FLM between 1.4 and 1.6. To use the FLM, multiply the lens' actual focal length by the FLM to see what its full-frame equivalent would be. In the prior example, a 35 mm lens on a camera with a 1.4 FLM is the same as a 49 mm (essentially a 50 mm) lens on a full-frame camera.

By conforming the full-frame sensor dimensions to 35mm film, manufacturers saved professional photographers a considerable amount of angst. They would not be forced to retire their inventory of perfectly good lenses when transitioning to a digital camera body or have to modify their composition techniques because trusted lenses no longer performed as expected.

FIGURE 10.10
In this image, the lens used to make the original 4 x 5" version was a 90 mm, which translates to wide-angle on a large-format camera. But as the highlighted boxes illustrate, that same lens would render a "normal" angle of view when attached to a medium format camera and a close-up view when used on a DSLR. *Source: Chris Walker.*

IMAGE RESOLUTION

The resolution of a digital camera or still image is determined by how many pixels the image sensor can produce. For example, the Canon PowerShot G16 is a 12-megapixel camera that, when set to its highest resolution, can produce a 4000 × 3000 pixel image. This is called *native resolution* because the camera is using all the pixels on the image sensor to produce the image. As the photographer, you can change the capture settings to a lower resolution such as 1600 × 1200 or 640 × 480. In response, the camera will use only a designated portion of the pixel array to form the image.

IMAGE ENCODING AND COMPRESSION

On consumer cameras, images are recorded using the popular JPEG compression codec. JPEG compression reduces the amount of space required to record an image to the memory card as well as the time it takes for the camera to process sensory data once the picture is snapped. Prosumer and professional cameras also support JPEG encoding, but both usually also provide the option of saving images in uncompressed formats like TIFF or Camera RAW. While these formats produce files that are significantly larger, they offer the advantage of preserving most or all of the original sensor data.

The Camera RAW format records a completely unprocessed version of the image as obtained by the sensor at the point of exposure. Professional photographers prefer the RAW file format because it allows them to retain maximum control of image processing during editing. JPEG and TIFF formatted files are processed prior to encoding, limiting the type of adjustments that can be made in image editing. Camera RAW is a proprietary standard that requires special software or plug-ins from the camera manufacturer in order to edit the image. While Camera RAW is a technically superior format, TIFF and JPEG images are much easier to work with, and their quality is acceptable for the vast majority of multimedia applications.

While the number of options varies by model and manufacturer, most digital cameras allow you to specify the amount of compression you want to apply to a JPEG image. For example, Canon offers three choices called *normal*, *fine*, and *superfine*. As the name implies, superfine produces the highest quality image by applying the smallest amount of compression. There's a dramatic difference between the file size of an image acquired at the smallest resolution and lowest quality JPEG setting and those at the highest quality setting. For example, if you take a picture with Canon EOS Rebel XS set to its lowest resolution (1936 × 1288) and JPEG setting, the resulting image file will be around 700 KB. The same image taken with the camera set to midrange resolution (2816 × 1880) and medium JPEG setting would yield a file of around 1.2 MB. If you were to use the highest resolution (3888 × 2592) and JPEG setting, the file would be around 3.8 MB. Switching the high-resolution setting to RAW bumps the file size up to almost 10 MB. As you can see, it's important to pay attention to the settings you use. Keeping a camera set to the highest resolution and best JPEG setting is normally a good choice, although using RAW offers advanced users more flexibility. See Figure 9.14 in the "Graphics" chapter for another example of how changing the resolution and JPEG setting affects image file size and the total number of images a memory card can store.

FLASHBACK
The Decisive Moment

For photographers who work on location, the two most important factors in image making are being there and knowing how to capitalize on the situation once you are. In terms of timing, Magnum photographer/founder Henri Cartier-Bresson (1908–2004), considered by many to be the father of photojournalism, believed in the latter with such conviction that he revived the term "the decisive moment" from the writings of a 17th-century French cardinal.

Photographically, *the decisive moment* is that instant when an action is at its peak, when it's stronger than it was the moment before or will be the moment after; it's that singular, perfect, narrow window of time in which the shutter should be released to best depict the emotion of an event. The strength of this moment can be seen through

(Continued)

FIGURE 10.11
In this set of images, the photographer came upon a couple at a county fair who were arguing. In the first of the 10 photographs (not shown) the young man is yelling at his girlfriend, who'd disappeared for an hour. In the final frame, the couple kissed. The first images held more aggression than desired, and the final seemed overtly sappy, so the ninth image, which held the anticipation of making up, became the chosen photograph in the sequence.
Source: Chris Walker.

anticipation, through the alignment of compositional elements, or in peak action (see Figure 10.11).

It took more than 100 years of photography for the term to be needed, but less than half that for it to become obsolete. In the early years of photography, images were exposed over a period of minutes—so timing was far less important than the photographer's location and composition were. Today we find that technology—the force that, through faster shutter speeds, once created the need for Bresson's statement—has brought us to a point in history where photographers no longer need to exercise such decisiveness in their timing.

Through the ability to extract still images from video, we will soon be freed from the necessity of precision timing, from the need to depress the shutter at the precise moment an action is at its zenith. Almost as retribution, though, we must now further challenge ourselves to be even more decisive in our selection of focal length, depth of field, and composition.

by Chris Walker

EXPOSURE

A digital camera creates a picture by exposing the image sensor to light. Underexposed images have a dark appearance and lack detail while overexposed images often contain bright spots and appear washed out. One of the most important tasks of the photographer is managing the exposure settings of the camera during image acquisition. *Exposure* is the product of two variables: the intensity of light (as controlled by the iris) and the duration of contact with the image sensor (as controlled by the speed of the shutter). This relationship, the *reciprocity law*, states that there is an inverse relationship between intensity and time and can be expressed mathematically as:

$$Exposure = Intensity \times Time$$

For example, setting the shutter speed to 1/250th and the aperture to f/8 results in the same exposure level as a setting of 1/125th at f/11 or 1/500th at f/5.6. In this example, doubling time while reducing the aperture by one full stop has the same negligible effect on exposure as halving the time of exposure while increasing the aperture by one full stop. As long as a change to one of the two variables is matched by a reciprocal change in the other, exposure remains constant.

FIGURE 10.12
Light bending as it passes through a lens or small opening is nothing new. The Chinese philosopher Mo Ti first noted this phenomenon 7,000 years ago when viewing images of a solar eclipse being projected on the ground through leaf gaps in overhead trees. So whether it's film, an image sensor, your hand, or a white card for viewing an eclipse, the only magic here lies in what we do with this fantastic medium.
Source: Chris Walker.

FIGURE 10.13
Left: This image was shot at 1/60th at f/22. Right: This one was shot at 1/1,000th at f/5.6. The overall amount of light striking the camera's sensor was virtually the same in each image, but the slower exposure time resulted in the image with the blurred ball.
Source: Chris Walker.

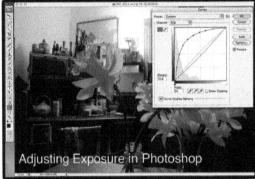

Original (underexposed)

FIGURE 10.14
Correct exposure can only be accomplished in the camera, but Photoshop and other programs allow for some adjustments to be made in postproduction. In the center frame, the Photoshop tool Curves was accessed and highlights and mid-tones were elevated. For the bottom image, the History Brush was used to return the area surrounding the lamp to its original tone, then Curves was again employed to add some magenta to the final color palate.
Source: Chris Walker.

Adjusting Exposure in Photoshop

Corrected Exposure

Measuring Light Intensity

Digital cameras have a built-in exposure meter that measures incoming light as it's reflected off objects in the camera's field of view. An *exposure meter* is an electronic instrument with a light-sensitive cell that's activated by partially depressing the camera's shutter button. When the camera is in an automatic shooting mode, the shutter and aperture settings will be set by the camera based on the meter's assessment of light intensity. The way a camera assesses the light intensity of a scene can vary. Most cameras offer a choice of three different metering methods in order to compensate for different lighting scenarios.

EVALUATIVE METERING MODE

With *evaluative metering*, the camera samples the intensity of light at multiple points in the image matrix and then combines the results with other camera data to determine the best exposure setting. Evaluative metering is the default method used on most cameras because it produces the best overall results, especially for scenes that are unevenly lit.

CENTER-WEIGHTED METERING MODE

Center-weighted metering is identical to the evaluative mode except that more weight is given to data from the center of the image when calculating the exposure settings. This method is recommended for scenes in which the main subject is backlit or surrounded by bright background objects.

SPOT METERING MODE

With *spot metering*, the camera calculates exposure based on the light intensity of the main subject located in the center of the screen. Spot metering is best for high-contrast scenes with varying levels of brightness.

GREAT IDEAS
Flash Control

Using the flash allows you to provide additional fill light for scenes where existing lighting is less than ideal. The range of a flash varies by manufacturer, but most are designed to work within 15 feet of the camera. Be careful when using a flash as it may wash out your image. Don't use a flash unless you really need it. Many cameras allow you to change the output of a flash incrementally from 100% (full), to 75%, 50%, 25%, and off. This feature is helpful when you want to remain close to the subject without overexposing the image or momentarily blinding your subjects. With most cameras, you normally have the option of selecting from a number of different flash modes.

- **Fill flash (always on):** In this mode, the camera fires the flash every time, even when the exposure meter indicates a sufficient level of natural light. Using a fill flash outdoors on a sunny day can help compensate for excessively bright sunlight, harsh shadows, and uneven backlighting (see Figure 10.15).
- **Auto flash:** In this mode, the camera meters the available light and only fires the flash when needed. Limiting the use of the flash helps conserve battery power.

(Continued)

FIGURE 10.15
Images made in direct sunlight can often benefit from a little judicious *fill flash*. The objective of using fill flash is to "fill" in the shadowed areas that may be too dark without it. Using too much fill, though, can unnaturally set your subject apart from the background. A good starting point is to set your flash to −1. If you're using a non-dedicated unit, try setting the ISO to a higher setting—either way, the flash will get the message that you desire less light on your scene than what it might want to give you.
Source: Chris Walker.

■ **Red-eye reduction:** In this mode, the red eyes caused by the reflection of the flash off the retina of the eye is reduced. When the flash is set to red-eye reduction mode, the camera fires a short burst of light followed by the actual flash. The short burst is intended to shut down the pupil of the eye, thus minimizing the kickback of reflected light. The closer the flash is to the lens, the more prone a camera is to producing red-eye. On professional cameras, the flash is farther away from the lens than on built-in systems and can often be detached and repositioned. In addition to controlling red-eye with the flash, you may also be able to reduce it by using a wide-angle lens, increasing the amount of existing lighting, or by moving the camera closer to the subject. In a worst-case scenario, you may be able to remove it using photo-editing software.

The Exposure Triangle

The term *exposure triangle* is widely used by photographers to refer to the three primary components of a camera system that a photographer adjusts to control exposure: 1) aperture, 2) ISO, or film speed, and 3) shutter speed (see Figure 10.16). These three settings interact with each other—so when you change one variable, you often have to change another to compensate. The combined values of all three parameters are represented numerically as the *exposure value* (EV). The larger the aperture, the more light strikes the image sensor and the greater potential there

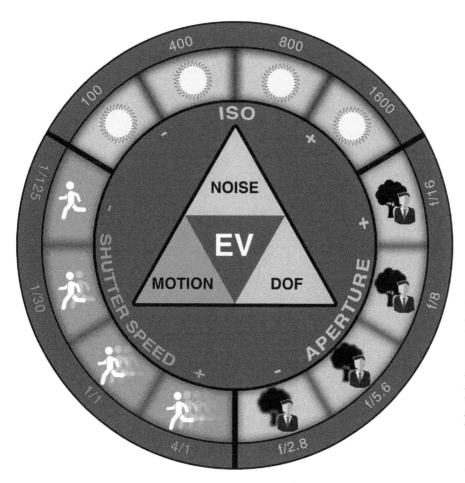

FIGURE 10.16
This illustration of the exposure triangle shows the relationship between ISO, shutter speed, and aperture, and how all three variables interact to achieve the exposure value for each shot.
Source: http://www. exposureguide.com; illustrator: Vic Costello.

will be for acquiring shallow depth of field. Increasing the ISO increases the light sensitivity of the image sensor (an advantage in low-light situations), but the image becomes noisier or grainier. And finally, the more you increase shutter speed, the greater detail you can achieve when shooting fast action but the more light you will need for achieving proper exposure. Professional photographers know how to manually adjust these controls and often prefer to do so in order to obtain a desired look or effect when shooting. A photographer can also choose to relegate control of these settings to the camera's exposure metering system by shooting in a completely automatic or semi-automatic mode.

APERTURE

On professional lenses, the aperture is adjusted by turning the innermost ring on the outside of the lens housing. A series of *f-stop* numbers are printed on the outside surface of the ring, indicating the size of the aperture. While shown as a whole number, an f-stop unit is actually a fraction used for calculating the physical diameter of the aperture. For example, an f-stop setting of f/16 means the diameter of the

Table 10.2	Diameter of the Aperture Obtained by Dividing the Focal Length of the Lens by the f-stop number		
	Focal Length of the Lens		
f-stop number	**18 mm**	**50 mm**	**300 mm**
2.8	6.429 mm	17.857 mm	107.143 mm
4	4.500 mm	12.500 mm	75.000 mm
5.6	3.214 mm	8.929 mm	53.571 mm
8	2.250 mm	6.250 mm	37.500 mm
11	1.636 mm	4.545 mm	27.273 mm
16	1.125 mm	3.125 mm	18.750 mm
22	0.818 mm	2.273 mm	13.636 mm

aperture is equal to 1/16th the focal length of the lens (see Table 10.2). To calculate the aperture of a 50 mm lens set to f/16, you would use the following formula:

$$focal\ length/f\text{-}stop\ number = aperture\ diameter$$
$$50\ mm/16 = 3.125\ mm$$

Typical f-stop positions include: f/32, f/22, f/16, f/11, f/8, f/5.6, f/4, f/2.8, f/2, and f/1.4, although you typically won't find a single lens that covers the entire range. Because the f-stop number is a fraction, the size of the aperture actually decreases as the f-stop number increases.

Opening the aperture by one full f-stop (e.g., changing from f/11 to f/8) doubles the size of the aperture and the amount of light striking the image sensor. Likewise, closing the aperture by one full stop (e.g., changing from f/1.4 to f/2) reduces the size of the aperture and the amount of incoming light by half. Some lenses allow the aperture to be adjusted in half-stop or third-stop increments for even greater control of light exposure.

Aperture strongly influences the relative amount of depth of field in a shot. To achieve shallow depth of field, use a low f-stop setting (wide aperture requires less light). To achieve great depth of field in a shot, use a higher f-stop setting (smaller opening requires more light).

ISO

One of the challenges of digital photography is that much of the terminology is rooted in film. One of the best examples of this is the continued use of the ISO Film Speed system. Originally based on a film's ability to respond to light, the ISO rating is now used to describe a sensor's ability to respond to light. The ISO designation follows a logarithmic scale, which means that each jump to a higher ISO number results in a doubling of the film's light sensitivity (see Table 10.3). This corresponds nicely to the f-stop scale, which works in precisely the same manner. All things being equal, increasing film speed by one ISO level has the same effect on exposure as opening the aperture by one full stop. As film speed increases,

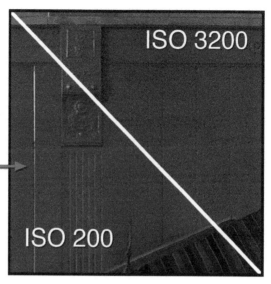

FIGURE 10.17
Electronic and analog media share many characteristics, including the degradation of image quality at higher ISOs. As the enlarged view illustrates, the discrepancies between ISOs 200 and 3200 are quite apparent. As technological improvements continue to be made, the distance in quality between low and high ISOs continues to shorten.
Source: Chris Walker.

Table 10.3	A Comparison of ISO to Light Sensitivity, Image Contrast, and Graininess		
ISO Film Speed Rating	**Light Sensitivity**	**Contrast**	**Image Grain**
50 ISO	low	very high	low
100 ISO	medium	high	medium
200 ISO	medium	medium	medium
400 ISO	high	medium	high
800 ISO	very high	low	very high

however, the sharpness and clarity of an image decreases, and your image will have a grainier, or "noisier," appearance (see Figure 10.17). For the cleanest images, it's best to shoot with the lowest possible film speed setting. Unless you choose to manually override the ISO setting of the camera, your camera will usually set your film speed automatically based on lighting conditions, flash settings, and other selected exposure settings.

SHUTTER SPEED

Shutter speed influences how motion is captured by the image sensor. Use slower shutter speed when subject motion is minimal, the light level is low, or you purposely want to create a motion blur effect (see Figure 10.18). Use a faster shutter speed when shooting fast-moving subjects, in settings with plenty of light, or when purposely trying to freeze action without compromising image clarity.

FIGURE 10.18
A motion blur was achieved in this image by following the taxi cab in motion using a slow shutter speed.

WHITE BALANCE

Our perception of colored objects in the natural world is affected by the type of light source used to illuminate them. Most light sources are not "true white" but rather an uneven mix of the primary color frequencies (red, blue, and green). For example, we know that under certain atmospheric conditions, the physical color of reflected sunlight can appear red, orange, white, yellow, or blue (see Figure 10.19). In the same way, there are many different types of artificial light sources (fluorescent, halogen, tungsten, etc.), each with its own unique color properties. Light sources are rated according to their color temperature on the Kelvin scale, so named for the British physicist William Thomson, 1st Baron Kelvin of Largs (1824–1907) (see Table 10.4).

While the human eye adjusts rather easily to variations in light, electronic image sensors must be calibrated to the color temperature of the light source they are exposed to in order to accurately capture the color of objects within the field of view. This process of calibration is called *white balance*. The white balance of a camera can be set manually by shooting a white object such as a blank sheet of paper while depressing the manual white balance button. Once a camera "sees" what white looks like under existing light, it can extrapolate the values of all of the other colors in the spectrum. Manual white balance is the most accurate way of calibrating the color space of a digital camera, especially when the source of light is mixed, such as an indoor scene with natural light pouring in from an open window. Keep in mind, though, that you must redo the white balance calibration each time the lighting condition in which you're shooting changes.

Digital cameras often provide white balance presets for several of the most common lighting conditions, including *daylight* and *cloudy* for outdoor situations and *tungsten* and *fluorescent* for indoors. However, if you forget to change a white balance preset when moving from one light source to another, the color of your newly acquired images will not be true (see Figure 10.20). For this reason, many people take the easy way out and just leave the camera set to *auto white balance* (AWB).

By now, we've become used to the fact that digital cameras include automatic settings for just about every control. While AWB works reasonably well in most cases,

FIGURE 10.19
This scene was shot late in the day under clear skies. The blue could have been natural had the exposure been longer, but the longer exposure would have caused the drifting fog to blur, so a bluish filter was used to emphasize the blue light while allowing an exposure time that still showed individual wisps of fog.
Source: Chris Walker.

Table 10.4	The Color Temperature of Common Indoor and Outdoor Lighting Sources (Kelvin Units)
Color Temperature	**Light Source**
1600 K	sunrise and sunset
1800 K	a candle
2800 K	tungsten lamp (ordinary household incandescent bulb)
3200 K	studio lamps, photofloods
4000 K	indoor fluorescent
5200 K	bright midday sun
5500 K	average daylight, electronic flash
6000 K	lightly overcast sky
6500 K	heavily overcast sky
7000 K	outdoor shade
8000 K	hazy sky
20000 K	deep blue clear sky

Source: http://en.Wikipedia.org.

FIGURE 10.20
Quality lighting is vital to good photography. In this comparison, the sequence of three images on the left were made at different times of the day; note that the brickwork on the building is reddest during the noon exposure and shifts as the day goes on due to the amount of blue, ambient light coming from the sky. In the images on the right (top to bottom), the windsurfer was shot moments after dawn, during "the golden hour"; the woman at the wood rack was shot at dusk, where you can see the sky light (blue) mixing with a mercury-vapor light coming from the left (green) and tungsten light from her patio and home (orange); the street festival image was balanced for the fluorescent lights in the background, but it also contains "bug lights" within the corn booth (yellow) and high pressure sodium lights from overhead (amber).
Source: Chris Walker.

you can usually get better results by using a white balance preset based on the type of light you are working with or by manually white balancing your camera.

FOCUS

The *focus control* is used to define the sharpness of an object within the frame by changing the distance between the optical elements of a lens. A camera's focus must be reset each time the distance between the camera and the subject physically changes. Holding the camera steady while depressing the shutter button will prevent unintentional blurring of the image upon capture.

Autofocus (AF)

When a camera is set to *autofocus* mode, it analyzes the area of a scene and then calculates the distance between the camera and the main subject. Point-and-shoot cameras normally use an active autofocus method in which an invisible infrared beam scans objects located within 25 feet of the lens. The camera computes subject distance by analyzing the time it takes for the light to be reflected back to the camera. DSLRs typically use a *passive autofocus* technique that's much more sophisticated and usually more accurate. With this approach, the camera uses a small sensor, called a charge-coupled device (CCD), to detect and analyze changes in the contrast of image pixels. *Active autofocusing* systems can be used in virtual darkness as they provide their own focusing light. Passive systems must have a sufficient amount of light and image contrast in order to work effectively.

AF TARGET POINT

By default, autofocus is usually set to a single target point located in the center of the image. When the main subject is positioned in the center of the frame, this works well. Simply set the focus and snap the image. However, a different focusing strategy must be employed when the subject is placed in an off-center position. With most cameras, this involves the following steps: 1) place the main subject in the center of the screen; 2) acquire and lock the focus by depressing the shutter button halfway; 3) reframe the main subject in an off-center position; and 4) fully depress the shutter button to capture the image. Many cameras provide options for acquiring focus with user-select, single-spot, or multi-spot target points.

While active and passive autofocusing systems have improved dramatically over the years, neither method is foolproof. At some point, autofocus will let you down as the camera miscalculates the proper focus setting. Problems are likely to occur in the following situations:

- When near and distant objects are mixed close together within the frame, the camera may be unable to determine which object in the composition to focus on.
- Moving objects like cars and bikes can confuse the autofocus sensor, causing a focus shift at the point of acquisition.
- Extremely bright lights or subject areas can make it difficult for the camera to lock onto a subject and acquire focus.
- Monochromatic scenes can lack the contrast necessary for acquiring an accurate focus.

> **GREAT IDEAS**
> Selective Focus
> Photographs are two-dimensional. They only have width and height. We infer depth based on visual clues, which can be created using a range of lighting, exposure, and focus techniques. *Selective focus* is a popular technique used by photographers to heighten the interest of an otherwise ordinary composition. Using selective focus, only one primary element in a scene is sharply in focus. The rest of the background and/or foreground elements of the scene are blurred, creating a sense of compositional depth (see Figure 10.21, right).

Manual Focus (MF)

On professional cameras with interchangeable lenses, focus can be acquired manually by rotating the innermost ring on the circumference of the lens. Turning the ring in either direction changes the sharpness of the image. On less expensive cameras, manual focus will be either unavailable or controlled through the use of a menu or button. The viewfinder usually displays an MF or AF as a reminder of which mode is currently active. Manual focus should be used whenever you are located more than 25 feet away from the subject or whenever the camera is unable to isolate the subject or acquire focus automatically.

DEPTH OF FIELD

Depth of field (DOF) refers to the area of a scene in front of and behind the main subject that is in focus. The term *great depth of field* is used to describe a photograph where the majority of the scene is sharply defined (see Figure 10.21, left). *Shallow depth of field* describes an image where noticeable portions of the foreground and/or background areas of a scene are out of focus (see Figure 10.21, right).

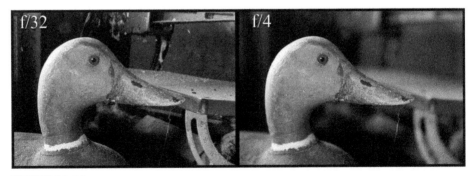

FIGURE 10.21
These images were made almost identically, with the only changes being the shutter speed and aperture. The aperture changes each in a way that alters its success through directing the viewer's gaze. While neither is necessarily "right," the image with less depth of field seems more successful, since in the one with greater depth the decoy's bill seems to be competing for attention with the tools in the background.
Source: Chris Walker.

Photographers will sometimes manipulate DOF to emphasize the focal point of a composition through visual contrast. Background elements can often steal attention away from the main subject in a photograph. For example, when an image is taken of a person positioned directly in front of a tree or wall, the subject and the background appear to merge. The lack of three-dimensional depth creates a flat image lacking in visual contrast. Decreasing DOF in a scene such as this deemphasizes the visual importance of the background by drawing the attention of the viewer to the portion of the scene that is in focus. In some cases, the photographer will use an exceptionally shallow depth of field, blurring the background to the point that it may be all but unrecognizable. In photography, this effect is often referred to as *bokeh* (BOH-ka), from a Japanese term meaning blur or haze.

The factors affecting DOF in an image are rather complex and would require more time than we have to go into here. In the simplest terms, it can be said that DOF is largely affected by three main variables: 1) the size of the lens aperture or f-stop setting; 2) the focal length of the lens; and 3) the distance from the camera to the subject.

Aperture Size

The size of the aperture is inversely related to the DOF of an image. As the size of the aperture decreases, DOF increases, causing more of the scene to appear in focus. As the aperture is enlarged, DOF decreases, creating greater contrast between foreground and background objects. In a brightly lit scene, the aperture is normally small, making it more difficult to acquire shallow depth of field. In situations like this, a larger aperture setting can be obtained by zooming in or by increasing the camera's shutter speed or decreasing the film speed (see Figure 10.22).

FIGURE 10.22
Depth of field is the front-to-back distance within a scene that appears to be in focus because of the aperture at which the image was made. In this comparison, the top image, shot at f/2.8, exhibits very shallow depth of field, while the bottom image, shot at f/22, exhibits maximum depth of field.
Source: Adam Bulgatz.

Focal Length

The focal length of the lens is also inversely related to DOF. As you zoom in on an image, the focal length of the lens increases while DOF decreases. For this reason, wide-angle shots such as landscapes and vistas often have a great depth of field, while narrow-angle shots acquired with a telephoto lens often have a shallow depth of field.

Subject/Camera Distance

The physical distance between the camera and the subject is the third variable affecting DOF in a composition. DOF increases with distance and decreases as you move the camera physically closer to the subject.

EXPOSURE MODES

Digital cameras feature a variety of exposure modes designed for many of the most common shooting conditions. The exposure mode options vary by camera, but they normally span a range from fully automatic, where control of image exposure is retained entirely by the camera, to fully manual, where the photographer assumes command of all exposure settings. A number of semi-automatic modes exist in between the two extremes, allowing the photographer and camera to share control of exposure settings.

Automatic Modes

FULLY AUTOMATIC MODE

When set to *fully automatic mode*, a camera will analyze the area of a scene and calculate the settings for shutter speed, aperture, ISO, white balance, focus, and flash. Depending on the quality of the camera, shooting in auto mode can produce good results under normal lighting conditions most of the time. While shooting in auto mode makes the camera easier to operate, it significantly reduces the photographer's role in the creative process.

FIGURE 10.23
On many DSLRs, the exposure mode can be quickly changed using a rotating dial such as this on the top of the camera.

PORTRAIT MODE

In *portrait mode*, the exposure controls of the camera are optimized for shooting close-ups with a shallow depth of field. The objective in this mode is to keep the subject in focus while blurring the background. The camera accomplishes this by raising the shutter speed in conjunction with widening the aperture. Portrait mode works best when the subject is tightly framed and there is considerable distance between the subject and the background. Shallow DOF is always more difficult to achieve when the subject is placed directly against the background.

LANDSCAPE MODE

Landscape mode is the opposite of portrait mode. In this mode, the exposure settings of the camera are optimized for shooting wide shots with a great depth of field. The objective in landscape mode is to keep as much of the scene as possible in focus. To accomplish this, the camera combines a small aperture with a slower shutter speed. As a result, in some cases, you may need to use a tripod to maintain a steady shot.

SPORTS MODE

Sports mode, or *action mode*, as it's sometimes called, favors a fast shutter speed and is recommended for shooting a moving subject within a scene. When capturing moving subjects during a bike race or soccer game, for example, a fast shutter speed is required in order to freeze the image without blurring. If the shutter speed is too slow, a motion blur will occur. When composing an action scene, a dramatic effect can be achieved by panning the camera along with the moving subject while depressing the shutter button. This technique produces a sharply defined subject while creating an intentional motion blur in the background (see Figure 10.24).

FIGURE 10.24
Sports mode is useful for stopping action and having enough depth of field left to make your images sharp. But sometimes it's good to experiment and "pan" a few frames. *Panning* is the process of selecting a slow shutter speed, such as 1/8th or 1/15th, and triggering the shutter while following the action. This method is not for the impatient; photographers who succeed at panning learn early on to shoot hard and edit harder.
Source: Chris Walker.

NIGHT MODE

Night mode uses a slow shutter speed combined with the flash when shooting a subject set against a dimly lit backdrop like a sunset or evening sky. The long exposure time allows the details of the background to remain correctly exposed during the firing of the flash to illuminate the subject. A tripod should be used in order to prevent unintentional blurring.

Tech Talk

Stitching Mode *Stitching mode* is used for acquiring a sequence of shots that can be joined together in editing to create a high-resolution segmented panorama (see Figure 10.25). After taking the first picture in stitch mode, the camera provides a split screen view of the previous shot and the currently framed scene to help you align the end of one frame with the beginning of the next. Many smartphone cameras and compacts offer a panorama mode to achieve a similar outcome. Instead of shooting multiple segmented images of a scene and stitching them together later in editing, your camera creates a single image on the fly as you pan slowly across the scene during exposure. Shooting in panorama mode is easy and can produce good results under the right conditions. However, it isn't really the same thing and can often lead to unintended visual artifacts. When done well, stitching produces more professional results without visual artifacts because much more original image data goes into the formation of the panorama.

FIGURE 10.25
Stitching mode can be used to take a series of photos that will be loaded into Photoshop, or an internal camera program, to "stitch" them together. The key to success lies in overlapping your images—between a third and a half of the area of the previous—so the computer can read the design of one image as it prepares to lace it together with the next one in the series. This stitched image, a tiny courtroom where Lincoln practiced law, is a composite of six vertical photos.
Source: Chris Walker.

Semi-Automatic Modes

APERTURE PRIORITY MODE

In *aperture priority mode*, the photographer determines the f-stop setting manually while the camera sets the remaining exposure variables. The main purpose of using this mode is to control for depth of field in a scene. However, unlike portrait or landscape modes, the photographer retains total control of the aperture.

SHUTTER PRIORITY MODE

In *shutter priority mode*, the photographer sets the shutter speed while the camera sets all the remaining exposure variables. This mode is used when the photographer wants to retain precise control of exposure time. For example, when shooting a waterfall, a slow shutter speed can be set in order to accentuate motion by blurring the water while the surrounding area of the scene remains sharp (see Figures 10.26–10.28). Using a fast shutter speed on the same scene can result in the effect of suspended droplets of water hovering in midair for heightened effect.

PROGRAM MODE

Some cameras offer a *program mode* setting in which the camera determines the correct settings for aperture and shutter speed while allowing the photographer access to other controls like ISO, white balance, flash, and so on.

Manual Mode

In *full manual mode*, the photographer has control of all the camera's exposure settings and related controls. While this mode requires the most skill and knowledge, it also allows for the greatest degree of creative control.

FIGURE 10.26
Shutter priority mode allows the photographer to choose a shutter speed and leaves it up to the camera's programming to choose the appropriate aperture. For this rainy afternoon, the shutter speed was approximately 12 seconds and the aperture was f/32.
Source: Chris Walker.

FIGURE 10.27
The length of exposure needed for this image ultimately gives the illusion of clouds or fog mingling among the rocks below. In reality, though, it's the frothy heads of crashing waves that have been rendered softly over the course of the 20-minute exposure, cumulatively being gathered as they blur and overlap on a single piece of film.
Source: Chris Walker.

FIGURE 10.28
By opting for a lengthy exposure, the water was allowed plenty of time to blur—about a minute—while the photographer's luck held out and very little wind stirred the leaves in the foreground.
Source: Chris Walker.

IMAGE STABILIZATION

Tripods, monopods, and other camera-mounting devices are used in still photography and video production to keep the camera stable when shooting and are covered in greater depth in chapter 13. Even the slightest movement of the camera during acquisition can result in a fuzzy image or a distracting visual shift when using a video camera. The potential for shakiness increases when the camera is set to a slow shutter speed and/or to a long focal length. Therefore, it's critical to stabilize the camera in low-light conditions or in situations where you are not close to the subject. In video production, shooting from a tripod should be considered the norm rather than the exception. Random or unmotivated camera movements are one of the telltale signs of an amateur production. While using a tripod adds another degree of difficulty to a production setup, having stable shots makes it worth the effort. In situations where using a tripod is not possible, you can help the situation by moving closer to the subject, adjusting the lens to a wide-angle setting, and supplementing existing light, particularly if it is a bit dark.

Video cameras often include a feature called *optical image stabilization* (OIS) that works by shifting the pixel matrix in the direction of camera movement in order to counteract the effects of camera motion. While it may work well under certain conditions, it is a digital effect, and its use can lead to the creation of unintended visual artifacts, making it a poor substitute for using a tripod.

SOLID-STATE MEMORY CARDS

The images captured by a digital camera are usually stored on a removable solid-state memory card. These cards can best be thought of as a temporary storage solution for digital images until they can be downloaded to a computer or transferred to a more secure location. Since the beginning of digital photography, a variety of different card formats have been introduced, leading to a confusing myriad of storage options. Since the cards are not interchangeable, it's important to know what type of flash memory card your camera uses and what capacity it supports.

The CompactFlash (CF) card format was introduced by SanDisk Corporation in 1994 and features a footprint that's a bit smaller than a matchbook and weighs only half an ounce. You can find CF memory cards in a range of storage capacities, including some that will hold over 100 GB of data.

The Secure Digital (SD) card format was developed jointly by Matsushita, SanDisk, and Toshiba and was released in 2000. SD cards are roughly half the size of CF cards and come in three main categories (according to storage capacity) as defined by the SD Association standards and specifications. *Standard Memory Cards* (SD) are the oldest and cheapest and have a capacity up to 2 GB. *High-Capacity Memory Cards* (SDHC) provide for data storage above 2 GB up to a maximum of 32 GB. *Extended Capacity Memory Cards* (SDXC) are rated above 32 GB up to a maximum of 2 TB (see Figure 10.29). Be careful, though, as older SD cameras and devices usually cannot use the newer SDHC or SDXC formats. Some devices, particularly mobile phones, use smaller versions of these SD formats under the labels miniSD, microSD, miniSDHC, microSDHC, and microSDXC.

SD cards are also rated for speed, primarily to help consumers know which cards are appropriate for video recording (see Table 10.5). SD Speed Class standards were established by the SD Association to support video recording to flash memory cards. The higher the SD classification number, the faster the speed of the card. When shooting video with a DSLR or video camera, be sure to consult the manual for the type of card to use. Class 2 cards are fine for general-purpose photography and standard-definition video recording but are limited in terms of capacity. Cards with a Class 4, 6, or 10 rating are designed for high-definition video recording. Class 10 is recommended for use with professional video cameras. UHS-1 and UHS-3 offer the best speed performance for professional HD and ultra HD production workflows.

FIGURE 10.29
Since 2000, when SD cards were first introduced, their capacity and speed have steadily increased. Because they vary so much in terms of format and class, be sure to read the fine print on the label to ensure you are getting the best card your device can support.
Source: SanDisk.

Table 10.5	SD Card Speed Class Standards		
	Mark	**Minimum Writing Speed**	**Application**
Speed Class	Class 2	2 MB/s	Digital photography and standard video recording (SD)
	Class 4	4 MB/s	HD and Full HD video recording
	Class 6	6 MB/s	
	Class 10	10 MB/s	Full HD video and HD still image continuous shooting
UHS Speed Class	UHS-1	10 MB/s	
	UHS-3	30 MB/s	2K and 4K video recording

Source: http://www.sdcard.org.

The **MultiMediaCard (MMC)** format was launched by Siemens AG and SanDisk in 1997. MMCs come in three different sizes, with the smallest version roughly the size of a postage stamp. SD has largely supplanted MMC in most new devices.

Sony developed the Memory Stick (MS) in 1998 as a proprietary format for their line of multimedia products. The Memory Stick Duo (MS Duo) is a variation of the MS, which is smaller in size.

FIGURE 10.30
For today's young generation of digital photographers who've never shot with film, the idea of manually loading a spool of 35 mm film into an analog camera must seem rather odd and old-fashioned. By comparison, inserting a solid-state memory card is a virtual "no-brainer."

TRANSFERRING AND MANAGING IMAGES

Most cameras made today have a USB port built into the camera for connecting directly to a computer to download images. Assuming that all the necessary hardware drivers are installed, your computer should automatically recognize a camera connection as soon as the cable is attached, the power is turned on, and the camera is placed in playback mode. If you have a computer with a built-in SD card reader, you can avoid cables altogether by removing the card from the camera and inserting it directly into the computer. In recent versions of Windows, connecting a camera should trigger the AutoPlay dialog box to open, which will present you with options for viewing, selecting, and downloading images from the camera's memory card to an attached hard drive. In Mac OS X, the default imaging software, iPhoto or Photos for OS X, will launch once a camera or SD card is detected, providing you with similar options as AutoPlay. Unless you specify a different location, both Windows and Mac systems will store your downloaded images by default in the Pictures library of the currently logged-in user. Likewise, both operating systems provide users with the option of manually downloading images from the camera (or memory card) to a designated folder or storage drive that is attached to the computer locally or remotely via the cloud or network connection.

Digital Image Management

Most people download images to a computer giving very little thought as to their location, organization, or potential retrievability. Without proper care, the My Photo or Pictures folder can quickly resemble the overstuffed family shoebox that's

Tech Talk

Metadata Every time an image is captured and saved by a digital camera, nonpicture information about the image is recorded and saved to the file header. This information is called *metadata* and includes things such as the date and time of image acquisition, the camera make and model number, image size, and values for exposure settings such as aperture, shutter speed, focal length, ISO, and, in some cases, GPS (Global Positioning Sys-tem) data. Most cameras today encode metadata using an international standard called the Exchangeable Image File Format (EXIF). Nearly all image-editing programs are capable of displaying EXIF metadata. In Photoshop, selecting **File>File Info** opens up a dialog window containing access to EXIF metadata along with a number of blank entry fields the photographer can use to attach more descriptive details to an image file (see Figure 10.31). Be

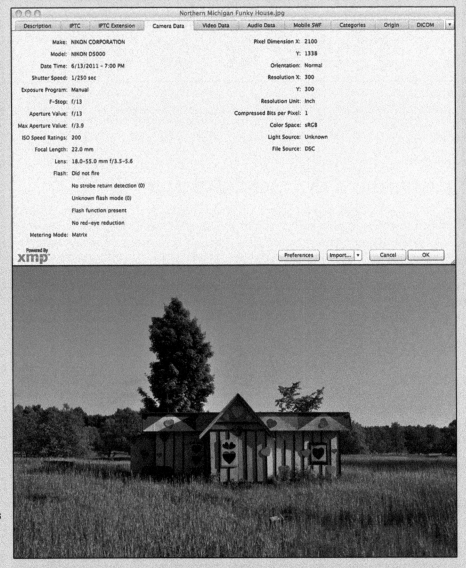

FIGURE 10.31
With each photograph, the camera gathers a significant amount of information, called metadata, that gets stored in the image file. In addition to a complete list of camera settings, some models even gather GPS data, allowing photographers to later identify locations or revisit them for subsequent shoots.
Source: Chris Walker.

careful about metadata. It often embeds a thumbnail of the original image that is not necessarily modified when you modify the actual image. This means that if you erase something from the image, it may still be visible in the thumbnail. If your camera has a GPS, you need to know that the GPS data is included in the image—something that is common on GPS-enabled smartphones. While software can use this information to help sort your images, it also means someone can easily find out where you took the image. Think before you release your images.

In 1979, the International Press Telecommunications Council (IPTC) developed a more extensive set of labeling attributes to give photographers the ability to add descriptive details about the origins and subject matter of an image to the file header. IPTC headers include a variety of informational fields such as object name and title; the city, state, and country of origin; credits; subject category, image caption, and keywords; and special instructions. Professional photographers, digital media producers, and large media organizations typically rely on some type of asset management system for logging, storing, and retrieving digital image files according to embedded IPTC metadata. Programs like Canto Cumulus and Extensis Portfolio provide a visual interface for logging images with IPTC tags, making it possible for content producers to locate and retrieve matching files using keywords and user-specified search criteria.

filled willy-nilly with 20 years of old photographs. And with digital images, the virtual shoebox is likely to become a cluttered mess all the more quickly. In order to effectively organize and manage an image library, the photographer should take the time to: 1) properly assign a descriptive name to each image file; 2) store related sets of images in topical subfolders; and 3) modify the metadata fields of an image file to include details about the picture's origins and subject matter. While this may seem like busywork, it is not. Asset management is an incredibly important part of any multimedia endeavor and invariably leads to a better workflow.

RENAMING IMAGES

Digital cameras usually assign rather meaningless names to image files. Renaming your image files is one of the first and most important things you can do to bring a sense of order and uniformity to a collection of related images. Programs such as Adobe Bridge and Apple's Aperture can help automate this process. When you rename the files, consider using a standard prefix for related images. For example, for a group of photos taken of Beth on her birthday in 2006, you could use beth_bd06_ as the prefix. As discussed in chapter 7, "Web Design," use lowercase names if you plan to use the images online. Similarly, use an underscore instead of a space when you want to separate the character elements in a file name. After establishing the prefix, you need to make the remaining part of the file names sequential. This is where using a program to automate the process really helps. In some cases, you may be able to use part of the file name generated by the camera. This is very helpful for preserving the chronological order of the collection.

IMAGE FOLDERS

Try to avoid the habit of storing all your digital images in a single master folder. As your image library grows, the folder will swell, and it will become increasingly difficult for you to navigate such a large collection of files in one location. A better method is to use subfolders to store related sets of images. Some of the same naming strategies we've discussed so far can be applied to the naming of image subfolders. Sorting images into subfolders according to project or client name, subject name, or event title will help alleviate a great deal of confusion and expedite locating image assets.

CHAPTER SUMMARY

A digital camera is one of many tools a multimedia producer can use to create visual assets for a project. The more knowledgeable you are about the imaging process, the more creative freedom you will be able to exercise during the acquisition of digital pictures. This chapter has focused primarily on the mechanical aspects of digital photography by discussing the operational function of imaging components and the management of exposure controls. As the photographer, the degree to which you retain control during the exposure process is determined by which shooting method or mode you adopt. In fully automatic mode, the camera retains total control of all the exposure variables. In manual mode, the photographer has more latitude and creative freedom but must also possess greater skill and knowledge about the camera, its operation, and intentional outcomes.

SECTION 4
Time-Based Media

11. Recording Formats and Device Settings   331
12. Audio Production   371
13. Video Production   403
14. Time-Based Editing   441

Shutterstock

CHAPTER 11

Recording Formats and Device Settings

The current saturation of relatively inexpensive multimedia communication tools holds tremendous potential for destroying the monopoly of ideas we have lived with for so long . . . A personal computer can be configured to act as a publishing house, a broadcast-quality TV studio, a professional recording studio, or the node in an international computer bulletin board system.

—Mark Dery, author and cultural critic (1993)

Chapter Highlights

This chapter examines:

- The evolution of analog and digital videotape recording formats
- The transition from tape-based recording formats to file-based recording formats
- Open and proprietary standards for encoding digital audio and video files
- The difference between compressed and uncompressed audio and video file formats
- FWIGSS—six basic camcorder settings everyone should understand

At some point in your multimedia endeavors you may find yourself having to operate a digital audio recorder or camcorder to record an interview or event. At the very least, you will be tasked to work with media file formats with strange looking extensions such as *.wav*, *.aif*, *.mp3*, *.mov*, *.m4v*, etc. and will be expected to know what they are and what to do with them. As the first of four chapters dealing with our final topic of time-based media, this chapter seeks to establish a foundation. Some of the questions we will tackle include: How are video images and audio signals recorded and stored as media files? What is the difference between a media container format and a codec? How do I know which recording format and settings to choose when my camera or audio recorder offers so many selections? Chapter 12 focuses on audio production and the equipment and techniques used for sound acquisition. Chapter 13 covers video production while chapter 14 wraps up the section with the topic of editing and motion graphics.

Key Terms

Advanced Audio Coding (AAC)
Advanced Video Coding (AVC)
AIFF (Audio Interchange File Format)
Audio Compression
AVCHD
Bit Depth
Bit Rate
Codec
Container Format
Dolby Digital (AC3)
DVD Video
Encoding
File-Based Recording
Follow Focus
FWIGSS
H.264/H.265
High-Definition Television (HD)
ISO/IEC/ITU (International Organization for Standardization/ International Electrotechnical Commission/ International Telecommunication Union)
Motion Pictures Experts Group (MPEG)
MP3
MPEG-1
MPEG-2
MPEG-4

Neutral Density Filter
Open Standard
Panasonic P2
  Memory Card
Professional Disc
Pulse-Code
  Modulation (PCM)
Quantization
QuickTime
Rack Focus
Record Format
Red Book Standard
Red Digital Cinema
Sample Rate
Sony SxS Memory
  Card
Ultra-High-Definition
  Television (Ultra HD)
Video Compression
Videotape
WAV (Waveform
  Audio File Format)
Zebra

LEGACY TELEVISION RECORDING FORMATS

In the early days of television broadcasting, programs were produced and transmitted simultaneously. During a "live" production, the audience would see the on-screen performance as it was carried out in real time, most likely in a remote television studio far away. Recording technologies, like videotape, that have long been associated with television and video production were not invented until long after television was established as a viable commercial enterprise.

Ampex Corporation invented the world's first open-reel audio tape recorder in 1948. Dubbed the Model 200, it was used by the American Broadcasting Company (ABC) for the tape-delayed transmission of *The Bing Crosby Show*. The event went down in history as the first tape-delayed broadcast of a radio program in the United States. It took Ampex another eight years to release the first commercial videotape recorder, the VRX-1000 (or Mark IV), which they introduced at the National Association of Radio and Television Broadcasters' convention in Chicago in 1956.

FIGURE 11.1
The popular children's program *Howdy Doody* was telecast by NBC from 1947 to 1960. Prior to the invention of video recording, programs like this one were produced and transmitted "live" to the home television audience.

Videotape

Unlike motion picture film, the frame and track regions on a magnetic tape are invisible to the human eye. But just because you can't see them doesn't mean they don't exist (see Figure 11.2). For recording purposes, videotape is divided into four tracks. The *video track* is the widest region and is used to store the picture portion of a television program. Videotape also contains two audio tracks. These *audio tracks* can be used in tandem for recording one two-channel stereo signal or separately for recording two monaural feeds. For example, in a two-person interview, the microphone input from Person A can be recorded to one track while the signal from Person B is routed to the second one.

The fourth region of a videotape is designated as the *control track*. To understand the purpose of the control track, it is helpful to draw a comparison to motion picture film. Film contains two lines of sprocket holes along each edge of the filmstrip. As a film is projected, moving gear-like wheels engage the sprocket holes to advance each frame of film to the next. The sprocket holes keep the film aligned and moving at the appropriate speed. Like film, videotape is in constant motion during record and playback modes. As the video and audio signals are recorded to tape, an electronic synch pulse is written to the control track to mark the location of each video frame. U.S. broadcast video systems traditionally generate 30 frames of picture information every second. The control track marks where these frames begin and end in order to ensure the videotape plays correctly.

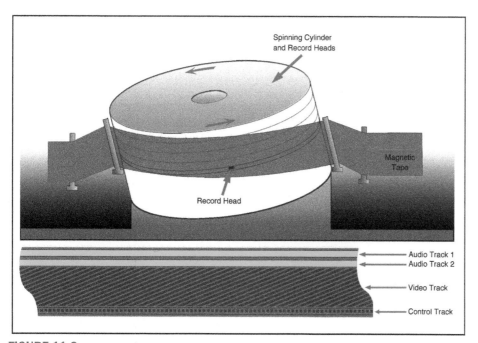

FIGURE 11.2
The surface area of a videotape is divided into linear regions called tracks. Most tape-based formats include one track for video, two tracks for audio, and one track for synchronization or control data.

Analog Tape Formats

The 1970s ushered in the era of electronic news gathering (ENG) and electronic field production (EFP) with the invention of the camcorder and a variety of consumer and professional videocassette tape formats such as VHS and U-matic. A chief disadvantage of analog tape formats was the problem of generation loss, which would occur whenever a program was copied from one tape to another. Since most editing at that time was performed machine to machine—basically through systematic dubbing from one videotape recorder (VTR) to another—generation loss was a pervasive concern. A copy of an analog tape was never as good as the original it was dubbed from. While in a first-generation dub (a copy of the original), the quality loss might not be too noticeable; signal degradation would get progressively worse with each additional dub to the next generation. Thus, a fourth-generation dub (a copy of a copy of a copy) looked far worse than one that was reproduced directly from the original.

Digital Tape Formats

The 1980s was marked by the digital revolution, which dramatically changed the nature of broadcast technologies and production workflows. Digital recording offered numerous advantages over earlier analog methods, but perhaps none was greater than the elimination of generation loss during editing and duplication. Digital VTRs recorded video and audio signals as discrete binary values that could be copied without error from one tape to the next. A data point was either a zero or a one, which meant that a copy of a copy of a copy would be virtually identical to the master recording every time.

All of the legacy analog formats and early digital formats recorded only in standard definition NTSC (National Television Standards Committee; 720 × 486) or PAL (Phase Alternating Line; 720 × 576). It wasn't until the mid- to late 1990s that professional high-definition (HD) tape formats became available, and initially, they were very expensive formats to work with. As an alternative to full-bandwidth HD formats such as D5HD and HDCAM, manufacturers discovered a way to record a low-resolution version of HD (1440 × 1080) on standard DV tape—a digital video tape format that sold for a fraction of the cost. This hybrid format, called HDV, appealed to many people working in the prosumer and educational markets and remained quite popular until the advent of high-definition file-based recording.

FIGURE 11.3
Tape formats are not interchangeable. The professional VTR on the left was designed specifically for use with Digital Betacam tapes, a format that is incompatible with the VHS recorder pictured right.

FIGURE 11.4
Over the years, videocassette tapes were produced in many different formats and sizes. Here, the full-size version of a Sony Betacam SP tape (purple) is compared to Panasonic's DVCPRO (yellow) and the popular consumer format MiniDV (red).

FLASHBACK

Timeline of Professional Videotape Formats

Analog Tape Formats

1971   U-matic 3/4-Inch

The Japanese consortium of Sony, JVC, and Matsushita (Panasonic) pioneer a new era of electronic news gathering (ENG) with their joint release of the U-matic videotape recording format. U-matic, better known as 3/4-inch, gave field producers the first viable alternative to a film-based production workflow.

1982   Sony Betacam and Panasonic M

Sony introduces Betacam, the first component video format designed specifically for professional use. In response, Panasonic releases the M format (or Recam). Both of these component formats used a new narrower tape medium that was only one-half inch thick. The M format proved largely unsuccessful.

1986   U-matic SP

Sony releases U-matic SP (for Superior Performance), which used chrome tape and enhanced signal processing to produce a better picture. It remained, however, a composite videotape format. U-matic is regarded as one of the most successful and longest lasting video formats of all time.

(Continued)

1986 *Betacam SP and MII*

Sony and Panasonic upgrade their professional line of recording formats with the release of Betacam SP and MII (pronounced *m-two*). While MII fared better than its predecessor (the failed M format), Betacam SP grew to become the dominant professional tape format throughout the 1990s.

Digital Standard-Definition Tape Formats

1986 *D1*

Sony and BTS bring the first digital tape format to market. Dubbed D1, the format provided a way for broadcasters to digitally write an uncompressed component NTSC video signal to tape. Unfortunately, D1 was a costly and inefficient format and had limited success.

1988 *D2*

Ampex and Sony introduce D2, the first digital tape format to be widely accepted by professional users.

1991 *D3*

Panasonic releases the D3 format. D3 decks were able to write uncompressed composite video to a one-half-inch-wide tape, the narrowest yet for a professional digital format.

1993 *Digital Betacam*

Sony unveils Digital Betacam (or Digibeta). Whereas their first attempt to design a digital component recorder proved a dismal failure, Digibeta proved a great success.

1994 *D5*

Panasonic introduces D5 for recording uncompressed digital component SD video.

1996 *Betacam SX*

Sony releases Betacam SX, a cheaper version of Digital Betacam specifically designed for those working in ENG.

Digital High-Definition Tape Formats

1994 *D5HD*

Panasonic introduces a high-definition companion product to D5.

1997 *HDCAM*

Sony releases HDCAM as a high-definition version of Digital Betacam, with the ability to record 1080i video at a native resolution of 1440 x 1080.

2001 *MPEG IMX*

Sony releases an advanced digital HD format that is fully compatible with the DTV (Digital Television) standard. It is also provided full support for all the legacy Betacam formats (Betacam, Betacam SP, Digital Betacam, and Beta SX).

DV Formats

1995 *DVCPRO*

Panasonic introduces this prosumer variant of the DV specification. DVCPRO was marketed to low-budget professional users (small market ENG news crews, etc.) looking for an alternative to expensive digital formats like Digital Betacam. Panasonic released DVCPRO50 as a high-end professional DV format two years later.

1997 *DVCAM*

Sony follows suit with its own professional format based on the DV standard.

2003 *HDV*

A consortium of four companies (Canon, JVC, Sharp, and Sony) introduce the HDV standard as a way to record HD video on a standard DV tape. To do so, they decreased the resolution of the HD image to 1440 x 1080. HDV provided an affordable way for low-budget professionals to begin working in HD.

FILE-BASED RECORDING FORMATS

While some people today still shoot on tape using older cameras that are rapidly becoming outdated, most consumers and professionals have embraced the shift to tapeless technologies that utilize solid-state media and file-based recording formats. With file-based recording, digital devices such as DSLRs (digital single lens reflex cameras), video camcorders, audio recorders, smartphones, and so forth encode audio and video signals directly to a flash drive or memory card as digital bitstreams enclosed in a wrapper or container file. A *bitstream* is a sequence of bits used to represent individual video or audio signals.

Codecs and Container Formats

The process of *encoding* is at the very heart of file-based recording. Without being overly technical, encoding is the method a device or software application uses to numerically represent a multimedia asset in binary form. An encoding algorithm, more commonly known as a *codec,* is a specially created *file format* used to arrange the underlying bits (zeros and ones) to conform to a particular standard. Decoding goes hand in hand with encoding. Your digital device or software app must be able to decode (or read) a file format in order to accurately play the contents back to you (see Figure 11.5). A codec, short for **co**der-**dec**oder, is said to be *supported* when a device or

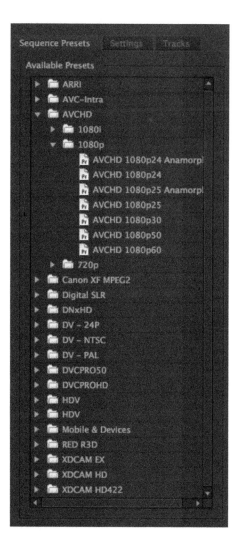

FIGURE 11.5

The sequence preset window in Adobe Premier Pro displays a long list of video formats it supports. While the choices may seem daunting at first, most of the time you will find yourself working with a handful of trusted video formats and codecs. So don't panic, you don't need to understand them all.

Source: Adobe product screenshot reprinted with permission from Adobe Systems Incorporated.

program is able to decode it and make sense of it and is *unsupported* when it is not able to do so. *Transcoding* is the process of converting a file from one format (or codec) to another; for example, converting a Microsoft Word document to PDF or a WAV audio file to MP3.

A *multimedia container* or *wrapper file* is used for bundling and storing the raw digital bitstreams that codecs create. For example, a digital stereo audio signal contains two bitstreams, one for the left channel and one for the right. An audio codec such as PCM is used to encode each bitstream while a container file such as WAV or AIFF keeps them together in a single data file. Each codec (and there are many of them) performs a single encoding/decoding function, while a container format can, and often does, support multiple codecs. Apple QuickTime is a popular container format. QuickTime supports a vast assortment of codecs, including these that are widely used in multimedia: 1) GIF, JPEG, PNG, and TIFF for graphics; 2) AIFF, AAC, MP3, and WAV for audio; and 3) AVCHD, DV, MPEG-4, H.264, and QuickTime Movie (.mov) for video (see Figure 11.6). Any file created with one of these QuickTime-supported codecs can be viewed using Apple's QuickTime Player or with a software program that supports QuickTime.

Hundreds of codecs have been developed for digital video and audio applications over the years. Some codecs, such as Dolby AC3 and WMA, are proprietary and may only work with certain programs or devices. Others, like MPEG-4, are supported by open standards, which means they are more universally accepted and supported. Some codecs are also designed to perform *compression*—the process of encoding or transcoding a data file using fewer bits. A compression codec is designed to reduce the file size of a digital asset without adversely affecting its resolution. The popular MP3 audio format is a compression codec that's used to reduce the size of a digital recording, thereby allowing you to fit thousands, rather than hundreds, of songs on your portable music player.

Media formats supported by QuickTime Player

QuickTime Player supports the following media file formats and codecs.

Below are the media formats and codecs that QuickTime Player can open in Mac OS X v10.6.x or later:

Media type	File formats	Codecs or components
Video	• QuickTime Movie (.mov) • MPEG-4 (.mp4, .m4v) • MPEG-2 (OS X Lion or later) • MPEG-1 • 3GPP • 3GPP2 • AVCHD (OS X Mountain Lion or later) • AVI (Motion JPEG only) • DV	• MPEG-2 (OS X Lion or later) • MPEG-4 (Part 2) • H.264 • H.263 • H.261 • Apple ProRes • Apple Pixlet • Animation • Cinepak • Component Video • DV • DVC Pro 50 • Graphics • Motion JPEG • Photo JPEG • Sorenson Video 2 • Sorenson Video 3
Audio	• iTunes Audio (.m4a, .m4b, .m4p) • MP3 • Core Audio (.caf) • AIFF • AU • SD2 • WAV • SND • AMR	• AAC (MPEG-4 Audio) • HE-AAC • Apple Lossless • MP3 • AMR Narrowband • MS ADPCM • QDesign Music 2 • Qualcomm PureVoice (QCELP) • IMA 4:1 • MACE 3:1 (Mac OS X v10.6.x only) • MACE 6:1 (Mac OS X v10.6.x only) • ALaw 2:1 • ULaw 2:1 • 24-Bit Integer • 32-Bit Integer • 32-Bit Floating Point • 64-Bit Floating Point

FIGURE 11.6
Apple continually updates this long list of video and audio file formats and codecs supported by its popular QuickTime Player.
Source: http://www.apple.com/support.

DIGITAL AUDIO ENCODING

Analog audio technologies like the phonograph and cassette tape recorder were designed to capture or reproduce the natural fluctuations of original sound waves from beginning to end without interruption. For example, when listening to a phonograph record, the stylus or needle remains in continuous contact with the vinyl disc as it spins on the turntable. There is a perfect one-to-one correlation between the modulation of the analog signal and the vibrations picked up by the stylus as it travels along a spiral path. Many audiophiles prefer analog recordings to digital recordings for the simple reason that they reproduce sound more organically, in much the same way that a human hears and processes sound (see Figure 11.7).

Pulse-Code Modulation

In order for sound to be understood by a computer, it must be converted from its native analog form to a digital format that can be represented with discrete numerical values. *Pulse-code modulation* (PCM) is one of the most common codecs used for recording audio as a digital stream of binary data. British engineer Alec Reeves conceived of PCM in 1937 as a way of reducing noise during the transmission of speech over long-distance telephone lines. His theory of PCM transmission relied on a process called sampling to transform a continuous signal into a sequence of discrete measurements occurring at regular intervals. Each measurement (or sample) represents one instance of a sound wave's properties at a single moment in time (see Figure 11.8). In digital recording, each sample is stored numerically as a binary string of zeros and ones. The fidelity of a PCM audio stream is determined by three variables: 1) sample rate, which specifies the number of samples recorded every second; 2) bit depth, which specifies the number of bits used to encode the value of each sample; and 3) bit rate, which specifies the number of bits per second transmitted during playback.

FIGURE 11.7
Audio recording technologies have changed often over the years. Physical media like vinyl records that you can hold and touch have been replaced with invisible data files that can be purchased online and downloaded to a portable MP3 player in a matter of seconds.

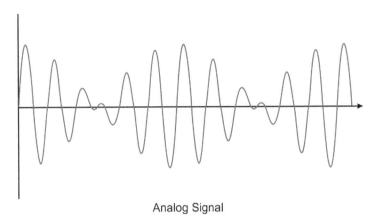

Analog Signal

FIGURE 11.8
Top: An analog audio signal is continuous, without interruption. Bottom: A digital audio signal is produced through sampling, a technique whereby sound is measured and recorded at discrete intervals across time.

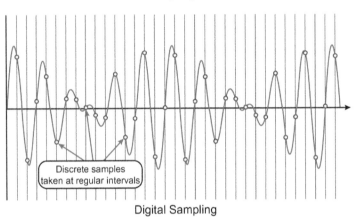

Discrete samples taken at regular intervals

Digital Sampling

SAMPLE RATE

The audio *sample rate* is designated in kilohertz (kHz) units. For example, a 48 kHz sample rate indicates that the recording was sampled 48,000 times per second. While working for Bell Laboratories, engineer Henry Nyquist discovered that the sample rate must be at least twice as large as the bandwidth (or frequency range) of the signal being recorded. Since human hearing has a frequency range of 20 Hz (hertz) to 20 kHz, a minimum sample rate of 40 kHz is required in order to effectively capture and encode all the frequencies within this range. If the sample rate is any lower than this, certain frequencies within the human hearing range may be lost during the recording process. If it is any higher, you're just wasting bits because the human ear cannot discern any notable differences in quality beyond this point. Because of Nyquist's work in sampling theory, 44.1 kHz eventually became the industry-standard sample rate for recorded music.

BIT DEPTH

Whereas sample rate largely impacts the frequency response of a digital recording, *bit depth* affects its dynamic range and the amount of noise and distortion introduced during the recording process. Each audio sample is stored as a binary sequence of zeros and ones. The bit depth setting determines how many zeros and ones are assigned to each sampling interval (usually either 16 or 24). The more bits you have to work with, the more descriptive the encoding can be to reflect the subtle fluctuations in the waveform's amplitude. *Quantization* is a term that's often associated with bit depth and is used to describe the mathematical process of assigning discrete numerical values to each voltage measurement.

An 8-bit sequence has 256 possibilities. A 16-bit sequence has 65,536 possibilities. And a 24-bit sequence can be arranged 16,777,216 different ways. The most common bit depth settings used in professional audio and video recording are 16 bit and 24 bit. While 24-bit recording is technically superior in terms of dynamic range, the higher bit depth also results in larger audio files. Large data files require more resources from your computer system and software when editing and mixing, potentially causing problems if your system isn't equipped to handle 24-bit audio processing. While the difference between 24 bits and 16 bits sounds relatively small, at a sample rate of 44,100 kHz, the amount of digital data stored every second becomes quite substantial. In a 16-bit/44.1 kHz audio recording (standard definition), 700,600 bits of uncompressed data are produced every second. In a 24-bit/96 kHz recording (high-definition), it jumps to more than 2.3 million bits per second.

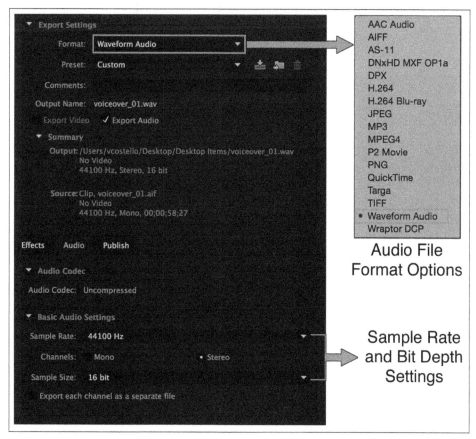

FIGURE 11.9
Adobe Media Encoder CC is a software product designed to transcode video and audio files into a different format. Here, an uncompressed AIFF audio file is being transcoded to a WAV file. The Export Settings properties window allows the user to specify a value for the following settings: 1) audio file format, 2) sample rate, 3) bit depth, and 4) mono or stereo sound.
Source: Adobe product screenshot reprinted with permission from Adobe Systems Incorporated.

FLASHBACK

The Red Book Standard

Sony and Philips are familiar names in the consumer electronics industry. They joined forces to create the audio compact disc format in 1980. In doing so, they developed the infamous "red book" standard for the audio compact disc (CD), which specifies a sample rate of 44.1 kHz and a bit depth of 16 bits. To this day, it remains the professional industry standard for distributing digitally recorded music to consumers on CD. No matter what the bit rate and sample rate are during production and editing, the final distribution file for your audio project should conform to 16 bit/44.1 kHz before being burned to a CD. In digital film and video production, a slightly higher sample rate of 48 kHz was adopted as the industry standard. This rate conforms to the encoding standards set by Philips, Sony, Toshiba, and Time Warner for the digital versatile disc (or DVD) recording platform in 1995. Because of this, camcorders are often programmed to encode the sound portion of a video recording at a sample rate of 48 kHz.

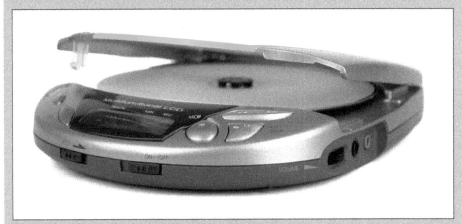

FIGURE 11.10
A portable compact disc player.

BIT RATE

With lossy compression formats such as MP3 and AAC, the number of bits assigned to each sample varies, making the concept of bit depth irrelevant. Instead, the number of bits available for encoding each sample is determined by the bit rate. *Bit rate* refers to the transmission speed of a compressed audio stream during playback—either locally or online in real time—and is expressed in *kilobits per second* (Kbps). In an MP3 audio recording, the bit rate has a user-defined range from 16 to 320 Kbps. The higher the bit rate, the better the quality of the recording. However, higher bit rates also produce larger files that require more transmission bandwidth and/or time to stream than files encoded at a lower bit rate. Setting the bit rate too high can hinder smooth playback of a recording that is being streamed in real time across a Wi-Fi or cellular network. Voice recordings retain more quality at lower bit rate settings than music. For music, 128 Kbps is considered the minimum threshold setting for hi-fidelity. For best results, choose a higher setting of 192 or

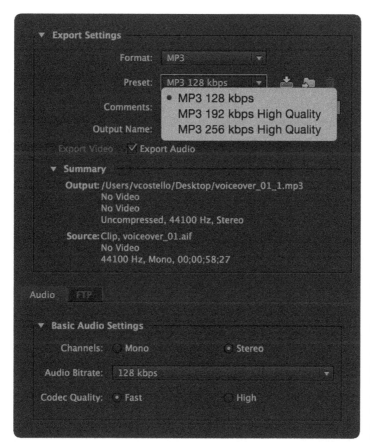

FIGURE 11.11
When Adobe Media Encoder is used to transcode an AIFF file to MP3, the basic audio settings look a little different. First, *sample rate* is no longer an option. This is because MP3s are almost always encoded at 44.1 kHz to conform to the industry standard for audio compact disc. Media Encoder assumes this, so no selection is required. Second, since lossy compression is being applied, *bit depth* is irrelevant. The only quality setting the user needs to be concerned with here is *bit rate*. *Source: Adobe product screenshot reprinted with permission from Adobe Systems Incorporated.*

256 Kbps. Most audio recorders and some cameras allow you to record sound in a compressed format. In such cases, you will find the bit rate setting in the system menu of the device. However, as a matter of best practice, avoid recording audio in a compressed file format. Instead, when given a choice, record audio uncompressed at the highest PCM resolution (AIFF or WAV). You'll be glad you did!

OPEN STANDARDS FOR VIDEO AND AUDIO ENCODING

An *open standard* is a publically released specification or set of specifications used in the design of a product, process, or protocol. You can think of them as rules that companies voluntarily choose to follow in order to make their products compatible with equipment or software made by others. For example, think about how convenient it is to be able to plug in your computer or smartphone charging cable to virtually any wall outlet. What if every hotel or university or business building installed a different type of wall outlet that wasn't supported by your device? You would be out of luck, or—at the very least—forced to carry around an adapter everywhere you went. In fact, when I travel to London, I do just that. I pack a universal power adapter because the electrical interface standards in the U.S. and the U.K. are incompatible.

Standardization makes life better and more predictable for everyone by reducing consumer confusion and creating a more level playing field for companies that design and manufacture similar products for everyday use. So where exactly do these standards come from? Largely, they are formed by consensus within international bodies and working groups made up of industry stakeholders and experts who share a common interest. The most well-known of these include: the International Electrotechnical Commission (IEC), the International Organization for Standardization (ISO), and the International Telecommunication Union (ITU). Together, they created the World Standards Cooperation in 2001 "to strengthen and advance the voluntary consensus-based international standards systems."[1]

In 1988, the ISO/IEC jointly established a working group called the Moving Picture Experts Group (MPEG) and tasked it with developing open standards for digital audio and video encoding. While MPEG, and other similar groups, have published a wide assortment of standards for digital audio and video encoding over the years, we'll touch on only a few of the most significant ones here.

MPEG-1 Audio Layer III (MP3)

MPEG's first set of standards was initially published in 1993 under the name MPEG-1. Part three of this five-part standard was released in 1995 specifying the details for three classes of lossy audio compression. The third class, formally termed *MPEG-1 Audio Layer III*, introduced the MP3 audio compression format. MP3 would eventually become one of the most widely known audio codecs in the world—its popularity heralded by the fact that it was the first digital format designed for encoding and storing music digitally on a portable audio player (see Figure 11.12). With this format, users could now compress a CD-quality audio track, originally distributed as an uncompressed WAV or AIF file, by a ratio

FIGURE 11.12
More than a decade after launching the original iPod player in 2001 (inset), Apple advertises the iPod touch on a double-decker bus in London, England (2012).
Source: Inset: Image courtesy of Apple, Inc.; Main image: Mira Agron/ Dreamstime.com.

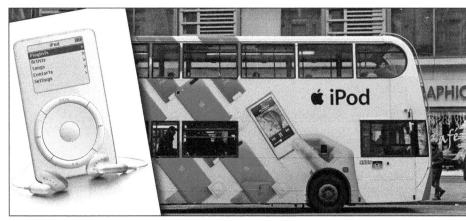

of 10:1. With such a drastic reduction in file size, consumers could now store roughly 10 times as many songs on a portable device. This was a key selling point for Apple when they released the first generation of the iPod portable MP3 player in 2001 and proudly flaunted the advertising slogan "1,000 songs in your pocket" (see Figure 11.12). The downside to lossy compression, of course, is that it results in a permanent loss of original file data. When you apply MP3 compression to a file, you invariably discard 90% of the original data in the sound file. An MP3 version, therefore, is significantly inferior in quality to the uncompressed original in terms of sound quality and fidelity. As time would later prove, however, consumers would be willing to accept this trade-off—more songs for an acceptable loss of quality—and many would never even notice the quality loss while listening through low-fidelity earbuds.

MPEG-2

In addition to MP3, MPEG-1 specified one of the first standards for encoding video, but because the image quality was so poor, its acceptance was short-lived. As a next step, the ISO/IEC released MPEG-2 in 1996. Specifically, MPEG-2 introduced H.262, an advanced format for encoding standard definition (SD) and HD video at a significantly higher bit rate then MPEG-1 allowed. MPEG-2 soon became the international standard for encoding SD video on a red-laser DVD. The new format paved the way for DVDs to eventually replace VHS tape as the primary distribution medium for home movies. MPEG-2 video was vastly superior to a VHS recording and, when combined with a DVD, came with many added benefits over videotape for the consumer (chapter menus, durability, random access to content, more storage capacity for bonus material, computer compatibility, etc.).

ADVANCED AUDIO CODING (AAC)

Audio compression was enhanced as well. With MPEG-2 came Advanced Audio Coding (AAC), a format that extended the stereo capabilities of MPEG-1 to multichannel surround sound. Dolby Digital (also known as AC3) is a widely popular multichannel surround sound standard capable of supporting up to 7.1 channels of audio. Dolby Digital 5.1 is a six-channel broadcast, cinema, and home theater standard that distributes audio to five normal-range speakers—three in the front (L-C-R) and two in the rear (L-R)—and one subwoofer (for low-frequency sounds). Dolby Digital 7.1 adds two additional side-mounted speakers (L-R) into the mix. AAC compression produces a superior quality recording and a smaller file size compared to MP3 files encoded at the same bit rate.

In addition to becoming the encoding standard for DVD video, MPEG-2 was incorporated into digital tape formats like HDV, XDCAM, tapeless video formats like MOD and TOD, and the terrestrial HDTV broadcasting standards ATSC (Advanced Television Systems Committee) and DVB (Digital Video Broadcasting). MPEG-2 is an evolving standard that has been amended several times since its initial public release.

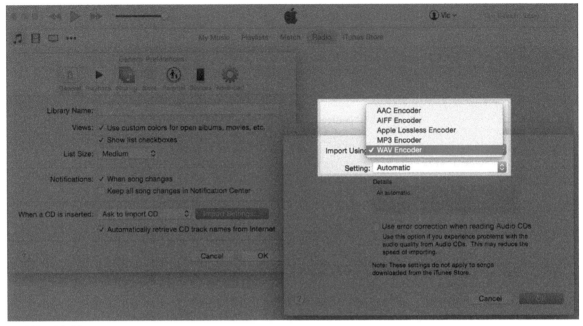

FIGURE 11.13
Apple iTunes includes a built-in audio encoder primarily for the purpose of converting uncompressed AIF and WAV files, such as those imported from an audio compact disc, to AAC or MP3. As shown here, you can specify a default codec in the application's general preferences menu.

MPEG-4

MPEG-4 is a more recent set of standards having to do with the compression and encoding of high-definition audio and video signals. Most likely, the video you shoot today with your smartphone, watch on a Blu-ray disc, stream from your Netflix or Hulu account, or publish to YouTube or Vimeo is encoded in a format prescribed by the now ubiquitous MPEG-4 standard. MPEG-4, like many open standards, has been modified and expanded many times. Like its predecessors, it is divided into multiple subsections called "parts," with each one specifying one particular aspect of the overall specification. From its inception in 1998 to 2014, MPEG-4 evolved into an extensive 30-part standard. The most important of these for audio and video professionals was introduced in 2003 and is called *MPEG-4 Part 10 Advanced Video Coding (AVC)*.

H.264/AVC

The MPEG-4 initiative led to the development of a largely universal format for encoding full-bandwidth HD video on a digital camera or camcorder (including mobile devices) and delivering it with efficiency to the home and mobile consumer across a Wi-Fi or cellular network. It serves equally well as both an acquisition format and a delivery format. Part 10 of the standard was truly revolutionary, as it introduced the *Advanced Video Coding* format, better known today as *H.264*, or generically as *MP4*. While people sometimes use the labels H.264 and MP4 interchangeably, technically, H.264 is the video compression codec and MP4 is the container format.

FIGURE 11.14
Adobe Media Encoder is used to transcode a QuickTime movie to MPEG-4/H.264. Encoding programs such as this allow users to control basic settings such as: 1) resolution (width x height), 2) frame rate, 3) field order (interlaced or progressive), 4) pixel aspect ratio, and 5) bit rate. These will be discussed in more detail later in the chapter.
Source: Adobe product screenshot reprinted with permission from Adobe Systems Incorporated.

As a codec, H.264 produces exceptional picture quality at a fraction of the file size of earlier methods of video encoding. At the time, keeping file size to a minimum was deemed critically important for speeding up the process of distributing video online and streaming it to users without unnecessarily long wait times or interruptions due to network congestion and buffering. The main reason you can view a video feed so quickly today on your Facebook page is because of the industry standard H.264 codec. Due to its immense popularity, H.264 quickly gained a following as one of the most widely adopted video compression formats of all time. Both ATSC and DVB have approved AVC for use in terrestrial HDTV broadcasting. The vast majority of digital cameras in use today support MPEG-4 encoding while nearly all video nonlinear editing (NLE) software programs support native capture and editing of MPEG-4–encoded media files. For the audio portion of a video recording, MPEG-4 carried forward the earlier specification from MPEG-2 for AAC compression.

Encoding for YouTube and Vimeo

MPEG-4 helped standardize the process of encoding video for use with online sharing services and is without question the best format to use when uploading a video to YouTube or Vimeo (see Figure 11.15). The compression guidelines for

YouTube

Advanced encoding settings

Recommended bitrates, codecs, and resolutions, and more

Container: .mp4

- No Edit Lists (or you may lose AV sync)
- moov atom at the front of the file (Fast Start)

Audio codec: AAC-LC

- Channels: Stereo or Stereo + 5.1
- Sample rate 96khz or 48khz

Video codec: H.264

- Progressive scan (no interlacing)
- High Profile
- 2 consecutive B frames
- Closed GOP. GOP of half the frame rate.
- CABAC
- Variable bitrate. No bitrate limit required, though we offer recommended bit rates below for reference
- Chroma subsampling: 4:2:0

FIGURE 11.15
YouTube recommends uploading video using the MPEG-4 (.mp4) container format and includes a detailed set of specifications on its website for properly encoding the video and audio portions of your program.
Source: http://www.support.google.com.

both services specify using MPEG-4 as the file format (or container file), the H.264 codec to encode video, and the AAC codec to encode audio.

High Efficiency Video Coding/H.265

While H.264/MPEG-4 AVC provides excellent encoding for standard high-definition video, it was not designed to handle the advanced bandwidth and compression requirements of ultra-high-definition television (*ultra HD* or *UHDTV*). Also known as *Next Generation Television*, UHDTV packs 4 to 16 times as many pixels into the image raster as standard HD. With the consumer electronics industry pushing for the rapid adoption and integration of 4K and 8K video systems, it should come as no surprise that the encoding formats are evolving once again. In 2013, the ISO/IEC MPEG and ITU-T Video Coding Experts Group (VCEG) jointly announced a new standard called High Efficiency Video Coding (HEVC). Dubbed H.265, the HEVC specification is the successor to H.264/MPEG-4 AVC, although it will take some time for manufactures to fully integrate this relatively new standard into new lines of equipment. HEVC/H.265 supports video resolutions up to 8K (8192 × 4320 pixels) and currently boasts twice the compression performance of its predecessor.

PROPRIETARY STANDARDS FOR VIDEO AND AUDIO ENCODING

A proprietary format is one designed or licensed to work only with specific equipment or computer software. As the chief pioneers and innovators of videotape recording, it's no surprise that Sony and Panasonic were likewise instrumental in leading the professional marketplace into a new era of tapeless recording. Together, they released three proprietary solid-state formats: Professional Disc, SxS, and P2. As proprietary card formats go, these are expensive high-end solutions—both in terms of the cost of the camera and the recording media they use. However, as one might expect, they are engineered to meet or exceed the high recording standards for broadcast television. As a result, proprietary formats such as these are typically more physically robust and yield higher quality results than consumer- or prosumer-grade cameras based on open standards. While these card formats are indeed proprietary, depending on the make and model of the device, the codec used by the camera to record video may or may not be proprietary. The cards are just the medium used to store the zeros and ones. It's the camera that determines which codec or format is used during recording.

SxS

Sony introduced XDCAM in 2003, a line of high-end cameras using Professional Disc, an optical recording medium like Blu-ray disc, capable of storing up to 50 GB of data. In 2007, Sandisk and Sony announced their joint release of the SxS (pro-nounced S-by-S) memory card specification. SxS is Sony's solid-state memory card format that combines high-speed flash memory with a standard PCI Express case (see Figure 11.16). Today, the vast majority of Sony's high-end camcorders record to SxS media. SxS-1 was introduced in 2009 as a less expensive alternative to the costly SxS cards. While cheaper, SxS-1 cards have a shorter life span, even though they are still rated to last five years under heavy use. The SxS Pro+ format came out in 2013 to support 4K video acquisition.

FIGURE 11.16
This Sony XDCAM EX professional camcorder records video to a proprietary SxS memory card.

P2

In 2004, Panasonic introduced P2, a solid-state memory card format for use with its top-of-the line broadcast cameras. A P2 card is made up of multiple SD cards enclosed in

FIGURE 11.17
Proprietary card formats like SxS and P2 are designed for professional users. These cards are significantly better than off-the-shelf SD memory cards, and as a result are more robust and reliable. They are also more expensive, a fact that puts them out of reach for many low-budget producers.

a PCMCIA card case. In 2012, Panasonic release a smaller version of the P2 standard called microP2, which is compatible with the SDHC/SDXC memory card specifications. A P2 camcorder can record to a microP2 card using a card adapter and firmware update.

RED

RED Digital Cinema cameras use proprietary solid-state drives (SSDs) to store 4K and higher-resolution recordings. The RED MINI-MAG SSD can store 512 GB of data while the larger REDMAG comes in three sizes: 48 GB, 64 GB, and 240 GB. All things being equal, these custom RED drives are more expensive than almost any other forms of proprietary media. But for filmmakers, the investment is quite reasonable once you factor in the cost savings of no longer shooting in film.

GREAT IDEAS
The RED Camera

The RED Digital Cinema Camera Company is a U.S. firm founded in 2005 that produces advanced high-resolution cameras used in professional filmmaking (see Figure 11.18). They released their first camera in 2007. Dubbed the RED ONE, it featured an advanced 4K image sensor (4096 x 2160) with more than four times the resolution of standard HD. While the RED ONE was not the world's first 4K camera, it was the first to provide a legitimate challenge to 35 mm film in terms of image quality. Since its introduction, hundreds of motion pictures and television shows have been shot digitally with various versions of the RED cinema camera, including Peter Jackson's popular trilogy *The Hobbit* (2012–2014).

FIGURE 11.18
A RED Scarlet 4K Digital Cinema Camera and a follow focus system (discussed later) are mounted to a portable shoulder rig.

AVCHD

In 2006, Sony and Panasonic jointly released AVCHD, a proprietary format based on the MPEG-4 specifications. AVCHD has been incorporated into a growing number of consumer, prosumer, and professional camcorders and has been licensed for use by other manufacturers, including Canon, JVC, and Hitachi. A consumer-grade version of the standard, called AVCHD Lite, has a maximum resolution of 720p and is often used in digital still cameras for shooting HD video.

Like many digital formats, AVCHD offers a broad set of parameters that can be individually set by the camera operator for defining how a video signal is encoded. These settings are often located in the menu system of the camera and may have different names and options depending on the manufacturer. For example, a user may select any combination of the AVCHD record options on a SonyHXR-NX70U camcorder shown in Table 11.1.

The video quality setting is similar to the JPEG compression setting on a digital still camera. Choosing the highest bit rate produces the best quality image with the least

Table 11.1	Sony HXR-NX70U Record Options			
Record Format	**Bit Rate (Quality)**	**Resolution**	**Aspect Ratio**	**Frame Rate**
High-Definition (HD)	FX – Highest (24 Mbps)	1920 x 1080	16:9	60i
	FH – High (17 Mbps)	1920 x 1080		60p
	HQ – Standard (9 Mbps)	1440 x 1080		24p
	LP – Long Time (5 Mbps)	1440 x 1080		
Standard Definition (SD)	HQ – Standard (9 Mbps)	720 x 480	4:3 or 16:9	60i

Table 11.2	A Comparison of Record Time (Minutes), Record Format, and Memory Card Capacity for the Sony HXR-NX70U		
	Memory Card Capacity		
HD Quality	**8 GB**	**16 GB**	**32 GB**
FX	40	80	170
FH	55	110	225
HQ	90	185	375
LP	145	295	590

Note: The approximate recording time (in minutes) for each of the four quality settings on the Sony HXR-NX70U camcorder. Actual time depends on other variables such as frame rate and method of recording audio (compressed or uncompressed).

amount of compression. However, the higher setting also reduces the amount of recordable material your memory card or drive can hold (see Table 11.2).

QuickTime

In addition to being a media player, Apple QuickTime is a multimedia container format that's been around since 1991. As noted earlier in this chapter, QuickTime supports a wide range of graphic, audio, and video codecs (see Figure 11.6). In fact, the MPEG-4 specification, which wasn't released until 10 years later, was based almost entirely on QuickTime. Because of QuickTime's native compatibility with MPEG-4, many cameras, editing applications, and encoding programs include both QuickTime/MOV and MP4 encoding options. The only tangible difference between the two is that the MOV version includes a QuickTime wrapper and *.mov* file extension while the other has an MPEG-4 wrapper and an *.mp4* file extension.

WAV and AIFF

The two most common container formats for professional audio recording are: 1) the Waveform Audio File Format (WAV) developed jointly by Microsoft and IBM and

2) the Audio Interchange File Format (AIFF) released by Apple. WAV and AIFF are very similar. They both contain raw uncompressed PCM audio streams. When an audio file is converted from WAV to AIFF or vice versa, the enclosed bitstreams are left alone. Only the container file or wrapper is modified. You may have noticed that when you insert an audio CD into a Windows PC, the track icon for each song appears as a WAV file. If you take the same CD and insert it into a Mac, the track icons will appear in the AIFF file format. While WAV and AIFF are rival proprietary container formats, they are largely interchangeable, and virtually all video and sound editing programs support both formats.

FORMATTING MEMORY CARDS

Most camcorders record to a removable memory card, such as Memory Stick or SD, or to an internal solid-state drive. With removable media, cards can be shared between users and devices to facilitate the quick and easy transfer of files. With an internal drive, the recorder must be physically connected to your computer, usually via a USB cable, in order to transfer files. Before you record your first shot, be sure to properly initialize or format the card or drive. This is especially important when using a memory card or recording device for the first time. As a matter of good practice, get in the habit of formatting your media at the beginning of each shoot or production day. Formatting is sort of like rebooting your computer—it's a simple step that helps ensure the recording process will go smoothly each and every time. Formatting will erase all the data on the card, so be sure to back up your card files to a dedicated hard drive after each recording session (see Figure 11.20). Formatting also creates the root directory and file system that may be required by your device for writing and reading media files and metadata. Figure 11.19 shows the root directory and file system used on AVCHD camcorders.

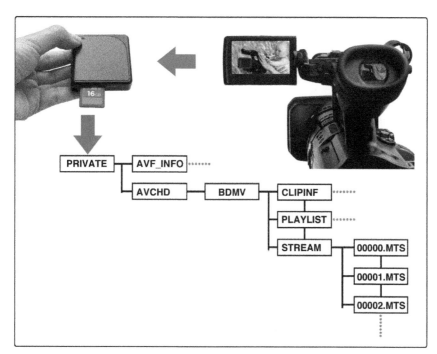

FIGURE 11.19
The AVCHD standard specifies this file directory structure for recording video and metadata to a solid-state memory card. It's important to keep this file structure intact. If any of the folder names is altered, your editing software may not be able to recognize the video files. With AVCHD, video files are saved to the STREAM folder in the .mts format (MPEG Transport Stream).

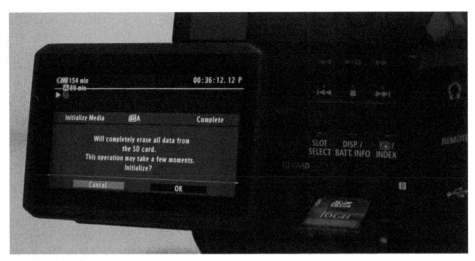

FIGURE 11.20
The menu system of a Canon C100 cinema camera displays a final warning that the initialize media function (or formatting procedure) will "completely erase" all the data on the card.

It's best to format a memory card using the actual device you are recording with and not on a standalone computer. After inserting the memory card, search the system menu for the media or card formatting option. For devices that allow you to record on either a memory card or an internal drive, you may be prompted to specify which media platform to format before performing the procedure.

DEVICE SETTINGS

Nearly every digital camera or audio recorder has built-in settings to control the operation of the device (see Figure 11.21). Sometimes these device settings are located on the camera body as switches, dials, buttons, and so on that you can physically move or turn to make a change (see Figure 11.22). This is particularly true of professional cameras and devices that are larger and have more surface area. More and more, however, especially as consumer electronics have become smaller in size, these settings are accessed through the system menu. Some devices have touch screen menus (like on your smartphone) while others provide buttons and scroll wheels to navigate through the various levels of menus and submenus. This chapter cannot possibly prepare you for all of the possible things you will run into, but it can highlight some of the most important device settings that are found on most audio and video recorders. For everything else, just remember that electronic devices almost always comes with a user's guide or manual—and these days, it isn't very difficult to find a PDF version of one waiting for you online. So be sure to spend time learning about your device's settings—how to access them, what they do, and how to control them for maximum effect.

FIGURE 11.21
FiLMiC Pro is a mobile video camera app that features many of the same device settings and controls found on professional camcorders. While this app is entirely touch screen driven, the inclusion of professional features such as these can transform a smartphone or tablet into a professional video acquisition tool.
Source: Courtesy of Cinegenix, LLC.

FIGURE 11.22
A number of important camera settings can be adjusted on the Canon C100 using external buttons or dials. Many of the ones pictured here will be explained later in the chapter: 1) focus mode switch (auto or manual), 2) image stabilization switch (on or off), 3) neutral density filter wheel, 4) exposure controls, 5) white balance presets and controls, and 6) zebra button (on or off).

Recording Format

As the first half of this chapter addressed, there are many file-based recording codecs and container formats to choose from when working with digital video and audio. The good news is that most of the guesswork has been done by the manufacturer of your device. As is often the case, you won't have to select a specific recording codec or container file because many devices only support one format. If given a choice, however, be sure to select the best quality format that's available. For example, if the audio recorder you're using allows you to record in either WAV or MP3, choose WAV because it is uncompressed and superior to MP3. Likewise, some cameras still give you the option to record in either standard definition or high-definition, and this choice affects which codec is used (MPEG-2 or MPEG-4). These days, I don't know what would possess anyone to choose the SD recording mode on an HD camera, but you may have a choice. My advice, choose HD!

Video Encoding Settings

After choosing your format, you will need to confirm the video encoding settings. Most cameras include menu settings for specifying resolution, scanning method, frame rate, and bit rate.

RESOLUTION OR FRAME SIZE

Resolution is the number of pixels in the digital frame. Most HD cameras offer two levels of resolution. The highest resolution (full bandwidth) for HD is 1920 × 1080 pixels. This option may be listed as *1080i* or *1080p* depending on the scanning method (*i*-interlaced or *p*-progressive). To conserve disk space, HD can be scaled down to the lower resolution of 1280 × 720 (shown as *720i* or *720p*). If you are shooting in SD, you may be able to choose between a standard 4:3 or widescreen 16:9 aspect ratio. Because of its large sensor size, a 4K camera includes many resolution options. In addition to standard HD resolutions such as 720i/p and 1080i/p, you should see options for 2K (2048 × 1080) and 4K (4096 × 2160). As with most of these choices, selecting the highest quality setting available is the best way to go as long as your recording media and postproduction software can handle it.

SCANNING METHOD

You usually have the option of recording *interlaced* or *progressive* frames during recording (refer back to chapter 9 for more about this). The legacy NTSC and PAL formats only supported interlaced scanning; however, HD supports both methods—even though broadcast transmission standards still call for interlaced scanning. Unless there is a specific request from the client or producer to record interlaced video, shooting in progressive mode is generally a safe bet. Progressive mode produces a sharper image overall and conforms more closely to current industry standards for electronic display screens and mobile devices. Converting interlaced video to progressive is easy. Most editing programs and software encoders provide a *de-interlace* option when exporting to your final distribution format. However, as a general rule, it's best to acquire video in the same format you plan to export it to when finished.

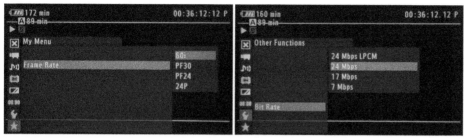

FIGURE 11.23
Users of the Canon C100 can specify the bit rate and frame rate they want to use in the camera's menu system.

FRAME RATE

In the United States, the standard *frame rate* for broadcast television transmissions is 30 or 24 frames per second (fps), which most digital cameras support. Filmmakers often prefer to shoot in 24p because it mirrors the native frame rate of motion picture film and creates a more film-like aesthetic. Again, the frame rate you use during recording can be changed later in postproduction, but every time you make a change to a video setting in post, you re-encode the video and potentially lose data from the original recording. Select the frame rate that best fits your final distribution format (see Figure 11.23, left).

BIT RATE

As in audio sampling (mentioned earlier), a separate *bit rate* setting determines the amount of compression that is applied algorithmically to the video stream. As you might expect, the higher the bit rate setting, the better the quality of the video and the larger the corresponding file will be (see Table 11.1). Most cameras offer a handful of bit rate compression settings listed either according to the actual bit rates (24 Mbps, 17 Mbps, 9 Mbps, and 5 Mbps) or by a qualitative scale of some sort (best quality, high quality, standard quality, long play). Choosing the highest bit rate ensures that your camera records the best image possible (see Figure 11.23, right).

Audio Encoding Settings

You will usually have the option of recording the audio portion of a video recording in one of three formats: 1) Linear PCM, 2) AAC, or 3) Dolby AC3. The uncompressed LPCM format is clearly the best choice over either of the compressed formats; however, when shooting at a higher video bit rate setting, your camera may force you to choose a compressed audio file format. Even so, these compression codecs are so good you needn't worry about this. If you use an external audio recorder such as the Zoom H4n, the same principle applies—select the highest quality uncompressed format available (in this case WAV). The H4n offers MP3 as an option, but it is intended primarily for long-play voice recordings (see Figure 11.24). A professional would never choose MP3 over WAV or AIFF. Also, if given a choice, be sure to select the highest settings on your device for sample rate, bit rate, and bit depth.

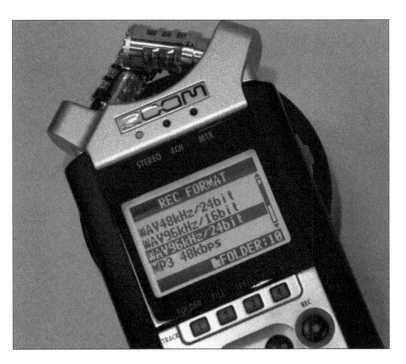

FIGURE 11.24
In the menu system of the Zoom H4n you can choose one of two formats (WAV or MP3) and various quality levels based on the user-defined sample rate and bit depth. The highest quality setting produces an uncompressed WAV file with a sample rate of 96 kHz and a bit depth of 24 bit.

After determining the recording format and encoding settings, it's time to move on to compose your shot and adjust the camera's image and sound recording properties for optimal picture and sound quality. Chapter 12 will focus more on shooting and producing techniques while the remainder of this chapter will address a basic set of important variables you need to know to operate a camcorder and acquire usable content.

FWIGSS

For a person new to video and filmmaking, it can be overwhelming trying to understand all the many buttons, dials, switches, symbols, connectors, functions, and menu settings on a digital camera or DSLR. For this reason, my colleagues and I employ the acronym **FWIGSS** to help students remember six basic camera functions that anyone operating a digital video camera must grasp in order to achieve professional results. Let's begin by unpacking this acronym to get our first glimpse of these six important control settings:

1. Focus
2. White Balance
3. Iris
4. Gain
5. Shutter Speed
6. Sound

While digital cameras offer many more features and functions than these, mastering FWIGSS will get you well underway to becoming a competent videographer. While some of these concepts were covered earlier in chapter 10, "Photography," this section will focus more on how they apply to the craft and techniques of video acquisition.

Think of FWIGSS as a basic *to-do* list that must be performed every time you set up a camera and begin recording. If you strike one shoot and set up 10 minutes later in a new location, be sure to go through the FWIGSS setup procedure again to help ensure consistent quality in your video and sound recordings. What follows may seem like a lot of steps and details to remember, but after you practice this workflow for a while, and learn how to adapt FWIGSS to your particular camera, you will be able to accomplish the basic setup procedures in just a few minutes every time.

Focus

Acquiring focus and maintaining it throughout the duration of a shot is a critical component of professional film and video acquisition. In chapter 10, this subject was discussed in terms of still photography, where focus only has to be maintained for a brief moment of time during exposure of a single frame. When shooting video, focus has to be maintained across time for the duration of a shot—which can last for several seconds or more—and adjusted on the fly to compensate for subjects that are in motion.

We refer to a camera image as *sharp* when the main subject within the frame is *in focus*. Foreground or background objects that appear along the z-axis may appear out of focus (depending on depth of field), but as long as the main subject is clearly defined, the image is in focus. A *soft* image is one where the subject or the entire frame is out of focus. Unintentionally blurry subjects are a visual distraction to the viewer and should be avoided at all cost.

Where you set the focus depends mainly on the distance between the camera and the main subject. In cases when the camera-subject distance is fixed throughout the duration of a shot, you only need to focus once to ensure the image remains in focus when zooming. However, if the distance between the camera and subject changes during a shot, such as in a soccer match where the goalie is sprinting away from the camera along the z-axis, you will need to ride the focus—a technique that involves continually adjusting focus on the fly while keeping the shot properly composed. Shooting moving subjects and keeping them in focus takes practice and requires considerably more skill than shooting in a setting where the camera and subject are fixed.

AUTOFOCUS AND MANUAL MODE

Nearly every camera comes equipped with an autofocusing (AF) system. Like other automatic features on a digital camera, autofocus is intended to make your life easier, giving you one less thing to worry about while composing and shooting video. As long as the lighting is good, the subject-camera distance is relatively stable, and there isn't a lot of visual complexity or movement within the frame, autofocus can yield acceptable results. So there's nothing innately wrong with using this feature, even if you are an aspiring professional. With AF turned on, the camera will automatically calculate the distance from the lens to the main subject and adjust the focus setting accordingly. However, you must remember that a camera is an electromechanical device that lacks any human capacity for intuition or judgment. It cannot think, only adjust as it was programmed to do based on its settings and the data it receives through its onboard systems. In certain situations where the variables are beyond those it was designed to handle, autofocus may create unintended visual artifacts or simply refuse to work at all. For instance:

FIGURE 11.25
For best results, set the camcorder to manual focus mode and follow these steps for setting the focus every time you change positions in relation to the subject.

- **AF may acquire focus on the wrong subject within the frame.** In a situation where there are two or more people in the frame, the AF sensor may not know which one to lock on to. By default, AF usually attempts to set focus in the center of the frame. However, if the subject you are shooting is off-center, using AF may not work. Refer back to chapter 10 on photography for more information about setting the AF target point.

- **AF may roll or shift as the subject moves within the frame.** If the scene you are shooting contains any subject movement or sudden lighting changes, AF may have trouble maintaining a lock on the main subject. In this situation, the image may suddenly and momentarily blur as the AF mechanism moves rapidly back and forth looking for a subject to acquire. Unintended AF roll or shift is a visual distraction that should be avoided.

- **AF may not be able to stay focused on highly reflective or complex subjects.** The busier the detail in a shot, the greater the opportunity for the AF sensor to get confused. Repeating patterns and glossy surfaces are just two examples of things that may prove too difficult for AF to handle.

- **AF may not work at all in low-light or low-contrast situations.** Nighttime shots and low-contrast settings make acquiring focus with AF extremely difficult.

As you get comfortable shooting with a video camera, try switching from AF to manual focus more often. It may take some practice getting the hang of it, but unless you are doing lots of action-oriented photography, shooting in manual focus (MF) mode isn't as hard as you may think—and doing so often leads to more satisfactory results.

Setting Focus in MF Mode

A common scenario for a videographer or filmmaker is shooting an interview where the camera and the subject are locked down in a fixed position. For example, consider a scenario where the subject is seated in a chair that is situated six feet from a camera mounted on a tripod. To set the focus, follow these steps (illustrated in Figure 11.25).

STEP 1: Compose your shot. Make sure the camera is set to MF mode.

STEP 2: Next, zoom in as far as you can on the subject's eyes.

STEP 3: Adjust the focus control until the eyes are sharply in focus. Moving quickly back and forth in smaller sweeps can help you identify the sweet spot more accurately.

STEP 4: Zoom back out to compose your shot.

You may now adjust the focal length of the lens to any position between a tight shot and a wide shot without losing focus. If at any point the distance between the camera and the subject changes, repeat these steps.

In this example, the subject's eyes lie along an invisible vertical plane that intersects with the z-axis. This is where we usually want the image to be the sharpest. I routinely set focus on the eyes because most of us are taught from childhood to look someone in the eyes when we are speaking with them. "The eyes are the window to your soul" goes the proverb, and it's the eyes upon which the viewer most often affixes his or her gaze.

FOCUS AND ZOOM CONTROLS

Focus and zoom controls vary depending upon the type of camera you are using. For cameras equipped with broadcast ENG/EFP lenses, DSLR lenses, or cinema lenses, focus is adjusted with the outer ring located closest to the front of the lens. Zooming is controlled with the middle ring or with the camera's servo control. The iris/aperture is adjusted with the ring closest to the rear of the lens. The placement of the focus control at the front of the lens enables a camera operator to support the front of the camera with one hand while simultaneously focusing. This location is particularly handy when making quick focus adjustments while walking or tracking moving subjects. Cheaper camcorders with built-in lenses may also come equipped with a focus ring on the lens while the least expensive compacts and smartphone cameras offer only touch screen control of these manual functions, if any at all.

Studio cameras and studio-configured cameras, such as those used at live events, feature rear controls for zoom and focus (see Figure 11.26). The zoom control is usually mounted to the right pan bar while the focus control is attached to the left. Mounting the controls on the pan bars allows the operator to tilt and pan the camera while simultaneously zooming and focusing as required.

Filmmakers will sometimes attach a *follow focus* system to a cinema lens in order to shift control of the focus to a more ergonomically friendly position on the side of the camera (see Figure 11.18). For example, on a dolly shot or walking shot, where the camera is physically transitioning from a wide angle to a tight shot of the subject, a second person (called a focus puller) can operate the focus control while the cinematographer concentrates on framing the subject. A follow focus system includes a large hand wheel and marking disk where focus marks can be applied with an erasable marker.

Pandering to an ever-savvy customer base of smartphone photographers and movie makers, developers of Android OS, Mac iOS, and Windows Phone OS now include support for manual focus mode in third-party smartphone camera apps. Unfortunately, controlling MF on a smartphone will likely require using an ergonomically unfriendly touch screen interface.

FIGURE 11.26
A camera operator uses the rear focus and zoom controls to maintain composition during a live television newscast.

FIGURE 11.27
The rack focus technique is used here to shift the focus in real time from the foreground subject to the background subject.

RACK FOCUS

Rack focus is a popular technique that shooters use to rapidly shift the viewer's attention from one subject to another along the z-axis (see Figure 11.27). With this technique, shallow depth of field is used to obtain a noticeable contrast between a sharply focused foreground subject and a soft or blurry background one (or vice versa). With the camera rolling and on the director's cue, the focus puller changes the focus setting until the sharp subject in the frame gradually turns soft and the soft subject gradually comes into focus. The viewer's gaze will naturally shift to the portion of the frame that is most clearly defined.

White Balance

Digital cameras are basically colorblind. In order to accurately capture true colors, the camera must be calibrated to a reference color. We use pure white as the reference color because white light contains the three primary colors in equal measure. Once a camera "knows" what white looks like under a specific lighting condition, it will be able to accurately reproduce all other colors under the same lighting conditions.

Since shots are often combined in editing to create scenes and sequences, it's important that related shots have matching color profiles. For this reason, great care should be given to set the camera's white balance whenever the lighting source or color temperature in a scene changes, regardless of whether or not the camera is physically moved. For starters, be sure to reset the white balance whenever you move the camera from an indoor location with artificial light to an outdoor venue with natural light or vice versa. But remember, the color properties of light can also vary within an indoor setting by type of lighting fixture or outdoors by atmospheric conditions or time of day. For example, fluorescent bulbs emit a different color temperature than tungsten light fixtures. Likewise, as the position of the sun changes throughout the day, the color temperature it emits also changes. For this reason, white balancing the camera and doing so often is important—and once you learn the steps, the procedure takes only seconds to complete.

WHITE BALANCE CONTROLS

Auto white balance (AWB) is a feature found on most digital cameras today. With AWB turned on, the camera assesses the light hitting the image sensor and calibrates accordingly. Under certain conditions and with a high-quality camera, AWB may work great most of the time, but it will not work consistently all the time. AWB will fail you at some point, which is why you should never use this feature when working on a professional project.

The next best option you may choose is to use the white balance presets. Many cameras include a switch or menu setting that allows you to select a broadly defined lighting scenario such as Sunny, Cloudy, Fluorescent, Tungsten, and so on. Presets will put you in the ballpark, but they may not fully compensate for the subtle variations in color temperature that may exist within a specific type of light.

The best option to choose, if your camera allows, is to perform a custom white balance (see Figure 11.28). To do so, follow these steps:

- Locate the white balance settings on your camera and select the manual or custom WB option. On higher-end cameras, WB controls are often found on the exterior of the camera body. On less expensive cameras, be prepared to delve into the onboard menu system.
- Have the subject or an assistant aim a white card or sheet of paper at the camera. The card should reflect the same light source hitting the subject.
- Zoom in on the card to fill 80%–100% of the frame with white. Be sure your exposure and focus settings are properly set. If the image is too dark or out of focus, the camera may not be able to perform the operation.
- Press and hold the Set button until the camera confirms that white balance has been acquired. If the color temperature has changed dramatically from the last time you performed a white balance, you may actually notice a color shift in the viewfinder. But don't worry if don't see a dramatic change. If you followed the procedure correctly, your camera is now set to reproduce the best color possible.

FIGURE 11.28
The videographer zooms in on a white card held by the subject to perform a white balance at the start of a recording session.

Iris

In chapter 10, we learned that *exposure* is the product of *light intensity* and time. Specifically, three variables continually interact to form what photographers call the exposure triangle: aperture, ISO/gain, and shutter speed. The first of these, aperture, is controlled by the camera's iris to regulate the amount of light hitting the image sensor. The aperture is an opening in the iris at the rear of the lens through which light passes. As with all the other functions discussed so far in this section, you can control this function manually or allow the camera to control it for you automatically. Which should you choose? Here, it really depends on your level of experience in photography or videography. If you are relatively inexperienced, you may be better off entrusting this control to your camera. For the most part, when it comes to automatic exposure controls, digital cameras are pretty good at calculating proper settings for exposure, especially when the subject is well lit.

Those of you with a more advanced understanding of lenses, cameras, and lighting may want to retain control of the iris function in order to achieve a specific look. For example, all things being equal, the size of the aperture affects the relative degree to which you achieve great or shallow depth of field. But here's the rub—there are many other variables to consider as well, such as sensor size, lens type, focal length, shutter speed, lighting, and so on. Learning how to master manual control of all these functions goes beyond the scope of this book. So don't be timid about experimenting with manual controls or deepening your knowledge through books and tutorials that go into much greater detail on this subject.

The key for beginners to understand is that proper exposure is essential to producing a professional-looking video image. Images that are too dark are called underexposed. Pictures that are too bright are overexposed. Work in well-lit areas until you develop the ability to compensate for darker settings or learn how to supplement poorly lit subjects with professional light kits or reflectors.

NEUTRAL DENSITY (ND) FILTERS

When shooting in a bright location such as the beach on a cloudless summer day, you may have difficulty keeping images from being overexposed, even with the aperture completely stopped down. For this reason, professional video cameras often include a built-in set of neutral density (ND) filters situated between the lens and the image sensor. You can think of an ND filter as a pair of sunglasses for your camera. It reduces the overall amount of light entering the camera without altering the color properties of the light. Hence, they are color neutral. There are also standalone ND filters designed to attach to the front of prime and zoom lenses using a threaded mount (see Figure 11.29). The use of an ND filter gives the photographer greater latitude in controlling the iris (as well as other exposure controls), especially in bright conditions—thereby helping prevent overexposure. ND filters come in many different styles. Some are solid while others are graduated. Variable ND filters, while more expensive, offer a range of light-reduction capability, typically from two to eight steps of light control. Solid ND filters reduce light by a fixed amount.

ZEBRA STRIPES

To assist you in monitoring exposure levels during recording, many cameras include a Zebra feature. With Zebra turned on, the viewfinder will display crosshatched diagonal lines, resembling Zebra stripes, over any portion of the image

FIGURE 11.29
Left: This neutral density filter kit contains three ND filters with varying degrees of exposure adjustment (2, 3, and 4 stops). Right: Filters such as these are designed with a threaded ring for quick connection to a compatible lens.

FIGURE 11.30
In the top image, the zebra lines tell us the image is grossly overexposed. The bottom image displays the same shot after correcting exposure. While the zebra lines have not entirely disappeared, the subject is now properly exposed as indicated by only a few minor hot spots in the lighter regions of the background.

that is overexposed (see Figure 11.30). The iris can then be adjusted up or down until the Zebra stripes either go away entirely or are barely visible, resulting in an image that is properly exposed. The Zebra setting corresponds to IRE units, a broadcast engineering standard for defining the relative range from black to white in a composite video signal. On the low end, a value of 7.5 IRE corresponds to video black, while on the other end of the continuum, a value of 100 IRE represents the peak white levels before clipping. To ensure that your video is legally *broadcast safe*, strive to keep the video levels within this range.

Professional NLE software includes a special type of oscilloscope known as a wave-form monitor that allows an editor to visually evaluate video levels in IRE units during postproduction. Aperture settings correspond to IRE units, with each f-stop equaling roughly 15 IRE units. The Zebra control can usually be set to one of two light-intensity thresholds: 70% or 100%. When set to 100%, the warning stripes appear whenever a portion of an image clips at 100 IRE. Under normal lighting conditions, white clothing or other white articles may register slightly higher than 100 IRE since they are the brightest objects within the frame, and this should be expected. The 70% threshold corresponds to the upper end of the range we normally expect for Caucasian skin tones (60–70 IRE). The use of this setting may help you optimize exposure when shooting human subjects with lighter skin tones. Zebra stripes are a visual aid to help ensure that video clipping does not occur and that your image is neither under- nor overexposed. They appear only in your viewfinder during recording and are not permanently recorded to the image file.

Gain

Shooting in a low-light situation can pose a challenge to both the still photographer and the videographer. If supplemental lighting is not available, the only option you may have to keep a shot from be underexposed, and potentially useless, is to increase the light sensitivity of your camera. Chapter 10 discussed the ISO system that was originally adopted for photographers as a way of rating the light sensitivity of photographic film. As a reminder, the higher the ISO rating, the more sensitive film is to light, but, also, the grainier the image will be when processed. With a digital camera, the electronic image sensor, which replaces physical film, can also be made more or less sensitive to light by turning a dial, flipping a switch, or changing a menu setting.

Video cameras traditionally provide a *gain* control with a three-position setting labeled 0 dB, +6 dB, and +12 dB. Gain works by amplifying the voltage level of the composite video signal, which explains why decibels are used as the unit of measure. Every 6 dB of gain doubles the light sensitivity of the image sensor as well as the amount of noise in the image. It also provides the equivalent of one full f-stop of light (or brightness) to the image. The optimal position for gain is 0 dB, which will render the cleanest image minus any visual noise due to amplification.

For all practical purposes, the ISO and gain controls perform the same function. However, because it has been around for so long, ISO is a much more familiar system to photographers and DPs who understand and know how use it in conjunction with the other two variables in the exposure triangle. The ISO standard also goes beyond the three simple gain settings found on most video cameras. For example, the Canon C100 has an ISO range from 320 to 80,000 in 1/3 step increments. As digital cameras keep improving, the nominal ISO setting continues to improve. This means that shooters can now go much higher up the ISO scale than previously before encountering noticeable noise or degradation in the video image. What gets a little confusing these days is that some hybrid cameras are equipped with both an ISO and gain setting. In the end, don't worry about it. Just remember that when you need a little extra punch of brightness in your dimly lit shot, you have these controls at your fingertips to make a difference and perhaps even save the day.

Shutter Speed

On a digital still camera, the shutter is a component that controls the duration of time that light accumulates on the image sensor during a single exposure. Shutter speed is the duration of the interval. On DSLRs, the shutter is a mechanical curtain that opens or closes to permit light to pass or block its transmission when the camera is set to still picture mode. On video cameras, compacts, and smartphones, or when DSLRs are set to video mode, the shutter is an electronic component that instructs the image sensor when to turn on and off. A shutter functions somewhat differently when recording video then when shooting still pictures. In still picture mode, the shutter opens only once per individual exposure. In video mode, the shutter opens and closes repeatedly at a constant rate, which may or may not correspond directly to the current frame rate of the camera.

Shutter speed is expressed as a fraction of second. For example, a shutter speed of 1/250 indicates that the shutter will open and close at a rate of 250 times per second during recording. For normal shooting situations, the general rule of thumb is that the denominator in the shutter speed fraction should be double the frame rate of your video. Since most video today is shot at 24, 25, or 30 frames per second (fps), this would suggest a corresponding default shutter speed of 1/48, 1/50, or 1/60. It's important to understand, however, that shooting at a different shutter speed than any of these defaults will not alter the frame rate of your recording.

As the third member of the exposure triangle, you can expect shutter speed to influence the amount of light coming into contact with the image sensor. Because the shutter momentarily impedes the flow of light to the image sensor, acting like a gate; increasing shutter speed decreases the amount of light hitting the sensor. To compensate, you can add more light, open up the aperture, increase the ISO/gain setting, or perform some combination of the three. Likewise, reducing shutter speed increases the amount of light striking the image sensor.

As in still photography, videographers use faster shutter speeds for capturing fast-moving subjects and action shots so that they appear sharply defined with little to no blurring. Choose a fast shutter speed when shooting sporting events and other activities where there is a relatively high degree of primary motion within the frame and plenty of light. Choose a slower shutter speed in low-light conditions and when the subject's movements are minimal.

Sound

Using the word *film* or *video* to describe the art of motion picture recording is a bit of a misnomer because it tends to emphasize the visual component of the craft at the expense of sound. It cannot be overstated how important the element of sound is in professional videography and filmmaking. In fact, because of huge advances in recent years in the performance capabilities of automated metering and exposure controls on digital cameras, it is not at all difficult, with decent lighting, for an amateur with little training to walk away with great looking video at the end of a shoot. Acquiring professional sound is usually another story. Much of what you need to understand about acquiring professional sound can be found in chapter 12, which focuses entirely on audio production. For now, I just want to focus on a few things to consider before pressing the record button.

CONNECTIONS AND SIGNAL FLOW

Camcorders typically come with a built-in microphone, which usually works well for recording natural sound. When shooting interviews, however, be sure to use an external microphone connected to the camera. Whether the microphone is wireless or wired doesn't matter, as long as it's a decent microphone rated for professional

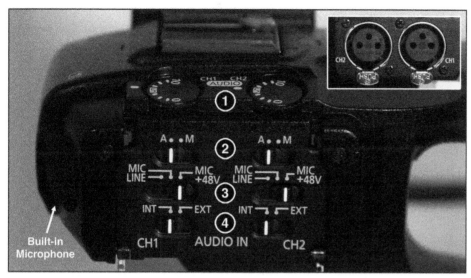

FIGURE 11.31
Audio signal flow and record levels on the Canon C100 are controlled here. As with most professional camcorders, up to two external microphones can be attached via the XLR connectors (see inset). Half the controls correspond to microphone input 1 while the other half are for input 2. 1) Record Level—use this control to set the record level when the A/M switch 2) is set to Manual. Monitor the VU meters on the viewfinder to determine the appropriate level. 3) Choose **LINE** when connecting a line-level device, such as an MP3 player, to a microphone input. Chose **MIC** when using a self-powered (dynamic) microphone. Choose **MIC +48V** when using a condenser microphone requiring phantom power. 4) Choose **INT** when using the camera's built-in microphone. Choose **EXT** to change the signal flow to an external microphone.

use. After connecting it to the camera, verify that the audio signal is registering on the camera's VU meter and that you are hearing it through your attached headphones. As stressed further in chapter 12, monitoring audio without headphones is not an option, unless you just don't care about obtaining best results or want to throw caution to the wind. Follow this checklist for ensuring quality audio acquisition and for problem-solving signal flow issues:

1. Choose a location relatively free of unwanted sources of background sounds that compete with or detract from the primary audio. A few examples of things to avoid include: air handling units, construction equipment/tools, crowds, fountains, high winds, traffic/vehicular noises (cars, planes, trains), speaker/PA (public address) systems, and so on. If a background sound is related to the subject of your interview/story, it may actually compliment the interview. Just make sure the subject's audio is the most prominent source in the mix and that it is audible and clearly distinguishable above any background sounds.
2. Listening through your headphones, make sure the audio signal is free of transmission noise caused by ground loops, RF (radio frequency) interference, phase cancelation, or electrical shorts such as: buzzes, crackling, hum, intermittent breakup, missing frequencies, static, and so on.

3. If the attached microphone has an on/off switch, make sure it is turned on.

4. Make sure the XLR cable connectors are fully seated on both ends to the corresponding jacks and securely locked in place.

5. If you are using a condenser microphone, verify that it has a working battery (typically AA) or that *phantom power* (if available) is turned on.

6. Confirm that the microphone preamp is set to an appropriate record level. The record level is visually represented by the VU meters and is indicative of what the camera "hears" and the amount of preamplification that is applied to the signal during recording. Make sure the signal is strong enough without clipping. Since most cameras feature two microphone inputs, be sure to set the record level that corresponds to the input number of the microphone you're adjusting.

7. Connect headphones to the input jack (usually color coded green) and set the headphone volume to an appropriate level. Remember, the headphone volume is what you hear and has no impact on the recorded audio signal.

8. After following these steps, if you are still experiencing problems, you may have a bad microphone or microphone cable. Try alternately swapping out the cable and microphone with another one in an effort to narrow down which component may be causing the problem.

9. Record a brief sound check with the subject while fine-tuning the record level. Play back the sound check while monitoring it through the headphones to make sure you are happy with the quality of the recording.

CHAPTER SUMMARY

Video recording began in 1956. Since that time, many formats have come and gone as engineers and product developers found newer and better ways to encode video and audio on magnetic tape or solid-state media. For many years, the recording device (the camera or VCR) was outfitted to work with a specific physical container such as a magnetic tape reel or plastic cassette. A videotape recording could be played back only on a corresponding VTR designed work with the same tape format.

The most significant development in recent years was the development of solid-state technologies that use file-based recording formats and codecs. Such formats have drastically reduced the cost of professional HD recording systems and the media we use to store digital files. However, because these formats are digital, there is hardly ever just one way to record or transcode a video or audio signal. You can't just turn the camera on, press the record button, and expect the best results. You need to know a lot more information related to recording formats, codecs, container files, resolutions, frame rates, sample rates, bit rates, and so forth in order to make informed judgments about the best resolution and quality for a given job or assignment. The more you know now, the better you will be able to adapt when everything changes once again—and the next generation of recording technologies emerge.

NOTE

1 http://www.worldstandardscooperation.org/

CHAPTER 12
Audio Production

The notion of media will be completely blended in one digital stream. Moving pictures and static pictures and text and audio—the mix of any of those will be commonplace. Imagine turning the pages of a magazine: every one of the images is a sound clip, and when you put your cursor over one of them, the audio comes. That's absolutely going to be happening in 15 years. Full convergence of media and television and computers.

—Jim Clark, computer scientist and founder of Silicon Graphics Inc. and Netscape (1994)

Key Terms
A/D Conversion
Amplitude
Audio
Automatic Gain
    Control (AGC)
Balanced Audio
Boom Pole
Clipping
Condenser
    Microphone
Decibel (dB)
Dynamic
    Microphone
Dynamic Range
Equalization (EQ)
Frequency
Gain
Handheld
    Microphone
Headphones
Lavalier
    Microphone
Microphone
Mini Plug
Monitoring
Over-Under Wrap
Phantom Power
Pitch
Plosives
Polar Pattern
Preamp
Proximity Effect
RCA Connector
Ribbon Microphone
Shotgun
    Microphone
Sound
Sound Pressure
    Wave
Three-Band Equalizer

Chapter Highlights

This chapter examines:
- The nature of sound and audio
- The audio chain and signal flow
- Microphone element designs, pickup patterns, and form factors
- Microphone placement and recording techniques
- Audio cables and connectors

SOUND AND AUDIO

This chapter examines sound, one of the key ingredients in the multimedia producer's recipe book. Sound is what we hear and can be featured in a standalone product, such as a song, a podcast, or a radio commercial, or it can be part of a larger product, such as the music or dialog in a feature-length film. Think about how boring video games would be without sound effects to go along with the movement of spacecraft and the explosion of weapons. In television production, the phrase *sound on tape* (SOT) is used to describe audio captured on location at the time of a video or film recording. For example, during the World Series, the sounds of the ball hitting the bat, the crowd cheering in the background, and the voices of the announcers calling the game, are synchronized in real time with camera shots of the runner rounding third base after hitting a home run. While the images and

TS/TRS (Tip and
  Sleeve/Tip, Ring,
  and Sleeve)
  Connector
Unbalanced Audio
VU (Volume-Unit)
  Meter
Windscreen
XLR Connector

sound of a live event are often acquired together, at the same moment, the work-flows for recording sound for use in a preproduced video or film are not necessarily the same, and it is important to understand the differences. This chapter focuses on the basic concepts, tools, and techniques you need to be aware of as you delve into sound acquisition, recording, and editing.

WHAT IS SOUND?

It's important to distinguish between the physical characteristics of sound as a phenomenon of nature and the process of audio production—the electronic capture and reproduction of sound. *Sound* is a natural phenomenon that involves pressure and vibration (see Figure 12.1). Understanding how sound and hearing work will help you

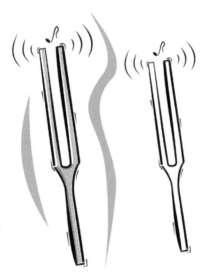

capture and produce better quality audio. What we perceive as sound traveling across time and distance is actually the invisible moving presence of a sound pressure wave. *Sound waves* are a special type of energy and require a molecular medium for propagation. They can travel though solids, gases, or liquids, but air molecules are the best transmission medium. Despite Hollywood's portrayal of loud space battles, sound cannot travel within the vacuum of space, and in reality, a ship exploding in space would not make a sound as there are no air molecules. We hear by discerning changes in the pressure and movement of the air particles around us. When a tree falls in the forest, the air molecules in its path are momentarily displaced. They are violently pushed out of the way to make room for the falling tree. This sets off a chain reaction as the energy of the initial force is passed along to neighboring molecules in all directions. Back and forth they go, oscillating until the energy that caused the disturbance dissipates.

FIGURE 12.1
Striking a tuning fork causes its two prongs to vibrate, which, in turn, produces a musical tone.

The best way to illustrate the movement of a sound pressure wave is to look at something more visible in nature. When you drop a small rock into a still pond, you see concentric ripples or waves traverse outward from the point of the disruption (see Figure 12.2). Here, water serves as the conduit for energy to flow away from the source. However, the actual water molecules travel only a tiny distance as they bounce back and forth transmitting the energy signature of the wave. As the wave travels further away from the source, the oscillations of the molecules begin to slow down until the pond is once again at rest.

FIGURE 12.2
Concentric ripples are the visible evidence of molecular vibration in water. Uniform waves progress outward in every direction as energy is released at the point of disturbance.

Tech Talk

Characteristics of a Sound Wave While sound is invisible to the eyes, two characteristics of a sound wave can be measured and visualized by digital recording devices and sound processing hardware and software. Amplitude and frequency are the observable dimensions of a sound pressure wave that we are most interested in (see Figure 12.3). *Amplitude* is a sound pressure wave's intensity, or dynamic pressure, and *frequency* is the wave's rate of vibration or oscillation. In hearing, we perceive amplitude as the relative loudness of a sound and frequency as its pitch.

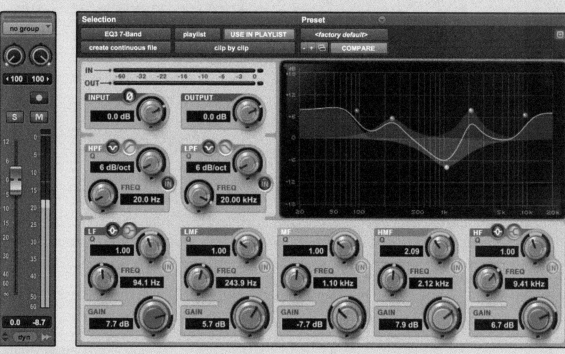

FIGURE 12.3
In Avid Pro Tools, a VU (volume-unit) meter (left) provides a visual reference of the amplitude of a sound source in decibels and a slider for increasing or decreasing its level. Likewise, the seven-band equalizer plug-in (right) visually displays the frequency range and numerous controls for adjusting each individual band.

Amplitude

The first thing we tend to notice about sound is how loud it is. Loud sounds capture our attention almost immediately, while soft sounds strain our senses or elude us entirely. Because sound waves are invisible to the human eye, we must use pictures to illustrate their physical qualities and characteristics (see Figure 12.4). A sound wave's height (amplitude) indicates the intensity or magnitude of the pressure wave. *Amplitude* is defined as the distance from the crest of the wave to the trough. The louder the sound, the greater the amplitude, and the taller its waveform. The amplitude of a sound is greatest near the source and diminishes over distance and time.

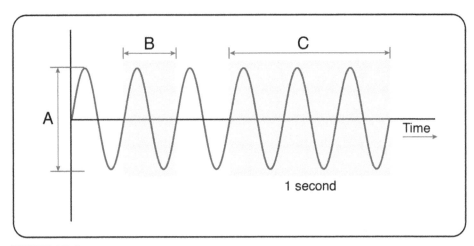

FIGURE 12.4
Sine waves are often used to visualize the repetitive oscillations of sound vibrations. A) *Amplitude* is represented by the height of the wave. B) *Wavelength* is the distance traveled during one complete vibration cycle. C) *Frequency* is the number of complete wave cycles that occur over a set period of time (usually measured in one-second intervals).

Amplitude is measured in decibel units. The decibel (dB) is a logarithmic unit of measurement used to quantify the sound pressure level (SPL) or magnitude of a sound wave in an acoustical space. Humans are capable of hearing a wide range of sounds, from 0 dB to 120 dB. A value of 0 dB represents the least audible sounds we can hear (just above silence). With each increase of 20 dB on the decibel scale, the amplitude and perceived loudness of sound increases 10 times. Thus, a 20 dB sound is 10 times louder than the faintest sound. A 40 dB sound source is 100 times louder than the faintest sound and 10 times louder than sound at 20 dB. When you reach 120 dB, the SPL is 1,000,000 times greater than the level of sound at 0 dB. While adapting to a logarithmic scale can be confusing at first, using a scale with a relatively small number of decibel units is easier to deal with than one with a million or more increments of variation.

The human threshold for pain begins around 140 dB, while permanent hearing loss occurs at 150 dB. Hearing loss most commonly results from repeated exposure to loud sounds over time. With the growing popularity of digital music and MP3 players, concern has emerged over the potentially damaging effects of listening repeatedly to loud music through headphones or earbuds. The close proximity of earbuds to the sensitive organs of the ear makes this an even greater concern and has prompted the makers of personal listening devices to offer volume-limit controls on their units. A volume limiter option allows users to set a maximum listening level based on decibels or the relative volume units of the device. While many factors can contribute to hearing loss or damage, setting a volume limit in place is advisable. By the way, that ringing you get in your ears after a concert—it's called *tinnitus* and can become permanent.

Tech Talk

Dynamic Range Loudness is rarely constant and tends to vary and fluctuate across time. For example, the human voice can quickly move from a whisper to a shout. Likewise, a classical composition can vary from quiet movements of reflection and solitude to intense moments of drama and passion. This difference in loudness, from the quietest point to the loudest, is called *dynamic range*.

Frequency

As sound waves pass through matter, the vibrating molecules experience three phases of movement (see Figure 12.5). As molecules move in an inward direction, they are pushed closer together, leading to an increase in molecular density and sound pressure. This is the *compression phase* and is represented by the portion of the waveform above the horizontal axis (time). The highest point of the waveform is called the *crest* and signifies the moment of greatest sound pressure. Once maximum compression has been reached, elasticity kicks in, causing the molecules to return to their original position. For a fraction of a second, the molecules are at rest as they change direction and begin moving outward. During the *rarefaction phase*, molecules are pulled apart, resulting in a decrease in molecular density and sound pressure. Rarefaction is denoted as the portion of the waveform below the horizontal axis. The lowest point on the waveform is called the *trough* and indicates the moment of lowest sound pressure.

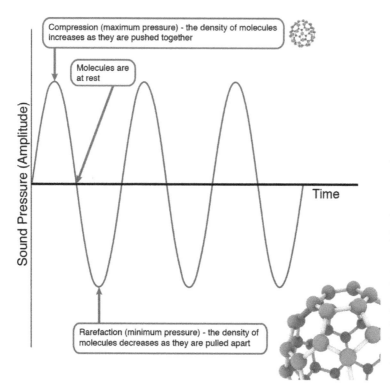

FIGURE 12.5
When the air molecules around us are energized by a sound pressure wave, they begin to oscillate, bouncing rapidly back and forth in unison. As molecules travel inward they are squeezed tightly together (*compression*); as they spring back in the opposite direction, they pull apart and spread out (*rarefaction*). At one brief moment in each wave cycle, when molecules change direction, they are briefly at rest.

Table 12.1	The Frequency Chart for a Six-String Acoustic Guitar	
String	**Note**	**Frequency**
6th	E	82 Hz
5th	A	110 Hz
4th	D	147 Hz
3rd	G	196 Hz
2nd	B	247 Hz
1st	E	330 Hz

The progression of a sound wave through one phase of rest, compression, and rarefaction is called a *cycle,* and a sound's frequency is based on its number of cycles per second. *Frequency* refers to a sound's relative low or high pitch. Frequency is measured in hertz (Hz), cycles per second. Every vibration has a unique frequency signature. A common frequency used in audio production for the purposes of calibration is the 1 kHz tone. By the way, 1 kHz is simply 1,000 Hz. Kilohertz (kHz) units can be used as an abbreviated way of referring to particularly high frequencies.

When individually plucked, the strings of an acoustic guitar in standard tuning create the frequencies, or pitch, shown in Table 12.1. Each string can be played separately, producing a single note or pitch. However, most of the time a musician will strike multiple strings at a time, thus creating diverse sounds and harmonics with complex frequency signatures. Most sounds in nature, including human speech, are likewise composed of multiple frequencies interacting together to produce an holistic aural impression.

People with normal hearing are capable of perceiving sound frequencies from 20 to 20,000 Hz. This range is often divided into three subgroups, or bands, called *bass,* *midrange,* and *treble.* The bass frequencies include lower pitch sounds in the range of 20–320 Hz. Midrange frequencies include medium pitch sounds falling between 320 and 5,120 Hz. Treble frequencies, high pitch sounds from 5,120 to 20,000 Hz, represent the largest segment of the human audio spectrum. While the treble range is the broadest, most of the frequencies required for understanding human speech fall in the midrange.

MICROPHONES

A *microphone* is a recording instrument used to convert sound waves into an electrical equivalent that can be stored, transmitted, and played back through an audio sound system. Some microphones are designed specifically for use in a studio environment, while others are optimized for field use. Likewise, some microphones are better for voice work while others are designed primarily for instrument recording. While there's often more than one clear-cut choice, it's important to understand the fundamental differences in microphone design in order to choose the most appropriate tool for the job.

GREAT IDEAS
Equalization

Sound systems often allow you to adjust the bass, midrange, and treble output of a program source or channel. This feature is known as a *three-band equalizer* (or EQ) and provides the user with separate controls for raising or lowering the gain of each frequency region or band (see Figure 12.6, top). For example, "rolling off" or "dialing down" the bass frequencies can add brightness and clarity to the sound signal. This can be helpful when listening to news or talk-radio channels, but for music, people often want to feel the deep and penetrating lower frequencies. In such cases, adding bass and rolling off the treble may be more to one's liking.

A three-band equalizer is simple and inexpensive, but it provides only global controls for adjusting the pitch of the recording or transmission. Professional recording studios and production facilities typically rely on more robust and sophisticated tools for adjusting EQ. The better systems break the frequency spectrum into many more bands (see Figure 12.6, bottom), allowing for precise isolation and manipulation of individual frequencies. You'll find a virtual version of this tool in most audio and video editing software.

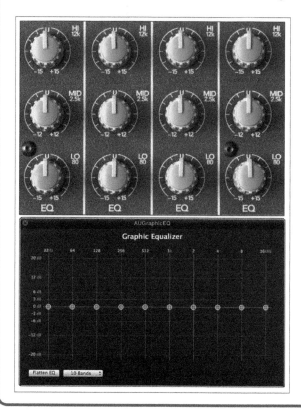

FIGURE 12.6
Top: A three-band equalizer, like the one pictured here, is a standard feature on most audio mixing consoles and on many electronic sound devices (car stereos, amplifiers, etc.). Bottom: A screenshot of the graphic equalizer in Final Cut Pro X. With this interface, users can select between 10 and 31 bands of equalization.

How Do Microphones Work?

While the digital revolution has radically transformed the design of nearly all the production assets in the multimedia toolkit, professional microphones remain largely analog devices that have changed very little in design over the past 30 years.

FIGURE 12.7
A boom arm and shock mount are used to support the microphone during this recording studio session. A pop filter is placed in front of the microphone to reduce plosives, vocal artifacts such as those infamous "popping *P*s."

The microphone's job is to convert the acoustical waveform signature of the sound wave into an electrical voltage signal bearing the amplitude and frequency imprint of the recorded sound, a process called *transduction*. The signal coming out of a microphone is called an *analog signal* because it is analogous to the variations in sound pressure and frequency present in the original sound wave. And like the original sound wave, analog recordings provide a continuous and uninterrupted representation of the original sound.

Microphones are generally classified according to three main features or characteristics: 1) transduction method, 2) polar pattern, and 3) form factor.

Classifying Microphones by Transducer Type

Microphones use a *transducer* element to capture sounds. The transducer contains a moving diaphragm or ribbon that vibrates when exposed to a sound and encodes a sound wave's strength and frequency into electricity by modulating the current. Based on transduction method, dynamic microphones and condenser microphones are the two most common types.

DYNAMIC MICROPHONE

A *dynamic microphone* uses acoustical energy and mechanical vibration as the means for producing the electromagnetic signal required for analog recording. Dynamic microphones do not require a power source. They are durable, relatively inexpensive, and moisture and shock resistant. Moving-coil and ribbon microphones are two

A. Dynamic Microphone

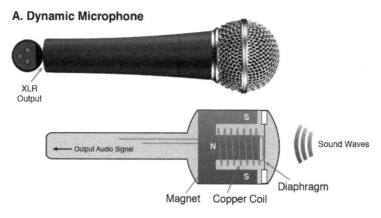

XLR
Output

Sound Waves

Output Audio Signal

Diaphragm

Magnet   Copper Coil

B. Condenser Microphone

Battery Compartment

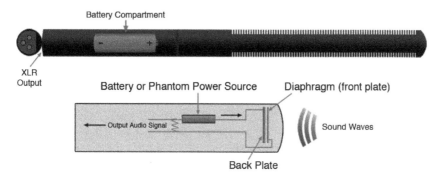

XLR
Output

Battery or Phantom Power Source   Diaphragm (front plate)

Output Audio Signal

Sound Waves

Back Plate

FIGURE 12.8
A) A dynamic
microphone is
less sensitive to
sound because
the transducer is
self-powered by the
sound of the subject's
voice. B) A condenser
microphone is
more sensitive to
sound because
the transducer is
powered by a battery
or phantom power
source.

of the most common types of dynamic microphones. Both rely on electromagnetic induction, which uses magnets to produce an electric current (see Figure 12.8, A).

Moving-Coil Microphone

In a *moving-coil microphone*, a diaphragm is attached to a coil (a metal core wrapped with copper wire) suspended in a magnetic field between the north and south poles of a fixed magnet. The diaphragm is a thin, circular membrane, typically made of paper, plastic, or metal. As the diaphragm vibrates, the coil oscillates in the magnetic field, producing a tiny current that's transmitted via copper wire to the microphone cable. The electromagnetic signal modulates in unison with the amplitude and frequency of the sound pressure wave, producing a copy of the original waveform.

Ribbon Microphone

A *ribbon microphone* uses a thin metal ribbon of corrugated metal, usually aluminum, as the transduction element. The ribbon is suspended in a magnetic field between the opposite poles of a fixed magnet and generates an electromagnetic current when it pulsates in the magnetic field. Ribbon microphones are technically superior to moving-coil designs because they respond to sound bidirectionally,

FIGURE 12.9
Vintage radio microphones like this one often have a ribbon transducer.

from both the front and the back of the element. While ribbon microphones are relatively expensive, broadcasting and recording professionals value them for their superior performance and natural sound reproduction. The metal elements in early ribbon microphones were quite delicate, and ribbon microphones had a reputation for being easy to damage. Newer ribbon microphones are more robust, though as with their predecessors, you need to be careful about picking up wind noise when using them outdoors (see Figure 12.9).

CONDENSER MICROPHONE

A *condenser microphone* uses a capacitor to record variations in amplitude and frequency. The capacitor has two parts, the back plate (containing the electric charge) and the diaphragm. As the diaphragm vibrates, the distance between it and the back plate changes, thus modulating the intensity of the voltage signal. Condenser microphones are much more sensitive to sound than dynamic microphones and as a result can be positioned farther from the source of the sound. Condenser microphones are separated into two groups based on diaphragm size. Large diaphragm condensers have a bigger form factor and are more often used in a studio recording environment, while small diaphragm condensers have a slender body profile and may be found in both field and studio environments (see Figure 12.8, B).

Condenser elements require a power source to supply the electric charge to the back plate. For this reason, condenser mics are often equipped with an attached battery pack or built-in power module. A single AA battery is usually all that's required. You can also power a condenser microphone with *phantom power*, an electric current that's transmitted to the microphone from an attached mixer or recording device (see Figure 12.10). Phantom power supplies a 48-volt (+48V) electric charge to the capacitor through the signal wires of the XLR cable connecting the microphone. Professional audio mixers/recorders and video cameras usually provide phantom power output. However, you may need to flip a switch or change a menu setting to activate it.

An *electret condenser* microphone is slightly different from a true condenser microphone in that the back plate is designed by the manufacturer to stay permanently charged, eliminating the need for a power source. Most professional condenser microphones in use today feature an electret condenser. And while the condenser may not need external power, most of these mics also contain an integrated preamp that requires a tiny amount of sustained voltage. For this reason, a battery or phantom power is still needed for the microphone to work.

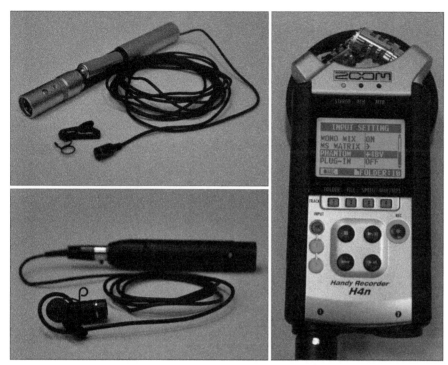

FIGURE 12.10
The two microphones on the left are condensers. However, the one pictured at the top can be powered with either a battery or phantom power. The microphone on the bottom does not have a battery compartment and must be powered by the camera or recorder it is connected to. Most professional recording devices can provide phantom power, but it must be turned on to work. The phantom power switch may be located on the outside of the unit or, as shown on the right, within the menu system of the device.

Classifying Microphones by Polar Pattern

Microphones are also classified according to their *polar pattern* (or *pickup pattern*). Polar pattern refers to how well a microphone picks up sound within 360 degrees of its central axis. Polar patterns are three-dimensional, so in effect, the sensitivity field includes the area above and below the microphone as well as to the right, left, front, and back. The narrower the pickup pattern, the more directional the microphone will be, and the more effective it will be in sensing sounds along the central axis. In short, the polar pattern of a microphone affects how you use it and under which circumstances the microphone will function at its best (see Figure 12.11).

OMNIDIRECTIONAL

The pickup pattern of an *omnidirectional microphone* is a sphere around the microphone, although not an entirely perfect one. In theory, these microphones respond equally to sound in all directions. In practice, however, the microphone body, particularly on handheld microphones, can block or obscure the path of a sound wave. This can shield the microphone from some frequencies. The smaller the microphone's

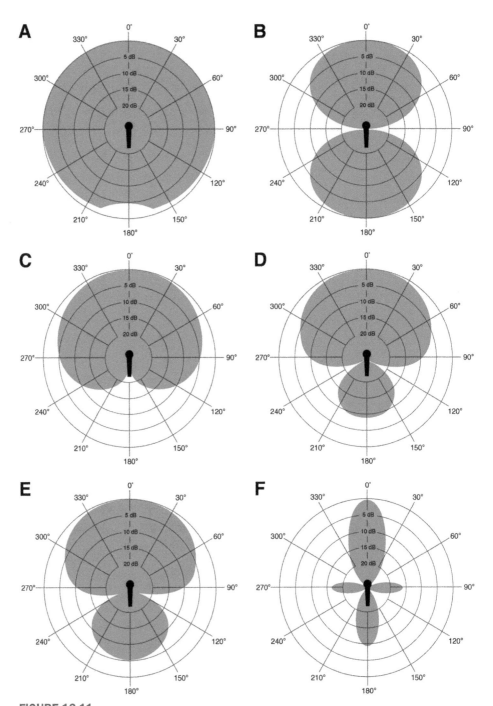

FIGURE 12.11
Six of the most common polar patterns: A) omnidirectional; B) bidirectional; C) cardioid;
D) supercardioid; E) hypercardioid; F) ultracardioid (or shotgun).

body, the less of a problem this is. Because they pick up sound from all directions, omnidirectional microphones are best used in situations where there is little to no ambient sound. You may also hear these microphones called *nondirectional*.

BIDIRECTIONAL

Bidirectional microphones pick up sound equally from the front and rear of the element. Most ribbon microphones are bidirectional. As a broadcast performance microphone, these are ideal for interviews where the host and guest are seated on opposite sides of a table or in situations where two people are required to share a single microphone.

CARDIOID (UNIDIRECTIONAL)

As the name implies, a *unidirectional microphone* picks up sound from only one direction. This makes it well suited for working in situations with lots of ambient (or background) sound. There are a number of variants of this type of microphone. *Cardioid microphones* have a unidirectional polar pattern with a heart-like shape (hence their name). This pickup pattern favors sounds coming from the front and sides up to 130 degrees. Cardioid microphones boast a relatively narrow pickup field and do a good job of rejecting ambient sound from the rear of the microphone. Cardioid microphones are ideal for recording single subjects and vocalists. Other members of the unidirectional family include *supercardioid*, *hypercardioid*, and *ultracardioid* (or *shotgun*) *microphones*. Each progression comes with a narrower pickup field and an expanded area of sound rejection from the rear of the microphone. The narrower the pickup pattern, the more deliberate the operator needs to be in aiming the microphone directly at the sound source during recording.

Classifying Microphones by Form Factor

Microphones come in many different shapes and sizes, but in terms of practical application, there are four microphone styles you will run into more than all the others: handheld, lavalier, shotgun, and boundary microphones (see Figure 12.12 and Figure 12.21). Once you are familiar with these, you will be ready to handle the vast majority of recording challenges with ease and confidence.

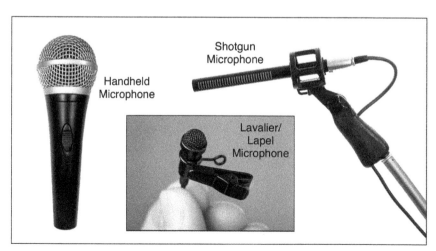

Shotgun Microphone

Handheld Microphone

Lavalier/ Lapel Microphone

FIGURE 12.12
Microphones are classified by form factor depending on the general purpose they are designed for.

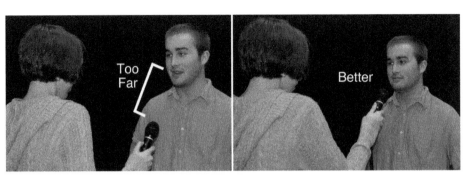

FIGURE 12.13
Television news reporters often use handheld microphones for conducting field interviews. Because handhelds are usually dynamic, they should be positioned no further than a few inches from the front of the subject's mouth.

HANDHELD MICROPHONE

Handheld microphones are designed for the talent or performer to hold during a recording session. Dynamic handheld microphones are ideal for rugged use and heavy handling, but they need to be held close to the subject's or talent's mouth in order to generate enough sound pressure for a good recording (see Figure 12.13). The rugged construction of dynamic handheld microphones minimizes noise caused by sudden movement, rough handling, or when passing the microphone along from person to person. Reporters rely on this type of microphone most often when recording a stand-up interview or conducting field interviews. If you are interviewing someone using a directional handheld microphone, remember that you need to aim it toward the other person when he or she is talking. Think about it as sharing an ice cream cone. If the other person is going to eat, you've got to put the cone in front of him or her.

Some handhelds are equipped with an electret condenser element. While this increases the microphone's sensitivity, it raises the risk of unwanted noise from outside forces. To reduce handling noise, condenser handheld microphones usually come with an internal shock mount. The shock mount suspends the element in midair with elastic bands, insulating it against sudden jarring movements.

Most handheld microphones are unidirectional. Handhelds work best when the microphone is positioned no further than six inches away from the mouth and slightly off-axis. Getting too close to the microphone grill (the shield) can produce annoying artifacts such as the infamous "popping *P*s" and other unpleasant plosives—the sound caused by releasing blocked air in speech, particularly from the pronunciation of the hard consonants *b, d, g, k, p,* and *t.* Remember, the microphone element is highly sensitive to sound pressure vibrations, and when a plosive ignites less than an inch away, vocal distortion and clipping are likely to occur. Using a windscreen or pop filter can reduce or eliminate vocal artifacts and wind noise (see Figure 12.14 and Figure 12.19).

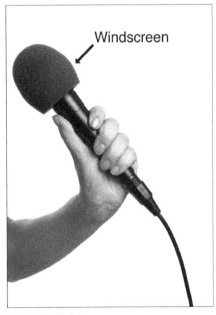

FIGURE 12.14
When using any microphone outdoors, it's a good idea to attach a windscreen.

Up until now, we have assumed that a handheld micro-phone must be held at all times. While this is a common approach in field productions, concerts, and the like, handhelds can also be attached to a floor stand, tabletop stand, podium, or boom arm using a microphone clip, gooseneck, or other adapter (see Figure 12.15). Secur-ing a handheld microphone to a stand or mount ensures hands-free operation and eliminates the risk of handling noise, unless of course the stand topples over or the talent swats the microphone. It happens!

The downside to using stands, or handheld micro-phones at all, lies in the fact that most inexperienced users (nonprofessionals) vehemently shy away from close contact with a microphone. Most people feel ner-vous around microphones and assume they will work just fine if positioned 10 feet away from them. So if the keynote speaker for the annual fundraising banquet is an engineer, doctor, lawyer, or accountant, and not a professional orator, you may need to remind him or her about the importance of moving in close to the microphone in order to be heard and obtain a usable recording. Even then, they may choose to ignore your instructions or simply forget them as the common fear of public speaking sets in. In either event, a better option awaits you in our discussion of the next form factor.

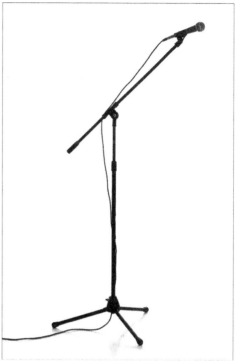

FIGURE 12.15
A handheld microphone is supported by a microphone stand for hands-free operation.

LAVALIER MICROPHONES

Unlike a handheld microphone, a *lavalier mic* is designed for hands-free opera-tion and is a popular choice for recording interviews. Also known as a lapel or lav microphone, this low-profile workhorse is designed with an electret condenser transducer element. Although they come in a variety of polar patterns, the most common ones have an omnidirectional, cardioid, or supercardioid element. Pro-fessional lav microphones usually require a battery pack or phantom power source.

Lavalier microphones are highly sensitive to sound and touch and should never be held by hand when recording. They are also not designed to be spoken into directly (on axis) at close range. Instead, lavs are designed to be attached to the subject's clothing three to six inches below the chin. Using a specially designed alligator clip, a lav can easily be attached to the front of a jacket, shirt, tie, or lapel. Because they are physically attached in one spot, the distance from the microphone to the source remains constant. Whether the subject is running, walking, sitting, or stand-ing, the position of a lavalier microphone, relative to the source, will not change. However, even when a lavalier is properly attached, you have to be careful. The tal-ent's physical actions (moving hands, feet, clothing, etc.) can cause unwanted noise if the microphone is suddenly bumped or jostled. Lavs are particularly popular with platform speakers who want the freedom to walk and talk at the same time without having to hold a microphone or stand behind a podium. They are also a good choice for recording interviews, especially when used indoors in a quiet

Tech Talk

The Proximity Effect The *proximity effect* is an acoustic phenomenon that boosts the bass frequencies of your voice as you move progressively closer to the microphone diaphragm. Next time you're in a recording studio, test this out by putting on a pair of headphones and listening to how your voice resonates more deeply as you narrow the gap between your mouth and the microphone. While the proximity effect is common with most unidirectional dynamic microphones, especially those with a single, large diaphragm, you'll particularly notice it with ribbon microphones, as both sides of the diaphragm are exposed to sound pressure. While you need to be close to a dynamic microphone when you use it, avoid leaning in too closely. When you are a quarter inch or closer to the microphone, it will lead to unnatural low-end distortion artifacts.

Whether the proximity effect is good or bad is simply a matter of taste and perspective. Radio disc jockeys, public-address announcers, and voice recording artists often get paid for having warm, larger-than-life voices. A professional can use the

proximity effect to his or her advantage to enhance the overall warmth and presence of a performance or to increase the power and delivery of certain words and phrases (see Figure 12.16). Over time, vocal artists develop an instinctive ability to control the proximity effect and to gauge when and how far to lean in on the microphone to mediate its intensity.

Too much bass, however, can muddy the audio. Overemphasized bass frequencies can cause the midrange and highs to be compressed, and the overall clarity and breadth of a vocal recording may suffer. Most professional microphones vulnerable to the proximity effect have a bass or low-frequency roll-off feature that gradually reduces the bass response as sound pressure increases. Mixers and recorders often include a similar control for attenuating (reducing) bass sounds or canceling out excessive low-end frequencies. Because of the popularity of the bass roll-off feature with recording engineers, this feature is sometimes even included on microphones, resulting in little to no proximity effect distortion.

FIGURE 12.16
A radio announcer is comfortable working closely to the microphone when speaking to her audience over the air.

setting (like a TV studio or office) and where the talent's physical movements won't interfere with a good recording.

Proper microphone placement is essential for a quality recording and optimizing the rejection of unwanted ambient sound. The microphone element should face upward toward the chin and be free of any obstructions from clothing and jewelry. Attaching a windscreen to the microphone capsule can help alleviate wind or breathing noise. Lavs should be positioned so the subject's voice projects directly over the top of the microphone. Most of the time, this means affixing it directly in the center of the upper body or chest. However, if the subject is turned off-axis to the camera, then the microphone should be positioned slightly to the left or right of center so that it remains directly under the mouth or chin of the subject.

To maintain a professional appearance, lavalier microphones should be properly dressed. Dressing a microphone involves making it as attractive and obscure as possible (see Figure 12.17). At all costs, be sure to avoid the rookie mistake of allowing the microphone cable to dangle down the front of the subject's shirt or blouse. This is a telltale sign of an amateur production. With just a little bit of effort, and discretion, the microphone cable can be rerouted out of sight beneath clothing or hidden behind a tie, lapel, jacket, or collar. Discretion is critical because working with people in a professional production setting requires sensitivity to cultural norms and rules of etiquette. While you need to keep these issues in mind whenever you are working, you need to be particularly cognizant of these issues when working with people from other cultures or with different genders.

In order to effectively hide the microphone cable, it may be necessary to conceal it under a shirt or blouse. Such a request needs to be made in a professional manner, with sensitivity to personal space and gender differences. Giving subjects clear instructions about microphone placement and offering them the option of moving to an offset

FIGURE 12.17
In the top two photos, the lavalier is improperly affixed to the subject. Take the time to properly position and dress a lavalier microphone, hiding the cable from view as best you can. Doing so will improves the quality of the recording and the appearance of the subject during an on-camera interview.

location (such as a dressing room or restroom) is often appreciated. However, do not assume the subject will know which way is up and which way is down. Do not expect the subject to understand the best technique for dressing the cable or assume he or she will have performed the task completely as instructed. In the end, this is your job, and before recording begins, you should make every effort to ensure the microphone has been properly attached, positioned, and dressed. Leave nothing to chance.

SHOTGUN MICROPHONES

Shotgun microphones are among the most directional microphones. They feature a condenser element with an extremely narrow pickup pattern—in supercardioid, hypercardioid, and ultracardioid varieties. They are so named because of their long and slender form factor, which resembles the general shape of a shotgun barrel. Shotguns microphones are housed in a cylindrical capsule with a small diaphragm. While they are relatively expensive, film and video producers like these microphones because of their versatility and usefulness in complicated mic situations, particularly those in which more than one person in a scene is speaking. The main advantage of using this type of microphone is that it can remain hidden out of sight, beyond the camera's field of view. Some shotgun microphones have interchangeable capsules that allow you to change the characteristics of the microphone on the fly.

Because of their narrow polar pattern, shotgun microphones need to be aimed in much the same way that a rifle has to be pointed toward its intended target. In a film-style recording setup, a shotgun is often mounted to a *boom* pole (or *fish pole*), a device that allows the audio operator to extend the microphone 6 to 12 feet into the scene where the actors are located (see Figure 12.18). It can also be attached to

FIGURE 12.18
A boom pole is used to position a shotgun microphone within a few feet of the subjects in this scene. The videographer works with the boom pole operator to ensure that the microphone does not dip down into the visible portion of the frame.

FIGURE 12.19
A pistol grip is used in lieu of a boom pole for acquiring the sound of footsteps on leaves. When using a shotgun microphone to acquire sound effects, the audio engineer usually wants to get the microphone as close to the source of the sound as possible.

a small *pistol grip* for handheld control (see Figure 12.19) or mounted directly on top of a video camera. Using a boom pole or pistol grip, the audio operator is able to keep the axis of the barrel continually aimed at the subject as dialog moves from one person to another or as sound traverses along a linear path. The boom pole operator monitors the recording with headphones to assist with maintaining the "sweet spot" where the microphone is positioned at its optimal best. Remember to make sure the microphone stays out of the shot when you use a boom pole (see Figure 12.20).

If you are working alone, you may not have a second set of hands to operate a boom pole or pistol grip. In such cases, attaching it to the camera will allow for hands-free operation. While mounting a shotgun microphone directly to a camera is sometimes less than ideal, this technique can produce good results as long as the distance between the sound source and the camera remains constant.

Whether attached to a camera, boom pole, or pistolgrip, shotguns need to be secured in a sturdy shock mount in order to reduce mechanical transmission noise. Since they use a condenser element, shotguns require a power source, either phantom power or a battery—typically found in a compartment at the end of the microphone capsule. While broadcast and film producers have been using shotgun-style microphones for years, they are now quite popular with corporate and low-budget productions. If you can only afford to have one microphone in your production arsenal, this is the one to choose.

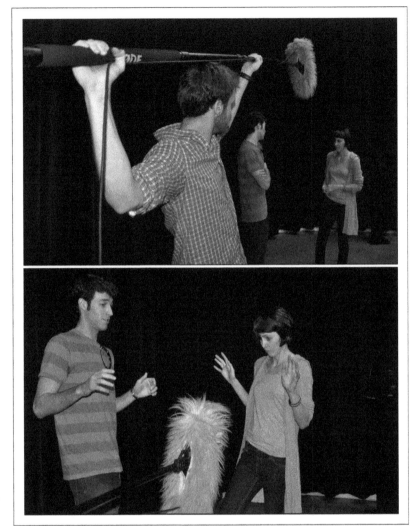

FIGURE 12.20
Different techniques can be used for positioning a microphone with a boom pole—either above the subjects or below them. Placing it too closely to the talent (bottom photo) can interfere with a performance or result in the microphone showing up on camera, thus ruining the take.

BOUNDARY MICROPHONES

Boundary microphones, also known as *pressure zone microphones* (PZMs), are condenser microphones intended to be placed on a flat surface, usually a table, ceiling, or wall. The enclosed PZM mic capsule is affixed above a metal baseplate and detects changes in the sound pressure waves within the air gap—an area called the pressure zone (see Figure 12.21). The design minimizes the effects of sound reflecting off other sources such as a wall by limiting the sound capture area. PZMs are usually used to record meetings and conferences and are good for recording multiple people at the same time. As you can see, they don't really look like what we typically think a microphone looks like. You can use this to your advantage—PZMs are less likely to make people nervous.

FIGURE 12.21
The Audio-Technica ES961 is a cardioid condenser boundary microphone designed for use on a flat surface such as a conference table or floor.
Source: http://audio-technica.com.

Built-in or External Microphones?

The microphones we've talked about so far have been external microphones that you attach to a recording device, but many devices have built-in microphones, including laptop computers, cameras, cell phones, and voice recorders. Most often, built-in microphones are low-end condenser microphones. After all, if you are using a microphone for a phone call or video chat, it just needs to be good enough to enable you to be clearly understood. As such, many built-in microphones are designed primarily for transmitting conversations, not recording them. There are, of course, exceptions. As a general rule, avoid using a built-in microphone for voice acquisition without testing it first.

Regardless of the quality of a built-in microphone, however, it has some inherent limitations. One of the most obvious ones is that it *is* built in. This means that in most cases the operator has little control over the positioning of the microphone, particularly with video cameras, and the closer the microphone is to the source, the better it will perform. Although professional external microphones are relatively more expensive, they are made with better transducers and components, and as such, there's simply no substitute for using one given a choice (see Figure 12.22). In fact, as a general rule in professional situations, you should avoid the temptation of ever using a built-in microphone to acquire primary audio content (actor dialog, voiceovers, interviews, etc.).

FIGURE 12.22
Left: The producer uses the built-in microphone on his digital audio recorder. Right: Here he uses the same recorder but attaches an external handheld microphone. All things being equal, you will achieve better results using a professional external microphone to conduct interviews.

WHY USE AN EXTERNAL MICROPHONE?

Here are four reasons for using a professional-grade external microphone instead of one that is built into the recording device:

1. You can select the best type of microphone from a vast assortment of professional microphones to fit the recording setting, subject, and application.
2. You will have greater control over the placement of the microphone and its proximity to the subject, irrespective of where the sound or video recording device is located.
3. All things being equal, a professional external microphone will have better sound recording specs than the built-in microphone attached to your device.
4. Professional external microphones use a balanced XLR connector, which is better for reducing RF interference and other types of transmission noise.

Wireless Microphones

Although most of the time you are working with audio you'll be running a wire directly from the microphone to your recorder or mixer, you'll occasionally need to use a wireless microphone, particularly if you have talent who likes to walk around the room a lot. In some cases, you can plug your regular microphone into a wireless transmitter—essentially a tiny radio station that will send the audio to a radio receiver—that you'll plug into your mixer or recorder (see Figure 12.23). You may lose some of your frequency range when you switch to wireless. Like all battery-operated equipment, make sure you keep fresh batteries on hand for the transmitter and the receiver. If you use more than one wireless microphone at a time, you'll have to make sure they aren't using the same radio frequency. Just as two radio stations can't broadcast on 88.1 FM at the same time, you can't have two wireless microphones operating on the same radio frequency. The better the system, the more frequency options you'll have. Remember, you may not be the only one using a wireless microphone at some locations.

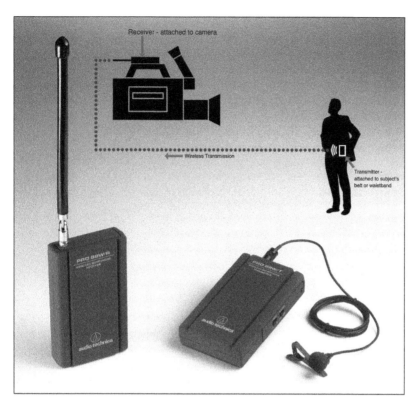

FIGURE 12.23
A wireless microphone like this one is designed for remote field production. The microphone and transmitter are attached to the subject. The receiver is attached to the camera.
Source: http://www.audio-technica.com.

Tech Talk

Synchronizing Video and Audio in Post Most DSLR cameras lack an XLR input for connecting a professional external microphone to the camera. Also absent from most of them is a built-in preamp for setting levels, a VU meter for monitoring, and, in some cases, a headphone jack for listening. For this reason, many low-budget filmmakers have adopted the old-school technique of recording video and audio on two separate devices. Portable and inexpensive field recorders like the Zoom H4 have grown immensely popular in recent years for just this purpose. The H4 is designed with dual XLR inputs, phantom power, high-definition sampling modes for recording uncompressed audio, and a host of other settings and features that professional videographers and audio engineers are used to having.

In order to align asynchronous video and audio clips in post, the camera needs to record a reference audio track for each shot. Fortunately, DSLRs capable of shooting video include a built-in microphone that can be used for this purpose.

At the beginning of each shot, a film slate or clapboard is positioned in front of the camera. Information can be written on the slate's white board as a visual reference to production details such as the shooting date and the scene, shot, and take numbers (see Figure 13.10). With the camera rolling, an assistant opens and closes the clap sticks to create a loud "slap" that will be used later as an audible cue for synchronizing the sound captured on the portable recorder with that picked up by the DSLR camera. Professional NLE software increasingly provides built-in tools for automated audio synching of clips in the timeline. A specialty software program such as *PluralEyes*, made by RedGiant, analyzes the audio waveforms of related clips and synchronizes them in seconds. Some manual refinement may be necessary, but in practice, automated synching is remarkably accurate when working with clips with good audio levels. Specialty software like PluralEyes is also handy for batch processing an entire collection of clips at the end of shoot prior to reviewing or editing them in post.

There are two basic transmitter types for professional equipment, UHF and VHF. Of the two options, UHF offers the most available frequencies. This may be helpful if you are using more than five wireless microphones at a time or are going to be in locations where others are using wireless microphones. On the other hand, UHF microphones are typically more expensive than VHF microphones. Be aware that some of the radio frequencies overlap with television station frequencies. Always test your equipment before you begin production. A third option for wireless is an *infrared transmitter*, which uses a beam of infrared light to send the signal. It's usually best to avoid infrared systems, as they require line-of-site transmission. If something gets between the transmitter and the receiver, it won't work, much like the remote control for your television. Infrared does have the advantage of being more secure—you can't pick it up from outside the room—and infrared transmitters typically don't interfere with each other.

USB Microphones

One of the challenges with the move toward a digital workflow involves recording audio directly into the computer. While you can plug some microphones directly into a computer, a better solution is to use an A/D, an analog-to-digital converter, which translates the analog input into a digital format. Using an A/D isolates the conversion process from the rest of the computer and lessens the chance of computer components such as the power supply introducing unwanted noise. Another option is to use a microphone with the A/D built into it. These microphones are often called USB microphones because they typically connect to the computer via a USB connector (see Figure 12.24)

FIGURE 12.24
A student uses a USB microphone connected to a computer to record a voiceover.

AUDIO CONNECTORS

Microphones may be connected to audio recording devices by a variety of cables and connectors. Professional microphones use balanced connectors, while consumer devices use unbalanced connectors.

Balanced Audio Connectors

Professional microphones and audio devices are connected using balanced cables and connectors (see Figure 12.25). A *balanced microphone cable* has three wires encased in an outer rubber sheath. Audio signals flow in a loop, from the microphone to the recorder, and then back again. In a balanced system, a pair of twisted wires is used for conducting the signal path. The current travels down the positive wire in one direction and returns on the negative wire in the opposite direction. Since the impedance or resistance of the current is the same in both directions, this is called a *balanced line* or *circuit*. The third wire in a balanced cable is called the *shield* or *ground*. The ground wire is designed to "shield" the audio signal from electrical interference that can distort or weaken it in any way. The shield's job is to eliminate noise (buzzes, hums, hisses, etc.) by keeping interference from coming into contact with the audio signal. While using balanced wiring doesn't guarantee total noise rejection, it offers the best solution for protecting the integrity of the signal path. Balanced audio cables can be run for long distances with good results. This is particularly helpful in large rooms, for fixed recording environments, or with live events and concerts, where recording equipment is kept at some distance from the microphones and talent.

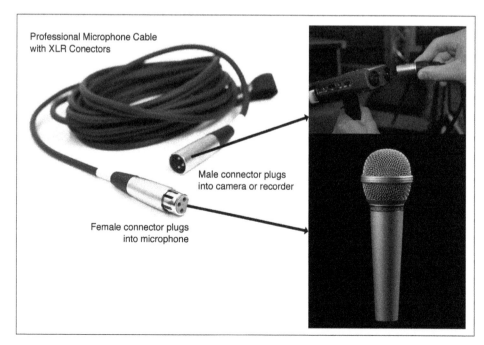

Professional Microphone Cable with XLR Conectors

Male connector plugs into camera or recorder

Female connector plugs into microphone

FIGURE 12.25
Professional microphones and recording systems are equipped with balanced XLR connectors.

XLR CONNECTORS

Balanced microphone cables usually have XLR connectors on each end of the wire. The female XLR connector attaches directly to the end of the microphone or power adapter, while the three-pin male connector plugs into the recorder or mixer. An XLR connector has a locking mechanism on the metal casing to keep it from coming loose during recording. To insert it, line up the pins and holes and push on the connector until you feel it snap in place. To disconnect it, press down on the safety lock while pulling back on the connector in a steady motion. Never pull directly on the cable wire when attempting to disconnect it. Doing so can weaken or sever the solder joint between the wire leads and the terminal posts, thus breaking the circuit and rendering the cable useless.

Unbalanced Audio Connectors

Most consumer microphones and electronic equipment use an unbalanced audio connector for patching analog sound sources. The male end of the connector is called the *plug* and the female end or receiving socket is referred to as the *jack*. An unbalanced cable uses two wires, a center conductor surrounded by a shield. The positive wire conducts the outbound signal flow, while the negative wire functions as both the return conduit and ground. Unbalanced cables are highly susceptible to interference when used across long distances. As a result, it's best to use them on patching runs of 20 feet or less.

TS AND TRS CONNECTORS

The quarter-inch phono plug has been around for over a century and uses a *tip and sleeve* (TS) design. This connector was originally made for the telephone industry for use by switchboard operators to patch telephone calls and is still used today for general-purpose audio patching. The tip conducts the positive phase of the audio signal while the sleeve carries the negative phase and serves as the ground. An insulator ring separates the tip conductor from the sleeve. The stereo version of this connector uses a *tip, ring, and sleeve* (TRS) design. While a stereo signal requires a third wire, the circuit remains unbalanced. Stereo quarter-inch phone plugs are used for connecting headphones to the output jack of a portable listening device or sound system. TRS cables can also be used to carry a balanced mono audio signal.

As electronics have gotten smaller, TS and TRS connectors have evolved as well. In addition to the traditional quarter-inch plug, both now come in an eighth-inch (3.5 mm) mini plug, used on most MP3 players and computers, and a 2.5 mm micro plug, which shows up on some mobile phones and other small devices. Adapters are available for converting any size of TS- or TRS-style connector to any other size (see Figure 12.26).

RCA CONNECTORS

In the early 1940s, the Radio Corporation of America designed the *RCA phono plug* for connecting phonographs (or record players) to amplifiers. Today, it is used for connecting both the audio and video signal paths of a diverse array of audiovisual (A/V) devices, including television monitors, gaming consoles, projectors, and numerous other things. RCA plugs are often color coded to match the receiving end of an RCA jack. Yellow designates the composite video channel, while red and white refer respectively to the right and left audio channels in a stereo system. You'll also find RCA plugs used for component video—a video format that uses separate cables for the red, green, and blue signals.

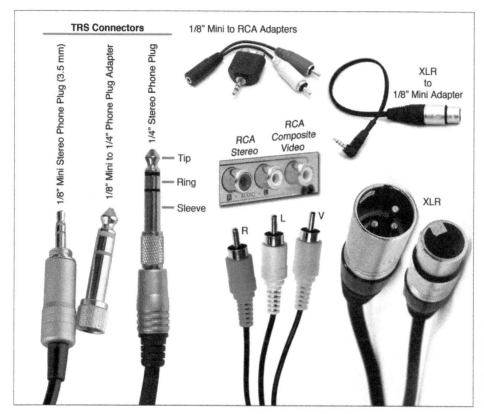

FIGURE 12.26
A wide variety of audio connectors and adapters are used in audio production. These are just a few you may run into.

ADAPTERS

While it's best to avoid using adapters, you'll sometimes need to use one for hooking up cables and devices with incompatible connectors, and it's a good idea to have some good-quality adapters in your audio kit. One of the problems you may run into is the need to mix balanced and unbalanced audio gear. For example, the external microphone jack on a consumer camcorder (if it has one at all) is likely going to be an eighth-inch mini plug. In order to use a professional microphone with a camera of this type, you'll need an XLR-to-mini plug adapter. Since the adapter is only traveling a short distance from the end of the microphone cable to the camera, you shouldn't have to worry too much about interference affecting the audio signal.

Still, adapters can complicate matters, as they introduce another potential failure point in the audio chain. If the adapter fails or comes undone, you'll lose your audio. To be safe, secure adapters with a small piece of gaffer tape to keep them from working lose during the recording. While gaffer tape looks similar to duct tape, don't confuse the two. Gaffer tape uses a different type of adhesive that doesn't leave a residue when you remove it. Mistake the two and you'll end up with messy gear. Make the mistake when taping cables down on a carpet and expect not to be invited back to the gig.

Cable Management 101

While a microphone cable may seem like a rather inconsequential item, the role it plays in protecting the integrity of signal flow in the audio chain is critical to the success of a production. When properly cared for, cables will last longer, perform better, and be easier to handle and use. It pays to invest some time to learn the art and science of proper cable care and management. One of the best things I learned during my first internship as a young college student was how to wrap and store cables properly. The crusty broadcast engineer I was assigned to work with made no bones about how pitifully poor my cable-wrapping technique was. While I had to endure a bit of public humiliation and some colorful expletives along the way, I have always been grateful to him for taking the time to teach me the importance of cable etiquette and, even more important, for imparting to me a healthy sense of pride in regard to the proper use and care of equipment.

The most important lesson in cable management is learning how to properly wrap and secure a cable when you're finished using it. Scrunching it up into a chaotic heap simply will not do. The next person who uses it will not appreciate the time he or she has to waste untangling the mess you created. Instead, cables should be carefully wrapped in a uniform coil, 12 to 24 inches in diameter (depending on the length of the cable). For short cables less than 50 feet, each loop should be comprised of 30–36 inches of wire. For longer cable runs, the loops can be larger. The important thing is consistency. As you wrap a cable, each loop should be roughly the same length in order to preserve the circular shape of the coil when finished.

Proper wrapping keeps cables from twisting, kinking, creasing, or bending, which can cause permanent damage to the encased wires or weaken them over time. Cables retain a "memory" based on good or bad patterns of repeated winding. In the long run, it's easier to wrap a cable properly every time than it is to retrain a gnarled cable that has been poorly managed or abused. Once kinks and twists have been introduced into cable memory, they are difficult to undo.

AUDIO MONITORING

One of the simplest recording scenarios is the one-person interview. All that's needed is a subject, a recording device (camcorder or audio recorder), a microphone, an XLR cable, and a set of headphones. The producer's goal is to acquire source material by interviewing the subject and recording his or her voice to disk. To achieve professional results, you need to monitor the audio signal as it is being recorded. Audio monitoring is a two-step process that includes 1) the objective act of measuring sound intensity and setting the record levels and 2) the subjective act of listening to the audio signal as it is being recorded.

Monitoring Record Levels Using a VU Meter (Step 1)

The electrical signal produced by a microphone is very weak and must be amplified during the recording process. Audio mixing consoles and recording devices have a built-in microphone preamp for boosting the strength of the signal for audio processing. The *preamp setting* (or *record level*) is controlled with buttons or dials on the recording equipment. In a stereo system, there are separate preamps and controls

Tech Talk

The Over-Under Wrap To prevent twists and kinks from developing, the method of *over-under wrapping* is used (see Figure 12.27). With this technique, each loop in the cable wrap is formed by twisting the wire in the opposite direction of the loop immediately before and after it. When the cable is unfurled, the alternating twists cancel each other out, allowing the cable to lie flat on the surface. Depending on whether you are right- or left-handed, the "over" loop runs in a clockwise or counterclockwise direction "over" the wire at the point where the loop began (Steps 1 and 2). The "under" loop runs the same way but is turned inward, causing it to twist in the opposite direction of the previous loop (Steps 3 and 4). In this pass, the cable is guided "under" the wire at the point where the loop began. This alternating pattern of over and under loops continues until the end of the cable is reached.

To complete the task, a cord or cable tie is used to secure the ends of the cable and keep the coil from coming undone. Once perfected, you will find that this technique can be used for all manner of video and audio cables. In fact, you may discover, as I have, that this method of coiling cables also works just as effectively on an extension cord or garden hose.

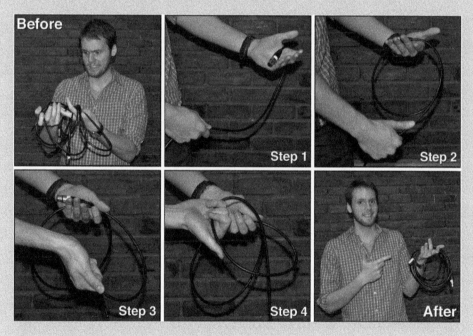

Before | Step 1 | Step 2 | Step 3 | Step 4 | After

FIGURE 12.27
Nobody likes working with a tangled cable. Here, a student uses the over-under wrap to properly coil a microphone cable.

for the left and right channels. As the recording engineer or operator, it's your job to monitor the amount of amplification that's applied to the microphone signal. The levels you choose will depend on many variables, including the strength of the subject's voice, the type of microphone being used, the distance from the subject to the microphone, and the amount of background noise in the interview setting. For example, a soft-spoken person usually requires more amplification than a person with a naturally loud delivery. On professional systems, the preamp can be controlled automatically using *automatic gain control* (AGC) or manually using the *volume-unit* (VU) meter and record level controls. Given a choice, most professionals prefer the manual method.

A VU meter displays the strength of the microphone signal (in decibel units) after it has passed through the preamp (see Figure 12.28). An analog VU meter has a typical range of –20 dB to +3 dB. A bouncing needle indicates the loudness of the signal as it modulates throughout the full dynamic range of the recording (from the quietest moments to the loudest ones). Digital VU meters vary in style. Most of them have a wider range on the low end, starting at –48 or –36 dB. Instead of a needle, they feature a row of colored LEDs.

On most VU meters, the region above 0 dB is color coded red to indicate that the signal is being overmodulated because of excessive amplification. While an occasional bounce into the lower region of the red scale usually isn't a problem, when too much amplification is applied, waveform distortion can occur, causing a phenomenon known as *clipping* (see Figure 12.29). Clipping permanently corrupts

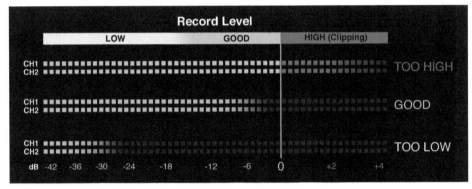

FIGURE 12.28
During a recording, try to keep the audio levels within the green portion of the scale, or good range, at roughly 50%–80%. Setting the record levels too high can produce clipping or distortion. Setting them too low will require you to amplify them in postproduction, introducing noise unnecessarily into the signal path.

FIGURE 12.29
Digital VU meters often include a clipping warning light that illuminates whenever sound levels exceed the distortion threshold. Sometimes, as shown here, the red area of the decibel scale is not displayed on a VU meter, perhaps to save space on a screen or visual interface. Instead, a clipping warning light may be all you have to work with to ensure that levels are kept from over-modulating.

the fidelity of the audio signal and cannot be repaired. For this reason, it is best to avoid pushing levels into the red at all. On the opposite end of the scale, you should also avoid setting the record level too low. A low audio signal will need to be boosted to acceptable levels in postproduction. Whenever you re-amplify a recorded audio signal, noise is introduced, and the quality of the original recording deteriorates. The lower your original record levels are, the more you will need to re-amplify them later. Maintaining proper levels throughout a recording session is key to obtaining professional results.

THE SOUND CHECK

Before starting the recording, conduct a *sound check* with your subject. Prompt the subject to speak in a normal tone of voice. Using the VU meter as a visual reference, adjust the record levels to the point where the loudest portions of their speech peak around 0 dB without going "into the red." After pressing "Record," continue monitoring the levels and adjusting them as necessary.

Monitoring with Headphones or Speakers (Step 2)

A VU meter gives you a visual reference of what the electronic recording device is "hearing" and is an objective indicator of the recorded signal's intensity. You also need to monitor a recording by *listening*—using your ears to assess and evaluate the aesthetic properties of the recording. Monitoring a live recording with headphones or near-field speakers allows you to hear the voice of your subject and any associated background sounds or noise as it is being recorded. The volume control on a recording device is used to raise and lower the headphone or control room level and has no effect on the actual recording. So just because the recording sounds *loud* to you in your ears doesn't mean the record levels are set properly. It might just be that the volume is set to the maximum level, leading to a false impression. As a matter of practice, set the record levels first and then adjust the volume of your headphones or speakers to the desired level.

HEADPHONES

It is worth investing in at least one set of good-quality headphones. Look for an over-the-ear rather than earbud design. Professional video cameras and field recorders will have headphone jacks that let you monitor your audio during the capture process—so get in the habit of always using headphones when you are working! Doing so will help you make sure nothing goes wrong with your audio. You can't rely on the VU meter alone to tell you if you are capturing good audio. It doesn't tell you if the audio signal is good or whether or not your microphone is working or picking up the main subject. You could just be picking up static or background noise. You might even be recording with the wrong microphone by mistake, for example, using an internal mic when you meant to be recording with an external mic. Try to keep the headphones on whenever you are capturing audio. Just because the audio sounded good when you started out doesn't mean it will sound good all the way through. Batteries die, cables get unplugged, and microphones can move or become detached. Oh, and cell phones can sometimes wreak havoc on your audio if you are not using RF-shielded microphones. You need to know if your audio has problems before you go back to the studio to edit.

Listen for potential audio problems—your headphones can help you here as well. Is your subject wearing metal bracelets that might clink together? What about background noise? Is the air conditioner making too much noise? What about that high-pitched electronic squeal from the video projector? Whenever possible, either eliminate the source of the unwanted sounds or find a better location. Whatever you do, don't just say, "I'll fix it in editing." There's a good chance you won't be able to, at least not easily, particularly if the noise is in the same frequency range as your talent's voice. Watch for echoes in a room and pay attention to where you set up your equipment. Try to avoid recording in the middle of a large room with hard walls—instead move to the side of the room. Look for things that will absorb rather than reflect sound. Recording on a busy street? Your headphones will help you make sure you've placed your microphone in a position to minimize the traffic noise.

CHAPTER SUMMARY

All too often, newcomers to multimedia production don't pay enough attention to the quality of their audio work, and it shows in the final product. To work in the industry, you need to understand the correct tool to use for a task. For audio, this means knowing which microphone to use when and what the relative advantages are for each type. As an example, we've seen that a ribbon microphone is great as a tabletop microphone for conducting an interview in a studio. On the other hand, it is not a great microphone for conducting an interview outdoors, as it is very susceptible to wind noise. Make sure you know when to use a balanced cable and when you can get away with using an unbalanced cable—the short answer is, use balanced whenever possible, but by all means keep your unbalanced cable runs to around 20 feet or less. Use professional-grade equipment whenever possible—this doesn't mean the most expensive, just good quality—and avoid internal microphones when possible. Oh, and don't forget your headphones. They really are one of the most important tools you've got, not only when you are editing audio but when you are capturing it as well. Few things are worse in audio production than coming back from an assignment and realizing that the battery died in your microphone three minutes into the interview and, because you weren't wearing headphones, you didn't realize it.

CHAPTER 13
Video Production

My movie is born first in my head, dies on paper; is resuscitated by the living persons and real objects I use, which are killed on film but, placed in a certain order and projected on to a screen, come to life again like flowers in water.

—Robert Bresson, French film director (1901–1999)

Chapter Highlights

This chapter examines:

- The variables affecting the camera's field of view (framing)
- The building blocks of film/visual grammar (frame, shot, scene, and sequence)
- Shot designations commonly used in video composition
- Three principles of motion in television and film
- Lighting techniques, instruments, and modification tools used

FILM OR VIDEO—WHAT'S THE DIFFERENCE?

Before the age of digital production, the terms *film* and *video* referred discretely to two specific analog methods for recording moving images. Film was an optical medium rooted in photography—one that relied on chemical processing of motion picture films and movie projectors for theatrical presentation. Video, on the other hand, was an electronic platform that relied on magnetic tape, optical disc, and television broadcasting for program distribution. Movies were shot on film while television shows were shot on tape. Today, while film is not entirely dead, it is no longer the sole medium for moviemaking and distribution. Likewise, videotape is nearing end-of-life as a recording medium for television. Increasingly, movies and documentaries are shot and distributed digitally from start to finish. I intentionally chose the term *video production* over *film production* for the title of this chapter because it is a broader and more encompassing term. Film, as a chemical acquisition format, has been largely supplanted by digital media and production workflows, while *film* as the art and craft of traditional moviemaking lives on (see Figure 13.1). As a medium, it is now

Key Terms

180-Degree Rule
Arc
B-Roll
Backlight
Close-Up (CU)
Coverage
Cross-Shot
Dolly
Establishing Shot
Falloff
Fill Light
Flag
Framing
Fresnel
Handheld Shot
Hard Light
Headroom
High-Angle Shot
Key Light
Lead Room
Low-Angle Shot
Master Shot
Medium Shot (MS)
Monopod
Natural Sound
Pan
Pedestal
Point of View
Primary Motion
Reflector
Scene
Scrim
Secondary Motion
Sequence
Shot/Shot List
Softbox
Soft Light
Sound Bite (SOT, or
  Sound on Tape)

Spill Light
Stand-Up
Take
Tertiary Motion
Three-Point Lighting
Tilt
Tripod
Truck
Two-Shot
Viewfinder
Voiceover (VO)
Wide Shot (WS)

THEN & NOW!

FIGURE 13.1
Film versus video. Left: The hand crank of a vintage motion picture camera is used for advancing motion picture *film* past the lens one frame at a time while exposing it to light. Right: Today, many motion pictures and documentaries are being shot digitally using a camera such as this 4K model manufactured by RED Digital Cinema.

culturally synonymous with video and is often used interchangeably to refer to the same thing. For example, when a new movie comes out, we refer to it as a film and to its director as a filmmaker, regardless of whether or not it was actually shot on film. Likewise, we go to the nearest Redbox to check out the latest Blu-ray video or to Netflix to stream the "video" version of a "film" online.

Regardless of whether we express it in terms of film or video, the production process is the proverbial cream in the Oreo cookie—sandwiched between the equally important, yet sometimes less exciting and more tedious, phases of preproduction and post. Remember the Three *P*s model discussed in chapter 3? This chapter focuses on the second *P*, *production*, while chapter 14 covers the third *P*, *postproduction*. As a reminder, *production* is the acquisition phase of a project, when the director or assistant director shouts "Roll tape!" or "Action!" Or when an actor or host delivers her carefully rehearsed lines—or when average or exceptional people reveal candid moments of insight to a reporter or a documentary filmmaker before a camera that's recording every word. Depending on the scale of the project, production can require the help of hundreds of people or a crew of only one. All it takes is one person with an idea in his or her head and the creativity and skill to capture real people, real objects, and real moments through which to tell a unique and compelling story on screen.

UNDERSTANDING HUMAN VISION

The physical universe where humans dwell is comprised of three-dimensional space. The first dimension is a horizontal plane. This is referred to as the *x-axis* in Cartesian geometry, but more often, it is described simply as width or length. The second dimension is the vertical plane, or *y-axis*. We call this dimension height. The third dimension, or *z-axis*, is depth. Imagine a taut string extending from the tip of your nose to the horizon. This is the z-axis, and it represents your direct line of sight. *Peripheral vision* is a term we use to describe the part of our vision that extends beyond the z-axis—to objects further to the left or right or up or down. The further peripheral objects lie outside of our direct gaze, the less likely we are to notice them. So while human vision tends to favor a wide-angle view of the world, objects that are more closely aligned to the z-axis are much more likely to grab and hold our attention. To compensate, our head and eyes move constantly in an effort to keep the people and objects we are most interested in following aligned with the z-axis.

FIELD OF VIEW

Any camera, whether it is used to obtain still or moving images, is an extension of the human eye and, as a result, sees only what the photographer allows it to see. Because a camera has no brain, and no ability to turn or move on its own without human assistance, it requires your hands, your feet, and your expertise to compose good shots. It is a tool—and you must learn how to use it well it if you intend to capture meaningful content that viewers will find engaging.

We refer to what the camera sees at any particular moment as the *field of view*, a concept that was first introduced in chapter 4. A photographer monitors the field of view using

FIGURE 13.2
Today, more and more people are shooting video on a mobile device, and when good principles are put into practice, professional results can be achieved. However, a rookie mistake that often occurs is when the shooter records video in portrait mode. While snapping vertical images with a phone is perfectly fine in still photography, video should be shot in landscape mode to conform it to the standard aspect ratio of television.

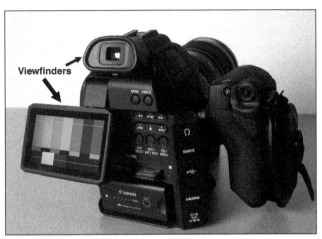

Viewfinders

FIGURE 13.3
Most video cameras have two viewfinders: 1) an electronic flat-screen monitor that can be viewed up close or from a short distance away, and 2) a near-field optical or electronic viewfinder that you monitor through one eye.

a *viewfinder* (see Figure 13.3). Professional video cameras typically have two electronic viewfinders: one is a near-field viewfinder that requires you to position one eye against a rubber eyepiece designed to shield the screen from sunlight and magnify the image. The second one is a small flat-screen monitor that can be viewed more easily at a distance. On DSLR (digital single lens reflex) cameras, an optical viewfinder permits through-the-lens viewing when composing and shooting still photos. When shooting video, you must use an electronic viewfinder—either one built into the camera or an external field monitor connected to an HDMI port or video output. Four variables work in conjunction to determine a camera's field of view: 1) camera location, 2) camera angle, 3) subject location, and 4) focal length.

Camera Location

The term *point of view* refers to the position of the camera in relation to the subject and is determined by physical location and angle. One of the first decisions a videographer makes on a shoot is where to set the camera. Beginners don't usually give this decision as much thought as they should and will often plop the camera and tripod down in the first place they come to that looks good. In short, don't overlook opportunities for giving your viewer a more interesting point of view. Before settling on a camera location, walk around, explore the possibilities, observe the effects of light and the interaction of foreground, mid-ground, and background to see which vantage point offers the greatest potential. With the z-axis in mind, give adequate thought to how the main subject of the composition interacts with competing visual elements such as other people, set pieces, props, and fixed or moving objects within the frame (see Figure 13.4). Moving the camera one foot to the left or two feet to the right, or sometimes even an inch or two, can make the difference between an average shot and one that is visually superior. Work to eliminate unsightly background mergers such as the proverbial tree branch, lamppost, or fence rail protruding awkwardly from the subject's head. Think of camera location as your first opportunity to simplify the shot by selectively cropping out unwanted visual elements from the frame with the goal of improving subject isolation and emphasis. Camera and subject location work somewhat in tandem. After fiddling with one you may have to adjust the other, then continue tweaking both until you achieve the shot you want.

When shooting in the field, you also need to consider lighting, which we'll look at in more detail later in this chapter. What time of day are you shooting, and where is the sun? Is it possible to position the camera in relation to the subject in a way that takes advantage of existing light? Normally, it's best to have the sun at your back and the camera pointing in the opposite direction. When shooting at night, consider the location of artificial light sources such as streetlamps and whether or

FIGURE 13.4
The subject/camera placement and z-axis depth improves as you move from top to the bottom in this series of images. Top: Placing the subject in front of a wall takes the z-axis out of play and can cause harsh background shadows. Middle: Z-axis depth is better in this image; however, the window appears to be growing out of the subject's head, and light from the fill light is reflecting off the glass. The bench in the background adds visual clutter. Bottom: Shallow depth of field enhances visual interest and draws attention to the main subject. There are no unsightly or awkward background mergers. Seating the subject at an angle is more dynamic.

not they can be used to enhance illumination of the subject or background or are best left alone because they present a visual distraction.

As a general rule for interviews, try to locate the camera within four to six feet of the subject. While you can stay further back and merely zoom in for a close-up, it's better to work from a distance that more closely resembles a real conversation. Interviewing a subject from across the room is unnatural and may contribute to greater discomfort or anxiety that gets captured by the camera and noticed by the viewer. The same is true when acquiring B-Roll. Unless you're filming an establishing shot of Mount Everest, an adult elephant, or something else of similar magnitude or scale, positioning the camera closer to the subject almost always leads to better results. Don't rely so much on your camera's zoom to fill the frame. Get in the habit of *zooming with your feet*. Move in closer to the subject! Remember, this is what you do in real life when you spot someone across a crowded room with whom you want to have a conversation. Instead of shouting from a distance, you walk over to the person in order to interact in a more personal and meaningful way. All things being equal, your camera will yield better shots when placed in close proximity to the subject rather than farther away.

GREAT IDEAS
The Sound Bite

A *sound bite* is a short candid excerpt taken from a longer interview or speech that is inserted into a video program or news package during the postproduction process. In television, a sound bite is denoted by the scriptwriting abbreviation SOT (pronounced *S-O-T*) for *sound on tape*. In radio broadcasting, a short interview segment is called *an actuality*. Television news reporters and producers rely heavily on sound bites as an essential component of journalistic storytelling. Sound bites are also regularly featured in documentary films, realty TV shows, and corporate and educational video programs. The practice of using sound bites as a structural component of a visual narrative is nearly ubiquitous. Occasionally, you may even see a "staged" interview sound bite in a motion picture or television commercial. Learning how to effectively set up and shoot an on-camera interview is one of the most essential skills for any aspiring producer or videographer.

GREAT IDEAS
B-Roll and Natural Sound

B-Roll is a term used to describe individual shots that are intentionally acquired to enhance or illustrate the audio portion of a visual narrative. B-Roll footage is used in editing to fill holes in the timeline where synchronized video is not included—for example, over a voiceover—or as a cover shot during a portion of a video sound bite. In narrative filmmaking, cut-ins and cutaways serve a similar function. The only difference is that B-Roll is usually shot candidly for unscripted programs while cut-ins and cutaways are generally scripted, staged, and performed by actors. B-Roll is often accompanied by *natural sound* (or nat sound). For example, in an on-camera sound bite, a tennis coach discusses her star player. As she is speaking, a B-Roll shot of the player practicing is inserted on top, replacing her image, while natural sound is heard in the background underneath the coach's voice (e.g., sounds of the ball striking the ground and hitting the racket, the scuffle of feet, and grunts from the player, etc.). Sound bites, B-Roll, and natural sound often go hand in hand and are the proverbial bread and butter of many video projects.

Camera Angle

Television reporters and documentary filmmakers routinely shoot from an eye-level camera angle during interviews because this position offers the least biased view of the subject (see Figure 13.5). As the saying goes, two people are said to see "eye to eye" when they agree with one another. Shooting at eye level helps maintain the viewer's perception of a level playing field—where the viewer perceives him- or herself as an equal participant in the exchange and no one has the upper hand. It is a neutral angle that helps mirror a natural and unbiased conversation (see Figure 13.5).

As humans, our normal or default angle of view is also from eye level, usually from a standing position five to six feet off the ground—a very ordinary vantage point that most amateurs default to when taking pictures. Great possibilities can emerge photographically as we break free of what feels easiest and most comfortable and begin experimenting with creative camera angles that reveal a more unique point of view. When shooting B-Roll or cutaways, try getting down low, even to ground level, or scaling to a height above the action—hovering over it from a bird's eye point of view. A *low-angle shot* is one where the camera is placed below the subject's eye-line,

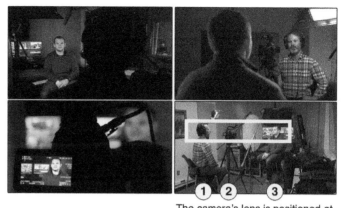

The camera's lens is positioned at eye level with both the interviewer and the interviewee.

FIGURE 13.5
Notice how the interviewer (1), the interviewee (3), and the camera (2) are positioned at eye level. This is the ideal setup for a journalistic-style on-camera interview. In a situation such as this, the interviewee is instructed to look at the interviewer/videographer and not directly at the camera. The videographer has positioned himself next to the camera where he can conduct the interview while monitoring video and audio signals during recording.

creating a sense from the viewer's perspective that he or she is looking up at the subject. A *high-angle shot* is just the opposite, with the camera pointing down from a position above the subject's eye-line. High- and low-angle shots are used often in the production of dramatic narrative films to intensify the emotion and energy of on-screen action. High-angle shots weaken the perceived status of on-camera subjects—whether they're characters in a movie, professional talent, or everyday people in candid or staged moments of life—making them appear more delicate, feeble, vulnerable, or helpless, while high-angle shots do just the opposite—rendering them more stout, confident, influential, or powerful. The more extreme the angle, the more intense the perceived feelings of relative strength and power.

Subject Location

You may or may not have as much influence in deciding subject location as you do for camera position or camera angle. For example, if you've set up a formal interview with a city councilwoman in her office, it would be inappropriate and presumptuous of you to show up and start rearranging the furniture. However, you can often make minor adjustments without asking permission and, as the producer, suggest the seating arrangement you think works best. You can also suggest an alternative room or setting for the interview that provides better aesthetics, lighting, and/or sound isolation. The worse thing the subject can say is no, so don't be afraid to try. Arrive early, if possible, to explore the location and to scout out alternative settings and backdrops. It is in your subject's best interest to trust your judgment because your subject shares your desire to make him or her look as good as possible on camera.

One of the best tips for subject placement is to extend the z-axis as much as possible. Try to position the subject at least six to eight feet away from walls or fixed backdrops. The greater the distance between the subject and background, the more opportunity you will have for composing a pleasing shot with shallow depth of field (see Figure 13.6). Pulling the subject away from walls also helps when

FIGURE 13.6
In this example, the videographer shot this interview sequence using various settings, angles, and compositional frames. The interview was composed as a medium shot that varied slightly across several takes (top panels). B-roll was acquired after the interview using a mix of medium and close-up shots (middle and bottom panels).

FIGURE 13.7
In this shot, the subject is heavily backlit, causing her to appear dark in contrast to the properly exposed background.

focusing lights—for example, giving you more flexibility to position a backlight and a greater opportunity to reduce or eliminate harsh shadows on the wall caused by the subject.

Finally, avoid placing the subject in front of a window or other highly reflective surface. Backlight from a window can often overpower the scene, producing a darkened and featureless silhouette of subject (see Figure 13.7). To reduce exterior light spilling into a room and mixing with other light sources, try to close doors and window shades. If you don't have a light kit with you, then look around to identify the best source(s) of available lighting. Where can you position the subject so he or she is properly lit from the front and backlight isn't a problem? Don't be afraid to ask if you can turn certain lights off and other lights on if available.

Focal Length

The final determinant of *field of view* is focal length. The variable focal length lens found on most video camcorders gives you latitude to fine tune your framing—by zooming from a narrow-angle to wide-angle view or to anywhere in between. Ultimately, it's the focal length of the lens that determines what portion of the viewable area of a scene is included in a shot and what is left out. Be sure to include sufficient white space in the frame to keep the image from looking cramped or cluttered, but not so much that emphasis on the subject is compromised or lost. Also, get in the habit of critically examining the outer edge of the frame to see where the cutoff lines are. Avoid dissecting people in half or eliminating key parts of an object that are needed to mentally complete the image—think back to the principle of psychological closure discussed in chapter 4. Be purposeful in your framing and continually ask yourself if the adjustment you just made improved the composition or took it down a notch. It should be obvious to the trained eye that each framing decision is deliberate, natural, and complimentary. Otherwise, it may be seen as a mistake or, at best, something not quite right or out of place.

While it's best practice to zoom with your feet rather than with the camera's zoom control, there are times when physical boundaries or rules can impose a limit on how close a camera can be placed to the subject. An obvious example is a sporting event, where cameras have to be located off the court or field of play. If you've been to a professional sporting event such as a football or baseball game, you may have noticed cameras in the stands or on the sidelines with giant box-shaped lenses attached (see Figure 13.8 and Figure 13.20). Professional zoom lenses such as these are very expensive but provide significantly greater magnification than lenses found on portable broadcast cameras and far more than a smartphone with its tiny built-in lens. At times when it's impossible to get physically close to your subject, be sure to bring along a long lens to compensate.

FIGURE 13.8
A professional broadcast lens is sometimes bigger than the camera, as this picture illustrates. Expensive long lenses like this one are used in sports broadcasting to acquire close-ups from a distant vantage point.

GREAT IDEAS
Ten Tips for Shooting an Effective Interview

1. **Position the camera, interviewer, and interviewee at eye level in relation to one another.** Doing this will ensure the interviewee's sight line (the direction of his/her gaze) is natural and non-distracting. If the interviewee has to look up or down at the interviewer (perhaps because one is sitting and the other is standing), the camera will capture this and the viewer will sense that something isn't right.

2. **Avoid placing the interviewee directly against a wall.** Placing the subject directly against a wall or backdrop eliminates the z-axis from play and visually flattens the shot by merging the background with the foreground. Ideally, try to keep at least six to eight feet of space between the subject and the background.

3. **Avoid placing the interviewee in front of a window.** Windows generally make for poor backdrops, especially when shooting on a bright day and into the sun. If the light spilling in through a window is more intense than the light illuminating the front of the subject, a darkened backlit image will result where facial details, shape, and depth are lost or diminished.

4. **Avoid swivel chairs.** The tendency when sitting in a swivel chair is to swivel, and often the person sitting in one doesn't even realize he or she is doing so. However, when you see a video image of someone bobbing back and forth in his or her seat or the subject's eyes darting back and forth unnaturally, it draws attention to itself and creates a distraction for the viewer.

5. **Follow the rule of thirds—place the subject to right or left of center.** Generally, placing the subject in the center of the screen is the weakest option. Cheating the subject to the left or right of center provides lead space between his or her nose and the edge of the screen (in the direction of the subject's sight line) and produces a stronger, more visually pleasing composition. Adjust headroom and lead room as appropriate.

6. **Have the subject look slightly off-axis to camera—never directly head-on.** There are times when it's appropriate for an on-camera subject to look head-on into the camera while addressing the viewer directly (e.g., TV newscaster, infomercial pitch person, game show host, etc.). However, in a journalistic-style interview, the interviewee should look slightly off-camera at the interviewer, maintaining eye contact as in a normal conversation. If others are present off-camera, be sure they do not compete for the interviewee's attention, potentially causing a noticeable break or shift in eye contact.

7. **Place the interviewer as close to the left or right side of the camera as possible.** The further away the interviewer is situated to the left or right of the camera, the more the interviewee's face will be angled away from the viewer—resulting in a profile shot. Shoot the interviewee as close to head-on as possible without he or she actually looking into the camera.

8. **Alternate shooting with the interviewer on both sides of the camera.** This is another way of saying mix it up. After shooting one interview with the interviewer positioned on the left side of the camera, shoot the next one from the other side. A simple tactic such as this can help reduce visual monotony and predictability in the final edited story.

9. **Eliminate distracting background mergers and clutter.** Pay attention to how the subject physically intersects with background elements in the scene. Through purposeful camera placement, subject placement, and framing, simplify the shot by removing any visual clutter that would otherwise compete with the main subject in the shot.

10. **Monitor audio and video recording.** Be sure to do a trial recording prior to the start of the interview and monitor video and audio signals during taping. Before you strike your equipment and leave, be sure to review recorded snippets of the interview to ensure you are happy with the results.

FIGURE 13.9
Prior to high-definition video, a heavily saturated red outfit such as the one worn by this television newscaster was considered taboo because it tended to bleed (or smear) on a low-resolution SD monitor. High-definition (HD) cameras handle color much better. Still, as a general rule, on-camera talent should avoid wearing predominantly black or white clothing. Because black is naturally dark and white is so highly reflective, using either color as the base color in a shot will negatively affect the exposure of mid-tone colors in the image. For best results go with natural mid-tone colors for clothing and avoid the extremes as much as possible.

FILM GRAMMAR

Motion picture films and television programs are developed on paper (in scripted form) long before the first frame of video is composed and shot. Thus, not surprisingly, the industry spawned its own grammatical conventions to describe the constituent parts of a visual narrative as denoted in scripts, storyboards, treatments, and the like. The term *film grammar* (or *visual grammar*) is an umbrella term used to metaphorically explain the basic structural elements of a visual narrative—in much the same way that the terms *letters*, *words*, *sentences*, and *paragraphs* are used to describe the essential components of written syntax. The four building blocks of film grammar are 1) frame, 2) shot, 3) scene, and 4) sequence.

Frame

A *frame* is a single still image. In the United States, video is typically shot at 24 frames per second (fps)—the traditional frame rate for motion picture film—while broadcast television programs are shot at 30 fps. Each frame contributes to the illusion of visual motion that we perceive as live action, as they are captured one by one and then projected rapidly before our eyes. A motion picture frame carries little meaning on its own when isolated from adjacent frames in a series. It is analogous to a letter in a written word—and has significance only within the larger context of that to which it is attached. We typically do not refer to individual frames in scripts unless they are still images, graphics, or "freeze frames" occurring over a designated span of time.

Shot

A *shot* is the smallest standalone component in a visual time-based narrative. It is analogous to a word in written grammar. The saying "a picture is worth a thousand words" suddenly comes to mind. By definition, a shot is a continuous live or recorded moving image taken from a single camera's point of view over time. The term *shot* derives from the early days of filmmaking when a camera operator turned a hand crank to manually advance the film frame by frame, through the gate and past the lens, where it was exposed to light for a fraction of a second (see Figure 13.1, left). Because the hand crank resembled those used on heavy artillery guns for rapidly firing a round of ammunition, the pioneers of filmmaking embraced the "shooting" metaphor to describe the mechanics of the moviemaking process. For this reason, a videographer or cinematographer is sometimes called a "shooter," and industry idioms such as "shooting a scene" and going on a "film shoot" are still used today.

The interval from the first turn of the hand crank to a complete stop represented a single shot. Today, in lieu of a hand crank, modern digital cameras are equipped with a record button. The shooter presses this button once to begin recording and a second time to stop. Each interval of recording (from start to stop) produces a single "shot" that is recorded to disk or memory card as a standalone file. The files are imported from the memory card into your editing program as *clips*. In postproduction, a shot is defined as the portion of a clip between two transition points on the timeline or, prior to an edit, as the segment marked by IN and OUT points in the source or preview monitor. In a live multi-camera production, a switcher is used to instantaneously transition from one shot to another using two or more cameras—with each one providing a different point of view.

The duration of a shot can be very brief, less than a fraction of a second, or it can span an interval of several seconds or more. Because viewers have a relatively short attention span these days, it's generally a good idea to transition from shot to shot quickly to maintain a pace that is visually stimulating and dynamic. When a single shot appears on the screen for too long (typically 10–15 seconds or longer), viewers can lose interest or stop watching.

TAKE

A *take* is a single recorded instance of a particular shot. A shooter may attempt a shot several times before he or she (or the director) is satisfied with the outcome. Each of these attempts is called a *take*, and at the end the shoot, the director has the job of sorting out the *good takes* from the *bad takes*, all of which have been recorded and saved to disk—along with a film slate reference for each scene, shot, and take number (see Figure 13.10). The best takes will make it into the final edited version of the production while the bad takes will likely never be seen by anyone else, unless, of course, the director creates a blooper reel comprised of the more humorous blunders and gaffes. Bloopers are a fun way of reminding the audience how much time, effort, and enjoyment goes on behind-the-scenes during the making of a film or television program. Multiple takes are most common in productions where an actor, host, or reporter must deliver a scripted performance from memory. Rarely does an actor nail a scene perfectly on the very first take. And even when they do, it certainly doesn't hurt to record a backup take or two for good measure.

FIGURE 13.10
A clapperboard is used to synchronize picture and sound for each recorded scene and shot. On a motion picture film set, the clapper loader or second assistant camera (2nd AC) is responsible for updating scene information on the film slate at the beginning of each take. For U.S. productions, the slate designation for the scene number is usually a number followed by a letter (as shown here). The number corresponds to the actual scene number in the script while the letter indicates the shot number in the scene.
Source: bepsy/Shutterstock.com.

Scene

A *scene* is an event within a film that takes place in a single location within a specific period of time. In grammatical terms, it is analogous to a sentence because it is comprised of multiple shots in the same way that words are combined to form sentences. Motion picture screenplays are divided into scenes because doing so makes it easier for a director to break down a long story into manageable parts during the production process. In a screenplay, the scenes are numbered consecutively from the beginning to the end of the script, and a *slug line* indicates whether the scene takes place inside (INT.) or outside (EXT.) and time of day (DAY or NIGHT). To illustrate, imagine a short film that has 12 scenes and three locations: an apartment, an office, and an outdoor café. Because of the time and the cost involved with setting up and striking each location, it would be terribly inefficient to shoot the scenes in the order they appear in the script. In fact, filming the scenes consecutively would require resetting three locations 12 different times. However, by organizing the scenes according to location and time of day, a more efficient and cost-effective production schedule can be put together involving only three setups and five days of shooting (see Table 13.1).

Table 13.1	Example Scene List and Production Schedule	
Scene Number	**Slug Line**	**Production Schedule**
1, 7, and 12	INT. ANITA'S APARTMENT - DAY	Days 1–2
4 and 8	INT. ANITA'S APARTMENT - NIGHT	Day 3
2, 6, 9, and 11	INT. OFFICE - DAY	Days 4–5
3, 5, and 10	EXT. CAFE - DAY	Day 6

Whether you're shooting a motion picture, documentary, corporate video, or news feature, organizing your project by scenes and locations will save you lots of time, frustration, and money.

Sequence

A *sequence* is an edited series of individual shots that promotes a sense of continuous action or narrative flow (see Figure 13.11). A sequence is analogous to a paragraph in written grammar. You can think of it as a mini-story embedded into a larger narrative. Think about a simple scene in a park where a mother and child approach a cart to purchase an ice cream cone. After completing the transaction, they both turn to walk away. A scene like this could be filmed as one long continuous shot taken from a stationary camera with a wide-angle lens. The downside to this approach is that a shot will present the action in real time and be limited to a fixed and distant point-of-view—one that's also lacking in visual variety and detail. Most people would find this pretty boring to watch, don't you think? Since there are three people in the scene (mother, child, and ice cream vendor), one or more of the subjects will have their back or side to the camera for most of the scene. The viewer will likely feel detached from this event as an outsider instead of an active participant who is emotionally engaged and drawn into the scene. As we'll see in a moment, a wide shot is good for establishing the setting of a new scene, but it's those specially crafted medium shots and close-ups, woven together into a sequence, that can rivet the viewer's attention and keep them engrossed in the story.

As an alternative, a scene such as this can be shot and put into a sequence using a variety of interrelated shots taken from different camera angles and points of view. Cinematographers use the term *coverage* to describe this practice. And the goal of coverage is not just to combine a bunch of random shots together to speed up the action, but to shoot and cut with intentionality and purpose, to enhance the story, and to keep the viewer engaged. A thoughtfully constructed sequence can intensify action, heighten emotion, and compress time. Instead of taking sixty seconds for the action to unfold in real time, an edited sequence can depict the same scene in half the time or less, while providing more information and detail about each of the subjects.

Narrative films are often shot with a single camera. Unfortunately, the camera can only be in one place at a time. In order to obtain multiple shots of a scene from

FIGURE 13.11
These still image frames were lifted from a one-minute student-produced motivational film for Everlast. The sequence cuts back and forth between two locations past and present—a makeshift gym in a barn (present) and a boxing ring (recent past)—as the main character recalls the details of his most recent triumph. The powerfully constructed sequence is set entirely to music and natural sound. Scanning these frames in order from left to right and from top to bottom, think about how shots can be woven together into a sequence to tell a story in a more interesting way while condensing time and intensifying action and emotion.
Source: Courtesy of Wilson Hester and Peter Walpole.

various camera positions, the actors must repeat the scene for as many different camera setups as the director calls for. Following each successful performance or iteration of a scene, there's usually a break, allowing time for the crew to reset the camera and lights for the next shot.

To illustrate, let's consider a very simple scenario involving two people seated in a dimly lit television studio (see Figure 13.12). In order to create a sequence

FIGURE 13.12
Top: A master shot or cover shot is produced by framing both subjects within the frame. Bottom left and right: Two matching cross-shots with complementary framing and lead room. In single-camera film production, a scene such as this one is performed and recorded at least three times—once from each camera position. In postproduction, the shots are interwoven to create a visually interesting and dynamic edited sequence.

using three different camera setups, the actors need to perform their lines at least three times with no mistakes. The first time the scene is performed, the camera will be set to a *two-shot* that clearly establishes both subjects in the frame (Figure 13.12, top). This shot is referred to as the *master shot* or *cover shot*. During the second performance, the camera will be moved to a new position and set to a medium or close-up shot of Person A (Figure 13.12, bottom left). For the final performance, the camera will be moved again and set to a medium or close-up shot of Person B (Figure 13.12, bottom right). The second and third shots, called *cross-shots*, normally exclude the second person from the frame and are composed as matching reverse images of one another. Person A is shot looking left to right (from the camera's perspective) with lead room on the right side of the frame. Person B is shot looking right to left with complimentary lead room on the left.

GREAT IDEAS

180-Degree Rule (Crossing the Line)

Screen direction refers to the direction subjects are facing as we look at them in the viewfinder or on a television monitor or movie screen. When shooting two people in a scene using three cameras or the single-camera *master shot/cross-shot* just described, you need to avoid accidentally reversing the screen direction of the subjects when cutting from the master shot to a cross-shot. In other words, in a cross-shot, the subject should face the same direction and be positioned on the same side of the screen as in the master shot. A reverse in screen direction in an edited sequence is a visual faux pas and looks like a mistake to the viewer. To avoid this potential pitfall, picture an imaginary line drawn through the middle of both subjects (see Figure 13.13). This imaginary vector is known as the *axis of action*, or simply *the line*. When shooting the scene, be sure to keep the camera or multiple cameras on the same side of this line at all times. This will preserve visual continuity during live switching or editing. At a televised football game or soccer match, the main stadium cameras are located on one side of the playing field only. Live switching of cameras placed on opposite sides of the field during the game would create the undesirable effect of instantly reversing the position of players and teams on the field. The solution? Don't cross the line!

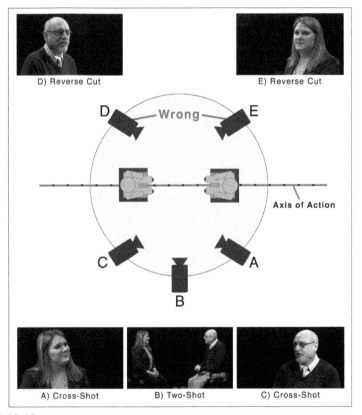

FIGURE 13.13

When filming a scene with multiple cameras or camera setups, be sure to shoot from the same side of the 180-line every time. Crossing the line will result a reverse shot, making it appear to the viewer that one of the subjects in the shot has suddenly switched positions or changed direction.

SHOT DESIGNATIONS

Shots vary according to how tightly the subject is framed within the scene. Some shots are very tightly framed, revealing only a tiny portion of the subject, while other shots are more loosely framed, providing a wider view of the subject while including nearby people and objects. Professionals will often describe how a subject is framed using industry-accepted shot designations or abbreviations, such as *wide shot* (WS) or *low-angle shot*. There are many of them, so for the sake of time and space, only a few of the most common ones will be covered in this section. Figure 13.14 includes a collection of studio- and field-produced shots and their corresponding designations. These will become familiar to you as you see them referenced in written scripts and storyboards or hear them talked about by others during a shoot.

Wide Shot (WS)	Medium Shot (MS)	Close-Up (CU)
Extreme Close-Up (XCU)	Two-Shot	Over the Shoulder Shot (OTS)
High-Angle Shot	Low-Angle Shot	Shallow Depth of Field
Establishing Shot	Wide Shot (WS)	Medium Shot (MS)
Close-Up (CU)	Extreme Close-Up (XCU)	Extreme Close-Up (XCU)

FIGURE 13.14
These examples of field- and studio-produced shots are just a glimpse of the many different ways to frame your subject.

Wide Shot

As the name implies, a *wide shot* (WS) or *long shot* (LS) captures a wide angle of view of a scene or person. The WS designation can be used for describing something grand, such as a panorama shot of Pike's Peak, or for an all-encompassing shot of a single human subject from head to toe. To be more precise, we could refer to the Pike's Peak example as an extreme wide shot (EWS). An extreme wide shot or extreme long shot (ELS) is sometimes called an *establishing shot*, particularly when it is used as the first shot in a sequence to "establish" a location or scene change. Establishing shots provide the viewer with a sense of place, helping the viewer develop a mental map of the physical occupants, space, and boundaries where the action is taking place. Establishing shots can vary in range and scope. For instance, to establish a scene in New York City, one could use an EWS of the Manhattan skyline, the Statue of Liberty, a subway station with a recognizable name, or performers masquerading as action heroes in Times Square or Central Park. The more recognizable the people, setting, or landmarks in an establishing shot, the more effective it will be as a visual cue for connecting viewers to the actual location, season, and time of day it represents. Complimentary wide shots are sometimes used as bookends at the opening and close of a sequence or movie as a way of visually indicating the beginning and end of a particular scene or story.

Medium Shot

A *medium shot* (MS) is a tighter composition that generally contains only a portion of the subject in the frame while allowing sufficient room for gestures, actions, or references to nearby people and objects just beyond view. The cutoff point for a medium shot can occur near the ankles, knees, waist, elbows, shoulders, or neck. However, be careful to avoid setting the bottom of the frame even with one of the body's natural joints. Instead, select a cutoff point that is slightly above or below the joint. Tighter medium shots are good for isolating a single subject while accentuating facial expressions, actions, and movement. More loosely framed medium shots permit other people and objects to reside within the frame simultaneously. For example, a medium two-shot might reveal two people interacting side-by-side from the waist up. Likewise, an *over-the-shoulder* (OTS) shot includes a portion of one person shot from behind as he or she interacts with the main subject who is facing the camera.

Close-Up

A *close-up* comes in two varieties: normal (CU) and extreme (XCU). As with all shot designations, these are relative labels that are somewhat subjective. A close-up to one person might be viewed as an extreme close-up to someone else. As far as human subjects go, a close-up takes us beyond the bust shot to a composition that fills the majority of the frame with the subject's head or face but may still include portions of the neck or upper torso. An extreme close-up moves in even tighter on the face or specific facial features such as the eyes or mouth. Extreme close-ups can focus attention on the actions and movements of hands, feet, eyes, and so on as well as on details found on objects and things in everyday life.

LEAD ROOM

Lead room (or nose room) is an area of visual white space between the subject and the edge of the frame (see Figure 13.15). It is used to indicate directional forces or to serve as a visual cue to an off-camera person or object. In the case of moving subjects such as bikes, cars, trains, and so on, lead space is added in front of the vehicle to help accentuate motion and infer directionality. The more the subject is turned in a profile position away from the camera, the more lead space is needed to compensate for the pull of visual forces exerted by the edge of the frame. When a subject looks directly at the camera, it's best to frame him or her in the center of the screen with an equal amount of white space to the left or right. In an interview, where the subject looks slightly off-axis to the left or right of the camera, he or she should be framed off-center with lead room added to the side of the frame the subject is angled toward. Lead room reminds the audience that someone else is present even though we cannot see any portion of the person within the frame.

HEADROOM

Headroom is the white space located between the top of a person's head or hairline and the top edge of the video frame. Unless you are composing an extreme close-up, it's generally a good idea to include at least a small amount of space above the subject's head (see Figure 13.16). The amount of headroom depends on the subject and the relative tightness of the shot. If the subject has a particularly high forehead

Lead Room

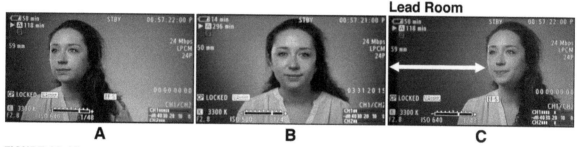

A   **B**   **C**

FIGURE 13.15
A) This shot illustrates improper lead room for a subject looking right to left. B) Center framing, with an equal amount of white space on both sides, is appropriate here since the subject is looking directly at the camera. C) This shot illustrates proper lead room for a subject looking right to left.

Headroom

A   **B**   **C**

FIGURE 13.16
A) This shot is framed with too much headroom. B) This shots lacks headroom entirely. 3) This shot illustrates proper headroom. The amount of headroom you include in a shot is often a matter of taste and personal preference. Over time, you will develop a sense of what works well and what doesn't for different subjects and settings. Think of these examples as benchmarks to give you an idea of how headroom can affect the overall composition of a shot.

FIGURE 13.17
These B-Roll shots were acquired during the performance of a percussion ensemble. Top: A wide shot (WS). Center: A medium shot (MS). Bottom: A close-up (CU). Individual shots such as these, reflecting diverse points of view, can be combined in editing to form a sequence.

and/or hairline, then little headroom, if any, may be called for. Remembering the rule of thirds may help. Frame your subject first with the eyes at or close to the upper horizontal line. Next examine the headroom and make adjustments from there.

Create a Shot List

Before heading out on a shoot, take time to think ahead and construct a *shot list*. This is particularly important when working on an unscripted project. Write down everything you can think of that visually relates to your story and think deeply about what shots might flow together in an edited sequence. At every location, be sure to acquire wide shots that can be used to establish or re-establish the setting throughout your story. If the scene is inside, be sure to get at least one exterior shot of the building or a familiar landmark. Shoot your interviews with care, and get lots of B-Roll from a variety of different wide, medium, and close-up views (see Figure 13.17). The more intentional you are in framing and acquiring diverse shots, the more you will have to work with as you assemble your project in post.

MOTION

As we learned in chapter 9, motion in television and film is a perceptual illusion achieved by rapidly projecting still images at a high frame rate (24 or 30 frames per second). Herb Zettl classifies the three principles of motion in video or film as: 1) primary motion, 2) secondary motion, and 3) tertiary motion.[1]

Primary Motion

Primary motion includes the physical on-screen movements of people, animals, and objects that take place in front of the camera during a shoot. It is the result of the natural and choreographed movements of subjects within the frame and includes the full gamut of on-screen movement—from high-energy shots of fast-moving vehicles, combatants embroiled in conflict, athletes in the heat of fierce competition, and so forth to the more muted or understated movements of a falling leaf, a flickering candle, or a twitching eyebrow. Primary motion is so named because, as Zettl notes, "it is, and should be, the prevalent motion in a scene." As a shooter, you should be continually looking for ways to capture primary motion, either through carefully choreographed performances from your actors or in the candid moments of real life, when filming average people performing extraordinary feats or simple mundane actions that are unusual or visually compelling.

ACTION, REACTION, AND INTERACTION

Newton's third law of physics states that "with every action there is an equal and opposite reaction." Thus, primary motion isn't manifested through action alone, but also through reaction and interaction. Action is expressed through the movements of people, animals, machines, or objects in a scene: a close-up of hands and fingers crafting a fishing lure, a medium shot of a skilled juggler tossing balls in a circular orbit, or a wide shot of a motorcycle stunt rider soaring through the air across a gaping canyon. A reaction shot captures the response of people or things affected by an initial force or action. Try not to limit yourself to the actions of the main subject alone. Pay attention to how others are being affected or moved. Consider the reaction of fans cheering and flailing wildly after their team scores the winning goal or the mixture of trust and apprehension on a child's face as dad lets go of the bicycle for the very first time. Work the scene, repositioning the camera often to capture motion (and emotion) that's related to the primary action or performance. Finally, look for ways to capture interaction within the frame by featuring two or more subjects whose actions are mutually intertwined or interdependent.

Secondary Motion

Secondary motion is produced by the physical movement of the camera or through zooming. Technically, it is independent of event motion and works best when performed in combination with primary motion occurring at the same time. An inexperienced shooter can easily get carried away overusing secondary motion—after all, panning, zooming, and moving around with a camera in tow is so much more exciting than simply pointing and shooting from a stationary position, right? However, secondary motion can easily become a visual distraction, especially when camera movements are unmotivated by the action unfolding within a scene. Secondary motion draws attention to itself and away from the story or subject whenever a viewer perceives it as random or accidental. When properly motivated and used in moderation, secondary motion appears natural and uncontrived. Done well, the viewer shouldn't even notice when the camera moves because the primary motion on screen calls for it and keeps it in check. For example, in a shot where the subject is walking toward the camera (primary motion), the shooter must zoom out or walk backward (secondary motion) to maintain consistent framing. Because a camera move like this is motivated by primary motion, it will be perceived as natural to the viewer and will draw little attention, if any, to itself.

I like to encourage my students to avoid secondary motion altogether at first, relying on it only in an offline capacity, as a tool for framing or recomposing a shot. Doing so forces someone new to shooting to observe and rely more fully on primary motion as the driving visual force in his or her story. The type of secondary motion you can achieve often depends on whether or not you are controlling the camera by hand or using a tripod or other device for stabilization.

HANDHELD MOTION

Due to their larger form factor, portable broadcast cameras are designed to be shoulder operated or *handheld*, providing adequate image stability for a trained shooter. In the hands of an inexperienced person, however, shooting handheld can result in shaky camerawork that looks unprofessional. The primary advantage of shooting handheld is speed. With only the camera to worry about, a shooter can quickly move from place to place within a scene, drastically reducing the amount of time it takes to set up and acquire shots from different positions. It also allows you to move in tight on your subject for compelling close-up shots and to rapidly angle low or high for shots that cannot be easily achieved with the camera attached to a tripod or other device.

One of my favorite handheld moves is to perform a walking shot while holding the camera slightly above the ground. Another popular handheld technique, known as a Dutch angle or Dutch tilt, involves shooting with the camera slanted sideways on a diagonal axis. A canted camera angle can produce tension, heighten drama, and

FIGURE 13.18
A student uses a freestanding monopod to stabilize a DSLR camera during a video shoot in Costa Rica. The lightweight size and portability of a monopod makes it a popular alternative to a tripod when using smaller cameras in remote regions.

intensify the primary motion of characters or subjects within the frame. To minimize camera shake while handholding the camera, get close to your subject and shoot with the lens set to the shortest focal length possible (wide angle of view). Trying to maintain a steady handheld shot while zoomed in tight on a subject is very difficult to do even with experience. You can also try turning on your camera's optical image stabilization (OIS) function, which is designed to digitally compensate for image jitter and shake caused by sudden unintended bumps or movement.

TRIPOD MOTION

Whenever possible, shoot from a tripod! A *tripod* is a three-legged support system designed to keep the camera at an appropriate working height while giving the photographer smoother control when framing and recording shots (see Figure 13.19). When using a tripod, the camera is attached to a tripod mounting plate, which in turn is attached to the tripod head using a quick-release mechanism that permits

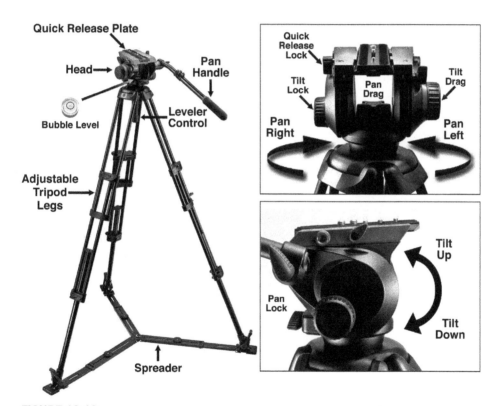

FIGURE 13.19
There's more to a professional tripod than you might think. Various controls are included to help you quickly change the camera's height and level the head. You can also vary the amount of tension using the pan and tilt drag controls or lock them down to keep the camera from moving. The pan handle is used for panning and tilting with one hand while controlling the camera with the other. The quick-release plate bolts to the bottom of the camera, allowing you to swiftly slide the camera on and off the head when changing locations.
Source: Manfrotto.

rapid connection and disconnection during a shoot. It's good practice to disconnect the camera from the tripod before moving it from one location to another. Also, be sure to level the tripod when placing it on uneven ground, otherwise you may end up with a crooked image. Most tripods include a leveling bubble at the base of head to take the guesswork out of balancing it in the field.

Pan and Tilt

A *pan* involves swiveling the camera left or right horizontally on a fixed pivot point. To pan left requires aiming the lens of the camera more to the shooter's left. Panning right swings the lens in the opposite direction. A *tilt* involves swiveling the camera up or down vertically on a fixed pivot point. To tilt up means to point the lens in a more upward direction while a tilt down requires moving it the other way.

PEDESTAL MOTION

Studio cameras are often mounted to a *pedestal* (see Figure 13.20). Unlike a tripod, a pedestal utilizes a single-column support system on wheels and is designed for use on smooth hard surfaces. In addition to accommodating simple pan and tilt moves, a pedestal allows you to move the entire camera up and down and along the floor in any direction.

Pedestal Up and Down

A camera pedestal is counter-balanced to allow it to move effortlessly up and down along a vertical shaft of pressurized gas. Whereas tilting forces the camera into an upward or downward angled view, a pedestal permits the camera to remain parallel to the floor as it is raised or lowered. The vertical range of a studio pedestal is only a few feet, yet this permits a camera operator to perform dramatic moving shots, especially when combined with other secondary motion.

A *dolly* move is achieved by rolling the entire camera and pedestal forward or backward in a relatively straight line. To dolly in is to move the camera closer to the subject while to dolly out is to pull back and away from the subject in the opposite direction. At first, you may think that a dolly move and a zoom are in essence the same thing—producing an identical motion effect. However, filmmakers favor dolly shots over zooming because the dolly produces movement that more closely mirrors human experience. A dolly visually captures the motion someone performs when physically moving closer or further away from another

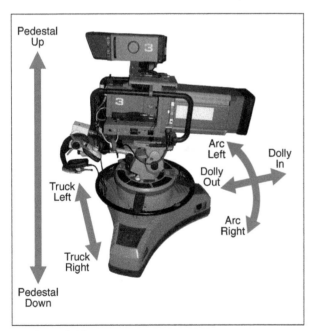

FIGURE 13.20
In addition to simple panning and tilting moves, a camera mounted to a studio pedestal can move laterally across the floor in any direction as well as vertically up or down.
Source: © Soundsnaps / Dreamstime.com - Studio TV Camera On Pedestal Photo.

person or object. With zooming, the camera remains stationary as the subject is brought closer into view through magnification. See the difference for yourself by performing a test using both techniques. After comparing the results on screen, I think you'll agree that the motion created by the dolly move looks more realistic.

Truck and Arc

A *truck* is a lateral movement of the entire camera from left to right (or vice versa) in a relatively straight line. An *arc* involves moving the entire camera to the left or right along a curved path. A director specifies the path of a truck or arc move with the commands truck left and truck right or arc left and arc right.

You do not have to use an expensive studio pedestal to attempt moving shots like these. They can be performed handheld and/or with the aid of a device like a shoulder rig, jib, Steadicam, dolly, or any other number of contraptions designed to facilitate smooth camera motion (see Figure 13.21 and Figure 13.22). When using a camera dolly, it helps to have track the dolly can ride on to minimize shock from uneven surfaces. There are many ways to improvise using inexpensive means and a little bit of creativity. You may be able achieve good results shooting from a car, cart, skateboard, wheel chair, and so on. Just be careful and use common sense.

FIGURE 13.21
Camera support systems such as these provide added stability for moving shots and come in many shapes and sizes. Top left: A *slider* provides lateral movement for the camera by gliding sideways on a three-foot rail support. Top right: A *shoulder rig* comes in handy when shooting handheld with a smaller camera such as this DSLR. Bottom left: A videographer sits atop a *platform dolly* designed to move smoothly along a curved linear track when pushed from behind. Bottom right: A *Steadicam Pilot* uses a gimbal stabilizing system to keep the shot steady during walking shot.

FIGURE 13.22
Filmmakers have increasingly taken to the skies as the tools of aerial photography have become more affordable. Here, the GoPro HERO3, a popular broadcast-quality point-of-view (POV) camera, is attached to a remote-controlled quadcopter to provide secondary motion from a bird's eye view. While this may look like child's play, it takes a skilled operator at the controls to acquire smooth shots. In addition, the Federal Aviation Administration (FAA) has instituted strict rules for the operation of unmanned aircraft for such purposes.

Also, make sure you have production assistants on hand to help spot you and the camera as you perform your moves.

Tertiary Motion

Tertiary motion, or "sequence motion," is achieved as shots and sequences are ordered and connected together in editing. Cutting back and forth from one shot to another produces visual energy in the form of tertiary motion. Dissolves, fades, wipes, page peels, key frame animation, and other types of computer-generated motion effects fall into this third and final category of motion. Tertiary motion is covered in more detail in chapter 14.

GREAT IDEAS
Ten Tips for Shooting Great B-Roll

1. **Use a tripod or other image stabilizer.** Unintentional motion artifacts captured by the camera are a visual distraction to the viewer and one of the first telltale signs of an amateur production. It is critically important to capture stable images. If you are new to video production, you probably won't have the experience or the type

of camera you need to shoot handheld shots effectively. Use a tripod whenever possible and avoid bumping or moving the camera when recording a shot. If you must shoot handheld, set your lens to a wide-angle setting and move in close to your subject. Shooting with a short focal length will enable you to acquire a more stable image.

2. **Shoot lots and lots of B-Roll.** A trusted video production adage says, "You can never get enough B-Roll." Be sure to work the shot, which means zooming with your feet and changing the camera position, angle, and framing often in order to acquire a wide variety of shots for every subject and activity. Record difficult shots multiple times until you are happy with the result. Assume that less than 30% of what you shoot will be good enough for inclusion in the story and that 70% or more will be unusable—left on the proverbial cutting room floor. Shoot far more than you can ever possibly imagine needing. Think of B-Roll shots as the individual building blocks of a larger sequence. Prepare a shot list prior to the shoot. Look for opportunities to shoot real people and subjects, doing interesting things, in candid moments of life.

3. **Record at least 5–10 seconds of each shot.** Set up your shot, press the record button, and let the camera do the rest—recording the shot without interruption. In editing, it is helpful to have handles on each shot, a second or two of pad at the beginning and end of a clip. Handles give an editor creative leeway when trimming clips or attaching transitions. Routinely shooting clips that are shorter than five seconds may create editing workflow challenges for you in postproduction.

4. **Avoid secondary motion—no zooming, panning, or tilting during a shot.** Especially when you are just starting out, use secondary motion only to frame and compose your shot. Look for interesting primary motion and let this be the star ingredient in your B-Roll. Properly composed static shots with compelling primary motion will serve you better in editing than long pans and zooms that are poorly executed.

5. **Use secondary motion only when it is motivated by primary motion.** Having just advised against using secondary motion at all, the fact is that sometimes it can't be helped. For example, when shooting athletic events, you often need to move the camera while recording in order to keep the subject properly framed. When the action calls for it, it is certainly okay to use secondary motion. However, practice how to zoom and pan and tilt smoothly before heading out to shoot your first volleyball match.

6. **Look for good sources of primary motion and natural sound.** Shoot subjects doing something interesting (action); shoot them in candid moments of reaction; shoot them interacting with others. Be sure to record natural sound when shooting B-roll.

7. **Get close to your subject—zoom with your feet.** Whenever possible, move around to get close to the action. Avoid shooting from a distance and from the default human position (eye level, standing up). Get down low. Get up high. Shoot over the shoulder and incorporate the z-axis.

8. **Shoot establishing shots to signal a location or scene change or introduce a sequence.** After shooting inside an office, get a shot from across the street of the building's exterior or the sign in front with the company name. Shoot recognizable landmarks that will help viewers quickly connect with the subject, story, or location.

9. **Fill the frame and make sure there is a clearly defined subject.** Some white space is good. If there's too much, however, the subject may not be obvious. Eliminate visual clutter. Shoot more close-ups and medium shots than wide shots.

10. **Incorporate the elements and principles of design (see chapter 4).** Shoot from an angle or Dutch tilt position to accentuate diagonal lines. Establish contrast and interest through the application of color, pattern, texture, and light. Make sure every shot is balanced. Look for ways to connote a sense of depth within the two-dimensional frame.

LIGHTING

The concept of lighting was introduced in chapter 4. Please take a moment to review this section before continuing here for a more detailed look at the application of lighting for film and video. Whether you're shooting interiors or exteriors, in natural or artificial light, or in daytime or at night, your subject should be properly lit for the camera. Lighting involves much more than illumination—ensuring that the subject is brightly lit; it helps enhance visual appearance, and, in the case of human subjects, it can be used to complement physical features such as skin tone, shape, texture, and depth (see Figure 13.23). Lighting can be used to direct the viewer's attention to a particular part of the frame by increasing the contrast between the bright and dark regions of the frame. Our attention is naturally drawn to the brighter areas of a visual image first. Lighting can also be used to enhance or change the color temperature in a scene to connote a desired mood or vibe (remember cool versus warm colors). To the viewer, lighting should look natural and appropriate to the setting and context of the visual experience—never contrived—lest it draw attention to itself.

Hard and Soft Light

Have you ever noticed that light bulbs often come in two varieties: clear and frosted. A clear bulb produces a *hard light*, which is brighter but also produces stronger reflections and harsher shadows with a more crisply defined edge. The unobstructed filament of a clear bulb is intense and overpowering in certain applications. A frosted bulb, on the other hand, produces *soft light*, which wraps itself more delicately around the subject. The translucent coating of a frosted bulb diffuses light—scattering it so it lands more evenly on the objects in its path while casting lighter shadows with softer edges.

The sun on a bright cloudless day is a hard light source. When the sky is overcast, the sun is transformed into a soft light. Clouds absorb sunlight and reflect a portion of it back into the atmosphere, thereby reducing the overall brightness or intensity of light reaching the surface. Clouds also act as a giant diffuser—scattering light so it falls more uniformly on the subject while reducing harsh shadows and

FIGURE 13.23
The image on the left was shot under overhead fluorescent lighting while the "warmer" image on the right was shot using a portable light kit and the technique of three-point lighting—and with the overhead lights turned off. The first image is relatively flat, while the second image is more saturated and has better contrast.

reflections. All things being equal, people look much better on camera when they are shot under cloudy skies then under direct intense sunlight. In the absence of clouds, you can move to a shady spot under a tree or in the shadow of a building or other tall structure. Sunlight now becomes a *reflected light* source, striking the subject indirectly from every angle as it ricochets off surrounding surfaces. Whenever light strikes an object, some of its energy is absorbed while the rest of it is reflected back out at an angle. Shiny light-colored surfaces such as tinted glass, white clothing, and silver sunshades reflect light better than dull dark-colored surfaces that tend to absorb more light than they give back. While on a sunny day a subject standing in the shade of a tree may be sufficiently illuminated for the camera, the image may appear flat or washed out—lacking detail and contrast. In such cases, supplementing natural light with artificial light or reflected light can help improve the shot. More on this later!

Angle of Light

The orientation of the sun changes throughout the day as it moves across the sky in a linear path. As a result, the angle of the light it casts also changes continually. At midday, when the sun is directly overhead, the shadows and reflections it casts are the harshest. Subjects tend to look better when the angle of a light source is at 45 degrees or less. In fact, photographers often speak of the golden hour, a brief window of time just after sunrise or before sunset each day, when exterior lighting is optimal. During the golden hour when the sun is near the horizon, it casts a reddish light, producing a warmer color cast on the subject and background than at other times of the day. Sunlight during the golden hour is also softer (less intense) and easier to work with. If you aren't interested in a warmer look, then add or subtract additional hours. Just remember, the closer to midday you get, the higher the angle of the sun will be, and the more difficulty you will have mitigating the undesirable consequences of direct sunlight at its worst. When working indoors, the 45-degree rule still holds. For best results, set the height of studio or stand-mounted lights so the angle of light in relation to the subject is roughly 45 degrees.

Light Modification Tools

Much of what we do when lighting a scene for film or video involves harnessing the power of light and controlling it to achieve an intended effect. For example, when shooting outdoors in bright sunshine, you can't just command the sun to move to a different angle or position or summon a cloud to come and soften the shadows. Instead, you must work with what you have and learn to apply some of the many tricks of the trade used by professionals to modify and control light to achieve a desired look. Let's take a look at three of the most common light modification techniques at your disposal: 1) block out unwanted light using a *flag*, 2) diffuse a hard light source using a *scrim*, or 3) redirect spill light using a *reflector* (see Figure 13.24).

FLAGS

A *flag* is used to block out direct light or prevent spill light from hitting your subject. It functions as a barrier obstructing the passage of light beyond a certain point. You can think of *spill light* as all the unwanted light in a scene that you would like

FIGURE 13.24
A flag, scrim, and reflector are mounted to C-stands and strategically positioned to help control and modify light for an on-camera interview.

to eliminate or redirect. Flags come in many sizes and are usually rectangular in shape. They are usually constructed of an opaque fabric, such as black duvetyne, that is stretched and mounted on a rigid frame. A flag works in much the same way as the sun visor in your car—as a shield for your eyes from blinding sunlight. A flag can be held by hand, but it is best to permanently affix it to a *C-stand*—a sturdy metal stand with an adjustable swing arm that allows for precise positioning of any type of light-modifying device. If you don't have access to a professional flag kit, you can improvise using cardboard, poster board, foamcore, or another solid material to block out incoming light. Many studio and kit lights come with barn doors to help contain or redirect spill light generated from the instrument. Functioning somewhat like a flag, barn doors are used to block light at the source—keeping it from spilling out haphazardly in all directions. A four-leaf barn door has movable metal plates protruding outward from the front of the light to the left, right, top, and bottom. Each leaf can swing independently, allowing for less or more blockage in all four directions.

SCRIMS

A *scrim* is a lightweight translucent material made of spun glass, fabric, plastic, or wire mesh that's placed in front of a light source to diffuse its beam. Unlike a flag, a scrim permits light to pass while softening the beam. Large scrims are typically mounted to a sturdy frame and positioned between the light source and the subject. Smaller scrims can be directly affixed to the front of a light fixture. Scrims come in different weights or densities to allow for variation in how much diffusion is applied. Large scrims can be mounted to a freestanding frame, providing wide coverage for a group shot or even large objects such as a boat or car. Like flags, they also come in smaller sizes for direct attachment to a C-stand. Scrim material can also be purchased in rolls, allowing you to cut it down to a specific size to cover the front of a light or slide into a gel frame. For example, small squares of scrim material can be attached directly to the barn doors of a light fixture using clothespins or metal clips. When using incandescent lights, be careful, though, as they can become extremely hot. For heat-generating lights such as these, be sure to use metal scrims (wire mesh) designed to slide in between the front of the lamp and the barn doors or heat-resistant scrim material and clips.

REFLECTORS

A *reflector* redirects spill light to fill in areas of the subject that are unevenly lit. For example, in a case where the subject is facing at an angle to the sun, one side of the face will be brighter than the other, resulting in an uneven wash and a high-contrast image. To compensate, a reflector can be used to redirect spill light back toward the underlit side of the face. A reflector can be constructed easily by wrapping a rigid section of cardboard in aluminum foil. A sheet of white foamcore or poster board can also serve as an excellent reflector, as does a collapsible sunshade like the ones found in an auto parts store. Professionally made reflectors are optimized for maximum reflection and are designed for robust use and portability. They usually come in silver, white, or gold and are often reversible to give you the option of more than one color. A gold reflector is used to add warmth to the subject. As you might expect, the larger the reflector, the more light you will be able to intercept and bounce back toward the subject. When shooting indoors, you can use physical light-colored surfaces (walls and ceilings) to bounce light indirectly on the subject. For example, instead of aiming a strong hard light directly at the subject, try bouncing it off the white ceiling tiles in a room. The ceiling, which is highly reflective, transforms the hard light into a softer fill light that more evenly covers the subject.

Lamp Technologies

The three most common types of lamps used in television studio and field lighting instruments are: 1) incandescent, 2) fluorescent, and 3) LED. Incandescent bulbs for television/video applications are color balanced at 3,200 K (Kelvin) for general-purpose indoor lighting. Fluorescent bulbs and LED lamps come in two varieties: 3,200 K (indoor) or 5,600 K (daylight).

INCANDESCENT LAMPS

The *incandescent light* has been around in various forms for many years. It is constructed of a glass or quartz bulb containing a wire filament that is heated by electricity to a high temperature to produce a bright glowing light. The bulb also contains an inert gas that prevents the filament from evaporating and the bulb from darkening over prolonged use. Most incandescent lighting instruments used in video production use tungsten-halogen bulbs (also called quartz lamps). The bulb is made of quartz,

GREAT IDEAS
Three-Point Lighting

The classic technique of *three-point lighting* is often employed when shooting a single-subject interview (see Figure 13.25 and Figure 13.26). It is sometimes called triangle lighting because the position of the three instruments around the subject tends to form an isosceles triangle. The *key light* is the brightest source and the main provider of subject illumination. The primary purpose of the key light is to "reveal the basic shape of the subject."[2]

FIGURE 13.25
In three-point lighting, the placement of the key light, fill light, and backlight forms a triangle around the subject.

The *fill light* is positioned at an opposite angle to the key light in front of the subject. It is intended to compensate for falloff by softening the dark shadows created by the key light without eliminating them entirely. Remember, we need some shadows to maintain a sense of depth and shape. *Falloff* is the degree to which the lit area of a subject transitions into shadow. The key light creates a fast falloff with bright areas offset quickly by harsh dark shadows. Sometimes, for dramatic effect, a director wants to achieve what is known as the chiaroscuro effect or low-key lighting, where one side of a person's face is brightly lit while the other side is masked in shadow. In such cases, the fill light is left out. Most of the time, however, the goal is to create a more natural on-camera look where the illumination of the subject is more balanced. The fill light, which is generally a soft light instrument, slows falloff and helps bring better contrast and balance to the image. The *backlight* helps separate the subject from the background by accentuating the contours of the subject's hair and shoulders. All three lights are aimed downward at the subject at roughly a 45-degree angle. A fourth light is sometimes added to light the background or set piece behind the subject.

FIGURE 13.26
This interview was shot using three-point lighting. As you can see, the fill light doesn't have to be an actual lighting instrument. Here, a reflector is used to bounce spill light to the left side of the subject's face to counteract falloff. Also, notice that the backlight does not have to be placed directly behind the subject to serve its intended purpose.

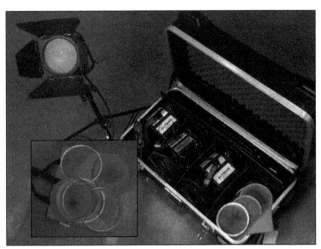

FIGURE 13.27
This portable light kit includes four 650-watt tungsten-halogen Fresnels. Each instrument includes a stand, a power cord, and a four-leaf barn door. An assortment of wire scrims is also included.

the filament is constructed of tungsten, and halogen gas is used to extend the life of the bulb (see Figure 13.27).

Incandescent lights generate lots of heat. For this reason, you need to exercise extreme caution when touching them if they are turned on or before they have completely cooled after being turned off. Experienced gaffers wear gloves to protect their hands from injury when working with incandescent lights. Care also must be taken not to jostle or bump a hot incandescent light. When the filament is hot, it is extremely fragile and can break with even the slightest agitation. It's best to wait until the lamp is completely cool before touching or moving it. For added incentive, remember that professional-grade incandescent bulbs are expensive compared to the consumer variety used in a household table lamp. A new quartz bulb can easily set you back $20–$40 depending on the model. Light kits often include spare bulbs because breakage and burnout are always a possibility and will often occur at the worst possible moment during a shoot. One last warning about incandescent bulbs—be careful not to touch the surface of the bulb when replacing it. Residual oil from your fingers can coat the outer shell of the bulb. When the lamp heats up, areas coated in oil can overheat, causing the lamp to fail or even shatter.

FLUORESCENT AND LED LAMPS

In recent years, new types of non-incandescent bulb technologies have evolved for professional video applications—namely fluorescents and LEDs. *Fluorescent* lamps are constructed of a low-pressure mercury-vapor gas-filled tube. When an electric charge is added to the mercury vapor, ultraviolet light is produced, causing the phosphor coating on the inside of the glass tube to glow and emit light. Fluorescent lights operate cool to the touch, have a long life, and are significantly more energy efficient than incandescent bulbs. However, because of their long tubular shape and the addition of a ballast to regulate current, fluorescent lighting fixtures are large and bulky in comparison to traditional instruments. Also, because fluorescent bulbs are coated, they naturally cast a soft light with a broad spread that cannot be focused. In order to provide sufficient illumination, fluorescent fixtures generally have to be placed close to the subject. This works exceptionally well when lighting a single-subject interview that is tightly framed; however, when lighting a wide area, fluorescents may not be the best choice—particularly if your goal is to keep the lights out of the shot. For many applications, including studio lighting, fluorescents are combined with focusable instruments (tungsten or LED) to create a more balanced and pleasing image with higher contrast.

LEDs are the latest innovation in video lighting, combining some of the best qualities of incandescent and fluorescent technologies. LED (light-emitting diode) lamps contain no filament or gas. Instead, they use a tiny electronic component called a diode, the simplest form of a semiconductor, to generate light when electrically charged. LED lighting instruments are extremely energy efficient, operate with very little heat, are lightweight and compact, can be dimmed without affecting color temperature, and are rated exceptionally high for durability and longevity. Depending on the design of the lighting instrument, LEDs can be used to generate an intense focusable hard light or a broad soft light—thus making them a versatile solution that can satisfy many types of video lighting needs. LEDs can be dimmed full range without affecting color temperature. Unfortunately, LEDs are also one of the most expensive lighting technologies currently available to video professionals.

Tech Talk

Lighting Instruments Film and television lighting instruments come in a variety of styles suited for different tastes, budgets, and uses (see Figure 13.29).

- **Fresnel:** A *Fresnel* is a focusable lighting instrument that allows the user to alter the angle of the beam across a range—from a narrow hard light to a broad softer light (see Figure 13.28). Inside the Fresnel's housing, the lamp connects to a movable platform that slides back and forth between a rear-mounted reflector and a front-mounted lens as the focusing knob is turned. The relative positions of the reflector and lens in relation to the lamp determine the intensity and angle of the beam at any particular point between spot and broad. Fresnels are often used as the key light in three-point lighting because they produce a relatively hard yet controllable beam. They often come equipped with a four-leaf barn door for controlling spill and a gel frame slot for holding metal scrims or colored gels.
- **Scoop:** If we compare a Fresnel to a spotlight, then a scoop is best thought of as a floodlight. A *scoop* is a bowl-shaped broad light instrument designed to cover a wide surface area. The lamp sits at the rear of the inside of a shiny scoop, which acts as a parabolic or ellipsoidal reflector to direct the beam. Since a scoop cannot be focused, the only way to control the spread of light it casts is to move it closer or further away from the subject. A scrim can be attached to the front of a scoop to further soften the throw.
- **Umbrella light:** An *umbrella light* is a standard lighting instrument (usually a Fresnel) that's designed to be connected to an attached umbrella with a shiny reflective surface. The umbrella captures the hard light emanating from the lamp and bounces it back out as a soft light in the opposite direction. An umbrella light is often used as the fill light in a three-point lighting setup.
- **Softbox:** A *softbox* is a variation of the umbrella light concept. It features a one-piece collapsible umbrella-like design with a curved reflective inside coating and a rectangular front. A diffusion scrim is stretched over the opening to create an even broad throw.
- **Camera light:** A *camera light* mounts to the top of a video camera. It is used more for convenience and

SPOT   FLOOD

FIGURE 13.28
A Fresnel lamp can be manually focused, altering the spread of light from a narrow beam (spot) to a broad beam (flood).

(Continued)

necessity than for creating a properly lit image, as lighting a subject directly head-on isn't usually very flattering. When shooting in dimly lit areas or at night, a camera light comes in handy and can often make the difference between acquiring an unusable shot and having something you can work with in post. For best results, use a camera light when you are within a short distance of the subject. Many LED camera lights come with a dimmer control and attachable scrims and color gels for greater lighting control.

FIGURE 13.29
A) Fresnel with barn door; B) scoop; C) umbrella light; D) softbox with detachable scrim; E) LED camera light with plastic diffuser; F) variable-color LED light with barn door.

CHAPTER SUMMARY

As with anything new, learning how to light and shoot video with professional results takes time, patience, and lots of practice. Before embarking on an actual project for school or work, practice shooting a simple interview and some accompanying B-Roll. Select a human subject; find a setting that is well lit, visually interesting, and relatively quiet; and shoot a five-minute interview with a properly framed close-up. Shoot from a tripod with the camera set at eye level, and use an external lavaliere microphone to capture sound if you have one. Be sure that it is properly attached (see chapter 12). Go through the FWIGSS setup procedures step by step (see chapter 11). Don't cut any corners. Play back the interview and critique your work. How did it turn out? Show it to a colleague or professor for feedback. Repeat the practice interview with a second subject and a third, each time building on previous experience while improving results. Once you are competent shooting an interview, practice moving the camera and resetting it quickly from one location to another while capturing B-Roll. Experiment with as many different camera positions and angles as you can as you practice getting more B-Roll than you can ever imagine needing. Keep shooting until you have completely worked the scene and exhausted all possibilities for shot composition and motion. Stop, critique your work, obtain feedback, and try again! If you commit yourself to practicing prior to an actual production, you will achieve better results and have much more confidence when the stakes are higher and a grade or a paid gig are on the line.

NOTES

1 Zettl, H. (2013). *Sight, sound and motion: Applied media aesthetics* (7th ed.). Boston, MA: Wadsworth.
2 Zettl, H. (2014). *Television production handbook* (12th ed.). Independence, KY: Cengage Learning.

CHAPTER 14
Time-Based Editing

As we get newer and better compression algorithms for video and still-frame images, we'll approach the next major leap in desktop computing: video on the desktop.

—**John C. Dvorak, technology journalist and radio broadcaster (1995)**

Chapter Highlights

This chapter examines:

- The use of nonlinear editing (NLE) in video and audio production
- The visual interface components in an NLE workspace
- Strategies for project organization and asset management
- Working with project media files and clips in a nondestructive editing environment
- General concepts and principles related to the aesthetics of editing

FROM LINEAR TO NONLINEAR EDITING

Video editing is the art of arranging static and time-based media assets into a linear form of presentation for the purpose of telling a story or communicating a message. The goal of editing is to produce a thoughtful narrative with a clear beginning, middle, and end. Audio editing is similar but with a focus on sound-based media elements only. Many of the basic editing techniques used in video postproduction are applicable to audio, particularly if you are using professional audio editing software such as Avid Pro Tools or Adobe Audition.

Motion picture editing began as a simple manual process. In the early days of film, an editor would review and edit footage using a hand-operated device (see Figure 14.1). Editing was performed by physically cutting film into sections, rearranging the pieces into a new linear order, and then splicing them together again using clear tape or another type of adhesive—hence the term *linear editing*. This method was also used in audio tape editing. You'll find that many of the terms used in digital audio and video editing today have their origins from this era, particularly the use of terms such as the *razor blade tool*—a reference to the traditional cutting

Key Terms
Action Safe
Alpha Channel
Audio Sweetening
Audio Track
Chroma Key
Clip
Color Correction
Compositing
Cut
Cutaway
Dissolve
Effect
Fade
Freeze Frame
IN and OUT Points
Jump Cut
Keying
Log and Capture
Matte
Mixing
Nonlinear Editing
 (NLE)
Playhead
Render
Rough Cut
Scratch Disk
Scrubbing
Slug
Sound Effects (SFX)
Split Edit
Three-Point Editing
Timecode
Timeline
Title
Title Safe
Transition
Video Track
Voiceover (VO)

FIGURE 14.1
Left: In the early days, motion picture editing required manually viewing, cutting, and splicing pieces of film together on an editing table to make a movie. Right: Today, film and video editing is done virtually using an NLE program such as Adobe Premiere Pro, Apple Final Cut Pro, or Avid Media Composer. There's no more mess and no more film left behind on the cutting room floor.

instrument—and the term *bins*—a virtual desktop alternative to the physical bins, such as repurposed coffee cans, that film editors once used to hold segments or clips of film.

While film editing began as a physical process, video editing started out as an electronic process. Unlike film, one cannot expose videotape to the light to view the transparent frames of each still image. Video images are processed electronically, which means that viewing and editing have to be done using electromechanical players, recorders, and monitors. In the beginning, video editing was nothing more than systematic duplication. Material was copied segment by segment from one videotape to another—a process known as *tape-to-tape* or *machine-to-machine editing*.

Machine-to-machine editing worked pretty well for many years. The simplest machine-to-machine editing system involved five pieces of equipment: 1) a playback deck (VCR) attached to 2) a source monitor for viewing; 3) a record deck attached to 4) program monitor for recording; and 5) an edit controller. The edit controller was connected to both decks, allowing the editor to control them remotely. To perform an edit, the editor would begin by "electronically" marking the beginning and end of a selected shot on the source deck. This involved shuttling the deck (moving or *scrubbing* the tape backward or forward), pausing it at a specific spot on the tape, and pressing physical buttons to mark the respective IN and OUT points. The editor would perform the same procedure to set an IN point on the record deck. Pushing one last button allowed the editor to preview or perform the edit. During the pre-roll phase, both machines would back up three to five seconds ahead of the designated IN points and then roll forward in unison. Once the IN point was reached on the record VCR, recording would begin and continue until the OUT point triggered the end of the edit.

This type of machine-to-machine editing configuration was sometimes called a *cuts-only system* because the only type of edit you could perform was a cut. If you wanted to create anything other than a straight cut, you had to use an *A/B Roll editing system*. The A/B Roll workstation had two source decks instead of one. The A-Deck was loaded with primary footage (interviews, scripted dialog, etc.) while the B-Deck contained secondary material (cover shots, establishing shots, cutaways, etc.) that would appear while the main person or character was talking on screen. By the way, this is where the familiar, yet sometimes confusing, term *B-Roll* originated.

The computerization of media has made machine-to-machine editing a thing of the past. The edit controller is no longer a physical device sitting on a tabletop, but rather software powered by a computer. Welcome to the age of nonlinear editing (NLE), where programs such as Adobe Premiere Pro, Avid Media Composer, and Apple Final Cut Pro are used by professional editors to craft their stories. For consumers, the marketplace offers a number of simple-to-learn NLEs such as Pinnacle Studio, Apple iMovie, and Windows Movie Maker. Professional NLE titles are designed for filmmakers and producers who require advanced tools to support more complex postproduction needs and workflows. Audio editing software comes in a similar range, from consumer-level software such as GarageBand and Audacity to professional-grade software such as Adobe Audition, Apple Logic Pro, or Avid Pro Tools.

BUILDING BLOCKS OF AN EDITED SEQUENCE

Most professionally produced television shows or video programs contain basic components that, when edited together, tell a story, communicate a message, or stimulate an emotion. Raw footage for a project is acquired during the production phase. The amount of raw footage you have depends on the type of project you are working on and your skill in keeping the number of "bad takes" to a minimum. For a 1-hour documentary, you may have 10 hours of source material (interviews, B-Roll, etc.) to work with. We refer to this as a *10 to 1 shooting ratio* (10:1) because the amount of source footage is 10 times greater than the length of the finished product. For a 60-second news package, an editor will often have much less footage to work with. Although the shooting ratio may remain the same at 10:1, given the shorter program length, the amount of actual footage drops to 10 minutes.

The media assets used to build an edited sequence typically fall into four main categories: 1) pre-scripted elements; 2) unscripted or post-scripted elements; 3) music and sound effects; and 4) graphics.

Pre-Scripted Elements

In a pre-scripted movie or television program, a written script is completed prior to the start of production. Feature films, television newscasts, dramas, sitcoms, commercials, and educational videos are traditionally pre-scripted—leaving it up to the writers to determine the on-camera action, narration, or dialog ahead of time during the pre-production phase of the project. In such cases, the script serves as a master blueprint for directing the on-camera performances of professional actors or talent. In postproduction, the same script will assist the editor in arranging shots and scenes into the predetermined linear presentation.

FIGURE 14.2
Television news anchors are able to maintain eye contact with the viewer by reading their scripts via a teleprompter mounted to the front of the camera.

In narrative filmmaking, actors are called to memorize their lines and rehearse them before the actual performance. Still, on-camera performances are rarely perfect, and directors will often ask talent to perform multiple takes of a scene before they are satisfied with the results. In some situations, such as in a game show, corporate video, or television newscast, scripted lines or dialog are performed using a teleprompter (see Figure 14.2). A *teleprompter* projects words onto an angled glass panel that's mounted in front of a television camera lens. It allows the talent to read their script while looking directly into the camera. Teleprompters are used often in studio productions (news, sports, talk shows, etc.) but can also be used in remote field production. While a teleprompter can eliminate or cut down on rehearsal time and speed up production, their use doesn't guarantee a perfect take. Reading from a teleprompter takes practice, and some people are naturally better at it than others.

Unscripted or Post-Scripted Elements

Nonfiction stories such as broadcast news packages and documentary films rely heavily on unscripted action (or candid footage) and post-scripted elements such as voiceovers or standups. Candid shots are unscripted, intended to capture the normal actions, speech, and sounds of real subjects and objects in their natural setting. Ideally, it means that nothing shot by the camera is intentionally scripted, staged, or performed. The camera is merely there to document reality. Whereas in scripted programs, shots are rather rigidly preplanned and constructed, here the camera is used to *capture* a story—as reflected through the actions, behaviors, thoughts, ideas, feelings, and expressions of everyday people, however ordinary or extraordinary they may be. Likewise, the written copy for voiceovers and standups is typically post-scripted—written after production has ceased and postproduction has begun in order to most accurately tell the story that unfolds. Four of the most common media assets used in editing non-fiction programs are: 1) sound bites, 2) B-Roll, 3) natural sound, and 4) voiceover.

SOUND BITES

Whereas interviews are shot or recorded during the production phase of a project, sound bites are "constructed" by editors during postproduction. A sound bite can be as short as a single word or several sentences long. The phrase *talking head* is used to describe an on-camera interview segment that goes on for too long, potentially causing the viewer or listener to lose interest and disengage from the message. The average length of a sound bite on network news programs is less than 10 seconds. As a rule of thumb, sound bites should be kept to under 20 seconds. Usually, the shorter, the better!

To avoid having a long sound bite of, say, 30 seconds, an editor can divide it in half, producing two shorter bites that are roughly 15 seconds each. The editor can then insert a stand-up, natural sound pop (or snippet), music, voiceover, or other sound bite in between the two halves as a narrative bridge, transition, or cutaway. With this technique, the content of the 30-second bite still gets communicated but in a more dynamic way by intercutting it with other elements.

Sound bites from different people can be combined through editing into a sequence to form a continuous thought or interwoven narrative. The rapid intercutting of shorter sound bites in combination with other program elements is a great way to keep an audience engaged in the program. A skillful editor can even join noncontiguous sound bites in such a way as to make the person speaking sound as if they are saying something entirely different. At such times, the editor is a potentially powerful gatekeeper and shaper of ideas and, as such, needs to follow the ethical standards and practices of the profession and the organization he or she works for. Nowhere is this more important than in journalism, where reporters are expected to uphold the virtues of truth, fairness, and objectivity. An editor at Comedy Central likely has more latitude and creative freedom in editing (under the cover of parody and satire) than a news editor working at CNN.

B-ROLL

B-Roll serves an important secondary role. It refers to video footage that's used to visually support the spoken word narrative. Visual storytellers and scriptwriters are often encouraged to "write to the pictures," which means making sure there is thoughtful harmony and synergy between what the viewer hears and what he or she sees on screen. For example, when a voiceover is added to a sequence, B-Roll is placed on top to visually illustrate the narrative content of the VO. Likewise, in an interview segment, B-Roll can be used, in part or in whole, to replace the shot of the person speaking, effectively converting an SOT into a VO. B-Roll includes specialty shots such as cut-ins and cutaways, which we will discuss later, graphics, animations, and other footage designed to visually enhance the audio portion of the program. For example, as a reporter is speaking off-camera about a local bank robbery, the viewer sees a sequence of B-Roll shots depicting the scene of the crime. A sequence like this might include material obtained from surveillance cameras along with other shots filmed during the aftermath of the event. There's a popular saying among shooters and editors that "you can never get enough B-Roll." The more B-Roll an editor has to work with, the more options he or she will have for improving a story's visual pace and structure.

NATURAL SOUND

Natural sound (also known as *nat sound* or *ambient sound*) is the synchronized audio portion of a video recording that is acquired when shooting B-Roll. For example, while shooting B-Roll of a mountain waterfall, be sure to record the sound of the water cascading over the rocks. This is natural sound, and it comes in handy when editing! For example, in a scene where a hiker speaks on camera during a 15-second sound bite, the editor inserts B-Roll of the waterfall for the last 5 seconds. The waterfall shot will have a greater impact on the viewer if nat sound is incorporated in the mix. When mixing the two sources, the audio levels for the hiker's SOT should be set to full (100%) and the audio levels for natural sound much lower (less than 50%). This will ensure natural sound stays in the background (where it normally belongs) and that it doesn't compete or interfere with the main audio source.

VOICEOVER (VO)

A *voiceover* (or *VO*) is a narrative device used to audibly support or describe the visual portion of a video program or segment. Recorded off-camera, a VO is the sound of the hidden announcer, storyteller, reporter, narrator, or host, who guides the audience through a program—filling in details while adding color and continuity to the linear presentation of visual information. Voiceovers are often used in conjunction with sound bites. In news reporting, the *VO-SOT* (pronounced VOH-soht) is a technique in which a television anchor reads a scripted story off-camera

---

GREAT IDEAS
The Stand-Up

In television, a *reporter stand-up* or *on-camera host* segment can be used as an alternative to a voiceover or in combination with it. For example, a reporter may choose to use a stand-up at the beginning and end of a story and voiceovers throughout the rest of the package. The best stand-ups add meaningful visual value to the story by providing something other than a good look at the reporter or host. A stand-up can be used to perform a visual demonstration, stress a key point, or take the viewer on a brief walking tour.

FIGURE 14.3
A TV reporter delivers an on-camera stand-up.

while related images and sounds appear on screen. *VO-SOT-VO* describes a fundamental editing technique where voiceovers and sound bites alternate to form the narrative structure of a linear story.

Music and Sound Effects

Music and sound effects are usually inserted into the timeline beneath the primary audio tracks containing sound bites (SOTs), VOs, and nat sound—giving the editor independent control over each track when mixing levels or adding audio processing effects such as compression and EQ. They should be imported into the NLE project bin in an uncompressed file format such as WAV or AIFF. If you import a compressed audio file, particularly a lossy file such as MP3, you will end up recompressing the audio when you export it at the end of the project, thus compromising its fidelity. Professionals usually avoid working with MP3 audio assets in video editing. MP3 is a consumer distribution format that is heavily compressed and technically inferior to WAV or AIFF.

Graphics

A *lower-third* is a television graphic used to identify the name of the person appearing or speaking on screen (see Figure 14.4, top). Sometimes the person's title, or, as in this case, email address, is included as well. As the name suggests, a lower-third is usually positioned in the lower-third area of the frame They are sometimes referred to as *supers* because they are typically superimposed over a background video source or graphic.

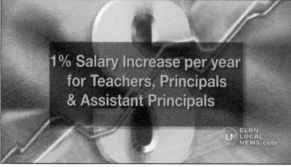

FIGURE 14.4
Top: A lower-third is superimposed over the background video to identify both newscasters. Bottom: Full-screen graphics, such as this one, fill the entire video frame.

A lower-third is placed on screen through a process called *keying*. Keying replaces the background pixels in a title graphic (known as the *alpha channel*) with video from another source. This technique is similar to the superimposition of a weather map behind the weathercaster during the evening news. The weathercaster usually stands in front of a green or blue wall. Using a technique called *chroma keying*, the colored wall is replaced with video of a weather graphic. For best results, the weathercaster cannot wear clothing containing the same color as the wall. Can you imagine what that would look like? Like the green or blue wall in a TV studio, the alpha channel serves as a mask, allowing a title to be seamlessly merged with the video beneath it.

Most NLE software programs make it relatively easy to create and insert a simple title graphic. However, when you want something more complex, you will want to turn to a graphic editing program such as Adobe Photoshop (see Figure 14.5) or to a motion graphics program such as Adobe After Effects. You can then use the NLE to import the graphic into the project as a standalone media asset. NLE programs recognize most common graphic file formats including JPEG, GIF, TIFF, and PNG. In fact, professional editing software usually allows you to import native Photoshop files (PSDs) directly into the project. When the NLE opens a PSD file, it converts each layer to a corresponding video track, allowing the editor to have independent control of each layered element in the timeline.

Television graphics come in all shapes, sizes, and formats. For example, an over-the-shoulder graphic appears at head level just to the left or right of a television anchor or host. Crawls scroll from right to left across the bottom of the screen with the latest stock information or school closings while credit rolls scroll vertically, identifying members of the cast and crew at the end of a television show or movie. A *full-screen graphic* fills the entire screen while a *bug* (a tiny network or station logo) takes up very little real estate in the corner of the screen (see Figure 14.4).

FIGURE 14.5
Adobe Photoshop includes several film and video presets. For an HD television program choose the one shown here. Film and video presets include visual guides to show the action and title safe areas.
Source: Adobe product screenshot reprinted with permission from Adobe Systems Incorporated.

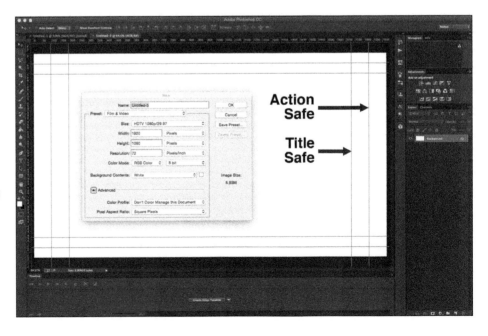

FIGURE 14.6
Adobe Premiere
Pro includes this
title generator for
composing on-screen
graphics. Notice the
title and action safe
guidelines displayed
in the design window
to aid in the placement
of text and graphics.
*Source: Adobe product
screenshot reprinted
with permission
from Adobe Systems
Incorporated.*

DESIGNING GRAPHICS FOR TELEVISION

When designing television graphics, keep in mind that viewers may be watching the video on a low-resolution screen or even in a small window on a computer monitor or digital device. Viewers have a short time in which to process visual information that flashes on the screen for only seconds at a time. Follow these tips when planning your graphics:

- **Avoid clutter.** Remember, less is more. Don't pack more information into the visual screen space than is absolutely necessary. Avoid long sentences and paragraphs. Instead, use short phrases or bulleted text whenever possible.
- **Use thick sans serif fonts.** Select high-density fonts with a thick stroke. Script fonts and other light stroke fonts do not translate well to video, where much of their detail is lost, making them hard to read and frustrating for the viewer.
- **Use large font sizes.** Use font size to denote visual hierarchy, but keep the sizes relatively large. It's better to use a readable font and break up information across several screens than to cram too much information into a single title screen or graphic.
- **Strive for good contrast.** If the background is dark, the foreground text should be light. Separate the text from the background by using drop shadows, stroke, light, and texture. Try using a high-contrast background graphic or colored box behind text instead of superimposing text directly over video and running the risk of making it hard to read.
- **Use video-friendly colors.** White and yellow are popular colors for screen text because they are easy to read against a dark background. Black also works quite well when placed over a white or light-colored background.

- **Margins and white space.** Stay within the *title safe area* of the frame—the area where titles will display well—and don't forget to leave white space. Most NLEs will show you the title safe area of the screen. You'll also see lines marking the *action safe* area. The reason for this is that older television sets didn't actually show the entire picture; a mask usually covered part of the picture tube, and some pixels along the outer edges were lost during broadcast transmission. While newer flat panel displays don't have this problem, it's still a good idea to pay attention to the positioning of titles and action within the frame as this will help ensure there is sufficient white space in the frame.

CONTINUITY EDITING

Combining shots in an edited sequence should be done in such a way that the linear presentation of visual and aural elements in a timeline is perceived as natural and coherent to the viewer. Bad edits can be disruptive to the narrative flow of a story, causing viewers to disconnect, get confused, lose their place, or stop watching altogether. There's a saying that "the best edits are the ones you never see." In other words, good edits are so seamless and logical that the viewer doesn't even notice when they occur. And this is what editors often hope to achieve. *Continuity editing* is a term used to describe a wide range of practices and techniques that editors use to achieve smooth and natural transitions from shot to shot over time. When edits are performed well, the narrative continuity of the story is enhanced—leading to a more satisfying and enriching experience for the viewer (see Figure 14.7).

Cut-Ins

The cut-in is a popular editing technique used in continuity editing. A *cut-in* directs the viewer's attention to a related object or alternative viewpoint within the current scene. For example, in a scene showing a woman stepping into an elevator, the sequence might begin with a wide shot of the elevator as the woman enters through the opening doors. She turns, glances down, and reaches out her hand, at which point we cut to a close-up shot of her finger pushing the button for the 10th floor. The cut-in of her finger may be framed from her point of view as if we are looking at it through her eyes or through the eyes of someone standing nearby. A cut-in is often shot as a close-up that guides the viewer's attention to a related element within the frame. Be careful when you are cutting your scene together. Avoid cutting between two shots that look almost the same. In doing so you run the risk of creating a *jump cut*—where the position of the main subject shifts suddenly on screen for no apparent reason. You'll see this error sometimes in news, when the video editor joins two non-adjacent sound bites together in the timeline. This is one of the reasons cut-ins (and cutaways) are so important. Editors often use them to cover or hide a jump cut by positioning them over a transition point on the video track above.

CUTTING ON ACTION

Cutting on action is a technique editors use to match continuous action in a scene as it unfolds across two sequential shots. In our previous example, the woman on

FIGURE 14.7
The film *Chariots of Fire* won an Oscar for Best Picture in 1981. The movie included a one-minute scene, pictured here with still images, of two athletes competing in the Great Court Run. The runner's goal was to complete one lap around the main college square before 12 strikes of the courtyard clock (roughly 43 seconds). The edited scene was comprised of 30+ shots from multiple camera angles. Through continuity editing, the director was able to portray the scene in real time with continuous action, an amazing feat considering the scene was likely shot using only one camera. Notice how many cut-ins are interspersed with shots of the runners.[1]

the elevator performs a simple action by reaching out her hand to push a button on the control panel. Cutting on action means the editor will cut from the wide-angle view to the close-up (or cut-in shot) while the hand is in motion. Typically, the best transition points occur at the apex of movement, when the action is most intense, and before the subject or object begins to decelerate or stop. The editor must ensure the last frame of the action in the first shot matches the first frame of the continuing action in the second shot. For example, if the right hand is used to extend the finger in the first shot, the right hand should be shown completing the action in the second shot. If the actor uses a different hand in the second shot, then a continuity error will occur, drawing attention to the edit and disrupting the viewer's attention.

GREAT IDEAS
Multi-Camera Editing (or Multi-Cam)

Multi-cam is a production and editing technique whereby shots of an event or scene are recorded simultaneously from multiple camera sources and then assembled in editing to resemble a *live* switched event or to produce a visually fast-paced sequence. Each *iso* (isolated) camera records a unique view of the action at a different angle and distance from the subject. After the shoot, footage from each camera is imported into the editing software, where the video and audio in each clip is then synchronized to a common master clip or sync source. In a professional multi-cam production, cameras are often synchronized to a timecode generator that produces a common reference signal that each camera records during the shoot. This is the most foolproof method for synchronizing multi-cam clips in postproduction. Unfortunately, many less expensive cameras are not designed to accept an external timecode signal. As an alternative, multi-cam producers must ensure that each camera records live audio of the event as it occurs. In a scene where there is no dialog or dominant sound source, you can use a clapboard to mark the beginning of a recording with a visual reference and an audible sound stamp. Professional NLE software—such as Adobe Premiere Pro, Avid Media Composer, and Apple Final Cut Pro—that supports multi-cam editing also includes tools for automated audio-based synching of *iso* footage obtained from multiple cameras (see Figure 14.8). Once all the clips have been synchronized, you can use your NLE's multi-cam editing mode to cut or transition from source to source (or clip to clip) in real time as though you were switching multiple cameras during a live event. The transition points between shots can then be tweaked and refined manually as desired.

FIGURE 14.8
Multi-cam editing in Adobe Premiere Pro. Six cameras were used to record this live band performance. A switched program feed was recorded on-site along with six ISO recording (one for each camera). In Adobe Premiere Pro, the six ISO camera recordings were imported into a multi-cam editing session and synchronized to the original switched recording of the event.
Source: Adobe product screenshot reprinted with permission from Adobe Systems Incorporated.

PROJECT ORGANIZATION AND ASSET MANAGEMENT

NLE Project Folder

At the end of production you will likely end up with a fair bit of footage and other project assets, and you need to know how to effectively organize and manage them. It helps to understand how your NLE software stores and saves project files. As a general rule, at the beginning of every new project, it's a good idea to create a master *project folder* to serve as the container for all the project files and assets associated with it. The project folder should contain the native project file generated by your NLE software and numerous topical subfolders for storing media content such as video, music sound effects, still images, titles, and so forth. In addition, NLE applications will often create additional subfolders for storing video and audio capture files, render files, and backup copies of the master project file. Again, each project you are currently working on should have its own designated project folder (see Figure 14.9).

Adobe Premiere Pro and the legacy version of Apple Final Cut Pro use the term *scratch disk* as the name of the interface component for setting up the name and location of the project folder and subfolders. Hence, the phrase "setting your scratch disks" is synonymous with the process of linking to or creating the project folder at the beginning of an editing session. In Avid Media Composer, the editor uses the "media creation settings" window to set up the name and location of the project

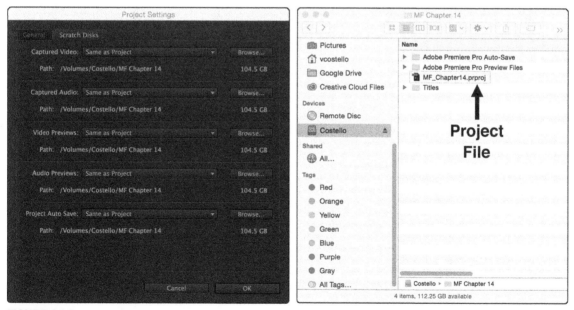

FIGURE 14.9
Left: Upon starting a new project in Adobe Premiere Pro, the editor is prompted to identify the scratch disk locations for the captured video and audio files, preview files, and backup files. All the media assets and project files associated with a video project should be stored in a master project root folder. This way, you will never lose track of files associated with your project. Right: Based on the information you provide in the scratch disk window, the program will create physical folders and files on your drive as shown.
Source: Adobe product screenshot reprinted with permission from Adobe Systems Incorporated.

FIGURE 14.10
The Adobe Premiere Pro interface is divided into four main regions. 1) The Source Monitor is used to preview media clips and to trim video and audio clips prior to inserting them in the timeline. 2) The Program Monitor displays video from the timeline during playback. 3) The Project Panel displays bins and image thumbnails for each asset associated with the project (video, audio, titles, sequences, etc.). Double-clicking on a clip loads it into the source monitor. 4) The Timeline is where you assemble your project—insert and order your clips; add titles, effects, and transitions; mix audio levels; render frames; and so on.
Source: Adobe product screenshot reprinted with permission from Adobe Systems Incorporated.

folder. Similarly, Avid Pro Tools refers to each project as a "session" and requires the user to create a "session folder" at the start of each new project. Whatever the name or approach, be sure you understand how to properly designate the name and location of your project folder. This step is critically important and, when done well, will save you a lot of time and potential frustration during the editing process. Also, consider using an external hard drive as your scratch disk instead of the one on your computer running the OS and NLE software. Using a dedicated external drive for your video project assets can help speed up performance and allow you to move your project easily from one computer to another. Once you've created the project folder, be sure not to move it or change its name. This goes for all the content within the project folder as well. Doing so can potentially confuse the NLE program, causing it to lose track of the media files and assets it needs to properly display and run your edited sequence.

NLE Project File

The *project file* is a proprietary data file used for keeping track of every detail associated with an NLE project. Once an editing project is created, it can be revisited in later sessions by double-clicking on the project file icon. The project file can be thought of as a set of instructions for playing media clips back in real time as an edited sequence.

Media Files and Media Clips

Media files are the raw project assets that are created or acquired prior to the start of an editing session. These include the actual video and audio files captured from tape or through direct transfer from a video camera, memory card, or other digital source. Media files are typically the largest file assets associated with an editing project. For example, digital video (DV) requires 1 GB of storage for every five minutes of recorded footage (or 250 MB per minute). High-definition video files consume an even larger amount of digital real estate, which is why high-capacity hard drives are so often used in editing.

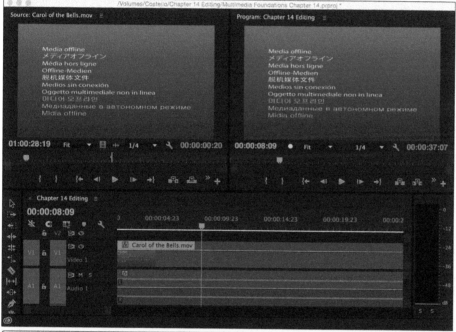

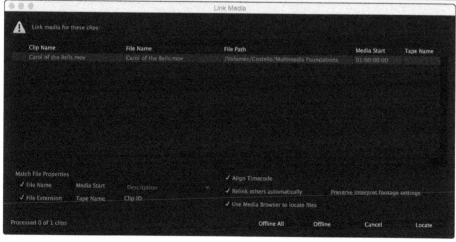

FIGURE 14.11
Top: Red is generally a bad color to see on a media clip or sequence. Here, in Adobe Premiere Pro, it signifies that a media file has gone offline. In other words, the *media file* associated with *media clip* in the timeline has either been deleted from the project's hard drive or moved to a new location—thus breaking the link that was established when the media was first imported. Bottom: The *Link Media* panel in Premiere Pro is used to locate and re-link the missing asset. *Source: Adobe product screenshot reprinted with permission from Adobe Systems Incorporated.*

Intermediate Formats A nonlinear editing system can experience problems and slowdowns when decoding highly compressed interframe video formats such as HDV, AVCHD, or H.264 on the fly. Depending on the speed of your system and NLE software, it is possible to edit interframe streams natively. However, to reduce the likelihood of playback artifacts or rendering slowdowns, editors will often convert interframe video to an intermediate format prior to editing. For example, in legacy versions of Final Cut Pro (version 7 and earlier), HDV footage is automatically upconverted to ProRes 4:2:2 during the log and capture process. ProRes is Apple's intermediate codec for editing uncompressed full-bandwidth (1920 x 1080) HD video. It is comparable to DNxHD, the intermediate codec used in Avid Media Composer. Like Avid, Adobe Premiere Pro includes DNxHD as an intermediate format. The intermediate codecs mentioned here use intraframe compression, which is easier to decode, but which also produces a transcoded file that will be considerably larger than the original source footage. By transcoding to an intraframe format for editing, playback and rendering artifacts are kept to a minimum and the editing process will typically go more smoothly.

When a media file is imported into an active NLE session, a clip is created and added to the media browser or project bin. A *clip* is a relatively small data file that "points" to a larger underlying media file that's stored on the hard drive. It functions as an alias or virtual representation of the real thing, and for this reason, it is sometimes called a *pointer file*. A clip can be placed in the timeline, trimmed, cut, and deleted without changing or destroying the actual media file it is linked with. A single clip can be added to the timeline sequence multiple times without adding significantly to the physical size of the project file. Each instance of a clip is a standalone digital asset that keeps track of the pointer data for a particular event in the edited sequence. You can delete a media clip from the bin without deleting the media file. While deleting it makes the clip icon disappear from view in the project window or browser, the actual media file is safe and sound in its original location on the hard drive. A *media file* can be reconnected with a *media clip* at any time though re-linking or by re-importing it into the project.

Capture and Render Files

Capture files are time-based media files that are created when footage is ingested into the computer through a connected camera or videotape recorder. The video and audio tracks recorded on tape exist as linear streams of digital information that are read and rendered in real time as the tape is played back. Capturing involves converting these time-based streams (or video and audio tracks) into a file-based format that can be read and processed by the NLE program. Once captured, a media file can be easily moved and copied, allowing it to be used in other projects or saved in a digital archive for retrieval at a later time.

LOGGING AND BATCH CAPTURING

With the *logging and batch capturing* method, an editor will preview footage prior to capturing. He or she works through the footage one scene at a time, stopping

FIGURE 14.12
This is the log and capture window in Adobe Premiere Pro. User-provided metadata can be attached to each imported clip using the data fields on the right.
Source: Adobe product screenshot reprinted with permission from Adobe Systems Incorporated.

at the beginning and end of each good take to set an IN and OUT point. In the logging fields, the editor can designate the tape or reel number, clip name, scene and take number, shot description, camera angle, and other notes or comments as desired. This information will be permanently attached as metadata to the captured media file. After viewing and logging the source footage, the editor will select the batch capture option. At this point, the NLE will proceed to capture each of the scenes specified in the editor's logging notes. The bad takes are skipped and the total capture time is cut down significantly, especially for big projects with hours and hours of footage. Batch capturing allows the editor to automate the capturing workflow, saving time and hard drive space, while tagging clips with descriptive information that will stay attached to the footage as long as it remains in its current digital form.

RENDERING

From time to time during every editing session, the software will need to create new video files in response to the placement of a transition, effect, filter, title, or multilayer composite. This process is called *rendering* (see Figure 14.13). For example,

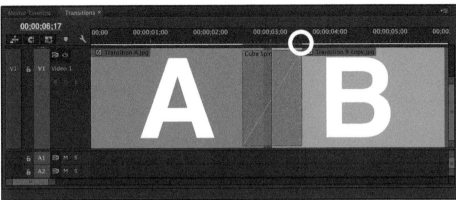

Unrendered Effects and Transitions (red and yellow)

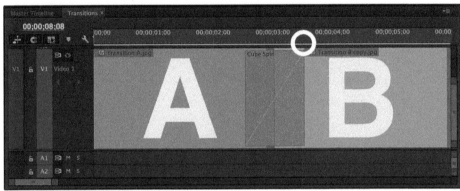

After Rendering (green)

FIGURE 14.13
Top: In Adobe Premiere Pro, a color-coded render bar appears near the top of the timeline to indicate whether or not the underlying clips have been rendered. When the bar is yellow or red, it means the frames associated with a particular clip, transition, or effect have not yet been rendered. Simple effects can be previewed in real time without rendering while more complex ones will need to be rendered first in order to view them smoothly or even at all. Bottom: The render bar turns green once rendering has been successfully completed.
Source: Adobe product screenshot reprinted with permission from Adobe Systems Incorporated.

when a one-second dissolve is attached to two adjacent clips in the timeline, a one-second video clip must be rendered to represent the visual effect.

You can render clips as you go or wait until the end of a project and render everything at once. The more complex the effects and transitions, the longer it will take for rendering to be performed. Depending on the speed of your computer, the NLE can often play back unrendered clips in real time. However, the display quality may be poor because the program has to process the transition or effect on the fly in real time. It's a good idea to stop occasionally throughout a session to render all the unrendered clips in the sequence.

FLASHBACK
NLE Pioneers

Avid Technology is one of the oldest developers of nonlinear editing software. Its flagship program, Media Composer, was released in 1989 and continues to be one of the most recognized NLE applications used in the motion picture and television industries. Adobe's NLE solution is called Premier Pro, which Adobe released in 1991. Adobe's chief competitor, Macromedia, was instrumental in developing a rival NLE called KeyGrip, a product designed to work natively with Apple QuickTime. KeyGrip was renamed Final Cut and eventually sold to Apple, who released it commercially as Final Cut Pro in 1999. While there are many professional NLE solutions to choose from, Avid Media Composer, Adobe Premiere Pro, and Apple Final Cut Pro have stood the test of time and remain three of the most recognized names in nonlinear video editing.

COMPONENTS OF AN NLE INTERFACE
Project Panel

The NLE project panel goes by different names. Look for a window or panel group that allows you to browse all your project media files that are stored on a local or attached hard drive, bins containing your media clips, and other tabs or sections granting you access to clip and sequence information, effects, and global project or session properties. Think of the project panel as command headquarters—the main portal and information vault for everything related to your project. In many respects, it serves a purpose very similar to the OS file browser on your computer—the Finder in Mac OS X or File Explorer on a Windows PC—but from within the application. Through it you can locate and import files into your project, open them in the source monitor, drag them to the timeline, search for and re-link missing clips, and keep track of where everything associated with your project is stored.

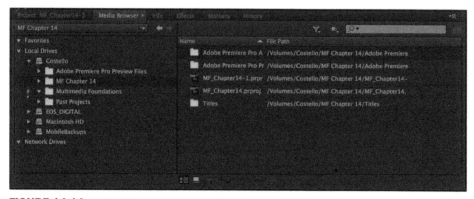

FIGURE 14.14
The Media Browser in Adobe Premiere Pro allows you to locate, view, import, and re-link media files stored on a physical hard drive from within the application.
Source: Adobe product screenshot reprinted with permission from Adobe Systems Incorporated.

Timeline

The *timeline* displays your edited sequence and the position of audio and video clips that are arranged and kept in order on linear regions called *tracks*. When a video clip is added to the timeline, the video portion of the clip is placed on a *video track* while the audio portion is inserted beneath it on an *audio track*. Audio tracks are normally grouped in linked stereo pairs. By default, the first track (or left channel) is sent to the left speaker and the second track (or right channel) is output to the right. Some NLEs combine the left and right audio channels into a single stereo track. When a synchronized video clip (such as an SOT) is placed on the timeline, it usually occupies three adjacent tracks (one video track and two audio tracks). If a single microphone was used in the recording, there will be only one channel of associated audio and thus only one corresponding audio track. A mono track can be easily converted to a dual mono pair by the NLE, sending it to both the left and right speakers.

When editing a video clip containing synchronized audio, you will often want to apply the same action simultaneously to both the video and audio portions of a clip. For example, when a clip is split in two using the splice or razor blade tool, the edit will typically affect all three tracks at once. Likewise, when you reposition a video clip within the timeline, the linked video and audio segments will travel together in tandem, allowing them to remain *in sync*. Problems can occur when video and audio become unsynchronized. Even a slight shift of only a few frames can affect lip-synching in an SOT, causing you and the audience to squirm in momentary discomfort.

Sometimes an editor will choose to unlink a clip in order to control the video and audio separately. For example, you may want to perform a *split edit* by assigning different IN and OUT points to the video and audio clips. This technique is commonly used when editing sound bites. With a split edit, the audience might see a person talking for one to two seconds before they actually hear him or her. Another use of this technique would be to show B-Roll during the first five seconds of a sound bite before cutting to a synchronized headshot of the person speaking. Split edits are performed routinely in editing and are extremely useful. Just remember to re-link the clips when you're finished working with them to prevent accidentally unsynchronizing them later.

In addition to synchronized clips, editors deal with a variety of standalone media assets. Digital images, for example, contain no corresponding audio. They are also static, meaning they have no duration (length), as compared to time-based media assets. Static clips like images, titles, backgrounds, and slugs (a solid black video frame) are automatically converted to time-based video clips when imported or created by the NLE software to allow them to be extended within the timeline to any length the editor desires.

VIDEO COMPOSITING AND AUDIO MIXING

Compositing is the process of combining two or more video tracks together to form a new image or visual effect. Video tracks are used in much the same way as layers in Photoshop to segregate clips into discrete editable regions, thereby allowing the editor to maintain individual control over the settings for each asset and its position in the timeline. In the timeline, tracks are viewed from the top down, meaning that a clip placed on video track 2 (V2) will partially or completely obscure the view of a clip placed beneath it on video track 1 (V1). Let's look at a few examples.

Example 1: A simple two-track composite: The editor begins by placing an SOT on V1, the first video track in the timeline. Next, he inserts a lower-third title graphic above the SOT on V2 (see Figure 14.15). At this point, the program monitor will display a composite image showing the title superimposed over the top of the person speaking. Because each element in the composite image resides on its own track, it can be edited independently without affecting other clips in the timeline.

Example 2: A five-track composite: In this example, a composite image is formed by vertically aligning five clips on adjacent tracks in an edited sequence (see Figure 14.16). First, a gradient background is inserted on V1. Next, a close-up shot of

FIGURE 14.15
Example 1: Adobe Premiere Pro is used to create a two-track composite image comprised of a video clip (V1) and lower-third title graphic (V2). *Source: Adobe product screenshot reprinted with permission from Adobe Systems Incorporated.*

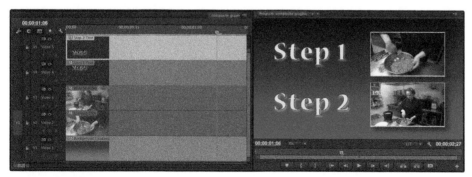

FIGURE 14.16
Example 2: The timeline shown on the left includes five video tracks containing media clips that are aligned to produce the composite graphic on the right. Each track contains one of the five elements used in the composite.
Source: Adobe product screenshot reprinted with permission from Adobe Systems Incorporated.

the host is inserted on V2 and then scaled down and positioned on the right side of the frame. This step is repeated for the wide shot, which is placed on V3. Finally, two text graphics are positioned on tracks V4 and V5 respectively. The composite image shows all five elements co-residing within the frame. Incidentally, the five elements do not have to appear or disappear at the same points in the timeline. The editor can choose a different IN and OUT point for each element. The possibilities are endless.

Mixing is the audio version of compositing. With mixing, multiple audio clips can be combined in an unlimited number of ways to form a complex aural experience. For example, in a motion picture film, an action sequence often contains multiple tracks of dialog, background sounds, music, and sound effects (SFX). Again, let's consider a common example.

Example 3: A four-track stereo mix: Here, we begin a sequence by placing an SOT on the timeline. The audio portion of the SOT resides on A1 (see Figure 14.17). Music is then added to A2 and placed beneath the tracks of the person speaking. In this example, the primary, or foreground audio, is being produced by the SOT. The editor wants it to stand out above the music and sets the A1 audio level to full (100%). Music is a background element and as such should not compete for the audience's attention. The editor adjusts A2 to a lower level that's more appropriate for a background source. As additional sources are added to the sequence, the editor will mix them accordingly until he or she achieves the intended balance and effect called for.

FIGURE 14.17
Example 3: The audio track mixer interface in Adobe Premiere Pro is used for mixing audio from the SOT on A1 with music on A2. The editor needs to set the level of each stereo track pair independently to achieve an aesthetically pleasing mix. Since the SOT is the main element, tracks A1 and A2 are set to normal levels (full). Notice how the music is set much lower to keep it from competing with the main spoken word audio.
Source: Adobe product screenshot reprinted with permission from Adobe Systems Incorporated.

Source and Program Monitors

The NLE interface contains two virtual television monitors. The *source monitor* (sometimes called the preview monitor) sits on the left and is used for reviewing project assets and trimming (shortening) and adjusting them before inserting them as clips on the timeline. Double-clicking on a clip in a bin or on the timeline typically opens it in the source monitor, where edits and changes can be performed. The source monitor can only hold one clip at a time. When you are done working on one, simply double-click on another clip to swap them out. The *program monitor* is positioned to the right and is linked to the timeline. As you play back or scan through an edited sequence in the timeline, the program monitor displays its contents. Likewise, as you scrub the program monitor playhead back and forth, the companion playhead in the timeline moves left and right in perfect unison. The source and program monitors contain a variety of identical virtual controls for viewing, playing, and marking clips.

TRANSPORT CONTROLS

The *transport controls* act in much the same way as the buttons on a VCR or DVD player, allowing you to scan the contents of a time-based media clip. The editor has access to familiar functions like play, pause, stop, rewind, and fast-forward. The transport controls can be activated through keyboard input as well. Experienced editors prefer using keyboard shortcuts because they're generally much quicker to execute than virtual controls. For example, most NLEs allow you to press the keys J, K, and L on your keyboard to scrub through a clip in reverse (J), to pause (K), and to scrub forward (L). *Jog* and *shuttle* are terms used to describe the speed at which you *scrub* (move) through a clip. Jog moves the playhead a few frames at a time or in slow-motion while shuttle advances it rapidly in either direction.

PLAYHEAD

The *playhead* defines your position in a time-based clip. You can scrub slowly or rapidly through a clip by dragging the playhead horizontally in either direction. *Audio scrubbing* allows you to hear the audio portion of a clip as you move the playhead back and forth and is a useful technique for locating sound artifacts or verbal stutters you want to eliminate or isolate in editing (such as um, uh, ah, etc.). The source monitor playhead allows you to scrub through the currently loaded clip. The program monitor playhead allows you to scrub through the entire length of the timeline. Because the program monitor is linked directly to the timeline, moving either playhead causes the other one to move in tandem.

TIMECODE FIELDS

Every frame of video is addressable via *timecode*. Whenever you mark an IN point or OUT point, the location is stored as a numerical series of eight digits denoting hours, minutes, seconds, and frames. A timecode display of 01:18:54:27 indicates a frame location of 1 hour, 18 minutes, 54 seconds, and 27 frames. This format is used to denote the duration of marked clips, transitions, and other program assets. For example, a one-second dissolve would appear as 00:00:01:00 in the duration field.

GREAT IDEAS
NLE Keyboard Shortcuts

Keyboard shortcuts like the ones listed here are relatively common in all NLE programs and help speed up the editing workflow

Keyboard Shortcut	Action
Space bar	Starts or stops the playhead (Play/Pause)
I key	Marks the IN point
O key	Marks the OUT point
J key	Plays backward—pressing multiple times speeds up scrubbing
K key	Stops playing
L key	Plays forward—pressing multiple times speeds up scrubbing
Home key	Moves playhead to the beginning of the sequence
End key	Moves playhead to the end of the sequence
Left/Right arrow	Nudges the playhead one frame to the left or right
Up/Down arrow	Moves the playhead forward or backward to the first or last frame of an adjacent clip

IMAGE FRAME

The largest area of a monitor control interface is reserved for the picture data. What you can do in this region is largely dependent on the features available to you inside your NLE software. Typically, you will be able to transform the size and aspect ratio of the image through scaling, cropping, and wireframe controls. A *wireframe* acts like a bounding box that allows you to freely transform video within the frame—whether it's rotating the image, changing the playback speed, adding a visual affect or filter, or otherwise altering a clip's movement or appearance.

When an audio asset is loaded into preview, the visual interface looks different. Instead of a video image you'll see an audio waveform. A *waveform* is a visual representation of the amplitude signature of the audio clip across time. The height of the waveform indicates the volume level. By looking at the waveform, you can often tell whether audio was recorded at an appropriate level or not (see Figure 14.18). Under-modulated audio (audio that is too soft) will have a short waveform height or perhaps none at all—simply a flat line. Overmodulated audio (audio that is too loud), which may be distorted, will have an intense waveform pattern that extends from the bottom of the track to the top (or from the "floor" to the "ceiling"). A waveform's fluctuations can provide the editor with a visual representation of timing and rhythm, which comes in handy when setting IN and

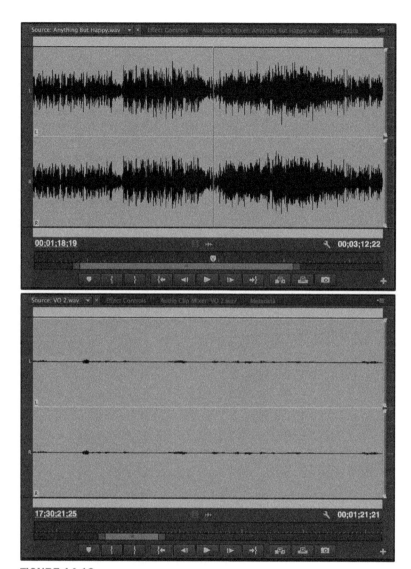

FIGURE 14.18
When audio is loaded into the source monitor in Adobe Premiere Pro, it appears on screen as
a virtual waveform. Top: Visually, this waveform suggests that the audio levels are properly set.
Bottom: This waveform looks relatively flat, suggesting the recording was severely under-modulated.
Source: Adobe product screenshot reprinted with permission from Adobe Systems Incorporated.

OUT points. In a music clip, the waveform can reveal the beat structure and tempo
of a selection, providing visual cues for determining transition points. In addition
to having a waveform on the timeline, audio and video editing software includes
a VU (volume-units) meter to let you monitor the loudness of a source objectively
in decibel units.

ADDING CLIPS TO THE TIMELINE

Video editing can be compared to the process of building a car on an assembly line. Before production can begin, all the individual automobile parts must be designed, constructed, and set out in proper order on an assembly line. The order of assembly is critically important, as a car is built from the inside out one part at a time. The chassis comes first and serves as the skeletal framework that all other parts connect to in one way or another. Tools are used to secure parts to the chassis. In editing, you can think of clips as car parts and the timeline as the chassis. Clips are constructed in the source monitor where they are trimmed and marked before inserting them into the timeline from end to end. Tools are used in editing to add clips to the timeline, move and trim clips, and modify their behavior. Program length is determined by the combined duration of all of the clips in the timeline from left to right.

There is no single prescribed method or workflow for constructing an edited sequence, as each genre and story have their own unique structure and content. However, the editing process usually starts with establishing a simple ordered sequence of clips from beginning to end and then going through it again and again in a series of passes to advance it from a simple rough cut to a polished finished edited master. Each pass is additive, building upon previous work performed during an earlier stage in the editing process. No matter what process you adopt, try to be systematic, orderly, and deliberate in how you edit and the workflows you employ. As an example, consider the following process involving six editing stages or passes.

First Pass—Construct the Primary Audio Narrative

The primary audio portion of a program is often constructed first by inserting the spoken word or performance-based segments of a story such as dialog, sound bites (SOTs), narration, and voiceovers into the timeline in sequential order from the beginning to the end. Think of audio as the wheels of the chassis on top of which everything else rides. The tracks in the timeline are even structured in this way, with video tracks located in the top half of the timeline and audio tracks below. Audio serves as a cue to help inform editing decisions—for example, where to position the beginning or end of a media clip. It's generally a bad idea to cut from one shot to another in the middle of a spoken word or sentence. Taking a cue from an SOT or music track, a better approach would be to time the cut to occur at a natural break in the conversation or in conjunction with a significant shift or transition in the tempo or rhythm of the audio soundtrack—such as during a pause or breath between spoken words or just before or after a sound effect, music stinger, or particular beat in a musical score.

Second Pass—Insert B-Roll and Natural Sound

With the primary audio portion of the narrative in place, you are ready to jump back to the head of the timeline to begin inserting B-Roll and natural sound. One purpose of B-Roll is to fill in holes in the video track where only audio currently exists—for example, above a voiceover or narration clip. Another use of B-Roll is to cover the video portion of a talking head (or SOT), in whole or in part, and to hide any visual jump cuts that resulted from cutting together non-adjacent segments of an audio interview.

Third Pass—Insert Titles and Graphics

Once all your video clips are in position in the timeline, you can begin inserting lower-thirds and graphics. If a title or graphic is to be superimposed with an underlying video clip, be sure to place it on the track immediately above the corresponding clip. If your project includes several lower-thirds—each identifying a different subject—then consider using the first title as a template for constructing the others. Doing so will ensure that the duration of your titles and their corresponding font and style attributes are consistent throughout the program. Begin by editing the first title and adding it to the timeline. Next, use the copy and paste function to duplicate the title clip. Open this clip in the title editor to change the text identifiers to match the second subject—repeating this step for as many titles you have in the project. This method is much faster than creating each individual title from scratch when you have a series of identically formatted graphics.

A graphic should appear on screen long enough for the viewer to read it. For lower-thirds, five to seven seconds generally does the trick. Also, it's good practice to establish the subject on screen for at least one second before superimposing the title. Likewise, take down the super before cutting to another shot. Finally, consider fading lower-thirds in and out rather than using a hard cut, as the gradual transition of a fade is far less abrupt.

Fourth Pass—Add Sound Effects and Music

Not every project requires music and sound effects, but when you want to include them in a project, it is usually better to hold off doing so until the basic structure of your story is sufficiently developed. An exception to this, of course, is a music video or a musical segment that is a part of a longer sequence. In such cases, a recorded song serves as the primary audio and needs to be placed on the timeline first before inserting video. This way the beat structure of the song can be used for timing the duration and placement of video clips and transitions. When using SFXs and music as a secondary or background audio source, they should be mixed with primary audio at an appropriate level so as not to compete with or distract from the main subject or message.

Fifth Pass—Add Transitions and Effects

Once all your clips have been inserted into the timeline and you are satisfied with their placement, you can begin the process of adding transitions and effects. Trimming and repositioning clips after transitions have been attached can be difficult and time-consuming, so it's best to add them near the backend of postproduction. Likewise, adding effects prematurely to clips—before you have to—can slow down the editing process. Effects usually require rendering, and the more effects accumulate as your timeline grows, the longer it can take to render them, and the more often you will find yourself having to pause from editing to do so.

Sixth Pass—Finishing Touches

Before closing out an editing project, there will be lots of nitty-gritty details to attend to. You will spend lots of time making minute adjustments to the placement of clips and the timing of transitions, titles, effects, and so forth as you work to refine and polish the overall presentation. You may also need to perform color correction to fix, enhance, or alter the color properties of video clips and their consistency across the length of your program. With audio, you will likely have to tweak levels and add sound processing filters and plug-ins to improve individual audio clips or the overall mix of the composite soundtrack. Finally, you will need to perform a final comprehensive rendering of every clip in the timeline before exporting the project to a distribution format.

GREAT IDEAS

Track Management

Table 14.1 shows an example of a track management scheme you could adopt for assigning video and audio tracks to specific types of content. Organizing your tracks this way will help keep your timeline looking logically ordered and uncluttered. It's a good practice to assign specific types of content to dedicated video and audio tracks and to be consistent throughout the project from beginning to end. Doing so will ensure your timeline is constructed in an orderly and logical manner, making it easier for you and others to navigate within it as the project sequence grows. Failing to properly manage your timeline—the placement of clips and the assignment of tracks—will result in a timeline or sequence that is visually cluttered, chaotic, and poorly constructed.

Table 14.1	Assigning Tracks in the Project Timeline
Video Track 3 (V3)	Titles/Graphics
Video Track 2 (V2)	B-Roll
Video Track 1 (V1)	SOT Video
Audio Track 1 (A1)	SOT Audio and Voiceovers (L)
Audio Track 2 (A2)	SOT Audio and Voiceovers (R)
Audio Track 3 (A3)	Natural Sound (L)
Audio Track 4 (A4)	Natural Sound (R)
Audio Track 5 (A5)	Sound Effects (L)
Audio Track 6 (A6)	Sound Effects (R)
Audio Track 7 (A7)	Music (L)
Audio Track 8 (A8)	Music (R)

FIGURE 14.19
This close-up view of the source monitor in Adobe Premiere Pro illustrates the process of trimming. The original video clip is 0002:56:00 in length. The editor isolates a 20-second sound bite by marking an IN point at the beginning of the sound bite and an OUT point at the end.
Source: Adobe product screenshot reprinted with permission from Adobe Systems Incorporated.

FIGURE 14.20
When the edit is performed, only the 20-second portion of the clip that's been marked will be inserted in the timeline. Trimming clips prior to putting them in the timeline is highly recommended. While you can also trim directly in the timeline, it is best to do so only to fine-tune your initial edit decisions.
Source: Adobe product screenshot reprinted with permission from Adobe Systems Incorporated.

THREE-POINT EDITING

Let's assume all the constituent parts for our video (our media clips) have been created and imported into the project window and have been properly logged, labeled, and organized. Where do we go from here? While it's possible to start dragging clips willy-nilly from the project bin into the timeline, this is a bad habit and promotes an unproductive workflow. The original media clips you acquired are raw and uncut—and should be marked and trimmed prior to inserting them in the timeline, not afterward. Instead, work through your footage methodically, opening your clips one at a time in the source monitor of your NLE. Here, you can preview them and make thoughtful decisions about what portion of each clip to include in the timeline. To illustrate, let's walk through the process of editing a basic sequence comprised of three clips: a voiceover, a sound bite, and a second voiceover. To do this, we'll use the standard editing technique of *three-point editing*. (**Note:** You can view this editing demonstration on the companion website for this textbook.)

Step 1: Set an IN Point and OUT Point in the Source Monitor

I begin by opening the voiceover clip in the source monitor. The clip is more than five minutes long and contains numerous voiceover segments along with several takes of each one. In the end, I will not use most of the content in this clip. I only need to extract a few choice sound bites for my project. I scrub the playhead to the first voiceover (VO #1) and set an **IN point** by pressing the *I* key on my keyboard. Next, I move the playhead to the end of VO #1 and set an **OUT point** by pressing the *O* key on my keyboard. The marked clip has a duration of 00:00:20:10 and is ready to be inserted into the timeline (see Figure 14.21, top).

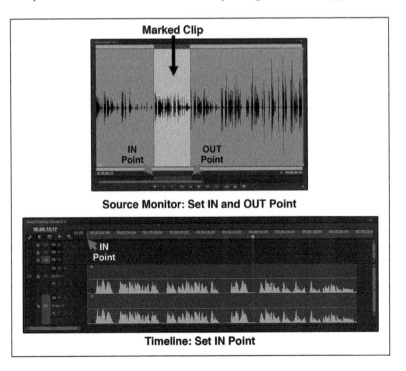

FIGURE 14.21
Top (Step 1): An IN and OUT point are set to mark the beginning and end of the 20-second clip in the source monitor. Bottom (Steps 2 and 3): An IN point is set on the timeline and then the edit is performed.
Source: Adobe product screenshot reprinted with permission from Adobe Systems Incorporated.

Step 2: Set an IN Point in the Timeline

Next, I change the focus of the NLE to the timeline by clicking on it. Since this is my first edit, setting the IN point is relatively easy. I advance the playhead one second into the timeline and press *I* on my keyboard to mark the **IN point** (see Figure 14.21, bottom). With three points marked, the NLE has enough information to automatically calculate the timeline OUT point. For this reason, I do not have to specify it. In fact, when using this method of editing, a fourth point is never required and should never be entered. Hence the term . . . three-point editing.

Step 3: Perform the Edit

With three points marked, I'm ready to perform the edit. Presto! Just like that, a new 30-second clip is added to the timeline at precisely the right spot (see Figure 14.21, bottom). The original three-minute clip remains in the project bin for future use and will remain visible in the source monitor until I load a different project asset. Keep in mind that the newly created clip is merely an alias, a visual representation of a pointer file that can be changed at any time without affecting the corresponding media file stored on my hard drive. I can work with the clip directly in the timeline—repositioning it or trimming it or extending it as required. I can also load it back into the source monitor by double-clicking on it. As your project evolves, the number of clips and aliases you have access to will steadily increase. You need to keep track of which clip is loaded into the source monitor at any one time. It's easy to get confused and make mistakes by inadvertently editing the wrong project asset or timeline clip.

Step 4: Repeat Steps 1 through 3 for SOT #2 and VO #2

The next step in this example is to repeat steps 1 through 3 for the remaining clips in the sequence (see Figure 14.22). On the timeline, the **IN point** for each subsequent edit will be the **OUT point** of the previous one. This will ensure that each clip is butted tightly against the other with no empty frames in between.

Step 5: Add B-Roll over VO Segments

Once the three clips have been added to my sequence, I return to the beginning of the timeline and start inserting B-Roll over each voiceover segment (see Figure 14.23). To keep from overwriting the voiceover clips on A1 and A2, natural sound is placed beneath these tracks on A3 and A4.

FIGURE 14.22
Step 4: Repeat the first three steps until you complete the first pass for a simple VO-SOT-VO sequence.
Source: Adobe product screenshot reprinted with permission from Adobe Systems Incorporated.

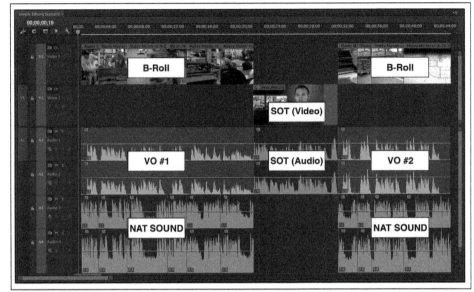

FIGURE 14.23
Step 5: The completed sequence with the inclusion of B-Roll and natural sound.
Source: Adobe product screenshot reprinted with permission from Adobe Systems Incorporated.

When editing B-Roll, I slightly modify my three-point editing technique. Since my goal now is to fill precise gaps or segments in the timeline sequence, I want to set **IN** and **OUT points** on the timeline first. Next, in the source monitor, I mark only an **IN point** to designate the starting frame of each B-Roll clip. The clip will end when it reaches the OUT point as designated on the timeline.

TRANSITIONS

A *transition* is a visual effect applied to the timeline at the beginning or end of a video or audio clip. Transitions are used to enhance the flow and rhythm of a project and to guide the viewer's senses through changes in the narrative structure of a story as it unfolds (see Figure 14.24).

Cut

The most common transition is called a *cut*. A cut is an instantaneous transition from the end of one shot to the beginning of another shot. Because of this, a cut has no duration per se. In fact, you can think of a cut as the invisible transition. Cuts are popular with editors because of their simplicity. When properly timed, the audience will hardly know a cut has occurred. As we've already discussed, however, cutting in the middle of a word or sentence, or on an awkward beat in the underscore, can disrupt continuity and be self-defeating. Most often, the editor's goal is to make the presence of a cut invisible to the audience. Remember, the best edits are often the ones you don't notice. Incidentally, the first beat of a bar, called the downbeat, is the strongest point in a melody line and a great location for the placement of a cut or other transition.

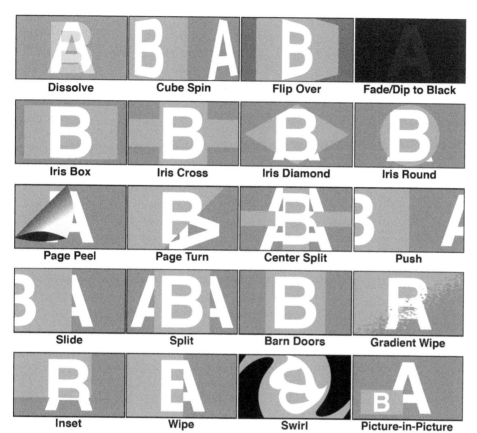

FIGURE 14.24
These icons represent many of the standard video transitions included in Adobe Premiere Pro CC.

Fade

The absence of picture data on a television screen is referred to as *black*. A *slug* is a media clip comprised entirely of black frames. A slug (of any length) can be inserted into the timeline as a clip separator—as a way of signaling a key transition or scene change—in much the same way that a lighting blackout is used during a theatrical production to herald the beginning or end of a scene or act. Programs usually begin and end in black with a *fade* providing the transition. A *fade up* is a gradual transition from black to a fully opaque television image, while a *fade down* is a gradual transition in the opposite direction. Video and audio fades often occur simultaneously. For example, in an end-of-program fade to black, the video image should reach 100% black at precisely the same time the audio signal is fully muted. For this reason, it is standard practice to use the same duration time for both the video and audio portions of a fade.

Dissolve

A *dissolve* is a gradual transition from one shot to another that is created by over-lapping the fade down of one clip with the fade up of the next adjacent clip in a sequence. Dissolves are less abrupt than cuts and are often used to signify a change in time, a change of location, or a change in tempo. Dissolves can be used to slow the pace of a program when a gentler timing structure or rhythm is called for. Short dissolves of less than 10 frames can be used in place of a cut to soften a transition without necessarily affecting an otherwise upbeat tempo. The longer the duration of a dissolve, the more dramatic and pronounced the effect.

Wipe

Most other transitions fall into the category of wipes or *3D effects*. A *wipe* uses a linear movement or sweeping pattern to transition from one image to another. For example a *vertical wipe* moves from the top of the frame down, or from the bottom of the frame up, as it overwrites the current image with new pixels. A *horizontal wipe* does the same thing by sweeping left to right or right to left. A *circle wipe* moves in a radial direction from the center of the image outward and vice versa. Wipes come in a virtually unlimited assortment of shapes and patterns. There are *checkerboard* wipes, *clock* wipes, and *slide* wipes, which push the entire frame of video off-screen. A *spin* wipe is used to rotate the video frame as it moves out of view, while an *explosion* wipe shatters the picture into pieces before sending them off in every direction. If your selection of wipes is limited, chances are that a third-party software developer has produced wipes for your NLE that can be obtained for free or purchased and downloaded for a fee.

Like wipes, *3D transitions* come in all shapes and sizes. Using powerful algorithms, video can be squished, stretched, warped, morphed, and distorted in any number of ways to achieve creative and unusual visual effects. *Page peel* transitions curl the edge of the video frame inward to simulate turning pages in a book. *Cube spin* transitions turn the video frame into a rotating object with multiple sides displaying different images or picture data. The list goes on and on.

Wipes and 3D transitions are visually very cool. They are fun to play with and can add legitimate value to a visual experience for the viewer. However, you must use them with caution. Anything you add into the video timeline should be motivated by the story and the impact you wish to make on the viewer. Simply throwing things into an edited sequence because you can, or because they look cool, is not necessarily going to make the end product look any more professional or be any more effective. In fact, it may backfire, producing a negative effect. Until you have more experience, stick with cuts and dissolves—and whatever you do, be consistent in terms of when and where you apply visual transitions. Do not use a pinwheel wipe in the first transition, a page peel in the second, and exploding video in the third. This sort of sporadic and random use of transitions will only confuse the viewer or overwhelm his or her visual senses. As we've said before, less is more!

Transition Properties

Once a transition has been added to the timeline, it becomes a customizable asset with properties that can be easily changed. Transition values are saved in a data file that's stored in the render folder. While most transitions will play back in real time, at some point before exporting your project, you will need to fully render them.

Once rendered, they will perform more smoothly and appear sharper when playing them in the timeline.

The most important property you need to pay attention to is the transition duration. *Duration* is the amount of time a transition takes to perform from beginning to end, as indicated in seconds and frames. The default transition in most programs is one second (or 30 frames). When adding a dissolve between two clips, I often use a 20-frame duration, which is roughly two-thirds of a second. This duration serves me well most of the time. For something particularly dramatic, I might use a longer increment of one to three seconds. Only rarely will I use anything longer. You need to remember that transitions take time to execute and that this can affect the runtime of your project, consuming precious seconds and minutes over the course of a long program. For example, in a 60-second commercial spot with 10 default transitions, one-sixth of the presentation will be taken up by transitions. The simple act of changing the default duration from one second to 15 frames will give you five additional seconds to work with. Think about it: 5 seconds in a 60-second spot is a lot of time.

In addition to the duration property, you can adjust a number of other variables. For example, you can change the direction of an edge wipe, causing it to start from the left, right, top, or bottom of the frame. The properties you have access to will depend on the transition you're working with. Each transition is unique and therefore has different parameters and values you can adjust or manipulate to change the way it performs.

When applying a transition, make sure the adjoining clips you're attaching it to are connected. If there's a gap between the two clips that you can't see—perhaps because you're zoomed out too far—then the transition may not attach. Zooming in to the timeline for a close-up view of the transition point is really helpful. Once attached, transitions become modular visual objects you can modify.

CHAPTER SUMMARY

Not surprisingly, you'll find that the NLE interface varies from program to program. What doesn't change, however, are good editing practices. For example, the technique of using a cutaway or B-Roll to mask a jump cut won't become irrelevant simply because you switch from Avid Media Composer to Adobe Premiere Pro—nor will it eradicate the need to carefully monitor your audio levels in post. For the most part, you will find that the core concepts and aesthetics of editing are the very things that influenced the design of whatever NLE you're using—along with the hodgepodge of tools and features they include. Most professional programs include a timeline for arranging clips linearly from beginning to end, a media browser or library to organize your project assets into bins, a source monitor to mark and trim clips, and a program monitor to review and keep track of your progress. While you need to become familiar with the operational features and functions of the NLE you're using, applying good practices and principles to your project—such as three-point editing—is far more important.

NOTE

1 Puttnam, D. (Producer), & Hudson, H. (Director). (1981). *Chariots of Fire* [Motion picture]. USA and Canada: 20th Century Fox.

Index

180-degree rule 420
35mm film 296, 301–2
3D *see* three-dimensional (3D)

above the fold 180, 181
A/B Roll editing system 443
absolute URL 219–20
accessibility: interfaces 196–8; web design 229–30
accordions: navigation 177, 178
action safe area 449, 450
active autofocusing 315
Adams, Ansel 84, 293
adapters: audio connectors 397
A/D conversion 394
additive color mixing 270
Adobe Illustrator 10, 101, 115, 252, 258, 266
Adobe Photoshop 10, 29–30, 32, 35–6, 48–9, 51, 258, 260, 448; application-specific shortcuts 61; Character panel 249; color picker 271; Glyphs panel 245; mockup 101–2; raster images 266; scaling 275; space 115, 117; system requirements for 50
Adobe Premiere Pro 10, 54, 337, 442–3, 449, 452–9, 461–2, 465, 469, 473, 475
Advanced Audio Coding (AAC) 345
Advanced Research Projects Agency (ARPA) 202
Advanced Video Coding (AVC) 346
aesthetics 113–14
agency: interactivity 168, 189
algorithm 28
aliasing 254, 276
alignment: principle of unity 130; text 257, 258
ALL CAPS: font styles 250–1
Allen, Paul 41
alpha channel 448
alt attributes 230
alternative text 197, 221, 230, 246, 251
alt tags 230
ambient sound 383, 386, 446

amplitude: sound 373–4
analog 28
analog signal: microphone 378
analog tape formats 334
analog television: legacy of 289
analysis: user-centered design 95–8
anchor 218
Android OS 39, 47–9, 172, 361
angle of view 121, 297–8, 299, 301, 409, 427
animated GIF 11
animation 11
anti-aliasing 254, 276
aperture 299; exposure 309–10
aperture priority mode: exposure modes 321
aperture size 317
app 25, 49
Apple Computer 42
Apple Final Cut Pro 10, 54, 442–3, 452–3, 459
Apple iCloud 70, 71
Apple iOS 47, 197
Apple Lisa 5, 56, 57
application software 48–9
APS-C (Advanced Photo System Type-C): image sensor 297–8, 300–2
arc: secondary motion 429–30
archives 185–6
ARPANET 202
ascender: letterform parts 240
ASCII (American Standard Code for Information Interchange) 44–5
ASP (Active Server Pages) 228
aspect ratio 116–17, 138, 283–4
asymmetrical balance 136–7
ATSC (Advanced Television Systems Committee) 290–1, 292, 345, 347
attribute: tag 205, 206, 208, 218, 221–2, 224
audience 21–4, 79–81, 81
audio 10–11; audio book 14; compression 344, 345; encoding settings 357–8; mixing 460–2; scrubbing 463; sweetening 92, 468

audio connectors: adapters 397; balanced 395–6; cable management 398; RCA connectors 396; tip, ring, and sleeve (TRS) 396; tip and sleep (TS) 396; unbalanced 396–7; XLR 396
Audio Interchange File Format (AIFF) 352–3
audio production: audio 371–2; audio connectors 395–8; audio monitoring 398–402; microphones 376–94; monitoring record levels using volume-unit (VU) meter 398–401; monitoring with headphones or speakers 401–2; over-under wrap 399; sound 371–6; sound check 401; *see also* microphones
audio track 333, 460; management 468
augmented reality (AR) 173–4, 175
autofocus 315
automatic gain control (AGC) 399
automatic modes: exposure 318–20
automation 32–4
auto white balance (AWB) 312, 363
AVCHD 338, 351–2, 353
Avid Media Composer 10, 54, 442–3, 452–3, 456, 459, 475
AV script 86–7
axis of action 420
axis of orientation 145

backlight 410–11, 436–7
Baidu Eye 175
balance: perceptual forces 136
balanced audio 395–6
bandwidth 73
baseline: letterform parts 240
baseline shift 253
batch computing 40
batch processing 34
benchmarking 97
Berners-Lee, Tim 11, 12, 15, 201, 202
beveling 125, 258; font transformations 259
bidirectional microphone 382, 383

bit (Binary digIT) 43
bit depth: digital audio 339–43, 357–8
bitmap image 266–7
bit rate 342–3; video encoding 357
bitstream 337
Blackletter typeface 241–2, 246
block-level elements 207, 208
blogging 17
Blu-ray disc 68
Blu-ray Disc Association 291
body copy: chunking 149
body tag: HTML document 206
boldface 240; font styles 249–50
boom pole 388–90
boot sequence 47
border property: tables and CSS box model 160, 161
boundary microphone 390
box model: Cascading Style Sheets (CSS) 161
breadcrumbs: navigation 176, 179–80
Bresson, Robert 403
brightness 127
broadcasting 22
B-roll 409, 410, 424; adding over voiceover segments 471–2; edited sequence 445–6; inserting 466–7; natural sound and 408; tips for shooting great 430–1
browsers 211–12
button 220, 222, 224, 227, 228
byte 44–5

cable management 398, 399
camera: angle 409; focal length 411–12; location 406–8; shot designations 421–4; subject location 409–11
Camera RAW 303
canted angle 122
capline 240
capture files 456–7
cardioid microphone 382, 383
card sorting 99–100
carousel interface: navigation 182–4
Cartier-Bresson, Henri 303
Cascading Style Sheets (CSS) 157, 159, 186, 198, 203–4; box model 161; controlling appearance 223–5; graphical user interfaces 169; menus 176
cells: tables 159
centered text 257, 258

center-weighted metering mode: measuring light intensity 307
central processing unit (CPU) 49, 51
character reference 210
checkboxes: forms 187
checkerboard wipe 474
chroma keying 448
chunking body copy 149
cinema standards: moving pictures 287–91
Clark, Jim 371
clickstream 189
client: 82–3; client team 95
clipping: audio monitoring 400
clip 455–6; adding to timeline 466–8
clock speed 51
clock wipe 474
close-up (CU) 422–4
cloud content management systems (CMS) 70–1
cloud storage 65, 71, 72
CMYK (Cyan, Magenta, Yellow and Black) color model 270
codec (coder-decoder) 337–8
collaborative filtering 189
color: additive mixing 270; correction 92, 468; design element 127–8; dimensions of 127; font 253; gradients 258; principle of emphasis 134; subtractive color mixing 270
color depth 270–1
color space 270–1
color temperature 124, 313
columns: grid 155; tables 159
command line interface (CLI) 55
communication 4, 6, 27–9, 31; S-M-C-R model of 79; see also visual communication
compact disc (CD-ROM) 66–8
Compact Flash (CF) card 323
compositing 460–1
composition 115; rule of thirds 138
compression 277–9; audio 344, 345; image 302–3; video 346–7
compression phase: frequency 375
computer: application software 48–9; connecting drives and devices 72–5; hardware and software 46–55; hardware basics 50–5; human interface 55–61; inside the box 49–50
computer graphics 263
condensed typeface: font styles 250

condenser microphone 379, 380
consumer cameras 294–5
consumer-generated media (CGM) 20
consumers 81
container format 331, 337–8, 346, 348, 352–3, 356
content and form 110, 112–13
content management system (CMS) 164
content sharing 17
continuation: perceptual forces 139
contrast: letterform parts 239–40; principle of emphasis 132–4
control track 333
copy: page layout 143
copyright 92
cosmetic customization 189
counter: letterform parts 240
counterform 240
coverage 417, 435
cover shot 408, 419, 443
creativity 78–9
crop factor 301
cropping 275
crossing the line 420
cross-shots 419, 420
C-stand 434
CTSS (Compatible Time Sharing System) 40
cube spin 474
cultural transcoding 36
customization 189–91
cut: video transitions 472
cutaway 408, 409, 443, 445, 450, 475
cut-ins 450–1
cuts-only editing system 443
cutting on action 450–1

data mining 170, 189
decibel (dB) 367, 373, 374, 400, 465
decisive moment 303–4
declarations: HTML document 206
decorative typefaces 244, 247
de-interlace 356
democratization of media 20
demographics 94
deployment: user-centered design 105
depth: principle of emphasis 134
depth of field (DOF) 134, 316–18
Dery, Mark 331
descender: letterform parts 240

design 98–105; mockup 101, 102, 103; prototype 104–5; user-centered 99–100; wireframe 100–101, 102, 103

designated market area (DMA) 21–2

design elements: color 127–8; composition 115; dot 118–19; form 123–5; line 120–2; pattern 126–7; positive and negative space 118; shape 122–3; space 115–18; texture 125–6; two-dimensional space (2D) 116–17

design principles: alignment 130; asymmetrical balance 136–7; balance 136; color 134; continuation 139; contrast and value 132–4; depth 134; emphasis 132–5; perception forces 136–40; proportion 134–5; proximity 129; psychological closure 140; repetition 130–1; rule of thirds 138; similarity 130, 131; symmetrical balance 136, 137; unity 128–31

device settings 354–8; acronym FWIGSS 358–70; audio encoding settings 357–8; bit rate 357; frame rate 357; frame size 356; recording format 356; resolution 356; scanning method 356; video encoding settings 356–7

digital audio encoding 339–43; pulse-code modulation 339–43

digital camera 293: acronym FWIGSS 358–70; DSLR 295; exposure 305–11; exposure modes 318–21; image folders 327–8; renaming images 327; solid-state memory cards 323–4; video cameras 296; see also imaging chain

Digital Cinema Initiatives, LLC (DCI) 291

digital files: cloud storage 71, 72; collaboration 72; file management 64; file sharing 71, 72; fixed storage 65; flash memory 68–9; magnetic storage 69–71; optical disk 66–8; removable storage 66; saving and managing 61–2, 65–72; storage solutions 65–72; synchronization 72

digital images: management 325, 327–8; metadata 326–7; transferring and managing 325–8

digital imaging 264–82: raster images 266, 267–80; vector graphics 266, 280–2

digital revolution 43–5; from bits to bytes 44–5

digital single lens reflex (DSLR) 294–7, 300–302, 393, 426, 429; autofocus 315; exposure mode 318; memory card 323; optical viewfinder 406; recording format 337; settings 58, 361, 367

digital tape formats 334

Digital Television (DTV) 289–90

digital versatile disc (DVD) 68, 92; menu 144, 165, 169; transport controls 463; video 342, 345

digital zoom 299

digitization 32

direct-attached storage (DAS) 65

director 90

display screen standards 282–4; aspect ratio 283–4, 285

dissolve: video transitions 473–4

distribution: text 257

dithering 280

Divine Proportion 151

Dolby Digital (AC3) 345

dolly: secondary motion 428–9

domain name 212–13

dot: design element 118–19

Dreamweaver 176, 203, 224, 228, 230–1, 240

dropdown lists: forms 187

dropdown menus 177, 178

drop shadow: font transformations 259, 260; graphic design 125, 134, 280; text 258, 449

DSLR see digital single lens reflex

dummy text 101, 161

duration: transition properties 475

Dutch tilt 122

DVB (Digital Video Broadcasting) 291, 345, 347

DVD see digital versatile disc (DVD)

Dvorak, John C. 441

dynamic microphone 378–9

dynamic page 164

dynamic range 375, 400

editing: nonlinear (NLE) 441–3; see also time-based editing

EDTV (enhanced definition television) 290

effects 467

electret condenser microphone 380

Electronic Numerical Integrator and Calculator (ENIAC) 40, 41

element: HTML 202, 204, 205–9, 216–17, 218, 221–2, 228–9

email: creating link in HTML 221

embossing 243, 259

emphasis 128, 132–5; color 134; contrast and value 132–4; depth 134; proportion 134–5

encoding 337

Engelbart, Douglas 3, 55

equalization: sound systems 377

establishing shot 408, 422, 431, 443

evaluative metering mode: measuring light intensity 307

EXIF (Exchangeable Image File Format) 326

executive producer 83

expanded typeface: font styles 250

exposure: aperture 309–10; digital camera 305–11; flash control 307–8; iris 364; measuring light intensity 307; meter 307; triangle 308–11; value 308, 309

exposure modes: action 319; aperture priority 321; automatic 318–20; digital camera 318–21; fully automatic 318; landscape 319; manual 321; night 320; portrait 319; program 321; semi-automatic 321; shutter priority 321, 322; sports 319

extreme wide shot (EWS) 422

fade: video transitions 473

falloff: lighting 125, 436–7

fat footer 181

faux font styles 248–9

favicons 279

feedback: soliciting and applying 194–5

Fetter, William 263

field: interlaced scanning 287

field of view 116, 405–12; camera angle 409; camera location 406–8; focal length 411–12; subject location 409–11

figure-ground: perceptual forces 134, 136, 139–40

file: file manager 62–3; format 337; management 64; naming conventions 214; sharing 71, 72; system 62–3

file-based recording formats 337–8

File Transfer Protocol (FTP) 201, 212, 213, 230–1

filler text 161
fill flash 307–8
fill light 407, 435, 436–7, 439
film 10, 368; video *vs.* 403–4
film grammar 414–19; frame 414; scene 416–17; sequence 417–19; shot 415; take 415
FiLMiC Pro 355
film speed 310–11, 317
Firewire 69, 73–4
firmware 46, 350
fisheye lens 297, 298, 301
fixed focal-length lenses 297–8
fixed layouts 164–5
fixed storage 65
flags: light modification tools 433–4
flash control 307–8
flash memory 68–9
F-layout 145–7
flicker fusion threshold 287–8
floating graphic 157
fluid layouts 165
fluorescent lamps 438–9
flush left 257, 258
focal length 304, 310, 317, 318; field of view 411–12
focal length multiplier (FLM) 301–2
focal point 128, 132, 138
focus: autofocus (AF) 315; autofocus and manual mode 359–61; camera functions 358, 359–62; manual 316; rack 362; zoom controls 361, 362
focus control 315–16
focus mode 315, 355
folders: managing digital files 56, 62, 64
follow focus 91, 351, 361
font 236; color 253; family 236, 237; management 254–5; size 251–2; transformations 258–9, 260
Font Book 255
font styles 248–55; ALL CAPS or SMALL CAPS 250–1; anti-aliasing 254; baseline shift 253, 254; boldface 249–50; condensed or expanded type 250; font color 253; italics 249–50; management 254–5; size 251–2; strikethrough 251; superscript/subscript 254; true and faux 248–9; underline 251
footers: website interface 180–1
form: content and form 110, 112–13; design element 123–5

formal balance 136
form factor: microphones 383–90
forms: interface component 187–8
frame: film grammar 41; image 116, 121, 136, 138, 464–5; raster scanning 285
frame rate 287, 290, 347, 352, 356, 357, 368; video encoding 357
frame size: video encoding 356
freeze frame 414
frequency: sound 374, 375–6
Fresnel: lighting instruments 438, 439, 440
f-stop 309–10
full-frame image sensor 300
full-screen graphic 448
fully automatic mode: exposure modes 318
functional customization 190
FWIGSS: acronym for digital device 358–70; focus 358, 359–62; gain 358, 367; iris 358, 364–7; shutter speed 358, 367–8; sound 358, 368–70; white balance 358, 362–3, 364

gain: camera function 358, 367; sound system 377
Garalde typeface 242
Garrett, Jesse James 81
Gates, Bill 41, 77, 113
geometric shapes 122, 123
Gestalt psychology 128, 139, 263
gestures 56, 171, 173, 175, 183
GIF 11, 32, 35, 63, 246, 338, 448; animated, 11; raster image format 266, 280
gigabyte 62
Golden Ratio 151
Google 9; Google Drive 70, 71; Google Glass 174, 175
Gothic 241
GPS (Global Positioning System) 173, 285
gradient fill: font transformations 259
graphical user interface (GUI) 55–7, 168
graphics 9–10, 263, 264, 467; designing for television 449–50; digital imaging 264–82; graphics card 54; graphics processing units (GPUs) 54–5; graphic vectors 139; video 447–50
grayscale 127

great depth of field 316
gridline 117, 153, 257
grid system 152–9; anatomy of 155; common structures 155–6; graph paper 153, 154; modular grid 158–9; multicolumn grid 156–7; single-column grid 156
Gutenberg diagram 145
Gutenberg, Johannes 235, 236–8, 241–2

halftone image 119
Hall, Justin Allyn 39
handheld microphone 384–5
handheld shot 426–7, 431
hard-disk drive (HDD) 65
hard light 125, 432–3
hardware 46; basics 50–5; CPU 51; inside the box 49–50; system memory 52–5
hashtag 9
HDTV (high-definition television) 290, 345, 347
head: HTML document 206
headings 149
headline 149
headphones: audio monitoring 401–2
headroom 423–4
hierarchy: visual 148; websites 214–15
high-angle shot 409, 421
high-key image 133
horizontal dropdown menus: navigation 177, 178
horizontal wipe 474
hue 127
human-computer interaction (HCI) 167
human interface: computers 55–61; graphical user interface (GUI) 55–7; keyboard 57–61; mouse 55–7
human interface device (HID) 55
Humanist typeface 242, 246
human vision: peripheral 405; understanding 404–5
hypercardioid microphone 382, 383
hyperlinks: adding image information 221–2; creating and managing 218–22; email links 221; linking images 221–2; linking to external sites 220; linking within the website 218–20; navigation bar 220

hypermedia 8
Hypertext Markup Language (HTML) 7, 168, 202; basic elements 205; body 206; declarations 206; demystifying code 202–9; head 206, 208; HTML5 202; sections of document 206
hypertext reference 218
Hypertext Transfer Protocol (HTTP) 212–13

IBM PC 41
illusion of apparent motion 287–8
image 263, 264
image frame 464–5
image optimization 279
image sensor 295, 296, 299, 300–4; compression 302–3; image encoding 302–3; image resolution 302; sensor size 300, 301
image stabilization: photography 322–3
imaging chain: compression 302–3; decisive moment 303–4; digital camera 296–304; image encoding 302–3; image resolution 302; image sensor 300–3; iris 299; ISO 310–11; lens 297–8; prime lenses 297–8; sensor size 300, 301; shutter 300; shutter speed 311; zoom lenses 298
implementation: user-centered design 105
incandescent lamps 435, 438
index page 202, 214, 215, 219
index vectors 139
informal balance 136
inline elements: HTML 207
inline graphic 157
inner glow: font transformations 259
IN points: video editing 442, 470–2
input prompt 188
inside stroke: font transformations 259
Institute of Electrical and Electronics Engineers (IEEE) 73, 74
intellectual property 92
interactive media 81
interactive multimedia 15
interactive web content 228–9
interactivity: user interfaces 167–8
interlaced scanning 286, 356
International Electrotechnical Commission (IEC) 62, 244, 344–5, 349

International Organization for Standardization (ISO) 93; ISO Film Speed system 310–11
International Telecommunication Union (ITU) 344, 348
Internet: history of 202
Internet Protocol (IP) address 213
interview: tips for shooting 412
IPTC (International Press Telecommunications Council) 327
iris 299; camera function 364–7
italics 240, 247; font styles 249–50

JavaScript 186, 202, 208, 220, 228
Jobs, Steve 41, 42, 167
JPEG (Joint Photographic Experts Group) 277–9, 279
jump drive 69
justification: text 257, 258

Kanizsa's triangle 141
Kay, Alan 42
kerning: character spacing 256
keyboard 57–61; basics 57, 58; character keys 58–9; function keys 60; keystroke combinations 60–1; modifier keys 59; shortcuts 60
keying 448
key light 436–7, 439
kickoff meeting 95
kilobyte 62
Kodak Corporation 294
Kuhn, Thomas 19

landscape mode: exposure modes 319
lavalier microphone 385–8
layout 143, 145–8; above the fold 180, 181; see also page layouts
leading: line spacing 256–7
lead room 422–3
learnability 191
LED (light-emitting diode) lamps 438–9, 440
legacy media 4–6, 18
legibility: text 238–9
lens: fisheye 298; prime 297–8; short 297; telephoto 297–8; variable focal-length 298; wide-angle 297; zoom 298, 299
letterform 235, 240
light: angle of 433; flags 433–4; fluorescent and LED lamps 438–9; hardness 125; incandescent lamps

435, 438; lamp technologies 435, 438–9; modification tools 433–5; scrims 434–5; three-point lighting 124–5, 432–9; color temperature 313; design element 124–6; hard 432–3; photography 314; reflected 433; soft 432–3
light intensity 124, 364
line: curved 121–2; design element 120–2; diagonal and straight 121
Local Area Network (LAN) 70
logging and batch capturing 456–7
long lenses 297–8
long shot 422
loudness 375
low-angle shot 409, 421
lower-third graphic 447
low-key image 133

machine-to-machine editing 442
Mac OS X Finder 62–3
macro lenses 298
magnetic storage 69–71
Manovich, Lev 27, 28, 30–2, 36
manual focus 316
manual mode: exposure modes 321
manuscript grid 156
Marcotte, Ethan 195
margins 155
mass audience 21
master shot 419, 420
McLuhan, Marshall 3, 36, 112–13
mean line: letterform parts 240
media clips 455–6
media files 455–6
media stickiness 168
medium 5, 112
medium shot (MS) 421, 422
megabyte 62
memory cards 68, 69; camera 324–5; comparison 352; file-based recording 337; formatting 353–4; media files 455; Panasonic P2 349–50; S-by-S 349; shot 415; solid-state 323–4
Memory Stick (MS) 68, 324
menus: horizontal dropdown 177, 178; navigation 176, 177, 178; vertical dropdown 177, 178
merging cells: tables 159–60
metadata 326–7
metering modes 307
microblogging 17
microcomputer 40–2

Micro Instrumentation and Telemetry Systems (MITS) 40
microphones: bidirectional 382, 383; boundary 390; built-in or external 391–2; cardioid 382, 383; classifying by form factor 383–90; classifying by polar pattern 381–3; classifying by transducer type 378–80; condenser 379, 380; dynamic 378–9; function 377–8; handheld 384–5; hypercardioid 382, 383; lavalier 385–8; moving-coil 379; omnidirectional 381, 382, 383; proximity effect 386; ribbon 379–80; shotgun 382, 383, 388–9; supercardioid 382, 383; ultracardioid 382, 383; unidirectional 382, 383; USB 394; wireless 392–4; *see also* audio production
microprocessor 29, 40, 51, 52
Microsoft 41; OneDrive 70, 71, 72; Windows 13, 50, 164
mini plug 396, 397
mixing: audio 460–2
mobile app 49
mobile operating systems 47–8
mockup 101, 102, 103
Modern typefaces 243, 247
modular grid 158–9
modules 155
monitoring: audio 398–402; headphones 401–2; using volume-unit (VU) meter 398–401
monopod 322, 426
monospaced 240
Moore, Gordon 52
Moore's law 52
Morse, Samuel 45
Mosaic browser 13, 14
motherboard 49
motion: primary 424–5; secondary 425–30; tertiary 430
motion graphics 11
motion tracking interfaces 173
motion vectors 139
mouse 55–7
moving-coil microphone 379
moving images: ASTC (Advanced Television Systems Committee) 290–1, 292; digital cinema standards 291; digital television 289–90; DVB (Digital Video Broadcasting) 291; fields 287; illusion of apparent motion

287–8; interlaced scanning 286; progressive scanning 286; raster scanning 285–7; television and cinema standards 287–91
MP3 (MPEG-1 audio layer III) 344–5
MPEG (Moving Picture Experts Group): high efficiency video coding/H.265 348–9; MPEG-1 audio layer III (MP3) 344–5; MPEG-2 345; MPEG-4 346–8
MS-DOS (MicroSoft-Disk Operating System) 42
multi-camera editing 452
multicolumn grid 156–7
multimedia 3–4; animation 11; audio 10–11; container 338; defined 6–7, 9–11; graphics 9–10; legacy 4–6; text 6–7, 9; video 10; web content 228–9
MultiMediaCard (MMC) 324
multi-touch interfaces 170, 199
music 447, 467

naming conventions: file 214
narrowcasting 24
native resolution 282, 302
natural sound 408, 431, 446; inserting 466–7
navigation: accordions 177, 178; menus 176, 177, 178; primary 176, 179; secondary 176; tabs 177, 179; user interface 175–9; website 213–15
navigation bar 220
negative space 118
Negroponte, Nicholas 25, 37, 43
Nelson, Ted 8
nesting: file management 64; tags 206, 207
network 201–2; servers 213; URL address 212–13
network-attached storage (NAS) 65, 70
network card 50
neutral density (ND) filters 365
new media 20, 25–36; automation 32–4; convergence 29–30; cultural transcoding 36; five principles of 28–36; numerical representation 28–9; structural modularity 30–2; variability 34–6
news aggregators 17
news producing 83–4
Next Generation Broadcast Television 291

night mode: exposure modes 320
NLE *see* nonlinear editing (NLE)
nonbreaking space 209, 210
nondestructive editing 441
nonlinear editing (NLE) 10, 441–3; adding clips to timeline 466–8; capture files 456–7; components of NLE interface 459–65; keyboard shortcuts 464; media files and media clips 455–6; pioneers 459; project file 454; project folder 453–9; project panel 459; render files 457–8; source and program monitors 463–5; timeline 460–2
normal lens 298
Norman, Don 77
novelty lenses 298
NTSC (National Television Standards Committee) 289, 290, 334, 336, 356
Nyquist, Henry 340

Oblique typeface 240
old media 4–6, 17–25, 27; characteristics of 19; consumer as producer 20; large audience 21–4; large organization 19–20; paradigm shift 19, 20; simultaneous delivery 25
Old Style typeface 241–2, 246
omnidirectional microphone 381–3
open standards: video and audio encoding 343–9
operating system software (OS) 41–2, 47–8
optical disk 66–8
optical drive 50
optical zoom 299
organic shapes 122–3
outer glow: font transformations 259
OUT points: video editing 442, 470–2
outside stroke: font transformations 259
over-the-shoulder shot 421, 422
over-under wrap 399

padding 157, 160, 161
page layouts 143; chunking 149; fixed layouts 164–5; F-layout 145–7; fluid layouts 165; grid system 152–9; Gutenberg diagram 145; headings 149, 150; organizing content on 143–4; static and dynamic pages 164; tables 159–60; Z-layout 147–8

page peel: video transitions 474
page templates 161–3
pagination 184–5
Palo Alto Research Center (PARC) 55, 56
PAL (Phase Alternating Line) 289, 334
pan: secondary motion 428
Panasonic P2 memory card 349–50
Pandora 17, 24
paradigm shift 19, 20
parallax scrolling 186
parent folder 64
parentheticals 85
passive autofocus 315
pattern: design element 126–7
pattern fill: font transformations 258
pedestal motion 428–30; dolly, truck and arc 429–30; pedestal up and down 428–9
perceptual forces 136–40; asymmetrical balance 136–7; balance 136; continuation 139; figure-ground 139–40; psychological closure 140; symmetrical balance 136, 137
peripheral vision 405
permissions: intellectual property 72
personal computer (PC): history of 39–43
personalization 188–9
perspective 121
phantom power 369, 370, 379–81, 385, 389, 393
photography 265, 293–6; analog 265; aperture size 317; consumer cameras 294–5; focus 315–16; image stabilization 322–3; prosumer and professional cameras 295–6; quality lighting 314; video cameras 296; white balance 312, 315; *see also* imaging chain
PHP (Hypertext Preprocessor) 228
pickup pattern 381
picture element 267
pistol grip 389
pitch 373, 376, 377
pixel 119; definition of 267
pixel count 272
pixel density 272–4
pixel dimensions 272
pixel perfect 283
pixel resolution 272–4
planning: preproduction 82–8

playhead 463
plosives 378, 384
plug-in 202, 211, 216, 228–9
PNG 32, 35–6, 266, 279, 338, 348
point 252
pointer file 456
point of view: camera location 406–8
point size: letterform parts 240, 252
polar pattern: microphones 381–3
portrait mode: exposure modes 319
positive space 118
postproduction 92, 93
posture: letterforms 240
preamp 380, 393, 398–400
preproduction: AV script format 86–7; corporate producing 82–4; entertainment and news producing 83–4; previsualization 84–8; screenplay format 88, 89; script 85–7, 88; storyboard 85, 86; treatment 85
pressure zone microphone (PZM) 390
previsualization 84–8, 85
primary motion 424–5
primary navigation 176, 179
primary optical area 145
prime lenses 297–8
producer 83–4
production: Three *Ps* model 88, 90–1, 404
production schedule 416, 417
Professional Disc 349
program mode: exposure modes 321
program monitor 463–5
progressive scanning 286, 356
project director 95
project file 454
project folder 453
project planning: audience 79–81; creativity 78–9; postproduction 82, 92, 93; preproduction 82–8; production 82, 88, 90–1; road map 77–81; users 81
project team 95
proportion: principle of emphasis 134–5
proprietary standards: video and audio encoding 349–53
prosumer 295–6
protocols: web design 201, 212–13, 219, 230
prototype 95, 101, 104–5
proximity: principle of unity 129

proximity effect 386
psychological closure: perceptual forces 140, 141
pulse-code modulation (PCM) 339–43; bit depth 340–1; bit rate 342–3; sample rate 340

quantization 341
quartz lamps 435, 438
QuickTime 15, 34, 338, 347, 352, 459

rack focus 362
radio buttons: forms 187
ragged right: text 257
RAM (random access memory) 49, 52–5
Rand, Paul 109
rarefaction phase: frequency 375–6
raster images: anti-aliasing 276; color space 270–1; compression 277–9; cropping 275; defining 272–4; digital imaging 266, 267–80; formats 279–80; pixel count 272, 273; pixel density 272–4; pixel dimensions 272; resampling 275, 276; resolution 269, 272–4; scaling 274, 275
raster scanning: moving images 285–7
RCA (Radio Corporation of America) connector 396, 397
readability: text 238–9
Reagan, Ronald 269
Real-Time Streaming Protocol (RTSP) 212
reciprocity law 305
recording formats 331; analog tape formats 334; device settings 354–8; digital audio encoding 339–43; digital tape formats 334; file-based 337–8; formatting memory cards 353–4; legacy television 332–5; timeline of videotape formats 335–7; videotape 333
record level 398–401
Red Book Standard 342
RED Digital Cinema Camera 296, 350, 351, 404
red-eye reduction 308
reflected light 433
reflector: light modification tools 365, 433, 434, 435, 437, 439
refresh rate 286
relative URL 219

removable storage 66
rendering 457–8
repetition: principle of unity 130–1
resampling: raster image 275, 276
resolution: dependent 266, 274; image 302; native 282; pixel 272–4; raster image 269; video encoding 356
responsive web design 195, 196
RGB (Red, Green and Blue) color model 270, 271
ribbon microphone 379–80
Rich Internet Applications (RIAs) 14–15
rich media 15
right-aligning: text 257, 258
Roche, Peter 269
Roman typeface 240
root folder 64, 213
rows: grids 155; tables 159
rule of thirds 138, 413

sample 28
sample rate 339–43, 357–58
sans serif typefaces 243
saturation 127
scaling: raster image 274, 275
scanning: moving images 285–7; video encoding 356
scene: film grammar 416–17
Schram, Wilber 79
Schremp, Rick 201
scoop: lighting instruments 439, 440
scratch disk 453
screen font 245, 254
screenplay 88, 89; script format 88, 89
scrims: light modification tools 434–5, 440
script: previsualization 85–7, 88
script typefaces 244, 247
scrubbing 442, 463–4
SDTV (Standard Definition Television) 290
search engine optimization (SEO) 7
SECAM (Sequential Color and Memory) 289
secondary motion 425–30
secondary navigation 176
Secure Digital (SD) card 323
selective focus 316
Semantic Web 15
semi-automatic modes: exposure modes 321
sequence: film grammar 417–19

sequence motion 430
serial bus 73
serif typefaces 240–3
server 201, 202; IP addresses 213; naming convention 214; network 212–13; uploading website to 230–1
shallow depth of field 316
Shannon, Claude 79
Shannon–Weaver model 79
shape: design element 122–3
Shneiderman, Ben 167
short lighting 125
short-range apparent motion 287
shot: film grammar 415; shot list 424
shot designations 421–4; close-up 422–4; medium shot 422; mix it up 424; wide shot 422
shotgun microphone 382, 383, 388–9
shutter 296, 298, 300
shutter priority mode: exposure modes 321, 322
shutter speed 298, 300, 326, 364, 367–8; camera function 358, 367–8
sidebar 146–7, 156
similarity: principle of unity 130, 131
single-column grid 156
site design 215
slab serif typefaces 243, 247
slide wipe: video transitions 474
slug 460, 473
slug line 416, 417
SMALL CAPS: font styles 250–1
smartphone 10, 12, 25, 29, 31, 37, 46–9
S-M-C-R model of communication 79
snapping 257, 258
social bookmarking 17
social media 9–10, 16–17
social networking 17
softbox: lighting instruments 439
soft light 432–3
software 46; app 25, 49; application 48–9; operating system 41–2, 47–8
solid-state hard drives (SSDs) 65
solid-state memory cards 323–4
Sony SxS Memory Card 349
sound 372–6; amplitude 373–4; audio and 371–2; camera function 358, 368–70; connections and signal flow 368–70; equalization 377; frequency 374, 375–6

sound bite 408, 445, 466
sound check 401
sound effects (SFX) 10, 92, 462, 467, 468
sound on tape (SOT) 371, 408, 460
sound pressure wave 372–5, 379, 390
source monitor 463–5
space: design element 115–18; negative 118; positive 118; two-dimensional (2D) 116–17; white 118
spatial zones 155
speakers: audio monitoring 401–2
spill light 433–4, 435, 437
splash page 164
split edit 460
splitting cells: tables 159–60
sports mode: exposure modes 319
spot metering mode: measuring light intensity 307
stand-up 384, 445, 446
static page 164
still image 264, 279, 296, 302; animation 11; frame 414, 418, 424, 442, 451; graphics 9
stitching mode 320
storage 65
storyboard: previsualization 85, 86
stress: letterform parts 239–40
strikethrough: font styles 251
stroke: font transformations 259, 260; letterform parts 239–40
structural modularity 30–2
style sheet 157, 159, 161, 169, 198
subscript 254
subtractive color mixing 270
supercardioid microphone 382, 383
superscript 254
super-telephoto lenses 298
symbol typefaces 244–5, 247
symmetrical balance 136–7
system memory (RAM) 49, 52–5; requirements for application software 54

tables 159–60; creating 222–3; defining 159; merging cells 159–60; splitting cells 159–60
tabs: navigation 177, 179
tag 7, 9, 204, 206–9; alt tags 230; anatomy of 208, 209; HTML 204, 205; HTML5 206, 207; lists 217, 218; nesting 206, 207; tag name 208

tailoring 188–91; customization 189–91; personalization 188–9
take: film grammar 415
Talbot, William Henry Fox 119
target audience 80
target market 80
telephoto lenses 297–8
teleprompter 444
television: designing graphics for 449–50; legacy of analog 289; standards for moving pictures 287–91
terabyte 62
tertiary motion 430
text: alignment 257, 258; character and line spacing 256–7; distribution 257; justification 257, 258; kerning 256; leading 256–7; legibility 238–9; multimedia 6–7, 9; readability 238–9; tracking 256; text fields 187, 188
texture: design element 125–6
text user interface (TUI) 56
theory of perceptual grouping 128
"think outside the box" 98
Thomson, William 312
three-band equalization 377
three-dimensional (3D) 122, 124; effects 474; modeling program 124; transition 474
three-point lighting 436–7
Three Ps model 82–2, 94; postproduction 92, 93; preproduction 82–8, 89; production 88, 90–1, 404
thumb drives 69
thumbnails 182, 183
Thunderbolt 69, 74–5
TIFF 277, 279, 303, 338, 448
tilt: secondary motion 428
time-based editing: adding clips to timeline 466–8; B-roll 445–6; building blocks of edited sequence 443–50; continuity editing 450–1; cut-ins 450–1; cuts 472; dissolve 473–4; editing scenario 470–2; face 473; graphics 447–50; multi-camera 452; music and sound effects 447; natural sound 446; NLE project folder 453–9; nonlinear editing (NLE) 441–3; pre-scripted elements 443–4; sound bites 445; track management 468; transition properties 474–5; transitions

472–5; unscripted or post-scripted elements 444–7; voiceover 446–7; wipe 474
timecode 463
timeline 460–2; adding clips to 466–8; IN point in 471
titles 467
title safe area 448, 450
tonal range 133
top-level domain (TLD) 212
touch user interfaces 170, 171
track: audio and video 460; management 468
tracking: character spacing 256
transcoding 338
transducer: microphones 378–80
transitional typefaces 242–3, 246, 247
transitions 472–5; adding 467; cut 472; dissolve 473–4; fade 473; properties 474–5; wipe 474
transport controls 463
treatment: previsualization 85
tripod 406, 427–8; handheld motion 426; image stabilization 322–3; shooting B-roll 430–1
trough: frequency 375–6
truck: secondary motion 429–30
true color 271
true font styles 248–9
TS/TRS (tip and sleeve/tip, ring, and sleeve) connectors 396, 397
tungsten lamps 312
two-dimensional space (2D) 116–17
two-shot 419, 422
type 235
typeface 237, 261; categorizing 241–6; characteristics 239–41, 246–7; computers and 245–6; decorative 244; posture 240; proportions and letterform parts 240–1; sans serif 243; script 244; serif 241–3; stroke, contrast, and stress 239; symbol 244–5; weight 240
typographic grid 152, 155, 159
typography 235–8

UHD (ultra-high-definition) 291
UHDTV (ultra-high-definition television) 348
UI components and features: accordions 177, 178; archives 185–6; breadcrumbs 179–80; carousels 182–4; footers 180–1; home links 179; horizontal

dropdown menus 177, 178; managing hierarchy 179–81; menus 176–7, 178; navigation 175–9; organizing content 181–6; pagination 184–5; primary navigation 176; secondary navigation 176; tabs 177, 179; thumbnails 182, 183; vertical dropdown menus 177, 178
ultracardioid microphone 382, 383
umbrella light: lighting instruments 439, 440
unbalanced audio 396–7
underline: font styles 251
unidirectional microphone 382, 383
Uniform Resource Locator (URL) 202; address on Web 212–13
unity 128–31; alignment 130; proximity 129; repetition 130–1; similarity 130, 131
usability 94, 191–5; efficiency 192; error management 192; feedback 194–5; learnability 191; memorability 192; satisfaction 192–3; testing 193–4
usability testing 94, 193–4
USB (Universal Serial Bus) 69, 73–5; drives 69; microphones 394; USB-C connector 74–5
user 81; experience 93, 95
user-centered design (UCD) 82, 93–105; analysis 95–8; card sorting 99–100; conducting research 97–8; deployment 105; identifying target users 96–7; implementation 105; mockup 101, 102, 103; needs assessment 96; prototype 104–5; putting principles into practice 95–105; specifying requirements 97; wireframe 101, 102, 103
User Experience Professionals Association (UXPA) 95
user-generated content (UGC) 20
user interface (UI): accessibility 196–8; augmented reality (AR) 173–4, 175; designer job post 169–70; graphical 168; interactivity 167–8; touch 170, 171; types of 168–74; voice 170, 172; see also UI components and features

Vail, Alfred 45
value: principle of emphasis 132–4
variable focal-length lens 298

vector graphics: digital imaging 266, 280–2
Venetian typefaces 242
vertical dropdown menus: navigation 177, 178
vertical wipe: video transitions 474
video 10, 368; adapter 54; blogging 17; cameras 296; card 49, 54; compositing 460–2; compression 346–7; encoding settings 356–7; film *vs.* 403–4
video and audio encoding: AIFF (Audio Interchange File Format) 352–3; AVCHD 351–2; high efficiency video coding/H.265 348–9; MEG-1 audio layer III (MP3) 344–5; MPEG-2 345; MPEG-4 346–8; open standards for 343–9; P2 349–50; proprietary standards for 349–53; QuickTime 352; RED Digital Cinema 350, 351; SxS 349; WAV (Waveform Audio File Format) 352–3
video production: 180-degree rule 420; B-roll 408, 430–1; crossing the line 420; field of view 405–12; film grammar 414–19; frame 414; lighting 432–9; lighting instruments 439–40; motion 424–30; natural sound 408; scene 416–17; sequence 417–19; shot 415; shot designations 421–4; sound bite 408; three-point lighting 436–7; tips for shooting B-roll 430–1; tips for shooting interview 412
videotape formats 333; timeline of 335–7
video track 333, 460; management 468
viewfinder 406
Vimeo 17, 346: encoding for 347–8
virtual private network (VPN) 70

visual communication 109–14; aesthetics 113–14; content and form 110, 112–13
visual grammar *see* film grammar
visual hierarchy 148
vlogging 17
voice interfaces 170, 172
voiceover (VO) 391, 394; B-roll 408, 445, 471–2; edited sequence 444–5; narrative device 446–7; sound bites 445; stand-up 446
VU (volume-unit) meter: monitoring record levels 398–401

Warnock, John 143
warping: font transformations 258
waveform 464–5
Waveform Audio File Format (WAV) 352–3
wavelength: sound 374
Weaver, Warren 79
WebAIM.org 230
Web design: accessibility issues 229–30; background and text colors 225; block quotes 217; characteristics of appearance 225–9; code compatibility 229–30; creating and managing hyperlinks 218–22; creating tables 222–3; file naming conventions 214; font type and style 226; headings 216–17; hierarchy 214–15; HTML5 elements 216; interactive and multimedia content 228–9; link characteristics 226–7; lists 217, 218; margins 225; marking up content 215–23; navigation 213–15; paragraphs 217; planning site structure 213–15; responsive 195, 196; root folder 213; site uniformity and consistency 215; uploading the site to server 230–1; usability 215

web-safe font 246
web user interfaces (WUIs) 168
Wertheimer, Max 128, 267
white balance: camera function 362–3, 364; controls 363, 364; photography 312, 315
white space 118
wide-angle lenses 297
widescreen 284
wide shot (WS) 421, 422
Windows File Explorer 62
windscreen 384, 386
wipe: video transitions 474
wireframe 100–1, 102, 103, 464–5
wireless microphone 392–4
World Wide Web (WWW) 4, 8, 11–12; browsers 211–12; demystifying code 202–9; history 202; HTML characters 210; HTML elements 205; network 212–13; three generations of 14–16
World Wide Web Consortium (W3C) 159, 202, 208, 211, 224, 229, 230
Wozniak, Steve 42
wrapper file 338
Wright, Charles 19, 25

x-axis 116
x-height: letterform parts 240
XLR connectors 396, 397

y-axis 116
YouTube 9, 17, 20, 23, 37, 48, 168, 191, 346, 347–8; encoding for 347–8

z-axis 117, 404–5, 407
zebra stripes 365–7
Zettl, Herb 424, 425
Z-layout 147–8
zoom lenses 298